...ore than twenty...
...ce in the compute...
...ged by Digital Research, Inc...
...rs of CP/M®, to customize CP/M...
...PC. Mr. Johnson-Laird is the p...
...d founder of Johnson-Laird,...
...l-C Software, Inc., two Portlan...
...on, software houses.

THE PROGRAMMER'S
CP/M® HANDBOOK

THE PROGRAMMER'S CP/M® HANDBOOK

Andy Johnson-Laird

Osborne/McGraw-Hill
Berkeley, California

Published by
Osborne/McGraw-Hill
2600 Tenth Street
Berkeley, California 94710
U.S.A.

For information on translations and book distributors outside of the U.S.A.,
please write to Osborne/McGraw-Hill at the above address.

CP/M is a registered trademark of Digital Research, Inc.
CP/M-86, MP/M-86, and MP/M II are trademarks of
    Digital Research, Inc.
Z80 is a registered trademark of Zilog, Inc.

THE PROGRAMMER'S CP/M® HANDBOOK

Copyright ©1983 by Osborne/McGraw-Hill. All rights reserved. Printed in the United States of America. Except as permitted under the Copyright Act of 1976, no part of this publication may be reproduced or distributed in any form or by any means, or stored in a data base or retrieval system, without the prior written permission of the publisher, with the exception that the program listings may be entered, stored, and executed in a computer system, but they may not be reproduced for publication.

1234567890 DODO 89876543

ISBN 0-88134-103-7 (Paperback Edition)
ISBN 0-88134-119-3 (Hardcover Edition)

Mary Borchers, Acquisitions Editor
Ralph Baumgartner, Technical Editor
Susan Schwartz, Copy Editor
Judy Wohlfrom, Text Design
Yashi Okita, Cover Design

Dedication

Several years ago I was told that "Perfection is an English education, an American salary, and a Japanese wife."

Accordingly, I wish to thank the members of Staff at Culford School in England, who gave me the English education, the people who work with me at Johnson-Laird Inc. and Control-C Software and our clients, who give me my American salary, and Mr. and Mrs. Kitagawa, who gave me Kay Kitagawa (who not only married me but took over where my English grammar left off).

A.J-L.

Acknowledgments

Although this book is not authorized or endorsed by Digital Research, I would like to express my thanks to Gary Kildall and Kathy Strutynski of Digital Research, and to Phil Nelson (formerly of Digital Research, now of Victor Technology) for their help in keeping me on the path to truth in this book. I would also like to thank Denise Penrose, Marty McNiff, Mary Borchers, and Ralph Baumgartner at Osborne/McGraw-Hill for their apparently inexhaustible patience.

A.J-L.

Contents

1	Introduction	1
2	The Structure of CP/M	5
3	The CP/M File System	17
4	The Console Command Processor (CCP)	45
5	The BASIC Disk Operating System	67
6	The BASIC Input/Output System	147
7	Building a New CP/M System	183
8	Writing an Enhanced BIOS	209
9	Dealing with Hardware Errors	295
10	Debugging a New CP/M System	319
11	Additional Utility Programs	371
12	Error Messages	449
A	ASCII Character Set	465
B	CP/M Command Summary	469
C	Summary of BDOS Calls	479
D	Summary of BIOS Calls	485
	Index	487

Outline of Contents
Notation
Example Programs on Diskette

Introduction

This book is a sequel to the *Osborne CP/M® User Guide* by Thom Hogan. It is a technical book written mainly for programmers who require a thorough knowledge of the internal structure of CP/M—how the various pieces of CP/M work, how to use CP/M as an operating system, and finally, how to implement CP/M on different computer systems. This book is written for people who

- Have been working with microcomputers that run Digital Research's CP/M operating system.
- Understand the internals of the microprocessor world—bits, bytes, ports, RAM, ROM, and other jargon of the programmer.
- Know how to write in assembly language for the Intel 8080 or Zilog Z80 Central Processing Unit (CPU) chips.

If you don't have this kind of background, start by getting practical experience on a system running CP/M and by reading the following books from Osborne/McGraw-Hill:

- *An Introduction to Microcomputers: Volume 1—Basic Concepts*
  This book describes the fundamental concepts and facts that you need to

know about microprocessors in order to program them. If you really need basics, there is a Volume 0 called *The Beginner's Book*.

- *8080A/8085 Assembly Language Programming*
  This book covers all aspects of writing programs in 8080 assembly language, giving many examples.
- *Osborne CP/M® User Guide (2nd Edition)*
  This book introduces the CP/M operating system. It tells you how to use CP/M as a tool to get things done on a computer.

The book you are reading now deals only with CP/M Version 2.2 for the 8080 or Z80 chips. At the time of writing, new versions of CP/M and MP/M (the multi-user, multi-tasking successor to CP/M) were becoming available. CP/M-86 and MP/M-86 for the Intel 8086 CPU chip and MP/M-II for the 8080 or Z80 chips had been released, with CP/M 3.0 (8080 or Z80) in the wings. The 8086, although related architecturally to the 8080, is different enough to make it impossible to cover in detail in this book; and while MP/M-II and MP/M-86 are similar to CP/M, they have many aspects that cannot be adequately discussed within the scope of this book.

Outline of Contents

This book explains topics as if you were starting from the top of a pyramid. Successive "slices" down the pyramid cover the same material but give more detail.

The first chapter includes a brief outline of the notation used in this book for example programs written in Intel 8080 assembly language and in the C programming language.

Chapter 2 deals with the structure of CP/M, describing its major parts, their positions in memory, and their functions.

Chapter 3 discusses CP/M's file system in as much detail as possible, given its proprietary nature. The directory entry, disk parameter block, and file organization are described.

Chapter 4 covers the Console Command Processor (CCP), examining the way in which you enter command lines, the CP/M commands built into the CCP, how the CCP loads programs, and how it transfers control to these programs.

Chapter 5 begins the programming section. It deals with the system calls your programs can make to the high-level part of CP/M, the Basic Disk Operating System (BDOS).

Chapters 6 through 10 deal with the Basic Input/Output System (BIOS). This is the part of CP/M that is unique to each computer system. It is the part that you as a programmer will write and implement for your own computer system.

Chapter 6 describes a standard implementation of the BIOS.

Chapter 7 describes the mechanism for rebuilding CP/M for a different configuration.

Chapter 8 tells you how to write an enhanced BIOS.

Chapter 9 takes a close look at how to handle hardware errors—how to detect and deal with them, and how to make this task easier for the person using the computer.

Chapter 10 discusses the problems you may face when you try to debug your BIOS code. It includes debugging subroutines and describes techniques that will save you time and suffering.

Chapter 11 describes several utility programs, some that work with the features of the enhanced BIOS in Chapter 8 and some that will work with all CP/M 2 implementations.

Chapter 12 concerns error messages and some oddities that you will discover, sometimes painfully, in CP/M. Messages are explained and some probable causes for strange results are documented.

The appendixes contain "ready-reference" information and summaries of information that you need at your side when designing, coding, and testing programs to run under CP/M or your own BIOS routines.

Notation

When you program your computer, you will be sitting in front of your terminal interacting with CP/M and the utility programs that run under it. The sections that follow describe the notation used to represent the dialog that will appear on your terminal and the output that will appear on your printer.

Console Dialog

This book follows the conventions used in the *Osborne CP/M User Guide*, extended slightly to handle more complex dialogs. In this book

- <name> means the ASCII character named between the angle brackets, < and >. For example, <BEL> is the ASCII Bell character, and <HT> is the ASCII Horizontal Tab Character. (Refer to Appendix A for the complete ASCII character set.)
- <cr> means to press the CARRIAGE RETURN key.
- 123 or a number without a suffix means a decimal number.
- 100B or a number followed by B means a binary number.
- 0A5H or a number followed by H means a hexadecimal number. A hexadecimal number starting with a letter is usually shown with a leading 0 to avoid confusion.

- ^x means to hold the CONTROL (CTRL) key down while pressing the x key.
- <u>Underline</u> is keyboard input you type. Output from the computer is shown without underlining.

Assembly Language Program Examples

This book uses Intel 8080 mnemonics throughout as a "lowest common denominator"—the Z80 CPU contains features absent in the 8080, but not vice versa. Output from Digital Research's ASM Assembler is shown so that you can see the generated object code as well as the source.

High-Level Language Examples

The utility programs described in Chapter 11 are written in C, a programming language which lends itself to describing algorithms clearly without becoming entangled in linguistic bureaucracy. Cryptic expressions have been avoided in favor of those that most clearly show how to solve the problem. Ample comments explain the code.

An excellent book for those who do not know how to program in C is *The C Programming Language* by Brian Kernighan and Dennis Ritchie (Prentice-Hall). Appendix A of this book is the C Reference Manual.

Example Programs on Diskette

Example programs in this book have been assembled with ASM and tested with DDT, Digital Research's Dynamic Debugging Tool. C examples were compiled using Leor Zolman's BDS C Compiler (Version 1.50) and tested using the enhanced BIOS described in Chapter 8.

All of the source code shown in this book is available on a single-sided, single-density, 8-inch diskette (IBM 3740 format). Please do *not* contact Osborne/McGraw-Hill to order this diskette. Call or write

Johnson-Laird, Inc.
Attn: The CP/M Programmer's Handbook Diskette
6441 SW Canyon Court
Portland, OR 97221
Tel: (503) 292-6330

The diskette is available for $50 plus shipping costs.

CP/M from Digital Research
The Pieces of CP/M
   CP/M Diskette Format
   Loading CP/M
   Console Command Processor
   Basic Disk Operating System
   Basic Input/Output System
   CCP, BDOS, and BIOS
      Interactions

The Structure of CP/M

This chapter introduces the pieces that make up CP/M—what they are and what they do. This bird's-eye view of CP/M will establish a framework to which later chapters will add more detailed information.

You may have purchased the standard version of CP/M directly from Digital Research, but it is more likely you received CP/M when you bought your microprocessor system or its disk drive system. Or, you may have purchased CP/M separately from a software distributor. In any case, this distributor or the company that made the system or disk drive will have already modified the standard version of CP/M to work on your specific hardware. Most manufacturers' versions of CP/M have more files on their system diskette than are described here for the standard Digital Research release.

Some manufacturers have rewritten all the documentation so that you may not have received any Digital Research CP/M manuals. If this is the case, you should order the complete set from Digital Research, because as a programmer, you will need to have them for reference.

CP/M from Digital Research

Digital Research provides a standard "vanilla-flavored" version of CP/M that will run only on the Intel Microcomputer Development System (MDS). The CP/M package from Digital Research contains seven manuals and an 8-inch, single-sided, single-density standard IBM 3740 format diskette.

The following manuals come with this CP/M system:

- *An Introduction to CP/M Features and Facilities.* This is a brief description of CP/M and the utility programs you will find on the diskette. It describes only CP/M version 1.4.

- *CP/M 2.0 User's Guide.* Digital Research wrote this manual to describe the new features of CP/M 2.0 and the extensions made to existing CP/M 1.4 features.

- *ED: A Context Editor for the CP/M Disk System.* By today's standards, ED is a primitive line editor, but you can still use it to make changes to files containing ASCII text, such as the BIOS source code.

- *CP/M Assembler (ASM).* ASM is a simple but fast assembler that can be used to translate the BIOS source code on the diskette into machine code. Since ASM is only a bare-bones assembler, many programmers now use its successor, MAC (also from Digital Research).

- *CP/M Dynamic Debugging Tool (DDT).* DDT is an extremely useful program that allows you to load programs in machine code form and then test them, executing the program either one machine instruction at a time or stopping only when the CPU reaches a specific point in the program.

- *CP/M Alteration Guide.* There are two manuals with this title, one for CP/M version 1.4 and the other for 2.0. Both manuals describe, somewhat cryptically, how to modify CP/M.

- *CP/M Interface Guide.* Again, there are two versions, 1.4 and 2.0. These manuals tell you how to write programs that communicate directly with CP/M.

The diskette supplied by Digital Research has the following files:

ASM.COM
    The CP/M assembler.

BIOS.ASM
    A source code file containing a sample BIOS for the Intel Microcomputer Development System (MDS). Unless you have the MDS, this file is useful only as an example of a BIOS.

CBIOS.ASM
   Another source code file for a BIOS. This one is skeletal: There are gaps so that you can insert code for your computer.

DDT.COM
   The Dynamic Debugging Tool program.

DEBLOCK.ASM
   A source code file that you will need to use in the BIOS if your computer uses sector sizes other than 128 bytes. It is an example of how to block and deblock 128-byte sectors to and from the sector size you need.

DISKDEF.LIB
   A library of source text that you will use if you have a copy of Digital Research's advanced assembler, MAC.

DUMP.ASM
   The source for an example program. DUMP reads a CP/M disk file and displays it in hexadecimal form on the console.

DUMP.COM
   The actual executable program derived from DUMP.ASM.

ED.COM
   The source file editor.

LOAD.COM
   A program that takes the machine code file output by the assembler, ASM, and creates another file with the data rearranged so that you can execute the program by just typing its name on the keyboard.

MOVCPM.COM
   A program that creates versions of CP/M for different memory sizes.

PIP.COM
   A program for copying information from one place to another (PIP is short for Peripheral Interchange Program).

STAT.COM
   A program that displays statistics about the CP/M and other information that you have stored on disks.

SUBMIT.COM
   A program that you use to enter CP/M commands automatically. It helps you avoid repeated typing of long command sequences.

SYSGEN.COM
   A program that writes CP/M onto diskettes.

XSUB.COM
   An extended version of the SUBMIT program. The files named previously

fall into two groups: One group is used only to rebuild CP/M, while the other set is general-purpose programming tools.

The Pieces of CP/M

CP/M is composed of the Basic Disk Operating System (BDOS), the Console Command Processor (CCP), and the Basic Input/Output System (BIOS).

On occasion you will see references in CP/M manuals to something called the FDOS, which stands for "Floppy Disk Operating System." This name is given to the portion of CP/M consisting of both the BDOS and BIOS and is a relic passed down from the original version. Since it is rarely necessary to refer to the BDOS and the BIOS combined as a single entity, no further references to the FDOS will be made in this book.

The BDOS and the CCP are the proprietary parts of CP/M. Unless you are willing to pay several thousand dollars, you cannot get the source code for them. You do not need to. CP/M is designed so that all of the code that varies from one machine to another is contained in the BIOS, and you do get the BIOS source code from Digital Research. Several companies make specialized BIOSs for different computer systems. In many cases they, as well as some CP/M hardware manufacturers, do not make the source code for their BIOS available; they have put time and effort into building their BIOS, and they wish to preserve the proprietary nature of what they have done.

You may have to build a special configuration of CP/M for a specific computer. This involves no more than the following four steps:

1. Make a version of the BDOS and CCP for the memory size of your computer.
2. Write a modified version of the BIOS that matches the hardware in your computer.
3. Write a small program to load CP/M into memory when you press the RESET button on your computer.
4. Join all of the pieces together and write them out to a diskette.

These steps will be explained in Chapters 7, 8, and 9.

In the third step, you write a small program that loads CP/M into memory when you press the RESET button on your computer. This program is normally called the bootstrap loader. You may also see it called the "boot" or even the "cold start" loader. "Bootstrap" refers to the idea that when the computer is first turned on, there is no program to execute. The task of getting that very first program into the computer is, conceptually, as difficult as attempting to pick yourself up off the ground by pulling on your own bootstraps. In the early days of computing, this operation was performed by entering instructions manually—setting large banks

Chapter 2: The Structure of CP/M   9

of switches (the computer was built to read the switches as soon as it was turned on). Today, microcomputers contain some small fragment of a program in "nonvolatile" read-only memory (ROM)—memory that retains data when the computer is turned off. This stored program, usually a Programmable Read Only Memory (PROM) chip, can load your bootstrap program, which in turn loads CP/M.

CP/M Diskette Format

The standard version of CP/M is formatted on an 8-inch, single-sided diskette. Diskettes other than this type will probably have different layouts; hard disks definitely will be different.

The physical format of the standard 8-inch diskette is shown in Figure 2-1. The

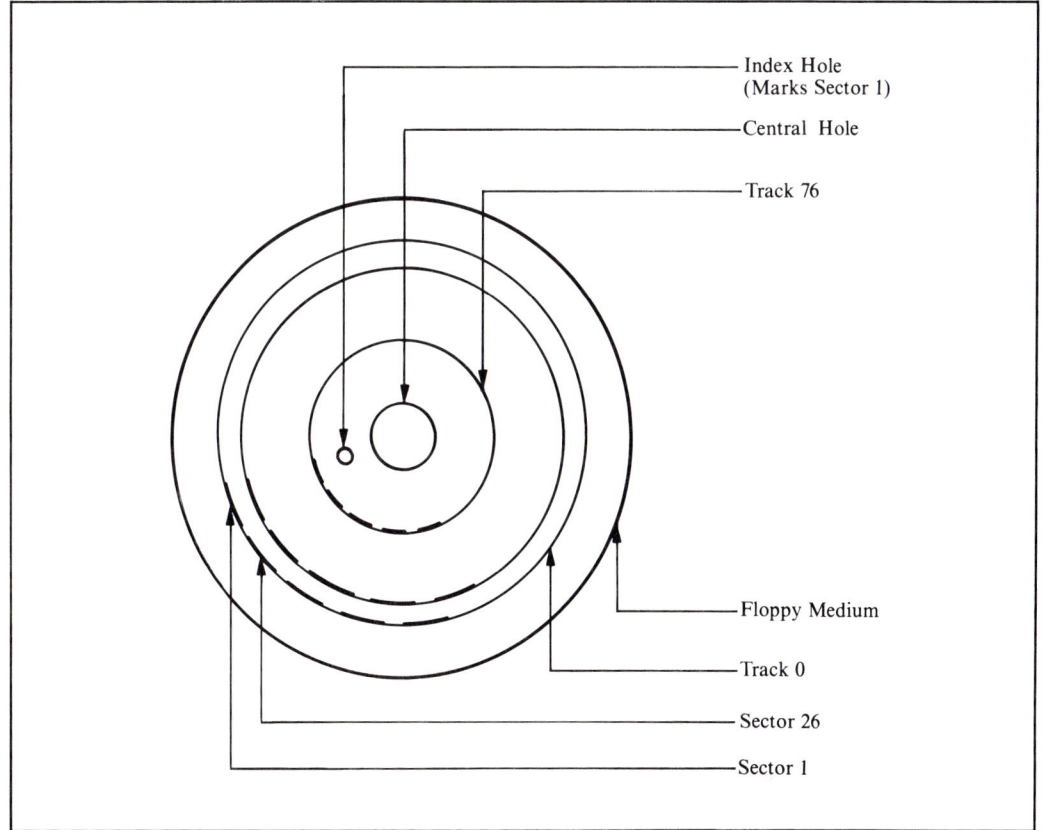

Figure 2-1.   Floppy disk layout

10   The CP/M Programmer's Handbook

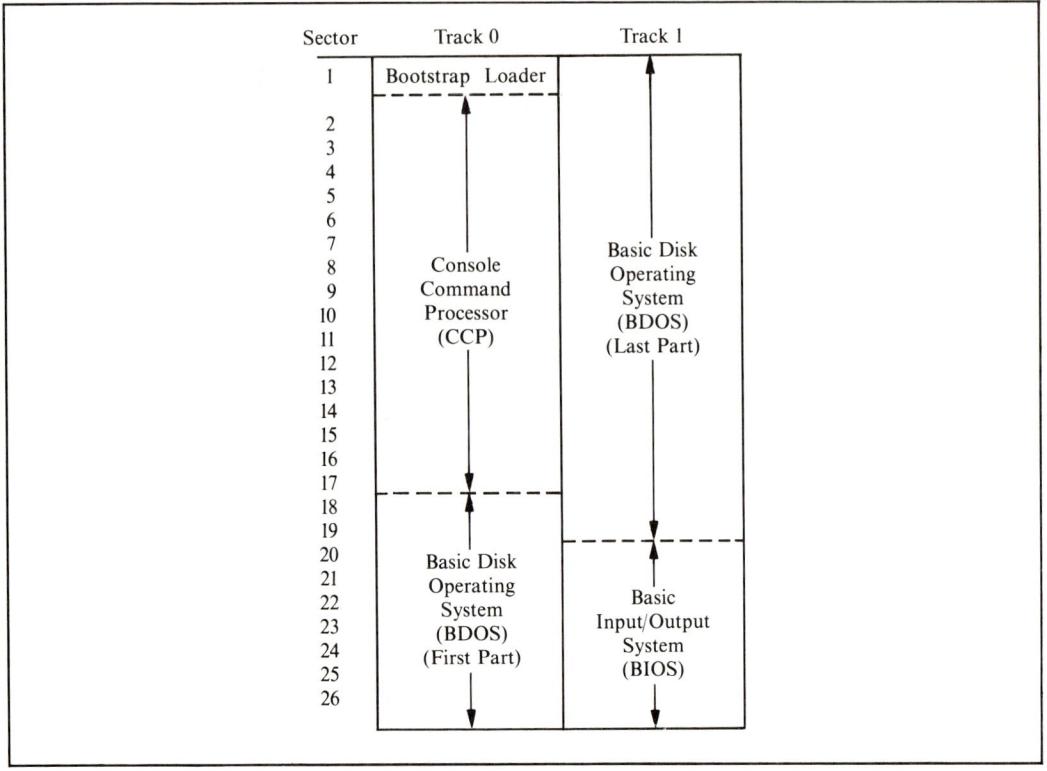

Figure 2-2.   Layout of CP/M on tracks 0 and 1 of floppy disk

diskette has a total of 77 concentric tracks numbered from zero (the outermost) to 76 (the innermost). Each of these tracks is divided radially into 26 sectors. These physical sectors are numbered from 1 to 26; physical sector zero does not exist. Each sector has enough space for 128 bytes of data.

Even when CP/M is implemented on a large hard disk with much larger sector sizes, it still works with 128-byte sectors. The BIOS has extra instructions that convert the *real* sectors into CP/M-style 128-byte sectors.

A final note on physical format: The soft-sectored, single-sided, single-density, 8-inch diskette (IBM 3740 format) is the *only* standard format. Any other formats will be unique to the hardware manufacturer that uses them. It is unlikely that you can read a diskette on one manufacturer's computer if it was written on another's, even though the formats appear to be the same. For example, a single-sided, double-density diskette written on an Intel Development System cannot be read on a Digital Microsystems computer even though both use double-density format. If you want to move data from one computer to another, use 8-inch, single-sided, single-density format diskettes, and it *should* work.

Chapter 2: The Structure of CP/M   **11**

In order to see how CP/M is stored on a diskette, consider the first two tracks on the diskette, track 0 and track 1. Figure 2-2 shows how the data is stored on these tracks.

Loading CP/M

The events that occur after you first switch on your computer and put the CP/M diskette into a disk drive are the same as those that occur when you press the RESET button—the computer generates a RESET signal.

The RESET button stops the central processor unit (CPU). All of the internals of the CPU are set to an initial state, and all the registers are cleared to zero. The program counter is also cleared to zero so that when the RESET signal goes away (it only lasts for a few milliseconds), the CPU starts executing instructions at location 0000H in memory.

Memory chips, when they first receive power, cannot be relied upon to contain any particular value. Therefore, hardware designers arrange for some initial instructions to be forced into memory at location 0000H and onward. It is this feat that is like pulling yourself up by your own bootstraps. How can you make the computer obey a particular instruction when there is "nothing" (of any sensible value) inside the machine?

There are two common techniques for placing preliminary instructions into memory:

Force-feeding

With this approach, the hardware engineer assumes that when the RESET signal is applied, some part of the computer system, typically the floppy disk controller, can masquerade as memory. Just before the CPU is unleashed, the floppy disk controller will take control of the computer system and copy a small program into memory at location 0000H and upward. Then the CPU is allowed to start executing instructions at location 0000H. The disk controller preserves the instructions even when power is off because they are stored in nonvolatile PROM-based firmware. These instructions make the disk controller read the first sector of the first track of the system diskette into memory and then transfer control to it.

Shadow ROM

This is a variation of the force-feeding technique. The hardware manufacturer arranges some ROM at location 0000H. There is also some normal read/write memory at location 0000H, but this is electronically disabled when the RESET signal has been activated. The CPU, unleashed at location 0000H, starts to execute the ROM instruction. The first act of the ROM program is to copy itself into read/write memory at some convenient location higher up in memory and transfer control of the machine up to this copy. Then the real memory at location 0000H can be turned on, the ROM turned off, and the first sector on the disk read in.

With either technique, the result is the same. The first sector of the disk is read into memory and control is transferred to the first instruction contained in the sector.

This first sector contains the main CP/M bootstrap program. This program initializes some aspects of the hardware and then reads in the remainder of track 0 and most of the sectors on track 1 (the exact number depends on the overall length of the BIOS itself). The CP/M bootstrap program will contain only the most primitive diskette error handling, trying to read the disk over and over again if the hardware indicates that it is having problems reading a sector.

The bootstrap program loads CP/M to the correct place in memory; the load address is a constant in the bootstrap. If you need to build a version of CP/M that uses more memory, you will need to change this load address inside the bootstrap as well as the address to which the bootstrap will jump when all of CP/M has been read in. This address too is a constant in the bootstrap program.

The bootstrap program transfers control to the first instruction in the BIOS, the cold boot entry point. "Cold" implies that the operation is starting cold from an empty computer.

The cold boot code in the BIOS will set up the hardware in your computer. That is, it programs the various chips that control the speed at which serial ports transmit and receive data. It initializes the serial port chips themselves and generally readies the computer system. Its final act is to transfer control to the first instruction in the BDOS in order to start up CP/M proper.

Once the BDOS receives control, it initializes itself, scans the file directory on the system diskette, and hands over control to the CCP. The CCP then outputs the "A>" prompt to the console and waits for you to enter a command. CP/M is then ready to do your bidding.

At this point, it is worthwhile to review which CP/M parts are in memory, where in memory they are, and what functions they perform.

This overview will look at memory first. Figure 2-3 shows the positions in memory of the Console Command Processor, the Basic Disk Operating System, and the Basic Input/Output System.

By touching upon these major memory components—the CCP, BDOS, and BIOS—this discussion will consider which modules interact with them, how requests for action are passed to them, and what functions they can perform.

Console Command Processor

As you can see in Figure 2-3, the CCP is the first part of CP/M that is encountered going "up" through memory addresses. This is significant when you consider that the CCP is only necessary in between programs. When CP/M is idle, it needs the CCP to interact with you, to accept your next command. Once CP/M has started to execute the command, the CCP is redundant; any console interaction will be handled by the program you are running rather than by the CCP.

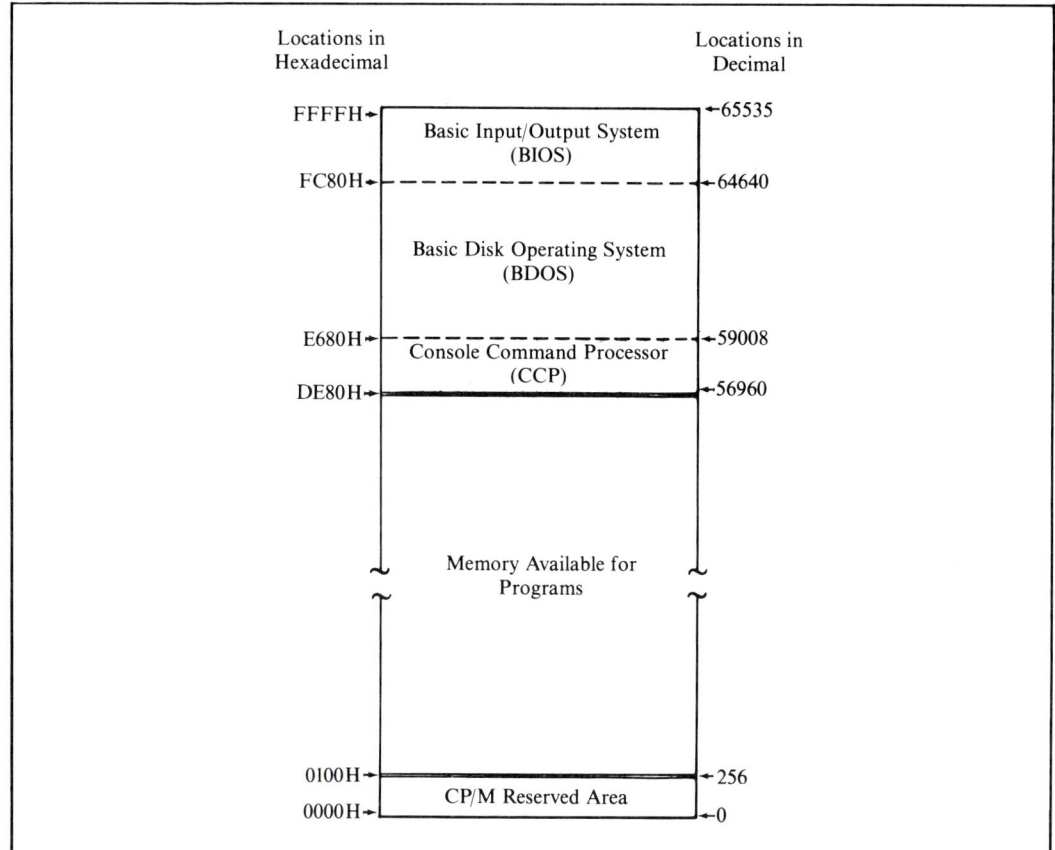

Figure 2-3. Memory layout with CP/M loaded

Therefore, the CCP leads a very jerky existence in memory. It is loaded when you first start CP/M. When you ask CP/M, via the CCP, to execute a program, this program can overwrite the CCP and use the memory occupied by the CCP for its own purposes. When the program you asked for has finished, CP/M needs to reload the CCP, now ready for its interaction with you. This process of reloading the CCP is known as a *warm boot*. In contrast with the cold boot mentioned before, the warm boot is not a complete "start from cold"; it's just a reloading of the CCP. The BDOS and BIOS are not touched.

How does a program tell CP/M that it has finished and that a warm boot must be executed? By jumping to location 0000H. While the BIOS was initializing itself during the cold boot routine, it put an instruction at location 0000H to jump to the warm boot routine, which is also in the BIOS. Once the BIOS warm boot routine has reloaded the CCP from the disk, it will transfer control to the CCP. (The cold and warm boot routines are discussed further in Chapter 6.)

This brief description indicates that every command you enter causes a program to be loaded, the CCP to be overwritten, the program to run, and the CCP to be reloaded when the program jumps to location 0000H on completing its task. This is not completely true. Some frequently needed commands reside in the CCP. Using one of these commands means that CP/M does not have to load anything from a diskette; the programs are already in memory as part of the CCP. These commands, known as "intrinsic" or "resident" commands, are listed here with a brief description of what they do. (All of them are described more thoroughly in Chapter 4.) The "resident" commands are

DIR	Displays which files are on a diskette
ERA	Erases files from a diskette
REN	Changes the names of files on diskette
TYPE	Displays the contents of text files on the console
SAVE	Saves some of memory as a file on diskette
USER	Changes User File Group.

Basic Disk Operating System

The BDOS is the heart of CP/M. The CCP and all of the programs that you run under CP/M talk to the BDOS for all their outside contacts. The BDOS performs such tasks as console input/output, printer output, and file management (creating, deleting, and renaming files and reading and writing sectors).

The BDOS performs all of these things in a rather detached way. It is concerned only with the logical tasks at hand rather than the detailed action of getting a sector from a diskette into memory, for example. These "low-level" operations are done by the BDOS in conjunction with the BIOS.

But how does a program work with the BDOS? By another strategically placed jump instruction in memory. Remember that the cold boot placed the jump to the BIOS warm boot routine in location 0000H. At location 0005H, it puts a jump instruction that transfers control up to the first instruction of the BDOS. Thus, any program that transfers control to location 0005H will find its way into the BDOS. Typically, programs make a CALL instruction to location 0005H so that once the BDOS has performed the task at hand, it can return to the calling program at the correct place. The program enlisting the BDOS's help puts special values into several of the CPU registers before it makes the call to location 0005H. These values tell the BDOS what operation is required and the other values needed for the specific operation.

Basic Input/Output System

As mentioned before, the BDOS deals with the input and output of information in a detached way, unencumbered by the physical details of the computer hardware. It is the BIOS that communicates directly with the hardware, the ports, and the peripheral devices wired to them.

This separation of *logical* input/output in the BDOS from the *physical* input/output in the BIOS is one of the major reasons why CP/M is so popular. It means that the same version of CP/M can be adapted for all types of computers, regardless of the oddities of the hardware design. Digital Research will tell you that there are over 200,000 computers in the world running CP/M. Just about all of them are running *identical* copies of the CCP and BDOS. Only the BIOS is different. If you write a program that plays by the rules and only interacts with the BDOS to get things done, it will run on almost all of those 200,000 computers without your having to change a single line of code.

You probably noticed the word "almost" in the last paragraph. Sometimes programmers make demands of the BIOS directly rather than the BDOS. This leads to trouble. The BIOS should be off limits to your program. You need to know what it is and how it works in order to build a customized version of CP/M, but you must *never* write programs that talk directly to the BIOS if you want them to run on other versions of CP/M.

Now that you understand the perils of talking to the BIOS, it is safe to describe how the BDOS communicates with the BIOS. Unlike the BDOS, which has a single entry point and uses a value in a register to specify the function to be performed, the BIOS has several entry points. The first few instructions in the BIOS are all independent entry points, each taking up three bytes of memory. The BDOS will enter the BIOS at the appropriate instruction, depending on the function to be performed. This group of entry points is similar in function to a railroad marshalling yard. It directs the BDOS to the correct destination in the BIOS for the function it needs to have done. The entry point group consists of a series of JUMP instructions, each one three bytes long. The group as a whole is called the BIOS jump table, or jump vector. Each entry point has a predefined meaning. These points are detailed and will be discussed in Chapter 6.

CCP, BDOS, and BIOS Interactions

Figure 2-4 summarizes the functions that the CCP, BDOS, and BIOS perform, the ways in which these parts of CP/M communicate among themselves, and the way in which one of your programs running under CP/M interacts with the BDOS.

16   The CP/M Programmer's Handbook

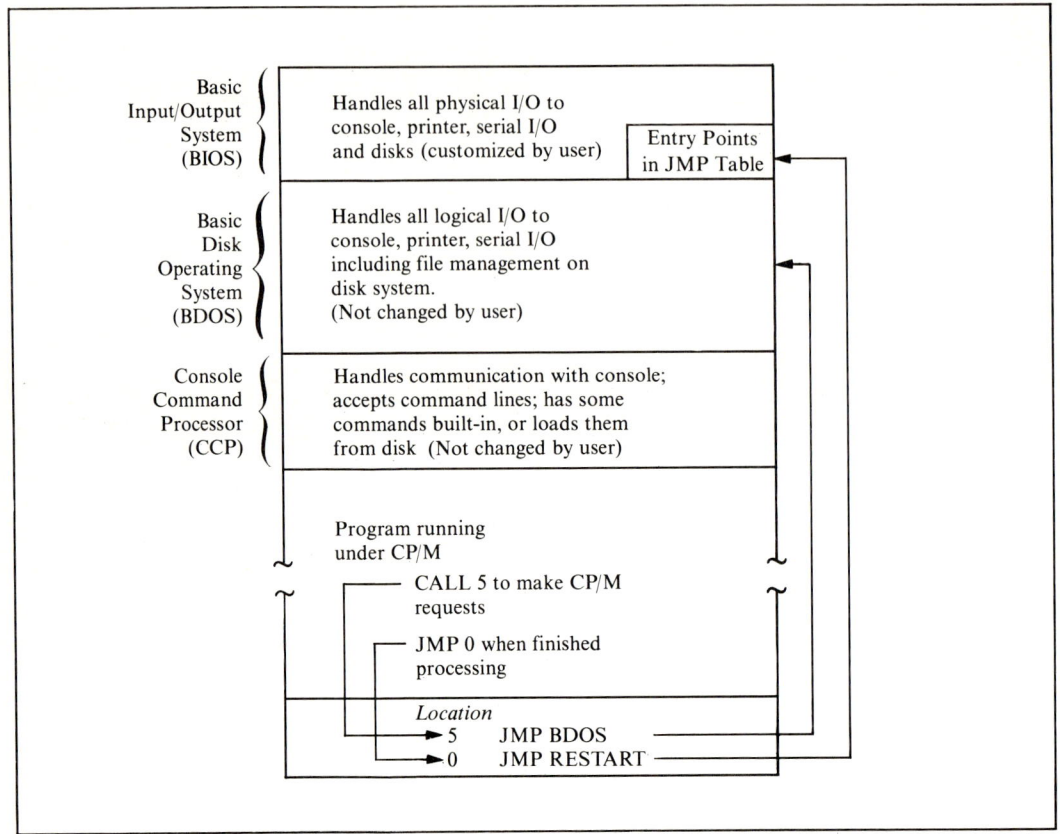

Figure 2-4.   CP/M's functional breakdown

How CP/M Views the Disk
The Making of a File
Disk Definition Tables
File Organizations

The CP/M File System

This chapter gives you a close look at the CP/M file system. The Basic Disk Operating System (BDOS) is responsible for this file system: It keeps a directory of the files on disk, noting where data are actually stored on the disk. Because the file system automatically keeps track of this information, you can ignore the details of which tracks and sectors on the disk have data for a given file.

How CP/M Views the Disk

To manage files on the disk, CP/M works with the disk in logical terms rather than in physical terms of tracks and sectors. CP/M treats the disk as three major areas.

These are the *reserved area*, which contains the bootstrap program and CP/M itself; the *file directory*, containing one or more entries for each file stored on the disk; and the *data storage area*, which occupies the remainder of the disk. You will be looking at how CP/M allocates the storage to the files as your programs create them.

The Basic Input/Output System (BIOS) has built-in tables that tell CP/M the respective sizes of the three areas. These are the *disk definition tables*, described later in this chapter.

Allocation Blocks

Rather than work with individual 128-byte sectors, CP/M joins several of these sectors logically to form an allocation block. Typically, an allocation block will contain eight 128-byte sectors (which makes it 1024 or 1K bytes long). This makes for easier disk manipulation because the magnitude of the numbers involved is reduced. For example, a standard 8-inch, single-density, single-sided floppy disk has 1950 128-byte sectors; hard disks may have 120,000 or more. By using allocation blocks that view the disk eight sectors at a time, the number of storage units to be managed is substantially reduced. The total number is important because numeric information is handled as 16-bit integers on the 8080 and Z80 microprocessors, and therefore the largest unsigned number possible is 0FFFFH (65,535 or 64K decimal).

Whenever CP/M refers to a specific allocation block, all that is needed is a simple number. The first allocation block is number 0, the next is number 1, and so on, up to the total remaining capacity of the disk.

The typical allocation block contains 1024 (1K) bytes, or eight 128-byte sectors. For the larger hard disks, the allocation block can be 16,384 (16K) bytes, which is 128 128-byte sectors. CP/M is given the allocation via an entry in the disk definition tables in the BIOS.

The size of the allocation block is not arbitrary, but it is a compromise. The originator of the working BIOS for the system—either the manufacturer or the operating system's designer—chooses the size by considering the total storage capacity of the disk. This choice is tempered by the fact that if a file is created with only a single byte of data in it, that file would be given a complete allocation block. Large allocation blocks can waste disk storage if there are many small files, but they can be useful when a few very large files are called for.

This can be seen better by considering the case of a 1K-byte allocation block. If you create a very small file containing just a single byte of data, you will have allocated an entire allocation block. The remaining 1023 bytes will not be used. You can use them by adding to the file, but when you first create this one-byte file, they will be just so much dead space. This is the problem: Each file on the disk will normally have one partly filled allocation block. If these blocks are very large, the amount of wasted (unused) space can be very large. With 16K-byte blocks, a 10-megabyte disk with only 3 megabytes of data on it could become logically full, with all allocation blocks allocated.

On the other hand, when you use large allocation blocks, CP/M's performance is significantly improved because the BDOS refers to the file directory less frequently. For example, it can read a 16K-byte file with only a single directory reference.

Therefore, when considering block allocation, keep the following questions in mind:

How big is the logical disk?
    With a larger disk, you can tolerate space wasted by incomplete allocation blocks.

What is the mean file size?
    If you anticipate many small files, use small allocation blocks so that you have a larger "supply" of blocks. If you anticipate a smaller number of large files, use larger allocation blocks to get faster file operations.

When a file is first created, it is assigned a single allocation block on the disk. Which block is assigned depends on what other files you already have on the disk and which blocks have already been allocated to them. CP/M maintains a table of which blocks are allocated and which are available. As the file accumulates more data, it will fill up the first allocation block. When this happens, CP/M will extend the file and allocate another block to it. Thus, as the file grows, it occupies more blocks. These blocks need not be adjacent to each other on the disk. The file can exist as a series of allocation blocks scattered all over the disk. However, when you need to see the entire file, CP/M presents the allocation blocks in the correct order. Thus, application programs can ignore allocation blocks. CP/M keeps track of which allocation blocks belong to each file through the file directory.

The File Directory

The *file directory* is sandwiched between the reserved area and the data storage area on the disk. The actual size of the directory is defined in the BIOS's disk definition tables. The directory can have some binary multiple of entries in it, with one or more entries for each file that exists on the disk. For a standard 8-inch floppy diskette, there will be room for 64 directory entries; for a hard disk, 1024 entries would not be unusual. Each directory entry is 32 bytes long.

Simple arithmetic can be used to calculate how much space the directory occupies on a standard floppy diskette. For example, for a floppy disk the formula is $64 \times 32 = 2048$ bytes = 2 allocation blocks of 1024 bytes each.

The directory entry contains the name of the file along with a list of the allocation blocks currently used by the file. Clearly, a single 32-byte directory entry cannot contain all of the allocation blocks necessary for a 5-megabyte file, especially since CP/M uses only 16 bytes of the 32-byte total for storage of allocation block numbers.

Extents

Often CP/M will need to control files that need many allocation blocks. It does this by creating more than one directory entry. Second and subsequent directory entries have the same file name as the first. One of the other bytes of the directory entry is used to indicate the directory entry sequence number. Each new directory entry brings with it a new supply of bytes that can be used to hold more allocation block numbers. In CP/M jargon, each directory entry is called an *extent*. Because the directory entry for each extent has 16 bytes for storing allocation block numbers, it can store either 16 one-byte numbers or 8 two-byte numbers. Therefore, the total number of allocation blocks possible in each extent is either 8 (for disks with more than 255 allocation blocks) or 16 (for smaller disks).

File Control Blocks

Before CP/M can do anything with a file, it has to have some control information in memory. This information is stored in a *file control block,* or FCB. The FCB has been described as a motel for directory entries—a place for them to reside when they are not at home on the disk. When operations on a file are complete, CP/M transforms the FCB back into a directory entry and rewrites it over the original entry. The FCB is discussed in detail at the end of this chapter.

As a summary, Figure 3-1 shows the relationships between disk sectors, allocation blocks, directory entries, and file control blocks.

The Making of a File

To reinforce what you already know about the CP/M file system, this section takes you on a "walk-through" of the events that occur when a program running under CP/M creates a file, writes data to it, and then *closes* the file.

Assume that a program has been loaded in memory and the CPU is about to start executing it. First, the program will declare space in memory for an FCB and will place some preset values there, the most important of which is the file name. The area in the FCB that will hold the allocation block numbers as they are assigned is initially filled with binary 0's. Because the first allocation block that is available for file data is block 1, an allocation block number of 0 will mean that no blocks have been allocated.

The program starts executing. It makes a call to the BDOS (via location 0005H) requesting that CP/M create a file. It transfers to the BDOS the address in memory of the FCB. The BDOS then locates an available entry in the directory, creates a new entry based on the FCB in the program, and returns to the program, ready to write data to the file. Note that CP/M makes no attempt to see if there is already a file of the same name on the disk. Therefore, most real-world programs precede a request to make a file with a request to delete any existing file of the same name.

The program now starts writing data to the file, 128-byte sector by 128-byte sector. CP/M does not have any provision for writing one byte at a time. It handles data sector-by-sector only, flushing sectors to the disk as they become full.

Chapter 3: The CP/M File System **21**

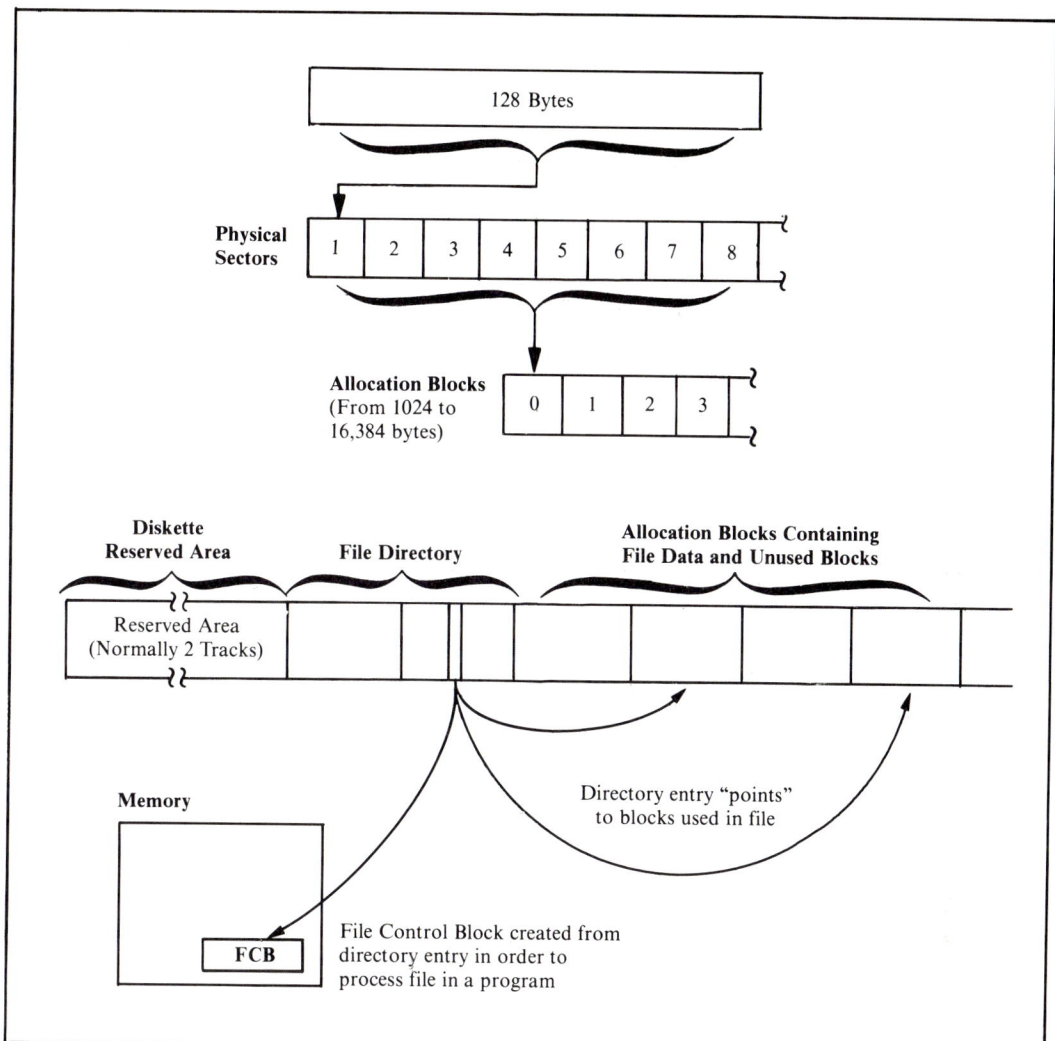

Figure 3-1. The hierarchical relationship between sectors, allocation blocks, directory entires, and FCBs

The first time a program asks CP/M (via a BDOS request) to write a sector onto the file on the disk, the BDOS finds an unused allocation block and assigns it to the file. The number of the allocation block is placed inside the FCB in memory. As each allocation block is filled up, a new allocation block is found and assigned, and its number is added to the list of allocation blocks inside the FCB. Finally, when the FCB has no more room for allocation block numbers, the BDOS

- Writes an updated directory entry out to the disk.

- Seeks out the next spare entry in the directory.
- Resets the FCB in memory to indicate that it is now working on the second extent of the file.
- Clears out the allocation block area in the FCB and waits for the next sector from the program.

Thus the process continues. New extents are automatically opened until the program determines that it is time to finish, writes the last sector out to the disk, and makes a BDOS request to close the file. The BDOS then converts the FCB into a final directory entry and writes to the directory.

Directory Entry

The directory consists of a series of 32-byte entries with one or more entries for each file on the disk. The total number of entries is a binary multiple. The actual number depends on the disk format (it will be 64 for a standard floppy disk and perhaps 2048 for a hard disk).

Figure 3-2 shows the detailed structure of a directory entry. Note that the description is actually Intel 8080 source code for the data definitions you would need in order to manipulate a directory entry. It shows a series of EQU instructions—*equate* instructions, used to assign values or expressions to a label, and in this case used to access an entry. It also shows a series of DS or *define storage* instructions used to declare storage for an entry. The comments on each line describe the function of each of the fields. Where data elements are less than a byte long, the comment identifies which bits are used.

As you study Figure 3-2, you will notice some terminology that as yet has not been discussed. This is described in detail in the sections that follow.

File User Number (Byte 0) The least significant (low order) four bits of byte 0 in the directory entry contain a number in the range 0 to 15. This is the *user number* in which the file belongs. A better name for this field would have been file group number. It works like this: Suppose several users are sharing a computer system with a hard disk that cannot be removed from the system without a lot of trouble. How can each user be sure not to tamper with other users' files? One simple way would be for each to use individual initials as the first characters of any file names. Then each could tell at a glance whether a file was another's and avoid doing anything to anyone else's files. A drawback of this scheme is that valuable character positions would be used in the file name, not to mention the problems resulting if several users had the same initials.

The file user number is prefixed to each file name and can be thought of as part of the name itself. When CP/M is first brought up, User 0 is the default user—the one that will be chosen unless another is designated. Any files created will go into the directory bearing the user number of 0. These files are referred to as being in user area 0. However, with a shared computer system, arrangements must be made for multiple user areas. The USER command makes this possible. User numbers and areas can range from 0 through 15. For example, a user in area 7 would not be able to get a directory of, access, or erase files in user area 5.

This user-number byte serves a second purpose. If this byte is set to a value of 0E5H, CP/M considers that the file directory entry has been deleted and completely ignores the remaining 31 bytes of data. The number 0E5H was not chosen whimsically. When IBM first defined the standard for floppy diskettes, they chose the binary pattern 11100101 (0E5H) as a good test pattern. A new floppy diskette formatted for use has nothing but bytes of 0E5H on it. Thus, the process of erasing a file is a "logical" deletion, where only the first byte of the directory entry is changed to 0E5H. If you accidentally delete a file (and provided that no other directory activity has occurred) it can be resurrected by simply changing this first byte back to a reasonable user number. This process will be explained in Chapter 11.

File Name and Type (Bytes 1 - 8 and 9 - 11)   As you can see from Figure 3-2, the file name in a directory entry is eight bytes long; the file type is three. These two fields are used to name a file unambiguously. A file name can be less than eight characters and the file type less than three, but in these cases, the unused character positions are filled with spaces.

Whenever file names and file types are written together, they are separated by a period. You do not need the period if you are not using the file type (which is the same as saying that the file type is all spaces). Some examples of file names are

```
READ. ME
LONGNAME.TYP
1
1.2
```

```
0000 =          FDE$USER        EQU     0       ;File user number (LS 4 bits)
0001 =          FDE$NAME        EQU     1       ;File name (8 bytes)
0009 =          FDE$TYP         EQU     9       ;File type
                                                ;Offsets for bits used in type
0009 =          FDE$RO          EQU     9       ;Bit 7 = 1 - Read only
000A =          FDE$SYS         EQU     10      ;Bit 7 = 1 - System status
000B =          FDE$CHANGE      EQU     11      ;Bit 7 = 0 = File Written To
                                                ;
000C =          FDE$EXTENT      EQU     12      ;Extent number
                                                ;13, 14 reserved for CP/M
000F =          FDE$RECUSED     EQU     15      ;Records used in this extent
0010 =          FDE$ABUSED      EQU     16      ;Allocation blocks used
                ;
                ;
                ;
0000            FD$USER:        DS              ;File user number
0001            FD$NAME:        DS      8       ;File name
0009            FD$TYP:         DS      3       ;File type
000C            FD$EXTENT:      DS      1       ;Extent
000D            FD$RESV:        DS      2       ;Reserved for CP/M
000F            FD$RECUSED:     DS      1       ;Records used in this extent
0010            FD$ABUSED:      DS      16      ;Allocation blocks used
```

Figure 3-2.   Data declarations for CP/M's file directory entries

A file name and type can contain the characters A through Z, 0 through 9, and some of the so-called "mark" characters such as "/" and "—". You can also use lowercase letters, but be careful. When you enter commands into the system using the CCP, it converts all lowercases to uppercases, so it will never be able to find files that actually have lowercase letters in their directory entries. Avoid using the "mark" characters excessively. Ones you can use are

! @ # $ % ( ) — + /

Characters that you must not use are

< > . , ; : = ? * [ ]

These characters are used by CP/M in normal command lines, so using them in file names will cause problems.

You can use odd characters in file names to your advantage. For example, if you create files with nongraphic characters in their names or types, the only way you can access these files will be from within programs. You cannot manipulate these files from the keyboard except by using ambiguous file names (described in the next section). This makes it more difficult to erase files accidentally since you cannot specify their names directly from the console.

Ambiguous File Names   CP/M has the capability to refer to one or more file names by using special "wild card" characters in the file names. The "?" is the main wildcard character. Whenever you ask CP/M to do something related to files, it will match a "?" with any character it finds in the file name. In the extreme case, a file name and type of "????????.???" will match with any and all file names.

As another example, all the chapters of this book were held in files called "CHAP1.DOC," "CHAP2.DOC," and so on. They were frequently referred to, however, as "CHAP??.DOC." Why two question marks? If only one had been used, for example, "CHAP?.DOC," CP/M would not have been able to match this with "CHAP10.DOC" nor any other chapter with two digits. The matching that CP/M does is strictly character-by-character.

Because typing question marks can be tedious and special attention must be paid to the exact number entered, a convenient shorthand is available. The asterisk character "*" can be used to mean "as many ?'s as you need to fill out the name or the type field." Thus, "????????.???" can be written "*.*" and "CHAP??.DOC" could also be rewritten "CHAP*.DOC."

The use of "*" is allowed only when you are entering file names from the console. The question mark notation, however, can be used for certain BDOS operations, with the file name and type field in the FCB being set to the "?" as needed.

File Type Conventions   Although you are at liberty to think up file names without constraint, file types are subject to convention and, in one or two cases, to the mandate of CP/M itself.

The types that will cause problems if you do not use them correctly are

.ASM
    Assembly language source for the ASM program

.MAC
    Macro assembly language

.HEX
    Hexadecimal file output by assemblers

.REL
    Relocatable file output by assemblers

.COM
    Command file executed by entering its name alone

.PRN
    Print file written to disk as a convenience

.LIB
    Library file of programs

.SUB
    Input for CP/M SUBMIT utility program

Examples of conventional file types are

.C
    C source code

.PAS
    Pascal source code

.COB
    COBOL source code

.FTN
    FORTRAN source code

.APL
    APL programs

.TXT
    Text files

.DOC
    Documentation files

.INT
    Intermediate files

.DTA
    Data files

.IDX
   Index files

.$$$
   Temporary files

The file type is also useful for keeping several copies of the same file, for example, "TEST.001," "TEST.002," and so on.

File Status   Each one of the states *Read-Only, System,* and *File Changed* requires only a single bit in the directory entry. To avoid using unnecessary space, they have been slotted into the three bytes used for the file type field. Since these bytes are stored as characters in ASCII (which is a seven-bit code), the most significant bit is not used for the file type and thus is available to show status.

Bit 7 of byte 9 shows Read-Only status. As its name implies, if a file is set to be Read-Only, CP/M will not allow any data to be written to the file or the file to be deleted.

If a file is declared to be System status (bit 7 of byte 10), it will not show up when you display the file directory. Nor can the file be copied from one place to another with standard CP/M utilities such as PIP unless you specifically ask the utility to do so. In normal practice, you should set your standard software tools and application programs to be both Read-Only and System status/Read-Only, so that you cannot accidentally delete them, and System status, so that they do not clutter up the directory display.

The File Changed bit (bit 7 of byte 11) is always set to 0 when you close a file to which you have been writing. This can be useful in conjunction with a file backup utility program that sets this bit to 1 whenever it makes a backup copy. Just by scanning the directory, this utility program can determine which files have changed since it was last run. The utility can be made to back up only those files that have changed. This is much easier than having to remember which files you have changed since you last made backup copies.

With a floppy disk system, there is less need to worry about backing up on a file-by-file basis—it is just as easy to copy the whole diskette. This system is useful, however, with a hard disk system with hundreds of files stored on the disk.

File Extent (Byte 12)   Each directory entry represents a file extent. Byte 12 in the directory entry identified the extent number. If you have a file of less than 16,384 bytes, you will need only one extent—number 0. If you write more information to thie file, more extents will be needed. The extent number increases by 1 as each new extent is created.

The extent number is stored in the file directory because the directory entries are in random sequence. The BDOS must do a sequential search from the top of the directory to be sure of finding any given extent of a file. If the directory is large, as it could be on a hard disk system, this search can take several seconds.

Reserved Bytes 13 and 14 These bytes are used by the proprietary parts of CP/M's file system. From your point of view, they will be set to 0.

Record Number (Byte 15) Byte 15 contains a count of the number of records (128-byte sectors) that have been used in the last partially filled allocation block referenced in this directory entry. Since CP/M creates a file sequentially, only the most recently allocated block is not completely full.

Disk Map (Bytes 16 - 31) Bytes 16–31 store the allocation block numbers used by each extent. There are 16 bytes in this area. If the total number of allocation blocks (as defined by you in the BIOS disk tables) is less than 256, this area can hold as many as 16 allocation block numbers. If you have described the disk as having more than 255 allocation blocks, CP/M uses this area to store eight two-byte values. In this case allocation blocks can take on much larger values.

A directory entry can store either 8 or 16 allocation block numbers. If the file has not yet expanded to require this total number of allocation blocks, the unused positions in the entry are filled with zeros. You may think this would create a problem because it appears that several files will have been allocated block 0 over and over. In fact, there is no problem because the file directory itself always occupies block 0 (and depending on its size several of the blocks following). For all practical purposes, block 0 "does not exist," at least for the storage of file data.

Note that if, by accident, the relationship between files and their allocation blocks is scrambled—that is, either the data in a given block is overwritten, or two or more active directory entries contain the same block number—CP/M cannot access information properly and the disk becomes worthless.

Several commercially available utility programs manipulate the directory. You can use them to inspect and change a damaged directory, reviving accidentally erased files if you need to. There are other utilities you can use to logically remove bad sectors on the disk. These utilities find the bad areas, work backward from the track and sector numbers, and compute the allocation block in which the error occurs. Once the block numbers are known, they create a dummy file, either in user area 15 or, in some cases, in an "impossible" user area (one greater than 15), that appears to "own" all the bad allocation blocks.

A good utility program protects the integrity of the directory by verifying that each allocation block is "owned" by only one directory entry.

Disk Definition Tables

As mentioned previously, the BIOS contains tables telling the BDOS how to view the disk storage devices that are part of the computer system. These tables are built *by you*. If you are using standard 8-inch, single-sided, single-density floppy diskettes, you can use the examples in the Digital Research manual *CP/M 2 Alteration Guide*. But if you are using some other, more complex system, you must make some careful judgments. Any mistakes in the *disk definition tables* can create serious problems, especially when you try to correct diskettes created using the erroneous tables. You, as a programmer, must ensure the correctness of the tables by being careful.

One other point before looking at table structures: Because the tables exist and define a particular disk "shape" does not mean that such a disk need necessarily be connected to the system. The tables describe *logical* disks, and there is no way for the physical hardware to check whether your disk tables are correct. You may have a computer system with a single hard disk, yet describe the disk as though it were divided into several *logical* disks. CP/M will view each such "disk" independently, and they should be thought of as separate disks.

Disk Parameter Header Table

This table is the starting point in the disk definition tables. It is the topmost structure and contains nothing but the addresses of other structures. There is one entry in this table for each logical disk that you choose to describe. There is an entry point in the BIOS that returns the address of the parameter header table for a specific logical disk.

An example of the code needed to define a disk parameter header table is shown in Figure 3-3.

Sector Skewing (Skewtable)   To define sector *skewing,* also called sector *interlacing,* picture a diskette spinning in a disk drive. The sectors in the track over which the head is positioned are passing by the head one after another—sector 1, sector 2, and so on—until the diskette has turned one complete revolution. Then the sequence repeats. A standard 8-inch diskette has 26 sectors on each track, and the disk spins at 360 rpm. One turn of the diskette takes 60/360 seconds, about 166 milliseconds per track, or 6 milliseconds per sector.

Now imagine CP/M loading a program from such a diskette. The BDOS takes a finite amount of time to read and process each sector since it reads only a single sector at a time. It has to make repeated reads to load a program. By the time the BDOS has read and loaded sector n, it will be too late to read sector n+1. This sector will have already passed by the head and will not come around for another 166 milliseconds. Proceeding in this fashion, almost 4½ seconds are needed to read one complete track.

This problem can be solved by simply numbering the sectors *logically* so that there are several physical sectors between each logical sector. This procedure, called *sector skewing* or *interlace,* is shown in Figure 3-4. Note that unlike physical sectors, logical sectors are numbered from 0 to 25.

Figure 3-4 shows the standard CP/M sector interlace for 8-inch, single-sided, single-density floppy diskettes. You see that logical sector 0 has six sectors between

```
                DPBASE:                         ;Base of the parameter header
                                                ; (used to access the headers)
    0000 1000           DW      SKEWTABLE       ;Pointer to logical-to-physical
                                                ; sector conversion table
    0002 0000           DW      0               ;Scratch pad areas used by CP/M
    0004 0000           DW      0
    0006 0000           DW      0
    0008 2A00           DW      DIRBUF          ;Pointer to Directory Buffer
                                                ; work area
    000A AA00           DW      DPB0            ;Pointer to disk parameter block
    000C B900           DW      WACD            ;Pointer to work area (used to
                                                ; check for changed diskettes)
    000E C900           DW      ALVEC0          ;Pointer to allocation vector
                ;
                ;
                ;       The following equates would normally be derived from
                ;       values found in the disk parameter Block.
                ;       They are shown here only for the sake of completeness.
                ;
    003F =      NODE    EQU     63              ;Number of directory entries 1
    00F2 =      NOAB    EQU     242             ;Number of allocation blocks
                ;
                ;       Example data definitions for those objects pointed
                ;       to by the disk parameter header
                ;
                SKEWTABLE:                      ;Sector skew table.
                                                ; Indexed by logical sector
    0010 01070D13       DB      01,07,13,19     ;Logical sectors 0,1,2,3
    0014 19050B11       DB      25,05,11,17     ;4,5,6,7
    0018 1703090F       DB      23,03,09,15     ;8,9,10,11
    001C 1502080E       DB      21,02,08,14     ;12,13,14,15
    0020 141A060C       DB      20,26,06,12     ;16,17,18,19
    0024 1218040A       DB      18,24,04,10     ;20,21,22,23
    0028 1016           DB      16,22           ;24,25
                ;
    002A        DIRBUF: DS      128             ;Directory buffer
    00AA        DPB0:   DS      15              ;Disk parameter block
                                                ;This is normally a table of
                                                ; constants.
                                                ;A dummy definition is shown
                                                ; here
    00B9        WACD:   DS      (NODE+1)/4      ;Work area to check directory
                                                ;Only used for removable media
    00C9        ALVEC0: DS      (NOAB/8)+1      ;Allocation vector #0
                                                ;Needs 1 bit per allocation
                                                ; block
```

Figure 3-3. Data declarations for a disk parameter header

it and logical sector 1. There is a similar gap between each of the logical sectors, so that there are six "sector times" (about 38 milliseconds) between two adjacent logical sectors. This gives ample time for the software to access each sector. However, several revolutions of the disk are still necessary to read every sector in turn. In Figure 3-4, the vertical columns of logical sectors show which sectors are read on each successive revolution of the diskette.

The wrong interlace can strongly affect performance. It is not a gradual effect, either; if you "miss" the interlace, the perceived performance will be very slow. In the example given here, six turns of the diskette are needed to read the whole track — this lasts one second as opposed to 4½ without any interlacing. But don't imagine that you can change the interlace with impunity; files written with one interlace stay that way. You must be sure to read them back with the same interlace with which they were written.

30 The CP/M Programmer's Handbook

Some disk controllers can simplify this procedure. When you format the diskette, they can write the sector addresses onto the diskette with the interlace already built in. When CP/M requests sector n, the controller's electronics wait until they see the requested sector's header fly by. They then initiate the read or write operation. In this case you can embed the interlace right into the formatting of the diskette.

Because the wrong interlace gives terrible performance, it is easy to know when you have the right one. Some programmers use the time required to format a diskette as the performance criterion to optimize the interlace. This is not good practice because under normal circumstances you will spend very little time formatting diskettes. The time spent loading a program would be a better arbiter, since far more time is spent doing this. You might argue that doing a file update would be even more representative, but most updates produce slow and sporadic disk activity. This kind of disk usage is not suitable for setting the correct interlace.

Hard disks do not present any problem for sector skewing. They spin at 3600 rpm or faster, and at that speed there simply is no interlace that will help. Some

Physical Sector	Logical Sector					
	Pass 1	Pass 2	Pass 3	Pass 4	Pass 5	Pass 6
1	0					
2				13		
3			9			
4						22
5		5				
6					18	
7	1					
8				14		
9			10			
10						23
11		6				
12					19	
13	2					
14				15		
15			11			
16						24
17		7				
18					20	
19	3					
20				16		
21			12			
22						25
23		8				
24					21	
25	4					
26				17		

NOTE: Additional sector between logical sectors 12 and 13

Figure 3-4.   Physical to logical sector skewing

tricks can be played to improve the performance of a hard disk—these will be discussed in the section called "Special Considerations for Hard Disks," later in this chapter.

To better understand these theories, study an example of the standard interlace table, or *skewtable*. Bear in mind that the code that will access this table will first be given a *logical* sector. It will then have to return the appropriate *physical* sector.

Figure 3-5 shows the code for the skew table and the code that can be used to access the table. The table is indexed by a logical sector and the corresponding table entry is the physical sector. You can see that the code assumes that the first *logical* sector assigned by CP/M will be sector number 0. Hence there is no need to subtract 1 from the sector number before using it as a table subscript.

Unused Areas in the Disk Parameter Header Table The three words shown as 0's in Figure 3-3 are used by CP/M as temporary variables during disk operations.

Directory Buffer (DIRBUF) The *directory buffer* is a 128-byte area used by CP/M to store a sector from the directory while processing directory entries. You only need one directory buffer; it can be shared by all of the logical disks in the system.

Disk Parameter Block (DPB0) The *disk parameter block* describes the particular characteristics of each logical disk. In general, you will need a separate parameter block for each *type* of logical disk. Logical disks can share a parameter block only if their

```
                    SKEWTABLE:                      ;Logical sector
      0000 01070D13         DB      01,07,13,19    ;0,1,2,3
      0004 19050B11         DB      25,05,11,17    ;4,5,6,7
      0008 1703090F         DB      23,03,09,15    ;8,9,10,11
      000C 1502080E         DB      21,02,08,14    ;12,13,14,15
      0010 141A060C         DB      20,26,06,12    ;16,17,18,19
      0014 1218040A         DB      18,24,04,10    ;20,21,22,23
      0018 1016             DB      16,22          ;24,25
                    ;
                    ;
                    ;       The code to translate logical sectors to physical
                    ;         sectors is as follows:
                    ;
                    ;       On entry, the logical sector will be transferred from
                    ;       CP/M as a 16-bit value in registers BC.
                    ;       CP/M also transfers the address of the skew table
                    ;       in registers DE (it finds the skew table by looking in
                    ;       the disk parameter header entry).
                    ;
                    ;       On return, the physical sector will be placed
                    ;       in registers HL.
                    ;
                    SECTRAN:
      001A EB               XCHG                   ;HL -> skew table base address
      001B 09               DAD     B              ;HL -> physical sector
                                                   ;       entry in skew table
      001C 6E               MOV     L,M            ;L = physical sector
      001D 60               MOV     H,0            ;HL = Physical Sector
      001E C9               RET                    ;Return to BDOS
```

Figure 3-5. Data declarations for the standard skewtable for standard diskettes

characteristics are identical. You can, for example, use a single parameter block to describe all of the single-sided, single-density diskette drives that you have in the system. However, you would need another parameter block to describe double-sided, double-density diskette drives. It is also rare to be able to share parameter blocks when a physical hard disk is split up into several logical disks. You will understand why after looking at the contents of a parameter block, described later in this chapter.

Work Area to Check for Changed Diskettes (WACD)   One of the major problems that CP/M faces when working with removable media such as floppy diskettes is that the computer operator, without any warning, can open the diskette drive and substitute a different diskette. On early versions of CP/M, this resulted in the newly inserted diskette being overwritten with data from the original diskette.

With the current version of CP/M, you can request that CP/M check if the diskette has been changed. Given this request, CP/M examines the directory entries whenever it has worked on the directory and, if it detects that the diskette has been changed, declares the whole diskette to be Read-Only status and inhibits any further writing to the diskette. This status will be in effect until the next warm boot operation occurs. A warm boot occurs whenever a program terminates or a CONTROL-C is entered to the CCP, resetting the operating system.

The value of WACD is the address of a buffer, or temporary storage area, that CP/M can use to check the directory. The length of this buffer is defined (somewhat out of place) in the disk parameter block.

Allocation Vector (ALVEC0)   CP/M views each disk as a set of allocation blocks, assigning blocks to individual files as those files are created or expanded, and relinquishing blocks as files are deleted.

CP/M needs some mechanism for keeping track of which blocks are used and which are free. It uses the *allocation vector* to form a *bit map*, with each bit in the map corresponding to a specific allocation block. The most significant bit (bit 7) in the first byte corresponds to the first allocation block, number 0. Bit 6 corresponds to block 1, and so on for the entire disk.

Whenever you request CP/M to use a logical disk, CP/M will *log in* the disk. This consists of reading down the file directory and, for each active entry or extent, interacting with the allocation blocks "owned" by that particular file extent. For each block number in the extent, the corresponding bit in the allocation vector is set to 1. At the end of this process, the allocation vector will accurately represent a map of which blocks are in use and which are free.

When CP/M goes looking for an unused allocation block, it tries to find one near the last one used, to keep the file from becoming too fragmented.

In order to reserve enough space for the allocation vector, you need to reserve one bit for each allocation block. Computing the number of allocation blocks is discussed in the section "Maximum Allocation Block Number," later in this chapter.

Disk Parameter Block

The *disk parameter block* in early versions of CP/M was built into the BDOS and was a closely guarded secret of the CP/M file system. To make CP/M adaptable to hard disk systems, Digital Research decided to move the parameter blocks out into the BIOS where everyone could adapt them. Because of the proprietary nature of CP/M's file system, you will still see several odd-looking fields, and you may find the explanation given here somewhat superficial. However, the lack of explanation in no way detracts from your ability to use CP/M as a tool.

Figure 3-6 shows the code necessary to define a parameter block for 8-inch, single-sided diskettes. This table is pointed to by—that is, its address is given in—an entry in the disk parameter header. Each of the entries shown in the disk parameter block is explained in the following sections.

Sectors Per Track This is the number of 128-byte sectors per track. The standard diskette shown in the example has 26 sectors. As you can see, simply telling CP/M that there are 26 sectors per track does not indicate whether the first sector is numbered 0 or 1. CP/M assumes that the first sector is 0; it is left to a sector translate subroutine to decipher which physical sector this corresponds to.

Hard disks normally have sector sizes larger than 128 bytes. This is discussed in the section on considerations for hard disks.

Block Shift, Block Mask, and Extent Mask These mysteriously named fields are used internally by CP/M during disk file operations. The values that you specify for them depend primarily on the size of the allocation block that you want.

Allocation block size can vary from 1024 bytes (1K) to 16,384 bytes (16K). There is a distinct trade-off between these two extremes, as discussed in the section on allocation blocks at the beginning of this chapter.

An allocation block size of 1024 (1K) bytes is suggested for floppy diskettes with capacities up to 1 megabyte, and a block size of 4096 (4K) bytes for larger floppy or hard disks.

```
           DPB0:
0000 1A00        DW    26              ;Sectors per track
0002 03          DB    3               ;Block shift
0003 07          DB    7               ;Block mask
0004 03          DB    3               ;Extent mask
0005 F200        DW    242             ;Max. allocation block number
0007 3F00        DW    63              ;Number of directory entries 1
0009 C0          DB    1100$0000B      ;Bit map for allocation blocks
000A 00          DB    0000$0000B      ; used for directory
000B 1000        DW    16              ;No. of bytes in dir. check buffer
000D 0200        DW    2               ;No. of tracks before directory
```

Figure 3-6. Data declarations for the disk parameter block for standard diskettes

If you can define which block size you wish to use, you can now select the values for the block shift and the block mask from Table 3-1.

Table 3-1. Block Shift and Mask Value

Allocation Block Size	Block Shift	Block Mask
1,024	3	7
2,048	4	15
4,096	5	31
8,192	6	63
16,384	7	127

Select your required allocation block size from the left-hand column. This tells you which values of block shift and mask to enter into the disk parameter block.

The last of these three variables, the *extent mask,* depends not only on the block size but also on the total storage capacity of the logical disk. This latter consideration is only important for computing whether or not there will be fewer than 256 allocation blocks on the logical disk. Just divide the chosen allocation block size into the capacity of the logical disk and check whether you will have fewer than 256 blocks.

Keeping this answer and the allocation block size in mind, refer to Table 3-2 for the appropriate value for the extent mask field of the parameter block. Select the appropriate line according to the allocation block size you have chosen. Then, depending on the total number of allocation blocks in the logical disk, select the extent mask from the appropriate column.

Table 3-2. Extent Mask Value

Allocation Block Size	Number of Allocation Blocks	
	1 to 255	256 and Above
1,024	0	(Impossible)
2,048	1	0
4,096	3	1
8,192	7	3
16,384	15	7

Maximum Allocation Block Number This value is the *number* of the last allocation block in the logical disk. As the first block number is 0, this value is *one less* than the total number of allocation blocks on the disk. Where only a partial allocation block exists, the number of blocks is rounded down.

Figure 3-7 has an example for standard 8-inch, single-sided, single-density diskettes. Note that CP/M uses two reserved tracks on this diskette format.

Number of Directory Entries Minus 1   Do not confuse this entry with the number of files that can be stored on the logical disk; it is only the number of *entries* (minus one). Each extent of each file takes one directory entry, so very large files will consume several entries. Also note that the value in the table is *one less* than the number of entries.

On a standard 8-inch diskette, the value is 63 entries. On a hard disk, you may want to use 1023 or even 2047. Remember that CP/M performs a sequential scan down the directory and this takes a noticeable amount of time. Therefore, you should balance the number of logical disks with your estimate of the largest file size that you wish to support.

As a final note, make sure to choose a number of entries that fits evenly into one or more allocation blocks. Each directory entry needs 32 bytes, so you can compute the number of bytes required. Make sure this number can be divided by your chosen allocation block size without a remainder.

Allocation Blocks for the Directory   This is a strange value; it is not a number, but a bit map. Looking at Figure 3-6, you see the example value written out in full as a binary value to illustrate how this value is defined. This 16-bit value has a bit set to 1 for each allocation block that is to be used for the file directory.

This value is derived from the number of directory entries you want to have on the disk and the size of the allocation block you want to use. One given, or

Physical characteristics:		Calculate:	
77	Tracks/Diskette	77	Tracks/Diskette
26	Sectors/Track	− 2	Tracks Reserved for CP/M
128	Bytes/Sector	75	Tracks for File Storage
2	Tracks Reserved for CP/M	×26	Number of Sectors
1024	Bytes/Allocation Block	1950	Sectors for File Storage
		×128	Bytes per Sector
		249,600	Bytes for File Storage
		÷1024	Bytes/Allocation Block
		243.75	Total Number of Allocation Blocks
		242	Number of the last allocation block (rounded and based on first block being Block 0)

Figure 3-7.   Computing the maximum allocation block number for standard diskettes

constant, in this derivation is that the size of each directory entry is 32 bytes.

In the example, 64 entries are required (remember the number shown is one less than the required value). Each entry has 32 bytes. The total number of bytes required for the directory thus is 64 times 32, or 2048 bytes. Dividing this by the allocation block size of 1024 indicates that two allocation blocks must be reserved for the directory. You can see that the example value shows this by setting the two most significant bits of the 16-bit value.

As a word of warning, do not be tempted to declare this value using a DW (define word) pseudo-operation. Doing so will store the value *byte-reversed*.

Size of Buffer for Directory Checking   As mentioned before in the discussion of the disk parameter header, CP/M can be requested to check directory entries whenever it is working on the directory. In order to do this, CP/M needs a buffer area, called the *work area to check for changed diskettes,* or WACD, in which it can hold working variables that keep a compressed record of what is on the directory. The length of this buffer area is kept in the disk parameter block; its address is specified in the parameter header. Because CP/M keeps a compressed record of the directory, you need only provide one byte for every four directory entries. You can see in Figure 3-6 that 16 bytes are specified to keep track of the 64 directory entries.

Number of Tracks Before the Directory   Figure 3-8 shows the layout of CP/M on a standard floppy diskette. You will see that the first two tracks are reserved, containing the initial bootstrap code and CP/M itself. Hence the example in Figure 3-6, giving the code for a standard floppy disk, shows two reserved tracks (the number of tracks before the directory).

This *track offset value*, as it is sometimes called, provides a convenient method of dividing a physical disk into several logical disks.

Special Considerations for Hard Disks

If you want to run CP/M on a hard disk, you must provide code and build tables that make CP/M work as if it were running on a very large floppy disk. You must even include 128-byte sectors. However, this is not difficult to do.

To adapt hard disks to the 128-byte sector size, you must provide code in the disk driver in your BIOS that will present the illusion of reading and writing 128-byte sectors even though it is really working on sectors of 512 bytes. This code is called the *blocking/deblocking* routine.

If hard disks have sector sizes other than 128 bytes, what of the number of sectors per track, and the number of tracks?

Hard disks come in all sizes. The situation is further confused by the disk controllers, the hardware that controls the disk. In many cases, you can think of the hard disk as just a series of sectors without any tracks at all. The controller, given a *relative* sector number by the BIOS, can translate this sector number into which track, read/write head (if there is more than one platter), and sector are actually being referenced.

Chapter 3: The CP/M File System **37**

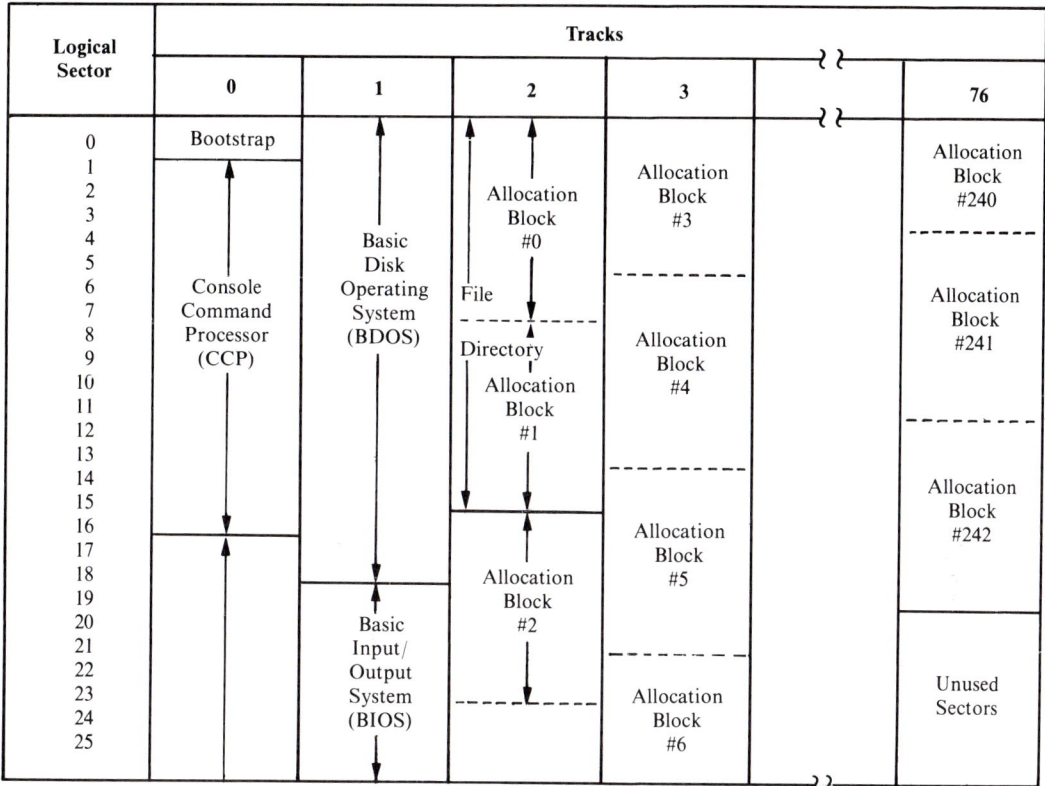

Figure 3-8. Layout of standard diskette

Furthermore, most hard disks rotate so rapidly that there is nothing to be gained by using a sector-skewing algorithm. There is just no way to read more than one physical sector per revolution; there is not enough time.

In many cases it is desirable to divide up a single, physical hard disk into several smaller, logical disks. This is done mainly for performance reasons: Several smaller disks, along with smaller directories, result in faster file operations.

The disk parameter header will have 0's for the skewtable entry and the pointer to the WACD buffer. In general, hard disks *cannot* be changed, at least not without turning off the power and swapping the entire disk drive. If you are using one of the new generation of removable hard disks, you will need to use the directory checking feature of CP/M.

The disk parameter block for a hard disk will be quite different from that used for a floppy diskette. The number of sectors per track needs careful consideration. Remember, this is the number of 128-byte sectors. The conversion from the physical sector size to 128-byte sectors will be done in the disk driver in the BIOS.

If you have a disk controller that works in terms of sectors and tracks, all you need do is compute the number of 128-byte sectors on each track. Multiply the number of physical sectors per track by their size in bytes and then divide the product by 128 to give the result as the number of 128-byte sectors per physical track.

But what of those controllers that view their hard disks as a series of sectors without reference to tracks? They obscure the fact that the sectors are arranged on concentric tracks on the disk's surface. In this case, you can play a trick on CP/M. You can set the "sectors per track" value to the number of 128-byte sectors that will fit into one of the disk's physical sectors. To do this, divide the physical sector size by 128. For example, a 512-byte physical sector size will give an answer of four 128-byte sectors per "track." You can now view the hard disk as having as many "tracks" as there are physical sectors. By using this method, you avoid having to do any kind of arithmetic on CP/M's sector numbers; the "track" number to which CP/M will ask your BIOS to move the disk heads will be the *relative physical sector*. Once the controller has read this physical sector for you, you can look at the 128-byte sector number, which will be 0, 1, 2, or 3 (for a 512-byte physical sector) in order to select which 128 bytes need to be moved in or out of the disk buffer.

The block shift, block mask, and extent mask will be computed as before. Use a 4096-byte allocation block size. This will yield a value of 5 for the block shift, 31 for the block mask, and given that you will have more than 256 allocation blocks for each logical disk, an extent mask value of 1.

The maximum allocation block number will be computed as before. Keep clear in your mind whether you are working with the number of physical sectors (which will be larger than 128 bytes) or with 128-byte sectors when you are computing the storage capacity of each logical disk.

The number of directory entries (less 1) is best set to 511 for logical disks of 1 megabyte and either 1023 or 2047 for larger disks. Remember that under CP/M version 2 you cannot have a logical disk larger than 8 megabytes.

The allocation blocks for the directory are also computed as described for floppy disks.

As a rule, the size of the directory check buffer (WADC) will be set to 0, since there is no need to use this feature on hard disk systems with fixed media.

The number of tracks before the directory (track offset) can be used to divide up the physical disk into smaller logical disks, as shown in Figure 3-9.

There is no rule that says the tracks before a logical disk's directory cannot be used to contain other complete logical disks. You can see this in Figure 3-9. CP/M behaves as if each logical disk starts at track 0 (and indeed they do), but by specifying increasingly larger numbers of tracks before each directory, the logical disks can be staggered across the available space on the physical disk.

Figure 3-10 shows the calculations involved in the first phase of building disk parameter blocks for the hard disk shown in Figure 3-9. The physical characteristics are those imposed by the design of the hard disk. As a programmer, you do not have any control over these; however, you can choose how much of the physical

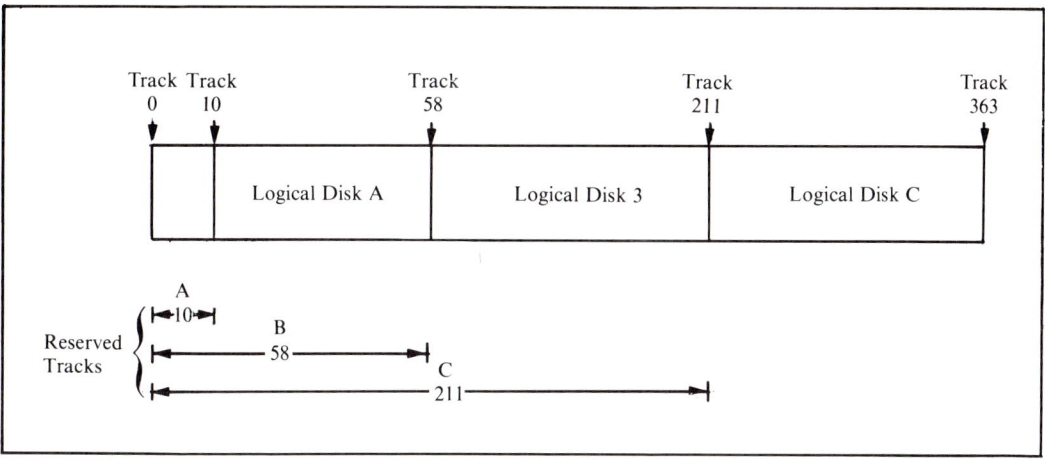

Figure 3-9. Dividing hard disks into logical disks

disk is assigned to each logical disk, the allocation block size, and the number of directory entries. You can see that logical disk A is much smaller than disks B and C, and that B and C are the same size. Disk A will be the systems disk from which most programs will be loaded, so its smaller directory size will make program loading much faster. The allocation block size for disk A is also smaller in order to reduce the amount of space wasted in partially filled allocation blocks.

Figure 3-10 also shows the calculations involved in computing the maximum allocation block number. Again, note that once the total number of allocation blocks has been computed, it is necessary to round it down in the case of any fractional components and then subtract 1 to get the maximum number (the first block being 0).

Figure 3-11 shows the actual values that will be put into the parameter blocks. It is assumed that the disk controller is one of those types that view the physical disk as a series of contiguous sectors and make no reference to tracks; the internal electronics and firmware in the controller take care of these details. For this reason, CP/M is told that each *physical* sector is a "track" in CP/M's terms. Each "track" has 512 bytes and can therefore store four 128-byte sectors. You can see this is the value that is in the sectors/"track" field.

The block shift and mask values are obtained from Table 3-1, using the allocation block size previously chosen. Then, with both the allocation block size and the maximum number of allocation blocks (see Figure 3-10), the extent mask can be obtained from Table 3-2. You can see in Figure 3-11 that extent mask values of 1 were obtained for all three logical disks even though two different allocation block sizes have been chosen, and even though disk A has less than 256 blocks and disks B and C have more.

40 The CP/M Programmer's Handbook

Physical Characteristics:		Calculate:		
364	Tracks/Disk			
20	Sectors/Track	**A:**	**B: and C:**	
512	Bytes/Sector	48	153	Tracks assigned to Disk
10,240	Bytes/Track	×10,240	×10,240	Bytes/Track
		491,520	1,566,720	Bytes/Disk
		÷ 2048	÷ 4096	Bytes/Allocation Block
Chosen Logical Characteristics:		240	382.5	Number of Allocation Blocks
		239	381	Maximum Block Number

	Tracks	Allocation Block Size
Reserved Area	10	n/a
Disk A:	48	2048
Disk B:	153	4096
Disk C:	153	4096

Figure 3-10. Computing the maximum allocation block number for a hard disk

```
DPBA:       DPBB:       DPBC:
  4           4           4         ;128-byte sectors/"track"
  4           5           5         ;Block shift
 15          31          31         ;Block mask
  1           1           1         ;Extent mask
239         381         381         ;Max. all. block #
255        1023        1023         ;No. of directory entries
11110000B 11111111B 11111111B       ;Bit Map for allocation blocks
00000000B 00000000B 00000000B       ; used for directory
  0           0           0         ;No. of bytes in dir.check buffer
 (10)       (58)        (211)       ;Actual tracks before directory
200        1160        4220         ;"Tracks" before directory
```

Figure 3-11. Disk parameter tables for a hard disk

The bit map showing how many allocation blocks are required to hold the file directory is computed by multiplying the number of directory entries by 32 and dividing the product by the allocation block size. This yields results of 4 for disk A and 8 for disks B and C. As you can see, the bit maps have the appropriate number of bits set.

Since most of the hard disks on the market today do not have removable media, the lengths of the directory checking buffer are set to 0.

The number of "tracks" before the directory requires a final touch of skullduggery. Having already indicated to CP/M that each "track" has four sectors, you need to continue in the same vein and express the number of real tracks before the directories in units of 512-byte physical sectors.

As a final note, if you are specifying these parameter blocks for a disk controller that requires you to communicate with it in terms of physical tracks and 128-byte sectors, then the number of sectors per track must be set to 80 (twenty

512-byte sectors per physical track). You would also have to change the number of tracks before the directory by stating the number of physical tracks (shown in parentheses on Figure 3-11).

Adding Additional Information to the Parameter Block

Normally, some additional information must be associated with each logical disk. For example, in a system that has several physical disks, you need to identify where each *logical* disk resides. You may also want to identify some other *physical* parameters, disk drive types, I/O port numbers, and addresses of driver subroutines.

You may be tempted to extend the disk parameter header entry because there is a separate header entry for each logical disk. But the disk parameter header is exactly 16 bytes long; adding more bytes makes the arithmetic that we need to use in the BIOS awkward. The best place to put these kinds of information is to *prefix* them to the front of each disk parameter block. The label at the front of the block must be left in the same place lest CP/M become confused. Only special additional code that you write will be "smart" enough to look *in front* of the block in order to find the additional parameter information.

File Organizations

CP/M supports two types of files: sequential and random. CP/M views both types as made up of a series of 128-byte *records*. Note that in CP/M's terms, a record is the same as a 128-byte sector. This terminology sometimes gets in the way. It may help to think of 128-byte sectors as *physical* records. Applications programs manipulate *logical* records that bear little or no relation to these physical records. There is code in the applications programs to manipulate logical records.

CP/M does not impose any restrictions on the contents of a file. In many cases, though, certain conventions are used when textual data is stored. Each line of text is terminated by ASCII CARRIAGE RETURN and LINE FEED. The last sector of a text file is filled with ASCII SUB characters; in hexadecimal this is 1AH.

File Control Blocks

In order to get CP/M to work on a file, you need to provide a structure in which both you and the BDOS can keep relevant details about the file, its name and type, and so on. The file control block (FCB) is a derivative of the file directory entry, as you can see in Figure 3-12. This figure shows both a series of equates that can be used to access an entry and a series of DB (define byte) instructions to declare an example.

The first difference you will see between the file directory entry and the FCB is that the very first byte is serving a different purpose. In the FCB, it is used to specify on which disk the file is to be found. You may recall that in the directory, this byte indicates the user number for a given entry. When you are actually processing files, the current user number is set either by the operator in a command from the console or by a BDOS function call; this predefines which subset of files in the directory will be processed. Therefore, the FCB does not need to keep track of the user number.

The disk number in the FCB's first byte is stored in an odd way. A value of 0 indicates to CP/M that it should look for the file on the current default disk. This default disk is selected either by an entry from the console or by making a specific BDOS call from within a program. In general, the default disk should be preset to the disk that contains the set of programs with which you are working. This avoids unnecessary typing on the keyboard when you want to load a program.

A disk number value other than 0 represents a letter of the alphabet based on a simple codification scheme of A = 1, B = 2, and so on.

As you can see from Figure 3-12, the file name and type must be set to the required values, and for sequential file processing, the remainder of the FCB can be set to zeros. Strictly speaking, the last three bytes of the FCB (the random record number and the random record overflow byte) need not even be declared if you are never going to process the file randomly.

This raises a subtle conceptual point. Random files are only random files because *you* process them randomly. Though this sounds like a truism, what it means is that CP/M's files are not intrinsically random or sequential. What they are depends on how you choose to process them at any given point. Therefore,

```
0000 =          FCBE$DISK       EQU     0       ;Disk drive (0 = default, 1=A)
0001 =          FCBE$NAME       EQU     1       ;File name (8 bytes)
0009 =          FCBE$TYP        EQU     9       ;File type
                                                ;Offsets for bits used in type
0009 =          FCBE$RO         EQU     9       ;Bit 7 = 1 - read only
000A =          FCBE$SYS        EQU     10      ;Bit 7 = 1 - system status
000B =          FCBE$CHANGE     EQU     11      ;Bit 7 = 0 - file written to
                                                ;
000C =          FCBE$EXTENT     EQU     12      ;Extent number
                                                ;13, 14 reserved for CP/M
000F =          FCBE$RECUSED    EQU     15      ;Records used in this extent
0010 =          FCBE$ABUSED     EQU     16      ;Allocation blocks used
0020 =          FCBE$SEQREC     EQU     32      ;Sequential rec. to read/write
0021 =          FCBE$RANREC     EQU     33      ;Random rec. to read/write
0023 =          FCBE$RANRECO    EQU     35      ;Random rec. overflow byte (MS)
                ;
                ;
0000 00         FCB$DISK:       DB      0               ;Search on default disk drive
0001 46494C454F FCB$NAME:       DB      'FILENAME'      ;File name
0009 545950     FCB$TYP:        DB      'TYP'           ;File type
000C 00         FCB$EXTENT:     DB      0               ;Extent
000D 0000       FCB$RESV:       DB      0,0             ;Reserved for CP/M
000F 00         FCB$RECUSED:    DB      0               ;Records used in this extent
0010 0000000000 FCB$ABUSED:     DB      0,0,0,0,0,0,0,0 ;Allocation blocks used
0018 0000000000                 DB      0,0,0,0,0,0,0,0
0020 00         FCB$SEQREC:     DB      0               ;Sequential rec. to read/write
0021 0000       FCB$RANREC:     DW      0               ;Random rec. to read/write
0023 00         FCB$RANRECO:    DB      0               ;Random rec. overflow byte (MS)
```

Figure 3-12.   Data declarations for the FCB

while the manner in which you process them will be different, there is nothing special built into the file that predicates how it will be used.

Sequential Files

A sequential file begins at the beginning and ends at the end. You can view it as a contiguous series of 128-byte "records."

In order to create a sequential file, you must declare a file control block with the required file name and type and request the BDOS to *create* the file. You can then request the BDOS to write, "record" by "record" (really 128-byte sector by 128-byte sector) into the file. The BDOS will take care of opening up new extents as it needs to. When you have written out all the data, you must make a BDOS request to close the file.

To read an existing file, you also need an FCB with the required file name and type declared. You then make a BDOS request to open the file for processing and a series of Read Sequential requests, each one bringing in the next "record" until either your program detects an end of file condition (by examining the data coming in from the file) or the BDOS discovers that there are no more sectors in the file to read. There is no need to close a file from which you have been reading data — but *do close it*. This is not necessary if you are going to run the program only under CP/M, but it is necessary if you want to run under MP/M (the multiuser version of CP/M).

What if you need to append further information to an existing file? One option is to create a new file, copy the existing file to the new one, and then start adding data to the end of the new file. Fortunately, with CP/M this is not necessary. In the FCB used to read a file, the name and the type were specified, but you can also specify the extent number. If you do, the BDOS will proceed to open (if it can find it) the extent number that you are asking for. If the BDOS opens the extent successfully, all you need do is check if the number of records used in the extent (held in the field FCB$RECUSED) is less than 128 (80H). This indicates the extent is not full. By taking this record number and placing it into the FCB$SEQREC (sequential record number) byte in the FCB, you can make CP/M *jump ahead* and start writing from the effective end of the file.

Random Files

Random files use a simple variation of the technique described above. The main difference is that the random record number must be set in the FCB. The BDOS automatically keeps track of file extents during Read/Write Random requests. (These requests are explained more fully in Chapter 5.)

Conceptually, random files need a small mind-twist. After creating a file as described earlier, you must set the random record number in the FCB before each Write Random request. This is the two-byte value called FCB$RANREC in Figure 3-12. Then, when you give the Write Random request to the BDOS, it will look at the record number; compute in which extent the record must exist; if necessary, create the directory entry for the extent; and finally, write out the data record. Using this scheme, you can dart backward and forward in the file putting records at random throughout the file space, with CP/M creating the necessary directory entries each time you venture into a part of the file that has not yet been written to.

The same technique is used to read a file randomly. You set the random record number in the FCB and then give a system call to the BDOS to open the correct extent and read the data. The BDOS will return an error if it cannot find the required extent or if the particular record is nonexistent.

Problems lie in wait for the unwary. Before starting to do any random reading or writing, you must open up the file at extent 0 even though this extent may not contain any data records. For a new file, this can be done with the Create File request, and for an existing file with the normal Open File request. If you create a *sparse* file, one that has gaps in between the data, you may have some problems manipulating the file. It will appear to have several extents, each one being partially full. This will fool some programs that normally process sequential files; they don't expect to see a partial extent except at the end of a file, and may treat the wrong spot as the end.

Functions of the CCP
    Editing the CCP Command Line
Built-In Commands
Program Loading
    Base Page
    Memory Dumps of the Base Page
    Processing the Command Tail
    Available Memory
    Communicating with the BIOS
    Returning to CP/M

The Console Command Processor (CCP)

The Console Command Processor processes commands that you enter from the console. As you may recall from the brief overview in Chapter 2, the CCP is loaded into memory immediately below the BDOS. In practice, many programs deliberately overwrite the CCP in order to use the memory it normally occupies. This gives these programs an additional 800H bytes (2K bytes).

When one of these "transient programs" terminates, it relinquishes control to the BIOS, which in turn reloads a fresh copy of the CCP from the system tracks of the disk back into memory and then transfers control to it. Consequently, the CCP leads a sporadic existence—an endless series of being loaded into memory, accepting a command from you at the console, being overwritten by the program you requested to be loaded, and then being brought back into memory when the program terminates.

This chapter discusses what the CCP does for you in those brief periods when it is in memory.

Functions of the CCP

Simply put, once the CCP has control of the machine, so do you. The CCP announces its presence by displaying a prompt of two characters: a letter of the alphabet for the current default disk drive and a "greater than" sign. In the example A>, the A tells you that the default disk drive is currently set to be logical drive A, and the ">," that the message was output by the CCP.

Once you see the prompt, the CCP is ready for you to enter a command line. A command line consists of two major parts: the name of the command and, optionally, some values for the command. This last part is known as the *command tail*.

The command itself can be one of two things: either the name of a file or the name of one of the frequently used commands built into the CCP.

If you enter the name of one of the built-in commands, the CCP does not need to go out to the disk system in order to load the command for execution. The executable code is already inside the CCP.

If the name of the command you entered does not match any of the built-in commands (the CCP has a table of their names), the CCP will search the appropriate logical disk drive for a file with a matching name and a file type of "COM" (which is short for command). You do not enter ".COM" when invoking a command—the CCP assumes a file type of "COM."

If you do not precede the name of the COM file with a logical disk drive specification, the CCP will search the current default drive. If you have prefixed the COM file's name with a specific logical drive, the CCP will look only on that drive for the program. For example, the command MYPROG will cause the CCP to look for a file called "MYPROG.COM" on the current default drive, whereas C:MYPROG would make the CCP search only on drive C.

If you enter a command name that matches neither the CCP's built-in command table nor the name of any COM file on the specified disk, the CCP will output the command name followed by a question mark, indicating it is unable to find the file.

Editing the CCP Command Line

The CCP uses a line buffer to store what you type until you strike either a CARRIAGE RETURN or a LINE FEED. If you make an error or change your mind, you can modify the incomplete command, even to the point of discarding it.

Chapter 4: The Console Command Processor (CCP)

You edit the command line by entering *control characters* from the console. Control characters are designated either by the combination of keys required to generate them from the keyboard or by their official name in the ASCII character set. For example, CONTROL-J is also known as CARRIAGE RETURN or CR.

Whenever CP/M has to represent control characters, the convention is to indicate the "control" aspect of a character with a caret ("^"). For example, CONTROL-A will appear as "^A", CONTROL-Z as "^Z", and so on. But if you press the CONTROL key with the normal shift key and the "6" key, this will produce a CONTROL-^ or "^^". The representation of control keys with the caret is only necessary when outputting to the console or the printer — internally, these characters are held as their appropriate binary values.

CONTROL-C: Warm Boot   If you enter a CONTROL-C as the first character of a command line, the CCP will initiate a warm boot operation. This operation resets CP/M completely, including the disk system. A fresh copy of the CCP is loaded into memory and the file directory of the current default disk drive is scanned, rebuilding the allocation bit map held in the BIOS (as discussed in Chapter 3).

The only time you would initiate a warm boot operation is after you have changed a diskette (or a disk, if you have removable media hard disks). Thus, CP/M will reset the disk system.

Note that a CONTROL-C only initiates a warm boot if it is the first character on a command line. If you enter it in any other position, the CCP will just echo it to the screen as "^C". If you have already entered several characters on a command line, use CONTROL-U or CONTROL-X to cancel the line, and then use CONTROL-C to initiate a warm boot. You can tell a warm boot has occurred because there will be a noticeable pause after the CONTROL-C before the next prompt is displayed. The system needs a finite length of time to scan the file directory and rebuild the allocation bit map.

CONTROL-E: Physical End-of-Line   The CONTROL-E command is a relic of the days of the teletype and terminals that did not perform an automatic carriage return and line feed when the cursor went off the screen to the right. When you type a CONTROL-E, CP/M sends a CARRIAGE RETURN/LINE FEED command to the console, but does not start to execute the command line you have typed thus far. CONTROL-E is, in effect, a *physical* end-of-line, not a *logical* one.

As you can see, you will need to use this command only if your terminal either overprints (if it is a hard copy device) or does not wrap around when the cursor gets to the right-hand end of the line.

CONTROL-H: Backspace   The CONTROL-H command is the ASCII backspace character. When you type it, the CCP will "destructively" backspace the cursor. Use it to correct typing errors you discover before you finish entering the command line. The last character you typed will disappear from the screen. The CCP does this by sending a three-character sequence of backspace, space, backspace to the console.

The CCP ignores attempts to backspace over its own prompt. It also takes care of backspacing over control characters that take two character positions on the line. The CCP sends the character sequence backspace, backspace, space, space, backspace, backspace, erasing both characters.

CONTROL-J: Line Feed/CONTROL-M: Carriage Return

The CONTROL-J command is the ASCII LINE FEED character; CONTROL-M is the CARRIAGE RETURN. Both of these characters terminate the command line. The CCP will then execute the command.

CONTROL-P: Printer Echo

The CONTROL-P command is used to turn on and off a feature called *printer echo*. When it is turned on, every character sent to the console is also sent to CP/M's list device. You can use this command to get a hard copy of information that normally goes only to the console.

CONTROL-P is a "toggle." The first time you type CONTROL-P it turns on printer echo; the next time you type CONTROL-P it turns off printer echo. Whenever CP/M does a warm boot, printer echo is turned off.

There is no easy way to know whether printer echo is on or off. Try typing a few CARRIAGE RETURNs, and see whether the printer responds; if it does not, type CONTROL-P and try again.

One of the shortcomings in most CP/M implementations is that the printer drivers (the software in the BIOS that controls or "drives" the printer) do not behave very intelligently if the printer is switched off or not ready when you or your program asks it to print. Under these circumstances, the software will wait forever and the system will appear to be dead. So if you "hang" the system in this way when you type a CONTROL-P, check that the printer is turned on and ready. Otherwise, you may have to reset the entire system.

CONTROL-R: Repeat Command Line

The CONTROL-R command makes the CCP repeat or retype the current input line. The CCP outputs a "#" character, a CARRIAGE RETURN/LINE FEED, and then the entire contents of the command line buffer. This is a useful feature if you are working on a teletype or other hard copy terminal and have used the RUB or DEL characters. Since these characters do not destructively delete a character, you can get a visually confusing line of text on the terminal. The CONTROL-R character gives you a fresh copy of the line without any of the logically deleted characters cluttering it up. In this way you can see exactly what you have typed into the command line buffer.

See the discussion of the RUB and DEL characters for an example of CONTROL-R in use.

CONTROL-S: Stop Screen Output

The CONTROL-S command is the ASCII XOFF (also called DC3) character; XOFF is an abbreviation for "Transmit Off." Typing CONTROL-S will temporarily stop output to the console. In a standard version of

CP/M, the CCP will resume output when *any* character is entered (including another CONTROL-S) from the console. Thus, you can use CONTROL-S as a toggle switch to turn console output on and off.

In some implementations of CP/M, the console driver itself (the low-level code in the BIOS that controls the console) will be maintaining a communication protocol with the console; therefore, a better way of resuming console output after pausing with a CONTROL-S is to use CONTROL-Q, the ASCII XON or "Transmit On" character. Entering a CONTROL-Q instead of relying on the fact that *any* character may be used to continue the output is a fail-safe measure.

The commands CONTROL-S and CONTROL-Q are most useful when you have large amounts of data on the screen. By "riding" the CONTROL-S and CONTROL-Q keys, you can let the data come to the screen in small bursts that you can easily scan.

CONTROL-U or CONTROL-X: Undo Command Line   The commands CONTROL-U and CONTROL-X perform the same function: They erase the current partially entered command line so that you can undo any mistakes and start over. The CONTROL-U command was originally intended for hard copy terminals. The CCP outputs a "#" character, then a CARRIAGE RETURN/LINE FEED, and then some blanks to leave the cursor lined up and ready for you to enter the next command line. It leaves what you originally entered in the previous line on the screen. The CONTROL-X command is more suited to screens; the CCP destructively backspaces to the beginning of the command line so that you can reenter it.

RUB or DEL: Delete Last Character   The rubout or delete function (keys marked RUB, RUBOUT, DEL, or DELETE) nondestructively deletes the last character that you typed. That is, it deletes the last character from the command line buffer and echoes it back to the console.

Here is an example of a command line with the last few characters deleted using the RUB key:

```
A>RUN PAYROLLLLORYAPSALES
             ^^^^^^^
             DELeted
```

You can see that the command line very quickly becomes unreadable. If you lose track of what are data characters and what has been deleted, you can use CONTROL-R to get a fresh copy of what is in the command line buffer.

The example above would then appear as follows:

```
A>RUN PAYROLLLLORYAPSALES#
  RUN SALES_
```

The "#" character is output by the CCP to indicate that the line has been repeated. The "_" represents the position of the cursor, which is now ready to continue with the command line.

Built-In Commands

When you enter a command line and press either CARRIAGE RETURN or LINE FEED, the CCP will check if the command name is one of the set of built-in commands. (It has a small table of command names embedded in it, against which the entered command name is checked.) If the command name matches a built-in one, the CCP executes the command immediately.

The next few sections describe the built-in commands that are available; however, refer to *Osborne CP/M User Guide,* second edition by Thom Hogan (Berkeley: Osborne/McGraw-Hill, 1982) for a more comprehensive discussion with examples of the various forms of each command.

X: — Changing Default Disk Drives   The default drive is the currently active drive that CP/M uses for all file access whenever you do not nominate a specific drive. If you wish to change the default drive, simply enter the new default drive's identifying letter followed by a colon. The CCP responds by changing the name of the disk that appears in the prompt line.

On hard disks, this simple operation may take a second or two to complete because the BDOS, requested by the CCP to log in the drive, must read through the disk directory and rebuild the allocation vector for the disk. If you have a diskette or a disk that is removable, changing it and performing a warm boot has the same effect of refreshing CP/M's image of which allocation blocks are used and which are available. It takes longer on a hard disk because, as a rule, the directories are much larger.

DIR — Directory of Files   In its simplest form, the DIR command displays a listing of the files set to Directory status in the current user number (or file group) on the current default drive. Therefore, when you do not ask for any files after the DIR command, a file name of "*.*" is assumed. This is a total wildcard, so all files that have not been given System status will be displayed. This is the only built-in command where an omitted file name reference expands to "all file names, all file types."

You can display the directory of a different drive by specifying the drive in the same command line as the DIR command.

You can qualify the files you want displayed by entering a unique or ambiguous file name or extension. Only those files that match the given file name specification will be displayed, and even then, only those files that are not set to System status will appear on the screen. (The standard CP/M utility program STAT can be used to change files from SYS to DIR status.)

Another side effect of the DIR command and files that are SYS status is best illustrated by an example. Imagine that the current logical drive B has two files on it called SYSFILE (which has SYS status) and NONSYS (which does not). Look at the following console dialog, in which user input is underlined:

```
B>DIR<cr>
B: NONSYS            SYSFILE does not show
B>DIR JUNK<cr>
NO FILE              JUNK does not exist
B>DIR SYSFILE<cr>
B>_
```

Do you see the problem? If a file is not on the disk, the CCP will display NO FILE (or NOT FOUND in earlier versions of CP/M). However, if the file *does* exist but is a SYS file, the CCP does not display it because of its status; nor does the CCP say NO FILE. Instead it quietly returns to the prompt. This can be confusing if you are searching for a file that happens to be set to SYS status. The only safe way to find out if the file does exist is to use the STAT utility.

ERA — Erase a File   The ERA command logically removes files from the disk (*logically* because only the file directory is affected; the actual data blocks are not changed).

The logical delete changes the first byte of each directory entry belonging to a file to a value of 0E5H. As you may recall from the discussion on the file directory entry in Chapter 3, this first byte usually contains the file user number. If it is set to 0E5H, it marks the entry as being deleted.

ERA makes a complete pass down the file directory to logically delete all of the extents of the file.

Unlike DIR, the ERA command does not assume "all files, all types" if you omit a file name. If it did, it would be all too easy to erase all of your files by accident. You must enter "*.*" to erase all files, and even then, you must reassure the CCP that you really want to erase all of them from the disk. The actual dialog looks like the following:

```
A>era b:*.*<cr>
ALL (Y/N)?y<cr>
A>_
```

If you change your mind at the last minute, you can press "n" and the CCP will not erase any files.

One flaw in CP/M is that the ERA command only asks for confirmation when you attempt to erase all of your files using a name such as "*.*" or "*.???". Consider the impact of the following command:

```
A>ERA *.C??<cr>
A>_
```

The CCP with no hesitation has wiped out all files that have a file type starting with the letter "C" in the current user number on logical disk A.

If you need to use an ambiguous file name in an ERA command, check which files you will delete by first using a STAT command with exactly the same ambiguous file name. STAT will show you all the files that match the ambiguous name, even those with SYS status that would not be displayed by a DIR command.

There are several utility programs on the market with names like UNERA or WHOOPS, which take an ambiguous file name and reinstate the files that you may have accidentally erased. A design for a version of UNERASE is discussed in Chapter 11.

If you attempt to erase a file that is not on the specified drive, the CCP will respond with a NO FILE message.

REN — Rename a File   The REN command renames a file, changing the file name, the file type, or both. In order to rename, you need to enter two file names, the new name and the current file name.

To remember the correct name format, think of the phrase *new = old*. The actual command syntax is

```
A>ren newfile.typ=oldfile.typ<cr>
A>_
```

You can use a logical disk drive letter to specify on which drive the file exists. If you specify the drive, you only need to enter it on one of the file names. If you enter the drive with both file names, it must be the same letter for both.

Unlike the previous built-in command, REN cannot be used with ambiguous file names. If you try, the CCP echoes back the ambiguous names and a question mark, as in the following dialog:

```
A>ren chap*.doc=chapter*.doc<cr>
CHAP*.DOC=CHAPTER*.DOC?
A>_
```

If the REN command cannot find the old file, it will respond NO FILE. If the new file already exists, the message FILE EXISTS will be displayed. If you receive a FILE EXISTS message and want to check that the new file does exist, remember that it is better to use the STAT command than DIR. The extant file may be declared to be SYS status and therefore will not appear if you use the DIR command.

TYPE — Type a Text File   The TYPE command copies the specified file to the console. You cannot use ambiguous file names, and you will need to press CONTROL-S if the file has more data than can fill one screen. With the TYPE command, the data in the file will fly past on the screen unless you stop the display by pressing CONTROL-S. Be careful, because if you type any other character, the TYPE command will abort and return control to the CCP.

Once you have had time to see what is displayed on the screen, you can press CONTROL-Q to resume the output of data to the console. With standard CP/M implementations, you will discover that any character can be used to restart the flow of data; however, use CONTROL-Q as a fail-safe measure. CONTROL-S (X-OFF) and CONTROL-Q (X-ON) conform to the standard protocol which should be used.

If you need to get hard copy output of the contents of the file, you should type a CONTROL-P command before you press the CARRIAGE RETURN at the end of the TYPE command line.

As you may have inferred, the TYPE command should only be used to output ASCII text files. If for some reason you use the TYPE command with a file that contains binary information, strange characters will appear on the screen. In fact, you may program your terminal into some state that can only be remedied by turning the power off and then on again. The general rule therefore is *only* use the TYPE command with ASCII text files.

SAVE — Save Memory Image on Disk   The SAVE command is the hardest of the CCP's commands to explain. It is more useful to the programmer than to a typical end user. The format of this command is

```
A>SAVE n FILENAME.TYP<cr>
A>_
```

The SAVE command creates a file of the specified name and type (or overwrites an existing file of this name and type), and writes into it the specified number n of memory pages. A page in CP/M is 256 (100H) bytes. The SAVE command starts writing out memory from location 100H, the start of the Transient Program Area (TPA). Before you use this command, you will normally have loaded a program into the TPA. The SAVE command does just what its name implies: It saves an image of the program onto a disk file.

More often than not, when you use the SAVE command the file type will be ".COM." With the file saved in this way, the CCP will be able to load and execute the file.

USER — Change User Numbers   As mentioned before, the directory of each logical disk consists of several directories that are physically interwoven but logically separated by the user number. When you use a specific user number, those files that were created when you were in another user number are logically not available to you.

The USER command provides a way for you to move from one user number to another. The command format is

```
A>USER n<cr>
A>_
```

where n can be any number from 0 to 15. Any other number will provoke the CCP to echoing back your entry, followed by a question mark.

But once you have switched back and forth between user numbers several times, it is easy to become confused about which user number you are in. The STAT command can be used to find the current user number. If you are in a user number that does not make a copy of STAT available to you however, all you can do is use the USER command to set yourself to another user number. You cannot find out which user number you were in; you can only tell the system the user number you want to go to.

In the custom BIOS systems discussed later, there is a way of displaying the current user number each time a warm boot occurs. If you are building a system in which you plan to utilize CP/M's user number features, you should give this display of the current user number serious thought. If you are in the wrong user number and erase files, you can create serious problems.

Some implementations of CP/M have modified the CCP so that the prompt shows the current user number as well as the default drive (similar to the prompt used in MP/M). However, this use of a nonstandard CCP is not a good practice. As a rule, customization should be confined to the BIOS.

Program Loading

The first area to consider when loading a program is the first 100H bytes of memory, called the *base page*. Several fields—units in this area of memory—are set to predetermined values before a program takes control.

To aid in this discussion, imagine a program called COPYFILE that copies one file to another. This program expects you to specify the source and destination file names on the command line. A typical command would read

```
A>copyfile tofile.typ fromfile.typ display
```

Notice the word "display." COPYFILE will, if you specify the "display" option, output the contents of the source file ("fromfile.typ") on the console as the transfer takes place.

When you press the CARRIAGE RETURN key at the end of the command line, the CCP will search the current default drive ("A" in the example) and load a file called COPYFILE.COM into memory starting at location 100H. The CCP then transfers control to location 100H—just past the base page—and COPYFILE starts executing.

Base Page

The base page normally starts from location 0000H in memory, but where there is other material in low memory addresses, it may start at a higher address. Figure 4-1 shows the assembly language code you will need to access the base page. RAM is assumed to start at location 0000H in this example.

Chapter 4: The Console Command Processor (CCP)   55

```
0000 =          RAM            EQU        0          ;Start of RAM (and the base page)
                                                     ;You may need to change this to
                                                     ; some other value (e.g. 4300H)
0000            ;              ORG        RAM        ;Set location counter to RAM base
0000            WARMBOOT:      DS         3          ;Contains a JMP to warm boot entry
                                                     ; in BIOS Jump vector table
                ;
0002 =          BIOSPAGE       EQU        RAM+2      ;BIOS Jump vector page
                ;
0003            IOBYTE:        DS         1          ;Input/output redirection byte
                ;
0004            CURUSER:       DS         1          ;Current user (bits 7-4)
0004 =          CURDISK        EQU        CURUSER    ;Default logical disk (bits 3-0)
                ;
0005            BDOSE:         DS         3          ;Contains a JMP to BDOS entry
0007 =          TOPRAM         EQU        BDOSE+2    ;Top page of usable RAM
                ;
0005C                          ORG        RAM+5CH    ;Bypass unused locations
                ;
005C            FCB1:          DS         16         ;File control block #1
                                                     ;Note: if you use this FCB here
                                                     ; you will overwrite FCB2 below.
                ;
006C            FCB2:          DS         16         ;File control block #2
                                                     ;You must move this to another
                                                     ; place before using it
                ;
0080                           ORG        RAM+80H    ;Bypass unused locations
                ;
                COMTAIL:                             ;Complete command tail
0080            COMTAIL$COUNT: DS         1          ;Count of the number of chars
                                                     ; in command tail (CR not incl.)
0081            COMTAIL$CHARS: DS         127        ;Characters in command tail
                                                     ; converted to uppercase and
                                                     ; without trailing carriage ret.
                ;
0080                           ORG        RAM+80H    ;Redefine command tail area
                ;
0080            DMABUFFER:     DS         128        ;Default "DMA" address used
                                                     ; as a 128-byte record buffer
                ;
0100                           ORG        RAM+100H   ;Bypass unused locations
                TPA:                                 ;Start of transient program area
                                                     ; into which programs are loaded.
```

Figure 4-1.   Base page data declarations

Some versions of CP/M, such as the early Heathkit/Zenith system, have ROM from location 0000H to 42FFH. Digital Research, responding to market pressure, produced a version of CP/M that assumed RAM starting at 4300H. If you have one of these systems, you must add 4300H to all addresses in the following paragraphs *except* for those that refer to addresses at the top of memory. These will not be affected by the presence of ROM in low memory.

The individual values used in fields in the base page are described in the following sections.

Warmboot   The three-byte *warmboot* field contains an instruction to jump up to the high end of RAM. This JMP instruction transfers control into the BIOS and triggers a warm boot operation. As mentioned before, a warm boot causes CP/M to reload the CCP and rebuild the allocation vector for the current default disk. If you need to cause a warm boot from within one of your assembly language programs, code

```
JMP   0              ;Warm Boot
```

BIOSPAGE   The BIOS has several different entry points; however, they are all clustered together at the beginning of the BIOS. The first few instructions of the BIOS look like the following:

```
JMP   ENTRY1
JMP   ENTRY2
JMP   ENTRY3         ;and so on
```

Because of the way CP/M is put together, the first jump instruction *always* starts on a page boundary. Remember that a page is 256 (100H) bytes of memory, so a page boundary is an address where the least significant eight bits are zero. For example, the BIOS jump vector (as this set of JMPs is called) may start at an address such as F200H or E600H. The exact address is determined by the size of the BIOS.

By looking at the BIOSPAGE, the most significant byte of the address in the warmboot JMP instruction, the page address of the BIOS jump vector can be determined.

IOBYTE   CP/M is based on a philosophy of separating the *physical* world from CP/M's own *logical* view of the world. This philosophy also applies to the character-oriented devices that CP/M supports.

The IOBYTE consists of four two-bit fields that can be used to assign a physical device to each of the logical ones. It is important to understand that the IOBYTE itself is just a passive data structure. Actual assignment occurs only when the physical device drivers examine the IOBYTE, interpreting its contents and selecting the correct physical drive for the cooperation of the BIOS. These device drivers are the low-level (that is, close to machine language) code in the BIOS that actually interfaces and controls the physical device.

The four *logical* devices that CP/M knows about are

1. *The console.* This is the device through which you communicate with CP/M. It is normally a terminal with a screen and a keyboard. The console is a bidirectional device: It can be used as a source for information (input) and a destination to which you can send information (output).

    In CP/M terminology, the console is known by the symbolic name of "CON:". Note the ":"—this differentiates the device name from a disk file that might be called "CON."

2. *The list device.* This is normally a printer of some sort and is used to make hard copy listings. CP/M views the printer as an output device only. This creates problems for printers that need to tell CP/M they are busy, but this

Chapter 4: The Console Command Processor (CCP)   **57**

problem can be remedied by adding code to the low-level printer driver.
CP/M's name for this logical device is "LST:".

3. *The paper tape reader.* It is unusual to find a paper tape reader in use today. Originally, CP/M ran on an Intel Microcomputer Development System called the MDS-800, and this system had a paper tape reader. This device can be used only as a source for information.
CP/M calls this logical device "RDR:".

4. *The paper tape punch.* This, too, is a relic from CP/M's early days and the MDS-800. In this case, the punch can be used only for output.
The logical device name used by CP/M is "PUN:".

The physical arrangement of the IOBYTE fields is shown in Figure 4-2.

Each two-bit field can take on one of four values: 00, 01, 10, and 11. The particular value can be interpreted by the BIOS to mean a specific physical device, as shown in Table 4-1.

Although the actual interpretation of the IOBYTE is performed by the BIOS, the STAT utility can set the IOBYTE using the logical and physical device names, and PIP (Peripheral Interchange Program) can be used to copy data from one device to another. In addition, you can write a program that simply changes the

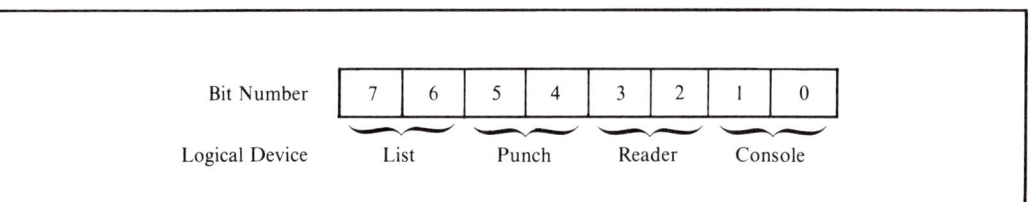

Figure 4-2. Arrangement of the IOBYTE

Table 4-1.   IOBYTE Values

Logical Device	Physical Device			
	00	01	10	11
Console (CON:)	TTY:	CRT:	BAT:	UC1:
Reader (RDR:)	TTY:	PTR:	UR1:	UR2:
Punch (PUN:)	TTY:	PTP:	UP1:	UP2:
List (LST:)	TTY:	CRT:	LPT:	UL1:

contents of the IOBYTE. But be careful: Changes in the IOBYTE take effect immediately.

The values in the IOBYTE have the following meanings:

Console (CON:)

    00   Teletype driver (TTY:)
              This driver is assumed to be connected to a hard copy device being used as the main console.

    01   CRT driver (CRT:)
              The driver is assumed to be connected to a CRT terminal.

    10   Batch mode (BAT:)
              This is a rather special case. It is assumed that appropriate drivers will be called so that console input comes from the logical reader (RDR:) and console output is sent to the logical list device (LST:).

    11   User defined console (UC1:)
              Meaning depends on the individual BIOS implementation. If, for example, you have a high-resolution graphics screen, you could arrange for this setting of the IOBYTE to direct console output to it. You might make console input come in from some graphic tablet, joystick, or other device.

Reader (RDR:)

    00   Teletype driver (TTY:)
              This refers to the paper tape reader device that was often found on teletype consoles.

    01   Paper tape reader (PTR:)
              This presumes some kind of high-speed input device connected to the system. Modern systems rarely have such a device, so this setting is often used to connect the logical reader to the input side of a communications line.

    10   User defined reader #1 (UR1:)

    11   User defined reader #2 (UR2:)
              Both of these settings can be used to direct the physical driver to some other specialized devices. These values are included only because they would otherwise have been unassigned. They are rarely used.

Punch (PUN:)

    00   Teletype driver (TTY:)
              This refers to the paper tape punch that was often found on teletype consoles.

    01   Paper tape punch (PTP:)

This presumes that there is some kind of high-speed paper tape punch connected to the system. Again, this is rarely the case, so this setting is often used to connect the logical punch to the output side of a communications line.

10   User defined punch #1 (UP1:)

11   User defined punch #2 (UP2:)
These two settings correspond to the two user defined readers, but they are practically never used.

List (LST:)

00   Teletype driver (TTY:)
Output will be printed on a teletype.

01   CRT driver (CRT:)
Output will be directed to the screen on a CRT terminal.

10   Line printer driver (LPT:)
Output will go to a high-speed printing device. Although the name *line printer* implies a specific type of hardware, it can be any kind of printer.

11   User defined list device (UL1:)
Whoever writes the BIOS can arrange for this setting to cause logical list device output to go to a device other than the main printer.

To repeat: The IOBYTE is not actually used by the main body of CP/M. It is just a passive data structure that can be manipulated by the STAT utility. Whether the IOBYTE has any effect depends entirely on the particular BIOS implementation.

CURUSER   The CURUSER field is the most significant four bits (high order nibble) of its byte. It contains the currently selected user number set by the CCP USER command, by a specific call to the BDOS, or by a program setting this nibble to the required value. This last way of changing user numbers may cause compatibility problems with future versions of CP/M, so use it only under controlled conditions.

CURDISK   The CURDISK field is the least significant four bits of the byte it shares with CURUSER. It contains a value of 0 if the current disk is A:, 1 if it is B:, and so on.
The CURDISK field can be set from the CCP, by a request to the BDOS, or by a program altering this field. The caveat given for CURUSER regarding compatibility also applies here.

BDOSE   This three-byte field contains an instruction to jump to the entry point of the BDOS. Whenever you want the BDOS to do something, you can transfer the request to the BDOS by placing the appropriate values in registers and making a CALL to this JMP instruction. By using a CALL, the return address will be placed on the stack. The subsequent JMP to the BDOS does not put any additional information onto the stack, which operates on a last-in, first-out basis; so when the system returns from the BDOS, it will return directly to your program.

TOPRAM   Because the BDOS, like the BIOS, starts on a page boundary, the most significant byte of the address of the BDOS entry tells you in which page the BDOS starts. You must subtract 1 from the value in TOPRAM to get the highest page number that you can use in your program. Note that when you use this technique, you assume that the CCP will be overwritten since it resides in memory just below the BDOS.

FCB1 and FCB2   As a convenience, the CCP takes the first two parameters that appear in the command tail (see next section), attempts to parse them as though they were file names, and places the results in FCB1 and FCB2. The results, in this context, mean that the logical disk letter is converted to its FCB representation, and the file name and type, converted to uppercase, are placed in the FCB in the correct bytes. In addition, any use of "*" in the file name is expanded to one or more question marks. For example, a file name of "abc*.*" will be converted to a name of "ABC?????" and type of "???".

Notice that FCB2 starts only 16 bytes above FCB1, yet a normal FCB is at least 33 bytes long (36 bytes if you want to use random access). In many cases, programs only require a single file name. Therefore, you can proceed to use FCB1 straight away, not caring that FCB2 will be overwritten.

In the case of the COPYFILE program example on previous pages, two file names are required. Before FCB1 can be used, the 16 bytes of FCB2 must be moved into a skeleton FCB that is declared in the body of COPYFILE itself.

COMTAIL   The command tail is everything on the command line *other* than the command name itself. For example, the command tail in the COPYFILE command line is shown here:

```
A>copyfile tofile.type fromfile.typ display
```

The CCP takes the command tail (converted to uppercase) and stores it in the COMTAIL area.

COMTAIL$COUNT   This is a single-byte binary count of the number of characters in the command tail. The count does *not* include a trailing CARRIAGE RETURN or a blank between the command name and the command tail. For example, if you enter the command line

```
A>PRINT ABC*.*
```

the COMTAIL$COUNT will be six, which is the number of characters in the string "ABC*.*".

COMTAIL$CHARS   These are the actual characters in the command tail. This field is not blank-filled, so you must use the COMTAIL$COUNT in order to detect the end of the command tail.

DMA$BUFFER   In Figure 4-1, the DMA$BUFFER is actually the same area of memory as the COMTAIL. This is a space-saving trick that works because most programs process the contents of the command tail before they do any disk input or output.

The DMA$BUFFER is a sector buffer (hence it has a length of 128 bytes). The use of the acronym DMA (direct memory access) refers back to the Intel MDS-800. This system had hardware that could move data to and from diskettes by going directly to memory, bypassing the CPU completely. The term is still used even though you may have a computer system that does not use DMA for its disk I/O. You can substitute the idea of "the address to/from which data is read/written" in place of the DMA concept.

You can request CP/M to use a DMA address other than DMA$BUFFER, but whenever the CCP is in control, the DMA address will be set back here.

TPA   This is the *transient program area* into which the CCP loads programs. The TPA extends up to the base of the BDOS.

The TPA is also the starting address for the memory image that is saved on disk whenever you use the CCP SAVE command.

Memory Dumps of the Base Page

The following are printouts showing the contents of the base page (the first 100H bytes of memory) as the COPYFILE program will see it.

This is an example of the first 16 bytes of memory:

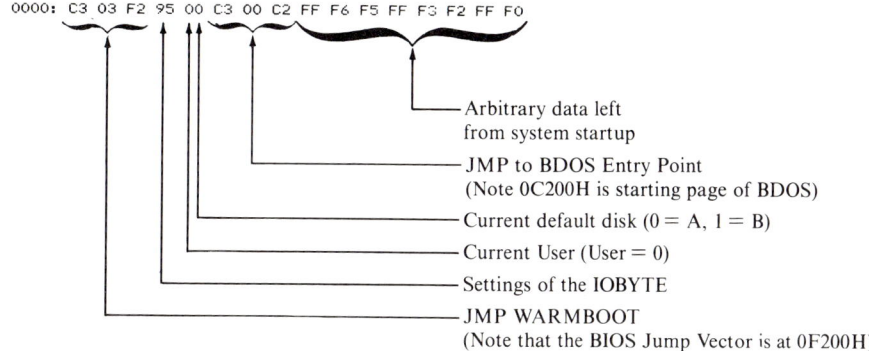

62   The CP/M Programmer's Handbook

The command line, as you recall, was

```
A>copyfile tofile.typ fromfile.typ display
```

The FCB1 and FCB2 areas will be set by the CCP as follows:

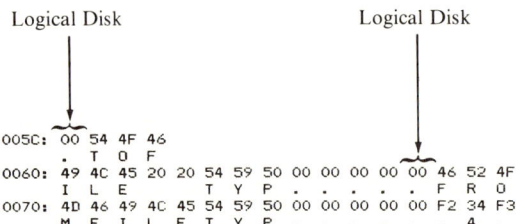

```
       Logical Disk                    Logical Disk

005C: 00 54 4F 46
       .  T  O  F
0060: 49 4C 45 20 20 54 59 50 00 00 00 00 00 46 52 4F
       I  L  E           T  Y  P              .  F  R  O
0070: 4D 46 49 4C 45 54 59 50 00 00 00 00 00 F2 34 F3
       M  F  I  L  E  T  Y  P  .  .  .  .  .     4  .
```

Since the logical disks were not specified in the file names in the command line, the CCP has set the disk code in both FCB1 and FCB2 to 00H, meaning "use the default disk." The file name and type have been converted to uppercase, separated, and put into the FCBs in their appointed places.

The complete command tail has been stored in COMTAIL as follows:

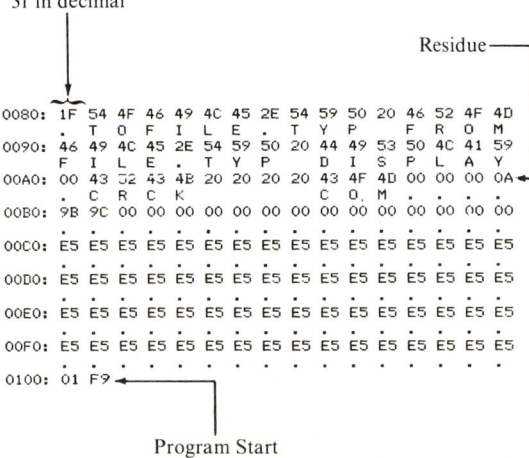

```
      31 in decimal                                Residue

0080: 1F 54 4F 46 49 4C 45 2E 54 59 50 20 46 52 4F 4D
       .  T  O  F  I  L  E  .  T  Y  P     F  R  O  M
0090: 46 49 4C 45 2E 54 59 50 20 44 49 53 50 4C 41 59
       F  I  L  E  .  T  Y  P     D  I  S  P  L  A  Y
00A0: 00 43 52 43 4B 20 20 20 20 43 4F 4D 00 00 00 0A
       .  C  R  C  K              C  O  M  .  .  .  .
00B0: 9B 9C 00 00 00 00 00 00 00 00 00 00 00 00 00 00
       .  .  .  .  .  .  .  .  .  .  .  .  .  .  .  .
00C0: E5 E5 E5 E5 E5 E5 E5 E5 E5 E5 E5 E5 E5 E5 E5 E5
00D0: E5 E5 E5 E5 E5 E5 E5 E5 E5 E5 E5 E5 E5 E5 E5 E5
00E0: E5 E5 E5 E5 E5 E5 E5 E5 E5 E5 E5 E5 E5 E5 E5 E5
00F0: E5 E5 E5 E5 E5 E5 E5 E5 E5 E5 E5 E5 E5 E5 E5 E5
0100: 01 F9

                   Program Start
```

You can see that the command tail length is 01FH (31 decimal). This is followed immediately by the command tail characters themselves. Note that the command tail stops at location 9FH. The remainder of the data that you can see is the residue of some previous directory operation by the CCP. You can see the file name CRCK.COM in a directory entry, followed by several 0E5Hs that are unused directory space.

Finally, at location 0100H are the first two bytes of the program.

Chapter 4: The Console Command Processor (CCP)   **63**

Processing the Command Tail

One of the first problems facing you if you write a program that can accept parameters from the command tail is to process the command tail itself, isolating each of the parameters. You should use a standard subroutine to do this. This subroutine splits the command line into individual parameters and returns a count of the number of parameters, as well as a pointer to a table of addresses. Each address in this table points in turn to a null-byte-terminated string. Each parameter is placed in a separate string.

Figure 4-3 contains the listing of this subroutine, CTP (Command Tail Processor).

```
        0100                      ORG     100H
        0100 CD3601   START:      CALL    CTP             ;Test bed for CTP
        0103 00                   NOP
                                  ; Remainder of your program
                      ;
                      ;           This subroutine breaks the command tail apart, placing
                      ;           each value in a separate string area.
                      ;
                      ;           Return parameters:
                      ;                   A = 0 - No error (Z flag set)
                      ;                   B = Count of number of parameters
                      ;                   HL -> Table of addresses
                      ;                           Each address points to a null-byte-
                      ;                           terminated parameter string.
                      ;                   If too many parameters are specified, then A = TMP
                      ;                   If a given parameter is too long, then A = PTL
                      ;                           and D points to the first character of the
                      ;                           offending parameter in the COMTAIL area.
                      ;
        0080 =        COMTAIL         EQU     80H             ;Command tail in base page
        0080 =        COMTAIL$COUNT   EQU     COMTAIL         ;Count of chars. in command tail
        0001 =        CTP$TMP         EQU     1               ;Too many parameters error code
        0002 =        CTP$PTL         EQU     2               ;Parameter too long error code
                      ;
                      PTABLE:                                 ;Table of pointers to parameters
        0104 0C01                     DW      P1              ; Parameter 1
        0106 1A01                     DW      P2              ; Parameter 2
        0108 2801                     DW      P3              ; Parameter 3
                                      ; <--- Add more parameter addresses here
        010A 0000                     DW      0               ; Terminator
                      ;
                      ;           Parameter strings.
                      ;           The first byte is 0 so that unused parameters appear
                      ;           to be null strings.
                      ;           The last byte of each is a 0 and is used to detect
                      ;           a parameter that is too long.
        010C 0001010101 P1:           DB      0,1,1,1,1,1,1,1,1,1,1,1,1,0 ;Param. 1 & terminator
        011A 0001010101 P2:           DB      0,1,1,1,1,1,1,1,1,1,1,1,1,0 ;Param. 2 & terminator
        0128 0001010101 P3:           DB      0,1,1,1,1,1,1,1,1,1,1,1,1,0 ;Param. 3 & terminator
                                      ; <--- Add more parameter strings here
                      ;
                      CTP:                                    ;Main entry point <<<<<
        0136 210401                   LXI     H,PTABLE        ;HL -> table of addresses
        0139 0E00                     MVI     C,0             ;Set parameter count
        013B 3A8000                   LDA     COMTAIL$COUNT   ;Character count
        013E B7                       ORA     A               ;Check if any params.
        013F C8                       RZ                      ;Exit (return params. already set)
        0140 E5                       PUSH    H               ;Save on top of stack for later
        0141 47                       MOV     B,A             ;B = COMTAIL char. count
        0142 218100                   LXI     H,COMTAIL+1     ;HL -> Command tail chars.
```

Figure 4-3.   Command Tail Processor (CTP)

```
                  CTP$NEXTP:                  ;Next parameter loop
0145 E3              XTHL                     ;HL -> Table of addresses
                                              ;Top of stack = COMTAIL ptr.
0146 5E              MOV    E,M               ;Get LS byte of param. addr.
0147 23              INX    H                 ;Update address pointer
0148 56              MOV    D,M               ;Get MS byte of param. addr.
                                              ;DE -> Parameter string (or is 0)
0149 7A              MOV    A,D               ;Get copy of MS byte of addr.
014A B3              ORA    E                 ;Combine MS and LS byte
014B CA8001          JZ     CTP$TMPX          ;Too many parameters--exit
014E 23              INX    H                 ;Update pointer to next address
014F E3              XTHL                     ;HL -> comtail
                                              ;Top of stack--update addr. ptr.
                                       ;At this point, we have
                                       ; HL -> next byte in command tail
                                       ; DE -> first byte of next parameter string
                  CTP$SKIPB:
0150 7E              MOV    A,M               ;Get next parameter byte
0151 23              INX    H                 ;Update command tail ptr.
0152 05              DCR    B                 ;Check if characters still remain
0153 FA7301          MB     CTPX              ;No, so exit
0156 FE20            CPI    ' '               ;Check if blank
0158 CA5001          JZ     CTP$SKIPB         ;Yes, so skip blanks
015B 0C              INR    C                 ;Increment parameter counter
                  CTP$NEXTC:
015C 12              STAX   D                 ;Store in parameter string
015D 13              INX    D                 ;Update parameter string ptr.
015E 1A              LDAX   D                 ;Check next byte
015F B7              ORA    A                 ;Check if terminator
0160 CA7A01          JZ     CTP$PTLX          ;Parameter too long exit
0163 AF              XRA    A                 ;Float a 00-byte at end of param.
0164 12              STAX   D                 ;Store in param. string
0165 7E              MOV    A,M               ;Get next character from tail
0166 23              INX    H                 ;Update command tail pointer
0167 05              DCR    B                 ;Check if characters still remain
0168 FA7301          JM     CTPX              ;No, so exit
016B FE20            CPI    ' '               ;Check if parameter terminator
016D CA4501          JZ     CTP$NEXTP         ;Yes, so move to next parameter
0170 C35C01          JMP    CTP$NEXTC         ;No, so store it in param. string
                  ;
                  CTPX:                       ;Normal exit
0173 AF              XRA    A                 ;A = 0 & Z-flag set
                  ;
                  CTPCX:                      ;Common exit code
0174 E1              POP    H                 ;Balance stack
0175 210401          LXI    H,PTABLE          ;Return ptr. to param. addr. table
0178 B7              ORA    A                 ;Ensure Z-flag set appropriately
0179 C9              RET
                  ;
                  CTP$PTLX:                   ;Parameter too long exit
017A 3E02            MVI    A,CTP$PTL         ;Set error code
017C EB              XCHG                     ;DE -> offending parameter
017D C37401          JMP    CTPCX             ;Common exit
                  ;
                  CTP$TMPX:                   ;Too many parameters exit
0180 3E01            MVI    A,CTP$TMP         ;Set error code
0182 C37401          JMP    CTPCX             ;Common exit
                  ;
0185                 END    START
```

Figure 4-3. Command Tail Processor (CTP) (continued)

Available Memory

Many programs need to use all of available memory, and so very early in the program they need to set the stack pointer to the top end of the available RAM. As mentioned before, the CCP can be overwritten as it will be reloaded on the next warm boot.

Figure 4-4 shows the code used to set the stack pointer. This code determines the amount of memory in the TPA and sets the stack pointer to the top of available RAM.

Communicating with the BIOS

If you are writing a utility program to interact with a customized BIOS, there will be occasions where you need to make a *direct* BIOS call. However, if your program ends up on a system running Digital Research's MP/M Operating System, you will have serious problems if you try to call the BIOS directly. Among other things, you will crash the operating system.

If you need to make such a call and you are aware of the dangers of using direct BIOS calls, Figure 4-5 shows you one way to do it.

Remember that the first instructions in the BIOS are the jump vector—a sequence of JMP instructions one after the other. Before you can make a direct call, you need to know the *relative page offset* of the particular JMP instruction you want to go to. The BIOS jump vector always starts on a page boundary, so all you need to know is the least significant byte of its address.

```
0007 =              TOPRAM  EQU   7         ;Most significant byte of
                    ;                                 BDOS entry point
0000 3A0700                 LDA   TOPRAM    ;Get MS byte of BDOS entry point
0003 3D                     DCR   A         ;Back off one page
0004 2EFF                   MVI   L,0FFH    ;Set LS byte of final address
0006 67                     MOV   H,A       ;HL = XXFFH
0007 F9                     SPHL            ;Set stack pointer from HL
```

Figure 4-4. Setting stack pointer to top of available RAM

```
                    ;       Use this technique only for CP/M utility programs.
                    ;       MP/M programs do not permit this.
                    ;
0009 =              CONIN    EQU   09H      ;Get console input character
                                            ; (It's the 4th jump in the vector)
0002 =              BIOSPAGE EQU   2        ;Address of BIOS page
                    ;
                    ;       At this point you make a direct CONIN
                    ;       CALL...
                    ;
0000 2E09                   MVI   L,CONIN   ;Get LS byte of CONIN entry point
0002 CD0500                 CALL  BIOS      ;Go to BIOS entry subroutine
                    ;... the rest of your program...
                    ;
                    ;
                    BIOS:
0005 3A0200                 LDA   BIOSPAGE  ;Get BIOS jump vector page
0008 67                     MOV   H,A       ;HL -> entry point
                                            ;(You set LS byte before coming here)
0009 E9                     PCHL            ;"Jump" to BIOS
                                            ;Your return address is already
                                            ; on the stack
```

Figure 4-5. Making a direct BIOS call

```
                        ;         Note: This example assumes you have not
                        ;         overwritten the CCP.
                        ;
        0100            ORG       100H        ;Start at TPA
                START:
        0100 210000     LXI       H,0         ;Save CCP's stack pointer
        0103 39         DAD       SP          ;By adding it to 0 in HL
        0104 220F01     SHLD      CCP$STACK
        0107 314101     LXI       SP,LOCAL$STACK
                        ;
                        ;   The main body of your program is here
                        ;
                        ;   ... and when you are ready to return
                        ;       to the CCP...
        010A 2A0F01     LHLD      CCP$STACK   ;Get CCP's stack pointer
        010D F9         SPHL                  ;Restore SP
        010E C9         RET                   ;Return to the CCP
                        ;
        010F            CCP$STACK:  DS   2    ;Save area for CCP SP
        0111                        DS   48   ;Local stack
                        LOCAL$STACK:
        0141            END       START
```

Figure 4-6.   Returning to CCP at program end

Returning to CP/M

Once your program has run, you will need to return control back to CP/M. If your program has not overwritten the CCP and has left the stack pointer as it was when your program was entered, you can return directly to the CCP using a RET instruction.

Figure 4-6 shows how a normal program would do this if you use a local stack, one within the program. The CCP stack is too small; it has room for only 24 16-bit values.

The advantage of returning directly to the CCP is speed. This is true especially on a hard disk system, where the time needed to perform a warm boot is quite noticeable.

If your program has overwritten the CCP, you have no option but to transfer control to location 0000H and let the warm boot occur. To do this, all you need do is execute

```
EXIT:   JMP   0          ;Warm Boot
```

(As a hint, if you are testing a program and it suddenly exits back to CP/M, the odds are that it has inadvertently blundered to location 0000H and executed a warm boot.)

What the BDOS Does
BDOS Function Calls
   Naming Conventions
   Making a BDOS Function Request

The Basic Disk Operating System

The Basic Disk Operating System is the real heart of CP/M. Unlike the Console Command Processor, it must be in memory all the time. It provides all of the input/output services to CP/M programs, including the CCP.

As a general rule, unless you are writing a system-dependent utility program, you should use the BDOS for *all* of your program's input/output. If you circumvent the BDOS you will probably create problems for yourself later.

What the BDOS Does

The BDOS does all of the system input/output for you. These services can be grouped into two types of functions:

Simple Byte-by-Byte I/O
   This is sending and receiving data between the computer system and its logical devices—the console, the "reader" and "punch" (or their substitutes), and the printer.

Disk File I/O
   This covers such tasks as creating new files, deleting old files, opening existing files, and reading and writing 128-byte long "records" to and from these files.

The remainder of this chapter explains each of the BDOS functions, shows how to make each operating system request, and gives additional information for each function. You should also refer to Digital Research's manual, *CP/M 2 Interface Guide,* for their standard description of these functions.

BDOS Function Calls

The BDOS function calls are described in the order of their function code numbers. Figure 5-1 summarizes these calls.

Naming Conventions

In practice, whenever you write programs that make BDOS calls, you should include a series of equates for the BDOS function code numbers. We shall be making reference to these values in subsequent examples, so they are shown in Figure 5-2 as they will appear in the programs.

The function names used to define the equates in Figure 5-2 are shorter than those in Figure 5-1 to strike a balance between the abbreviated function names used in Digital Research's documentation and the need for clearer function descriptions.

Making a BDOS Function Request

All BDOS functions are requested by issuing a CALL instruction to location 0005H. You can also request a function by transferring control to location 0005H with the return address on the stack.

In order to tell the BDOS what you need it to do, you must arrange for the internal registers of the CPU to contain the required information before the CALL instruction is executed.

Function Code	Description
	Simple Byte-by-Byte I/O
0	Overall system and BDOS reset
1	Read a byte from the console keyboard
2	Write a byte to the console screen
3	Read a byte from the logical reader device
4	Write a byte to the logical punch device
5	Write a byte to the logical list device
6	Direct console I/O (no CCP-style editing)
7*	Read the current setting of the IOBYTE
8*	Set a new value of the IOBYTE
9	Send a "$"-terminated string to the console
10	Read a string from the console into a buffer
11	Check if a console key is waiting to be read
12	Return the CP/M version number
	Disk File I/O
13	Reset disk system
14	Select specified logical disk drive
15	Open specified file for reading/writing
16	Close specified file after reading/writing
17	Search file directory for first match with filename
18	Search file directory for next match with filename
19	Delete (erase) file
20	Read the next "record" sequentially
21	Write the next "record" sequentially
22	Create a new file with the specified name
23	Rename a file to a new name
24	Indicate which logical disks are active
25	Return the current default disk drive number
26	Set the DMA address (read/write address)
27	Return the address of an allocation vector
28*	Set specified logical disk drive to Read-Only status
29	Indicate which disks are currently Read-Only status
30	Set specified file to System or Read-Only status
31	Return address of disk parameter block (DPB)
32*	Set/Get the current user number
33	Read a "record" randomly
34	Write a "record" randomly
35	Return logical file size (even for random files)
36	Set record number for the next random read/write
37	Reset specified drive
40	Write a "record" randomly with zero fill

*These do not work under MP/M.

Figure 5-1. BDOS function calls

```
0000 =          B$SYSRESET    EQU    0     ;System Reset
0001 =          B$CONIN       EQU    1     ;Read Console Byte
0002 =          B$CONOUT      EQU    2     ;Write Console Byte
0003 =          B$READIN      EQU    3     ;Read "Reader" Byte
0004 =          B$PUNOUT      EQU    4     ;Write "Punch" Byte
0005 =          B$LISTOUT     EQU    5     ;Write Printer Byte
0006 =          B$DIRCONIO    EQU    6     ;Direct Console I/O
0007 =          B$GETIO       EQU    7     ;Get IOBYTE
0008 =          B$SETIO       EQU    8     ;Set IOBYTE
0009 =          B$PRINTS      EQU    9     ;Print Console String
000A =          B$READCONS    EQU    10    ;Read Console String
000B =          B$CONST       EQU    11    ;Read Console Status
000C =          B$GETVER      EQU    12    ;Get CP/M Version Number
000D =          B$DSKRESET    EQU    13    ;Disk System Reset
000E =          B$SELDSK      EQU    14    ;Select Disk
000F =          B$OPEN        EQU    15    ;Open File
0010 =          B$CLOSE       EQU    16    ;Close File
0011 =          B$SEARCHF     EQU    17    ;Search for First Name Match
0012 =          B$SEARCHN     EQU    18    ;Search for Next Name Match
0013 =          B$ERASE       EQU    19    ;Erase (delete) File
0014 =          B$READSEQ     EQU    20    ;Read Sequential
0015 =          B$WRITESEQ    EQU    21    ;Write Sequential
0016 =          B$CREATE      EQU    22    ;Create File
0017 =          B$RENAME      EQU    23    ;Rename File
0018 =          B$GETACTDSK   EQU    24    ;Get Active (Logged-in) Disks
0019 =          B$GETCURDSK   EQU    25    ;Get Current Default Disk
001A =          B$SETDMA      EQU    26    ;Set DMA (Read/Write) Address
001B =          B$GETALVEC    EQU    27    ;Get Allocation Vector Address
001C =          B$SETDSKRO    EQU    28    ;Set Disk to Read Only
001D =          B$GETRODSKS   EQU    29    ;Get Read Only Disks
001E =          B$SETFAT      EQU    30    ;Set File Attributes
001F =          B$GETDPB      EQU    31    ;Get Disk Parameter Block Address
0020 =          B$SETGETUN    EQU    32    ;Set/Get User Number
0021 =          B$READRAN     EQU    33    ;Read Random
0022 =          B$WRITERAN    EQU    34    ;Write Random
0023 =          B$GETFSIZ     EQU    35    ;Get File Size
0024 =          B$SETRANREC   EQU    36    ;Set Random Record Number
0025 =          B$RESETD      EQU    37    ;Reset Drive
0028 =          B$WRITERANZ   EQU    40    ;Write Random with Zero-Fill
```

Figure 5-2. Equates for BDOS function code numbers

The function code number of the specific function call you want performed must be in register C.

If you need to hand a single-byte value to the BDOS, such as a character to be sent to the console, then you must arrange for this value to be in register E. If the value you wish to pass to the BDOS is a 16-bit value, such as the address of a buffer or a file control block (FCB), this value must be in register pair DE.

When the BDOS hands back a single-byte value, such as a keyboard character or a return code indicating the success or failure of the function you requested, it will be returned in register A. When the BDOS returns a 16-bit value, it will be in register pair HL.

On return from the BDOS, registers A and L will contain the same value, as will registers B and H. This odd convention stems from CP/M's origins in PL/M (Programming Language/Microprocessor), a language used by Intel on their MDS system. Thus, PL/M laid the foundations for what are known as "register calling conventions."

Chapter 5: The Basic Disk Operating System

The BDOS makes no guarantee about the contents of the other registers. If you need to preserve a value that is in a register, either store the value in memory or push it onto the stack. The BDOS uses its own stack space, so there is no need to worry about it consuming your stack.

To sum up, when you make a function request to the BDOS that requires a byte value, the code and the required entry and exit parameters will be as follows:

```
MVI     C,FUNCTION$CODE         ;C = function code
MVI     E,SINGLE$BYTE           ;E = single byte value
CALL    BDOS                    ;Location 5
                                ;A = return code or value
                                ;or HL = return value
```

For those function requests that need to have an address passed to the BDOS, the calling sequence is

```
MVI     C,FUNCTION$CODE         ;C = function code
LXI     D,ADDRESS               ;DE = address
CALL    BDOS                    ;Location 5
                                ;A = return code or value
                                ;or HL = return value
```

If a function request involves disk files, you will have to tell the BDOS the address of the FCB that you have created for the file. (Refer back to Chapter 3 for descriptions of the FCB.)

Many file processing functions return a value in register A that is either 0FFH, indicating that the file named in the FCB could not be found, or equal to a value of 0, 1, 2, or 3. In the latter case, the BDOS is returning what is called a "directory code." The number is the directory entry number that the BDOS matched to the file name in your FCB. At any given moment, the BDOS has a 128-byte sector from the directory in memory. Each file directory entry is 32 bytes, so four of them (numbered 0, 1, 2, and 3) can be processed at a time. The directory code indicates which one has been matched to your FCB.

References to CP/M "records" in the following descriptions mean 128-byte sectors. Do not confuse them with the logical records used by applications programs. Think of CP/M records as 128-byte sectors throughout.

Function 0: System Reset

Function Code: C = 00H
Entry Parameters: None
Exit Parameters: Does not return

Example

```
0000 =              B$SYSRESET  EQU     0           ;System Reset
0005 =              BDOS        EQU     5           ;BDOS entry point

0000 0E00                       MVI     C,B$SYSRESET    ;Set function code
0002 C30500                     JMP     BDOS            ;Note: you can use a JMP since
                                                        ; you don't get control back
```

Purpose The system reset function makes CP/M do a complete reset, exactly the same as the warm boot function invoked when you transfer control to the WARM-BOOT point (refer to Figure 4-1).

In addition to resetting the BDOS, this function reloads the CCP, rebuilds the allocation vectors for the currently logged disks, sets the DMA address (used by CP/M to address the disk read/write buffer) to 80H, marks all disks as being Read/Write status, and transfers control to the CCP. The CCP then outputs its prompt to the console.

Notes This function is most useful when you are working in a high-level language that does not permit a jump instruction to an absolute address in memory. Use it when your program has finished and you need to return control back to CP/M.

Function 1: Read Console Byte

Function Code: C = 01H
Entry Parameters: None
Exit Parameters: A = Data byte from console

Example

```
0001 =          B$CONIN         EQU     1       ;Console input
0005 =          BDOS            EQU     5       ;BDOS entry

0000 0E01                       MVI     C,B$CONIN    ;Get function code
0002 CD0500                     CALL    BDOS
```

Purpose This function reads the next byte of data from the console keyboard and puts it into register A. If the character input is a graphic character, it will be echoed back to the console. The only control characters that are echoed are CARRIAGE RETURN, LINE FEED, BACKSPACE, and TAB. In the case of a TAB character, the BDOS outputs as many spaces as are required to move the cursor to the next multiple of eight columns. All of the other control characters, including CONTROL-C, are input but are not echoed.

This function also checks for CONTROL-S (XOFF) to see if console output should be suspended, and for CONTROL-P (printer echo toggle) to see if console output should also be sent to the list device. If CONTROL-S is found, further output will be suspended until you type another character. CONTROL-P will enable the echoing of console output the first time it is pressed and disable it the second time.

If there is no incoming data character, this function will wait until there is one.

Notes This function often hinders rather than helps, because it echoes the input. Whenever you need console input at the byte-by-byte level, you will usually want to suppress this echo back to the console. For instance, you may know that the "console" is actually a communications line such as a modem. You may be trying to accept a password that should not be echoed back. Or you may need to read a cursor control character that would cause an undesirable side effect on the terminal if echoed there.

In addition, if you need more than a single character from the console, your program will be easier to use if the person at the console can take full advantage of the CCP-style line editing. This can best be done by using the Read Console String function (code 10, 0AH).

Read Console String also is more useful for single character input, especially when you are expecting a "Y" or "N" (yes or no) response. If you use the Read Console Byte function, the operator will have only one chance to enter the data. When you use Read Console String, however, users have the chance to type one character, change their minds, backspace, and type another character.

Function 2: Write Console Byte

Function Code: C = 02H
Entry Parameters: E = Data byte to be output
Exit Parameters: None

Example

```
0002 =                B$CONOUT    EQU     2           ;Write Console Byte
0005 =                BDOS        EQU     5           ;BDOS entry

0000 0E02                         MVI     C,B$CONOUT  ;Function code
0002 1E2A                         MVI     E,'*'       ;E = data byte to be output
0004 CD0500                       CALL    BDOS
```

Purpose This function outputs the data byte in register E to the console. As with function 1, if the data byte is a TAB character, it will be expanded by the BDOS to the next column that is a multiple of eight. The BDOS also checks to see if there is an incoming character, and if there is, checks to see if it is a CONTROL-S (in which case console output is suspended) or CONTROL-P (in which case echoing of console output to the printer is toggled on or off).

Notes You may have problems using this function to output cursor-addressing control sequences to the console. If you try to output a true binary cursor address to position 9, the BDOS will interpret this as a TAB character (ASCII code 9) and dutifully replace it with zero to eight blanks. If you need to output binary values, you must set the most significant bit of the character (use an ORI 80H, for example) so that it will not be taken as the ASCII TAB.

Here are two general-purpose subroutines that you will need for outputting messages. The first one, shown in Figure 5-3, outputs a null-byte-terminated message from a specified address. The second, in Figure 5-4, does essentially the same thing *except* that the message string follows immediately after the call to the subroutine.

```
                        ;MSGOUT (message out)
                        ;Output null-byte-terminated message.

                        ;Calling sequence
                        ;       MESSAGE:        DB      'Message',0
                        ;       :
                        ;       LXI     H,MESSAGE
                        ;       CALL    MSGOUT

                        ;Exit Parameters
                        ;       HL -> Null byte terminator

        0002 =          B$CONOUT        EQU     2       ;Write Console Byte
        0005 =          BDOS            EQU     5       ;BDOS entry point

                        MSGOUT:
        0000 7E         MOV     A,M             ;Get next byte for output
        0001 B7         ORA     A
        0002 C8         RZ                      ;Return when null-byte
        0003 23         INX     H               ;Update message pointer
        0004 E5         PUSH    H               ;Save updated pointer
        0005 5F         MOV     E,A             ;Ready for BDOS
        0006 0E02       MVI     C,B$CONOUT
        0008 CD0500     CALL    BDOS
        000B E1         POP     H               ;Recover message pointer
        000C C30000     JMP     MSGOUT          ;Go back for next character
```

Figure 5-3.   Write console byte example, output null-byte terminated message from specified address

```
                        ;MSGOUTI (message out in-line)
                        ;Output null-byte-terminated message that
                        ;follows the CALL to MSGOUTI.

                        ;Calling sequence
                        ;       CALL    MSGOUTI
                        ;       DB      'Message',0
                        ;       ... next instruction

                        ;Exit Parameters
                        ;       HL -> instruction following message

        0002 =          B$CONOUT        EQU     2       ;Write Console Byte
        0005 =          BDOS            EQU     5       ;BDOS entry point

                        MSGOUTI:
        0000 E1         POP     H               ;HL -> message
        0001 7E         MOV     A,M             ;Get next data byte
        0002 23         INX     H               ;Update message pointer
        0003 B7         ORA     A               ;Check if null byte
        0004 C20800     JNZ     MSGOUTIC        ;No, continue
        0007 E9         PCHL                    ;Yes, return to next instruction
                                                ; after in-line message

                        MSGOUTIC:
        0008 E5         PUSH    H               ;Save message pointer
        0009 5F         MOV     E,A             ;Ready for BDOS
        000A 0E02       MVI     C,B$CONOUT      ;Function code
        000C CD0500     CALL    BDOS
        000F C30000     JMP     MSGOUTI         ;Go back for next char.
```

Figure 5-4.   Write console byte example, output null-byte terminated message following call to subroutine

Function 3: Read "Reader" Byte

        Function Code: C = 03H
        Entry Parameters: None
        Exit Parameters: A = Character input

Example

```
0003 =              B$READIN     EQU    3          ;Read "Reader" Byte
0005 =              BDOS         EQU    5          ;BDOS entry

0000 0E03                        MVI    C,B$READIN ;Function code
0002 CD0500                      CALL   BDOS       ;A = reader byte
```

Purpose   This function reads the next character from the logical "reader" device into register A. In practice, the physical device that is accessed depends entirely on how your BIOS is configured. In some systems, there is no reader at all; this function will return some arbitrary value such as 1AH (the ASCII CONTROL-Z character, used by CP/M to denote "End of File").

Control is not returned to the calling program until a character has been read.

Notes   Since the physical device (if any) used when you issue this request depends entirely on your particular BIOS, there can be no default standard for all CP/M implementations. This is one of the weaker parts of the BDOS.

You should "connect" the reader device by means of BIOS software to a serial port that can be used for communication with another system. This is only a partial solution to the problem, however, because this function call does not return control to your program until an incoming character has been received. There is no direct way that you can "poll" the reader device to see if an incoming character has been received. Once you make this function call, you lose control until the next character arrives; there is no function corresponding to the Read Console Status (function code 11, 0BH) that will simply read status and return to your program.

One possible solution is to build a timer into the BIOS reader driver that returns control to your program with a dummy value in A if a specified period of time goes by with no incoming character. But this brings up the problem of what dummy value to use. If you ever intend to send and receive files containing pure binary information, there is no character in ASCII that you might not encounter in a legitimate context. Therefore, any dummy character you might choose could also be true data.

The most cunning solution is to arrange for one setting of the IOBYTE (which controls logical-device-to-physical-device mapping) to connect the console to the serial communication line. This done, you can make use of the Read Console Status function, which will return not the physical console status but the serial line status. Your program can then act appropriately if no characters are received within a specified time. Figure 5-11 shows a subroutine that uses this technique in the Set IOBYTE function (code 8, 08H).

Figure 5-5 shows an example subroutine to read lines of data from the reader device. It reads characters from the reader, stacking them in memory until either a LINE FEED or a specified number of characters has been received. Note that CARRIAGE RETURNS are ignored, and the input line is terminated by a byte of 00H. The convention of 00H-byte terminated strings and no CARRIAGE RETURNS is used because it makes for much easier program logic. It also conforms to the conventions of the C language.

```
                        ;RL$RDR
                        ;Read line from reader device.
                        ;Carriage returns are ignored, and input terminates
                        ;when specified number of characters have been read
                        ;or a line feed is input.

                        ;Note: Potential weakness is that there is no
                        ;timeout in this subroutine. It will wait forever
                        ;if no more characters arrive at the reader device.

                        ;Calling sequence
                        ;        LXI       H,BUFFER
                        ;        LXI       B,MAXCOUNT
                        ;        CALL      RL$RDR

                        ;Exit Parameters
                        ;        HL -> 00H byte terminating string
                        ;        BC = residual count (0 if max. chars. read)
                        ;        E = last character read

     0003 =             B$READIN       EQU       3           ;Reader input
     0005 =             BDOS           EQU       5           ;BDOS entry point

     000D =             CR             EQU       0DH         ;Carriage return
     000A =             LF             EQU       0AH         ;Line feed (terminator)
                        RL$RDR:
     0000 79                           MOV       A,C         ;Check if count 0
     0001 B0                           ORA       B           ;If count 0 on entry, fake
     0002 5F                           MOV       E,A         ; last char. read (00H)
     0003 CA2000                       JZ        RL$RDRX     ;Yes, exit
     0006 C5                           PUSH      B           ;Save max. chars. count
     0007 E5                           PUSH      H           ;Save buffer pointer
                        RL$RDRI:                             ;Loop back here to ignore
     0008 0E03                         MVI       C,B$READIN
     000A CD0500                       CALL      BDOS        ;A = character input
     000D 5F                           MOV       E,A         ;Preserve copy of chars.
     000E FE0D                         CPI       CR          ;Check if carriage return
     0010 CA0800                       JZ        RL$RDRI     ;Yes, ignore it
     0013 E1                           POP       H           ;Recover buffer pointer
     0014 C1                           POP       B           ;Recover max. Count
     0015 FE0A                         CPI       LF          ;Check if line feed
     0017 CA2000                       JZ        RL$RDRX     ;Yes, exit
     001A 77                           MOV       M,A         ;No, store char. in buffer
     001B 23                           INX       H           ;Update buffer pointer
     001C 0B                           DCX       B           ;Downdate count
     001D C30000                       JMP       RL$RDR      ;Loop back for next char.
                        RL$RDRX:
     0020 3600                         MVI       M,0         ;Null-byte-terminate buffer
     0022 C9                           RET
```

Figure 5-5.   Read line from reader device

Function 4: Write "Punch" Byte

        Function Code: C = 04H
        Entry Parameters: E = Byte to be output
        Exit Parameters: None

Example

```
0004 =              B$PUNOUT        EQU     4           ;Write "Punch" Byte
0005 =              BDOS            EQU     5

0000 0E04           MVI     C,B$PUNOUT          ;Function code
0002 1E2A           MVI     E,'*'               ;Data byte to output
0004 CD0500         CALL    BDOS
```

Purpose   This function is a counterpart to the Read "Reader" Byte described above. It outputs the specified character from register E to the logical punch device. Again, the actual physical device used, if any, is determined by the BIOS. There is no set standard for this device; in some systems the punch device is a "bit bucket," so called because it absorbs all data that you output to it.

Notes   The problems and possible solutions discussed under the Read "Reader" Byte function call also apply here. One difference, of course, is that this function outputs data, so the problem of an indefinite loop waiting for the next character is less likely to occur. However, if your punch device is connected to a communications line, and if the output hardware is not ready, the BIOS line driver will wait forever. Unfortunately, there is no legitimate way to deal with this problem since the BDOS does not have a function call that checks whether a logical device is ready for output.

    Figure 5-6 shows a useful subroutine that outputs a 00H-byte terminated string to the punch. Wherever it encounters a LINE FEED, it inserts a CARRIAGE RETURN into the output data.

Function 5: Write List Byte

        Function Code: C = 05H
        Entry Parameters: E = Byte to be output
        Exit Parameters: None

Example

```
0005 =              B$LSTOUT        EQU     5           ;Write List Byte
0005 =              BDOS            EQU     5

0000 0E05           MVI     C,B$LSTOUT          ;Function code
0002 1E2A           MVI     E,'*'               ;Data byte to output
0004 CD0500         CALL    BDOS
```

Purpose   This function outputs the specified byte in register E to the logical list device. As with the reader and the punch, the physical device used depends entirely on the BIOS.

```
                    ;WL$PUN
                    ;Write line to punch device. Output terminates
                    ;when a 00H byte is encountered.
                    ;A carriage return is output when a line feed is
                    ;encountered.

                    ;Calling sequence
                    ;       LXI     H,BUFFER
                    ;       CALL    WL$PUN

                    ;Exit parameters
                    ;       HL -> 00H byte terminator

0004 =              B$PUNOUT        EQU     4
0005 =              BDOS            EQU     5

000D =              CR              EQU     0DH     ;Carriage return
000A =              LF              EQU     0AH     ;Line feed

                    WL$PUN:
0000 E5                     PUSH    H               ;Save buffer pointer
0001 7E                     MOV     A,M             ;Get next character
0002 B7                     ORA     A               ;Check if 00H
0003 CA2000                 JZ      WL$PUNX         ;Yes, exit
0006 FE0A                   CPI     LF              ;Check if line feed
0008 CC1600                 CZ      WL$PUNLF        ;Yes, O/P CR
000B 5F                     MOV     E,A             ;Character to be output
000C 0E04                   MVI     C,B$PUNOUT      ;Function code
000E CD0500                 CALL    BDOS            ;Output character
0011 E1                     POP     H               ;Recover buffer pointer
0012 23                     INX     H               ;Increment to next char.
0013 C30000                 JMP     WL$PUN          ;Output next char

                    WL$PUNLF:                       ;Line feed encountered
0016 0E04                   MVI     C,B$PUNOUT      ;Function code
0018 1E0D                   MVI     E,CR            ;Output a CR
001A CD0500                 CALL    BDOS
001D 3E0A                   MVI     A,LF            ;Recreate line feed
001F C9                     RET                     ;Output LF

                    WL$PUNX:                        ;Exit
0020 E1                     POP     H               ;Balance the stack
0021 C9                     RET
```

Figure 5-6.   Write line to punch device

Notes   One of the major problems associated with this function is that it does not deal with error conditions very intelligently. You cannot be sure which physical device will be used as the logical list device, and most standard BIOS implementations will cause your program to wait forever if the printer is not ready or has run out of paper. The BDOS has no provision to return any kind of error status to indicate that there is a problem with the list device. Therefore, the BIOS will have to be changed in order to handle this situation.

Figure 5-7 is a subroutine which outputs data to the list device. As you can see, this is essentially a repeat of Figure 5-6, which performs the same function for the logical punch device.

Chapter 5: The Basic Disk Operating System

```
                    ;WL$LST
                    ;Write line to list device. Output terminates
                    ;when a 00H byte is encountered.
                    ;A carriage return is output when a line feed is
                    ;encountered.

                    ;Calling sequence
                    ;       LXI     H,BUFFER
                    ;       CALL    WL$LST

                    ;Exit parameters
                    ;       HL -> 00H byte terminator

        0005 =      B$LSTOUT        EQU     5
        0005 =      BDOS            EQU     5

        000D =      CR              EQU     0DH     ;Carriage return
        000A =      LF              EQU     0AH     ;Line feed

                    WL$LST:
        0000 E5             PUSH    H               ;Save buffer pointer
        0001 7E             MOV     A,M             ;Get next character
        0002 B7             ORA     A               ;Check if 00H
        0003 CA2000         JZ      WL$LSTX         ;Yes, exit
        0006 FE0A           CPI     LF              ;Check if line feed
        0008 CC1600         CZ      WL$LSTLF        ;Yes, O/P CR
        000B 5F             MOV     E,A             ;Character to be output
        000C 0E05           MVI     C,B$LSTOUT      ;Function code
        000E CD0500         CALL    BDOS            ;Output character
        0011 E1             POP     H               ;Recover buffer pointer
        0012 23             INX     H               ;Update to next char.
        0013 C30000         JMP     WL$LST          ;Output next char.

                    WL$LSTLF:                       ;Line feed encountered
        0016 0E05           MVI     C,B$LSTOUT      ;Function code
        0018 1E0D           MVI     E,CR            ;Output a CR
        001A CD0500         CALL    BDOS
        001D 3E0A           MVI     A,LF            ;Recreate line feed
        001F C9             RET                     ;Output LF

                    WL$LSTX:                        ;Exit
        0020 E1             POP     H               ;Balance the stack
        0021 C9             RET
```

Figure 5-7. Write line to list device

Function 6: Direct Console I/O

Function Code: C = 06H
Entry Parameters: E = 0FFH for Input
                   E = Other than 0FFH for output
Exit Parameters: A = Input byte or status

Example

```
        0006 =      B$DIRCONIO      EQU     6       ;Direct (raw) Console I/O
        0005 =      BDOS            EQU     5       ;BDOS entry point

                                                    ;Example of console input

        0000 0E06           MVI     C,B$DIRCONIO    ;Function code
        0002 1EFF           MVI     E,0FFH          ;0FFH means input
        0004 CD0500         CALL    BDOS            ;A = 00 if no char. waiting
                                                    ;A = NZ if character input
```

```
                                                    ;Example of console output
0007 0E06           MVI       C,B$DIRCONIO          ;Function code
0009 1E2A           MVI       E,'*'                 ;Not 0FFH means output char.
000B CD0500         CALL      BDOS
```

Purpose   This function serves double duty: it both inputs and outputs characters from the console. However, it bypasses the normal control characters and line editing features (such as CONTROL-P and CONTROL-S) normally associated with console I/O. Hence the name "direct" (or "unadorned" as Digital Research describes it). If the value in register E is *not* 0FFH, then E contains a valid ASCII character that is output to the console. The logic used is most easily understood when written in pseudo-code:

```
if this is an input request (E = 0FFH)
    {
    if console status indicates a character is waiting
        {
        read the char from the console and
        return to caller with char in A
        }
    else (no input character waiting) and
        return to caller with A = 00
    }
else (output request)
    {
    output the char in E to the console and
    return to caller
    }
```

Notes   This function works well provided you never have to send a value of 0FFH or expect to receive a value of 00H. If you do need to send or receive pure binary data, you cannot use this function, since these values are likely to be part of the data stream.

To understand why you might want to send and receive binary data, remember that the logical "reader" does not have any method for you to check its status to see if an incoming character has arrived. All you can do is attempt to read a character (Read Reader Byte, function code 3). However, the BDOS will not give control back to you until a character arrives (which could be a very long time). One possibility is to logically assign the console to a communications line by the use of the IOBYTE (or some similar means) and then use this Direct I/O call to send and receive data to and from the line. Then you could indeed "poll" the communications line and avoid having your program go into an indefinite wait for an incoming character. An example subroutine using this technique is shown in Figure 5-11 under Set IOBYTE (function code 8).

Figure 5-8 shows a subroutine that uses the Direct Console Input and Output. Because this example is more complex than any shown so far, the code used to check the subroutine has also been included.

Function 7: Get IOBYTE Setting

Function Code: C = 07H
Entry Parameters: None
Exit Parameters: A = IOBYTE current value

```
                    ;---------------------------------------------------------
                    ;TESTBED CODE
                    ;Because of the complexity of this subroutine, the
                    ; actual testbed code has been left in this example.
                    ; It assumes that DDT or ZSID
                    ; will be used for checkout.
                    ;---------------------------------------------------------
                            IF      1                   ;Change to IF 0 to disable testbed
0100                        ORG     100H
0100 C31101                 JMP     START               ;Bypass "variables" setup by DDT
0103 00     OPTIONS:        DB      0                   ;Option flags
0104 41454900 TERMS:        DB      'A','E','I',0       ;Terminators
0108 05     BUFFER          DB      5                   ;Max. characters in buffer
0109 00                     DB      0                   ;Actual count
010A 6363636363             DB      99,99,99,99,99      ;Data bytes
010F 6363                   DB      99,99
            START:
0111 210801                 LXI     H,BUFFER            ;Get address of buffer
0114 110401                 LXI     D,TERMS             ;Address of terminator table
0117 3A0301                 LDA     OPTIONS             ;Get options set by DDT
011A 47                     MOV     B,A                 ;Put in correct register
011B CD2B01                 CALL    RCS                 ;Enter subroutine
011E CD3800                 CALL    38H                 ;Force DDT breakpoint
0121 C31101                 JMP     START               ;Test again
                            ENDIF                       ;End of testbed

            ;RCS: Read console string (using raw input)
            ;Reads a string of characters into a memory
            ; buffer using raw input.

            ;Supports options:
            ;       o to echo characters or not (when echoing,
            ;           a carriage return will be echoed followed
            ;           by line feed)
            ;       o warm boot on input of control-C or not
            ;       o terminating input either on:
            ;           o max. no of chars input
            ;           o matching terminator character

            ; Calling Sequence
            ;       LXI     H,BUFFER
            ;                       Buffer has structure:
            ;                               BUFFER: DB      10      Max. size
            ;                                       DB      0       Actual Read
            ;                                       DS      10+1    Buffer area
            ;       MVI     B,OPTIONS       Options required
            ;                               (see equates)
            ;       LXI     D,TERMS         Pointer to 00H-byte
            ;                               terminated Chars,
            ;                               any one of which is a
            ;                               terminator.
            ;       CALL    RCS

            ; Exit Parameters
            ;       BUFFER: Updated with data bytes and actual
            ;               character count input.
            ;               (Does not include the terminator).
            ;       A = Terminating Code
            ;               0 =     Maximum number of characters input.
            ;               NZ =    Terminator character found.

0001 =      RCS$ECHO        EQU     0000$0001B          ;Input characters to be echoed
0002 =      RCS$ABORT       EQU     0000$0010B          ;Abort on Control-C
0004 =      RCS$FOLD        EQU     0000$0100B          ;Fold lowercase to uppercase
0008 =      RCS$TERM        EQU     0000$1000B          ;DE -> term. char. set

0006 =      B$DIRCONIO      EQU     6                   ;Direct console I/O
0005 =      BDOS            EQU     5                   ;BDOS entry point

0003 =      CTL$C           EQU     03H                 ;Control-C
000D =      CR              EQU     0DH                 ;Carriage return
```

Figure 5-8. Read/write string from/to console using raw I/O

```
000A =              LF              EQU     0AH         ;Line feed
0008 =              BS              EQU     08H         ;Backspace

                    RCS$ST:                             ;Internal standard terminator table
0124 0D                             DB      0DH         ;Carriage return
0125 0A                             DB      0AH         ;Line feed
0126 00                             DB      0           ;End of table

                    RCS$BSS:                            ;Destructive backspace sequence
0127 08200800                       DB      BS,' ',BS,0

                    RCS:                                ;<<<<< Main entry
012B 23                             INX     H           ;HL -> actual count
012C 3600                           MVI     M,0         ;Reset to initial state
012E 2B                             DCX     H           ;HL -> max. count

                    RCS$L:
012F E5                             PUSH    H           ;Save buffer pointer
0130 CD9201                         CALL    RCS$GC      ;Get character and execute:
                                                        ; ECHO, ABORT, and FOLD options
                                                        ;C = character input
0133 E1                             POP     H           ;Recover buffer pointer
0134 3E08                           MVI     A,RCS$TERM  ;Check if user-specified terminator
0136 A0                             ANA     B           ;B = options
0137 C23D01                         JNZ     RCS$UST     ;User specified terminators
013A 112401                         LXI     D,RCS$ST    ;Standard terminators

                    RCS$UST:
013D CDD401                         CALL    RCS$CT      ;Check for terminator
0140 CA4C01                         JZ      RCS$NOTT    ;Not terminator
0143 47                             MOV     B,A         ;Preserve terminating char.

                    RCS$MCI:                            ;(Max. char. input shares this code)
0144 0E00                           MVI     C,0         ;Terminate buffer
0146 CD7F01                         CALL    RCS$SC      ;Save character
0149 78                             MOV     A,B         ;Recover terminating char.
014A B7                             ORA     A           ;Set flags
014B C9                             RET

                    RCS$NOTT:                           ;Not a terminator
014C 3E08                           MVI     A,BS        ;Check for backspace
014E B9                             CMP     C
014F CA6001                         JZ      RCS$BS      ;Backspace entered
0152 CD7F01                         CALL    RCS$SC      ;Save character in buffer
0155 CD8B01                         CALL    RCS$UC      ;Update count
0158 C22F01                         JNZ     RCS$L       ;Not max. so get another char.
015B 0600                           MVI     B,0         ;Fake terminating char.
015D C34401                         JMP     RCS$MCI     ;A = 0 for max. chars. input

                    RCS$BS:                             ;Backspace entered
0160 E5                             PUSH    H           ;Save buffer pointer
0161 23                             INX     H           ;HL -> actual count
0162 35                             DCR     M           ;Back up one
0163 FA7A01                         JM      RCS$NBS     ;Check if count negative
0166 212701                         LXI     H,RCS$BSS   ;HL -> backspacing sequence
0169 3E01                           MVI     A,RCS$ECHO  ;No, check if echoing
016B A0                             ANA     B           ;BS will have been echoed if so
016C CA7001                         JZ      RCS$BSNE    ;No, input BS not echoed
016F 23                             INX     H           ;Bypass initial backspace

                    RCS$BSNE:
0170 C5                             PUSH    B           ;Save options and character
0171 D5                             PUSH    D           ;Save terminator table pointer
0172 CDF601                         CALL    WCS         ;Write console string
0175 D1                             POP     D           ;Recover terminator table pointer
0176 C1                             POP     B           ;Recover options and character
0177 C37B01                         JMP     RCS$BSX     ;Exit from backspace logic

                    RCS$NBS:
017A 34                             INR     M           ;Reset count to 0

                    RCS$BSX:
017B E1                             POP     H           ;Recover buffer pointer
017C C32F01                         JMP     RCS$L       ;Get next character
```

Figure 5-8.   (Continued)

Chapter 5: The Basic Disk Operating System

```
                    RCS$SC:                  ;Save character in C in buffer
                                             ;HL -> buffer pointer
    017F D5         PUSH    D                ;Save terminator table pointer
    0180 E5         PUSH    H                ;Save buffer pointer
    0181 23         INX     H                ;HL -> actual count in buffer
    0182 5E         MOV     E,M              ;Get actual count
    0183 1C         INR     E                ;Count of 0 points to first data byte
    0184 1600       MVI     D,0              ;Make word value of actual count
    0186 19         DAD     D                ;HL -> next free data byte
    0187 71         MOV     M,C              ;Save data byte away
    0188 E1         POP     H                ;Recover buffer pointer
    0189 D1         POP     D                ;Recover terminator table
    018A C9         RET                      ; pointer

                    RCS$UC:                  ;Update buffer count and check for max.
                                             ;Return Z set if = to max., NZ
                                             ; if not HL -> buffer on entry
    018B E5         PUSH    H                ;Save buffer pointer
    018C 7E         MOV     A,M              ;Get max. count
    018D 23         INX     H                ;HL -> actual count
    018E 34         INR     M                ;Increase actual count
    018F BE         CMP     M                ;Compare max. to actual
    0190 E1         POP     H                ;Recover buffer pointer
    0191 C9         RET                      ;Z-flag set

                    RCS$GC:                  ;Get character and execute
                                             ; ECHO, ABORT and FOLD options
    0192 D5         PUSH    D                ;Save terminator table pointer
    0193 E5         PUSH    H                ;Save buffer pointer
    0194 C5         PUSH    B                ;Save option flags

    0195 0E06       RCS$WT: MVI     C,B$DIRCONIO    ;Function code
    0197 1EFF       MVI     E,OFFH           ;Specify input
    0199 CD0500     CALL    BDOS
    019C B7         ORA     A                ;Check if data waiting
    019D CA9501     JZ      RCS$WT           ;Go back and wait
    01A0 C1         POP     B                ;Recover option flags
    01A1 4F         MOV     C,A              ;Save data byte
    01A2 3E02       MVI     A,RCS$ABORT      ;Check if abort option enabled
    01A4 A0         ANA     B
    01A5 CAAE01     JZ      RCS$NA           ;No abort
    01A8 3E03       MVI     A,CTL$C          ;Check for control-C
    01AA B9         CMP     C
    01AB CA0000     JZ      0                ;Warm boot

    01AE 3E04       RCS$NA: MVI     A,RCS$FOLD      ;Check if folding enabled
    01B0 A0         ANA     B
    01B1 C4E501     CNZ     TOUPPER          ;Convert to uppercase
    01B4 3E01       MVI     A,RCS$ECHO       ;Check if echo required
    01B6 A0         ANA     B
    01B7 CAD101     JZ      RCS$NE           ;No echo required
    01BA C5         PUSH    B                ;Save options and character
    01BB 59         MOV     E,C              ;Move character for output
    01BC 0E06       MVI     C,B$DIRCONIO     ;Function code
    01BE CD0500     CALL    BDOS             ;Echo character
    01C1 C1         POP     B                ;Recover options and character
    01C2 3E0D       MVI     A,CR             ;Check if carriage return
    01C4 B9         CMP     C
    01C5 C2D101     JNZ     RCS$NE           ;No
    01C8 C5         PUSH    B                ;Save options and character
    01C9 0E06       MVI     C,B$DIRCONIO     ;Function code
    01CB 1E0A       MVI     E,LF             ;Output line feed
    01CD CD0500     CALL    BDOS
    01D0 C1         POP     B                ;Recover options and character

                    RCS$NE:
    01D1 E1         POP     H                ;Recover buffer pointer
    01D2 D1         POP     D                ;Recover terminator table
    01D3 C9         RET                      ;Character in C
```

Figure 5-8. (Continued)

```
                RCS$CT:                     ;Check for terminator
                                            ;C = character just input
                                            ;DE -> 00-byte character
                                            ; string of term. chars.
                                            ;Returns Z status if no
                                            ; match found, NZ if found
                                            ; (with A = C = terminating
                                            ; character)
01D4 D5                 PUSH    D           ;Save table pointer

                RCS$CTL:
01D5 1A                 LDAX    D           ;Get next terminator character
01D6 B7                 ORA     A           ;Check for end of table
01D7 CAE201             JZ      RCS$CTX     ;No terminator matched
01DA B9                 CMP     C           ;Compare to input character
01DB CAE201             JZ      RCS$CTX     ;Terminator matched
01DE 13                 INX     D           ;Move to next terminator
01DF C3D501             JMP     RCS$CTL     ; loop to try next character in table

                RCS$CTX:                    ;Check terminator exit
01E2 B7                 ORA     A           ;At this point, A will either
                                            ; be 0 if the end of the
                                            ; table has been reached, or
                                            ; NZ if a match has been
                                            ; found. The Z-flag will be
                                            ; set.
01E3 D1                 POP     D           ;Recover table pointer
01E4 C9                 RET

                ;TOUPPER - Fold lowercase letters to upper
                ;   C = Character on entry and exit
                TOUPPER:
01E5 3E60               MVI     A,'a'-1     ;Check if folding needed
01E7 B9                 CMP     C           ;Compare to input char.
01E8 D2F501             JNC     TOUPX       ;No, char. is < or = "a"-1
01EB 3E7A               MVI     A,'z'       ;Maybe, char. is = or > "a"
01ED B9                 CMP     C
01EE DAF501             JC      TOUPX       ;No, char. is > "z"
01F1 3EDF               MVI     A,0DFH      ;Fold character
01F3 A1                 ANA     C
01F4 4F                 MOV     C,A         ;Return folded character
                TOUPX:
01F5 C9                 RET

                ;WCS - Write console string (using raw I/O)
                ;Output terminates when a 00H byte is encountered.
                ;A carriage return is output when a line feed is
                ;encountered.

                ;Calling sequence
                ;       LXI     H,BUFFER
                ;       CALL    WCS

                ;Exit parameters
                ;       HL -> 00H byte terminator
                WCS:
01F6 E5                 PUSH    H           ;Save buffer pointer
01F7 7E                 MOV     A,M         ;Get next character
01F8 B7                 ORA     A           ;Check if 00H
01F9 CA1602             JZ      WCSX        ;Yes, exit
01FC FE0A               CPI     LF          ;Check if line feed
01FE CC0C02             CZ      WCSLF       ;Yes, output a carriage return
0201 5F                 MOV     E,A         ;Character to be output
0202 0E06               MVI     C,B$DIRCONIO ;Function code
0204 CD0500             CALL    BDOS        ;Output character
0207 E1                 POP     H           ;Recover buffer pointer
0208 23                 INX     H           ;Update to next char.
0209 C3F601             JMP     WCS         ;Output next char.
                WCSLF:                      ;Line feed encountered
020C 0E06               MVI     C,B$DIRCONIO ;Function code
```

Figure 5-8.   (Continued)

```
020E 1E0D           MVI     E,CR        ;Output a CR
0210 CD0500         CALL    BDOS
0213 3E0A           MVI     A,LF        ;Recreate line feed
0215 C9             RET                 ;Output LF

            WCSX:                       ;Exit
0216 E1             POP     H           ;Balance the stack
0217 C9             RET
```

Figure 5-8. (Continued)

Example

```
0007 =      B$GETIO     EQU     7       ;Get IOBYTE
0005 =      BDOS        EQU     5       ;BDOS entry point

0000 0E07               MVI     C,B$GETIO   ;Function code
0002 CD0500             CALL    BDOS        ;A = IOBYTE
```

Purpose This function places the current value of the IOBYTE in register A.

Notes As we saw in Chapter 4, the IOBYTE is a means of associating CP/M's logical devices (console, reader, punch, and list) with the physical devices supported by a particular BIOS. Use of the IOBYTE is completely optional. CP/M, to quote from the Digital Research *CP/M 2.0 Alteration Guide,* "...tolerate[s] the existence of the IOBYTE at location 0003H."

In practice, the STAT utility provided by Digital Research does have some features that set the IOBYTE to different values from the system console.

Figure 5-9 summarizes the IOBYTE structure. A more detailed description was given in Chapter 4.

Each two-bit field can take on one of four values: 00, 01, 10, and 11. The value can be interpreted by the BIOS to mean a specific physical device, as shown in Table 4-1.

Figure 5-10 has equates that are used to refer to the IOBYTE. You can see that the values shown are declared using the SHL (shift left) operator in the Digital Research Assembler. This is just a reminder that the values are structured this way in the IOBYTE itself.

```
                    +-------+-------+-------+-------+
            Bit No. | 7 : 6 | 5 : 4 | 3 : 2 | 1 : 0 |
                    +-------+-------+-------+-------+
     Logical Device   List    Punch   Reader  Console
```

Figure 5-9. The IOBYTE structure

```
;IOBYTE equates
;These are for accessing the IOBYTE.

;Mask values to isolate specific devices.
;(These can also be inverted to preserve all BUT the
; specific device)

0003 =          IO$CONM EQU     0000$0011B      ;Console mask
000C =          IO$RDRM EQU     0000$1100B      ;Reader mask
0030 =          IO$PUNM EQU     0011$0000B      ;Punch mask
00C0 =          IO$LSTM EQU     1100$0000B      ;List mask

                                                ;Console values
0000 =          IO$CTTY EQU     0               ;Console -> TTY:
0001 =          IO$CCRT EQU     1               ;Console -> CRT:
0002 =          IO$CBAT EQU     2               ;Console input <- RDR:
                                                ;Console output -> LST:
0003 =          IO$CUC1 EQU     3               ;Console -> UC1: (user console 1)

                                                ;Reader values
0000 =          IO$RTTY EQU     0 SHL 2         ;Reader <- TTY:
0004 =          IO$RRDR EQU     1 SHL 2         ;Reader <- RDR:
0008 =          IO$RUR1 EQU     2 SHL 2         ;Reader <- UR1: (user reader 1)
000C =          IO$RUR2 EQU     3 SHL 2         ;Reader <- UR2: (user reader 2)

                                                ;Punch values
0000 =          IO$PTTY EQU     0 SHL 4         ;Punch -> TTY:
0010 =          IO$PPUN EQU     1 SHL 4         ;Punch -> PUN:
0020 =          IO$PUP1 EQU     2 SHL 4         ;Punch -> UP1: (user punch 1)
0030 =          IO$PUP2 EQU     3 SHL 4         ;Punch -> UP2: (user punch 2)

                                                ;List values
0000 =          IO$LTTY EQU     0 SHL 6         ;List -> TTY:
0040 =          IO$LCRT EQU     1 SHL 6         ;List -> CRT:
0080 =          IO$LLPT EQU     2 SHL 6         ;List -> LPT: (physical line printer)
00C0 =          IO$LUL1 EQU     3 SHL 6         ;List -> UL1: (user list 1)
```

Figure 5-10.   IOBYTE equates

Function 8: Set IOBYTE

    Function Code: C = 08H
    Entry Parameters: E = New IOBYTE value
    Exit Parameters: None

Example   This listing shows you how to assign the logical reader device to the BIOS's console driver. It makes use of some equates from Figure 5-10.

```
0007 =          B$GETIO         EQU     7               ;Get IOBYTE
0008 =          B$SETIO         EQU     8               ;Set IOBYTE
0005 =          BDOS            EQU     5               ;BDOS entry point

000C =          IO$RDRM         EQU     0000$1100B      ;Reader bit mask
0008 =          IO$RUR1         EQU     2 SHL 2         ;User reader select

                                ;This example shows how to assign the logical
                                ;reader to the user-defined reader #1 (UR1:)

0100                            ORG     100H
0100 0E07                       MVI     C,B$GETIO       ;First, get current IOBYTE
```

Chapter 5: The Basic Disk Operating System

```
0102 CD0500              CALL    BDOS
0105 E6F3                ANI     (NOT IO$RDRM) AND 0FFH ;Preserve all but
                                                       ; reader bits
0107 F608                ORI     IO$RUR1         ;OR in new setting
0109 5F                  MOV     E,A             ;Ready for set IOBYTE
010A 0E08                MVI     C,B$SETIO       ;Set new value
010C CD0500              CALL    BDOS
```

Purpose This function sets the IOBYTE to a new value which is given in register E. Because of the individual bit fields in the IOBYTE, you will normally use the Get IOBYTE function, change some bits in the current value, and then call the Set IOBYTE function.

Notes You can use the Set IOBYTE, Get IOBYTE, and Direct Console I/O functions together to create a small program that transforms your computer system into a "smart" terminal. Any data that you type on your keyboard can be sent out of a serial communications line to another computer, and any data received on the line can be sent to the screen.

Figure 5-11 shows this program and illustrates the use of all of these functions.

For this program to function correctly, your BIOS must check the IOBYTE and detect whether the logical console is connected to the physical console (with the IOBYTE set to TTY:) or to the input side of the serial communications line (with the IOBYTE set to RDR:).

Figure 5-11 shows how to use the Get and Set IOBYTE functions to make a simple terminal emulator. For this example to work, the BIOS must detect the Console Value as 3 (IO$CUC1) and connect Console Status, Input, and Output functions to the communications line.

```
0006 =                   B$DIRCONIO      EQU     6           ;Direct console input/output
0007 =                   B$GETIO         EQU     7           ;Get IOBYTE
0008 =                   B$SETIO         EQU     8           ;Set IOBYTE
000B =                   B$CONST         EQU     11          ;Get console status (sneak preview)
0005 =                   BDOS            EQU     5           ;BDOS entry point

0003 =                   IO$CONM EQU     0000$0011B          ;Console mask for IOBYTE
0001 =                   IO$CCRT EQU     1                   ;Console -> CRT:
0003 =                   IO$CUC1 EQU     3                   ;Console -> user console #1
                         TERM:
0000 CD2A00                      CALL    SETCRT              ;Connect console -> CRT:

                         TERM$CKS:
0003 CD5200                      CALL    CONST               ;Get CRT status
0006 CA2400                      JZ      TERM$NOKI           ;No console input
0009 CD4B00                      CALL    CONIN               ;Get keyboard character
000C CD3000                      CALL    SETCOMM             ;Connect console -> comm. line
000F CD4500                      CALL    CONOUT              ;Output to comm. line

                         TERM$CCS:                           ;Check comm. status
0012 CD5200                      CALL    CONST               ;Get "console" status
0015 CA0000                      JZ      TERM                ;No incoming comm. character
0018 CD4B00                      CALL    CONIN               ;Get incoming comm. character
```

Figure 5-11. Simple terminal emulator

```
              001B CD2A00            CALL    SETCRT         ;Connect console -> CRT:
              001E CD4500            CALL    CONOUT         ;Output to CRT
              0021 C30300            JMP     TERM$CKS       ;Loop back to check keyboard status
                         TERM$NOKI:
              0024 CD3000            CALL    SETCOMM        ;Connect console -> comm. line
              0027 C31200            JMP     TERM$CCS       ;Loop back to check comm. status
                         SETCRT:                            ;Connect console -> CRT:
              002A F5                PUSH    PSW            ;Save possible data character
              002B 0601              MVI     B,IO$CCRT      ;Connect console -> CRT:
              002D C33300            JMP     SETCON         ;Common code
                         SETCOMM:                           ;Connect console -> comm. line
              0030 F5                PUSH    PSW            ;Save possible data character
              0031 0603              MVI     B,IO$CUC1      ;Connect console -> comm. line
                                                            ;Drop into SETCON
                         SETCON:                            ;Set console device
                                                            ;New code in B (in bits 1,0)
              0033 C5                PUSH    B              ;Save code
              0034 0E07              MVI     C,B$GETIO      ;Get current IOBYTE
              0036 CD0500            CALL    BDOS
              0039 E6FC              ANI     (NOT IO$CONM) AND 0FFH  ;Preserve all but console
              003B C1                POP     B              ;Recover required code
              003C B0                ORA     B              ;OR in new bits
              003D 5F                MOV     E,A            ;Ready for setting
              003E 0E08              MVI     C,B$SETIO      ;Function code
              0040 CD0500            CALL    BDOS
              0043 F1                POP     PSW            ;Recover possible data character
              0044 C9                RET
                         CONOUT:
              0045 5F                MOV     E,A            ;Get data byte for output
              0046 0E06              MVI     C,B$DIRCONIO   ;Function code
              0048 C30500            JMP     BDOS           ;BDOS returns to CONOUT's caller
                         CONIN:
              004B 0E06               MVI    C,B$DIRCONIO   ;Function code
              004D 1EFF               MVI    E,0FFH         ;Indicate console input
              004F C30500             JMP    BDOS           ;BDOS returns to CONIN's caller
                         CONST:
              0052 0E0B               MVI    C,B$CONST      ;Function code
              0054 CD0500             CALL   BDOS
              0057 B7                 ORA    A              ;Set Z-flag to result
              0058 C9                 RET
```

Figure 5-11. (Continued)

Function 9: Display "$"-Terminated String

Function Code: C = 09H
Entry Parameters: DE = Address of first byte of string
Exit Parameters: None

Example

```
              0009 =         B$PRINTS     EQU     9       ;Print $-Terminated String
              0005 =         BDOS         EQU     5       ;BDOS entry point

              000D =         CR           EQU     0DH     ;Carriage return
              000A =         LF           EQU     0AH     ;Line feed
              0009 =         TAB          EQU     09H     ;Horizontal tab
```

Chapter 5: The Basic Disk Operating System 89

```
0000 0D0A095468MESSAGE:     DB      CR,LF,TAB,'This is a message',CR,LF,'$'
0017 0E09             MVI     C,B$PRINTS      ;Function code
0019 110000           LXI     D,MESSAGE       ;Pointer to message
001C CD0500           CALL    BDOS
```

Purpose   This function outputs a string of characters to the console device. The address of this string is in registers DE. You must make sure that the last character of the string is "$"; the BDOS uses this character as a marker for the end of the string. The "$" itself does not get output to the console.

While the BDOS is outputting the string, it expands tabs as previously described, checks to see if there is an incoming character, and checks for CONTROL-S (XOFF, which stops the output until another character is entered) or CONTROL-P (which turns on or off echoing of console characters to the printer).

Notes   One of the biggest drawbacks of this function is its use of "$" as a terminating character. As a result, you cannot output a string with a "$" in it. To be truly general-purpose, it would be better to use a subroutine that used an ASCII NUL (00H) character as a terminator, and simply make repetitive calls to the BDOS CONOUT function (code 2). Figure 5-3 is an example of such a subroutine.

Figure 5-12 shows an example of a subroutine that outputs one of several messages. It selects the message based on a message code that you give it as a parameter. Therefore, it is useful for handling error messages; the calling code can pass it an 8-bit error code. You may find it more flexible to convert this subroutine to using 00H-byte-terminated messages using the techniques shown in Figure 5-3.

```
;OM (Output message)
;This subroutine selects one of several messages based on
; the contents of the A register on entry. It then displays
; this message on the console.

;Each message is declared with a "$" as its last character.
; If the A register contains a value larger than the number
; of messages declared, OM will output "Unknown Message".

;As an option, OM can output carriage return / line feed
; prior to outputting the message text.

;Entry parameters
;       HL -> message table
;               This has the form :
;                       DB      3       ;Number of messages in table
;                       DW      MSG0    ;Address of text (A = 0)
;                       DW      MSG1    ;(A = 1)
;                       DW      MSG2    ;(A = 2)
;
;       MSG0:   DB      'Message text$'
;                       ...etc.
;               A = Message code (from 0 on up)
;               B = Output CR/LF if non-zero
```

Figure 5-12.   Display $-terminated message on console

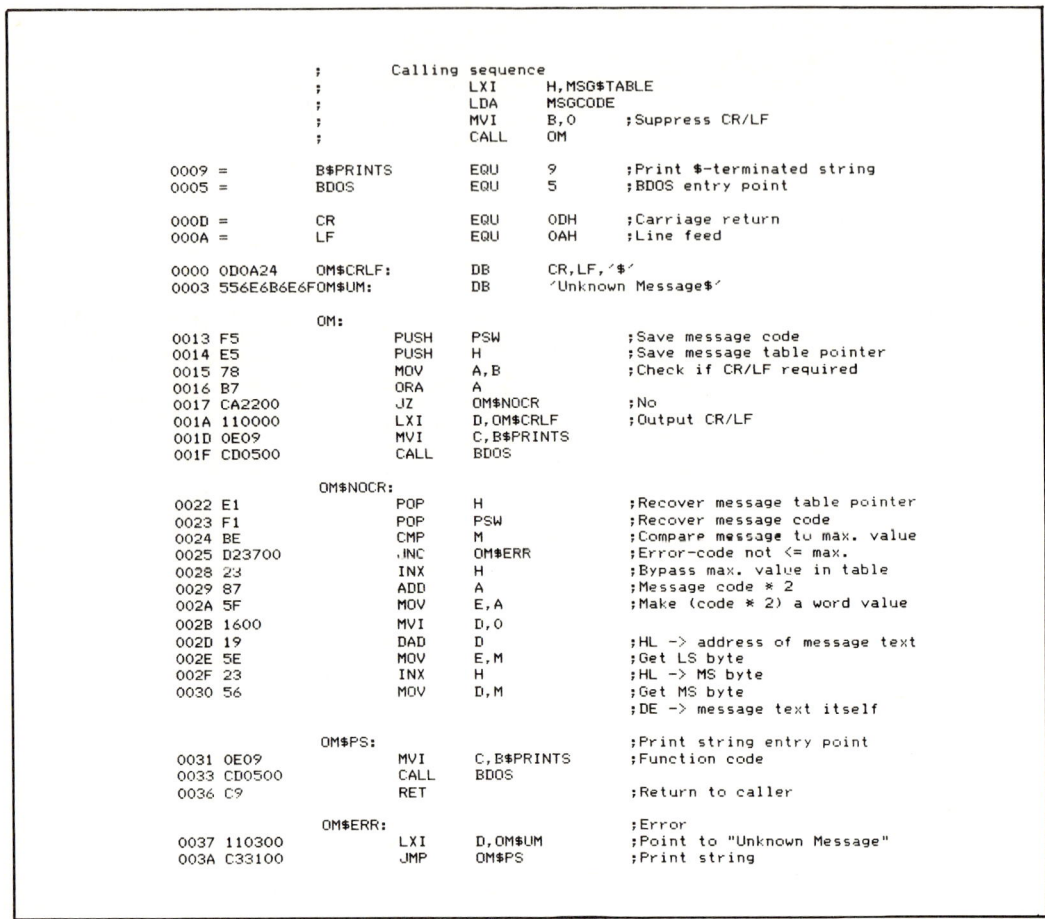

Figure 5-12. (Continued)

Function 10: Read Console String

Function Code: C = 0AH
Entry Parameters: DE = Address of string buffer
Exit Parameters: String buffer with console bytes in it

Example

```
000A =           B$READCONS      EQU     10      ;Read Console String
0005 =           BDOS            EQU     5       ;BDOS entry point
```

```
0050 =              BUFLEN      EQU     80              ;Buffer length
                    BUFFER:                             ;Console input buffer
0000 50             BUFMAXCH:   DB      BUFLEN          ;Max. no. of characters in
                                                        ; buffer
0001 00             BUFACTCH:   DB      0               ;Actual no. of characters input
0002                BUFCH:      DS      BUFLEN          ;Buffer characters
0052 0E0A                       MVI     C,B$READCONS    ;Function code
0054 110000                     LXI     D,BUFFER        ;Pointer to buffer
0057 CD0500                     CALL    BDOS
```

Purpose   This function reads a string of characters from the console device and stores them in a buffer (address in DE) that you define. Full line editing is possible: the operator can backspace, cancel the line and start over, and use all the normal control functions. What you will ultimately see in the buffer is the final version of the character string entered, without any of the errors or control characters used to do the line editing.

The buffer that you define has a special format. The first byte in the buffer tells the BDOS the maximum number of characters to be accepted. The second byte is reserved for the BDOS to tell you how many characters were actually placed in the buffer. The following bytes contain the characters of the string.

Character input will cease either when a CARRIAGE RETURN is entered or when the maximum number of characters, as specified in the buffer, has been received. The CARRIAGE RETURN is not stored in the buffer as a character—it just serves as a terminator.

If the first character entered is a CARRIAGE RETURN, then the BDOS sets the "characters input" byte to 0. If you attempt to input more than the maximum number of characters, the "characters input" count will be the same as the maximum value allowed.

Notes   This function is useful for accepting console input, especially because of the line editing that it allows. It should be used even for single-character responses, such as "Y/N" (yes or no), because the operator can type "Y", backspace, and overtype with "N". This makes for more "forgiving" programs, tolerant of humans who change their minds.

Figure 5-13 shows an example subroutine that uses this function. It accepts console input, matches the input against a table, and transfers control to the appropriate subroutine. Many interactive programs need to do this; they accept an operator command and then transfer control to the appropriate command processor to deal with that command.

This example also includes two other subroutines that are useful in their own right. One compares null-byte-terminated strings (FSCMP), and the other converts, or "folds," lowercase letters to uppercase (FOLD).

```
;RSA
;Return subprocessor address
;This subroutine returns one of several addresses selected
; from a table by matching keyboard input against specified
; strings. It is normally used to switch control to a
; particular subprocessor according to an option entered
; by the operator from the keyboard.
;
;Character string comparisons are performed with case-folding;
; that is, lowercase letters are converted to uppercase.
;
;If the operator input fails to match any of the specified
; strings, then the carry flag is set. Otherwise, it is
; cleared.

;Entry parameters
;       HL -> Subprocessor select table
;               This has the form :
;               DW      TEXT0,SUBPROC0
;               DW      TEXT1,SUBPROC1
;               DW      0       ;Terminator
;       TEXT0:  DB      'add',0 ;00H-byte terminated
;       TEXT1:  DB      'subtract',0
;       SUBPROC0:
;               Code for processing ADD function.
;       SUBPROC1:
;               Code for processing SUBTRACT function.

;Exit parameters
;       DE -> operator input string (00H-terminated
;               input string).
;       Carry Clear, HL -> subprocessor.
;       Carry Set, HL = 0000H.

;Calling sequence
;       LXI     H,SUBPROCTAB    ;Subprocessor table
;       CALL    RSA
;       JC      ERROR           ;Carry set only on error
;       LXI     D,RETURN        ;Fake CALL instruction
;       PUSH    D               ;Push return address on stack
;       PCHL                    ;"CALL" to subprocessor
;       RETURN:
```

```
000A =          B$READCONS  EQU     10          ;Read console string into buffer
0005 =          BDOS        EQU     5           ;BDOS entry point

0050 =          RSA$BL      EQU     80          ;Buffer length
0000 50         RSA$BUF:    DB      RSA$BL      ;Max. no. of characters
0001 00         RSA$ACTC:   DB      0           ;Actual no. of characters
0002            RSA$BUFC:   DS      RSA$BL      ;Buffer characters
0052 00                     DB      0           ;Safety terminator

                RSA:
0053 2B                     DCX     H           ;Adjust Subprocessor pointer
0054 2B                     DCX     H           ; for code below
0055 E5                     PUSH    H           ;Top of stack (TOS) -> subproc. table - 2
0056 0E0A                   MVI     C,B$READCONS ;Function code
0058 110000                 LXI     D,RSA$BUF   ;DE -> buffer
005B CD0500                 CALL    BDOS        ;Read operator input and
                                                ; Convert to 00H-terminated
005E 210100                 LXI     H,RSA$ACTC  ;HL -> actual no. of chars. input
0061 5E                     MOV     E,M         ;Get actual no. of chars. input
0062 1600                   MVI     D,0         ;Make into word value
0064 23                     INX     H           ;HL -> first data character
0065 19                     DAD     D           ;HL -> first UNUSED character in buffer
0066 3600                   MVI     M,0         ;Make input buffer 00H terminated

                RSA$ML:                         ;Compare input to specified values
                                                ; Main loop
0068 E1                     POP     H           ;Recover subprocessor table pointer
0069 23                     INX     H           ;Move to top of next entry
006A 23                     INX     H           ;HL -> text address
006B 5E                     MOV     E,M         ;Get text address
```

Figure 5-13. Read console string for keyboard options

```
006C 23              INX     H
006D 56              MOV     D,M             ;DE -> text

006E 7A              MOV     A,D             ;Check if at end of subprocessor table
006F B3              ORA     E
0070 CA8500          JZ      RSA$NFND        ;Match not found

0073 23              INX     H               ;HL -> subprocessor address
0074 E5              PUSH    H               ;Save ptr. to subprocessor table
0075 210200          LXI     H,RSA$BUFC      ;HL -> input characters
0078 CD8A00          CALL    FSCMP           ;Folded string compare
007B C26800          JNZ     RSA$ML          ;No match, move to next entry
007E E1              POP     H               ;Match found, recover subprocessor ptr.
007F 5E              MOV     E,M             ;Get actual subprocessor address
0080 23              INX     H
0081 56              MOV     D,M             ;DE -> Subprocessor code
0082 EB              XCHG                    ;HL -> Subprocessor code
0083 B7              ORA     A               ;Clear carry (match found)
0084 C9              RET

             RSA$NFND:
0085 210000          LXI     H,0             ;Indicate no match found
0088 37              STC                     ;Set carry
0089 C9              RET

             ;FSCMP
             ;Compare folded (lowercase to upper) string.
             ;This subroutine compares two 00H-byte terminated
             ;strings and returns with the condition flags set
             ;to indicate their relationship.

             ;Entry parameters
             ;      DE -> string 1
             ;      HL -> string 2

             ;Exit parameters
             ;      Flags set (based on string 1 - string 2, on a
             ;      character-by-character basis)

                     FSCMP:
008A 1A              LDAX    D               ;Get string 1 character
008B CD9E00          CALL    FOLD            ;Fold to uppercase
008E F5              PUSH    PSW             ;Save string 1 character
008F 7E              MOV     A,M             ;Get string 2 character
0090 CD9E00          CALL    FOLD            ;Fold to uppercase
0093 47              MOV     B,A             ;Save string 2 character
0094 F1              POP     PSW             ;Recover string 1 character
0095 B8              CMP     B               ;String 1 - string 2
0096 C0              RNZ                     ;Return if not equal
0097 B7              ORA     A               ;Equal, so check if end of strings
0098 C8              RZ                      ;Yes
0099 13              INX     D               ;No, update string 1 pointer
009A 23              INX     H               ; and string 2 pointer
009B C38A00          JMP     FSCMP           ;Check next character

             ;FOLD
             ;Folds a lowercase letter (a-z) to uppercase (A-Z)
             ;The character to be folded is in A on entry and on exit.

                     FOLD:
009E 4F              MOV     C,A             ;Preserve input character
009F 3E60            MVI     A,'a'-1         ;Check if folding needed
00A1 B9              CMP     C               ;Compare to input character
00A2 D2AF00          JNC     FOLDX           ;No, char. is <= "a"
00A5 3E7A            MVI     A,'z'           ;Check if < "z"
00A7 B9              CMP     C
00A8 DAAF00          JC      FOLDX           ;No, char. is > "z"
00AB 3EDF            MVI     A,0DFH
00AD A1              ANA     C               ;Fold character
00AE C9              RET

                     FOLDX:
00AF 79              MOV     A,C             ;Recover original input char.
00B0 C9              RET
```

Figure 5-13. (Continued)

Function 11: Read Console Status

        Function Code: C = 0BH
        Entry Parameters: None
        Exit Parameters: A = 00H if no incoming data byte
                               A = 0FFH if incoming data byte

Example

```
000B =              B$CONST       EQU     11        ;Get Console Status
0005 =              BDOS          EQU     5         ;BDOS entry point

0000 0E0B                         MVI     C,B$CONST ;Function code
0002 CD0500                       CALL    BDOS      ;A = 00 if no character waiting
                                                    ;A = 0FFH if character waiting
```

Purpose   This function tells you whether a console input character is waiting to be processed. Unlike the Console Input functions, which will wait until there is input, this function simply checks and returns immediately.

Notes   Use this function wherever you want to interrupt an executing program if a console keyboard character is entered. Just put a Console Status call in the main loop of the program. Then, if the program detects that keyboard data is waiting, it can take the appropriate action. Normally this would be to jump to location 0000H, thereby aborting the current program and initiating a warm boot.

Figure 5-11 is an example subroutine that shows how to use this function.

Function 12: Get CP/M Number

        Function Code: C = 0CH
        Entry Parameters: None
        Exit Parameters: HL = Version number code

Example

```
000C =              B$GETVER      EQU     12        ;Get CP/M Version Number
0005 =              BDOS          EQU     5         ;BDOS entry point

0000 0E0C                         MVI     C,B$GETVER ;Function code
0002 CD0500                       CALL    BDOS       ;H = 00 for CP/M
                                                     ;L = version (e.g. 22H for 2.2)
```

Purpose   This function tells you which version of CP/M you are currently running. A two-byte value is returned:

        H = 00H for CP/M, H = 01H for MP/M

        L = 00H for all releases before CP/M 2.0

        L = 20H for CP/M 2.0, 21H for 2.1, 22H for 2.2, and so on for any subsequent releases.

This information is of interest only if your program has some version-specific logic built into it. For example, CP/M version 1.4 does not support the same Random File Input/Output operations that CP/M 2.2 does. Therefore, if your program uses Random I/O, put this check at the beginning to ensure that it is indeed running under the appropriate version of CP/M.

Notes Figure 5-14 is a subroutine that checks the current CP/M version number, and, if it is not CP/M 2.2, displays an explanatory message on the console and does a warm boot by jumping to location 0000H.

Function 13: Reset Disk System

    Function Code: C = 0DH
    Entry Parameters: None
    Exit Parameters: None

```
                    ;CCPM
                    ;Check if CP/M
                    ;This subroutine determines the version number of the
                    ;operating system and, if not CP/M version 2, displays
                    ;an error message and executes a warm boot.

                    ;Entry and exit parameters
                    ;       None

                    ;Calling sequence
                    ;       CALL     CCPM          ;Warm boots if not CP/M 2

       0009 =       B$PRINTS        EQU     9        ;Display $-terminated string
       000C =       B$GETVER        EQU     12       ;Get version number
       0005 =       BDOS            EQU     5        ;BDOS entry point

       000D =       CR              EQU     0DH      ;Carriage return
       000A =       LF              EQU     0AH      ;Line feed

       0000 0D0A    CCPMM:  DB      CR,LF
       0002 5468697320     DB      'This program can only run under CP/M version 2.'
       0031 0D0A24         DB      CR,LF,'$'
                    CCPM:
       0034 0E0C            MVI     C,B$GETVER   ;Get version number
       0036 CD0500          CALL    BDOS
       0039 7C              MOV     A,H          ;H must be 0 for CP/M
       003A B7              ORA     A
       003B C24700          JNZ     CCPME        ;Must be MP/M
       003E 7D              MOV     A,L          ;L = version number of CP/M
       003F E6F0            ANI     0F0H         ;Version number in MS nibble
       0041 FE20            CPI     20H          ;Check if version 2
       0043 C24700          JNZ     CCPME        ;Must be an earlier version
       0046 C9              RET                  ;Yes, CP/M version 2
                    CCPME:                       ;Error
       0047 0E09            MVI     C,B$PRINTS   ;Display error message
       0049 110000          LXI     D,CCPMM
       004C CD0500          CALL    BDOS
       004F C30000          JMP     0            ;Warm boot
```

Figure 5-14. Determine the CP/M version number

Example

```
000D =          B$DSKRESET      EQU     13          ;Reset Disk System
0005 =          BDOS            EQU     5           ;BDOS entry point

0000 0E0D                       MVI     C,B$DSKRESET ;Function code
0002 CD0500                     CALL    BDOS
```

Purpose This function requests CP/M to completely reset the disk file system. CP/M then resets its internal tables, selects logical disk A as the default disk, resets the DMA address back to 0080H (the address of the buffer used by the BDOS to read and write to the disk), and marks all logical disks as having Read/Write status.

The BDOS will then have to log in each logical disk as each disk is accessed. This involves reading the entire file directory for the disk and rebuilding the allocation vectors (which keep track of which allocation blocks are free and which are used for file storage).

Notes This function lets you change the diskettes under program control. If the operator were to simply change diskettes, without CP/M knowing about it, the next access to the (now different) diskette would force CP/M to declare the disk Read-Only, thwarting any further attempts to write on the diskette. If you need to reset one or two disks, rather than the entire disk system, look ahead to the Reset Disk function (code 37) described at the end of this chapter.

Figure 5-15 shows a simple subroutine that outputs a message on the console, requesting that the diskette in a specified drive be changed. It then issues a Reset Disk function call to make sure that CP/M will log in the diskette on the next access to the drive.

```
                ;CDISK
                ;Change disk
                ;This subroutine displays a message requesting the
                ;user to change the specified logical disk, then waits
                ;for a carriage return to be pressed. It then issues
                ;a Disk Reset and returns to the caller.

                ;Entry parameters
                ;       A = Logical disk to be changed (A = 0, B = 1)

                ;Exit parameters
                ;       None

                ;Calling sequence
                ;       MVI     A,0             ;Change drive A:
                ;       CALL    CDISK

000D =          B$DSKRESET      EQU     13      ;Disk Reset function code
0009 =          B$PRINTS        EQU     9       ;Print $-terminated string
0001 =          B$CONIN         EQU     1       ;Get console input
0005 =          BDOS            EQU     5       ;BDOS entry point
```

Figure 5-15. Reset requested disk drive

Chapter 5: The Basic Disk Operating System

```
            000D =                  CR          EQU     0DH
            000A =                  LF          EQU     0AH
            0000 0D0A436861 CDISKM: DB          CR,LF,'Change logical disk '
            0016 00           CDISKD: DB        0
            0017 3A20616E64        DB           ': and press Carriage Return to continue$'
                             CDISK:
            003F C640                ADI        'A'-1                ;Convert to letter
            0041 321600              STA        CDISKD               ;Store in message
            0044 0E09                MVI        C,B$PRINTS           ;Display message
            0046 110000              LXI        D,CDISKM
            0049 CD0500              CALL       BDOS
                             CDISKW:
            004C 0E01                MVI        C,B$CONIN            ;Get keyboard character
            004E CD0500              CALL       BDOS
            0051 FE0D                CPI        CR
            0053 C24C00              JNZ        CDISKW
            0056 0E0D                MVI        C,B$DSKRESET         ;Now reset disk system
            0058 CD0500              CALL       BDOS
            005B C9                  RET
```

Figure 5-15.   Reset requested disk drive (continued)

Function 14: Select Logical Disk

      Function Code: C = 0EH
      Entry Parameters: E = Logical Disk Code
                                      00H = Drive A
                                      01H = Drive B and so on
      Exit Parameters: None

Example

```
            000E =               B$SELDSK    EQU     14           ;Select Logical Disk
            0005 =               BDOS        EQU     5            ;BDOS entry point

            0000 0E0E            MVI     C,B$SELDSK       ;Function code
            0002 1E00            MVI     E,0              ;E = 0 for A:, 1 for B: etc.
            0004 CD0500          CALL    BDOS
```

Purpose   This function makes the logical disk named in register E the default disk. All subsequent references to disk files that do not specify the disk will use this default.

                When you reference a disk file that *does* have an explicit logical disk in its name you do not have to issue another Select Disk function; the BDOS will take care of that for you.

Notes   Notice the way in which the logical disk is specified in register E. It is not the same as the disk drive specification in the first byte of the file control block. In the FCB, a value of 00H is used to mean "use the current default disk" (as specified in the last Select Disk call or by the operator on the console). With this function, a value of 00H in register A means that A is the selected drive, a value of 01H means drive B, and so on to 0FH for drive P, allowing 16 drives in the system.

If you select a logical disk that does not exist in your computer system, the BDOS will display the following message:

```
BDOS Err on J: Select
```

If you type a CARRIAGE RETURN in order to proceed, the BDOS will do a warm boot and transfer control back to the CCP. To avoid this, you must rely on the computer operator not to specify nonexistent disks or build into your program the knowledge of how many logical disk drives are on the system.

Another problem with this function is that you cannot distinguish a logical disk for which the appropriate tables have been built into the BIOS, but for which there is no physical disk drive. The BDOS does not check to see if the drive is physically present when you make the Select Disk call. It merely sets up some internal values ready to access the logical disk. If you then attempt to access this nonexistent drive, the BIOS will detect the error. What happens next is completely up to the BIOS. The standard BIOS will return control to the BDOS, indicating an error condition. The BDOS will output the message

```
BDOS Err on C: Bad Sector
```

You then have a choice. You can press CARRIAGE RETURN, in which case the BDOS will ignore the error and attempt to continue with whatever appears to have been read in. Or you can enter a CONTROL-C, causing the program to abort and CP/M to perform a warm boot.

Note that the Select Disk function does not return any values. If your program gets control back, you can assume that the logical disk you asked for at least has tables declared for it.

Function 15: Open File

Function Code: C = 0FH
Entry Parameters: DE = Address of file control block
Exit Parameters: A = Directory code

Example

```
000F =              B$OPEN          EQU     15              ;Open File
0005 =              BDOS            EQU     5               ;BDOS entry point
                    FCB:                                    ;File control block
0000 00             FCB$DISK:       DB      0               ;Search on default disk drive
0001 46494C454E     FCB$NAME:       DB      'FILENAME'      ;File name
0009 545950         FCB$TYP:        DB      'TYP'           ;File type
000C 00             FCB$EXTENT:     DB      0               ;Extent
000D 0000           FCB$RESV:       DB      0,0             ;Reserved for CP/M
000F 00             FCB$RECUSED:    DB      0               ;Records used in this extent
0010 0000000000     FCB$ABUSED:     DB      0,0,0,0,0,0,0,0 ;Allocation blocks used
0018 0000000000
0020 00             FCB$SEQREC:     DB      0               ;Sequential rec. to read/write
```

Chapter 5: The Basic Disk Operating System 99

```
0021 0000        FCB$RANREC:    DW    0        ;Random rec. to read/write
0023 00          FCB$RANRECO:   DB    0        ;Random rec. overflow byte (MS)

0024 0E0F                       MVI   C,B$OPEN ;Function code
0026 110000                     LXI   D,FCB    ;DE -> File control block
0029 CD0500                     CALL  BDOS     ;A = 0FFH if file not found
```

Purpose This function opens a specified file for reading or writing. The FCB, whose address must be in register DE, tells CP/M the user number, the logical disk, the file name, and the file type. All other bytes of the FCB will normally be set to 0.

The code returned by the BDOS in register A indicates whether the file has been opened successfully. If A contains 0FFH, then the BDOS was unable to find the correct entry in the directory. If A = 0, 1, 2, or 3, then the file has been opened.

Notes The Open File function searches the entire file directory on the specified logical disk looking for the file name, type, and extent specified in the FCB; that is, it is looking for an exact match for bytes 1 through 14 of the FCB. The file name and type may be ambiguous; that is, they may contain "?" characters. In this case, the BDOS will open the first file in the directory that matches the ambiguous name in the FCB. If the file name or type is shorter than eight or three characters respectively, then the remaining characters must be filled with blanks.

When the BDOS searches the file directory, it expects to find an *exact* match with each character of the file name and type, including lowercase letters or nongraphic characters. However, the BDOS uses only the least significant seven bits of each character—the most significant bit is used to indicate special file status characteristics, or *attributes*.

By matching the file extent as well as the name and type, you can, if you wish, open the file at some point other than its beginning. For normal sequential access, you would not usually want to do this, but if your program can predict which file extent is required, this is a method of moving directly to it.

It is also possible to open the same file more than once. Each instance requires a separate FCB. The BDOS is not aware that this is happening. It is really only safe to do this when you are reading the file. Each FCB can be used to read the file independently.

Once the file has been found in the directory, the number of records and the allocation blocks used are copied from the directory entry into the FCB (bytes 16 through 31). If the file is to be accessed sequentially from the beginning of the file, the current record (byte 32) must be set to zero by your program.

The value returned in register A is the relative directory entry number of the entry that matched the FCB. As previously explained, the buffer that CP/M uses holds a 128-byte record from the directory with four directory entries numbered 0, 1, 2, and 3. This *directory code* is returned by almost all of the file-related BDOS functions, but under normal circumstances you will be concerned only with whether the value returned in A is 0FFH or not.

Figure 5-16 shows a subroutine that takes a 00H-byte terminated character string, creates a valid FCB, and then opens the specified file. Shown as part of this example is the subroutine BF (Build FCB). It performs the brunt of the work of converting a string of ASCII characters into an FCB-style disk, file name, and type.

```
                        ;OPENF
                        ;Open File

                        ;Given a pointer to a 00H-byte-terminated file name,
                        ;and an area that can be used for a file control
                        ;block, this subroutine builds a valid file control
                        ;block and attempts to open the file.

                        ;If the file is opened, it returns with the carry flag clear.
                        ;If the file cannot be opened, this subroutine returns
                        ;with the carry flag set.

                        ;Entry parameters
                        ;       DE -> 36-byte area for file control block
                        ;       HL -> 00H-byte terminated file name of the
                        ;              form {disk:} Name {.typ}
                        ;              (disk and typ are optional)

                        ;Exit parameters
                        ;       Carry clear : File opened correctly.
                        ;       Carry set   : File not opened.

                        ;Calling Sequence
                        ;       LXI     D,FCB
                        ;       LXI     H,FNAME
                        ;       CALL    OPENF
                        ;       JC      ERROR
                        ;where
                        ;FCB:    DS      36              ;Space for file control block
                        ;FNAME:  DB      'A:TESTFILE.DAT',0

        000F =          B$OPEN  EQU     15              ;File Open function code
        0005 =          BDOS    EQU     5               ;BDOS entry point

                        OPENF:
        0000 D5                 PUSH    D               ;Preserve pointer to FCB
        0001 CD0C00             CALL    BF              ;Build file control block
        0004 0E0F               MVI     C,B$OPEN
        0006 D1                 POP     D               ;Recover pointer to FCB
        0007 CD0500             CALL    BDOS
        000A 17                 RAL                     ;If A=0FFH, carry set
                                                        ;otherwise carry clear
        000B C9                 RET

                        ;BF
                        ;Build file control block
                        ;This subroutine formats a 00H-byte-terminated string
                        ;(presumed to be a file name) into an FCB, setting
                        ;the disk and file name and type and clearing the
                        ;remainder of the FCB to 0's.

                        ;Entry parameters
                        ;       DE -> file control block (36 Bytes)
                        ;       HL -> file name string (00H-byte-terminated)

                        ;Exit parameters
                        ;       The built file control block
                        ;Calling sequence
                        ;       LXI     D,FCB
                        ;       LXI     H,FILENAME
                        ;       CALL    BF

                        BF:
```

Figure 5-16. Open file request

Chapter 5: The Basic Disk Operating System 101

```
        000C 23              INX     H               ;Check if 2nd char. is ":"
        000D 7E              MOV     A,M             ;Get character from file name
        000E 2B              DCX     H               ;HL -> now back at 1st char.
        000F FE3A            CPI     ':'             ;If ":", then disk specified
        0011 C21C00          JNZ     BF$ND           ;No disk
        0014 7E              MOV     A,M             ;Get disk letter
        0015 E61F            ANI     0001$1111B      ;A (41H) -> 1, B (42H) -> 2 ...
        0017 23              INX     H               ;Bypass disk letter
        0018 23              INX     H               ;Bypass ":"
        0019 C31D00          JMP     BF$SD           ;Store disk in FCB
                     BF$ND:
        001C AF              XRA     A               ;No disk present
                                                     ;Indicate default disk
                     BF$SD:
        001D 12              STAX    D               ;Store disk in FCB
        001E 13              INX     D               ;DE -> 1st char. of name in FCB
        001F 0E08            MVI     C,8             ;File name length
        0021 CD3700          CALL    BF$GT           ;Get token
                                                     ;Note -- at this point, BF$GT
                                                     ;will have advanced the string
                                                     ;pointer to either a "." or
                                                     ;00H byte
        0024 FE2E            CPI     '.'             ;Check terminating character
        0026 C22A00          JNZ     BF$NT           ;No file type specified
        0029 23              INX     H               ;Bypass "." in file name
                     BF$NT:
        002A 0E03            MVI     C,3             ;File type length
        002C CD3700          CALL    BF$GT           ;Get token
                                                     ;Note -- if no file type is
                                                     ;present BF$GT will merely
                                                     ;spacefill the FCB
        002F 0600            MVI     B,0             ;0-fill the remainder of the FCB
        0031 0E18            MVI     C,24            ;36 - 12 (disk, name, type = 12 chars.)
        0033 CD6400          CALL    BF$FT           ;Re-use fill token S/R
        0036 C9              RET
        ;BF$GT
        ;Build FCB -- get token

        ;This subroutine scans a file name string,
        ;placing characters into a file control block.
        ;On encountering a terminator character ("." or 00H),
        ;the remainder of the token is space filled.
        ;If an "*" is encountered, the remainder of the token
        ;is filled with "?".

        ;Entry parameters
        ;       DE -> Into file control block
        ;       HL -> Into file name string
        ;       C = Maximum no. of characters in token

        ;Exit parameters
        ;       File control block contains next token
        ;       A = Terminating character
                     BF$GT:
        0037 7E              MOV     A,M             ;Get next string character
        0038 B7              ORA     A               ;Check if end of string
        0039 CA5700          JZ      BF$SFT          ;Yes, space fill token
        003C FE2A            CPI     '*'             ;Check if ?-fill required
        003E CA5C00          JZ      BF$QFT          ;Yes, fill with ?
        0041 FE2E            CPI     '.'             ;Assume current token is file
                                                     ;name
                                                     ;Check if file type coming up
                                                     ;(If current token is file
                                                     ;type this check is
                                                     ;benignly redundant)
        0043 CA5700          JZ      BF$SFT          ;Yes, space fill token
        0046 12              STAX    D               ;None of the above, so store
                                                     ;in FCB
        0047 13              INX     D               ;Update FCB pointer
        0048 23              INX     H               ;Update string pointer
```

Figure 5-16. (Continued)

```
                    0049 0D              DCR      C              ;Countdown on token length
                    004A C23700          JNZ      BF$GT          ;Still more characters to go
                         BF$SKIP:                                 ;Skip chars. until "." or 00H
                    004D 7E              MOV      A,M            ;Get next string character
                    004E B7              ORA      A              ;Check if 00H
                    004F C8              RZ                      ;Yes
                    0050 FE2E            CPI      '.'            ;Check if "."
                    0052 C8              RZ                      ;Yes
                    0053 23              INX      H              ;Update string pointer (only)
                    0054 C34D00          JMP      BF$SKIP        ;Try next character
                         BF$SFT:                                  ;Space fill token
                    0057 0620            MVI      B,' '
                    0059 C36400          JMP      BF$FT          ;Common fill token code
                                                                  ;BF$FT returns to caller
                         BF$QFT:                                  ;Question mark fill token
                    005C 063F            MVI      B,'?'
                    005E CD6400          CALL     BF$FT          ;Common fill token code
                    0061 C34D00          JMP      BF$SKIP        ;Bypass multiple "*" etc.
                         BF$FT:                                   ;Fill token
                    0064 F5              PUSH     PSW            ;Save terminating character
                    0065 78              MOV      A,B            ;Get fill characer
                         BF$FTL:                                  ;Inner loop
                    0066 12              STAX     D              ;Store in FCB
                    0067 13              INX      D              ;Update FCB Pointer
                    0068 0D              DCR      C              ;Downdate residual count
                    0069 C26600          JNZ      BF$FTL         ;Keep going
                    006C F1              POP      PSW            ;Recover terminating character
                    006D C9              RET
```

Figure 5-16.   (Continued)

Function 16: Close File

Function Code: C = 10H
Entry Parameters: DE = Address of file control block
Exit Parameters: A = Directory code

Example

```
              0010 =         B$CLOSE        EQU      16         ;Close File
              0005 =         BDOS           EQU      5          ;BDOS entry point

              0000          FCB:            DS       36         ;File control block

              0024 0E10                     MVI      C,B$CLOSE  ;Function code
              0026 110000                   LXI      D,FCB      ;DE -> File control block
              0029 CD0500                   CALL     BDOS       ;A = 0,1,2,3 if successful
                                                                ;A = 0FFH if file name not
                                                                ; in directory
```

Purpose   This function terminates the processing of a file to which you have written information. Under CP/M you do not need to close a file that you have been reading. However, if you ever intend for your program to function correctly under MP/M (the multi-user version of CP/M) you should close all files regardless of their use.

The Close File function, like Open File, returns a directory code in the A register. Register A will contain 0FFH if the BDOS could not close the file successfully. If A is 0, 1, 2, or 3, then the file has been closed.

Notes   When the BDOS closes a file to which data has been written, it writes the current contents of the FCB out to the disk directory, updating an existing directory entry by matching the disk, name, type, and extent number in the same manner that the Open File function does.

Note that the BDOS does not transfer the last record of the file to the disk during the close operation. It merely updates the file directory. You must arrange to flush any partly filled record to the disk. If the file that you have created is a standard CP/M ASCII text file, you must arrange to fill the unused portion of the record with the standard 1AH end-of-file characters as CP/M expects, as explained in the section on the Write Sequential function (code 21).

Function 17: Search for First Name Match

Function Code: C = 11H
Entry Parameters: DE = Address of file control block
Exit Parameters: A = Directory code

Example

```
0011 =              B$SEARCHF       EQU     17              ;Search First
0005 =              BDOS            EQU     5               ;BDOS entry point

                    FCB:                                    ;File control block
0000 00             FCB$DISK:       DB      0               ;Search on default disk drive
0001 46494C453FFCB$NAME:            DB      'FILE????'      ;Ambiguous file name
0009 543F50         FCB$TYP:        DB      'T?P'           ;Ambiguous file type
000C 00             FCB$EXTENT:     DB      0               ;Extent
000D 0000           FCB$RESV:       DB      0,0             ;Reserved for CP/M
000F 00             FCB$RECUSED:    DB      0               ;Records used in this extent
0010 0000000000FCB$ABUSED:          DB      0,0,0,0,0,0,0,0 ;Allocation blocks used
0018 0000000000                     DB      0,0,0,0,0,0,0,0
0020 00             FCB$SEQREC:     DB      0               ;Sequential rec. to read/write
0021 0000           FCB$RANREC:     DW      0               ;Random rec. to read/write
0023 00             FCB$RANRECO:    DB      0               ;Random rec. overflow byte (MS)

0024 0E11                           MVI     C,B$SEARCHF     ;Function code
0026 110000                         LXI     D,FCB           ;DE -> File control block
0029 CD0500                         CALL    BDOS            ;A = 0,1,2,3.
                                                            ;(A * 32) + DMA -> directory
                                                            ; entry
                                                            ;A = 0FFH if file name not
                                                            ; found
```

Purpose   This function scans down the file directory for the first entry that matches the file name, type, and extent in the FCB addressed by DE. The file name, type, and extent may contain a "?" (ASCII 3FH) in one or more character positions. Where a "?" occurs, the BDOS will match *any* character in the corresponding position in the file directory. This is known as ambiguous file name matching.

The first byte of an FCB normally contains the logical disk number code. A value of 0 indicates the default disk, while 1 means disk A, 2 is B, and so on up to a possible maximum of 16 for disk P. However, if this byte contains a "?", the BDOS will search the default logical disk and will match the file name and type regardless of the user number. This function is normally used in conjunction with the Search Next function (which is described immediately after this function). Search First, in the process of matching a file, leaves certain variables in the BDOS set, ready for a subsequent Search Next.

Both Search First and Search Next return a directory code in the A register. With Search First, A = 0FFH when no files match the FCB; if a file match is found, A will have a value of 0, 1, 2, or 3.

Notes To locate the particular directory entry that either the Search First or Search Next function matched, multiply the directory code returned in A by the length of a directory entry (32 bytes). This is easily done by adding the A register to itself five times (see the code in Figure 5-17 near the label GNFC). Then add the DMA address to get the actual address where the matched directory entry is stored.

There are many occasions when you may need to write a program that will accept an ambiguous file name and operate on all of the file names that match it. (The DIR and ERA commands built into the CCP are examples that use ambiguous file names.) To do this, you must use several BDOS functions: the Set DMA Address function (code 26, described later in this chapter), this function (Search First), and Search Next (code 18). All of this is shown in the subroutine given in Figure 5-17.

```
;GNF
;This subroutine returns an FCB setup with either the
;first file matched by an ambiguous file name, or (if
;specified by entry parameter) the next file name.

;Note : this subroutine is context sensitive. You must
;        not have more than one ambiguous file name
;        sequence in process at any given time.

;>>>    Warning : This subroutine changes the DMA address
;>>>              inside the BDOS.

;Entry parameters
;       DE -> Possibly ambiguous file name
;             (00-byte terminated)
;             (Only needed for FIRST request)
;       HL -> File control block
;       A = 0  : Return FIRST file name that matches
;         = NZ : Return NEXT file name that matches

;Exit parameters
;Carry set : A = FF, no file name matches
;            A not = 0FFH, error in input file name
;Carry clear : FCB setup with next name
;              HL -> Directory entry returned
;                    by Search First/Next

;Calling sequence
;       LXI     D,FILENAME
;       LXI     H,FCB
```

Figure 5-17. Search first/next calls for ambiguous file name

```
                    ;           MVI     A,0         ;or MVI A,1 for NEXT
                    ;           CALL    GNF

        0011 =      B$SEARCHF   EQU     17          ;Search for first file name
        0012 =      B$SEARCHN   EQU     18          ;Search for next file name
        001A =      B$SETDMA    EQU     26          ;Set up DMA address
        0005 =      BDOS        EQU     5           ;BDOS entry point

        0080 =      GNFDMA      EQU     80H         ;Default DMA address
        000D =      GNFSVL      EQU     13          ;Save length (no. of chars to move)
        0024 =      GNFFCL      EQU     36          ;File control block length
        0000        GNFSV:      DS      GNFSVL      ;Save area for file name/type

                    GNF:
        000D E5                 PUSH    H           ;Save FCB pointer
        000E D5                 PUSH    D           ;Save file name pointer
        000F F5                 PUSH    PSW         ;Save first/next flag

        0010 118000             LXI     D,GNFDMA    ;Set DMA to known address
        0013 0E1A               MVI     C,B$SETDMA  ;Function code
        0015 CD0500             CALL    BDOS
        0018 F1                 POP     PSW         ;Recover first/next flag
        0019 E1                 POP     H           ;Recover file name pointer
        001A D1                 POP     D           ;Recover FCB pointer
        001B D5                 PUSH    D           ;Resave FCB pointer

        001C B7                 ORA     A           ;Check if FIRST or NEXT
        001D C23E00             JNZ     GNFN        ;NEXT
        0020 CD9300             CALL    BF          ;Build file control block
        0023 E1                 POP     H           ;Recover FCB pointer (to balance stack)
        0024 D8                 RC                  ;Return if error in file name
        0025 E5                 PUSH    H           ;Resave FCB pointer

                                                    ;Move ambiguous file name to
                                                    ;save area
                                                    ;HL -> FCB
        0026 110000             LXI     D,GNFSV     ;DE -> save area
        0029 0E0D               MVI     C,GNFSVL    ;Get save length
        002B CD8A00             CALL    MOVE
        002E D1                 POP     D           ;Recover FCB pointer
        002F D5                 PUSH    D           ;and resave

        0030 0E11               MVI     C,B$SEARCHF ;Search FIRST
        0032 CD0500             CALL    BDOS
        0035 E1                 POP     H           ;Recover FCB pointer
        0036 FEFF               CPI     0FFH        ;Check for error
        0038 CA7D00             JZ      GNFEX       ;Error exit
        003B C35D00             JMP     GNFC        ;Common code

                    GNFN:                           ;Execute search FIRST to re-
                                                    ;establish contact with
                                                    ;previous file
                                                    ;User's FCB still has
                                                    ;name/type in it
        003E CD7F00             CALL    GNFZF       ;Zero-fill all but file name/type
        0041 D1                 POP     D           ;Recover FCB address
        0042 D5                 PUSH    D           ;and resave
        0043 0E11               MVI     C,B$SEARCHF ;Re-find the file
        0045 CD0500             CALL    BDOS
        0048 D1                 POP     D           ;Recover FCB pointer
        0049 D5                 PUSH    D           ;and resave
        004A 210000             LXI     H,GNFSV     ;Move file name from save area
                                                    ;into FCB
        004D 0E0D               MVI     C,GNFSVL    ;Save area length
        004F CD8A00             CALL    MOVE

        0052 0E12               MVI     C,B$SEARCHN ;Search NEXT
        0054 CD0500             CALL    BDOS
        0057 E1                 POP     H           ;Recover FCB address
        0058 FEFF               CPI     0FFH        ;Check for error
        005A CA7D00             JZ      GNFEX       ;Error exit

                    GNFC:
        005D E5                 PUSH    H           ;Save FCB address
        005E 87                 ADD     A           ;Multiply BDOS return code * 32
```

Figure 5-17. (Continued)

```
     005F 87              ADD     A               ;* 4
     0060 87              ADD     A               ;* 8
     0061 87              ADD     A               ;* 16
     0062 87              ADD     A               ;* 32
     0063 218000          LXI     H,GNFDMA        ;HL -> DMA address
     0066 5F              MOV     E,A             ;Make (code * 32) a word value
                                                  ;in DE
     0067 1600            MVI     D,0
     0069 19              DAD     D               ;HL -> file's directory entry

                                                  ;Move file name into FCB
     006A D1              POP     D               ;Recover FCB address
     006B E5              PUSH    H               ;Save directory entry pointer
     006C D5              PUSH    D               ;and resave
     006D 0E0D            MVI     C,GNFSVL        ;Length of save area
     006F CD8A00          CALL    MOVE
     0072 3A0000          LDA     GNFSV           ;Get disk from save area
     0075 D1              POP     D               ;Recover FCB address
     0076 12              STAX    D               ;Overwrite user number in FCB

                                                  ;Set up to zero-fill tail end
                                                  ;of FCB
     0077 CD7F00          CALL    GNFZF           ;Zero-fill
     007A E1              POP     H               ;Recover directory entry
                                                  ;pointer
     007B AF              XRA     A               ;Clear carry
     007C C9              RET

               GNFEX:
     007D 37              STC                     ;Set carry to indicate error
     007E C9              RET

               ;GNFZF
               ;Get next file -- zero fill
               ;This subroutine zero-fills the bytes that follow the
               ;file name and type in an FCB.

               ;Entry parameters
               ;     DE -> file control block

               GNFZF:
     007F 210D00          LXI     H,GNFSVL        ;Bypass area that holds file name
     0082 19              DAD     D               ;HL -> FCB + GNFSVL
     0083 54              MOV     D,H             ;DE -> FCB + GNFSVL
     0084 5D              MOV     E,L
     0085 13              INX     D               ;DE -> FCB + GNFSVL + 1
     0086 3600            MVI     M,0             ;FCB + GNFSVL = 0
     0088 0E17            MVI     C,GNFFCL-GNFSVL ;Remainder of file control block

               ;Drop into MOVE
               ;Spread 0's through remainder
               ;of FCB

               ;MOVE
               ;This subroutine moves C bytes from HL to DE.

               MOVE:
     008A 7E              MOV     A,M             ;Get source byte
     008B 12              STAX    D               ;Save destination byte
     008C 13              INX     D               ;Increment destination pointer
     008D 23              INX     H               ;Increment source pointer
     008E 0D              DCR     C               ;Decrement count
     008F C28A00          JNZ     MOVE            ;Go back for more
     0092 C9              RET

               ;BF
               ;Build file control block

               ;This subroutine formats a 00H-byte terminated string

               ;(presumed to be a file name) into an FCB, setting the
               ;disk and file name and type, and clearing the
               ;remainder of the FCB to 0's.
```

Figure 5-17. (Continued)

```
                        ;Entry parameters
                        ;       DE -> File control block (36 bytes)
                        ;       HL -> File name string (00H-byte-terminated)

                        ;Exit parameters
                        ;       The built file control block

                        ;This subroutine is shown in full in Figure 5-16

        0093 C9         BF:     RET                     ;Dummy subroutine for this example
```

Figure 5-17. (Continued)

Function 18: Search for Next Name Match

Function Code: C = 12H
Entry Parameters: None (assumes previous Search First call)
Exit Parameters: A = Directory code

Example

```
        0012 =          B$SEARCHN       EQU     18      ;Search Next
        0005 =          BDOS            EQU     5       ;BDOS entry point

        0000 0E12                       MVI     C,B$SEARCHN     ;Function code
                                                                ;Note: No FCB pointer
                                                                ;You must precede this call
                                                                ; with a call to Search First
        0002 CD0500                     CALL    BDOS            ;A = 0,1,2,3
                                                                ;(A * 32) + DMA -> directory
                                                                ; entry
                                                                ;A = 0FFH if file name not
                                                                ; found
```

Purpose   This function searches down the file directory for the *next* file name, type, and extent that match the FCB specified in a previous Search First function call.

Search First and Search Next are the only BDOS functions that must be used together. As you can see, the Search Next function does not require an FCB address as an input parameter—all the necessary information will have been left in the BDOS on the Search First call.

Like Search First, Search Next returns a directory code in the A register; in this case, if A = 0FFH, it means that there are no *more* files that match the file control block. If A is not 0FFH, it will be a value of 0, 1, 2, or 3, indicating the relative directory entry number.

Notes   There are two ways of using the Search First/Next calls. Consider a simple file copying program that takes as input an ambiguous file name. You could scan the file directory, matching all of the possible file names, possibly displaying them on the console, and storing the names of the files to be copied in a table inside your program. This would have the advantage of enabling you to present the file names to the operator before any copying occurred. You could even arrange for the operator to select which files to copy on a file-by-file basis. One disadvantage would be that you could not accurately predict how many files might be selected. On some hard disk systems you might have to accommodate several thousand file names.

The alternative way of handling the problem would be to match one file name, copy it, then match the next file name, copy it, and so on. If you gave the operator the choice of selecting which files to copy, this person would have to wait at the terminal as each file was being copied, but the program would not need to have large table areas set aside to hold file names. This solution to the problem is slightly more complicated, as you can see from the logic in Figure 5-17.

The subroutine in Figure 5-17, Get Next File (GNF), contains all of the necessary logic to search down a directory for both alternatives described. It does require that you indicate *on entry* whether it should search for the first or next file match, by setting A to zero or some nonzero value respectively.

You can see from Figure 5-17 that whenever the subroutine is called to get the *next* file, you must execute a Search First function to re-find the previous file. Only then can a Search Next be issued.

As with all functions that return a directory code in A, if this value is not 0FFH, it will be the relative directory entry number in the directory record currently in memory. This directory record will have been read into memory at whatever address was specified at the last Set DMA Address function call (code 26, 1AH). Notwithstanding its odd name, the DMA Address is simply the address into which any record input from disk will be placed. If the Set DMA Address function has not been used to change the value, then the CP/M default DMA address, location 0080H, will be used to hold the directory record.

The actual code for locating the address of the particular directory entry matched by the Search First/Next functions is shown in Figure 5-17 near the label GNFC. The method involves multiplying the directory code by 32 and then adding this product to the current DMA address.

Function 19: Erase (Delete) File

Function Code: C = 13H
Entry Parameters: DE = Address of file control block
Exit Parameters: A = Directory code

Example

```
0013  =              B$ERASE       EQU      19         ;Erase File
0005  =              BDOS          EQU      5          ;BDOS entry point
                     FCB:                              ;File control block
0000  00             FCB$DISK:     DB       0          ;Search on default disk drive
0001  3F3F4C454E     FCB$NAME:     DB       '??LENAME'    ;Ambiguous file name
0009  3F5950         FCB$TYP:      DB       '?YP'         ;Ambiguous file type
000C  00             FCB$EXTENT:   DB       0          ;Extent
```

Chapter 5: The Basic Disk Operating System

```
            000D 0000          FCB$RESV:      DB    0,0             ;Reserved for CP/M
            000F 00            FCB$RECUSED:   DB    0               ;Records used in this extent
            0010 0000000000FCB$ABUSED:        DB    0,0,0,0,0,0,0,0 ;Allocation blocks used
            0018 0000000000                   DB    0,0,0,0,0,0,0,0
            0020 00            FCB$SEQREC:    DB    0               ;Sequential rec. to read/write
            0021 0000          FCB$RANREC:    DW    0               ;Random rec. to read/write
            0023 00            FCB$RANRECO:   DB    0               ;Random rec. overflow byte (MS)

            0024 0E13                         MVI   C,B$ERASE       ;Function code
            0026 110000                       LXI   D,FCB           ;DE -> file control block
            0029 CD0500                       CALL  BDOS            ;A = 0FFH if file not found
```

Purpose This function logically deletes from the file directory files that match the FCB addressed by DE. It does so by replacing the first byte of each relevant directory entry (remember, a single file can have several entries, one for each extent) by the value 0E5H. This flags the directory entry as being available for use.

Notes Like the previous two functions, Search First and Search Next, this function can take an ambiguous file name and type as part of the file control block, but unlike those functions, the logical disk select code cannot be a "?".

This function returns a directory code in A in the same way as the previous file operations.

Function 20: Read Sequential

Function Code: C = 14H
Entry Parameters: DE = Address of file control block
Exit Parameters: A = Directory code

Example

```
            0014 =             B$READSEQ      EQU   20              ;Read Sequential
            0005 =             BDOS           EQU   5               ;BDOS entry point

                               FCB:                                 ;File control block
            0000 00            FCB$DISK:      DB    0               ;Search on default disk drive.
            0001 46494C454EFCB$NAME:          DB    'FILENAME'      ;file name
            0009 545950        FCB$TYP:       DB    'TYP'           ;File type
            000C                              DS    24              ;Set by file open

                                                                    ;Record will be read into
                                                                    ; address set by prior SETDMA
                                                                    ; call
            0024 0E14                         MVI   C,B$READSEQ     ;Function code
            0026 110000                       LXI   D,FCB           ;DE -> File control block
            0029 CD0500                       CALL  BDOS            ;A = 00 if operation successful
                                                                    ;A = nonzero if no data in
                                                                    ; file
```

Purpose This function reads the next record (128-byte sector) from the designated file into memory at the address set by the last Set DMA function call (code 26, 1AH). The record read is specified by the FCB's sequential record field (FCB$SEQREC in the example listing for the Open File function, code 15). This field is incremented by 1 so that a subsequent call to Read Sequential will get the next record from the file. If the end of the current extent is reached, then the BDOS will

```
                ;GETC
                ;This subroutine gets the next character from a
                ;sequential disk file. It assumes that the file has
                ;already been opened.

                ;>>>    Note : this subroutine changes CP/M's DMA address.

                ;Entry parameters
                ;       DE -> file control block

                ;Exit parameters
                ;       A = next character from file
                ;           (= 0FFH on physical end of file)
                ;           Note : 1AH is normal EOF character for
                ;                  ASCII Files.

                ;Calling sequence
                ;       LXI     DE,FCB
                ;       CALL    GETC
                ;       CPI     1AH
                ;       JZ      EOFCHAR
                ;       CPI     0FFH
                ;       JZ      ACTUALEOF

0014 =          B$READSEQ   EQU     20          ;Read sequential
001A =          B$SETDMA    EQU     26          ;Set DMA address
0005 =          BDOS        EQU     5           ;BDOS entry point

0080 =          GETCBS  EQU     128             ;Buffer size
0000            GETCBF: DS      GETCBS          ;Declare buffer
0080 00         GETCCC: DB      0               ;Char. count (initially
                                                ;"empty")

                GETC:
0081 3A8000             LDA     GETCCC          ;Check if buffer is empty
0084 B7                 ORA     A
0085 CA9900             JZ      GETCFB          ;Yes, fill buffer

                GETCRE:                         ;Re-entry point after buffer filled
0088 3D                 DCR     A               ;No, downdate count
0089 328000             STA     GETCCC          ;Save downdated count

008C 47                 MOV     B,A             ;Compute offset of next
                                                ;character
008D 3E7F               MVI     A,GETCBS-1      ;By subtracting
008F 90                 SUB     B               ;(buffer size -- downdated count)
0090 5F                 MOV     E,A             ;Make result into word value
0091 1600               MVI     D,0
0093 210000             LXI     H,GETCBF        ;HL -> base of buffer
0096 19                 DAD     D               ;HL -> next character in buffer
0097 7E                 MOV     A,M             ;Get next character
0098 C9                 RET

                GETCFB:                         ;Fill buffer
0099 D5                 PUSH    D               ;Save FCB pointer
009A 110000             LXI     D,GETCBF        ;Set DMA address to buffer
009D 0E1A               MVI     C,B$SETDMA      ;function code
009F CD0500             CALL    BDOS
00A2 D1                 POP     D               ;Recover FCB pointer
00A3 0E14               MVI     C,B$READSEQ     ;Read sequential "record" (sector)
00A5 CD0500             CALL    BDOS
00A8 B7                 ORA     A               ;Check if read unsuccessful (A = NZ)
00A9 C2B400             JNZ     GETCX           ;Yes
00AC 3E80               MVI     A,GETCBS        ;Reset count
00AE 328000             STA     GETCCC
00B1 C38800             JMP     GETCRE          ;Re-enter subroutine

                GETCX:                          ;Physical end of file
00B4 3EFF               MVI     A,0FFH          ;Indicate such
00B6 C9                 RET
```

Figure 5-18. Read next character from sequential disk file

automatically open the next extent and reset the sequential record field to 0, ready for the next Read function call.

The file specified in the FCB must have been readied for input by issuing an Open File (code 15, 0FH) or a Create File (code 22, 16H) BDOS call.

The value 00H is returned in A to indicate a successful Read Sequential operation, while a nonzero value shows that the Read could not be completed because there was no data in the next record, as at the end of file.

Notes   Although it is not immediately obvious, you can change the sequential record number, FCB$SEQREC, and within a given extent, read a record at random. If you want to access any given record within a file, you must compute which extent that record would be in and set the extent field in the file control block (FCB$EXTENT) before you open the file. Thus, although the function name implies sequential access, in practice you can use it to perform a simple type of random access. If you need to do true random access, look ahead to the Random Read function (code 33), which takes care of opening the correct extent automatically.

Figure 5-18 shows an example of a subroutine that returns the data from a sequential file byte-by-byte, reading in records from the file as necessary. This subroutine, GETC, is useful as a low-level "primitive" on which you can build more sophisticated functions, such as those that read a fixed number of characters or read characters up to a CARRIAGE RETURN/LINE FEED combination.

When you read data from a CP/M text file, the normal convention is to fill the last record of the file with 1AH characters (CONTROL-Z). Therefore, two possible conditions can indicate end-of-file: either encountering a 1AH, or receiving a return code from the BDOS function (in the A register) of 0FFH. However, if the file that you are reading is not an ASCII text file, then a 1AH character has no special meaning—it is just a normal data byte in the body of the file.

Function 21: Write Sequential

```
Function Code:      C = 15H
Entry Parameters:   DE = Address of file control block
Exit Parameters:    A = Directory code
```

Example

```
0015 =              B$WRITESEQ   EQU    21           ;Write Sequential
0005 =              BDOS         EQU    5            ;BDOS entry point

                    FCB:                             ;File control block
0000 00             FCB$DISK:    DB     0            ;Search on default disk drive
0001 46494C454E     FCB$NAME:    DB     'FILENAME'   ;file name
0009 545950         FCB$TYP:     DB     'TYP'        ;File type
000C                             DS     24           ;Set by Open or Create File

                                                     ;Record must be in address
                                                     ; set by prior SETDMA call
0024 0E15                        MVI    C,B$WRITESEQ ;Function code
0026 110000                      LXI    D,FCB        ;DE -> File control block
0029 CD0500                      CALL   BDOS         ;A = 00H if operation
                                                     ; successful
                                                     ;A = nonzero if disk full
```

Purpose This function writes a record from the address specified in the last Set DMA (code 26, 1AH) function call to the file defined in the FCB. The sequential record number in the FCB (FCB$SEQREC) is updated by 1 so that the next call to Write Sequential will write to the next record position in the file. If necessary, a new extent will be opened to receive the new record.

This function is directly analogous to the Read Sequential function, writing instead of reading. The file specified in the FCB must first be activated by an Open File (code 15, 0FH) or create File call (code 22, 16H).

A directory code of 00H is returned in A to indicate that the Write was successful; a nonzero value is returned if the Write could not be completed because the disk was full.

Notes As with the Read Sequential function (code 20, 14H), you can achieve a simple form of random writing to the file by manipulating the sequential record number (FCB$SEQREC). However, you can only overwrite *existing* records in the file, and if you want to move to another extent, you must close the file and reopen it with the FCB$EXTENT field set to the correct value. For true random writing to the file, look ahead to the Write Random function (code 34, 22H). This takes care of opening or creating the correct extent of the file automatically.

The only logical error condition that can occur when writing to a file is insufficient room on the disk to accommodate the next extent of the file. Any hardware errors detected will be handled by the disk driver built into the BIOS or BDOS.

Figure 5-19 shows a subroutine, PUTC, to which you can pass data a byte at a time. It assembles this data into a buffer, making a call to Write Sequential whenever the buffer becomes full. You can see that provision is made in the entry parameters (by setting register B to a nonzero value) for the subroutine to fill the remaining unused characters of the buffer with 1AH characters. You must do this to denote the end of an ASCII text file.

Function 22: Create (Make) File

    Function Code: C = 16H
    Entry Parameters: DE = Address of file control block
    Exit Parameters: A = Directory code

Example

```
0016 =              B$CREATE      EQU     22          ;File Create
0005 =              BDOS          EQU     5,          ;BDOS entry point

                    FCB:                              ;File control block
0000 00             FCB$DISK:     DB      0           ;Search on default disk drive
0001 46494C454E     FCB$NAME:     DB      'FILENAME'  ;file name
0009 545950         FCB$TYP:      DB      'TYP'       ;File type
000C 00             FCB$EXTENT:   DB      0           ;Extent
```

Chapter 5: The Basic Disk Operating System

```
000D 0000          FCB$RESV:       DB      0,0             ;Reserved for CP/M
000F 00            FCB$RECUSED:    DB      0               ;Records used in this extent
0010 0000000000    FCB$ABUSED:     DB      0,0,0,0,0,0,0,0 ;Allocation blocks used
0018 0000000000
0020 00            FCB$SEQREC:     DB      0               ;Sequential rec. to read/write
0021 0000          FCB$RANREC:     DW      0               ;Random rec. to read/write
0023 00            FCB$RANRECO:    DB      0               ;Random rec. overflow byte (MS)

                                                           ;Note : file to be created
                                                           ;must not already exist....
0024 0E16          MVI     C,B$CREATE                      ;Function code
0026 110000        LXI     D,FCB                           ;DE -> file control block
0029 CD0500        CALL    BDOS                            ;A = 0,1,2,3 if operation
                                                           ; successful
                                                           ;A = 0FFH if directory full
```

```
                   ;PUTC
                   ;This subroutine either puts the next character out
                   ;to a sequential file, writing out completed "records"
                   ;(128-byte sectors) or, if requested to, will fill the
                   ;remainder of the current "record" with 1AH's to
                   ;indicate end of file to CP/M.

                   ;Entry parameters
                   ;       DE -> File control block
                   ;       B = 0, A = next data character to be output
                   ;       B /= 0, fill the current "record" with 1AH's

                   ;Exit parameters
                   ;       none.

                   ;Calling sequence
                   ;       LXI     D,FCB
                   ;       MVI     B,0     ;Not end of file
                   ;       LDA     CHAR
                   ;       CALL    PUTC
                   ;  or
                   ;       LXI     D,FCB
                   ;       MVI     B,1     ;Indicate end of file
                   ;       CALL    PUTC

0015 =             B$WRITESEQ  EQU  21     ;Write sequential
001A =             B$SETDMA    EQU  26     ;Set DMA address
0005 =             BDOS        EQU  5      ;BDOS entry point

0080 =             PUTCBS  EQU     128             ;Buffer size
0000               PUTCBF: DS      PUTCBS          ;Declare buffer
0080 00            PUTCCC: DB      0               ;Char. count (initially "empty")
                   PUTC:
0081 D5            PUSH    D                       ;Save FCB address
0082 F5            PUSH    PSW                     ;Save data character
0083 78            MOV     A,B                     ;Check if end of file requested
0084 B7            ORA     A
0085 C29900        JNZ     PUTCEF                  ;Yes
0088 CDC300        CALL    PUTCGA                  ;No, get address of next free byte
                                                   ;HL -> next free byte
                                                   ;E = Current char. count (as
                                                   ; well as A)
008B F1            POP     PSW                     ;Recover data character
008C 77            MOV     M,A                     ;Save in buffer
008D 7B            MOV     A,E                     ;Get current character count
008E 3C            INR     A                       ;Update character count
008F FE80          CPI     PUTCBS                  ;Check if buffer full
0091 CAA900        JZ      PUTCWB                  ;Yes, write buffer
0094 328000        STA     PUTCCC                  ;No, save updated count
0097 D1            POP     D                       ;Dump FCB address for return
0098 C9            RET
```

Figure 5-19. Write next character to sequential disk file

```
                PUTCEF:                      ;End of file
0099 F1                 POP     PSW          ;Dump data character
009A CDC300             CALL    PUTCGA       ;HL -> next free byte
                                             ;A = current character count

                PUTCCE:                      ;Copy EOF character
009D FE80               CPI     PUTCBS       ;Check for end of buffer
009F CAA900             JZ      PUTCWB       ;Yes, write out the buffer
00A2 361A               MVI     M,1AH        ;No, store EOF in buffer
00A4 3C                 INR     A            ;Update count
00A5 23                 INX     H            ;Update buffer pointer
00A6 C39D00             JMP     PUTCCE       ;Continue until end of buffer

                PUTCWB:                      ;Write buffer
00A9 AF                 XRA     A            ;Reset character count to 0
00AA 328000             STA     PUTCCC
00AD 110000             LXI     D,PUTCBF
00B0 0E1A               MVI     C,B$SETDMA   ;Set DMA address -> buffer
00B2 CD0500             CALL    BDOS
00B5 D1                 POP     D            ;Recover FCB address
00B6 0E15               MVI     C,B$WRITESEQ ;Write sequential record
00B8 CD0500             CALL    BDOS
00BB B7                 ORA     A            ;Check if error
00BC C2C000             JNZ     PUTCX        ;Yes if A = NZ
00BF C9                 RET                  ;No, return to caller

                PUTCX:                       ;Error exit
00C0 3EFF               MVI     A,0FFH       ;Indicate such
00C2 C9                 RET

                PUTCGA:                      ;Return with HL -> next free char.
                                             ;and A = current char. count
00C3 3A8000             LDA     PUTCCC       ;Get current character count
00C6 5F                 MOV     E,A          ;Make word value in DE
00C7 1600               MVI     D,0
00C9 210000             LXI     H,PUTCBF     ;HL -> Base of buffer
00CC 19                 DAD     D            ;HL -> next free character
00CD C9                 RET
```

Figure 5-19.   Write next character to sequential disk file (continued)

Purpose   This function creates a new file of the specified name and type. You must first ensure that no file of the same name and type already exists on the same logical disk, either by trying to open the file (if this succeeds, the file already exists) or by unconditionally erasing the file.

In addition to creating the file and its associated file directory entry, this function also effectively opens the file so that it is ready for records to be written to it.

This function returns a normal directory code if the file creation has completed successfully or a value of 0FFH if there is insufficient disk or directory space.

Notes   Under some circumstances, you may want to create a file that is slightly more "secure" than normal CP/M files. You can do this by using either lowercase letters or nongraphic ASCII characters such as ASCII NUL (00H) in the file name or type. Neither of these classes of characters can be generated from the keyboard; in the first case, the CCP changes all lowercase characters to uppercase, and in the second, it rejects names with odd characters in them. Thus, computer operators

Chapter 5: The Basic Disk Operating System

cannot erase such a file because there is no way that they can create the same file name from the CCP.

The converse is also true; the only way that you can erase these files is by using a program that *can* set the exact file name into an FCB and then issue an Erase File function call.

Note that this function cannot accept an ambiguous file name in the FCB.

Figure 5-20 shows a subroutine that creates a file only after it has erased any existing files of the same name.

Function 23: Rename File

    Function Code: C = 17H
    Entry Parameters: DE = Address of file control block
    Exit Parameters: A = Directory code

Example

```
0017 =              B$RENAME    EQU    23        ;Rename file
0005 =              BDOS        EQU    5         ;BDOS entry point

                    FCB:                         ;File control block
0000 00                         DB     0         ;Search on default disk drive
0001 4F4C444E41                 DB     'OLDNAME '          ;File name
0009 545950                     DB     'TYP'     ;File type
000C 00000000                   DB     0,0,0,0
```

```
                    ;CF
                    ;Create file
                    ;This subroutine creates a file. It erases any
                    ;previous file before creating the new one.

                    ;Entry parameters
                    ;       DE -> File control block for new file

                    ;Exit parameters
                    ;       Carry clear if operation successful
                    ;         (A = 0,1,2,3)
                    ;       Carry set if error (A = 0FFH)

                    ;Calling sequence
                    ;       LXI     D,FCB
                    ;       CALL    CF
                    ;       JC      ERROR

0013 =              B$ERASE     EQU    19        ;Erase file
0016 =              B$CREATE    EQU    22        ;Create file
0005 =              BDOS        EQU    5         ;BDOS entry point

                    CF:
0000 D5                         PUSH   D         ;Preserve FCB pointer
0001 0E13                       MVI    C,B$ERASE ;Erase any existing file
0003 CD0500                     CALL   BDOS
0006 D1                         POP    D         ;Recover FCB pointer
0007 0E16                       MVI    C,B$CREATE ;Create (and open new file)
0009 CD0500                     CALL   BDOS
000C FEFF                       CPI    0FFH      ;Carry set if OK, clear if error
000E 3F                         CMC              ;Complete to use Carry set if Error
000F C9                         RET
```

Figure 5-20.   Create file request

```
0010 00                         DB      0           ;FCB + 16
0011 4E45574E41                 DB      'NEWNAME '  ;File name
0019 545950                     DB      'TYP'       ;File type
001C 00000000                   DB      0,0,0,0

0020 0E17             MVI       C,B$RENAME  ;Function code
0022 110000           LXI       D,FCB       ;DE -> file control block
0025 CD0500           CALL      BDOS        ;A = 00H if operation succesful
                                            ;A = 0FFH if file not found
```

Purpose   This function renames an existing file name and type to a new name and type. It is unusual in that it uses a single FCB to store both the old file name and type (in the first 16 bytes) and the new file name and type (in the second 16 bytes).

This function returns a normal directory code if the file rename was completed successfully or a value of 0FFH if the old file name could not be found.

Notes   The Rename File function only checks that the old file name and type exist; it makes no check to ensure that the new name and type combination does not already exist. Therefore, you should try to open the new file name and type. If you succeed, do not attempt the rename operation. CP/M will create more than one file of the same name and type, and you stand to lose the information in both files as you attempt to sort out the problem.

For security, you can also use lowercase letters and nongraphic characters in the file name and type, as described under the File Create function (code 22, 16H) above.

Never use ambiguous file names in a rename operation; it produces strange effects and may result in files being irreparably damaged. This function will change *all* occurrences of the old file name to the new name.

Figure 5-21 shows a subroutine that will accept an existing file name and type and a new name and type and rename the old to the new. It checks to make sure that the new file name does not already exist, returning an error code if it does.

Function 24: Get Active Disks (Login Vector)

    Function Code: C = 18H
    Entry Parameters: None
    Exit Parameters: HL = Active disk map (login vector)

Example

```
0018 =       B$GETACTDSK    EQU    24       ;Get Active Disks
0005 =       BDOS           EQU    5        ;BDOS entry point

                                            ;Example of getting active
                                            ; disk function code
0000 0E18                   MVI    C,B$GETACTDSK
0002 CD0500                 CALL   BDOS     ;HL = active disk bit map
                                            ;Bits are = 1 if disk active
                                            ;Bits 15 14 13 ... 2 1 0
                                            ;Disk P  O  N ... C B A
```

Purpose   This function returns a bit map, called the *login vector,* in register pair HL, indicating which logical disk drives have been selected since the last warm boot or

```
                        ;RF
                        ;Rename file
                        ;This subroutine renames a file.
                        ;It uses the BF (build FCB) subroutine shown in Figure 5.16

                        ;Entry parameters
                        ;       *** No case-folding of file names occurs ***
                        ;       HL -> old file name (00-byte terminated)
                        ;       DE -> new file name (00-byte terminated)

                        ;Exit parameters
                        ;       Carry clear if operation successful
                        ;               (A = 0,1,2,3)
                        ;       Carry set if error
                        ;               A = 0FEH if new file name already exists
                        ;               A = 0FFH if old file name does not exist

                        ;Calling sequence
                        ;       LXI     H,OLDNAME       ;HL -> old name
                        ;       LXI     D,NEWNAME       ;DE -> new name
                        ;       CALL    RF
                        ;       JC      ERROR

000F =                  B$OPEN          EQU     15      ;Open file
0017 =                  B$RENAME        EQU     23      ;Rename file
0005 =                  BDOS            EQU     5       ;BDOS entry point

0000 0000000000 RFFCB:  DW      0,0,0,0,0,0,0   ;1 1/2 FCB's long
0010 0000000000         DW      0,0,0,0,0,0,0,0
0020 0000000000         DW      0,0,0,0,0,0,0,0
0030 000000             DW      0,0,0

                RF:
0036 D5                 PUSH    D               ;Save new name pointer
0037 110000             LXI     D,RFFCB         ;Build old name FCB
                                                ;HL already -> old name
003A CD5D00             CALL    BF

003D E1                 POP     H               ;Recover new name pointer
003E 111000             LXI     D,RFFCB+16      ;Build new name in second part of file
0041 CD5D00             CALL    BF              ;control block

0044 111000             LXI     D,RFFCB+16      ;Experimentally try
0047 0E0F               MVI     C,B$OPEN        ;to open the new file
0049 CD0500             CALL    BDOS            ;to ensure it does
004C FEFF               CPI     0FFH            ;not already exist
004E 3EFE               MVI     A,0FEH          ;Assume error (flags unchanged)
0050 D8                 RC                      ;Carry set if A was 0,1,2,3

0051 110000             LXI     D,RFFCB
0054 0E17               MVI     C,B$RENAME      ;Rename the file
0056 CD0500             CALL    BDOS
0059 FEFF               CPI     0FFH            ;Carry set if OK, clear if error
005B 3F                 CMC                     ;Invert to use carry, set if error
005C C9                 RET

                        ;BF
                        ;Build file control block
                        ;This subroutine formats a 00H-byte terminated string
                        ;(presumed to be a file name) into an FCB, setting the
                        ;disk and the file name and type, and clearing the
                        ;remainder of the FCB to 0's.

                        ;Entry parameters
                        ;       DE -> file control block (36 bytes)
                        ;       HL -> file name string (00H-byte terminated)

                        ;Exit parameters
                        ;       The built file control block.

                        ;Calling sequence
                        ;       LXI     D,FCB
                        ;       LXI     H,FILENAME
                        ;       CALL    BF

                BF:
005D C9                 RET             ;Dummy subroutine : see Figure 5.16.
```

Figure 5-21.   Rename file request

Reset Disk function (code 13, 0DH). The least significant bit of L corresponds to disk A, while the highest order bit in H maps disk P. The bit corresponding to the specific logical disk is set to 1 if the disk has been selected or to 0 if the disk is not currently on-line.

Logical disks can be selected programmatically through any file operation that sets the drive field to a nonzero value, through the Select Disk function (code 14, 0EH), or by the operator entering an "X:" command where "X" is equal to A, B, ..., P.

Notes   This function is intended for programs that need to know which logical disks are currently active in the system—that is, those logical disks which have been selected.

Function 25: Get Current Default Disk

Function Code: C = 19H
Entry Parameters: None
Exit Parameters: A = Current disk
                   (0 = A, 1 = B, ..., F = P)

Example

```
0019 =              B$GETCURDSK     EQU     25              ;Get Current Disk
0005 =              BDOS            EQU     5               ;BDOS entry point

0000 0E19                           MVI     C,B$GETCURDSK   ;Function code
0002 CD0500                         CALL    BDOS            ;A = 0 if A:, 1 if B: ...
```

Purpose   This function returns the current default disk set by the last Select Disk function call (code 14, 0EH) or by the operator entering the "X:" command (where "X" is A, B, ..., P) to the CCP.

Notes   This function returns the current default disk in coded form. Register A = 0 if drive A is the current drive, 1 if drive B, and so on. If you need to convert this to the corresponding ASCII character, simply add 41H to register A.

Use this function when you convert a file name and type in an FCB to an ASCII string in order to display it. If the first byte of the FCB is 00H, the current default drive is to be used. You must therefore use this function to determine the logical disk letter for the default drive.

Function 26: Set DMA (Read/Write) Address

Function Code: C = 1AH
Entry Parameters: DE = DMA (read/write) address
Exit Parameters: None

Example

```
001A =              B$SETDMA        EQU     26              ;Set DMA Address
0005 =              BDOS            EQU     5               ;BDOS entry point
```

```
0000            SECBUFF:        DS      128     ;Sector buffer

0080 0E1A                       MVI     C,B$SETDMA      ;Function code
0082 110000                     LXI     D,SECBUFF       ;Pointer to buffer
0085 CD0500                     CALL    BDOS
```

Purpose   This function sets the BDOS's direct memory access (DMA) address to a new value. The name is an historic relic dating back to the Intel Development System on which CP/M was originally developed. This machine, by virtue of its hardware, could read data from a diskette directly into memory or write data to a diskette directly from memory. The name *DMA address* now applies to the address of the buffer to and from which data is transferred whenever a diskette Read, Write, or directory operation is performed.

Whenever CP/M first starts up (cold boot) or a warm boot or Reset Disk operation occurs, the DMA address is reset to its default value of 0080H.

Notes   No function call can tell you the current value of the DMA address. All you can do is make a Set DMA function call to ensure that it is where you want it.

Once you have set the DMA address to the correct place for your program, it will remain set there until another Set DMA call, Reset Disk, or warm boot occurs.

The Read and Write Sequential and Random operations use the current setting of the DMA address, as do the directory operations Search First and Search Next.

Function 27: Get Allocation Vector

Function Code: C = 1BH
Entry Parameters: None
Exit Parameters: HL = Address of allocation vector

Example

```
001B =          B$GETALVEC      EQU     27      ;Get Allocation Vector Address
0005 =          BDOS            EQU     5       ;BDOS entry point

0000 0E1B                       MVI     C,B$GETALVEC    ;Function code
0002 CD0500                     CALL    BDOS            ;HL -> Base address of
                                                ;       allocation vector
```

Purpose   This function returns the base, or starting, address of the allocation vector for the currently selected logical disk. This information, indicating which parts of the disk are assigned, is used by utility programs and the BDOS itself to determine how much unused space is on the logical disk, to locate an unused allocation block in order to extend a file, or to relinquish an allocation block when a file is deleted.

Notes   Digital Research considers the actual layout of the allocation vector to be proprietary information.

Function 28: Set Logical Disk to Read-Only Status

Function Code: C = 1CH
Entry Parameters: None
Exit Parameters: None

Example

```
001C =            B$SETDSKRO       EQU    28      ;Set disk to Read Only
                                                  ; function code
0005 =            BDOS             EQU    5       ;BDOS entry point
                                                  ;Sets disk selected by prior
                                                  ;Select disk function call
0000 0E1C                          MVI    C,B$SETDSKRO  ;Function code
0002 CD0500                        CALL   BDOS
```

Purpose   This function logically sets the currently selected disk to a Read-Only state. Any attempts to execute a Write Sequential or Write Random function to the selected disk will be intercepted by the BDOS, and the following message will appear on the console:

BDOS Err on X: R/O

where X: is the selected disk.

Notes   Once you have requested Read-Only status for the currently selected logical disk, this status will persist even if you proceed to select other logical disks. In fact, it will remain in force until the next warm boot or Reset Disk System function call.

Digital Research documentation refers to this function code as Disk Write Protect. The Read-Only description is used here because it corresponds to the error message produced if your program attempts to write on the disk.

Function 29: Get Read-Only Disks

Function Code: C = 1DH
Entry Parameters: None
Exit Parameters: HL = Read-Only disk map

Example

```
001D =            B$GETRODSKS      EQU    29      ;Get Read Only disks
0005 =            BDOS             EQU    5       ;BDOS entry point

0000 0E19                          MVI    C,B$GETRODSKS  ;Function code
0002 CD0500                        CALL   BDOS            ;HL = Read Only disk bit map
                                                          ;Bits are = 1 if disk Read Only
                                                          ;Bits 15 14 13 ... 2 1 0
                                                          ;Disk  P  O  N ... C B A
```

Purpose   This function returns a bit map in registers H and L showing which logical disks in the system have been set to Read-Only status, either by the Set Logical

Disk to Read-Only function call (code 28, 1CH), or by the BDOS itself, because it detected that a diskette had been changed.

The least significant bit of L corresponds to logical disk A, while the most significant bit of H corresponds to disk P. The bit corresponding to the specific logical disk is set to 1 if the disk has been set to Read-Only status.

Function 30: Set File Attributes

Function Code: C = 1EH
Entry Parameters: DE = Address of FCB
Exit Parameters: A = Directory code

Example

```
001E =          B$SETFAT        EQU     30              ;Set File Attribute
0005 =          BDOS            EQU     5               ;BDOS entry point

                FCB:                                    ;File control block
0000 00         FCB$DISK:       DB      0               ;Search on default disk drive
0001 46494C454E FCB$NAME:       DB      'FILENAME'      ;File name
0009 D4         FCB$TYP:        DB      'T'+80H         ;Type with R/O
                                                        ; attribute
000A 5950                       DB      'YP'
000C 0000000000                 DW      0,0,0,0,0,0,0,0,0,0

0022 0E1E                       MVI     C,B$SETFAT      ;Function code
0024 110000                     LXI     D,FCB           ;DE -> file control block
                                                        ;MS bits set in file name/type
0027 CD0500                     CALL    BDOS            ;A = 0FFH if file not found
```

Purpose This function sets the bits that describe attributes of a file in the relevant directory entries for the specified file. Each file can be assigned up to 11 file attributes. Of these 11, two have predefined meanings, four others are available for you to use, and the remaining five are reserved for future use by CP/M.

Each attribute consists of a single bit. The most significant bit of each byte of the file name and type is used to store the attributes. The file attributes are known by a code consisting of the letter "f" (for file name) or "t" (for file type), followed by the number of the character position and a single quotation mark. For example, the Read-Only attribute is t1'.

The significance of the attributes is as follows:

- f1' to f4'   Available for you to use
- f5' to f8'   Reserved for future CP/M use
- t1'   Read-Only File attribute
- t2'   System File attribute
- t3'   Reserved for future CP/M use

Attributes are set by presenting this function with an FCB in which the unambiguous file name has been preset with the most significant bits set appropriately. This function then searches the directory for a match and changes the matched entries to contain the attributes which have been set in the FCB.

The BDOS will intercept any attempt to write on a file that has the Read-Only attribute set. The DIR command in the CCP does not display any file with System status.

Notes   You can use the four attributes available to you to set up a file security system, or perhaps to flag certain files that must be backed up to other disks. The Search First and Search Next functions allow you to view the complete file directory entry, so your programs can test the attributes easily.

The example subroutines in Figures 5-22 and 5-23 show how to set file attributes (SFA) and get file attributes (GFA), respectively. They both use a bit map in which the most significant 11 bits of the HL register pair are used to indicate the corresponding high bits of the 11 characters of the file name/type combination. You will also see some equates that have been declared to make it easier to manipulate the attributes in this bit map.

```
                ;SFA
                ;Set file attributes
                ;This subroutine takes a compressed bit map of all the
                ;file attribute bits, expands them into an existing
                ;file control block and then requests CP/M to set
                ;the attributes in the file directory.

                ;Entry parameters
                ;      DE -> file control block
                ;      HL = bit map. Only the most significant 11
                ;           bits are used. These correspond directly
                ;           with the possible attribute bytes.

                ;Exit parameters
                ;      Carry clear if operation successful (A = 0,1,2,3)
                ;      Carry set if error (A = 0FFH)

                ;Calling sequence
                ;      LXI     D,FCB
                ;      LXI     H,0000$0000$1100$0000B    ;Bit Map
                ;      CALL    SFA
                ;      JC      ERROR

                                        ;File Attribute Equates
8000 =          FA$F1   EQU     1000$0000$0000$0000B    ;F1' - F4'
4000 =          FA$F2   EQU     0100$0000$0000$0000B    ;Available for use by
2000 =          FA$F3   EQU     0010$0000$0000$0000B    ; application programs
1000 =          FA$F4   EQU     0001$0000$0000$0000B

0800 =          FA$F5   EQU     0000$1000$0000$0000B    ;F5' - F8'
0400 =          FA$F6   EQU     0000$0100$0000$0000B    ;Reserved for CP/M
0200 =          FA$F7   EQU     0000$0010$0000$0000B
0100 =          FA$F8   EQU     0000$0001$0000$0000B

0080 =          FA$T1   EQU     0000$0000$1000$0000B    ;T1' -- read/only file
0080 =          FA$RO   EQU     FA$T1
0040 =          FA$T2   EQU     0000$0000$0100$0000B    ;T2' -- system files
0040 =          FA$SYS  EQU     FA$T2
0020 =          FA$T3   EQU     0000$0000$0010$0000B    ;T3' -- reserved for CP/M

001E =          B$SETFAT EQU    30      ;Set file attributes
0005 =          BDOS    EQU     5       ;BDOS entry point
```

Figure 5-22.   Set file attributes

Chapter 5: The Basic Disk Operating System   **123**

```
                SFA:
0000 D5                 PUSH    D               ;Save FCB pointer
0001 13                 INX     D               ;HL -> 1st character of file name
0002 0E0B               MVI     C,8+3           ;Loop count for file name and type
                SFAL:                           ;Main processing loop
0004 AF                 XRA     A               ;Clear carry and A
0005 29                 DAD     H               ;Shift next MS bit into carry
0006 CE00               ACI     0               ;A = 0 or 1 depending on carry
0008 0F                 RRC                     ;Rotate LS bit of A into MS bit
0009 47                 MOV     B,A             ;Save result (00H or 80H)
000A EB                 XCHG                    ;HL -> FCB character
000B 7E                 MOV     A,M             ;Get FCB character
000C E67F               ANI     7FH             ;Isolate all but attribute bit
000E B0                 ORA     B               ;Set attribute with result
000F 77                 MOV     M,A             ;and store back into FCB
0010 EB                 XCHG                    ;DE -> FCB, HL = remaining bit map
0011 13                 INX     D               ;DE -> next character in FCB
0012 0D                 DCR     C               ;Downdate character count
0013 C20400             JNZ     SFAL            ;Loop back for next character
0016 0E1E               MVI     C,B$SETFAT      ;Set file attribute function code
0018 D1                 POP     D               ;Recover FCB pointer
0019 CD0500             CALL    BDOS
001C FEFF               CPI     0FFH            ;Carry set if OK, clear if error
001E 3F                 CMC                     ;Invert to use carry set if error
001F C9                 RET
```

Figure 5-22.   Set file attributes (continued)

```
                        ;GFA
                        ;Get file attributes
                        ;This subroutine finds the appropriate file using a
                        ;search for First Name Match function rather than opening
                        ;the file. It then builds a bit map of the file attribute
                        ;bits in the file name and type. This bit map is then ANDed
                        ;with the input bit map, and the result is returned in the
                        ;zero flag. The actual bit map built is also returned in case
                        ;more complex check is required.

                        ;>>>    Note: This subroutine changes the CP/M DMA address.

                        ;Entry parameters
                        ;       DE -> File control block
                        ;       HL = Bit map mask to be ANDed with attribute
                        ;            results

                        ;Exit parameters
                        ;       Carry clear, operation successful
                        ;               Nonzero status set to result of AND between
                        ;               input mask and attribute bits set.
                        ;               HL = Unmasked attribute bytes set.
                        ;       Carry set, file could not be found

001A =                  B$SETDMA    EQU     26      ;Set DMA address
0011 =                  B$SEARCHF   EQU     17      ;Search for first entry to match
0005 =                  BDOS        EQU     5       ;BDOS entry point
0080 =                  GFADMA      EQU     80H     ;Default DMA address

                        ;Calling sequence
                        ;       LXI     D,FCB
                        ;       LXI     H,0000$0000$1100$0000B   ;Bit map
                        ;       CALL    GFA
                        ;       JC      ERROR

                                                    ;File attribute equates
8000 =                  FA$F1       EQU     1000$0000$0000$0000B    ;F1' - F5'
4000 =                  FA$F2       EQU     0100$0000$0000$0000B    ;Available for use by
```

Figure 5-23.   Get file attributes

```
2000 =          FA$F3    EQU     0010$0000$0000$0000B    ;Application programs
1000 =          FA$F4    EQU     0001$0000$0000$0000B

0800 =          FA$F5    EQU     0000$1000$0000$0000B    ;F6' - F8'
0400 =          FA$F6    EQU     0000$0100$0000$0000B    ;Reserved for CP/M
0200 =          FA$F7    EQU     0000$0010$0000$0000B
0100 =          FA$F8    EQU     0000$0001$0000$0000B

0080 =          FA$T1    EQU     0000$0000$1000$0000B    ;T1' -- read/only file
0080 =          FA$RO    EQU     FA$T1
0040 =          FA$T2    EQU     0000$0000$0100$0000B    ;T2' -- system files
0040 =          FA$SYS   EQU     FA$T2
0020 =          FA$T3    EQU     0000$0000$0010$0000B    ;T3' -- reserved for CP/M

                GFA:
0000 E5                  PUSH    H                       ;Save AND-mask
0001 D5                  PUSH    D                       ;Save FCB pointer
0002 0E1A                MVI     C,B$SETDMA              ;Set DMA to default address
0004 118000              LXI     D,GFADMA                ;DE -> DMA address
0007 CD0500              CALL    BDOS

000A D1                  POP     D                       ;Recover FCB pointer
000B 0E11                MVI     C,B$SEARCHF             ;Search for match with name
000D CD0500              CALL    BDOS
0010 FEFF                CPI     0FFH                    ;Carry set if OK, clear if error
0012 3F                  CMC                             ;Invert to use set carry if error
0013 DA4100              JC      GFAX                    ;Return if error
                                                         ;Multiply by 32 to get offset into DMA buffer
0016 87                  ADD     A                       ;* 2
0017 87                  ADD     A                       ;* 4
0018 87                  ADD     A                       ;* 8
0019 87                  ADD     A                       ;* 16
001A 87                  ADD     A                       ;* 32
001B 5F                  MOV     E,A                     ;Make into a word value
001C 1600                MVI     D,0
001E 218000              LXI     H,GFADMA                ;HL -> DMA address
0021 19                  DAD     D                       ;HL -> Directory entry in DMA buffer
0022 23                  INX     H                       ;HL -> 1st character of file name
0023 EB                  XCHG                            ;DE -> 1st character of file name

0024 0E0B                MVI     C,8+3                   ;Count of characters in file name and type
0026 210000              LXI     H,0                     ;Clear bit map
                GFAL:                                    ;Main loop
0029 1A                  LDAX    D                       ;Get next character of file name
002A E680                ANI     80H                     ;Isolate attribute bit
002C 07                  RLC                             ;Move MS bit into LS bit
002D B5                  ORA     L                       ;OR in any previously set bits
002E 6F                  MOV     L,A                     ;Save result
002F 29                  DAD     H                       ;Shift HL left one bit for next time
0030 13                  INX     D                       ;DE -> next character in file name, type
0031 0D                  DCR     C                       ;Downdate count
0032 C22900              JNZ     GFAL                    ;Go back for next character

0035 29                  DAD     H                       ;Left justify attribute bits in HL
0036 29                  DAD     H                       ;MS attribute bit will already be in
0037 29                  DAD     H                       ;bit 11 of HL, so only 4 shifts are
0038 29                  DAD     H                       ;necessary

0039 D1                  POP     D                       ;Recover AND-mask
003A 7A                  MOV     A,D                     ;Get MS byte of mask
003B A4                  ANA     H                       ;AND with MS byte of result
003C 47                  MOV     B,A                     ;Save interim result
003D 7B                  MOV     A,E                     ;Get LS byte of mask
003E A5                  ANA     L                       ;AND with LS byte of result
003F B0                  ORA     B                       ;Combine two results to set Z flag

0040 C9                  RET
                GFAX:                                    ;Error exit
0041 E1                  POP     H                       ;Balance stack
0042 C9                  RET
```

Figure 5-23.   Get file attributes (continued)

Function 31: Get Disk Parameter Block Address

Function Code: C = 1FH
Entry Parameters: None
Exit Parameters: HL = Address of DPB

Example

```
001F =          B$GETDPB        EQU     31          ;Get Disk Parameter Block
                                                    ; Address
0005 =          BDOS            EQU     5           ;BDOS entry point

                                                    ;Returns DPB address of
                                                    ; logical disk previously
                                                    ; selected with a Select
                                                    ; Disk function.
0000 0E1F                       MVI     C,B$GETDPB  ;Function code
0002 CD0500                     CALL    BDOS        ;HL -> Base address of current
                                                    ; disk's parameter block
```

Purpose This function returns the address of the disk parameter block (DPB) for the last selected logical disk. The DPB, explained in Chapter 3, describes the physical characteristics of a specific logical disk—information mainly of interest for system utility programs.

Notes The subroutines shown in Figure 5-24 deal with two major problems. First, given a track and sector number, what allocation block will they fall into? Converseley, given an allocation block, what is its starting track and sector?

These subroutines are normally used by system utilities. They first get the DPB address using this BDOS function. Then they switch to using direct BIOS calls to perform their other functions, such as selecting disks, tracks, and sectors and reading and writing the disk.

The first subroutine, GTAS (Get Track and Sector), in Figure 5-24, takes an allocation block number and converts it to give you the starting track and sector number. GMTAS (Get Maximum Track and Sector) returns the maximum track and sector number for the specified disk. GDTAS (Get Directory Track and Sector) tells you not only the starting track and sector for the file directory, but also the number of 128-byte sectors in the directory.

Note that whenever a track number is used as an entry or an exit parameter, it is an absolute track number. That is, the number of reserved tracks on the disk before the directory has already been added to it.

GNTAS (Get Next Track and Sector) helps you read sectors sequentially. It adds 1 to the sector number, and when you reach the end of a track, updates the track number by 1 and resets the sector number to 1.

GAB (Get Allocation Block) is the converse of GTAS (Get Track and Sector). It returns the allocation block number, given a track and sector.

Finally, Figure 5-24 includes several useful 16-bit subroutines to divide the HL register pair by DE (DIVHL), to multiply HL by DE (MULHL), to subtract DE from HL (SUBHL—this can also be used as a 16-bit compare), and to shift HL right one bit (SHLR). The divide and multiply subroutines are somewhat primitive, using iterative subtraction and addition, respectively. Nevertheless, they do perform their role as supporting subroutines.

126 The CP/M Programmer's Handbook

```
                ;Useful subroutines for accessing the data in the
                ;disk parameter block
000E =          B$SELDSK    EQU     14          ;Select Disk function code
001F =          B$GETDPB    EQU     31          ;Get DPB address
0005 =          BDOS        EQU     5           ;BDOS entry point

                ;It makes for easier, more compact code to copy the
                ;specific disk parameter block into local variables
                ;while manipulating the information.
                ;Here are those variables --

                DPB:                            ;Disk parameter block
0000 0000       DPBSPT: DW      0               ;128-byte sectors per track
0002 00         DPBBS:  DB      0               ;Block shift
0003 00         DPBBM:  DB      0               ;Block mask
0004 00         DPBEM:  DB      0               ;Extent mask
0005 0000       DPBMAB: DW      0               ;Maximum allocation block number
0007 0000       DPBNOD: DW      0               ;Number of directory entries - 1
0009 0000       DPBDAB: DW      0               ;Directory allocation blocks
000B 0000       DPBCBS: DW      0               ;Check buffer size
000D 0000       DPBTBD: DW      0               ;Tracks before directory (reserved tracks)

000F =          DPBSZ   EQU     $-DPB           ;Disk parameter block size

                ;GETDPB
                ;Gets disk parameter block
                ;This subroutine copies the DPB for the specified
                ;logical disk into the local DPB variables above.

                ;Entry parameters
                ;       A = Logical disk number (A: = 0, B: = 1...)

                ;Exit parameters
                ;       Local variables contain DPB

                GETDPB:
000F 5F                 MOV     E,A             ;Get disk code for select disk
0010 0E0E               MVI     C,B$SELDSK      ;Select the disk
0012 CD0500             CALL    BDOS
0015 0E1F               MVI     C,B$GETDPB      ;Get the disk parameter base address
0017 CD0500             CALL    BDOS            ;HL -> DPB
001A 0E0F               MVI     C,DPBSZ         ;Set count
001C 110000             LXI     D,DPB           ;Get base address of local variables

                GDPBL:                          ;Copy DPB into local variables
001F 7E                 MOV     A,M             ;Get byte from DPB
0020 12                 STAX    D               ;Store into local variable
0021 13                 INX     D               ;Update local variable pointer
0022 23                 INX     H               ;Update DPB pointer
0023 0D                 DCR     C               ;Downdate count
0024 C21F00             JNZ     GDPBL           ;Loop back for next byte
0027 C9                 RET

                ;GTAS
                ;Get track and sector (given allocation block number)

                ;This subroutine converts an allocation block into a
                ;track and sector number -- note that this is based on
                ;128-byte sectors.

                ;>>>>>  Note: You must call GETDPB before
                ;>>>>>        you call this subroutine

                ;Entry parameters
                ;       HL = allocation block number

                ;Exit parameters
                ;       HL = track number
                ;       DE = sector number

                ;Method :
                ;In mathematical terms, the track can be derived from:
                ;Trk = ((allocation block * sec. per all. block) / sec. per trk)
                ;         + tracks before directory
```

Figure 5-24. Accessing disk parameter block data

```
                    ;The sector is derived from:
                    ;Sec = ((allocation block * sec. per all. block) modulo/
                    ;          sec. per trk) + 1
                    GTAS:
    0028 3A0200         LDA     DPBBS           ;Get block shift -- this will be 3 to
                                                ;7 depending on allocation block size
                                                ;It will be used as a count for shifting
                    GTASS:
    002B 29             DAD     H               ;Shift allocation block left one place
    002C 3D             DCR     A               ;Decrement block shift count
    002D C22B00         JNZ     GTASS           ;More shifts required
    0030 EB             XCHG                    ;DE = all. block * sec. per block
                                                ;i.e. DE = total number of sectors
    0031 2A0000         LHLD    DPBSPT          ;Get sectors per track
    0034 EB             XCHG                    ;HL = sec. per trk, DE = tot. no. of sec.
    0035 CD8F00         CALL    DIVHL           ;BC = HL/DE, HL = remainder
                                                ;BC = track, HL = sector
    0038 23             INX     H               ;Sector numbering starts from 1
    0039 EB             XCHG                    ;DE = sector, HL = track
    003A 2A0D00         LHLD    DPBTBD          ;Tracks before directory
    003D 09             DAD     B               ;DE = sector, HL = absolute track
    003E C9             RET

                    ;GMTAS
                    ;Get maximum track and sector

                    ;This is just a call to GTAS with the maximum
                    ;allocation block as the input parameter

                    ;>>>>> Note: You must call GETDPB before
                    ;>>>>>       you call this subroutine

                    ;Entry parameters: none

                    ;Exit parameters:
                    ;     HL = maximum track number
                    ;     DE = maximum sector
                    GMTAS:
    003F 2A0500         LHLD    DPBMAB          ;Get maximum allocation block
    0042 C32800         JMP     GTAS            ;Return from GTAS with parameters in HL and DE

                    ;GDTAS
                    ;Get directory track and sector

                    ;This returns the START track and sector for the
                    ;file directory, along with the number of sectors
                    ;in the directory.

                    ;>>>>> Note: You must call GETDPB before
                    ;>>>>>       you call this subroutine

                    ;Entry parameters: none

                    ;Exit parameters:
                    ;     BC = number of sectors in directory
                    ;     DE = directory start sector
                    ;     HL = directory start track
                    GDTAS:
    0045 2A0700         LHLD    DPBNOD          ;Get number of directory entries - 1
    0048 23             INX     H               ;Make true number of entries
                                                ;Each entry is 32 bytes long, so to
                                                ;convert to 128 byte sectors, divide by 4
    0049 CDD000         CALL    SHLR            ;/ 2 (by shifting HL right one bit)
    004C CDD000         CALL    SHLR            ;/ 4
    004F E5             PUSH    H               ;Save number of sectors
    0050 210000         LXI     H,0             ;Directory starts in allocation block 0
    0053 CD2800         CALL    GTAS            ;HL = track, DE = sector
    0056 C1             POP     B               ;Recover number of sectors
    0057 C9             RET
```

Figure 5-24. (Continued)

```
;GNTAS
;Get NEXT track and sector

;This subroutine updates the input track and sector
;by one, incrementing the track and resetting the
;sector number as required.

;>>>>>    Note: You must call GETDPB before
;>>>>>          you call this subroutine

; Note: you must check for end of disk by comparing
;       the track number returned by this subroutine
;       to that returned by by GMTAS + 1. When
;       equality occurs, the end of disk has been reached.

;Entry parameters
;       HL = current track number
;       DE = current sector number

;Exit parameters
;       HL = updated track number
;       DE = updated sector number

            GNTAS:
0058 E5             PUSH    H               ;Save track
0059 13             INX     D               ;Update sector
005A 2A0000         LHLD    DPBSPT          ;Get sectors per track
005D CDC900         CALL    SUBHL           ;HL = HL - DE
0060 E1             POP     H               ;Recover current track
0061 D0             RNC                     ;Return if updated sector <= sec. per trk.
0062 23             INX     H               ;Update track if upd. sec > sec. per trk.
0063 110100         LXI     D,1             ;Reset sector to 1
0066 C9             RET

;GAB
;Get allocation block

;This subroutine returns an allocation block number
;given a specific track and sector. It also returns
;the offset down the allocation block at which the
;sector will be found. This offset is in units of
;128-byte sectors.

;>>>>>    Note: You must call GETDPB before
;>>>>>          you call this subroutine

;Entry parameters
;       HL = track number
;       DE = sector number

;Exit parameters
;       HL = allocation block number

;Method
;The allocation block is formed from:
;AB = (sector + ((track - tracks before directory)
;       * sectors per track)) / log2 (sectors per all. block)

;The sector offset within allocation block is formed from:
;Offset = (sector + ((track - tracks before directory)
;         * sectors per track)) / AND (sectors per all. block - 1)

            GAB:
0067 D5             PUSH    D               ;Save sector
0068 EB             XCHG                    ;DE = track
0069 2A0D00         LHLD    DPBTBD          ;Get no. of tracks before directory
006C EB             XCHG                    ;DE = no. of tracks before dir. HL = track
006D CDC900         CALL    SUBHL           ;HL = HL - DE
                                            ;HL = relative track within logical disk
0070 EB             XCHG                    ;DE = relative track
0071 2A0000         LHLD    DPBSPT          ;Get sectors per track
0074 CDA400         CALL    MULHL           ;HL = HL * DE
                                            ;HL = number of sectors
0077 EB             XCHG                    ;DE = number of sectors
```

Figure 5-24. (Continued)

```
            0078 E1              POP     H               ;Recover sector
            0079 2B              DCX     H               ;Make relative to 0
            007A 19              DAD     D               ;HL = relative sector
            007B 3A0300          LDA     DPBBM           ;Get block mask
            007E 47              MOV     B,A             ;Ready for AND operation
            007F 7D              MOV     A,L             ;Get LS byte of relative sector
            0080 A0              ANA     B               ;AND with block mask
            0081 F5              PUSH    PSW             ;A = sector displacement
            0082 3A0200          LDA     DPBBS           ;Get block shift
            0085 4F              MOV     C,A             ;Make into counter
                        GABS:                            ;Shift loop
            0086 CDD000          CALL    SHLR            ;HL shifted right (divided by 2)
            0089 0D              DCR     C               ;Count down
            008A C28600          JNZ     GABS            ;Shift again if necessary
            008D F1              POP     PSW             ;Recover offset
            008E C9              RET

                    ;Utility subroutines
                    ;These perform 16-bit arithmetic on the HL register pair.

                    ;DIVHL
                    ;Divides HL by DE using an iterative subtract.
                    ;In practice, it uses an iterative ADD of the complemented divisor.

                    ;Entry parameters
                    ;       HL = dividend
                    ;       DE = divisor

                    ;Exit parameters
                    ;       BC = quotient
                    ;       HL = remainder
                        DIVHL:
            008F D5              PUSH    D               ;Save divisor
                                                         ;Note : 2's complement is formed by
                                                         ;inverting all bits and adding 1.
            0090 7B              MOV     A,E
            0091 2F              CMA                     ;Complement divisor (for iterative
            0092 5F              MOV     E,A             ;ADD later on)
            0093 7A              MOV     A,D             ;Get MS byte
            0094 2F              CMA                     ;Complement it
            0095 57              MOV     D,A
            0096 13              INX     D               ;Make 2's complement
                                                         ;Now, subtract negative divisor until
                                                         ;dividend goes negative, counting the number
                                                         ;of times the subtract occurs
            0097 010000          LXI     B,0             ;Initialize quotient
                        DIVHLS:                          ;Subtract loop
            009A 03              INX     B               ;Add 1 to quotient
            009B 19              DAD     D               ;"Subtract" divisor
            009C DA9A00          JC      DIVHLS          ;Dividend not yet negative
                                                         ;Dividend now negative, quotient 1 too large
            009F 0B              DCX     B               ;Correct quotient
                                                         ;Compute correct remainder
            00A0 EB              XCHG                    ;DE = remainder - divisor
            00A1 E1              POP     H               ;Recover positive divisor
            00A2 19              DAD     D               ;HL = remainder
            00A3 C9              RET                     ;BC = quotient, HL = remainder

                    ;MULHL
                    ;Multiply HL * DE using iterative ADD.

                    ;Entry parameters
                    ;       HL = multiplicand
                    ;       DE = multiplier

                    ;Exit parameters
                    ;       HL = product
                    ;       DE = multiplier
                        MULHL:
            00A4 C5              PUSH    B               ;Save user register
                                                         ;Check if either multiplicand
                                                         ; or multiplier is 0
```

Figure 5-24. (Continued)

```
00A5 7C              MOV     A,H
00A6 B5              ORA     L
00A7 CAC400          JZ      MULHLZ          ;Yes, fake product
00AA 7A              MOV     A,D
00AB B3              ORA     E
00AC CAC400          JZ      MULHLZ          ;Yes, fake product
                                             ;This routine will be faster if
                                             ; the smaller value is in DE
00AF 7A              MOV     A,D             ;Get MS byte of current DE value
00B0 BC              CMP     H               ;Check which is smaller
00B1 DAB500          JC      MULHLN          ;C set if D < H, so no exchange
00B4 EB              XCHG
             MULHLN:
00B5 42              MOV     B,D             ;BC = multiplier
00B6 4B              MOV     C,E
00B7 54              MOV     D,H             ;DE = HL = multiplicand
00B8 5D              MOV     E,L
00B9 0B              DCX     B               ;Adjust count as
                                             ;1 * multiplicand = multiplicand
             MULHLA:                         ;ADD loop
00BA 78              MOV     A,B             ;Check if all iterations completed
00BB B1              ORA     C
00BC CAC700          JZ      MULHLX          ;Yes, exit
00BF 19              DAD     D               ;HL = multicand + multiplicand
00C0 0B              DCX     B               ;Countdown on multiplier - 1
00C1 C3BA00          JMP     MULHLA          ;Loop back until all ADDs done
             MULHLZ:
00C4 210000          LXI     H,0             ;Fake product as either multiplicand
                                             ; or multiplier is 0
             MULHLX:
00C7 C1              POP     B               ;Recover user register
00C8 C9              RET

;SUBHL
;Subtract HL - DE

;Entry parameters
;       HL = subtrahend
;       DE = subtractor

;Exit parameters
;       HL = difference

             SUBHL:
00C9 7D              MOV     A,L             ;Get LS byte
00CA 93              SUB     E               ;Subtract without regard to carry
00CB 6F              MOV     L,A             ;Put back into difference
00CC 7C              MOV     A,H             ;Get MS byte
00CD 9A              SBB     D               ;Subtract including carry
00CE 67              MOV     H,A             ;Move back into difference
00CF C9              RET

;SHLR
;Shift HL right one place (dividing HL by 2)

;Entry parameters
;       HL = value to be shifted

;Exit parameters
;       HL = value/2

             SHLR:
00D0 B7              ORA     A               ;Clear carry
00D1 7C              MOV     A,H             ;Get MS byte
00D2 1F              RAR                     ;Bit 7 set from previous carry,
                                             ; bit 0 goes into carry
00D3 67              MOV     H,A             ;Put shift MS byte back
00D4 7D              MOV     A,L             ;Get LS byte
00D5 1F              RAR                     ;Bit 7 = bit 0 of MS byte
00D6 6F              MOV     L,A             ;Put back into result
00D7 C9              RET
```

Figure 5-24. (Continued)

Function 32: Set/Get User Number

        Function Code: C = 20H
        Entry Parameters: E = 0FFH to get user number, or
                                E = 0 to 15 to set user number
        Exit Parameters: A = Current user number if E was 0FFH

Example

```
0020 =              B$SETGETUN      EQU     32          ;Set/Get User Number
0005 =              BDOS            EQU     5           ;BDOS entry point

                                                        ;To set user number
0000 0E20           MVI             C,B$SETGETUN        ;Function code
0002 1E0F           MVI             E,15                ;Required user number
0004 CD0500         CALL            BDOS                ;To get user number
0007 0E20           MVI             C,B$SETGETUN        ;Function code
0009 1EFF           MVI             E,0FFH              ;Indicate request to GET
000B CD0500         CALL            BDOS                ;A = Current user no. (0 -- 15)
```

Purpose   This subroutine either sets or gets the current user number. The current user number determines which file directory entries are matched during all disk file operations.

When you call this function, the contents of the E register specify what action is to be taken. If E = 0FFH, then the function will return the current user number in the A register. If you set E to a number in the range 0 to 15 (that is, a valid user number), the function will set the current user number to this value.

Notes   You can use this function to share files with other users. You can locate a file by attempting to open a file and switching through all of the user numbers. Or you can share a file in another user number by setting to that number, operating on the file, and then reverting back to the original user number.

If you do change the current user number, make provisions in your program to return to the original number before your program terminates. It is disconcerting for computer operators to find that they are in a different user number after a program. Files can easily be damaged or accidentally erased this way.

Function 33: Read Random

        Function Code: C = 21H
        Entry Parameters: DE = Address of FCB
        Exit Parameters: A = Return code

Example

```
0021 =              B$READRAN       EQU     33          ;Read Random
0005 =              BDOS            EQU     5           ;BDOS entry point

                    FCB:                                ;File control block
0000 00             FCB$DISK:       DB      0           ;Search on default disk drive
0001 46494C454E     FCB$NAME:       DB      'FILENAME'  ;File name
0009 545950         FCB$TYP:        DB      'TYP'       ;File type
```

```
000C 00              FCB$EXTENT:     DB      0                   ;Extent
000D 0000            FCB$RESV:       DB      0,0                 ;Reserved for CP/M
000F 00              FCB$RECUSED:    DB      0                   ;Records used in this extent
0010 0000000000      FCB$ABUSED:     DB      0,0,0,0,0,0,0,0     ;Allocation blocks used
0018 0000000000                      DB      0,0,0,0,0,0,0
0020 00              FCB$SEQREC:     DB      0                   ;Sequential rec. to read/write
0021 0000            FCB$RANREC:     DW      0                   ;Random rec. to read/write
0023 00              FCB$RANRECO:    DB      0                   ;Random rec. overflow byte (MS)

0024 D204            RANRECNO:       DW      1234                ;Example random record number

                                                                 ;Record will be read into
                                                                 ; address set by prior
                                                                 ; SETDMA call
0026 2A2400                          LHLD    RANRECNO            ;Get random record number
0029 222100                          SHLD    FCB$RANREC          ;Set up file control block
002C 0E21                            MVI     C,B$READRAN         ;Function code
002E 110000                          LXI     D,FCB               ;DE -> file control block
0031 CD0500                          CALL    BDOS                ;A = 00 if operation successful
                                                                 ;A = nonzero if no data in
                                                                 ; file specifically:
                                                                 ;A = 01 -- attempt to read
                                                                 ;         unwritten record
                                                                 ;    03 -- CP/M could not
                                                                 ;         close current extent
                                                                 ;    04 -- attempt to read
                                                                 ;         unwritten extent
                                                                 ;    06 -- attempt to read
                                                                 ;         beyond end of disk
```

Purpose   This function reads a specific CP/M record (128 bytes) from a random file—that is, a file in which records can be accessed directly. It assumes that you have already opened the file, set the DMA address using the BDOS Set DMA function, and set the specific record to be read into the random record number in the FCB. This function computes the extent of the specified record number and attempts to open it and read the correct CP/M record into the DMA address.

The random record number in the FCB is three bytes long (at relative bytes 33, 34, and 35). Byte 33 is the least significant byte, 34 is the middle byte, and 35 the most significant. CP/M uses only the most significant byte (35) for computing the overall file size (function 35). You must set this byte to 0 when setting up the FCB. Bytes 33 and 34 are used together for the Read Random, so you can access from record 0 to 65535 (a maximum file size of 8,388,480 bytes).

This function returns with A set to 0 to indicate that the operation has been completed successfully, or A set to a nonzero value if an error has occurred. The error codes are as follows:

A = 01 (attempt to read unwritten record)

A = 03 (CP/M could not close current extent)

A = 04 (attempt to read unwritten extent)

A = 06 (attempt to read beyond end of disk)

Unlike the Read Sequential BDOS function (code 20, 14H), which updates the current (sequential) record number in the FCB, the Read Random function leaves the record number unchanged, so that a subsequent Write Random will replace the record just read.

You can follow a Read Random with a Write Sequential (code 21, 15H). This

Chapter 5: The Basic Disk Operating System   **133**

will rewrite the record just read, but will then update the sequential record number. Or you may choose to use a Read Sequential after the Read Random. In this case, the same record will be reread and the sequential record number will be incremented. In short, the file can be sequentially read or written once the Read Random has been used to position to the required place in the file.

Notes   To use the Read Random function, you must first open the *base extent* of the file, that is, extent 0. Even though there may be no actual data records in this extent, opening permits the file to be processed correctly.

One problem that is not immediately obvious with random files is that they can easily be created with gaps in the file. If you were to create the file with record number 0 and record number 5000, there would be no intervening file extents. Should you attempt to read or copy the file sequentially, even using CP/M's file copy utility, only the first extent (and in this case, record 0) would get copied. A Read Sequential function would return an "end of file" error after reading record 0. You must therefore be conscious of the type of the file that you try and read.

See Figure 5-26 for an example subroutine that performs Random File Reads and Writes. It reads or writes records of sizes other than 128 bytes, where necessary reading or writing several CP/M records, prereading them into its own buffer when the record being written occupies only part of a CP/M record. It also contains subroutines to produce a 32-bit product from multiplying HL by DE (MLDL—Multiply double length) and a right bit shift for DE, HL (SDLR—Shift double length right).

Function 34: Write Random

```
Function Code:     C = 22H
Entry Parameters:  DE = Address of file control block
Exit Parameters:   A = Return code
```

Example

```
0022 =              B$WRITERAN   EQU   34              ;Write Random
0005 =              BDOS         EQU   5               ;BDOS entry point

                    FCB:                               ;File control block
0000 00             FCB$DISK:    DB    0               ;Search on default disk drive
0001 46494C454E     FCB$NAME:    DB    'FILENAME'      ;File name
0009 545950         FCB$TYP:     DB    'TYP'           ;File type
000C 00             FCB$EXTENT:  DB    0               ;Extent
000D 0000           FCB$RESV:    DB    0,0             ;Reserved for CP/M
000F 00             FCB$RECUSED: DB    0               ;Records used in this extent
0010 0000000000     FCB$ABUSED:  DB    0,0,0,0,0,0,0,0 ;Allocation blocks used
0018 0000000000                  DB    0,0,0,0,0,0,0,0
0020 00             FCB$SEQREC:  DB    0               ;Sequential rec. to read/write
0021 0000           FCB$RANREC:  DW    0               ;Random rec. to read/write
0023 00             FCB$RANRECO: DB    0               ;Random rec. overflow byte (MS)

0024 D204           RANRECNO:    DW    1234            ;Example random record number

                                                       ;Record will be written from
                                                       ; address set by prior
                                                       ; SETDMA call
```

```
0026  2A2400         LHLD    RANRECNO        ;Get random record number
0029  222100         SHLD    FCB$RANREC      ;Set up file control block
002C  0E22           MVI     C,B$WRITERAN    ;Function code
002E  110000         LXI     D,FCB           ;DE -> file control block
0031  CD0500         CALL    BDOS            ;A = 00 if operation successful
                                             ;A = nonzero if no data in file
                                             ;  specifically:
                                             ;A = 03 -- CP/M could not
                                             ;          close current extent
                                             ;    05 -- directory full
                                             ;    06 -- attempt to write
                                             ;          beyond end of disk
```

Purpose   This function writes a specific CP/M record (128 bytes) into a random file. It is initiated in much the same way as the companion function, Read Random (code 33, 21 H). It assumes that you have already opened the file, set the DMA address to the address in memory containing the record to be written to disk, and set the random record number in the FCB to the specified record being written. This function also computes the extent in which the specified record number lies and opens the extent (creating it if it does not already exist). The error codes returned in A by this call are the same as those for Read Random, with the addition of error code 05, which indicates a full directory.

Like the Read Random (but unlike the Write Sequential), this function does not update the logical extent and sequential (current) record number in the FCB. Therefore, any subsequent sequential operation will access the record just written by the Read Random call, but these functions will update the sequential record number. The Write Random can therefore be used to position to the required place in the file, which can then be accessed sequentially.

Notes   In order to use the Write Random, you must first open the base extent (extent 0) of the file. Even though there may be no data records in this extent, opening permits the file to be processed correctly.

As explained in the notes for the Read Random function, you can easily create a random file with gaps in it. If you were to create a file with record number 0 and record number 5000, there would be no intervening file extents.

Figure 5-25 shows an example subroutine that creates a random file (CRF) but avoids this problem. You specify the number of 128-byte CP/M records in the file. The subroutine creates the file and then writes zero-filled records throughout. This makes it easier to process the file and permits standard CP/M utility programs to copy the file because there is a data record in every logical record position in the file. It is no longer a "sparse" file.

Figure 5-26 shows a subroutine that ties the Read and Write Random functions together. It performs Random Operations (RO). Unlike the standard BDOS functions that operate on 128-byte CP/M records, RO can handle arbitrary record size from one to several thousand bytes. You specify the relative record number of your record, not the CP/M record number (RO computes this). RO also prereads a CP/M record when your logical record occupies part of a 128-byte record, either because your record is less than 128 bytes or because it spans more than one

```
                        ;CRF
                        ;Create random file
                        ;This subroutine creates a random file. It erases any previous
                        ;file before creating the new one, and then writes 0-filled
                        ;records throughout the entire file.

                        ;Entry parameters
                        ;       DE -> file control block for new file
                        ;       HL = Number of 128-byte CP/M records to be
                        ;            zero-filled.

                        ;Exit parameters
                        ;       Carry clear if operation successful (A = 0,1,2,3)
                        ;       Carry set if error (A = 0FFH)

                        ;Calling sequence
                        ;       LXI     D,FCB
                        ;       CALL    CRF
                        ;       JC      ERROR

0013 =                  B$ERASE     EQU     19          ;Erase file
0016 =                  B$CREATE    EQU     22          ;Create file
001A =                  B$SETDMA    EQU     26          ;Set DMA address
0015 =                  B$WRITESEQ  EQU     21          ;Write sequential record
0005 =                  BDOS        EQU     5           ;BDOS entry point

                        CRFBUF:                         ;Zero-filled buffer
0000 0000000000         DW    0,0,0,0,0,0,0,0,0,0,0,0,0,0,0,0,0,0,0,0,0,0,0,0,0,
                              0,0,0
0032 0000000000         DW    0,0,0,0,0,0,0,0,0,0,0,0,0,0,0,0,0,0,0,0,0,0,0,0,0,
                              0,0,0
0064 0000000000         DW    0,0,0,0,0,0,0,0,0,0,0,0,0,0

0080 0000    CRFRC:     DW    0                         ;Record count

             CRF:
0082 228000             SHLD    CRFRC                   ;Save record count
0085 D5                 PUSH    D                       ;Preserve FCB pointer
0086 0E13               MVI     C,B$ERASE               ;Erase any existing file
0088 CD0500             CALL    BDOS
008B D1                 POP     D                       ;Recover FCB pointer
008C D5                 PUSH    D                       ; and resave
008D 0E16               MVI     C,B$CREATE              ;Create (and open new file)
008F CD0500             CALL    BDOS
0092 FEFF               CPI     0FFH                    ;Carry set if OK, clear if error
0094 3F                 CMC                             ;Complete to use carry set if error
0095 D1                 POP     D                       ;Recover FCB address
0096 D8                 RC                              ;Return if error
0097 D5                 PUSH    D                       ;Resave FCB pointer

0098 0E1A               MVI     C,B$SETDMA              ;Set DMA address to 0-buffer
009A 110000             LXI     D,CRFBUF
009D CD0500             CALL    BDOS
00A0 D1                 POP     D                       ;Recover FCB pointer

             CRFL:
00A1 2A8000             LHLD    CRFRC                   ;Get record count
00A4 7D                 MOV     A,L
00A5 B4                 ORA     H                       ;Check if count now zero
00A6 C8                 RZ                              ;Yes, exit
00A7 2B                 DCX     H                       ;Downdate count
00A8 228000             SHLD    CRFRC                   ;Save count
00AB D5                 PUSH    D                       ;Resave FCB address
00AC 0E15               MVI     C,B$WRITESEQ            ;Write sequentially
00AE CD0500             CALL    BDOS

00B1 D1                 POP     D                       ;Recover FCB
00B2 C3A100             JMP     CRFL                    ;Write next record
```

Figure 5-25.   Create random file

128-byte sector. The subroutine suppresses this preread if you happen to use a record size that is some multiple of 128 bytes. In this case, your records will fit exactly onto a 128-byte record, so there will never be some partially occupied 128-byte sector.

This example also contains subroutines to produce a 32-bit product from multiplying HL by DE (MLDL—Multiply double length) and a right bit shift for DE, HL (SDLR—Shift double length right).

```
              ;RO
              ;Random operation (read or write)

              ;This subroutine reads or writes a random record from a file.
              ;The record length can be other than 128-bytes. This
              ;subroutine computes the start CP/M record (which
              ;is 128 bytes), and, if reading, performs a random read
              ;and moves the user-specified record into a user buffer.
              ;If necessary, more CP/M records will be read until the complete
              ;user-specified record has been input.
              ;For writing, if the size of the user-specified record is not an exact
              ;multiple of CP/M records, the appropriate sectors will be preread.
              ;It is not necessary to preread when the user-specified record
              ;is an exact CP/M record, nor when subroutine is processing
              ;CP/M records entirely spanned by a user-specified record.

              ;Entry parameters
              ;      HL -> parameter block of the form:
              ;              DB      0           ;0FFH when reading, 00H for write
              ;              DW      FCB         ;Pointer to FCB
              ;              DW      RECNO       ;User record number
              ;              DW      RECSZ       ;User record size
              ;              DW      BUFFER      ;Pointer to buffer of
              ;                                  ; RECSZ bytes in length
              ;Exit parameters
              ;      A = 0 if operation completed (and user record
              ;              copied into user buffer)
              ;          1 if attempt to read unwritten CP/M record
              ;          3 if CP/M could not close an extent
              ;          4 if attempt to read unwritten extent
              ;          5 if CP/M could not create a new extent
              ;          6 if attempt to read beyond end of disk

              ;Calling sequence
              ;      LXI     H,PARAMS            ;HL -> parameter block
              ;      CALL    RO
              ;      ORA     A                   ;Check if error
              ;      JNZ     ERROR

0021  =       FCBE$RANREC   EQU     33          ;Offset of random record no. in FCB
001A  =       B$SETDMA      EQU     26          ;Set the DMA address
0021  =       B$READRAN     EQU     33          ;Read random record
0028  =       B$WRITERANZ   EQU     40          ;Write random record with zero-fill
                                                ; previously unallocated allocation
                                                ; blocks
0005  =       BDOS          EQU     5           ;BDOS entry point

              ROPB:                             ;Parameter block image
0000 00       ROREAD: DB    0                   ;NZ when reading, Z when writing
0001 0000     ROFCB:  DW    0                   ;Pointer to FCB
0003 0000     ROURN:  DW    0                   ;User record number
0005 0000     ROURL:  DW    0                   ;User record length
0007 0000     ROUB:   DW    0                   ;Pointer to user buffer
0009  =       ROPBL   EQU   $-ROPB              ;Parameter block length

0009 0000     ROFRP:  DW    0                   ;Pointer to start of user record fragment
                                                ; in first CP/M-record read in
```

Figure 5-26. Read/Write variable length records randomly

```
        000B 00           ROFRL:   DB    0         ;Fragment length
        000C 0000         RORNP:   DW    0         ;Record number pointer (in user FCB)
        000E 00           ROWECR:  DB    0         ;NZ when writing user records that are an
                                                   ; exact super-multiple of CP/M-record (and
                                                   ; therefore no preread is required)

        000F              ROBUF:   DS    128       ;Buffer for CP/M record

                          RO:
        008F 110000                LXI   D,ROPB    ;DE -> local parameter block
        0092 0E09                  MVI   C,ROPBL   ;Parameter block length
        0094 CDFE01                CALL  MOVE      ;Move C bytes from HL to DE

                                   ;To compute offset of user record in CP/M record,
                                   ; compute the relative BYTE offset of the start
                                   ; of the user record within the file (i.e.
                                   ; user record number * record size). The least
                                   ; significant 7 bits of this product give the
                                   ; byte offset of the start of the user record.
                                   ;The product / 128 (shifted left 7 bits) gives the
                                   ;CP/M record number of the start of the user record.

        0097 2A0500                LHLD  ROURL     ;Get user record length
        009A 7D                    MOV   A,L       ;Get LS bytes of user rec. length
        009B E67F                  ANI   7FH       ;Check if exact multiple of 128
        009D B7                    ORA   A         ;(i.e. exact CP/M records)
        009E 3E00                  MVI   A,0       ;A = 0, flags unchanged
        00A0 C2A400                JNZ   RONE      ;Not exact CP/M records
        00A3 3D                    DCR   A         ;A =FF

                          RONE:
        00A4 320E00                STA   ROWECR    ;Set write-exact-CP/M-records flag
        00A7 EB                    XCHG            ;DE = user record length
        00A8 2A0300                LHLD  ROURN     ;Get user record number
        00AB CDB801                CALL  MLDL      ;DE,HL = HL * DE
                                                   ;DE,HL = user-record byte offset in file
        00AE D5                    PUSH  D         ;Save user-record byte offset
        00AF E5                    PUSH  H
        00B0 7D                    MOV   A,L       ;Get LS byte of product
        00B1 E67F                  ANI   7FH       ;Isolate byte offset within

        00B3 4F                    MOV   C,A       ;CP/M record
        00B4 0600                  MVI   B,0       ;Make into word value
        00B6 210F00                LXI   H,ROBUF   ;Get base address of local buffer
        00B9 09                    DAD   B         ;HL -> Start of fragment in buffer
        00BA 220900                SHLD  ROFRP     ;Save fragment pointer

                                   ;Compute maximum fragment length that could reside in
                                   ;remainder of CP/M record, based on the offset in the
                                   ;CP/M record where the fragment starts.

        00BD 47                    MOV   B,A       ;Take copy of offset in CP/M record
        00BE 3E80                  MVI   A,128     ;CP/M record size
        00C0 90                    SUB   B         ;Compute 128 - offset
        00C1 320B00                STA   ROFRL     ;Assume this is the fragment length

                                   ;If the user record length is less than the assumed
                                   ; fragment length, use it in place of the result above

        00C4 47                    MOV   B,A       ;Get copy of assume frag. length
        00C5 3A0600                LDA   ROURL+1   ;Get MS byte of user record length
        00C8 B7                    ORA   A         ;If NZ, rec. len. must be > 128
        00C9 C2D600                JNZ   ROFLOK    ;So fragment length is OK
        00CC 3A0500                LDA   ROURL     ;Still a chance that rec. len.
        00CF B8                    CMP   B         ; less than fragment len.
        00D0 D2D600                JNC   ROFLOK    ;NC if user rec. len. => frag. len.
        00D3 320B00                STA   ROFRL     ;User rec. len. < frag. len. so
                                                   ; reset fragment length to smaller
                          ROFLOK:
        00D6 3A0E00                LDA   ROWECR    ;Get exact CP/M record flag
        00D9 47                    MOV   B,A       ;for ANDing with READ flag
        00DA 3A0000                LDA   ROREAD    ;Get read operation flag
        00DD 2F                    CMA             ;Invert so NZ when writing
```

Figure 5-26. (Continued)

```
00DE A0                  ANA   B              ;Form logical AND
00DF 320E00              STA   ROWECR         ;Save back in flag

                                              ;Recover the double length byte offset within the file
                                              ;of the start of the user record. Shift 7 places right
                                              ;to divide by 128 and get the CP/M record number for
                                              ;the start of the user record.

00E2 E1                  POP   H              ;Recover user rec. byte offset
00E3 D1                  POP   D
00E4 0E07                MVI   C,7            ;Count for shift right
                ROS:
00E6 CDF101              CALL  SDLR           ;DE,HL = DE,HL / 2
00E9 0D                  DCR   C
00EA C2E600              JNZ   ROS

00ED 7A                  MOV   A,D            ;Error if DE still NZ after
00EE B3                  ORA   E              ; division by 128.
00EF C2AC01              JNZ   ROERO

                                              ;Set CP/M record number in FCB
00F2 EB                  XCHG                 ;DE = CP/M record number
00F3 2A0100              LHLD  ROFCB          ;Get pointer to FCB
00F6 012100              LXI   B,FCBE$RANREC  ;Offset of random record no. in FCB
00F9 09                  DAD   B              ;HL -> ran. rec. no. in FCB
00FA 220C00              SHLD  RORNP          ;Save record number pointer
00FD 73                  MOV   M,E            ;Store LS byte
00FE 23                  INX   H
00FF 72                  MOV   M,D            ;Store MS byte

0100 0E1A                MVI   C,B$SETDMA     ;Set DMA address to local buffer
0102 110F00              LXI   D,ROBUF
0105 CD0500              CALL  BDOS

0108 3A0E00              LDA   ROWECR         ;Bypass preread if exact sector write
010B B7                  ORA   A
010C C21F01              JNZ   ROMNF

010F 2A0100              LHLD  ROFCB          ;Get pointer to FCB
0112 EB                  XCHG                 ;DE -> FCB
0113 0E21                MVI   C,B$READRAN    ;Read random function
0115 CD0500              CALL  BDOS

0118 FE05                CPI   5              ;Check if error code < 5
011A DCAF01              CC    ROCIE          ;Yes, check if ignorable error
                                              ; (i.e. error reading unwritten part
                                              ; of file for write operation preread)
011D B7                  ORA   A              ;Check if error
011E C0                  RNZ                  ;Yes

                ROMNF:                        ;Move next fragment
011F 2A0700              LHLD  ROUB           ;Get pointer to user buffer
0122 EB                  XCHG                 ;DE -> user buffer
0123 2A0900              LHLD  ROFRP          ;HL -> start of user rec. in local buffer
0126 3A0B00              LDA   ROFRL          ;Get fragment length
0129 4F                  MOV   C,A            ;Ready for MOVE

012A 3A0000              LDA   ROREAD         ;Check if reading
012D B7                  ORA   A
012E C23201              JNZ   RORD1          ;Yes, so leave DE, HL unchanged
0131 EB                  XCHG                 ;Writing, so swap source and destination
                                              ;DE -> start of user rec. in local buffer
                                              ;HL -> user buffer
                RORD1:
0132 CDFE01              CALL  MOVE           ;Reading - fragment local -> user buffer
                                              ;Writing - fragment user -> local buffer
0135 3A0000              LDA   ROREAD         ;Check if writing
0138 B7                  ORA   A
0139 CA3D01              JZ    ROWR1          ;Writing, so leave HL -> user buffer
013C EB                  XCHG                 ;HL -> next byte in user buffer
                ROWR1:
013D 220700              SHLD  ROUB           ;Save updated user buffer pointer
0140 3A0000              LDA   ROREAD         ;Check if reading
```

Figure 5-26. (Continued)

```
0143 B7              ORA     A
0144 C25001          JNZ     RORD3           ;Yes, bypass write code

0147 0E28            MVI     C,B$WRITERANZ   ;Write random
0149 2A0100          LHLD    ROFCB           ;Get address of FCB
014C EB              XCHG                    ;DE -> FCB
014D CD0500          CALL    BDOS

            RORD3:   ;Compute residual length of user record as yet unmoved.
                     ;If necessary (because more data needs to be transferred)
                     ;more CP/M records will be read. In this case
                     ;the start of the fragment will be offset 0. The fragment
                     ;length depends on whether the user record finishes within
                     ;the next sector or spans it. If the residual length of the
                     ;user record is > 128, the fragment length will be set to
                     ;128.

0150 2A0500          LHLD    ROURL           ;Get residual user rec. length
0153 3A0B00          LDA     ROFRL           ;Get fragment length just moved
0156 5F              MOV     E,A             ;Make into a word value
0157 1600            MVI     D,0
0159 CDEA01          CALL    SUBHL           ;Compute ROURL - ROFRL
015C 7C              MOV     A,H             ;Check if result 0
015D B5              ORA     L
015E C8              RZ                      ;Return when complete USER
                                             ; record has been transferred
015F 220500          SHLD    ROURL           ;Save downdated residual rec. length
0162 4D              MOV     C,L             ;Assume residual length < 128
0163 118000          LXI     D,128           ;Check if residual length is < 128
0166 CDEA01          CALL    SUBHL           ;HL = HL - DE
0169 FA6E01          JM      ROLT128         ;negative if < 128
016C 0E80            MVI     C,128           ;=> 128, so set frag.length to 128
            ROLT128:
016E 79              MOV     A,C
016F 320B00          STA     ROFRL           ;Fragment length now is either 128
                                             ; if more than 128 bytes left to input
                                             ; in user record, or just the right
                                             ; number of bytes (< 128) to complete
                                             ; the user record.
0172 210F00          LXI     H,ROBUF         ;All subsequent CP/M records will start
0175 220900          SHLD    ROFRP           ; at beginning of buffer

                                             ;Update random record number in FCB
0178 2A0C00          LHLD    RORNP           ;HL -> random record number in user FCB
017B 5E              MOV     E,M             ;Increment the random record number
017C 23              INX     H               ;HL -> MS byte of record number
017D 56              MOV     D,M             ;Get MS byte
017E 13              INX     D               ;Update record number itself
017F 7A              MOV     A,D             ;Check if record now 0
0180 B3              ORA     E
0181 C28701          JNZ     ROSRN           ;No, so save record number
0184 3E06            MVI     A,6             ;Indicate "seek past end of disk"
0186 C9              RET                     ;Return to user
            ROSRN:
0187 72              MOV     M,D             ;Save record number
0188 2B              DCX     H               ;HL -> LS byte
0189 73              MOV     M,E

                                             ;If writing, check if preread required
018A 3A0E00          LDA     ROWECR          ;Check if exact CP/M record write
018D B7              ORA     A
018E C21F01          JNZ     ROMNF           ;Yes, go move next fragment

0191 3A0000          LDA     ROREAD          ;If reading, perform read unconditionally
0194 B7              ORA     A
0195 C2A001          JNZ     RORD2

0198 3A0B00          LDA     ROFRL           ;For writes, bypass preread if
019B FE80            CPI     128             ; whole CP/M-record is to be overwritten
019D CA1F01          JZ      ROMNF           ; (fragment length = 128)
            RORD2:
01A0 0E21            MVI     C,B$READRAN     ;Read the next CP/M record
01A2 2A0100          LHLD    ROFCB           ; in sequence
```

Figure 5-26. (Continued)

```
01A5 EB              XCHG                   ;DE -> FCB
01A6 CD0500          CALL    BDOS
01A9 C31F01          JMP     ROMNF          ;Go back to move next fragment

             ROERO:                         ;Error because user record number
                                            ; * User record length / 128 gives
                                            ; a CP/M record number > 65535.
01AC 3E04            MVI     A,4            ;Indicate "attempt to read unwritten
01AE C9              RET                    ; extent"

             ROCIE:                         ;Check ignorable error (preread
                                            ; for write operation)
01AF 47              MOV     B,A            ;Save original error code
01B0 3A0000          LDA     ROREAD         ;Check if read operation
01B3 B7              ORA     A
01B4 78              MOV     A,B            ;Restore original error code but
                                            ; leave flags unchanged
01B5 C0              RNZ                    ;Return if reading
01B6 AF              XRA     A              ;Fake "no error" indicator
01B7 C9              RET

             ;MLDL
             ;Multiply HL * DE using iterative ADD with product
             ;returned in DE,HL.
             ;Entry parameters
             ;        HL = multiplicand
             ;        DE = multiplier

             ;Exit parameters
             ;        DE,HL = product
             ;        DE    = multiplier

             MLDL:
01B8 010000          LXI     B,0            ;Put 0 on top of stack
01BB C5              PUSH    B              ; to act as MS byte of product
                                            ;Check if either multiplicand
                                            ; or multiplier is 0
01BC 7C              MOV     A,H
01BD B5              ORA     L
01BE CAE501          JZ      MLDLZ          ;Yes, fake product
01C1 7A              MOV     A,D
01C2 B3              ORA     E
01C3 CAE501          JZ      MLDLZ          ;Yes, fake product

                                            ;This routine will be faster if
                                            ; the smaller value is in DE
01C6 7A              MOV     A,D            ;Get MS byte of current DE value
01C7 BC              CMP     H              ;Check which is smaller
01C8 DACC01          JC      MLDLNX         ;C set if D < H, so no exchange
01CB EB              XCHG
             MLDLNX:
01CC 42              MOV     B,D            ;BC = multiplier
01CD 4B              MOV     C,E

01CE 54              MOV     D,H            ;DE = HL = multiplicand
01CF 5D              MOV     E,L

01D0 0B              DCX     B              ;Adjust count as
                                            ; 1 * multiplicand = multiplicand
             MLDLA:                         ;ADD loop
01D1 78              MOV     A,B            ;Check if all iterations completed
01D2 B1              ORA     C
01D3 CAE801          JZ      MLDLX          ;Yes, exit
01D6 19              DAD     D              ;HL = multicand + multiplicand
01D7 E3              XTHL                   ;HL = MS bytes of result, TOS = part prod.
01D8 7D              MOV     A,L            ;Get LS byte of top half of product
01D9 CE00            ACI     0              ;Add one if carry set
01DB 6F              MOV     L,A            ;Replace
01DC 7C              MOV     A,H            ;Repeat for MS byte
01DD CE00            ACI     0
01DF 67              MOV     H,A
01E0 E3              XTHL
01E1 0B              DCX     B              ;Countdown on multiplier - 1
01E2 C3D101          JMP     MLDLA          ;Loop back until all ADDs done
```

Figure 5-26.   (Continued)

```
                        MLDLZ:
        01E5 210000             LXI     H,0             ;Fake product as either multiplicand
                                                        ; or multiplier is 0

                        MLDLX:
        01E8 D1                 POP     D               ;Recover MS part of product
        01E9 C9                 RET


                        ;SUBHL
                        ;Subtract HL - DE.

                        ;Entry parameters
                        ;       HL = subtrahend
                        ;       DE = subtractor

                        ;Exit parameters
                        ;       HL = difference

                        SUBHL:
        01EA 7D                 MOV     A,L             ;Get LS byte
        01EB 93                 SUB     E               ;Subtract without regard to carry
        01EC 6F                 MOV     L,A             ;Put back into difference
        01ED 7C                 MOV     A,H             ;Get MS byte
        01EE 9A                 SBB     D               ;Subtract including carry
        01EF 67                 MOV     H,A             ;Move back into difference
        01F0 C9                 RET

                        ;SDLR
                        ;Shift DE,HL right one place (dividing DE,HL by 2)

                        ;Entry parameters
                        ;       DE,HL = value to be shifted

                        ;Exit parameters
                        ;       DE,HL = value / 2

                        SDLR:
        01F1 B7                 ORA     A               ;Clear carry
        01F2 EB                 XCHG                    ;Shift DE first
        01F3 CDF701             CALL    SDLR2
        01F6 EB                 XCHG                    ;Now shift HL

                                                        ;Drop into SDLR2 with carry
                                                        ; set correctly from LS bit
                                                        ; of DE
                                                        ;Shift HL right one place
                        SDLR2:
        01F7 7C                 MOV     A,H             ;Get MS byte
        01F8 1F                 RAR                     ;Bit 7 set from previous carry,
                                                        ;Bit 0 goes into carry
        01F9 67                 MOV     H,A             ;Put shift MS byte back
        01FA 7D                 MOV     A,L             ;Get LS byte
        01FB 1F                 RAR                     ;Bit 7 = bit 0 of MS byte
        01FC 6F                 MOV     L,A             ;Put back into result
        01FD C9                 RET


                        ;MOVE
                        ;Moves C bytes from HL to DE

                        MOVE:
        01FE 7E                 MOV     A,M             ;Get source byte
        01FF 12                 STAX    D               ;Store in destination
        0200 13                 INX     D               ;Update destination pointer
        0201 23                 INX     H               ;Update source pointer
        0202 0D                 DCR     C               ;Downdate count
        0203 C2FE01             JNZ     MOVE            ;Get next byte
        0206 C9                 RET
```

Figure 5-26. (Continued)

Function 35: Get File Size

        Function Code: C = 23H
        Entry Parameters: DE = Address of FCB
        Exit Parameters: Random record field set in FCB

Example

```
0023 =                B$GETFSIZ     EQU     35            ;Get Random File LOGICAL size
0005 =                BDOS          EQU     5             ;BDOS entry point
                      FCB:                                ;File control block
0000 00               FCB$DISK:     DB      0             ;Search on default disk drive
0001 46494C454E       FCB$NAME:     DB      'FILENAME'    ;File name
0009 545950           FCB$TYP:      DB      'TYP'         ;File type
000C 00               FCB$EXTENT:   DB      0             ;Extent
000D 0000             FCB$RESV:     DB      0,0           ;Reserved for CP/M
000F 00               FCB$RECUSED:  DB      0             ;Records used in this extent
0010 0000000000       FCB$ABUSED:   DB      0,0,0,0,0,0,0,0 ;Allocation blocks used
0018 0000000000       
0020 00               FCB$SEQREC:   DB      0             ;Sequential rec. to read/write
0021 0000             FCB$RANREC:   DW      0             ;Random rec. to read/write
0023 00               FCB$RANRECO:  DB      0             ;Random rec. overflow byte (MS)

0024 0E23                           MVI     C,B$GETFSIZ   ;Function code
0026 110000                         LXI     D,FCB         ;DE -> file control block
0029 CD0500                         CALL    BDOS
002C 2A2100                         LHLD    FCB$RANREC    ;Get random record number
                                                          ;HL = LOGICAL file size
                                                          ; i.e. the record number of the
                                                          ; last record
```

Purpose   This function returns the virtual size of the specified file. It does so by setting the random record number (bytes 33-35) in the specified FCB to the maximum 128-byte record number in the file. The virtual file size is calculated from the record address of the record following the end of the file. Bytes 33 and 34 form a 16-bit value that contains the record number, with overflow indicated in byte 35. If byte 35 is 01, this means that the file has the maximum record count of 65,536.

If the function cannot find the file specified by the FCB, it returns with the random record field set to 0.

You can use this function when you want to add data to the end of an existing file. By calling this function first, the random record bytes will be set to the end of file. Subsequent Write Random calls will write out records to this preset address.

Notes   Do not confuse the virtual file size with the actual file size. In a random file, if you write just a single CP/M record to record number 1000 and then call this function, it will return with the random record number field set in the FCB to 1000—even though only a single record exists in the file.

For sequential files, this function returns the number of records in the file. In this case, the virtual and actual file sizes coincide.

Function 36: Set Random Record Number

        Function Code: C = 24H
        Entry Parameters: DE = Address of FCB
        Exit Parameters: Random record field set in FCB

Chapter 5: The Basic Disk Operating System **143**

Example

```
0024 =           B$SETRANREC   EQU   36         ;Set Random Record Number
0005 =           BDOS          EQU   5          ;BDOS entry point

                 FCB:                           ;File control block
0000 00          FCB$DISK:     DB    0          ;Search on default disk drive
0001 46494C454E  FCB$NAME:     DB    'FILENAME' ;File name
0009 545950      FCB$TYP:      DB    'TYP'      ;File type
000C 00          FCB$EXTENT:   DB    0          ;Extent
000D 0000        FCB$RESV:     DB    0,0        ;Reserved for CP/M
000F 00          FCB$RECUSED:  DB    0          ;Records used in this extent
0010 0000000000  FCB$ABUSED:   DB    0,0,0,0,0,0,0,0 ;Allocation blocks used
0018 0000000000                DB    0,0,0,0,0,0,0
0020 00          FCB$SEQREC:   DB    0          ;Sequential rec. to read/write
0021 0000        FCB$RANREC:   DW    0          ;Random rec. to read/write
0023 00          FCB$RANRECO:  DB    0          ;Random rec. overflow byte (MS)

                                                ;... file opened and read
                                                ; or written sequentially...

0024 0E24        MVI    C,B$SETRANREC           ;Function code
0026 110000      LXI    D,FCB                   ;DE -> file control block
0029 CD0500      CALL   BDOS
002C 2A2100      LHLD   FCB$RANREC              ;Get random record number
                                                ;HL = random record number
                                                ; that corresponds to the
                                                ; sequential progress down
                                                ; the file.
```

Purpose This function sets the random record number in the FCB to the correct value for the last record read or written sequentially to the file.

Notes This function provides you with a convenient way to build an index file so that you can randomly access a sequential file. Open the sequential file, and as you read each record, extract the appropriate key field from the data record. Make the BDOS Set Random Record request and create a new data record with just the key field and the random record number. Write the new data record out to the index file.

Once you have done this for each record in the file, your index file provides a convenient method, given a search key value, of finding the appropriate CP/M record in which the data lies.

You can also use this function as a means of finding out where you are currently positioned in a sequential file—either to relate a CP/M record number to the position, or simply as a place-marker to allow a repositioning to the same place later.

Function 37: Reset Logical Disk Drive

Function Code: C = 25H
Entry Parameters: DE = Logical drive bit map
Exit Parameters: A = 00H

Example

```
0025 =           B$RESETD      EQU   37         ;Reset Logical Disks
0005 =           BDOS          EQU   5          ;BDOS entry point
```

144 The CP/M Programmer's Handbook

```
                                                ;DE = Bit map of disks to be
                                                ; reset
                                                ;Bits are = 1 if disk to be
                                                ; reset
                                                ;Bits 15 14 13 ... 2 1 0
                                                ;Disk  P  O  N ... C B A
        0000 110200       LXI    D,0000$0000$0000$0010B  ;Reset drive B:
        0003 0E25         MVI    C,B$RESETD              ;Function code
        0005 CD0500       CALL   BDOS
```

Purpose This function resets individual disk drives. It is a more precise version of the Reset Disk System function (code 13,0DH), in that you can set specific logical disks rather than all of them.

The bit map in DE shows which disks are to be reset. The least significant bit of E represents disk A, and the most significant bit of D, disk P. The bits set to 1 indicate the disks to be reset.

Note that this function returns a zero value in A in order to maintain compatibility with MP/M.

Notes Use this function when only specific diskettes need to be changed. Changing a diskette without requesting CP/M to log it in will cause the BDOS to assume that an error has occurred and to set the new diskette to Read-Only status as a protective measure.

Function 40: Write Random with Zero-fill

Function Code: C = 28H
Entry Parameters: DE = Address of FCB
Exit Parameters: A = Return Code

Example

```
0028 =              B$WRITERANZ   EQU   40             ;Write Random with Zero-Fill
0005 =              BDOS          EQU   5              ;BDOS entry point
                    FCB:                               ;File control block
0000 00             FCB$DISK:     DB    0              ;Search on default disk drive
0001 46494C454E     FCB$NAME:     DB    'FILENAME'     ;File name
0009 545950         FCB$TYP:      DB    'TYP'          ;File type
000C 00             FCB$EXTENT:   DB    0              ;Extent
000D 0000           FCB$RESV:     DB    0,0            ;Reserved for CP/M
000F 00             FCB$RECUSED:  DB    0              ;Records used in this extent
0010 0000000000     FCB$ABUSED:   DB    0,0,0,0,0,0,0,0 ;Allocation blocks used
0018 0000000000                   DB    0,0,0,0,0,0,0,0
0020 00             FCB$SEQREC:   DB    0              ;Sequential rec. to read/write
0021 0000           FCB$RANREC:   DW    0              ;Random rec. to read/write
0023 00             FCB$RANRECO:  DB    0              ;Random rec. overflow byte (MS)

0024 D204           RANRECNO:     DW    1234           ;Example random record number
                                                       ;Record will be written from
                                                       ; address set by prior
                                                       ; SETDMA call
0026 2A2400         LHLD   RANRECNO        ;Get random record number
0029 222100         SHLD   FCB$RANREC      ;Set up file control block
002C 0E28           MVI    C,B$WRITERANZ   ;Function code
002E 110000         LXI    D,FCB           ;DE -> file control block
0031 CD0500         CALL   BDOS            ;A = 00 if operation successful
```

```
;A = nonzero if no data in file
; specifically :
;A = 03 -- CP/M could not
;         close current extent
;     05 -- directory full
;     06 -- attempt to write
;         beyond end of disk
```

Purpose This function is an extension to the Write Random function described previously. In addition to performing the Write Random, it will also fill each new allocation block with 00H's. Digital Research added this function to assist Microsoft with the production of its COBOL compiler—it makes the logic of the file handling code easier. It also is an economical way to completely fill a random file with 00H's. You need only write one record per allocation block; the BDOS will clear the rest of the block for you.

Notes Refer to the description of the Write Random function (code 34).

The BIOS Components
The BIOS Entry Points
Bootstrap Functions
Character Input/Output Functions
Disk Functions
Calling the BIOS Functions Directly
Example BIOS

The Basic Input/Output System

This chapter takes a closer look at the Basic Input/Output System (BIOS). The BIOS provides the software link between the Console Command Processor (CCP), the Basic Disk Operating System (BDOS), and the physical hardware of your computer system. The CCP and BDOS interact with the parts of your computer system only as logical devices. They can therefore remain unchanged from one computer system to the next. The BIOS, however, is customized for your particular type of computer and disk drives. The only predictable part of the BIOS is the way in which it interfaces to the CCP and BDOS. This must remain the same no matter what special features are built into the BIOS.

The BIOS Components

A standard BIOS consists of low-level subroutines that drive four types of physical devices:

- Console: CP/M communicates with the outside world via the console. Normally this will be a video terminal or a hard-copy terminal.
- "Reader" and "punch": These devices are normally used to communicate between computer systems—the names "reader" and "punch" are just historical relics from the early days of CP/M.
- List: This is a hard-copy printer, either letter-quality or dot-matrix.
- Disk drives: These can be anything from the industry standard single-sided, single-density, 8-inch floppy diskette drives to hard disk drives with capacities of several hundred megabytes.

The BIOS Entry Points

The first few instructions of the BIOS are all jump (JMP) instructions. They transfer control to the 17 different subroutines in the BIOS. The CCP and the BDOS, when making a specific request of the BIOS, do so by transferring control to the appropriate JMP instruction in this BIOS *jump table* or *jump vector*. The BIOS jump vector always starts at the beginning of a 256-byte page, so the address of the first jump instruction is always of the form xx00H, where "xx" is the page address. Location 0000H to 0002H has a jump instruction to the second entry of the BIOS jump vector—so you can always find the page address of the jump vector by looking in location 0002H.

Figure 6-1 shows the contents of the BIOS jump vector along with the page-relative address of each jump. The labels used in the jump instructions have been adopted by convention.

The following sections describe the functions of each of the BIOS's main subroutines. You should also refer to Digital Research's manual *CP/M 2.0 Alteration Guide* for their description of the BIOS routines.

Bootstrap Functions

There are two bootstrap functions. The cold bootstrap loads the entire CP/M operating system when the system is either first turned on or reset. The warm bootstrap reloads the CCP whenever a program branches to location 0000H.

```
xx00H    JMP   BOOT      ;"Cold" (first time) bootstrap
xx03H    JMP   WBOOT     ;"Warm" bootstrap
xx06H    JMP   CONST     ;Console input status
xx09H    JMP   CONIN     ;Console input
xx0CH    JMP   CONOUT    ;Console output
xx0FH    JMP   LIST      ;List output
xx12H    JMP   PUNCH     ;"Punch" output
xx15H    JMP   READER    ;"Reader" input
xx18H    JMP   HOME      ;Home disk heads (to track 0)
xx1BH    JMP   SELDSK    ;Select logical disk
xx1EH    JMP   SETTRK    ;Set track number
xx21H    JMP   SETSEC    ;Set sector number
xx24H    JMP   SETDMA    ;Set DMA address
xx27H    JMP   READ      ;Read (128-byte) sector
xx2AH    JMP   WRITE     ;Write (128-byte) sector
xx2DH    JMP   LISTST    ;List device output status
xx30H    JMP   SECTRAN   ;Sector translate
```

Figure 6-1. Layout of the standard BIOS jump vector

BOOT: "Cold" Bootstrap

The BOOT jump instruction is the first instruction executed in CP/M. The bootstrap sequence must transfer control to the BOOT entry point in order to bring up CP/M. In general, a PROM receives control either when power is first applied or after you press the RESET button on the computer. This reads in the CP/M loader on the first sector of the physical disk drive chosen to be logical disk A. This CP/M loader program reads the binary image of the CCP, BDOS, and BIOS into memory at some predetermined address. Then it transfers control to the BOOT entry point in the BIOS jump vector.

This BOOT routine must initialize all of the required computer hardware. It sets up the baud rates for the physical console (if this has not already been done during the bootstrap sequence), the "reader," "punch," and list devices, and the disk controller. It must also set up the base page of memory so that there is a jump at location 0000H to the warm boot entry point in the BIOS jump vector (at xx03H) and a jump at location 0005H to the BDOS entry point.

Most BOOT routines sign on by displaying a short message on the console, indicating the current version of CP/M and the computer hardware that this BIOS can support.

The BOOT routine terminates by transferring control to the start of the CCP + 6 bytes (the CCP has its own small jump vector at the beginning). Just before the BOOT routine jumps into the CCP, it sets the C register to 0 to indicate that logical disk A is to be the default disk drive. This is what causes "A>" to be the CCP's initial prompt.

The actual CCP entry point is derived from the base address of the BIOS. The CCP and BDOS together require 1E00H bytes of code, so the first instruction of the CCP starts at BIOS −1E00H.

WBOOT: "Warm" Bootstrap

Unlike the "cold" bootstrap entry point, which executes only once, the WBOOT or warm boot routine will be executed every time a program terminates by jumping to location 0000H, or whenever you type a CONTROL-C on the console as the first character of an input line.

The WBOOT routine is responsible for reloading the CCP into memory. Programs often use all of memory up to the starting point of the BDOS, overwriting the CCP in the process. The underlying philosophy is that while a program is executing, the CCP is not needed, so the program can use the memory previously occupied by the CCP. The CCP occupies 800H (2048) bytes of memory—and this is frequently just enough to make the difference between a program that cannot run and one that can.

A few programs that are self-contained and do not require the BDOS's facilities will also overwrite the BDOS to get another 1600H (5632) bytes of memory. Therefore, to be really safe, the WBOOT routine should read in both the CCP and the BDOS. It also needs to set up the two JMPs at location 0000H (to WBOOT itself) and at location 0005H (to the BDOS). Location 0003H should be set to the initial value of the IOBYTE if this is implemented in the BIOS.

As its last act, the WBOOT routine sets register C to indicate which logical disk is to be selected (C=0 for A, 1 for B, and so on). It then transfers control into the CCP at the first instruction in order to restart the CCP. Again, the actual address is computed based on the knowledge that the CCP starts 1E00H bytes lower in memory than the base address of the BIOS.

Character Input/Output Functions

Character input/output functions deal with logical devices: the console, "reader," "punch," and list devices. Because these logical devices can in practice be connected by software to one of several physical character I/O devices, many BIOS's use CP/M's IOBYTE features to assign logical devices to physical ones.

In this case, each of the BIOS functions must check the appropriate bit fields of the IOBYTE (see Figure 4-2 and Table 4-1) to transfer control to the correct physical device *driver* (program that controls a physical device).

CONST: Console Input Status

CONST simply returns an indicator showing whether there is an incoming character from the console device. The convention is that A=0FFH if a character is waiting to be processed, A=0 if one is not. Note that the zero flag need not be set to reflect the contents of the A register—it is the contents that are important.

CONST is called by the CCP whenever the CCP is in the middle of an operation that can be interrupted by pressing a keyboard character.

Chapter 6: The Basic Input/Output System   **151**

The BDOS will call CONST if a program makes a Read Console Status function call (B$CONST, code 11, 0BH). It is also called by the console input BIOS routine, CONIN (described next).

CONIN: Console Input

CONIN reads the next character from the console to the A register and sets the most significant (parity) bit to 0.

Normally, CONIN will call the CONST routine until it detects A = 0FFH. Only then will it input the data character and mask off the parity bit.

CONIN is called by the CCP and by the BDOS when a program executes a Read Console Byte function (B$CONIN, code 1).

CONOUT: Console Output

CONOUT outputs the character (in ASCII) in register C to the console. The most significant (parity) bit of the character will always be 0.

CONOUT must first check that the console device is ready to receive more data, delaying if necessary until it is, and only then sending the character to the device.

CONOUT is called by the CCP and by the BDOS when a program executes a Write Console Byte function (B$CONOUT, code 2).

LIST: List Output

LIST is similar to CONOUT except that it sends the character in register C to the list device. It too checks first that the list device is ready to receive the character.

LIST is called by the CCP in response to the CONTROL-P toggle for printer echo of console output, and by the BDOS when a program makes a Write Printer Byte or Display String call (B$LISTOUT and B$PRINTS, codes 5 and 9).

PUNCH: "Punch" Output

PUNCH sends the character in register C to the "punch" device. As mentioned earlier, the "punch" is rarely a real paper tape punch. In most BIOS's, the PUNCH entry point either returns immediately and is effectively a null routine, or it outputs the character to a communications device, such as a modem, on your computer.

PUNCH must check that the "punch" device is indeed ready to accept another character for output, and must wait if it is not.

Digital Research's documentation states that the character to be output will always have its most significant bit set to 0. This is not true. The BDOS simply transfers control over to the PUNCH entry point in the BIOS; the setting of the most significant bit will be determined by the program making the BDOS function request (B$PUNOUT, code 4). This is important because the requirement of a zero would preclude being able to send pure binary data via the BIOS PUNCH function.

READER: "Reader" Input

As with the PUNCH entry point, the READER entry point rarely connects to a real paper tape reader.

The READER function must return the next character from the reader device in the A register, waiting, if need be, until there is a character.

Digital Research's documentation again says that the most significant bit of the A register must be 0, but this is not the case if you wish to receive pure binary information via this function.

READER is called whenever a program makes a Read "Reader" Byte function request (B$READIN, code 3).

Disk Functions

All of the disk functions that follow were originally designed to operate on the 128-byte sectors used on single-sided, single-density, 8-inch floppy diskettes that were standard in the industry at the time. Now that CP/M runs on many different types of disks, some of the BIOS disk functions seem strange because most of the new disk drives use sector sizes other than 128 bytes.

To handle larger sector sizes, the BIOS has some additional code that makes the BDOS respond as if it were still handling 128-byte sectors. This code is referred to as the *blocking/deblocking* code. As its name implies, it blocks together several 128-byte "sectors" and only writes to the disk when a complete *physical* sector has been assembled. When reading, it reads in a physical sector and then deblocks it, handing back several 128-byte "sectors" to the BDOS.

To do all of this, the blocking/deblocking code uses a special buffer area of the same size as the physical sectors on the disk. This is known as the host disk buffer or HSTBUF. Physical sectors are read into this buffer and written to the disk from it.

In order to optimize this blocking/deblocking routine, the BIOS has code in it to reduce the number of times that an actual disk read or write occurs. A side effect is that at any given moment, several 128-byte "sectors" may be stored in the HSTBUF, waiting to be written out to the disk when HSTBUF becomes full. This sometimes complicates the logic of the BIOS disk functions. You cannot simply select a new disk drive, for example, when the HSTBUF contains data destined for another disk drive. You will see this complication in the BIOS only in the form of added logical operations; the BIOS disk functions rarely trigger immediate physical operations. It is easier to understand these BIOS functions if you consider that they make *requests*—and that these requests are satisfied only when it makes sense to do so, taking into account the blocking/deblocking logic.

HOME: Home Disk

HOME sets the requested track and sector to 0.

SELDSK: Select Disk

SELDSK does not do what its name implies. It does not (and must not) physically select a logical disk. Instead, it returns a pointer in the HL register pair to the disk parameter header for the logical disk specified in register C on entry. C = 0 for drive A, 1 for drive B, and so on. SELDSK also stores this code for the requested disk to be used later in the READ and WRITE functions.

If the logical disk code in register C refers to a nonexistent disk or to one for which no disk parameter header exists, then SELDSK must return with HL set to 0000H. Then the BDOS will output a message of the form

```
"BDOS Err on X: Select"
```

Note that SELDSK not only does not select the disk, but also does not indicate whether or not the requested disk is physically present—merely whether or not there are disk tables present for the disk.

SELDSK is called by the BDOS either during disk file operations or by a program issuing a Select Disk request (B$SELDSK, code 14).

SETTRK: Set Track

SETTRK saves the requested disk track that is in the BC register pair when SETTRK gets control. Note that this is an absolute track number; that is, the number of reserved tracks before the file directory will have been added to the track number relative to the start of the logical disk.

The number of the requested track will be used in the next BIOS READ or WRITE function (described later in this chapter).

SETTRK is called by the BDOS when it needs to read or write a 128-byte sector. Legitimate track numbers are from 0 to 0FFFFH (65,535).

SETSEC: Set Sector

SETSEC is similar to SETTRK in that it stores the requested sector number for later use in BIOS READ or WRITE functions. The requested sector number is handed to SETSEC in the A register; legitimate values are from 0 to 0FFH (255).

The sector number is a logical sector number. It does not take into account any sector skewing that might be used to improve disk performance.

SETSEC is called by the BDOS when it needs to read or write a 128-byte sector.

SETDMA: Set DMA Address

SETDMA saves the address in the BC register pair in the requested DMA address. The next BIOS READ or WRITE function will use the DMA address as a pointer to the 128-byte sector buffer into which data will be read or from which data will be written.

The default DMA address is 0080H. SETDMA is called by the BDOS when it needs to READ or WRITE a 128-byte sector.

READ: Read Sector

READ reads in a 128-byte sector provided that there have been previous BIOS function calls to

SELDSK — "select" the disk

SETDMA — set the DMA address

SETTRK — set the track number

SETSEC — set the sector number.

Because of the blocking/deblocking code in the BIOS, there are frequent occasions when the requested sector will already be in the host buffer (HSTBUF), so that a physical disk read is not required. All that is then required is for the BIOS to move the appropriate 128 bytes from the HSTBUF into the buffer pointed at by the DMA address.

Only during the READ function will the BIOS normally communicate with the physical disk drive, selecting it and seeking to read the requested track and sector. During this process, the READ function must also handle any hardware errors that occur, trying an operation again if a "soft," or recoverable, error occurs.

The READ function must return with the A register set to 00H if the read operation is completed successfully. If the READ function returns with the A register set to 01H, the BDOS will display an error message of the form

```
BDOS Err on X: Bad Sector
```

Under these circumstances, you have only two choices. You can enter a CARRIAGE RETURN, ignore the fact that there was an error, and attempt to make sense of the data in the DMA buffer. Or you can type a CONTROL-C to abort the operation, perform a warm boot, and return control to the CCP.

As you can see, CP/M's error handling is not particularly helpful, so most BIOS writers add more sophisticated error recovery right in the disk driver. This can include some interaction with the console so that a more determined effort can be made to correct errors or, if nothing else, give you more information as to what has gone wrong. Such error handling is discussed in Chapter 9.

If you are working with a hard disk system, the BIOS driver must also handle the management of bad sectors. You cannot simply replace a hard disk drive if one or two sectors become unreadable. This bad sector management normally requires that a directory of "spare" sectors be put on the hard disk before it is used to store data. Then, when a sector is found to be bad, one of the spare sectors is substituted in its place. This is also discussed in Chapter 9.

WRITE: Write Sector

WRITE is similar to READ but with the obvious difference that data is transferred from the DMA buffer to the specified 128-byte sector. Like READ, this function requires that the following function calls have already been made:

SELDSK — "select" the disk
SETDMA — set the DMA address
SETTRK — set the track number
SETSEC — set the sector number.

Again, it is only in the WRITE routine that the driver will start to talk directly to the physical hardware, selecting the disk unit, track, and sector, and transferring the data to the disk.

With the blocking/deblocking code, the BDOS optimizes the number of disk writes that are needed by indicating in register C the type of disk write that is to be performed:

0 = normal sector write
1 = write to file directory sector
2 = write to sector of previously unused allocation block.

Type 0 occurs whenever the BDOS is writing to a data sector in an already used allocation block. Under these circumstances, the disk driver must preread the appropriate host sector because there may be previously stored information on it.

Type 1 occurs whenever the BDOS is writing to a file directory sector — in this case, the BIOS must not defer writing the sector to the disk, as the information is too valuable to hold in memory until the HSTBUF is full. The longer the information resides in the HSTBUF, the greater the chance of a power failure or glitch, making file data already physically written to the disk inaccessible because the file directory is out of date.

Type 2 occurs whenever the BDOS needs to write to the first sector of a previously unused allocation block. Unused, in this context, includes an allocation block that has become available as a result of a file being erased. In this case, there is no need for the disk driver to preread an entire host-sized sector into the HSTBUF, as there is no data of value in the physical sector.

As with the READ routine, the WRITE function returns with A set to 00H if the operation has been completed successfully. If the WRITE function returns with A set to 01H, then the BDOS will display the *same* message as for READ:

```
BDOS Err on X: Bad Sector
```

You can see now why most BIOS writers add extensive error-recovery and user-interaction routines to their disk drivers.

For hard disk systems, some disk drivers are written so that they automatically "spare out" a failing sector, writing the data to one of the spare sectors on the disk.

LISTST: List Status

As you can tell from its position in the list of BIOS functions, the LISTST function was a latecomer. It was added when CP/M was upgraded from version 1.4 to version 2.0.

This function returns the current status of the list device, using the IOBYTE if necessary to select the correct physical device. It sets the A register to 0FFH if the list device can accept another character for output or to 00H if it is not ready.

Digital Research's documentation states that this function is used by the DESPOOL utility program (which allows you to print a file "simultaneously" with other operations) to improve console response during its operation, and that it is acceptable for the routine always to return 00H if you choose not to implement it fully.

Unfortunately, this statement is wrong. Many other programs use the LISTST function to "poll" the list device to make sure it is ready, and if it fails to come ready after a predetermined time, to output a message to the console indicating that the printer is not ready. If you ever make a call to the BDOS list output functions, Write Printer Byte and Print String (codes 5 and 9), and the printer is not ready, then CP/M will wait forever—and your program will have lost control so it cannot even detect that the problem has occurred. If LISTST always returns a 00H, then the printer will always appear not to be ready. Not only does this make nonsense out of the LISTST function, but it also causes a stream of false "Printer not Ready" error messages to appear on the console.

SECTRAN: Sector Translate

SECTRAN, given a logical sector number, locates the correct physical sector number in the sector translate table for the previously selected (via SELDSK) logical disk drive.

Note that both logical and physical sector numbers are 128-byte sectors, so if you are working with a hard disk system, it is not too efficient to impose a sector interlace at the 128-byte sector level. It is better to impose the sector interlace right inside the hard disk driver, if at all; in general, hard disks spin so rapidly that CP/M simply cannot take advantage of sector interlace.

The BDOS hands over the logical sector number in the BC register pair, with the address of the sector translate table in the DE register pair. SECTRAN must return the physical sector number in HL.

If SECTRAN is to be a null routine, it must move the contents of BC to HL and return.

Calling the BIOS Functions Directly

As a general rule, you should not make direct calls to the BIOS. To do so makes your programs less transportable from one CP/M system to the next. It precludes being able to run these programs under MP/M, which has a different form of BIOS called an extended I/O system, or XIOS.

There are one or two problems, however, that can only be solved by making direct BIOS calls. These occur in utility programs that, for example, need to make direct access to the CP/M file directory, or need to access some "private" jump instructions which have been added to the standard BIOS jump vector.

If you really do need direct access to the BIOS, Figure 6-2 shows an example subroutine that does this. It requires that the A register contain a BIOS function code indicating the offset in the jump vector of the jump instruction to which control is to be passed.

```
                ;       Equates for use with BIOS subroutine
                ;
0003 =          WBOOT   EQU     03H     ;Warm boot
0006 =          CONST   EQU     06H     ;Console status
0009 =          CONIN   EQU     09H     ;Console input
000C =          CONOUT  EQU     0CH     ;Console output
000F =          LIST    EQU     0FH     ;Output to list device
0012 =          PUNCH   EQU     12H     ;Output to punch device
0015 =          READER  EQU     15H     ;Input from reader
0018 =          HOME    EQU     18H     ;Home selected disk to track 0
001B =          SELDSK  EQU     1BH     ;Select disk
001E =          SETTRK  EQU     1EH     ;Set track
0021 =          SETSEC  EQU     21H     ;Set sector
0024 =          SETDMA  EQU     24H     ;Set DMA address
0027 =          READ    EQU     27H     ;Read 128-byte sector
002A =          WRITE   EQU     2AH     ;Write 128-byte sector
002D =          LISTST  EQU     2DH     ;Return list status
0030 =          SECTRAN EQU     30H     ;Sector translate
                ;
                                        ;Add further "private" BIOS codes here
                ;
                ;       BIOS
                ;       This subroutine transfers control to the appropriate
                ;       entry in the BIOS Jump Vector, based on a code number
                ;       handed to it in the L register.
                ;
                ;       Entry parameters
                ;
                ;       L = Code number (which is in fact the page-relative
                ;               address of the correct JMP instruction within
                ;               the jump vector)
                ;       All other registers are preserved and handed over to
                ;               the BIOS routine intact.
                ;
                ;       Exit parameters
                ;
```

Figure 6-2. BIOS equates

```
                        ;       This routine does not CALL the BIOS routine, therefore
                        ;       when the BIOS routine RETurns, it will do so directly
                        ;       to this routine's caller.
                        ;
                        ;       Calling sequence
                        ;
                        ;                       MVI     L,Code$Number
                        ;                       CALL    BIOS
                        ;
                        BIOS:
0000 F5                         PUSH    PSW             ;Save user's A register
0001 3A0200                     LDA     0002H           ;Get BIOS JMP vector page from
                                                        ;  warm boot JMP
0004 67                         MOV     H,A             ;HL -> BIOS JMP vector entry
0005 F1                         POP     PSW             ;Recover user's A register
0006 E9                         PCHL                    ;Transfer control into the BIOS routine
```

Figure 6-2.   BIOS equates (continued)

```
            Line Numbers    Functional Component or Routine
            0072-0116       BIOS Jump Vector
            0120-0270       Initialization Code
            0275-0286       Display Message
            0289-0310       Enter CP/M
            0333-0364       CONST - Console Status
            0369-0393       CONIN - Console Input
            0397-0410       CONOUT - Console Output
            0414-0451       LISTST - List Status
            0456-0471       LIST - List Output
            0476-0492       PUNCH - Punch Output
            0496-0511       READER - Reader Input
            0516-0536       IOBYTE Driver Select
            0540-0584       Device Control Tables
            0589-0744       Low-level Drivers for Console, List, etc.
            0769-0824       Disk Parameter Header Tables
            0831-0878       Disk Parameter Blocks
            0881-0907       Other Disk data areas
            0910-0955       SELDSK - Select Disk
            0958-0964       SETTRK - Set Track
            0967-0973       SETSEC - Set Sector
            0978-0984       SETDMA - Set DMA Address
            0987-1025       Sector Skew Tables
            1028-1037       SECTRAN - Logical to Physical Sector translation
            1041-1056       HOME - Home to Track 0
            1059-1154       Deblocking Algorithm data areas
            1157-1183       READ - Read 128-byte sector
            1185-1204       WRITE - Write 128-byte sector
            1206-1378       Deblocking Algorithm
            1381-1432       Buffer Move
            1435-1478       Deblocking subroutines
            1481-1590       8" Floppy Physical Read/Write
            1595-1681       5 1/4" Floppy Physical Read/Write
            1685-1764       WBOOT - Warm Boot
```

Figure 6-3.   Functional Index to Figure 6-4

Example BIOS

The remainder of this chapter is devoted to an example BIOS listing. This actual working BIOS shows the overall structure and interface to the individual BIOS subroutines.

Unlike most BIOS's, this one has been written specifically to be understood easily. The variable names are uncharacteristically long and descriptive, and each block of code has commentary to put it into context.

Each source line has been sequentially numbered (an infrequently used option that Digital Research's Assembler, ASM, permits). Figure 6-3 contains a functional index to the BIOS as a whole so that you can find particular functions in the listing in Figure 6-4 by line number.

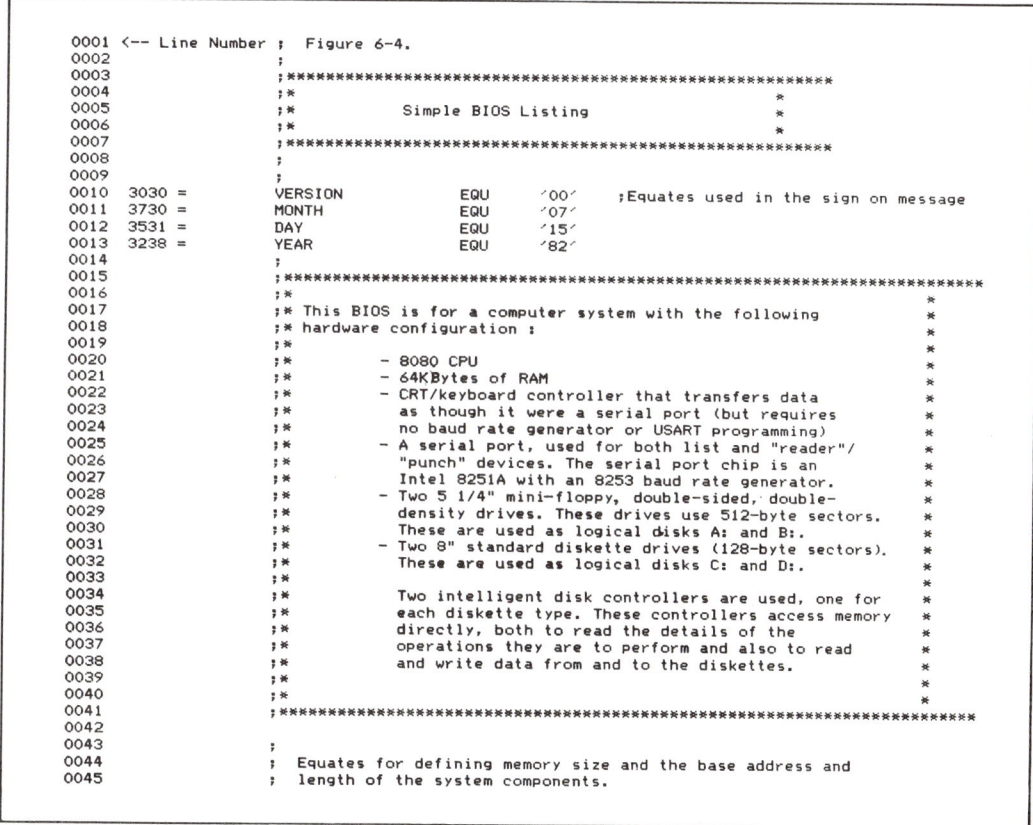

```
0001 <-- Line Number ;  Figure 6-4.
0002                  ;
0003                  ;*************************************************************
0004                  ;*                                                           *
0005                  ;*              Simple BIOS Listing                          *
0006                  ;*                                                           *
0007                  ;*************************************************************
0008                  ;
0009                  ;
0010 3030 =           VERSION         EQU     '00'    ;Equates used in the sign on message
0011 3730 =           MONTH           EQU     '07'
0012 3531 =           DAY             EQU     '15'
0013 3238 =           YEAR            EQU     '82'
0014                  ;
0015                  ;*************************************************************
0016                  ;*                                                           *
0017                  ;* This BIOS is for a computer system with the following     *
0018                  ;* hardware configuration :                                  *
0019                  ;*                                                           *
0020                  ;*      - 8080 CPU                                           *
0021                  ;*      - 64KBytes of RAM                                    *
0022                  ;*      - CRT/keyboard controller that transfers data        *
0023                  ;*        as though it were a serial port (but requires      *
0024                  ;*        no baud rate generator or USART programming)       *
0025                  ;*      - A serial port, used for both list and "reader"/    *
0026                  ;*        "punch" devices. The serial port chip is an        *
0027                  ;*        Intel 8251A with an 8253 baud rate generator.      *
0028                  ;*      - Two 5 1/4" mini-floppy, double-sided, double-      *
0029                  ;*        density drives. These drives use 512-byte sectors. *
0030                  ;*        These are used as logical disks A: and B:.         *
0031                  ;*      - Two 8" standard diskette drives (128-byte sectors).*
0032                  ;*        These are used as logical disks C: and D:.         *
0033                  ;*                                                           *
0034                  ;*        Two intelligent disk controllers are used, one for *
0035                  ;*        each diskette type. These controllers access memory*
0036                  ;*        directly, both to read the details of the          *
0037                  ;*        operations they are to perform and also to read    *
0038                  ;*        and write data from and to the diskettes.          *
0039                  ;*                                                           *
0040                  ;*                                                           *
0041                  ;*************************************************************
0042                  ;
0043                  ;
0044                  ; Equates for defining memory size and the base address and
0045                  ; length of the system components.
```

Figure 6-4. Simple BIOS listing

```
0046            ;
0047   0040 =   Memory$Size        EQU      64          ;Number of Kbytes of RAM
0048            ;
0049            ; The BIOS Length must be determined by inspection.
0050            ; Comment out the ORG BIOS$Entry line below by changing the first
0051            ; character to a semicolon. (This will make the Assembler start
0052            ; the BIOS at location 0.) Then assemble the BIOS and round up to
0053            ; the nearest 100H the address displayed on the console at the end
0054            ; of the assembly.
0055            ;
0056   0900 =   BIOS$Length        EQU      0900H
0057            ;
0058   0800 =   CCP$Length  EQU    0800H    ;Constant
0059   0E00 =   BDOS$Length        EQU      0E00H       ;Constant
0060            ;
0061   0008 =   Overall$Length     EQU      ((CCP$Length + BDOS$Length + BIOS$Length) / 1024) + 1
0062            ;
0063   E000 =   CCP$Entry   EQU    (Memory$Size - Overall$Length) * 1024
0064   E806 =   BDOS$Entry  EQU    CCP$Entry + CCP$Length + 6
0065   F600 =   BIOS$Entry  EQU    CCP$Entry + CCP$Length + BDOS$Length
0066            ;
0067            ;
0068            ;
0069
0070   F600              ORG      BIOS$Entry    ;Assemble code at BIOS address
0071            ;
0072            ; BIOS jump vector
0073            ; Control will be transferred to the appropriate entry point
0074            ; from the CCP or the BDOS, both of which compute the relative
0075            ; address of the BIOS jump vector in order to locate it.
0076            ; Transient programs can also make direct BIOS calls transferring
0077            ; control to location xx00H, where xx is the value in location
0078            ; 0002H.
0079            ;
0080   F600 C3F9F6       JMP      BOOT          ;Cold boot -- entered from CP/M bootstrap loader
0081                     Warm$Boot$Entry:       ; Labelled so that the initialization code can
0082                                            ; put the warm boot entry address down in location
0083                                            ; 0001H and 0002H of the base page
0084   F603 C329FE       JMP      WBOOT         ;Warm boot -- entered by jumping to location 0000H.
0085                                            ; Reloads the CCP which could have been
0086                                            ; overwritten by previous program in transient
0087                                            ; program area
0088   F606 C362F8       JMP      CONST         ;Console status -- returns A = 0FFH if there is a
0089                                            ; console keyboard character waiting
0090   F609 C378F8       JMP      CONIN         ;Console input -- returns the next console keyboard
0091                                            ; character in A
0092   F60C C386F8       JMP      CONOUT        ;Console output -- outputs the character in C to
0093                                            ; the console device
0094   F60F C3ACF8       JMP      LIST          ;List output -- outputs the character in C to the
0095                                            ; list device
0096   F612 C3BCF8       JMP      PUNCH         ;Punch output -- outputs the character in C to the
0097                                            ; logical punch device
0098   F615 C3CDF8       JMP      READER        ;Reader input -- returns the next input character from
0099                                            ; the logical reader device in A
0100   F618 C3D3FB       JMP      HOME          ;Homes the currently selected disk to track 0
0101   F61B C32BFB       JMP      SELDSK        ;Selects the disk drive specified in register C and
0102                                            ; returns the address of the disk parameter header
0103   F61E C358FB       JMP      SETTRK        ;Sets the track for the next read or write operation
0104                                            ; from the BC register pair
0105   F621 C35EFB       JMP      SETSEC        ;Sets the sector for the next read or write operation
0106                                            ; from the A register
0107   F624 C365FB       JMP      SETDMA        ;Sets the direct memory address (disk read/write)
0108                                            ; address for the next read or write operation
0109                                            ; from the DE register pair
0110   F627 C3FBFB       JMP      READ          ;Reads the previously specified track and sector from
0111                                            ; the selected disk into the DMA address
0112   F62A C315FC       JMP      WRITE         ;Writes the previously specified track and sector onto
0113                                            ; the selected disk from the DMA address
0114   F62D C394F8       JMP      LISTST        ;Returns A = 0FFH if the list device can accept
0115                                            ; another output character
0116   F630 C3CDFB       JMP      SECTRAN       ;Translates a logical sector into a physical one
0117            ;
0118            ;
0119            ;
0120            ; The cold boot initialization code is only needed once.
```

Figure 6-4.   (Continued)

Chapter 6: The Basic Input/Output System **161**

```
0121                   ;   It can be overwritten once it has been executed.
0122                   ;   Therefore, it is "hidden" inside the main disk buffer.
0123                   ;   When control is transferred to the BOOT entry point, this
0124                   ;   code will be executed, only being overwritten by data from
0125                   ;   the disk once the initialization procedure is complete.
0126                   ;
0127                   ;   To hide code in the buffer, the buffer is first declared
0128                   ;   normally. Then the value of the location counter following
0129                   ;   the buffer is noted. Then, using an ORG (ORiGin) statement, the
0130                   ;   location counter is "wound back" to the start of the buffer
0131                   ;   again and the initialization code written normally.
0132                   ;   At the end of this code, another ORG statement is used to
0133                   ;   set the location counter back as it was after the buffer had
0134                   ;   been declared.
0135                   ;
0136                   ;
0137   0200 =          Physical$Sector$Size    EQU     512       ;This is the actual sector size
0138                                                             ;for the 5 1/4" mini-floppy diskettes.
0139                                                             ;The 8" diskettes use 128-byte sectors.
0140                                                             ;Declare the physical disk buffer for the
0141                                                             ;5 1/4" diskettes
0142   F633            Disk$buffer:    DS      Physical$Sector$Size
0143                   ;
0144                                                             ;Save the location counter
0145   F833 =          After$Disk$Buffer  EQU   $                ;$ = Current value of location counter
0146                   ;
0147   F633                                    ORG     Disk$Buffer      ;Wind the location counter back
0148                   ;
0149                   Initialize$Stream:  ;This stream of data is used by the
0150                                       ;initialize subroutine. It has the following
0151                                       ;format:
0152                                       ;
0153                                       ;       DB      Port number to be initialized
0154                                       ;       DB      Number of bytes to be output
0155                                       ;       DB      xx,xx,xx,xx data to be output
0156                                       ;        :
0157                                       ;
0158                                       ;       DB      Port number of 00H terminator
0159                                       ;
0160                                       ;Note : On this machine, the console port does
0161                                       ;       not need to be initialized. This has
0162                                       ;       already been done by the PROM bootstrap code.
0163                                       ;
0164                                                             ;Initialize the 8251A USART used for
0165                                                             ;   the list and communications devices.
0166   F633 ED         DB      Communication$Status$Port         ;Port number
0167   F634 06         DB      6                                 ;Number of bytes
0168   F635 00         DB      0                                 ;Get chip ready to be programmed by
0169   F636 00         DB      0                                 ;  sending dummy data out to it
0170   F637 00         DB      0
0171   F638 42         DB      0100$0010B                        ;Reset and raise data terminal ready
0172   F639 6E         DB      01$10$11$10B                      ;1 stop bit, no parity, 8 bits per character
0173                                                             ;  baud rate divide factor of 16.
0174   F63A 25         DB      0010$0101B                        ;Raise request to send, and enable
0175                                                             ;  transmit and receive.
0176                   ;
0177                                                             ;Initialize the 8253 programmable interval
0178                                                             ;  timer used to generate the baud rate for
0179                                                             ;  the 8251A USART
0180   F63B DF         DB      Communication$Baud$Mode           ;Port number
0181   F63C 01         DB      1                                 ;Number of bytes
0182   F63D B6         DB      10$11$011$0B                      ;Select counter 2, load LS byte first,
0183                                                             ;  Mode 3 (for baud rates), binary count.
0184                   ;
0185   F63E DE         DB      Communication$Baud$Rate           ;Port number
0186   F63F 02         DB      2                                 ;Number of bytes
0187   F640 3800       DW      0038H                             ;1200 baud (based on 16X divide-down selected
0188                                                             ;  in the 8251A USART)
0189                   ;
0190   F642 00         DB      0                                 ;Port number of 0 terminates
0191                   ;
0192                   ;
0193                   ;  Equates for the sign-on message
0194                   ;
0195   000D =          CR  EQU     0DH                           ;Carriage return
```

Figure 6-4. (Continued)

```
0196   000A =              LF       EQU      0AH              ;Line feed
0197                                ;
0198                                Signon$Message:            ;Main sign-on message
0199   F643 43502F4D20     DB       'CP/M 2.2.'
0200   F64C 3030           DW       VERSION                   ;Current version number
0201   F64E 20             DB       ' '
0202   F64F 3037           DW       MONTH                     ;Current date
0203   F651 2F             DB       '/'
0204   F652 3135           DW       DAY
0205   F654 2F             DB       '/'
0206   F655 3832           DW       YEAR
0207   F657 0D0A0A         DB       CR,LF,LF
0208   F65A 53696D706C     DB       'Simple BIOS',CR,LF,LF
0209   F668 4469736B20     DB       'Disk configuration :',CR,LF,LF
0210   F67F 2020202020     DB       '   A: 0.35 Mbyte 5" Floppy',CR,LF
0211   F69D 2020202020     DB       '   B: 0.35 Mbyte 5" Floppy',CR,LF,LF
0212   F6BC 2020202020     DB       '   C: 0.24 Mbyte 8" Floppy',CR,LF
0213   F6DA 2020202020     DB       '   D: 0.24 Mbyte 8" Floppy',CR,LF
0214                                ;
0215   F6F8 00             DB       0
0216                                ;
0217   0004 =              Default$Disk     EQU      0004H    ;Default disk in base page
0218                                ;
0219                                BOOT:    ;Entered directly from the BIOS JMP vector.
0220                                         ;Control will be transferred here by the CP/M
0221                                         ;  bootstrap loader.
0222                                         ;The initialization state of the computer system
0223                                         ;  will be determined by the
0224                                         ;  PROM bootstrap and the CP/M loader setup.
0225                                         ;
0226                                         ;Initialize system.
0227                                         ;This routine uses the Initialize$Stream
0228                                         ;  declared above.
0229   F6F9 F3             DI                                 ;Disable interrupts to prevent any
0230                                         ; side effects during initialization.
0231   F6FA 2133F6         LXI      H,Initialize$Stream       ;HL -> Data stream
0232                                ;
0233                                Initialize$Loop:
0234   F6FD 7E             MOV      A,M                       ;Get port number
0235   F6FE B7             ORA      A                         ;If 00H, then initialization complete
0236   F6FF CA13F7         JZ       Initialize$Complete
0237   F702 320AF7         STA      Initialize$Port           ;Set up OUT instruction
0238   F705 23             INX      H                         ;HL -> Count of number of bytes to output
0239   F706 4E             MOV      C,M                       ;Get byte count
0240                                ;
0241                                Initialize$Next$Byte:
0242   F707 23             INX      H                         ;HL -> Next data byte
0243   F708 7E             MOV      A,M                       ;Get next data byte
0244   F709 D3             DB       OUT                       ;Output to correct port
0245                                Initialize$Port:
0246   F70A 00             DB       0                         ;<- Set above
0247   F70B 0D             DCR      C                         ;Count down
0248   F70C C207F7         JNZ      Initialize$Next$Byte      ;Go back if more bytes
0249   F70F 23             INX      H                         ;HL -> Next port number
0250   F710 C3FDF6         JMP      Initialize$Loop           ;Go back for next port initialization
0251                                ;
0252                                Initialize$Complete:
0253                                ;
0254
0255   F713 3E01           MVI      A,00$00$00$01B            ;Set IOBYTE to indicate terminal
0256   F715 320300         STA      IOBYTE                    ; is to act as console
0257
0258   F718 2143F6         LXI      H,Signon$Message          ;Display sign-on message on console
0259   F71B CD33F8         CALL     Display$Message
0260                                ;
0261
0262   F71E AF             XRA      A                         ;Set default disk drive to A:
0263   F71F 320400         STA      Default$Disk
0264   F722 FB             EI                                 ;Interrupts can now be enabled
0265
0266   F723 C340F8         JMP      Enter$CPM                 ;Complete initialization and enter
0267                                         ; CP/M by going to the Console Command
0268                                         ; Processor.
0269                                ;
0270                                ; End of cold boot initialization code
0271                                ;
```

Figure 6-4. (Continued)

```
0272   F833                    ORG      After$Disk$Buffer      ;Reset location counter
0273                     ;
0274                     ;
0275                            Display$Message:     ;Displays the specified message on the console.
0276                                                 ;On entry, HL points to a stream of bytes to be
0277                                                 ; output. A 00H-byte terminates the message.
0278   F833 7E                 MOV      A,M                    ;Get next message byte
0279   F834 B7                 ORA      A                      ;Check if terminator
0280   F835 C8                 RZ                              ;Yes, return to caller
0281   F836 4F                 MOV      C,A                    ;Prepare for output
0282   F837 E5                 PUSH     H                      ;Save message pointer
0283   F838 CD86F8             CALL     CONOUT                 ;Go to main console output routine
0284   F83B E1                 POP      H                      ;Recover message pointer
0285   F83C 23                 INX      H                      ;Move to next byte of message
0286   F83D C333F8             JMP      Display$Message        ;Loop until complete message output
0287                     ;
0288                     ;
0289                            Enter$CPM: ;This routine is entered either from the cold or warm
0290                                       ; boot code. It sets up the JMP instructions in the
0291                                       ;  base page, and also sets the high-level disk driver's
0292                                       ;  input/output address (also known as the DMA address).
0293                     ;
0294   F840 3EC3              MVI      A,JMP                  ;Get machine code for JMP
0295   F842 320000            STA      0000H                  ;Set up JMP at location 0000H
0296   F845 320500            STA      0005H                  ; and at location 0005H
0297                     ;
0298   F848 2103F6            LXI      H,Warm$Boot$Entry      ;Get BIOS vector address
0299   F84B 220100            SHLD     0001H                  ;Put address at location 0001H
0300
0301   F84E 2106E8            LXI      H,BDOS$Entry           ;Get BDOS entry point address
0302   F851 220600            SHLD     6                      ;Put address at location 0005H
0303                     ;
0304   F854 018000            LXI      B,80H                  ;Set disk I/O address to default
0305   F857 CD65FB            CALL     SETDMA                 ;Use normal BIOS routine
0306                     ;
0307   F85A FB                EI                              ;Ensure interrupts are enabled
0308   F85B 3A0400            LDA      Default$Disk           ;Transfer current default disk to
0309   F85E 4F                MOV      C,A                    ; Console Command Processor
0310   F85F C300E0            JMP      CCP$Entry              ;Transfer to CCP
0311                     ;
0312                     ;
0313                     ;   Serial input/output drivers
0314                     ;
0315                     ;   These drivers all look at the IOBYTE at location
0316                     ;   0003H, which will have been set by the cold boot routine.
0317                     ;   The IOBYTE can be modified by the STAT utility, by
0318                     ;   BDOS calls, or by a program that puts a value directly
0319                     ;   into location 0003H.
0320                     ;
0321                     ;   All of the routines make use of a subroutine, Select$Routine,
0322                     ;   that takes the least significant two bits of the A register
0323                     ;   and uses them to transfer control to one of the routines whose
0324                     ;   address immediately follows the call to Select$Routine.
0325                     ;   A second entry point, Select$Routine$21, uses bits
0326                     ;   2 and 1 to do the same job -- this saves some space
0327                     ;   by avoiding an unnecessary instruction.
0328                     ;
0329   0003 =                  IOBYTE   EQU      0003H         ;I/O redirection byte
0330                     ;
0331                     ;
0332                     ;
0333                            CONST:                        ;Get console status
0334                                                          ;Entered directly from the BIOS JMP vector
0335                                                          ; and returns a parameter that reflects whether
0336                                                          ; there is incoming data from the console.
0337                                                          ;
0338                                                          ;A = 00H (zero flag set) if no data
0339                                                          ;A = 0FFH (zero flag clear) if data
0340                                                          ;
0341                                                          ;CONST will be called by programs that
0342                                                          ; make periodic checks to see if the computer
0343                                                          ; operator has pressed any keys -- for example,
0344                                                          ; to interrupt an executing program.
0345                                                          ;
0346   F862 CD6AF8            CALL     Get$Console$Status     ;Return A = zero or nonzero
0347                                                          ;According to status, then convert
```

Figure 6-4. (Continued)

```
0348                                          ; to return parameter convention.
0349    F865 B7         ORA     A             ;Set flags to reflect status
0350    F866 C8         RZ                    ;If 0, no incoming data
0351    F867 3EFF       MVI     A,0FFH        ;Otherwise return A = 0FFH to
0352    F869 C9         RET                   ;  indicate incoming data
0353                    ;
0354                    Get$Console$Status:
0355    F86A 3A0300     LDA     IOBYTE        ;Get I/O redirection byte
0356                                          ;Console is selected according to
0357                                          ;  bits 1,0 of IOBYTE
0358    F86D CDDCF8     CALL    Select$Routine ;Select appropriate routine
0359                                          ;These routines return to the caller
0360                                          ;  of Get$Console$Status.
0361    F870 F6F8       DW      Teletype$In$Status      ;00 <- IOBYTE bits 1,0
0362    F872 FCF8       DW      Terminal$In$Status      ;01
0363    F874 02F9       DW      Communication$In$Status ;10
0364    F876 08F9       DW      Dummy$In$Status         ;11
0365                    ;
0366                    ;
0367                    ;
0368                    ;
0369                    CONIN:                ;Get console input character
0370                                          ;Entered directly from the BIOS JMP vector;
0371                                          ;  returns the next data character from the
0372                                          ;  Console in the A register. The most significant
0373                                          ;  bit of the data character will be 0, except
0374                                          ;  when "reader" (communication port) input has
0375                                          ;  been selected. In this case, the full eight bits
0376                                          ;  of data are returned to permit binary data to be
0377                                          ;  received.
0378                                          ;
0379                                          ;Normally, this routine will be called after
0380                                          ;  a call to CONST has indicated that a data character
0381                                          ;  is ready, but whenever the CCP or the BDOS can
0382                                          ;  proceed no further until console input occurs,
0383                                          ;  then CONIN will be called without a preceding
0384                                          ;  CONST call.
0385                                          ;
0386    F878 3A0300     LDA     IOBYTE        ;Get I/O redirection byte
0387    F87B CDDCF8     CALL    Select$Routine ;Select correct CONIN routine
0388                                          ;These routines return directly
0389                                          ;  to CONIN's caller.
0390    F87E 20F9       DW      Teletype$Input       ;00 <- IOBYTE bits 1,0
0391    F880 26F9       DW      Terminal$Input       ;01
0392    F882 2FF9       DW      Communication$Input  ;10
0393    F884 35F9       DW      Dummy$Input          ;11
0394                    ;
0395                    ;
0396                    ;
0397                    CONOUT:               ;Console output
0398                                          ;Entered directly from BIOS JMP vector;
0399                                          ;  outputs the data character in the C register
0400                                          ;  to the appropriate device according to bits
0401                                          ;  1,0 of IOBYTE
0402                                          ;
0403    F886 3A0300     LDA     IOBYTE        ;Get I/O redirection byte
0404    F889 CDDCF8     CALL    Select$Routine ;Select correct CONOUT routine
0405                                          ;These routines return directly
0406                                          ;  to CONOUT's caller.
0407    F88C 38F9       DW      Teletype$Output       ;00 <- IOBYTE bits 1,0
0408    F88E 3EF9       DW      Terminal$Output       ;01
0409    F890 44F9       DW      Communication$Output  ;10
0410    F892 4AF9       DW      Dummy$Output          ;11
0411                    ;
0412                    ;
0413                    ;
0414                    LISTST:               ;List device (output) status
0415                                          ;Entered directly from the BIOS JMP vector;
0416                                          ;  returns in A list device status that
0417                                          ;  indicates whether the list device can accept
0418                                          ;  another output character. The IOBYTE's bits
0419                                          ;  7,6 determine the physical device used.
0420                                          ;
0421                                          ;A = 00H (zero flag set): cannot accept data
0422                                          ;A = 0FFH (zero flag clear): can accept data
0423                                          ;
```

Figure 6-4. (Continued)

```
0424                                    ;Digital Research's documentation indicates
0425                                    ; that you can always return with A = 00H
0426                                    ; ("Cannot accept data") if you do not wish to
0427                                    ; implement the LISTST routine. This is NOT TRUE.
0428                                    ;If you do not wish to implement the LISTST routine
0429                                    ; always return with A = 0FFH ("Can accept data").
0430                                    ;The LIST driver will then take care of things rather
0431                                    ; than potentially hanging the system.
0432                                    ;
0433  F894  CD9CF8      CALL    Get$List$Status ;Return A = zero or nonzero
0434                                    ;  according to status, then convert
0435                                    ;  to return parameter convention
0436  F897  B7          ORA     A       ;Set flags to reflect status
0437  F898  C8          RZ              ;If 0, cannot accept data for output
0438  F899  3EFF        MVI     A,0FFH  ;Otherwise return A = 0FFH to
0439  F89B  C9          RET             ; indicate can accept data for output
0440                    ;
0441                    Get$List$Status:
0442  F89C  3A0300      LDA     IOBYTE  ;Get I/O redirection byte
0443  F89F  07          RLC             ;Move bits 7,6 to 1,0
0444  F8A0  07          RLC
0445  F8A1  CDDCF8      CALL    Select$Routine ;Select appropriate routine
0446                                    ;These routines return directly
0447                                    ; to Get$List$Status's caller.
0448  F8A4  0BF9        DW      Teletype$Out$Status      ;00 <- IOBYTE bits 1,0
0449  F8A6  11F9        DW      Terminal$Out$Status      ;01
0450  F8A8  17F9        DW      Communication$Out$Status ;10
0451  F8AA  1DF9        DW      Dummy$Out$Status         ;11
0452
0453                    ;
0454                    ;
0455                    ;
0456                    LIST:           ;List output
0457                                    ;Entered directly from BIOS JMP vector;
0458                                    ; outputs the data character in the C register
0459                                    ; to the appropriate device according to bits
0460                                    ; 7,6 of IOBYTE
0461                                    ;
0462  F8AC  3A0300      LDA     IOBYTE  ;Get I/O redirection byte
0463  F8AF  07          RLC             ;Move bits 7,6 to 1,0
0464  F8B0  07          RLC
0465  F8B1  CDDCF8      CALL    Select$Routine ;Select correct LIST routine
0466                                    ;These routines return directly
0467                                    ; to LIST's caller.
0468  F8B4  38F9        DW      Teletype$Output      ;00 <- IOBYTE bits 1,0
0469  F8B6  3EF9        DW      Terminal$Output      ;01
0470  F8B8  44F9        DW      Communication$Output ;10
0471  F8BA  4AF9        DW      Dummy$Output         ;11
0472
0473                    ;
0474                    ;
0475                    ;
0476                    PUNCH:          ;Punch output
0477                                    ;Entered directly from BIOS JMP vector;
0478                                    ; outputs the data character in the C register
0479                                    ; to the appropriate device according to bits
0480                                    ; 5,4 of IOBYTE
0481                                    ;
0482  F8BC  3A0300      LDA     IOBYTE  ;Get I/O redirection byte
0483  F8BF  0F          RRC             ;Move bits 5,4 to 2,1
0484  F8C0  0F          RRC
0485  F8C1  0F          RRC
0486  F8C2  CDDDF8      CALL    Select$Routine$21 ;Select correct PUNCH routine
0487                                    ;These routines return directly
0488                                    ; to PUNCH's caller.
0489  F8C5  38F9        DW      Teletype$Output      ;00 <- IOBYTE bits 1,0
0490  F8C7  4AF9        DW      Dummy$Output         ;01
0491  F8C9  44F9        DW      Communication$Output ;10
0492  F8CB  3EF9        DW      Terminal$Output      ;11
0493                    ;
0494                    ;
0495                    ;
0496                    READER:         ;Reader input
0497                                    ;Entered directly from BIOS JMP vector;
0498                                    ; inputs the next data character from the
0499                                    ; reader device into the A register
```

Figure 6-4. (Continued)

166 The CP/M Programmer's Handbook

```
0500                                          ;The appropriate device is selected according
0501                                          ; to bits 3,2 of IOBYTE.
0502                                          ;
0503    F8CD 3A0300         LDA     IOBYTE              ;Get I/O redirection byte
0504    F8D0 0F             RRC                         ;Move bits 3,2 to 2,1
0505    F8D1 CDDDF8         CALL    Select$Routine$21   ;Select correct READER routine
0506                                                    ;These routines return directly
0507                                                    ; to READER's caller.
0508    F8D4 38F9           DW      Teletype$Output        ;00 <- IOBYTE bits 1,0
0509    F8D6 4AF9           DW      Dummy$Output           ;01
0510    F8D8 44F9           DW      Communication$Output   ;10
0511    F8DA 3EF9           DW      Terminal$Output        ;11
0512
0513                        ;
0514                        ;
0515                        ;
0516                        Select$Routine:     ;Transfers control to a specified address
0517                                            ; following its calling address according to
0518                                            ; the value of bits 1,0 in A.
0519    F8DC 07             RLC                 ;Shift select values into bits 2,1
0520                                            ; in order to do word arithmetic
0521                        ;
0522                        Select$Routine$21:  ;Entry point to select routine selection bits
0523                                            ; are already in bits 2,1
0524    F8DD E606           ANI     0000$0110B  ;Isolate just bits 2,1
0525    F8DF E3             XTHL                ;HL -> first word of addresses after
0526                                            ; CALL instruction
0527    F8E0 5F             MOV     E,A         ;Add on selection value to address table
0528    F8E1 1600           MVI     D,0         ; base
0529    F8E3 19             DAD     D           ;HL -> selected routine address
0530                                            ;Get routine address into HL
0531    F8E4 7E             MOV     A,M         ;LS byte
0532    F8E5 23             INX     H           ;HL -> MS byte
0533    F8E6 66             MOV     H,M         ;MS byte
0534    F8E7 6F             MOV     L,A         ;HL -> routine
0535    F8E8 E3             XTHL                ;Top of stack -> routine
0536    F8E9 C9             RET                 ;Transfer to selected routine
0537                        ;
0538                        ;
0539                        ;
0540                        ;   Input/Output Equates
0541                        ;
0542    00ED =              Teletype$Status$Port        EQU     0EDH
0543    00EC =              Teletype$Data$Port          EQU     0ECH
0544    0001 =              Teletype$Output$Ready       EQU     0000$0001B     ;Status mask
0545    0002 =              Teletype$Input$Ready        EQU     0000$0010B     ;Status mask
0546                        ;
0547    0001 =              Terminal$Status$Port        EQU     01H
0548    0002 =              Terminal$Data$Port          EQU     02H
0549    0001 =              Terminal$Output$Ready       EQU     0000$0001B     ;Status mask
0550    0002 =              Terminal$Input$Ready        EQU     0000$0010B     ;Status mask
0551                        ;
0552    00ED =              Communication$Status$Port   EQU     0EDH
0553    00EC =              Communication$Data$Port     EQU     0ECH
0554    0001 =              Communication$Output$Ready  EQU     0000$0001B     ;Status mask
0555    0002 =              Communication$Input$Ready   EQU     0000$0010B     ;Status mask
0556                        ;
0557    00DF =              Communication$Baud$Mode     EQU     0DFH           ;Mode Select
0558    00DE =              Communication$Baud$Rate     EQU     0DEH           ;Rate Select
0559                        ;
0560                        ;
0561                        ;   Serial device control tables
0562                        ;
0563                        ;   In order to reduce the amount of executable code,
0564                        ;   the same low-level driver code is used for all serial ports.
0565                        ;   On entry to the low-level driver, HL points to the
0566                        ;   appropriate control table.
0567                        ;
0568                        Teletype$Table:
0569    F8EA ED             DB      Teletype$Status$Port
0570    F8EB EC             DB      Teletype$Data$Port
0571    F8EC 01             DB      Teletype$Output$Ready
0572    F8ED 02             DB      Teletype$Input$Ready
0573                        ;
0574                        Terminal$Table:
0575    F8CE 01             DB      Terminal$Status$Port
```

Figure 6-4. (Continued)

Chapter 6: The Basic Input/Output System   **167**

```
0576  F8EF 02           DB      Terminal$Data$Port
0577  F8F0 01           DB      Terminal$Output$Ready
0578  F8F1 02           DB      Terminal$Input$Ready
0579                    ;
0580                    Communication$Table:
0581  F8F2 ED           DB      Communication$Status$Port
0582  F8F3 EC           DB      Communication$Data$Port
0583  F8F4 01           DB      Communication$Output$Ready
0584  F8F5 02           DB      Communication$Input$Ready
0585                    ;
0586                    ;
0587                    ;
0588                    ;
0589                    ;   The following routines are "called" by Select$Routine
0590                    ;   to perform the low-level input/output
0591                    ;
0592                    Teletype$In$Status:
0593  F8F6 21EAF8       LXI     H,Teletype$Table    ;HL -> control table
0594  F8F9 C34BF9       JMP     Input$Status        ;Note use of JMP. Input$Status
0595                                                ; will execute the RETurn.
0596                    ;
0597                    Terminal$In$Status:
0598  F8FC 21EEF8       LXI     H,Terminal$Table    ;HL -> control table
0599  F8FF C34BF9       JMP     Input$Status        ;Note use of JMP. Input$Status
0600                                                ; will execute the RETurn.
0601                    ;
0602                    Communication$In$Status:
0603  F902 21F2F8       LXI     H,Communication$Table ;HL -> control table
0604  F905 C34BF9       JMP     Input$Status        ;Note use of JMP. Input$Status
0605                                                ; will execute the RETurn.
0606                    ;
0607                    Dummy$In$Status:                ;Dummy status, always returns
0608  F908 3EFF         MVI     A,0FFH              ; indicating incoming data is ready
0609  F90A C9           RET
0610                    ;
0611                    ;
0612                    Teletype$Out$Status:
0613  F90B 21EAF8       LXI     H,Teletype$Table    ;HL -> control table
0614  F90E C356F9       JMP     Output$Status       ;Note use of JMP. Output$Status
0615                                                ; will execute the RETurn.
0616                    ;
0617                    Terminal$Out$Status:
0618  F911 21EEF8       LXI     H,Terminal$Table    ;HL -> control table
0619  F914 C356F9       JMP     Output$Status       ;Note use of JMP. Output$Status
0620                                                ; will execute the RETurn.
0621                    ;
0622                    Communication$Out$Status:
0623  F917 21F2F8       LXI     H,Communication$Table ;HL -> control table
0624  F91A C356F9       JMP     Output$Status       ;Note use of JMP. Output$Status
0625                                                ; will execute the RETurn.
0626                    ;
0627                    Dummy$Out$Status:               ;Dummy status, always returns
0628  F91D 3EFF         MVI     A,0FFH              ; indicating ready for output
0629  F91F C9           RET
0630                    ;
0631                    ;
0632                    Teletype$Input:
0633  F920 21EAF8       LXI     H,Teletype$Table    ;HL -> control table
0634  F923 C360F9       JMP     Input$Data          ;Note use of JMP. Input$Data
0635                                                ; will execute the RETurn.
0636                    ;
0637                    Terminal$Input:
0638  F926 21EEF8       LXI     H,Terminal$Table    ;HL -> control table
0639                                                ; will execute the RETurn.
0640  F929 CD60F9       CALL    Input$Data          ;** Special case **
0641                                                ;Input$Data will return here
0642  F92C E67F         ANI     7FH                 ; so that parity bit can be set 0
0643  F92E C9           RET
0644                    ;
0645                    Communication$Input:
0646  F92F 21F2F8       LXI     H,Communication$Table ;HL -> control table
0647  F932 C360F9       JMP     Input$Data          ;Note use of JMP. Input$Data
0648                                                ; will execute the RETurn.
0649                    ;
0650                    Dummy$Input:                    ;Dummy input, always returns
0651  F935 3E1A         MVI     A,1AH               ; indicating CP/M end of file
```

Figure 6-4.   (Continued)

```
0652  F937 C9                RET
0653                       ;
0654                       ;
0655                       ;
0656                       ;
0657                       Teletype$Output:
0658  F938 21EAF8            LXI     H,Teletype$Table        ;HL -> control table
0659  F93B C370F9            JMP     Output$Data             ;Note use of JMP. Output$Data
0660                                                         ; will execute the RETurn.
0661                       ;
0662                       Terminal$Output:
0663  F93E 21EEF8            LXI     H,Terminal$Table        ;HL -> control table
0664                                                         ; will execute the RETurn.
0665  F941 C370F9            JMP     Output$Data             ;Note use of JMP. Output$Data
0666                                                         ; will execute the RETurn.
0667                       ;
0668                       Communication$Output:
0669  F944 21F2F8            LXI     H,Communication$Table   ;HL -> control table
0670  F947 C370F9            JMP     Output$Data             ;Note use of JMP. Output$Data
0671                                                         ; will execute the RETurn.
0672                       ;
0673                       Dummy$Output:                     ;Dummy output, always discards
0674  F94A C9                RET                             ; the output character
0675                       ;
0676                       ;
0677                       ;
0678                       ;
0679                       ; These are the general purpose low-level drivers.
0680                       ; On entry, HL points to the appropriate control table.
0681                       ; For output, the C register contains the data to be output.
0682                       ;
0683                       Input$Status:                     ;Return with A = 00H if no incoming data,
0684                                                         ; otherwise A = nonzero.
0685  F94B 7E                MOV     A,M                     ;Get status port
0686  F94C 3250F9            STA     Input$Status$Port       ;*** Self-modifying code ***
0687  F94F DB                DB      IN                      ;Input to A from correct status port
0688                       ;
0689                       Input$Status$Port:
0690  F950 00                DB      00                      ;<- Set above
0691  F951 23                INX     H                       ;Move HL to point to input data mask
0692  F952 23                INX     H
0693  F953 23                INX     H
0694  F954 A6                ANA     M                       ;Mask with input status
0695  F955 C9                RET
0696                       ;
0697                       ;
0698                       Output$Status:                    ;Return with A = 00H if not ready for output
0699                                                         ; otherwise A = nonzero.
0700  F956 7E                MOV     A,M                     ;Get status port
0701  F957 325BF9            STA     Output$Status$Port      ;*** Self-modifying code ***
0702  F95A DB                DB      IN                      ;Input to A from correct status port
0703                       ;
0704                       Output$Status$Port:
0705  F95B 00                DB      00                      ;<- Set above
0706  F95C 23                INX     H                       ;Move HL to point to output data mask
0707  F95D 23                INX     H
0708  F95E A6                ANA     M                       ;Mask with output status
0709  F95F C9                RET
0710                       ;
0711                       ;
0712                       Input$Data:                       ;Return with next data character in A.
0713                                                         ;Wait for status routine to indicate
0714                                                         ; incoming data.
0715  F960 E5                PUSH    H                       ;Save control table pointer
0716  F961 CD4BF9            CALL    Input$Status            ;Get input status in zero flag
0717  F964 E1                POP     H                       ;Recover control table pointer
0718  F965 CA60F9            JZ      Input$Data              ;Wait until incoming data
0719  F968 23                INX     H                       ;HL -> data port
0720  F969 7E                MOV     A,M                     ;Get data port
0721  F96A 326EF9            STA     Input$Data$Port         ;*** Self-modifying code ***
0722  F96D DB                DB      IN                      ;Input to A from correct data port
0723                       ;
0724                       Input$Data$Port:
0725  F96E 00                DB      0                       ;<- Set above
0726  F96F C9                RET
0727                       ;
```

Figure 6-4.   (Continued)

Chapter 6: The Basic Input/Output System **169**

```
0728                   ;
0729                   Output$Data:                    ;Output the data character in the C register.
0730                                                   ;Wait for status routine to indicate device
0731                                                   ; ready to accept another character
0732   F970 E5              PUSH    H                  ;Save control table pointer
0733   F971 CD56F9          CALL    Output$Status      ;Get output status in zero flag
0734   F974 E1              POP     H                  ;Recover control table pointer
0735   F975 CA70F9          JZ      Output$Data        ;Wait until ready for output
0736   F978 23              INX     H                  ;HL -> output port
0737   F979 7E              MOV     A,M                ;Get output port
0738   F97A 327FF9          STA     Output$Data$Port        ;*** Self-modifying code ***
0739   F97D 79              MOV     A,C                ;Get data character to be output
0740   F97E D3              DB      OUT                ;Output data to correct port
0741                   ;
0742                   Output$Data$Port:
0743   F97F 00              DB      0                  ;<- Set above
0744   F980 C9              RET
0745                   ;
0746                   ;
0747                   ; High level diskette drivers
0748                   ;
0749                   ; These drivers perform the following functions:
0750                   ;
0751                   ;    SELDSK   Select a specified disk and return the address of
0752                   ;             the appropriate disk parameter header
0753                   ;    SETTRK   Set the track number for the next read or write
0754                   ;    SETSEC   Set the sector number for the next read or write
0755                   ;    SETDMA   Set the DMA (read/write) address for the next read or write.
0756                   ;    SECTRAN  Translate a logical sector number into a physical
0757                   ;    HOME     Set the track to 0 so that the next read or write will
0758                   ;             be on Track 0
0759                   ;
0760                   ; In addition, the high-level drivers are responsible for making
0761                   ; the 5 1/4" floppy diskettes that use a 512-byte sector appear
0762                   ; to CP/M as though they used a 128-byte sector. They do this
0763                   ; by using what is called blocking/deblocking code,
0764                   ; described in more detail later in this listing,
0765                   ; just prior to the code itself.
0766                   ;
0767                   ;
0768                   ;
0769                   ; Disk parameter tables
0770                   ;
0771                   ; As discussed in Chapter 3, these describe the physical
0772                   ; characteristics of the disk drives. In this example BIOS,
0773                   ; there are two types of disk drives; standard single-sided,
0774                   ; single-density 8", and double-sided, double-density 5 1/4"
0775                   ; diskettes.
0776                   ;
0777                   ; The standard 8" diskettes do not need to use the blocking/
0778                   ; deblocking code, but the 5 1/4" drives do. Therefore an additional
0779                   ; byte has been prefixed to the disk parameter block to
0780                   ; tell the disk drivers each logical disk's physical
0781                   ; diskette type, and whether or not it needs deblocking.
0782                   ;
0783                   ;
0784                   ; Disk definition tables
0785                   ;
0786                   ; These consist of disk parameter headers, with one entry
0787                   ; per logical disk driver, and disk parameter blocks, with
0788                   ; either one parameter block per logical disk or the same
0789                   ; parameter block for several logical disks.
0790                   ;
0791                   ;
0792                   Disk$Parameter$Headers:                  ;Described in Chapter 3
0793                   ;
0794                                 ;Logical Disk A: (5 1/4" Diskette)
0795   F981 6BFB           DW      Floppy$5$Skewtable         ;5 1/4" skew table
0796   F983 0000000000     DW      0,0,0                      ;Reserved for CP/M
0797   F989 C1F9           DW      Directory$Buffer
0798   F98B 42FA           DW      Floppy$5$Parameter$Block
0799   F98D 61FA           DW      Disk$A$Workarea
0800   F98F C1FA           DW      Disk$A$Allocation$Vector
0801                   ;
0802                                 ;Logical Disk B: (5 1/4" Diskette)
0803   F991 6BFB           DW      Floppy$5$Skewtable         ;Shares same skew table as A:
```

Figure 6-4. (Continued)

170 The CP/M Programmer's Handbook

```
0804   F993 0000000000    DW      0,0,0                           ;Reserved for CP/M
0805   F999 C1F9          DW      Directory$Buffer                ;Share same buffer as A:
0806   F99B 42FA          DW      Floppy$5$Parameter$Block        ;Same DPB as A:
0807   F99D 81FA          DW      Disk$B$Workarea                 ;Private work area
0808   F99F D7FA          DW      Disk$B$Allocation$Vector        ;Private allocation vector
0809                      ;
0810                                      ;Logical Disk C: (8" Floppy)
0811   F9A1 B3FB          DW      Floppy$8$Skewtable              ;8" skew table
0812   F9A3 0000000000    DW      0,0,0                           ;Reserved for CP/M
0813   F9A9 C1F9          DW      Directory$Buffer                ;Share same buffer as A:
0814   F9AB 52FA          DW      Floppy$8$Parameter$Block
0815   F9AD A1FA          DW      Disk$C$Workarea                 ;Private work area
0816   F9AF EDFA          DW      Disk$C$Allocation$Vector        ;Private allocation vector
0817                      ;
0818                                      ;Logical Disk D: (8" Floppy)
0819   F9B1 6BFB          DW      Floppy$5$Skewtable              ;Shares same skew table as A:
0820   F9B3 0000000000    DW      0,0,0                           ;Reserved for CP/M
0821   F9B9 C1F9          DW      Directory$Buffer                ;Share same buffer as A:
0822   F9BB 52FA          DW      Floppy$8$Parameter$Block        ;Same DPB as C:
0823   F9BD B1FA          DW      Disk$D$Workarea                 ;Private work area
0824   F9BF 0CFB          DW      Disk$D$Allocation$Vector        ;Private allocation vector
0825
0826                      ;
0827                      ;
0828   F9C1              Directory$Buffer:  DS     128
0829                      ;
0830                      ;
0832                      ;
0833                      ;       Disk Types
0834                      ;
0835   0001 =             Floppy$5         EQU     1              ;5 1/4" mini floppy
0836   0002 =             Floppy$8         EQU     2              ;8" floppy (SS SD)
0837                      ;
0838                      ;       Blocking/deblocking indicator
0839                      ;
0840   0080 =             Need$Deblocking  EQU     1000$0000B     ;Sector size > 128 bytes
0841                      ;
0842                      ;
0843                      ;       Disk parameter blocks
0844                      ;
0845                      ;       5 1/4" mini floppy
0846                      ;
0847                                                              ;Extra byte prefixed to indicate
0848                                                              ; disk type and blocking required
0849   FA41 81            DB      Floppy$5 + Need$Deblocking
0850                     Floppy$5$Parameter$Block:
0851   FA42 4800          DW      72                              ;128-byte sectors per track
0852   FA44 04            DB      4                               ;Block shift
0853   FA45 0F            DB      15                              ;Block mask
0854   FA46 01            DB      1                               ;Extent mask
0855   FA47 AE00          DW      174                             ;Maximum allocation block number
0856   FA49 7F00          DW      127                             ;Number of directory entries - 1
0857   FA4B C0            DB      1100$0000B                      ;Bit map for reserving 1 alloc. block
0858   FA4C 00            DB      0000$0000B                      ; for file directory
0859   FA4D 2000          DW      32                              ;Disk changed work area size
0860   FA4F 0100          DW      1                               ;Number of tracks before directory
0861                      ;
0862                      ;
0863                      ;       Standard 8" Floppy
0864                                                              ;Extra byte prefixed to DPB for
0865                                                              ; this version of the BIOS
0866   FA51 02            DB      Floppy$8                        ;Indicates disk type and the fact
0867                                                              ; that no deblocking is required
0868                     Floppy$8$Parameter$Block:
0869   FA52 1A00          DW      26                              ;Sectors per track
0870   FA54 03            DB      3                               ;Block shift
0871   FA55 07            DB      7                               ;Block mask
0872   FA56 00            DB      0                               ;Extent mask
0873   FA57 F200          DW      242                             ;Maximum allocation block number
0874   FA59 3F00          DW      63                              ;Number of directory entries - 1
0875   FA5B C0            DB      1100$0000B                      ;Bit map for reserving 2 alloc. blocks
0876   FA5C 00            DB      0000$0000B                      ; for file directory
0877   FA5D 1000          DW      16                              ;Disk changed work area size
0878   FA5F 0200          DW      2                               ;Number of tracks before directory
0879                      ;
0880                      ;
```

Figure 6-4.   (Continued)

Chapter 6: The Basic Input/Output System

```
0881                    ; Disk work areas
0882                    ;
0883                    ; These are used by the BDOS to detect any unexpected
0884                    ; change of diskettes. The BDOS will automatically set
0885                    ; such a changed diskette to read-only status.
0886                    ;
0887 FA61               Disk$A$Workarea:     DS      32       ; A:
0888 FA81               Disk$B$Workarea:     DS      32       ; B:
0889 FAA1               Disk$C$Workarea:     DS      16       ; C:
0890 FAB1               Disk$D$Workarea:     DS      16       ; D:
0891                    ;
0892                    ;
0893                    ; Disk allocation vectors
0894                    ;
0895                    ; These are used by the BDOS to maintain a bit map of
0896                    ; which allocation blocks are used and which are free.
0897                    ; One byte is used for eight allocation blocks, hence the
0898                    ; expression of the form (allocation blocks/8)+1.
0899                    ;
0900 FAC1               Disk$A$Allocation$Vector   DS    (174/8)+1     ; A:
0901 FAD7               Disk$B$Allocation$Vector   DS    (174/8)+1     ; B:
0902                    ;
0903 FAED               Disk$C$Allocation$Vector   DS    (242/8)+1     ; C:
0904 FB0C               Disk$D$Allocation$Vector   DS    (242/8)+1     ; D:
0905                    ;
0906                    ;
0907 0004  =            Number$of$Logical$Disks           EQU    4
0908                    ;
0909                    ;
0910                    SELDSK:                      ;Select disk in C
0911                                                 ;C = 0 for drive A, 1 for B, etc.
0912                                                 ;Return the address of the appropriate
0913                                                 ; disk parameter header in HL, or 0000H
0914                                                 ; if the selected disk does not exist.
0915                    ;
0916 FB2B 210000        LXI     H,0                  ;Assume an error
0917 FB2E 79            MOV     A,C                  ;Check if requested disk valid
0918 FB2F FE04          CPI     Number$of$Logical$Disks
0919 FB31 D0            RNC                          ;Return if > maximum number of disks
0920                    ;
0921 FB32 32EAFB        STA     Selected$Disk        ;Save selected disk number
0922                                                 ;Set up to return DPH address
0923 FB35 6F            MOV     L,A                  ;Make disk into word value
0924 FB36 2600          MVI     H,0
0925                                                 ;Compute offset down disk parameter
0926                                                 ; header table by multiplying by
0927                                                 ; parameter header length (16 bytes)
0928 FB38 29            DAD     H                    ; *2
0929 FB39 29            DAD     H                    ; *4
0930 FB3A 29            DAD     H                    ; *8
0931 FB3B 29            DAD     H                    ; *16
0932 FB3C 1181F9        LXI     D,Disk$Parameter$Headers      ;Get base address
0933 FB3F 19            DAD     D                    ;DE -> Appropriate DPH
0934 FB40 E5            PUSH    H                    ;Save DPH address
0935                    ;
0936                                                 ;Access disk parameter block
0937                                                 ; to extract special prefix byte that
0938                                                 ; identifies disk type and whether
0939                                                 ; deblocking is required
0940                                                 ;
0941 FB41 110A00        LXI     D,10                 ;Get DPB pointer offset in DPH
0942 FB44 19            DAD     D                    ;DE -> DPB address in DPH
0943 FB45 5E            MOV     E,M                  ;Get DPB address in DE
0944 FB46 23            INX     H
0945 FB47 56            MOV     D,M
0946 FB48 EB            XCHG                         ;DE -> DPB
0947 FB49 2B            DCX     H                    ;DE -> prefix byte
0948 FB4A 7E            MOV     A,M                  ;Get prefix byte
0949 FB4B E60F          ANI     0FH                  ;Isolate disk type
0950 FB4D 32FAFB        STA     Disk$Type            ;Save for use in low-level driver
0951 FB50 7E            MOV     A,M                  ;Get another copy of prefix byte
0952 FB51 E680          ANI     Need$Deblocking      ;Isolate deblocking flag
0953 FB53 32F9FB        STA     Deblocking$Required  ;Save for use in low-level driver
0954 FB56 E1            POP     H                    ;Recover DPH pointer
0955 FB57 C9            RET
0956                    ;
```

Figure 6-4. (Continued)

```
0957                    ;
0958                    ;   Set logical track for next read or write
0959                    ;
0960                    SETTRK:
0961   FB58 60           MOV     H,B                     ;Selected track in BC on entry
0962   FB59 69           MOV     L,C
0963   FB5A 22EBFB       SHLD    Selected$Track          ;Save for low-level driver
0964   FB5D C9           RET
0965                    ;
0966                    ;
0967                    ;   Set logical sector for next read or write
0968                    ;
0969                    ;
0970                    SETSEC:                          ;Logical sector in C on entry
0971   FB5E 79           MOV     A,C
0972   FB5F 32EDFB       STA     Selected$Sector         ;Save for low-level driver
0973   FB62 C9           RET
0974                    ;
0975                    ;
0976                    ;   Set disk DMA (input/output) address for next read or write
0977                    ;
0978   FB63 0000         DMA$Address:    DW      0       ;DMA address
0979                    ;
0980                    SETDMA:                          ;Address in BC on entry
0981   FB65 69           MOV     L,C                     ;Move to HL to save
0982   FB66 60           MOV     H,B
0983   FB67 2263FB       SHLD    DMA$Address             ;Save for low-level driver
0984   FB6A C9           RET
0985                    ;
0986                    ;
0987                    ;   Translate logical sector number to physical
0988                    ;
0989                    ;   Sector translation tables
0990                    ;   These tables are indexed using the logical sector number,
0991                    ;   and contain the corresponding physical sector number.
0992                    ;
0993                    Floppy$5$Skewtable:              ;Each physical sector contains four
0994                                                     ; 128-byte sectors.
0995                            ;       Physical 128b   Logical 128b    Physical 512-byte
0996   FB6B 00010203     DB      00,01,02,03     ;00,01,02,03     0  )
0997   FB6F 10111213     DB      16,17,18,19     ;04,05,06,07     4  )
0998   FB73 20212223     DB      32,33,34,35     ;08,09,10,11     8  )
0999   FB77 0C0D0E0F     DB      12,13,14,15     ;12,13,14,15     3  ) Head
1000   FB7B 1C1D1E1F     DB      28,29,30,31     ;16,17,18,19     7  ) 0
1001   FB7F 08090A0B     DB      08,09,10,11     ;20,21,22,23     2  )
1002   FB83 18191A1B     DB      24,25,26,27     ;24,25,26,27     6  )
1003   FB87 04050607     DB      04,05,06,07     ;28,29,30,31     1  )
1004   FB8B 14151617     DB      20,21,22,23     ;32,33,34,35     5  )
1005                    ;
1006   FB8F 24252627     DB      36,37,38,39     ;36,37,38,39     0  ]
1007   FB93 34353637     DB      52,53,54,55     ;40,41,42,43     4  ]
1008   FB97 44454647     DB      68,69,70,71     ;44,45,46,47     8  ]
1009   FB9B 30313233     DB      48,49,50,51     ;48,49,50,51     3  ] Head
1010   FB9F 40414243     DB      64,65,66,67     ;52,53,54,55     7  ] 1
1011   FBA3 2C2D2E2F     DB      44,45,46,47     ;56,57,58,59     2  ]
1012   FBA7 3C3D3E3F     DB      60,61,62,63     ;60,61,62,63     6  ]
1013   FBAB 28292A2B     DB      40,41,42,43     ;64,65,66,67     1  ]
1014   FBAF 38393A3B     DB      56,57,58,59     ;68,69,70,71     5  ]
1015                    ;
1016                    ;
1017                    Floppy$8$Skewtable:              ;Standard 8" Driver
1018                            ;       01,02,03,04,05,06,07,08,09,10   Logical sectors
1019   FBB3 01070D1319   DB      01,07,13,19,25,05,11,17,23,03   ;Physical sectors
1020                    ;
1021                            ;       11,12,13,14,15,16,17,18,19,20   Logical sectors
1022   FBBD 090F150208   DB      09,15,21,02,08,14,20,26,06,12   ;Physical sectors
1023                    ;
1024                            ;       21,22,23,24,25,26               Logical sectors
1025   FBC7 1218040A10   DB      18,24,04,10,16,22               ;Physical sectors
1026                    ;
1027                    ;
1028                    SECTRAN:                         ;Translate logical sector into physical
1029                                                     ;On entry, BC = logical sector number
1030                                                     ;          DE -> appropriate skew table
1031                    ;
1032                                                     ;on exit, HL = physical sector number
```

Figure 6-4.   (Continued)

```
1033 FBCD EB            XCHG                         ;HL -> skew table base
1034 FBCE 09            DAD      B                   ;Add on logical sector number
1035 FBCF 6E            MOV      L,M                 ;Get physical sector number
1036 FBD0 2600          MVI      H,0                 ;Make into a 16-bit value
1037 FBD2 C9            RET
1038                    ;
1039                    ;
1040                    ;
1041               HOME:                              ;Home the selected logical disk to track 0.
1042                                                  ;Before doing this, a check must be made to see
1043                                                  ; if the physical disk buffer has information
1044                                                  ; that must be written out. This is indicated by
1045                                                  ; a flag, Must$Write$Buffer, set in the
1046                                                  ; deblocking code.
1047                    ;
1048 FBD3 3AE9FB        LDA      Must$Write$Buffer   ;Check if physical buffer must
1049 FBD6 B7            ORA      A                   ; be written out to disk
1050 FBD7 C2DDFB        JNZ      HOME$No$Write
1051 FBDA 32E8FB        STA      Data$In$Disk$Buffer ;No, so indicate that buffer
1052                                                  ; is now unoccupied.
1053               HOME$No$Write:
1054 FBDD 0E00          MVI      C,0                 ;Set to track 0 (logically --
1055 FBDF CD58FB        CALL     SETTRK              ; no actual disk operation occurs)
1056 FBE2 C9            RET
1057
1058                    ;
1059                    ; Data written to or read from the mini-floppy drive is transferred
1060                    ; via a physical buffer that is actually 512 bytes long (it was
1061                    ; declared at the front of the BIOS and holds the "one-time"
1062                    ; initialization code used for the cold boot procedure).
1063                    ;
1064                    ; The blocking/deblocking code attempts to minimize the amount
1065                    ; of actual disk I/O by storing the disk, track, and physical sector
1066                    ; currently residing in the Physical Buffer. If a read request is for
1067                    ; a 128-byte CP/M "sector" that already is in the physical buffer,
1068                    ; then no disk access occurs.
1069                    ;
1070                    ;
1071 0800 =         Allocation$Block$Size   EQU    2048
1072 0012 =         Physical$Sec$Per$Track  EQU    18
1073 0004 =         CPM$Sec$Per$Physical    EQU    Physical$Sector$Size/128
1074 0048 =         CPM$Sec$Per$Track       EQU    CPM$Sec$Per$Physical*Physical$Sec$Per$Track
1075 0003 =         Sector$Mask             EQU    CPM$Sec$Per$Physical-1
1076 0002 =         Sector$Bit$Shift        EQU    2          ;LOG2(CPM$Sec$Per$Physical)
1077                    ;
1078                                       ;These are the values handed over by the BDOS
1079                                       ; when it calls the WRITE operation.
1080                                       ;The allocated/unallocated indicates whether the
1081                                       ; BDOS is set to write to an unallocated allocation
1082                                       ; block (it only indicates this for the first
1083                                       ; 128-byte sector write) or to an allocation block
1084                                       ; that has already been allocated to a file.
1085                                       ;The BDOS also indicates if it is set to write to
1086                                       ; the file directory.
1087                    ;
1088 0000 =         Write$Allocated         EQU    0
1089 0001 =         Write$Directory         EQU    1
1090 0002 =         Write$Unallocated       EQU    2
1091                    ;
1092 FBE3 00        Write$Type:             DB     0         ;Contains the type of write
1093                                                          ; indicated by the BDOS.
1094                    ;
1095                    ;
1096               In$Buffer$Dk$Trk$Sec:                      ;Variables for physical sector
1097                                                          ; currently in Disk$Buffer in memory
1098 FBE4 00        In$Buffer$Disk:         DB     0         ; These are moved and compared
1099 FBE5 0000      In$Buffer$Track:        DW     0         ; as a group, so do not alter
1100 FBE7 00        In$Buffer$Sector:       DB     0         ; these lines.
1101                    ;
1102 FBE8 00        Data$In$Disk$Buffer:    DB     0         ;When nonzero, the disk buffer has
1103                                                          ; data from the disk in it.
1104 FBE9 00        Must$Write$Buffer:      DB     0         ;Nonzero when data has been
1105                                                          ; written into Disk$Buffer but
1106                                                          ; not yet written out to disk
1107                    ;
1108               Selected$Dk$Trk$Sec:                       ;Variables for selected disk, track, and sector
```

Figure 6-4. (Continued)

```
1109                                          ; (Selected by SELDSK, SETTRK,and SETSEC)
1110  FBEA 00      Selected$Disk:        DB    0      ; These are moved and
1111  FBEB 0000    Selected$Track:       DW    0      ; compared as a group so
1112  FBED 00      Selected$Sector:      DB    0      ; do not alter order.
1113
1114  FBEE 00      Selected$Physical$Sector: DB 0     ;Selected physical sector derived
1115                                                  ; from selected (CP/M) sector by
1116                                                  ; shifting it right the number of
1117                                                  ; of bits specified by
1118                                                  ; Sector$Bit$Shift
1119                         ;
1120  FBEF 00      Selected$Disk$Type:   DB    0      ;Set by SELDSK to indicate either
1121                                                  ; 8" or 5 1/4" floppy
1122  FBF0 00      Selected$Disk$Deblock: DB   0      ;Set by SELDSK to indicate whether
1123                                                  ; deblocking is required.
1124
1125
1126               Unallocated$Dk$Trk$Sec:            ;Parameters for writing to a previously
1127                                                  ; unallocated allocation block.
1128  FBF1 00      Unallocated$Disk:     DB    0      ; These are moved and compared
1129  FBF2 0000    Unallocated$Track:    DW    0      ; as a group so do not alter
1130  FBF4 00      Unallocated$Sector:   DB    0      ; these lines.
1131
1132  FBF5 00      Unallocated$Record$Count: DB 0     ;Number of unallocated "records"
1133                                                  ; in current previously unallocated
1134                                                  ; allocation block.
1135
1136  FBF6 00      Disk$Error$Flag:      DB    0      ;Nonzero to indicate an error
1137                                                  ; that could not be recovered
1138                                                  ; by the disk drivers. BDOS will
1139                                                  ; output a "bad sector" message.
1140                         ;
1141                         ;Flags used inside the deblocking code
1142
1143  FBF7 00      Must$Preread$Sector:  DB    0      ;Nonzero if a physical sector must
1144                                                  ; be read into the disk buffer
1145                                                  ; either before a write to an
1146                                                  ; allocated block can occur, or
1147                                                  ; for a normal CP/M 128-byte
1148                                                  ; sector read
1149  FBF8 00      Read$Operation:       DB    0      ;Nonzero when a CP/M 128-byte
1150                                                  ; sector is to be read
1151  FBF9 00      Deblocking$Required:  DB    0      ;Nonzero when the selected disk
1152                                                  ; needs deblocking (set in SELDSK)
1153  FBFA 00      Disk$Type:            DB    0      ;Indicates 8" or 5 1/4" floppy
1154                                                  ; selected (set in SELDSK).
1155                         ;
1156                         ;
1157                         ; Read in the 128-byte CP/M sector specified by previous calls
1158                         ; to select disk and to set track and sector. The sector will be read
1159                         ; into the address specified in the previous call to set DMA address.
1160                         ;
1161                         ; If reading from a disk drive using sectors larger than 128 bytes,
1162                         ; deblocking code will be used to "unpack" a 128-byte sector from
1163                         ; the physical sector.
1164                         READ:
1165  FBFB 3AF9FB          LDA   Deblocking$Required   ;Check if deblocking needed
1166  FBFE B7              ORA   A                     ;(flag was set in SELDSK call)
1167  FBFF CA52FD          JZ    Read$No$Deblock       ;No, use normal nondeblocked
1168
1169                                    ;The deblocking algorithm used is such
1170                                    ; that a read operation can be viewed
1171                                    ; up until the actual data transfer as
1172                                    ; though it was the first write to an
1173                                    ; unallocated allocation block.
1174  FC02 AF              XRA   A                              ;Set the record count to 0
1175  FC03 32F5FB          STA   Unallocated$Record$Count ;  for first "write"
1176  FC06 3C              INR   A                              ;Indicate that it is really a read
1177  FC07 32F8FB          STA   Read$Operation        ;   that is to be performed
1178  FC0A 32F7FB          STA   Must$Preread$Sector   ;  and force a preread of the sector
1179                                                   ;  to get it into the disk buffer
1180  FC0D 3E02            MVI   A,Write$Unallocated   ;Fake deblocking code into responding
1181  FC0F 32E3FB          STA   Write$Type            ;  as if this is the first write to an
1182                                                   ;  unallocated allocation block.
1183  FC12 C36EFC          JMP   Perform$Read$Write    ;Use common code to execute read
```

Figure 6-4. (Continued)

```
1184                    ;
1185                    ;   Write a 128-byte sector from the current DMA address to
1186                    ;   the previously selected disk, track, and sector.
1187                    ;
1188                    ;   On arrival here, the BDOS will have set register C to indicate
1189                    ;   whether this write operation is to an already allocated allocation
1190                    ;   block (which means a preread of the sector may be needed),
1191                    ;   to the directory (in which case the data will be written to the
1192                    ;   disk immediately), or to the first 128-byte sector of a previously
1193                    ;   unallocated allocation block (in which case no preread is required).
1194                    ;
1195                    ;   Only writes to the directory take place immediately. In all other
1196                    ;   cases, the data will be moved from the DMA address into the disk
1197                    ;   buffer, and only written out when circumstances force the
1198                    ;   transfer. The number of physical disk operations can therefore
1199                    ;   be reduced considerably.
1200                    ;
1201                    WRITE:
1202   FC15 3AF9FB      LDA     Deblocking$Required        ;Check if deblocking is required
1203   FC18 B7          ORA     A                          ;(flag set in SELDSK call)
1204   FC19 CA4DFD      JZ      Write$No$Deblock
1205
1206   FC1C AF          XRA     A                          ;Indicate that a write operation
1207   FC1D 32F8FB      STA     Read$Operation             ; is required (i.e. NOT a read)
1208   FC20 79          MOV     A,C                        ;Save the BDOS write type
1209   FC21 32E3FB      STA     Write$Type
1210   FC24 FE02        CPI     Write$Unallocated          ;Check if the first write to an
1211                                                       ;  unallocated allocation block
1212   FC26 C237FC      JNZ     Check$Unallocated$Block    ;No, check if in the middle of
1213                                                       ;  writing to an unallocated block
1214                                                       ;Yes, first write to unallocated
1215                                                       ;  allocation block -- initialize
1216                                                       ;  variables associated with
1217                                                       ;  unallocated writes.
1218   FC29 3E10        MVI     A,Allocation$Block$Size/128  ;Get number of 128-byte
1219                                                       ;  sectors and
1220   FC2B 32F5FB      STA     Unallocated$Record$Count   ;  set up a count.
1221                    ;
1222   FC2E 21EAFB      LXI     H,Selected$Dk$Trk$Sec      ;Copy disk, track, and sector
1223   FC31 11F1FB      LXI     D,Unallocated$Dk$Trk$Sec   ;  into unallocated variables
1224   FC34 CD35FD      CALL    Move$Dk$Trk$Sec
1225                    ;
1226                    ;   Check if this is not the first write to an unallocated
1227                    ;   allocation block -- if it is, the unallocated record count
1228                    ;   has just been set to the number of 128-byte sectors in the
1229                    ;   allocation block.
1230                    ;
1231                    Check$Unallocated$Block:
1232   FC37 3AF5FB      LDA     Unallocated$Record$Count
1233   FC3A B7          ORA     A
1234   FC3B CA66FC      JZ      Request$Preread            ;No, this is a write to an
1235                                                       ;  allocated block
1236                                                       ;Yes, this is a write to an
1237                                                       ;  unallocated block
1238   FC3E 3D          DCR     A                          ;Count down on number of 128-byte sectors
1239                                                       ;  left unwritten to in allocation block
1240   FC3F 32F5FB      STA     Unallocated$Record$Count   ;  and store back new value.
1241
1242   FC42 21EAFB      LXI     H,Selected$Dk$Trk$Sec      ;Check if the selected disk, track,
1243   FC45 11F1FB      LXI     D,Unallocated$Dk$Trk$Sec   ;  and sector are the same as for
1244   FC48 CD29FD      CALL    Compare$Dk$Trk$Sec         ;  those in the unallocated block.
1245   FC4B C266FC      JNZ     Request$Preread            ;No, a preread is required
1246                                                       ;Yes, no preread is needed.
1247                                                       ;Now is a convenient time to
1248                                                       ;  update the current sector and see
1249                                                       ;  if the track also needs updating.
1250                    ;
1251                                                       ;By design, Compare$Dk$Trk$Sec
1252                                                       ;  returns with
1253                                                       ;    DE -> Unallocated$Sector
1254   FC4E EB          XCHG                               ;    HL -> Unallocated$Sector
1255   FC4F 34          INR     M                          ;Update Unallocated$Sector
1256   FC50 7E          MOV     A,M                        ;Check if sector now > maximum
1257   FC51 FE48        CPI     CPM$Sec$Per$Track          ;  on a track
1258   FC53 DA5FFC      JC      No$Track$Change            ;No (A < M)
1259                                                       ;Yes,
```

Figure 6-4. (Continued)

```
1260  FC56 3600            MVI     M,0                          ;Reset sector to 0
1261  FC58 2AF2FB          LHLD    Unallocated$Track            ;Increase track by 1
1262  FC5B 23              INX     H
1263  FC5C 22F2FB          SHLD    Unallocated$Track
1264                       ;
1265                       No$Track$Change:
1266                                                            ;Indicate to later code that
1267                                                            ;  no preread is needed.
1268  FC5F AF              XRA     A
1269  FC60 32F7FB          STA     Must$Preread$Sector          ;Must$Preread$Sector=0
1270  FC63 C36EFC          JMP     Perform$Read$Write
1271                       ;
1272                       Request$Preread:
1273  FC66 AF              XRA     A                            ;Indicate that this is not a write
1274  FC67 32F5FB          STA     Unallocated$Record$Count     ;  into an unallocated block.
1275  FC6A 3C              INR     A
1276  FC6B 32F7FB          STA     Must$Preread$Sector          ;Indicate that a preread of the
1277                                                            ;  physical sector is required.
1278                       ;
1279                       ;
1280                       Perform$Read$Write:                  ;Common code to execute both reads and
1281                                                            ;  writes of 128-byte sectors.
1282  FC6E AF              XRA     A                            ;Assume that no disk errors will
1283  FC6F 32F6FB          STA     Disk$Error$Flag              ;  occur
1284
1285  FC72 3AEDFB          LDA     Selected$Sector              ;Convert selected 128-byte sector
1286  FC75 1F              RAR                                  ;  into physical sector by dividing by 4
1287  FC76 1F              RAR
1288  FC77 E63F            ANI     3FH                          ;Remove any unwanted bits
1289  FC79 32EEFB          STA     Selected$Physical$Sector
1290                       ;
1291  FC7C 21E8FB          LXI     H,Data$In$Disk$Buffer        ;Check if disk buffer already has
1292  FC7F 7E              MOV     A,M                          ;  data in it.
1293  FC80 3601            MVI     M,1                          ;(Unconditionally indicate that
1294                                                            ;  the buffer now has data in it)
1295  FC82 B7              ORA     A                            ;Did it indeed have data in it?
1296  FC83 CAA3FC          JZ      Read$Sector$into$Buffer      ;No, proceed to read a physical
1297                                                            ;  sector into the buffer.
1298                                                            ;The buffer does have a physical sector
1299                                                            ;  in it.
1300                                                            ;  Note: The disk, track, and PHYSICAL
1301                                                            ;  sector in the buffer need to be
1302                                                            ;  checked, hence the use of the
1303                                                            ;  Compare$Dk$Trk subroutine.
1304                       ;
1305
1306  FC86 11E4FB          LXI     D,In$Buffer$Dk$Trk$Sec       ;Check if sector in buffer is the
1307  FC89 21EAFB          LXI     H,Selected$Dk$Trk$Sec        ;  same as that selected earlier
1308  FC8C CD24FD          CALL    Compare$Dk$Trk               ;Compare ONLY disk and track
1309  FC8F C29CFC          JNZ     Sector$Not$In$Buffer         ;No, it must be read in
1310
1311  FC92 3AE7FB          LDA     In$Buffer$Sector             ;Get physical sector in buffer
1312  FC95 21EEFB          LXI     H,Selected$Physical$Sector
1313  FC98 BE              CMP     M                            ;Check if correct physical sector
1314  FC99 CAB1FC          JZ      Sector$In$Buffer             ;Yes, it is already in memory
1315                       ;
1316                       Sector$Not$In$Buffer:
1317                                                            ;No, it will have to be read in
1318                                                            ;  over current contents of buffer
1319  FC9C 3AE9FB          LDA     Must$Write$Buffer            ;Check if buffer has data in that
1320  FC9F B7              ORA     A                            ;  must be written out first
1321  FCA0 C495FD          CNZ     Write$Physical               ;Yes, write it out
1322                       ;
1323                       Read$Sector$into$Buffer:
1324  FCA3 CD11FD          CALL    Set$In$Buffer$Dk$Trk$Sec     ;Set in buffer variables from
1325                                                            ;  selected disk, track, and sector
1326                                                            ;  to reflect which sector is in the
1327                                                            ;  buffer now
1328  FCA6 3AF7FB          LDA     Must$Preread$Sector          ;In practice, the sector need only
1329  FCA9 B7              ORA     A                            ;  be physically read in if a preread
1330                                                            ;  is required
1331  FCAA C49AFD          CNZ     Read$Physical                ;Yes, preread the sector
1332  FCAD AF              XRA     A                            ;Reset the flag to reflect buffer
1333  FCAE 32E9FB          STA     Must$Write$Buffer            ;  contents.
1334                       ;
1335                       Sector$In$Buffer:                    ;Selected sector on correct track and
```

Figure 6-4.   (Continued)

```
1336                                                 ;  disk is already in the buffer.
1337                                                 ;Convert the selected CP/M (128-byte)
1338                                                 ;  sector into a relative address down
1339                                                 ;  the buffer.
1340    FCB1 3AEDFB        LDA     Selected$Sector   ;Get selected sector number
1341    FCB4 E603          ANI     Sector$Mask       ;Mask off only the least significant bits
1342    FCB6 6F            MOV     L,A               ;Multiply by 128 by shifting 16-bit value
1343    FCB7 2600          MVI     H,0               ;  left 7 bits
1344    FCB9 29            DAD     H                 ;* 2
1345    FCBA 29            DAD     H                 ;* 4
1346    FCBB 29            DAD     H                 ;* 8
1347    FCBC 29            DAD     H                 ;* 16
1348    FCBD 29            DAD     H                 ;* 32
1349    FCBE 29            DAD     H                 ;* 64
1350    FCBF 29            DAD     H                 ;* 128
1351                       ;
1352    FCC0 1133F6        LXI     D,Disk$Buffer     ;Get base address of disk buffer
1353    FCC3 19            DAD     D                 ;Add on sector number * 128
1354                                                 ;HL -> 128-byte sector number start
1355                                                 ;  address in disk buffer
1356    FCC4 EB            XCHG                      ;DE -> sector in disk buffer
1357    FCC5 2A63FB        LHLD    DMA$Address       ;Get DMA address set in SETDMA call
1358    FCC8 EB            XCHG                      ;Assume a read operation, so
1359                                                 ;  DE -> DMA address
1360                                                 ;  HL -> sector in disk buffer
1361    FCC9 0E10          MVI     C,128/8           ;Because of the faster method used
1362                                                 ;  to move data in and out of the
1363                                                 ;  disk buffer, (eight bytes moved per
1364                                                 ;  loop iteration) the count need only
1365                                                 ;  be 1/8th of normal.
1366                                                 ;At this point -
1367                                                 ;    C = loop count
1368                                                 ;    DE -> DMA address
1369                                                 ;    HL -> sector in disk buffer
1370    FCCB 3AF8FB        LDA     Read$Operation    ;Determine whether data is to be moved
1371    FCCE B7            ORA     A                 ;  out of the buffer (read) or into the
1372    FCCF C2D7FC        JNZ     Buffer$Move       ;  buffer (write)
1373                                                 ;Writing into buffer
1374                                                 ;  (A must be 0 get here)
1375    FCD2 3C            INR     A                 ;Set flag to force a write
1376    FCD3 32E9FB        STA     Must$Write$Buffer ;  of the disk buffer later on.
1377    FCD6 EB            XCHG                      ;Make DE -> sector in disk buffer
1378                                                 ;    HL -> DMA address
1379                       ;
1380                       ;
1381                       Buffer$Move:              ;The folowing move loop moves eight bytes
1382                                                 ;  at a time from (HL) to (DE), C contains
1383                                                 ;  the loop count.
1384    FCD7 7E            MOV     A,M               ;Get byte from source
1385    FCD8 12            STAX    D                 ;Put into destination
1386    FCD9 13            INX     D                 ;Update pointers
1387    FCDA 23            INX     H
1388    FCDB 7E            MOV     A,M               ;Get byte from source
1389    FCDC 12            STAX    D                 ;Put into destination
1390    FCDD 13            INX     D                 ;Update pointers
1391    FCDE 23            INX     H
1392    FCDF 7E            MOV     A,M               ;Get byte from source
1393    FCE0 12            STAX    D                 ;Put into destination
1394    FCE1 13            INX     D                 ;Update pointers
1395    FCE2 23            INX     H
1396    FCE3 7E            MOV     A,M               ;Get byte from source
1397    FCE4 12            STAX    D                 ;Put into destination
1398    FCE5 13            INX     D                 ;Update pointers
1399    FCE6 23            INX     H
1400    FCE7 7E            MOV     A,M               ;Get byte from source
1401    FCE8 12            STAX    D                 ;Put into destination
1402    FCE9 13            INX     D                 ;Update pointers
1403    FCEA 23            INX     H
1404    FCEB 7E            MOV     A,M               ;Get byte from source
1405    FCEC 12            STAX    D                 ;Put into destination
1406    FCED 13            INX     D                 ;Update pointers
1407    FCEE 23            INX     H
1408    FCEF 7E            MOV     A,M               ;Get byte from source
1409    FCF0 12            STAX    D                 ;Put into destination
1410    FCF1 13            INX     D                 ;Update pointers
```

Figure 6-4. (Continued)

```
1411   FCF2  23           INX     H
1412   FCF3  7E           MOV     A,M              ;Get byte from source
1413   FCF4  12           STAX    D                ;Put into destination
1414   FCF5  13           INX     D                ;Update pointers
1415   FCF6  23           INX     H
1416
1417   FCF7  0D           DCR     C                ;Count down on loop counter
1418   FCF8  C2D7FC       JNZ     Buffer$Move      ;Repeat until CP/M sector moved
1419                                               ;
1420   FCFB  3AE3FB       LDA     Write$Type       ;If write to directory, write out
1421   FCFE  FE01         CPI     Write$Directory  ; buffer immediately
1422   FD00  3AF6FB       LDA     Disk$Error$Flag  ;Get error flag in case delayed write or read
1423   FD03  C0           RNZ                      ;Return if delayed write or read
1424                                               ;
1425   FD04  B7           ORA     A                ;Check if any disk errors have occurred
1426   FD05  C0           RNZ                      ;Yes, abandon attempt to write to directory
1427                                               ;
1428   FD06  AF           XRA     A                ;Clear flag that indicates buffer must be
1429   FD07  32E9FB       STA     Must$Write$Buffer ; written out
1430   FD0A  CD95FD       CALL    Write$Physical   ;Write buffer out to physical sector
1431   FD0D  3AF6FB       LDA     Disk$Error$Flag  ;Return error flag to caller
1432   FD10  C9           RET
1433                                               ;
1434
1435                      Set$In$Buffer$Dk$Trk$Sec:    ;Indicate selected disk, track, and
1436                                                   ; sector now residing in buffer
1437   FD11  3AEAFB       LDA     Selected$Disk
1438   FD14  32E4FB       STA     In$Buffer$Disk
1439
1440   FD17  2AEBFB       LHLD    Selected$Track
1441   FD1A  22E5FB       SHLD    In$Buffer$Track
1442
1443   FD1D  3AEEFB       LDA     Selected$Physical$Sector
1444   FD20  32E7FB       STA     In$Buffer$Sector
1445
1446   FD23  C9           RET
1447                                               ;
1448                      Compare$Dk$Trk:          ;Compares just the disk and track
1449                                               ; pointed to by DE and HL
1450   FD24  0E03         MVI     C,3              ;Disk (1), track (2)
1451   FD26  C32BFD       JMP     Compare$Dk$Trk$Sec$Loop ;Use common code
1452
1453                      Compare$Dk$Trk$Sec:      ;Compares the disk, track, and sector
1454                                               ; variables pointed to by DE and HL
1455   FD29  0E04         MVI     C,4              ;Disk (1), track (2), and sector (1)
1456                      Compare$Dk$Trk$Sec$Loop:
1457   FD2B  1A           LDAX    D                ;Get comparitor
1458   FD2C  BE           CMP     M                ;Compare with comparand
1459   FD2D  C0           RNZ                      ;Abandon comparison if inequality found
1460   FD2E  13           INX     D                ;Update comparitor pointer
1461   FD2F  23           INX     H                ;Update comparand pointer
1462   FD30  0D           DCR     C                ;Count down on loop count
1463   FD31  C8           RZ                       ;Return (with zero flag set)
1464   FD32  C32BFD       JMP     Compare$Dk$Trk$Sec$Loop
1465                                               ;
1466                                               ;
1467                      Move$Dk$Trk$Sec:         ;Moves the disk, track, and sector
1468                                               ; variables pointed at by HL to
1469                                               ; those pointed at by DE
1470   FD35  0E04         MVI     C,4              ;Disk (1), track (2), and sector (1)
1471                      Move$Dk$Trk$Sec$Loop:
1472   FD37  7E           MOV     A,M              ;Get source byte
1473   FD38  12           STAX    D                ;Store in destination
1474   FD39  13           INX     D                ;Update pointers
1475   FD3A  23           INX     H
1476   FD3B  0D           DCR     C                ;Count down on byte count
1477   FD3C  C8           RZ                       ;Return if all bytes moved
1478   FD3D  C337FD       JMP     Move$Dk$Trk$Sec$Loop
1479                                               ;
1480                                               ;
1482                                               ;
1483                      ; There are two "smart" disk controllers on this system, one
1484                      ; for the 8" floppy diskette drives, and one for the 5 1/4"
1485                      ; mini-diskette drives.
1486                      ;
1487                      ; The controllers are "hard-wired" to monitor certain locations
```

Figure 6-4. (Continued)

```
1488            ;  in memory to detect when they are to perform some disk
1489            ;  operation. The 8" controller monitors location 0040H, and
1490            ;  the 5 1/4" controller monitors location 0045H. These are
1491            ;  called their disk control bytes. If the most significant
1492            ;  bit of a disk control byte is set, the controller will
1493            ;  look at the word following the respective control bytes.
1494            ;  This word must contain the address of a valid disk control
1495            ;  table that specifies the exact disk operation to be performed.
1496            ;
1497            ;  Once the operation has been completed, the controller resets
1498            ;  its disk control byte to 00H. This indicates completion
1499            ;  to the disk driver code.
1500            ;
1501            ;  The controller also sets a return code in a disk status block --
1502            ;  both controllers use the SAME location for this; 0043H.
1503            ;  If the first byte of this status block is less than 80H, then
1504            ;  a disk error has occurred. For this simple BIOS, no further details
1505            ;  of the status settings are relevant. Note that the disk controller
1506            ;  has built-in retry logic -- reads and writes are attempted ten
1507            ;  times before the controller returns an error.
1508            ;
1509            ;  The disk control table layout is shown below. Note that the
1510            ;  controllers have the capability for control tables to be
1511            ;  chained together so that a sequence of disk operations can
1512            ;  be initiated. In this BIOS this feature is not used. However,
1513            ;  the controller requires that the chain pointers in the
1514            ;  disk control tables be pointed back to the main control bytes
1515            ;  in order to indicate the end of the chain.
1516            ;
1517  0040  =   Disk$Control$8         EQU    40H      ;8" control byte
1518  0041  =   Command$Block$8        EQU    41H      ;Control table pointer
1519            ;
1520  0043  =   Disk$Status$Block      EQU    43H      ;8" AND 5 1/4" status block
1521            ;
1522  0045  =   Disk$Control$5         EQU    45H      ;5 1/4" control byte
1523  0046  =   Command$Block$5        EQU    46H      ;Control table pointer
1524
1525            ;
1526            ;  Floppy Disk Control Tables
1527            ;
1528  FD40 00   Floppy$Command:        DB     0        ;Command
1529  0001  =   Floppy$Read$Code       EQU    01H
1530  0002  =   Floppy$Write$Code      EQU    02H
1531  FD41 00   Floppy$Unit:           DB     0        ;Unit (drive) number = 0 or 1
1532  FD42 00   Floppy$Head:           DB     0        ;Head number = 0 or 1
1533  FD43 00   Floppy$Track:          DB     0        ;Track number
1534  FD44 00   Floppy$Sector:         DB     0        ;Sector number
1535  FD45 0000 Floppy$Byte$Count:     DW     0        ;Number of bytes to read/write
1536  FD47 0000 Floppy$DMA$Address:    DW     0        ;Transfer address
1537  FD49 0000 Floppy$Next$Status$Block: DW  0        ;Pointer to next status block
1538                                                   ;  if commands are chained.
1539  FD4B 0000 Floppy$Next$Control$Location: DW 0     ;Pointer to next control byte
1540                                                   ;  if commands are chained.
1541            ;
1542            ;
1543            ;
1544            Write$No$Deblock:                      ;Write contents of disk buffer to
1545                                                   ;  correct sector.
1546  FD4D 3E02   MVI    A,Floppy$Write$Code           ;Get write function code
1547  FD4F C354FD JMP    Common$No$Deblock             ;Go to common code
1548            Read$No$Deblock:                       ;Read previously selected sector
1549                                                   ;  into disk buffer.
1550  FD52 3E01   MVI    A,Floppy$Read$Code            ;Get read function code
1551            Common$No$Deblock:
1552  FD54 3240FD STA    Floppy$Command                ;Set command function code
1553                                                   ;Set up nondeblocked command table
1554  FD57 218000 LXI    H,128                         ;Bytes per sector
1555  FD5A 2245FD SHLD   Floppy$Byte$Count
1556  FD5D AF     XRA    A                             ;8" floppy only has head 0
1557  FD5E 3242FD STA    Floppy$Head
1558            ;
1559  FD61 3AEAFB LDA    Selected$Disk                 ;8" Floppy controller only has information
1560                                                   ;  on units 0 and 1 so Selected$Disk must
1561                                                   ;  be converted
1562  FD64 E601  ANI     01H                           ;Turn into 0 or 1
1563  FD66 3241FD STA    Floppy$Unit                   ;Set unit number
```

Figure 6-4. (Continued)

```
1564                                    ;
1565   FD69 3AEBFB      LDA     Selected$Track
1566   FD6C 3243FD      STA     Floppy$Track        ;Set track number
1567                                    ;
1568   FD6F 3AEDFB      LDA     Selected$Sector
1569   FD72 3244FD      STA     Floppy$Sector       ;Set sector number
1570                                    ;
1571   FD75 2A63FB      LHLD    DMA$Address         ;Transfer directly between DMA address
1572   FD78 2247FD      SHLD    Floppy$DMA$Address  ; and 8" controller.
1573                                    ;
1574                                    ;The disk controller can accept chained
1575                                    ; disk control tables, but in this case,
1576                                    ; they are not used, so the "Next" pointers
1577                                    ; must be pointed back at the initial
1578                                    ; control bytes in the base page.
1579   FD7B 214300      LXI     H,Disk$Status$Block       ;Point next status back at
1580   FD7E 2249FD      SHLD    Floppy$Next$Status$Block  ; main status block
1581                                    ;
1582   FD81 214000      LXI     H,Disk$Control$8           ;Point next control byte
1583   FD84 224BFD      SHLD    Floppy$Next$Control$Location ; back at main control byte
1584                                    ;
1585   FD87 2140FD      LXI     H,Floppy$Command    ;Point controller at control table
1586   FD8A 224100      SHLD    Command$Block$8
1587                                    ;
1588   FD8D 214000      LXI     H,Disk$Control$8    ;Activate controller to perform
1589   FD90 3680        MVI     M,80H               ; operation.
1590   FD92 C3F7FD      JMP     Wait$For$Disk$Complete
1591
1592                                    ;
1593                                    ;
1594                    Write$Physical:              ;Write contents of disk buffer to
1595                                                 ; correct sector.
1596
1597   FD95 3E02        MVI     A,Floppy$Write$Code ;Get write function code
1598   FD97 C39CFD      JMP     Common$Physical     ;Go to common code
1599                    Read$Physical:              ;Read previously selected sector
1600                                                 ; into disk buffer.
1601   FD9A 3E01        MVI     A,Floppy$Read$Code  ;Get read function code
1602                                    ;
1603                    Common$Physical:
1604   FD9C 3240FD      STA     Floppy$Command      ;Set command table
1605
1606                                    ;
1607   FD9F 3AFAFB      LDA     Disk$Type           ;Get disk type (set in SELDSK)
1608   FDA2 FE01        CPI     Floppy$5            ;Confirm it is a 5 1/4" Floppy
1609   FDA4 CAADFD      JZ      Correct$Disk$Type   ;Yes
1610   FDA7 3E01        MVI     A,1                 ;No, indicate disk error
1611   FDA9 32F6FB      STA     Disk$Error$Flag
1612   FDAC C9          RET
1613                    Correct$Disk$Type:          ;Set up disk control table
1614                                    ;
1615   FDAD 3AE4FB      LDA     In$Buffer$Disk      ;Convert disk number to 0 or 1
1616   FDB0 E601        ANI     1                   ; for disk controller
1617   FDB2 3241FD      STA     Floppy$Unit
1618
1619   FDB5 2AE5FB      LHLD    In$Buffer$Track     ;Set up track number
1620   FDB8 7D          MOV     A,L                 ;Note: This is single byte value
1621   FDB9 3243FD      STA     Floppy$Track        ; for the controller.
1622
1623                                    ;The sector must be converted into a
1624                                    ; head number and sector number.
1625                                    ; Sectors 0 - 8 are head 0, 9 - 17
1626                                    ; are head 1
1627   FDBC 0600        MVI     B,0                 ;Assume head 0
1628   FDBE 3AE7FB      LDA     In$Buffer$Sector    ;Get physical sector number
1629   FDC1 4F          MOV     C,A                 ;Save copy in case it is head 0
1630   FDC2 FE09        CPI     9                   ;Check if < 9
1631   FDC4 DACBFD      JC      Head$0              ;Yes it is < 9
1632   FDC7 D609        SUI     9                   ;No, modify sector number back
1633                                                 ; in the 0 - 8 range.
1634   FDC9 4F          MOV     C,A                 ;Put sector in B
1635   FDCA 04          INR     B                   ;Set to head 1
1636                    Head$0:
1637   FDCB 78          MOV     A,B                 ;Set head number
1638   FDCC 3242FD      STA     Floppy$Head
1639   FDCF 79          MOV     A,C                 ;Set sector number
```

Figure 6-4. (Continued)

```
1640   FDD0 3C        INR     A                        ; (physical sectors start at 1)
1641   FDD1 3244FD    STA     Floppy$Sector
1642                                                   ;
1643   FDD4 210002    LXI     H,Physical$Sector$Size   ;Set byte count
1644   FDD7 2245FD    SHLD    Floppy$Byte$Count
1645                                                   ;
1646   FDDA 2133F6    LXI     H,Disk$Buffer            ;Set transfer address to be
1647   FDDD 2247FD    SHLD    Floppy$DMA$Address       ;  disk buffer
1648                                                   ;
1649                                                   ;As only one control table is in
1650                                                   ; use, close the status and busy
1651                                                   ; chain pointers back to the
1652                                                   ; main control bytes.
1653   FDE0 214300    LXI     H,Disk$Status$Block
1654   FDE3 2249FD    SHLD    Floppy$Next$Status$Block
1655   FDE6 214500    LXI     H,Disk$Control$5
1656   FDE9 224BFD    SHLD    Floppy$Next$Control$Location
1657                                                   ;
1658   FDEC 2140FD    LXI     H,Floppy$Command         ;Set up command block pointer
1659   FDEF 224600    SHLD    Command$Block$5
1660                                                   ;
1661   FDF2 214500    LXI     H,Disk$Control$5         ;Activate 5 1/4" disk controller
1662   FDF5 3680      MVI     M,80H
1663                                                   ;
1664                  Wait$For$Disk$Complete:          ;Wait until Disk Status Block indicates
1665                                                   ; operation complete, then check
1666                                                   ; if any errors occurred.
1667                                                   ;On entry HL -> disk control byte
1668   FDF7 7E        MOV     A,M                      ;Get control byte
1669   FDF8 B7        ORA     A
1670   FDF9 C2F7FD    JNZ     Wait$For$Disk$Complete   ;Operation still not yet done
1671                                                   ;
1672   FDFC 3A4300    LDA     Disk$Status$Block        ;Complete -- now check status
1673   FDFF FE80      CPI     80H                      ;Check if any errors occurred
1674   FE01 DA09FE    JC      Disk$Error               ;Yes
1675   FE04 AF        XRA     A                        ;No
1676   FE05 32F6FB    STA     Disk$Error$Flag          ;Clear error flag
1677   FE08 C9        RET
1678                  Disk$Error:
1679   FE09 3E01      MVI     A,1
1680   FE0B 32F6FB    STA     Disk$Error$Flag          ;Set disk-error flag nonzero
1681   FE0E C9        RET
1682                                                   ;
1683                                                   ;
1684                                                   ;
1685                  ;  Disk control table images for warm boot
1686                                                   ;
1687                  Boot$Control$Part$1:
1688   FE0F 01        DB      1                        ;Read function
1689   FE10 00        DB      0                        ;Unit (drive) number
1690   FE11 00        DB      0                        ;Head number
1691   FE12 00        DB      0                        ;Track number
1692   FE13 02        DB      2                        ;Starting sector number
1693   FE14 0010      DW      8*512                    ;Number of bytes to read
1694   FE16 00E0      DW      CCP$Entry                ;Read into this address
1695   FE18 4300      DW      Disk$Status$Block        ;Pointer to next status block
1696   FE1A 4500      DW      Disk$Control$5           ;Pointer to next control table
1697                  Boot$Control$Part2:
1698   FE1C 01        DB      1                        ;Read function
1699   FE1D 00        DB      0                        ;Unit (drive) number
1700   FE1E 01        DB      1                        ;Head number
1701   FE1F 00        DB      0                        ;Track number
1702   FE20 01        DB      1                        ;Starting sector number
1703   FE21 0006      DW      3*512                    ;Number of bytes to read
1704   FE23 00F0      DW      CCP$Entry + (8*512)      ;Read into this address
1705   FE25 4300      DW      Disk$Status$Block        ;Pointer to next status block
1706   FE27 4500      DW      Disk$Control$5           ;Pointer to next control table
1707                                                   ;
1708                                                   ;
1709                                                   ;
1710                                                   ;
1711                  WBOOT:                           ;Warm boot entry
1712                                                   ;On warm boot, the CCP and BDOS must be reloaded
1713                                                   ; into memory. In this BIOS, only the 5 1/4"
1714                                                   ; diskettes will be used. Therefore this code
```

Figure 6-4. (Continued)

```
1715                                    ; is hardware specific to the controller. Two
1716                                    ; prefabricated control tables are used.
1717    FE29 318000         LXI     SP,80H
1718    FE2C 110FFE         LXI     D,Boot$Control$Part1    ;Execute first read of warm boot
1719    FE2F CD3BFE         CALL    Warm$Boot$Read          ;Load drive 0, track 0,
1720                                                        ;  head 0, sectors 2 to 8
1721    FE32 111CFE         LXI     D,Boot$Control$Part2    ;Execute second read
1722    FE35 CD3BFE         CALL    Warm$Boot$Read          ;Load drive 0, track 0,
1723                                                        ;  head 1, sectors 1 - 3
1724    FE38 C340F8         JMP     Enter$CPM               ;Set up base page and enter CCP
1725                        ;
1726                        Warm$Boot$Read:                 ;On entry, DE -> control table image
1727                                                        ;This control table is moved into
1728                                                        ;  the main disk control table and
1729                                                        ;  then the controller activated.
1730    FE3B 2140FD         LXI     H,Floppy$Command        ;HL -> actual control table
1731    FE3E 224600         SHLD    Command$Block$5         ;Tell the controller its address
1732                                                        ;Move the control table image
1733                                                        ;  into the control table itself
1734    FE41 0E0D           MVI     C,13                    ;Set byte count
1735                        Warm$Boot$Move:
1736    FE43 1A             LDAX    D                       ;Get image byte
1737    FE44 77             MOV     M,A                     ;Store into actual control table
1738    FE45 23             INX     H                       ;Update pointers
1739    FE46 13             INX     D
1740    FE47 0D             DCR     C                       ;Count down on byte count
1741    FE48 C243FE         JNZ     Warm$Boot$Move          ;Continue until all bytes moved
1742                        ;
1743    FE4B 214500         LXI     H,Disk$Control$5        ;Activate controller
1744    FE4E 3680           MVI     M,80H
1745                        Wait$For$Boot$Complete:
1746    FE50 7E             MOV     A,M                     ;Get status byte
1747    FE51 B7             ORA     A                       ;Check if complete
1748    FE52 C250FE         JNZ     Wait$For$Boot$Complete  ;No
1749                                                        ;Yes, check for errors
1750    FE55 3A4300         LDA     Disk$Status$Block
1751    FE58 FE80           CPI     80H
1752    FE5A DA5EFE         JC      Warm$Boot$Error         ;Yes, an error occurred
1753    FE5D C9             RET
1754                        ;
1755                        Warm$Boot$Error:
1756    FE5E 2167FE         LXI     H,Warm$Boot$Error$Message
1757    FE61 CD33F8         CALL    Display$Message
1758    FE64 C329FE         JMP     WBOOT                   ;Restart warm boot
1759                        ;
1760                        Warm$Boot$Error$Message:
1761    FE67 0D0A576172     DB      CR,LF,'Warm Boot Error - retrying...',CR,LF,0
1762                        ;
1763                        ;
1764    FE89                END     ;Of simple BIOS listing
```

Figure 6-4. (Continued)

The Major Steps
Building Your First System
Using SYSGEN to Write
  CP/M to Disk
Using DDT to Build the
  CP/M Memory Image
The CP/M Bootstrap Loader
Using MOVCPM to Relocate the
  CCP and BDOS
Putting It All Together

Building a New CP/M System

This chapter describes how to build a version of CP/M with your own BIOS built into it. It also shows you how to put CP/M onto a floppy disk and how to write a bootstrap loader to bring CP/M into memory.

The manufacturer of your computer system plays a significant role in building a new CP/M system. Several of CP/M's utility programs may be modified by manufacturers to adapt them to individual computer systems. Unfortunately, not all manufacturers customize these programs. You should therefore invest some time in studying the documentation provided with your system to see what and how much customizing may have already been done. You should also assemble and print out listings of all assembly language source files from your CP/M release diskette.

It is impossible to predict the details of customization and special procedures that the manufacturer may have installed on your particular system. Therefore, this chapter describes first the overall mechanism of building a CP/M system, and second the details of building a CP/M system around the example BIOS shown in the previous chapter as Figure 6-4.

The Major Steps

Building a new CP/M system consists of the following major steps:

- Create a new or modified BIOS with the appropriate device drivers in it. Assemble this so that it will execute at the top end of memory (by using an *origin* statement (ORG) to set the location counter).

- Create new versions of the CCP and BDOS with all addresses in the instructions changed so that they will be correctly located in memory just below the new BIOS. Digital Research provides a special utility called MOVCPM to do this.

- Create or modify a CP/M bootstrap loader that will be loaded by the firmware that executes when you first switch on your computer (or press the RESET button). Normally, the CP/M bootstrap loader executes in the low-address end of memory. The exact address and the details of any hardware initialization that it must perform will depend entirely on your particular computer system.

- Using Digital Research standard utility programs, bring the bootstrap loader, the CCP and BDOS, and the BIOS together in the low part of memory. Then write this new version of CP/M onto a disk in the appropriate places. Again, depending on the design of your computer system, you may be able to use the standard utility program, SYSGEN, to write the entire CP/M *image* onto disk. Otherwise you may have to write a special program to do this.

When CP/M is already running on your computer system and you want to add new features to the BIOS, all you need to do is change the BIOS and rebuild the system. The CCP and BDOS will need to be moved down in memory if the changes expand the BIOS significantly. If this happens, you will have to make minor changes in the bootstrap loader so that it reads the new CP/M image into memory at a lower address and transfers control to the correct location (the first instruction of the BIOS jump vector).

Building Your First System

The first time that you build CP/M, it is a good idea to make no changes to the BIOS at all. Simply reassemble the BIOS source code and proceed with the system build. Then, if the new system does not run, you know that it must be something in the procedure you used rather than any new features or modification to the BIOS source code. Changes in the BIOS could easily obscure any problems you have with the build procedure itself.

The Ingredients

To build CP/M, you will need the following files and utility programs:

- The assembly language source code for your BIOS. Check your CP/M release diskette for a file with a name like CBIOS.ASM (Customized Basic Input/Output System). Some manufacturers do not supply you with the source code for their BIOS; it may be sold separately or not released at all. If you cannot get hold of the source code, the only way that you can add new features to the BIOS is by writing the entire BIOS from scratch.

- The source code for the CP/M bootstrap loader. This too may be on the release diskette or available separately from your computer's manufacturer.

- The Digital Research assembler, which converts source code into machine language in hexadecimal form. This program, called ASM.COM, will be on your CP/M release diskette. Equivalent assemblers, such as Digital Research's macro-assemblers MAC and RMAC or Microsoft's M80, can also be used.

- The Digital Research utility called MOVCPM, which prepares a memory image of the CCP and BDOS with all addresses adjusted to the right values.

- The Digital Research debugging utility, called DDT (Dynamic Debugging Tool), or the more enhanced version for the Z80 CPU chip, ZSID (Z80 Symbolic Interactive Debugger). DDT is used to read in the various program files and piece together a memory image of the CP/M system.

- The Digital Research utility program SYSGEN. This writes the composite memory image of the bootstrap, CCP, BDOS, and BIOS onto the disk. SYSGEN was designed to work on floppy disk systems. If your computer uses a hard disk, you may have a program with a name like PUTCPM or WRITECPM that performs the same function.

The Ultimate Goal

In Figure 6-4, lines 0044 to 0065, you can see the equates that define the base addresses for the CCP, the BDOS, and the BIOS. Figure 7-1 shows how the top of memory will look when this version of CP/M has been loaded into memory.

Life would be simple if you could build this image in memory at the addresses shown and write the image out to disk. Building this image, however, would probably overwrite the version of CP/M that you were operating since it too lives at the top of memory. Therefore, the goal is to create a replica of this image lower down in memory, but with all the instruction addresses set to *execute* at the addresses shown in Figure 7-1.

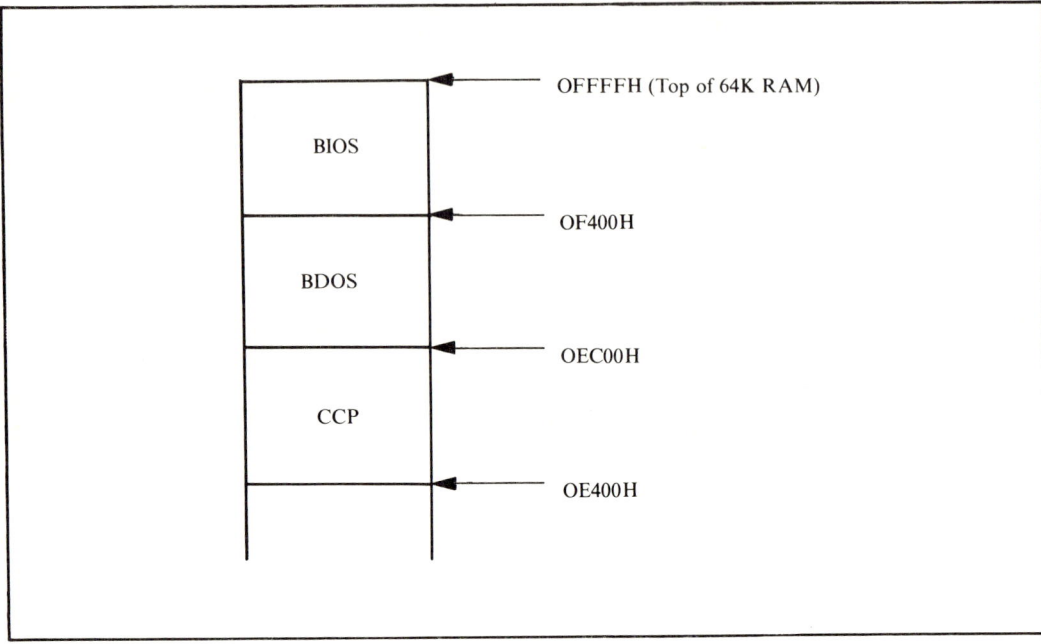

Figure 7-1.   Memory layout of CP/M

Using SYSGEN to Write CP/M to Disk

The SYSGEN utility writes a memory image onto a specified logical disk. It can use a memory image that you arrange to be in memory before you invoke SYSGEN, or you can direct SYSGEN to read in a disk file that contains the image. You can also use SYSGEN to transport an existing CP/M system from one diskette to another by directing it to load the CP/M image from one diskette into memory and then to write that image out to another diskette.

Check the documentation supplied by your computer's manufacturer to make sure that you can use SYSGEN on your system. SYSGEN, as released by Digital Research, is constructed to run on 8-inch, single-sided, single-density diskettes. If your system does not use these standard diskettes, SYSGEN must be customized to your disk system.

When SYSGEN loads a CP/M image into memory, it will place the bootstrap, CCP, BDOS, and BIOS at the predetermined addresses shown in Figure 7-2, regardless of where this CP/M originated.

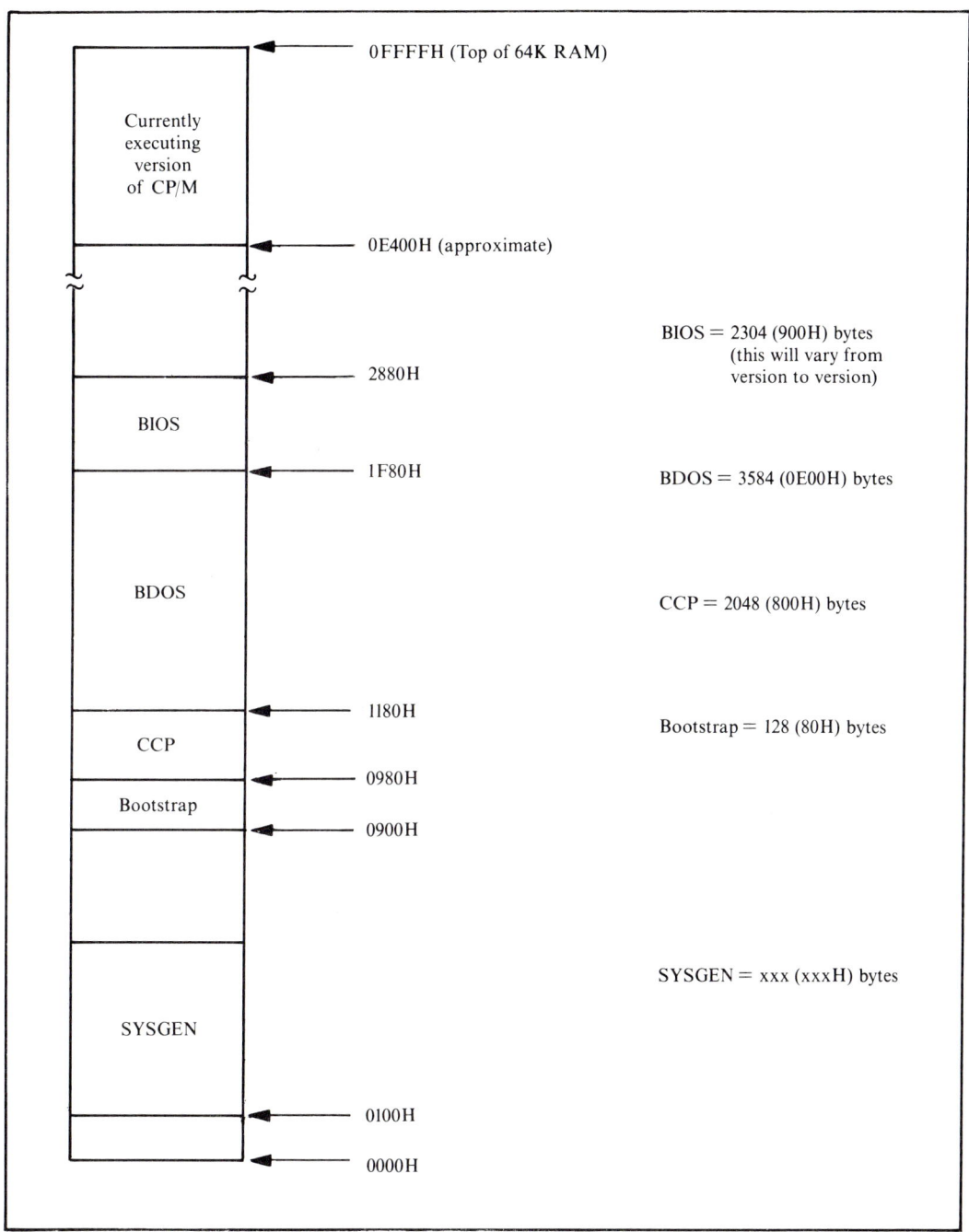

Figure 7-2. SYSGEN's memory layout

You can see that the *relative* arrangement between the components has not changed; the whole image has simply been moved down in memory well below the currently executing version of CP/M. The bootstrap has been added to the picture just beneath the CCP.

The SYSGEN utility writes this image onto a floppy diskette starting at sector 1 of track 0 and continuing to sector 26 on track 1. Refer back to Figure 2-2 to see the layout of CP/M on a standard 8-inch, single-sided, single-density diskette.

If you request SYSGEN to read the memory image from a file (which you do by calling SYSGEN with the file name on the same line as the SYSGEN call), then SYSGEN presumes that you have previously created the correct memory image and saved it (with the SAVE command). SYSGEN then skips over the first 16 sectors of the file so as to avoid overwriting itself.

Here is an example of how to use SYSGEN to move the CP/M image from one diskette to another:

```
A>SYSGEN<CR>
SYSGEN VER 2.0
SOURCE DRIVE NAME (OR RETURN TO SKIP) A
SOURCE ON A:, THEN TYPE RETURN <cr>
FUNCTION COMPLETE
DESTINATION DRIVE NAME (OR RETURN TO REBOOT) B
DESTINATION ON B: THEN TYPE RETURN <cr>
FUNCTION COMPLETE
DESTINATION DRIVE NAME (OR RETURN TO REBOOT) <cr>
A>_
```

As you can see, SYSGEN gives you the choice of specifying the source drive name or typing CARRIAGE RETURN. If you enter a CARRIAGE RETURN, SYSGEN assumes that the CP/M image is already in memory. Note that you need to call up SYSGEN only once to write out the same CP/M image to more than one disk.

A larger than standard BIOS can cause difficulties in using SYSGEN. The standard SYSGEN format only allows for six 128-byte sectors to contain the BIOS, so if your BIOS is larger than 768 (300H) bytes, it will be a problem. The CP/M image will not fit on the first two tracks of a standard 8-inch diskette.

Nowadays it is rare to find an 8-inch floppy diskette system where you must load CP/M from a single-sided, single-density diskette. Most systems now use double-sided or double-density diskettes as the normal format, but can switch to single-sided, single-density diskettes to interchange information with other computer systems.

Because there is no "standard" format for 8-inch, double-sided and double-density diskettes, you probably won't be able to read diskettes written on systems of a different make or model. Therefore, you need only be concerned about using a disk layout that will keep your disks compatible with other machines that are exactly the same as yours.

This is also true if you have 5 1/4-inch diskettes. There is no industry standard for these either, so your main consideration is to place the file directory in the same place as it will be on diskettes written by other users of your model of computer. You must also be sure to use the same sector skewing. Otherwise, you will get a garbled version whenever you try to read files originating on other systems.

With the higher capacity diskettes, you can reserve more space to hold the CP/M image on the diskette. For example, in the case of the BIOS shown in Figure 6-4, the CP/M image is written to a 5 1/4-inch, double-sided, double-density diskette using 512-byte sectors. Figure 7-3 shows the layout of this diskette. Note that the bootstrap loader is placed in a 512-byte sector all by itself. Doing so makes the bootstrap code and warm boot code in the BIOS much simpler.

The memory image must be altered to reflect the fact that the bootstrap now occupies an entire 512-byte sector. Rather than change all of the addresses, the bootstrap is loaded into memory 384 (180H) bytes lower, so that it ends at the same address as before. Figure 7-4 shows the revised memory image.

Writing a PUTCPM Utility

Because the example system uses 5 1/4-inch floppy diskettes with 512-byte sectors, the standard version of SYSGEN cannot be used to write the CP/M image onto a diskette. You will have to use a functional replacement provided by your computer's manufacturer or develop a small utility program to do the job.

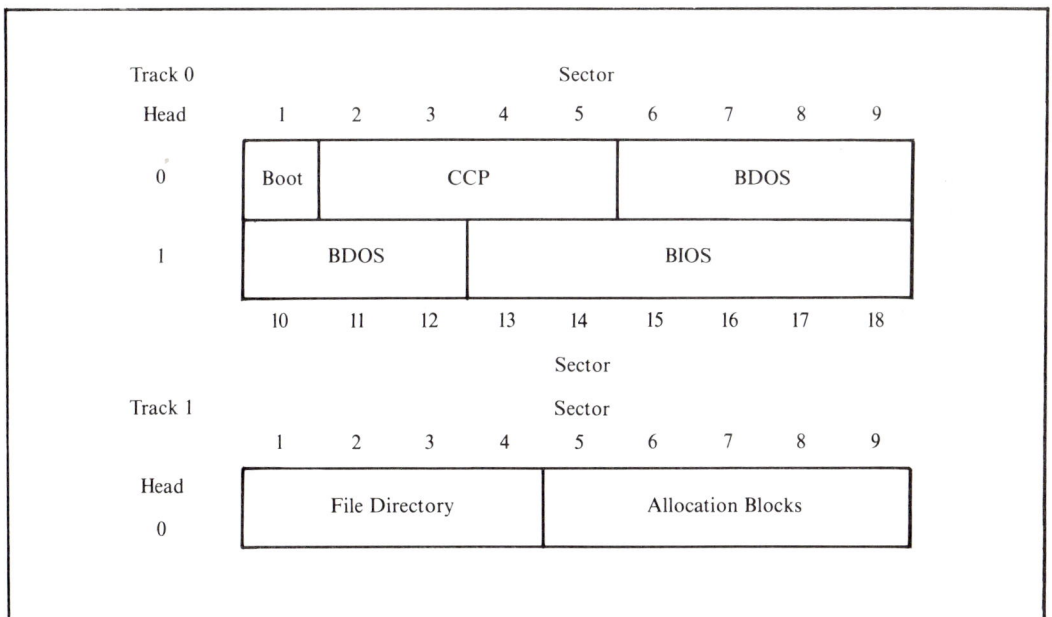

Figure 7-3. Disk layout for example BIOS on 5 1/4-inch diskettes

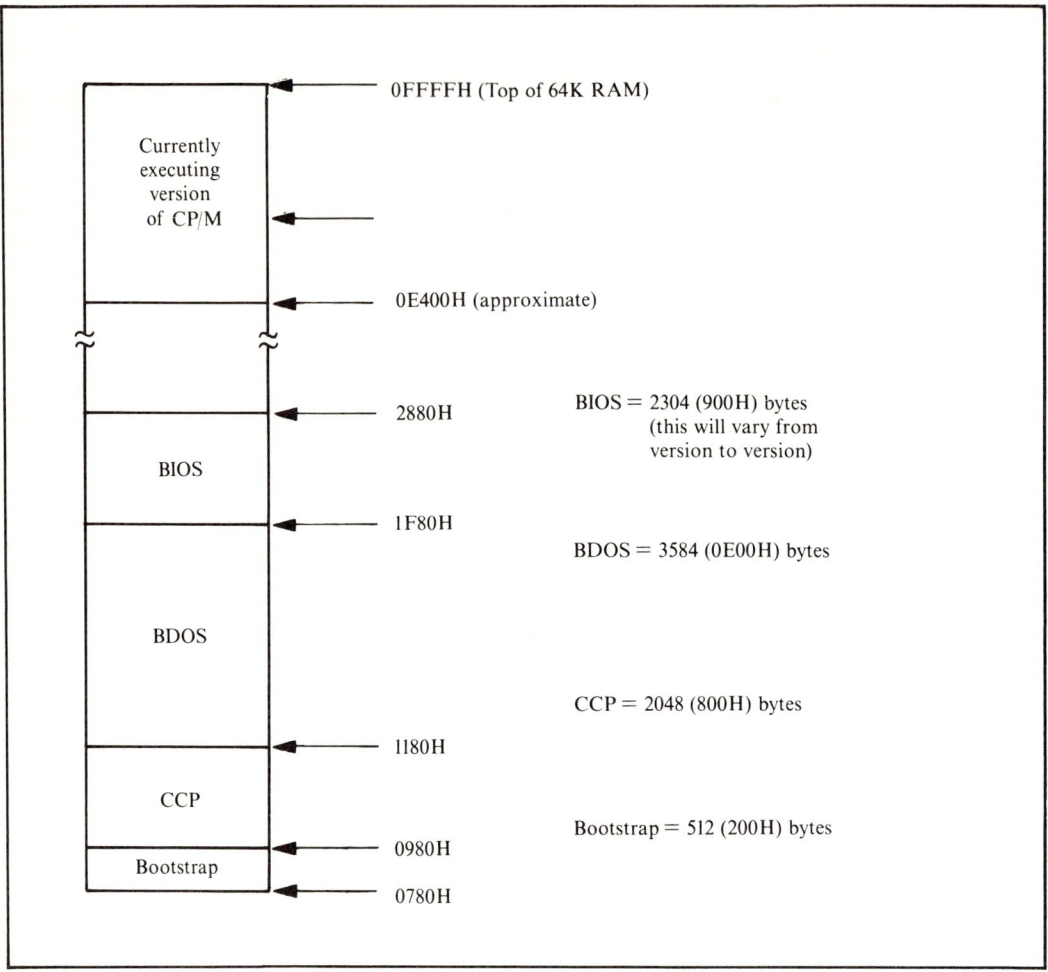

Figure 7-4. Addresses for example BIOS image

Figure 7-5 shows an example of such a program. It is written in a general-purpose way, so that you may be able to use it for your system by changing the equates at the front of the program to reflect the specifics of your disk drives.

Note that there are two problems to be solved. First, the area of the disk on which the CP/M image resides cannot be accessed by the BDOS, as it is outside the file system area on the disk. Second, it is rare to write the CP/M image onto the disk with any kind of sector skewing; to do so would slow down the loading process. In any case, skewing would be redundant, since the loader is doing no processing other than reading the disk and can therefore read the disk without skewing.

```
                ;       This program writes out the CP/M cold boot loader,
                ;       CCP, BDOS, and BIOS to a floppy diskette. It runs
                ;       under CP/M as a normal transient program.
                ;
3130 =          Version         EQU     '01'    ;Equates used in the sign-on
                                                ; message
3730 =          Month           EQU     '07'
3432 =          Day             EQU     '24'
3238 =          Year            EQU     '82'
                ;
                ;
                ;       The actual PUTCPMF5.COM program consists of this code,
                ;       plus the BOOTF5.HEX, CCP, BDOS, and BIOS.
                ;
                ;       When this program executes, the memory image should
                ;       look like this:
                ;
                ;               Component       Base Address
                ;               BIOS            1F80H
                ;               BDOS            1180H
                ;               CCP             0980H
                ;               BOOTF5          0780H
                ;
                ;       The components are produced as follows:
                ;
                ;               BIOS.HEX        By assembling source code
                ;               BDOS  )         From a CPMnn.COM file output
                ;               CCP   )           by MOVCPM and SAVEd on disk
                ;               BOOTF5.HEX      By assembling source code
                ;
                ;       The components are pieced together using DDT with the
                ;       following commands:
                ;
                ;               DDT CPMnn.COM
                ;               IPUTCPMF5.HEX
                ;               R                       (Reads in this program)
                ;               IBOOTF5.HEX
                ;               R680                    (Reads in BOOT at 0780H)
                ;               IBIOS.HEX
                ;               R2980                   (Reads in BIOS at 1F80H)
                ;               GO                      (Exit from DDT)
                ;               SAVE 40 PUTCPMF5.COM    (Create final .COM file)
                ;
                ;       The actual layout of the diskette is as follows:
                ;
                ; Track 0
                ;                       Sector
                ;               1     2     3     4     5     6     7     8     9
                ; Head          +-----+-----+-----+-----+-----+-----+-----+-----+-----+
                ;   0           |Boot |<======= CCP =======>|<======= BDOS =======|
                ;               +-----+-----+-----+-----+-----+-----+-----+-----+-----+
                ;   1           |====== BDOS ====>|<============= BIOS =============>|
                ;               +-----+-----+-----+-----+-----+-----+-----+-----+-----+
                ;              10    11    12    13    14    15    16    17    18
                ;                                       Sector
                ;
                ;       Equates for defining memory size and the base address and
                ;       length of the system components
                ;
0040 =          Memory$Size     EQU     64      ;Number of Kbytes of RAM
                ;
                ;       The BIOS Length must match that declared in the BIOS.
0900 =          BIOS$Length     EQU     0900H
                ;
0200 =          Boot$Length     EQU     512
0800 =          CCP$Length      EQU     0800H   ;Constant
0E00 =          BDOS$Length     EQU     0E00H   ;Constant
                ;
1F00 =          Length$In$Bytes EQU     CCP$Length + BDOS$Length + BIOS$Length
                ;
0780 =          Start$Image     EQU     980H - Boot$Length      ;Address of CP/M image
2100 =          Length$Image    EQU     Length$In$Bytes + Boot$Length
                ;
                ;
```

Figure 7-5.   Example PUTCPM

```
                ;       Disk characteristics
                ;
                ;       These equates describe the physical characteristics of
                ;       the floppy diskette so that the program can move from
                ;       one sector to the next, updating the track and resetting
                ;       the sector when necessary.
                ;
0001 =          First$Sector$on$Track    EQU     1
0012 =          Last$Sector$on$Track     EQU     18
0009 =          Last$Sector$on$Head$0    EQU     9
0200 =          Sector$Size              EQU     512
                ;
                ;       Controller characteristics
                ;
                ;       On this computer system, the floppy disk controller can write
                ;       multiple sectors in a single command. However, in order
                ;       to produce a more general example it is shown only reading one
                ;       sector at a time.
                ;
0001 =          Sectors$Per$Write        EQU     1
                ;
                ;       Cold boot characteristics
                ;
0000 =          Start$Track              EQU     0       ;Initial values for CP/M image
0001 =          Start$Sector             EQU     1       ;= " =
0011 =          Sectors$To$Write         EQU     (Length$Image + Sector$Size - 1) / Sector$Size
                ;


0009 =          B$PRINTS                 EQU     9       ;Print string terminated by $
0005 =          BDOS                     EQU     5       ;BDOS entry point
                ;
                ;
'0100                   ORG     100H
                Put$CPM:
0100 C33F01             JMP     Main$Code       ;Enter main code body
                                                ;For reasons of clarity, the main
                                                ; data structures are shown before the
                                                ; executable code.
000D =          CR      EQU     0DH             ;Carriage return
000A =          LF      EQU     0AH             ;Line feed
                ;
                Signon$Message:
0103 0D0A507574         DB      CR,LF,'Put CP/M on Diskette'
0119 0D0A               DB      CR,LF
011B 5665727369         DB      'Version '
0123 3031               DW      Version
0125 20                 DB      ' '
0126 3037               DW      Month
0128 2F                 DB      '/'
0129 3234               DW      Day
012B 2F                 DB      '/'
012C 3832               DW      Year
012E 0D0A24             DB      CR,LF,'$'

                ;
                ;       Disk control tables
                ;
0045 =          Disk$Control$5    EQU   45H     ;5 1/4" control byte
0046 =          Command$Block$5   EQU   46H     ;Control table pointer
0043 =          Disk$Status       EQU   43H     ;Completion status
                ;
                ;
                ;       The command table track and DMA$Address can also be used
                ;       as working storage and updated as the load process
                ;       continues. The sector in the command table cannot be
                ;       used directly as the disk controller requires it to be
                ;       the sector number on the specified head.(1 -- 9) rather
                ;       than the sector number on track. Hence a separate variable
                ;       must be used.
                ;
```

Figure 7-5.   (Continued)

```
0131 01          Sector:          DB    Start$Sector
                 ;
0132 02          Command$Table:   DB    02H              ;Command -- Write
0133 00          Unit:            DB    0                ;Unit (drive) number = 0 or 1
0134 00          Head:            DB    0                ;Head number = 0 or 1
0135 00          Track:           DB    Start$Track      ;Used as working variable
0136 00          Sector$on$head:  DB    0                ;Converted by low-level driver
0137 0002        Byte$Count:      DW    Sector$Size * Sectors$Per$Write
0139 8007        DMA$Address:     DW    Start$Image
013B 4300        Next$Status:     DW    Disk$Status      ;Pointer to next status block
                                                         ;  if commands are chained
013D 4500        Next$Control:    DW    Disk$Control$5   ;Pointer to next control byte
                                                         ;  if commands are chained
                 Main$Code:
013F 310001              LXI     SP,Put$CPM       ;Stack grows down below code

0142 110301              LXI     D,Signon$Message ;Sign on
0145 0E09                MVI     C,B$PRINTS       ;Print string until $
0147 CD0500              CALL    BDOS

014A 213201              LXI     H,Command$Table  ;Point the disk controller at
014D 224600              SHLD    Command$Block$5  ;  the command block

0150 0E11                MVI     C,Sectors$To$Write ;Set sector count
                 Write$Loop:
0152 CD7C01              CALL    Put$CPM$Write    ;Write data onto diskette
0155 0D                  DCR     C                ;Downdate sector count
0156 CA0000              JZ      0                ;Warm boot

0159 213101              LXI     H,Sector         ;Update sector number
015C 3E01                MVI     A,Sectors$Per$Write ;  by adding on number of sectors
015E 86                  ADD     M                ;  by controller
015F 77                  MOV     M,A              ;Save result
0160 3E13                MVI     A,Last$Sector$On$Track + 1 ;Check if at end of track
0162 BE                  CMP     M
0163 C26F01              JNZ     Not$End$Track

0166 3601                MVI     M,First$Sector$On$Track ;Yes, reset to beginning
0168 2A3501              LHLD    Track            ;Update track number
016B 23                  INX     H
016C 223501              SHLD    Track
                 Not$End$Track:
016F 2A3901              LHLD    DMA$Address      ;Update DMA address
0172 110002              LXI     D,Sector$Size * Sectors$Per$Write
0175 19                  DAD     D
0176 223901              SHLD    DMA$Address
0179 C35201              JMP     Write$Loop       ;Write next block
                 ;
                 Put$CPM$Write:
                                                  ;At this point, the description of the
                                                  ; operation required is in the variables
                                                  ; contained in the command table, along
                                                  ; with the sector variable.
017C C5                  PUSH    B                ;Save sector count in C

                 ;----- Change this routine to match the disk controller in use -----

017D 0600                MVI     B,0              ;Assume head 0
017F 3A3101              LDA     Sector           ;Get requested sector
0182 4F                  MOV     C,A              ;Take a copy of it
0183 FE0A                CPI     Last$Sector$on$Head$0+1 ;Check if on head 1
0185 DA8C01              JC      Head$0           ;No
0188 D609                SUI     Last$Sector$on$Head$0 ;Bias down for head 1
018A 4F                  MOV     C,A              ;Save copy
018B 04                  INR     B                ;Set head 1
                 Head$0:
018C 78                  MOV     A,B
018D 323401              STA     Head             ;Get head
0190 79                  MOV     A,C
0191 323601              STA     Sector$On$Head   ;Get sector
```

Figure 7-5. (Continued)

```
            0194 214500              LXI      H,Disk$Control$5        ;Activate controller
            0197 3680                MVI      M,80H
                              Wait$For$Boot$Complete:
            0199 7E                  MOV      A,M                     ;Get status byte
            019A B7                  ORA      A                       ;Check if complete
            019B C29901              JNZ      Wait$For$Boot$Complete  ;No
                                                                      ;Yes, check for errors
            019E 3A4300              LDA      Disk$Status
            01A1 FE80                CPI      80H
            01A3 DAA801              JC       Put$CPM$Error           ;Yes, an error occurred
                              ;------ End of physical write routine ------
            01A6 C1                  POP      B                       ;Recover sector count in C
            01A7 C9                  RET
                              ;
                              Put$CPM$Error:
            01A8 11B301              LXI      D,Put$CPM$Error$Message
            01AB 0E09                MVI      C,B$PRINTS              ;Print string until $
            01AD CD0500              CALL     BDOS                    ;Output error message
            01B0 C33F01              JMP      Main$Code               ;Restart the loader
                              ;
                              Put$CPM$Error$Message:
            01B3 0D0A457272          DB       CR,LF,'Error in writing CP/M - retrying...',CR,LF,'$'
            01DB                     END      Put$CPM
```

Figure 7-5. (Continued)

Using DDT to Build the CP/M Memory Image

DDT, the Digital Research debug program, is used to read files of type ".COM" and ".HEX" into memory. Understanding the internal structure of these file types is important, both to understand what DDT can do and to understand how the MOVCPM utility can effectively change a machine code file so that it can be executed at a new address in memory.

".COM" File Structure

A COM file is a memory image. It is a replica of the bit patterns that are to be created when the file is loaded into memory. COM files are normally designed to load at location 100H upwards. No internal structure to the file requires this, however, so if you know what the contents of a COM file are, there is nothing to preclude you from loading it into memory starting at some address other than 100H.

As you may recall from the description of the CCP in Chapter 4, the SAVE command built into the CCP allows you to create a COM file by specifying the number of 256-byte "pages" of memory and the name of the file. The CCP will write out an exact image of memory from location 100H up.

".HEX" File Structure

HEX files are output by the assembler. They contain an ASCII character representation of hexadecimal values. For example, the contents of a single byte of memory with the binary value 10101111 would be represented by two ASCII characters, A F, in a HEX file.

The HEX file has a higher level structure than just a series of ASCII characters however. Each line of ASCII characters is terminated by CARRIAGE RETURN/LINE FEED. The overall structure is shown in Figure 7-6.

The most important aspect of a HEX file is that each line contains the address at which the data bytes are loaded. Each line is processed independently, so the load addresses of succeeding lines need not be in order.

DDT can read in a HEX file at an address different from the address where the code must be in order to execute. For example, you can read in the HEX file of the BIOS at the correct place for the memory image (shown in Figure 7-4). There are two ways of using DDT to read in a COM or HEX file. You can specify the name of the file on the same command line with DDT. For example:

```
A>DDT B:XYZ.HEX<cr>     <- Call up DDT with file name
DDT VERS 2.0            <- DDT signs on
NEXT  PC
0180  0100              <- ... and displays next free byte
                           and entry point address
                        <- ... and prompts for a commmand
```

The advantage of this method of loading a file is that you can specify which logical disk is to be searched for the file. The second way of using DDT is to load DDT first, and then, when it has given its prompt, specify the file name and request that DDT load it like this:

```
-Ifilename.typ<cr>      <- Enter the file name and type
-R<cr>                  <- Read in the file
```

The "I" command initializes the default file control block in the base page (at location 005CH) with the file name and type; it does *not* set up the logical disk. If you need to do this, you must set the first byte of the default FCB manually like this:

```
-Ifilename.typ<cr>      <- Specify file name
-S5C<cr>                <- "S"et location 5C
005C 00 02<cr>          <- Was 00, you enter 02<cr>
005D 41 .<cr>           <- Enter "." to terminate
-R<cr>                  <- Read in the file
```

Location 005CH should be set to 01H for Drive A, 02H for B, and so on.

The "R" command will read in HEX files to the *execution* addresses specified in each line of the HEX file, so be careful—if you forget to put an ORG (origin)

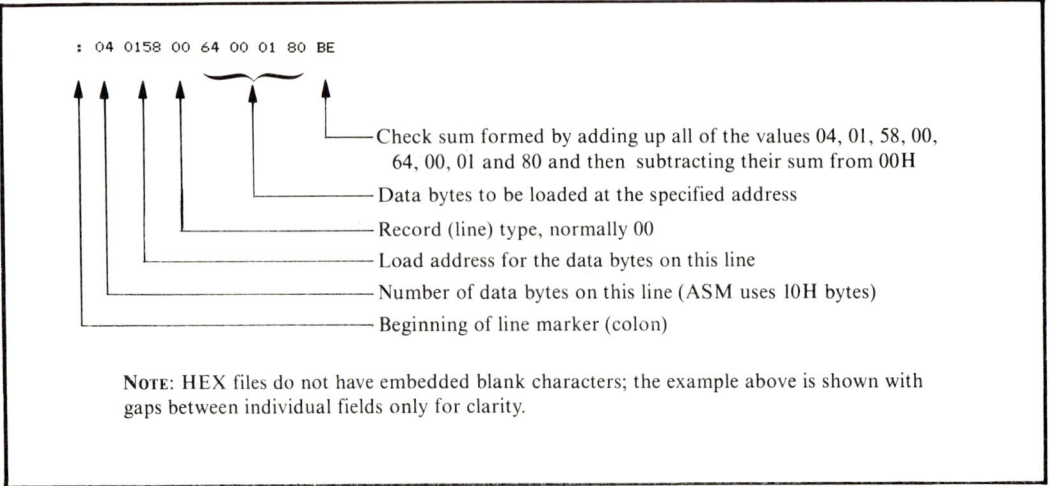

Figure 7-6. Example line from HEX file

statement at the front of the assembly language source code, reading in the resultant HEX file will overwrite location 0000H on up, destroying the contents of the base page. Similarly, if you were trying to read in the HEX file for a BIOS, there is an excellent chance that you will overwrite the currently executing CP/M system.

DDT reacts to the file type you enter as part of the file name. For file types other than .HEX, DDT loads the file starting at location 0100H on up.

The "R" command can also be used to read files into memory at different addresses. You do this by typing a hexadecimal number immediately after the R, with no intervening punctuation. For HEX files, the number that you enter is added to the address in each line of the HEX file and the sum is used as the address into which the data bytes are loaded. The data bytes themselves are not changed, just the load address.

For COM files, the number that you enter is added to 0100H and the sum is used as the starting address for loading the file.

The sum is performed as 16-bit, unsigned arithmetic with any carry ignored, so you can load a BIOS HEX file into low memory by using the "R" command with what is called an "offset value."

If a HEX file has been assembled to execute at address "exec," and you need to use DDT to read in this file to address "load," you need to solve the following equation:

offset = load − exec.

DDT's "H" command performs hexadecimal arithmetic. It calculates and displays the sum of and difference between two hexadecimal values. For example,

Chapter 7: Building a New CP/M System   **197**

the BIOS in Figure 6-4 has been assembled to *execute* at location 0F600H, but needs to be *loaded* into memory at location 1F80H. Here is how to compute the correct offset for the "R" command:

```
-H1F80,F600<cr>          <- Use the H command
1580,2980                <- Sum, difference
```

Thus, to read in the BIOS HEX file called FIG6-4.HEX at location 1F80H, you would enter the following commands to DDT:

```
-IFIG6-4.HEX<cr>         <- Specify file name and type
-R2980<cr>               <- Load at 0F600H + 2980H (= 1F80H)
```

In this way, using DDT, you can read in the HEX files for both the BIOS and the bootstrap loader.

The CP/M Bootstrap Loader

The bootstrap loader is brought into memory by PROM-based firmware in the computer system. It loads in the CCP, BDOS, and BIOS and then transfers control to the cold boot entry point in the BIOS—the first jump instruction in the BIOS jump vector.

The bootstrap loader is a stand-alone program; it cannot make use of any CP/M functions because no part of CP/M is in memory when the bootstrap loader is needed. The firmware in the PROM that loaded the bootstrap may contain some subroutines that can be used by the bootstrap, but this will vary from system to system.

Figure 7-7 shows the bootstrap code for the example BIOS (from Figure 6-4). This code has been written in a general way, so that you can adapt it to your system. The disk controller on the example system can in fact read in multiple sectors from the disk, but for generality the code shown reads in only one sector at a time. This considerably increases the time it takes to load CP/M, but does make the bootstrap loader more general.

Note that almost the first thing that the bootstrap does is to output to the console a sign-on message. Not only does this confirm the version number, but it shows that the bootstrap has been successfully loaded.

The PROM-based code has been designed to load the CP/M bootstrap into location 100H, allowing the code to be debugged as though it were a normal transient program, albeit with minor changes to the address at which it loads the CP/M image from disk. Clearly, this feature is not very helpful if CP/M is being brought up for the first time on a computer system. It helps a great deal, however, if you need to modify the bootstrap or add the capability to boot your system from a new type of disk drive.

```
                ;       Example CP/M cold bootstrap loader
                ;
                ;       This program is written out to track 0, head 0, sector 1
                ;       by the PUTCPMF5 program.
                ;       It is loaded into memory at location 100H on up by the
                ;       PROM-based bootstrap mechanism that gets control of the
                ;       CPU on power up or system reset.
                ;
3130 =          Version         EQU     '01'    ;Equates used in the sign-on message
3730 =          Month           EQU     '07'
3432 =          Day             EQU     '24'
3238 =          Year            EQU     '82'
                ;
0000 =          Debug           EQU     0       ;Set nonzero to debug as normal
                                                ; transient program
                ;
                ;       The actual layout of the diskette is as follows :
                ;
                ; Track 0                       Sector
                ;            1     2     3     4     5     6     7     8     9
                ; Head     +-----+-----+-----+-----+-----+-----+-----+-----+-----+
                ;   0      |Boot |<======= CCP =======>|<======= BDOS =======>|
                ;          +-----+-----+-----+-----+-----+-----+-----+-----+-----+
                ;   1      |====== BDOS ====>|<============= BIOS ===========>|
                ;          +-----+-----+-----+-----+-----+-----+-----+-----+-----+
                ;           10    11    12    13    14    15    16    17    18
                ;                                Sector
                ;
                ;       Equates for defining memory size and the base address and
                ;       length of the system components.
                ;
0040 =          Memory$Size     EQU     64      ;Number of Kbytes of RAM
                ;
                ;       The BIOS Length must match that declared in the BIOS.
                ;
0900 =          BIOS$Length     EQU     0900H
                ;
0800 =          CCP$Length      EQU     0800H   ;Constant
0E00 =          BDOS$Length     EQU     0E00H   ;Constant
                ;
0008 =          Length$In$K     EQU     ((CCP$Length + BDOS$Length + BIOS$Length) / 1024) + 1
1F00 =          Length$In$Bytes EQU     CCP$Length + BDOS$Length + BIOS$Length
                ;
                        IF              NOT Debug
E000 =          CCP$Entry       EQU     (Memory$Size - Length$In$K) * 1024
                        ENDIF
                        IF      Debug
                CCP$Entry       EQU     3980H   ;Read into a lower address.
                                                ;This address is chosen to be above
                                                ; the area into which DDT initially loads
                                                ; and the 980H makes the addresses similar
                                                ; to the SYSGEN values so that the memory
                                                ; image can be checked with DDT.
                        ENDIF
                ;
E806 =          BDOS$Entry      EQU     CCP$Entry + CCP$Length + 6
F600 =          BIOS$Entry      EQU     CCP$Entry + CCP$Length + BDOS$Length
                ;
                ;       Disk characteristics
                ;
                ;       These equates describe the physical characteristics of
                ;       the floppy diskette so that the program can move from
                ;       one sector to the next, updating the track and resetting
                ;       the sector when necessary.
                ;
0001 =          First$Sector$on$Track   EQU     1
0012 =          Last$Sector$on$Track    EQU     18
0009 =          Last$Sector$on$Head$0   EQU     9
0200 =          Sector$Size             EQU     512
                ;
                ;       Controller characteristics
                ;
```

Figure 7-7. Example CP/M cold bootstrap loader

Chapter 7: Building a New CP/M System

```
                        ;       On this computer system, the floppy disk controller can read
                        ;       multiple sectors in a single command. However, in order to
                        ;       produce a more general example it is shown only reading one
                        ;       sector at a time.
                        ;
0001 =                  Sectors$Per$Read        EQU     1
                        ;
                        ;
                        ;       Cold boot characteristics
                        ;
0000 =                  Start$Track             EQU     0               ;Initial values for CP/M image
0002 =                  Start$Sector            EQU     2               ;= " =
0010 =                  Sectors$To$Read         EQU     (Length$In$Bytes + Sector$Size - 1) / Sector$Size
                        ;
                        ;
                        ;
0100                            ORG     100H
                        Cold$Boot$Loader:
0100 C34001                     JMP     Main$Code               ;Enter main code body
                                                                ;For reasons of clarity, the main
                                                                ; data structures are shown before the
                                                                ; executable code.
000D =                  CR      EQU     0DH                     ;Carriage return
000A =                  LF      EQU     0AH                     ;Line feed
                        ;
                        Signon$Message:
0103 0D0A43502F                 DB      CR,LF,'CP/M Bootstrap Loader'
                                IF      Debug
                                DB      ' (Debug)'
                                ENDIF
011A 0D0A                       DB      CR,LF
011C 5665727369                 DB      'Version '
0124 3031                       DW      Version
0126 20                         DB      ' '
0127 3037                       DW      Month
0129 2F                         DB      '/'
012A 3234                       DW      Day
012C 2F                         DB      '/'
012D 3832                       DW      Year
012F 0D0A00                     DB      CR,LF,0

                        ;
                        ;       Disk Control Tables
                        ;
0045 =                  Disk$Control$5  EQU     45H             ;5 1/4" control byte
0046 =                  Command$Block$5 EQU     46H             ;Control table pointer
0043 =                  Disk$Status     EQU     43H             ;Completion status
                        ;
                        ;
                        ;       The command table track and DMA$Address can also be used
                        ;       as working storage and updated as the load process
                        ;       continues. The sector in the command table cannot be
                        ;       used directly as the disk controller requires it to be
                        ;       the sector number on the specified head (1 -- 9) rather
                        ;       than the sector number on track. Hence a separate variable
                        ;       must be used.
                        ;
0132 02                 Sector:         DB      Start$Sector
                        ;
0133 01                 Command$Table:  DB      01H             ;Command -- read
0134 00                 Unit:           DB      0               ;Unit (drive) number = 0 or 1
0135 00                 Head:           DB      0               ;Head number = 0 or 1
0136 00                 Track:          DB      Start$Track     ;Used as working variable
0137 00                 Sector$on$head: DB      0               ;Converted by low-level driver
0138 0002               Byte$Count:     DW      Sector$Size * Sectors$Per$Read
013A 00E0               DMA$Address:    DW      CCP$Entry
013C 4300               Next$Status:    DW      Disk$Status     ;Pointer to next status block
                                                                ; if commands are chained.
013E 4500               Next$Control:   DW      Disk$Control$5  ;Pointer to next control byte
                                                                ; if commands are chained.

                        Main$Code:
0140 310001                     LXI     SP,Cold$Boot$Loader     ;Stack grows down below code
```

Figure 7-7. (Continued)

```
0143 210301            LXI     H,Signon$Message        ;Sign on
0146 CDD901            CALL    Display$Message

0149 213301            LXI     H,Command$Table         ;Point the disk controller at
014C 224600            SHLD    Command$Block$5         ;  the command block

014F 0E10              MVI     C,Sectors$To$Read       ;Set sector count
               Load$Loop:
0151 CD7B01            CALL    Cold$Boot$Read          ;Read data into memory
0154 0D                DCR     C                       ;Downdate sector count
                       IF      NOT Debug
0155 CA00F6            JZ      BIOS$Entry              ;Enter BIOS when load done
                       ENDIF
                       IF      Debug
                       JZ      0                       ;Warm boot
                       ENDIF

0158 213201            LXI     H,Sector                ;Update sector number
015B 3E01              MVI     A,Sectors$Per$Read      ;  by adding on number of sectors
015D 86                ADD     M                       ;  by controller
015E 77                MOV     M,A                     ;Save result
015F 3E13              MVI     A,Last$Sector$On$Track + 1  ;Check if at end of track
0161 BE                CMP     M
0162 C26E01            JNZ     Not$End$Track

0165 3601              MVI     M,First$Sector$On$Track ;Yes, reset to beginning
0167 2A3601            LHLD    Track                   ;Update track number
016A 23                INX     H
016B 223601            SHLD    Track
               Not$End$Track:
016E 2A3A01            LHLD    DMA$Address             ;Update DMA Address
0171 110002            LXI     D,Sector$Size * Sectors$Per$Read
0174 19                DAD     D
0175 223A01            SHLD    DMA$Address
0178 C35101            JMP     Load$Loop               ;Read next block
               ;
               Cold$Boot$Read:                         ;At this point, the description of the
                                                       ; operation required is in the variables
                                                       ; contained in the command table, along
                                                       ; with the sector variable.

017B C5                PUSH    B                       ;Save sector count in C
               ;------ Change this routine to match the disk controller in use ------

017C 0600              MVI     B,0                     ;Assume head 0
017E 3A3201            LDA     Sector                  ;Get requested sector
0181 4F                MOV     C,A                     ;Take a copy of it
0182 FE0A              CPI     Last$Sector$on$Head$0+1 ;Check if on head 1
0184 DA8B01            JC      Head$0                  ;No
0187 D609              SUI     Last$Sector$on$Head$0   ;Bias down for head 1
0189 4F                MOV     C,A                     ;Save copy
018A 04                INR     B                       ;Set head 1
               Head$0:
018B 78                MOV     A,B                     ;Get head
018C 323501            STA     Head
018F 79                MOV     A,C                     ;Get sector
0190 323701            STA     Sector$On$Head

0193 214500            LXI     H,Disk$Control$5        ;Activate controller
0196 3680              MVI     M,80H

               Wait$For$Boot$Complete:
0198 7E                MOV     A,M                     ;Get status byte
0199 B7                ORA     A                       ;Check if complete
019A C29801            JNZ     Wait$For$Boot$Complete  ;No
                                                       ;Yes, check for errors
019D 3A4300            LDA     Disk$Status
01A0 FE80              CPI     80H
01A2 DAA701            JC      Cold$Boot$Error         ;Yes, an error occurred

               ;------ End of physical read routine ------
```

Figure 7-7.   (Continued)

```
                01A5 C1                 POP     B                       ;Recover sector count in C
                01A6 C9                 RET
                                ;
                                        Cold$Boot$Error:
                01A7 21B001             LXI     H,Cold$Boot$Error$Message
                01AA CDD901             CALL    Display$Message         ;Output error message
                01AD C34001             JMP     Main$Code               ;Restart the loader
                                ;
                                        Cold$Boot$Error$Message:
                01B0 0D0A426F6F         DB      CR,LF,'Bootstrap Loader Error - retrying...',CR,LF,0
                                ;
                                ;       Equates for Terminal Output
                                ;
                0001 =                  Terminal$Status$Port    EQU     01H
                0002 =                  Terminal$Data$Port      EQU     02H
                                ;
                0001 =                  Terminal$Output$Ready   EQU     0000$0001B
                                ;
                                ;
                                        Display$Message:        ;Displays the specified message on the console.
                                                                ;On entry, HL points to a stream of bytes to be
                                                                ;output. A 00H-byte terminates the message.
                01D9 7E                 MOV     A,M             ;Get next message byte
                01DA B7                 ORA     A               ;Check if terminator
                01DB C8                 RZ                      ;Yes, return to caller
                01DC 4F                 MOV     C,A             ;Prepare for output
                                        Output$Not$Ready:
                01DD DB01               IN      Terminal$Status$Port    ;Check if ready for output
                01DF E601               ANI     Terminal$Output$Ready
                01E1 CADD01             JZ      Output$Not$Ready        ;No, wait
                01E4 79                 MOV     A,C                     ;Get data character
                01E5 D302               OUT     Terminal$Data$Port      ;Output to screen

                01E7 23                 INX     H                       ;Move to next byte of message
                01E8 C3D901             JMP     Display$Message ;Loop until complete message output

                                                                ;The PROM-based bootstrap loader checks
                                                                ; to see that the characters "CP/M"
                                                                ; are on the diskette bootstrap sector
                                                                ; before it transfers control to it.
                02E0                    ORG     2E0H
                02E0 43502F4D           DB      'CP/M'
                02E4                    END     Cold$Boot$Loader
```

Figure 7-7. (Continued)

In this case, the bootstrap code must be loaded at location 0780H, not the normal 0980H, because the bootstrap takes a complete 512-byte sector (200H). The same principle applies in determining the offset value to be used with DDT's "R" command to read the bootstrap HEX file, namely:

offset = load address − execution address.

In this case, the values are the following:

0680H = 0780H − 0100H

Using MOVCPM to Relocate the CCP and BDOS

MOVCPM builds a CP/M memory image at the correct locations for SYSGEN, but with the instructions modified to execute at a specific address. Inside MOVCPM is not only a complete replica of CP/M, but also enough information to tell MOVCPM which bytes of which instructions need be changed whenever the execution address of the image needs to be moved.

MOVCPM, as released from Digital Research, contains the bootstrap and BIOS for an Intel MDS-800 computer along with the generic CCP and BDOS. Unless you have an MDS-800, all you use is the CCP and BDOS. Some manufacturers have customized MOVCPM to include the correct bootstrap and BIOS for their own computers; consult their documentation to see if this applies to your computer system.

When you invoke MOVCPM, you have the following options:

- MOVCPM<cr>
  MOVCPM will relocate its built-in copy of CP/M to the top of available memory and will then transfer control to this new image of CP/M. Unless your manufacturer has included the correct BIOS into MOVCPM, using this option will cause an immediate system crash.

- MOVCPM nn<cr>
  This is similar to the option above, except that MOVCPM assumes that *nn*K bytes of memory are available and will relocate the CP/M image to the top of that before transferring control. Again, this will crash the system unless the correct BIOS has been installed into MOVCPM.

- MOVCPM * *<cr>
  MOVCPM will adjust all of the internal addresses inside the CP/M image so that the image could execute at the top of available memory, but instead of actually putting this image at the top of memory, MOVCPM will leave it in low memory at the correct place for SYSGEN to write it onto a disk. The SAVE command could also preserve the image on a disk.

- MOVCPM *nn* *<cr>
  MOVCPM proceeds as above for the "* *" option except that the CP/M image is modified to execute at the top of *nn*K.

MOVCPM has a fundamental problem. The *nn* value indicates that the top of available memory is computed, assuming that your BIOS is small—less that 890 (380H) bytes. If your BIOS is larger (as is the case with the example in Figure 6-4), then you will have to reduce the value of "*nn*" artificially.

Figure 7-8 shows the relationship between the size of the BIOS and the "*nn*" value to use with MOVCPM. It also shows, for different lengths of BIOS, the BIOS base address, the offset value to be used in DDT to read in the BIOS to location 1F80H (preparatory to using SYSGEN or PUTCPM to write it out), and also the base addresses for the CCP and the BDOS. The base address of the BDOS indicates how much memory is available for loading transient programs, as the CCP can be overwritten if necessary.

The numbers in Figure 7-8 are based on the assumption that you have 64K of memory in your computer system. If this is not the case, then proceed as follows:

Chapter 7: Building a New CP/M System **203**

1. Convert the amount of memory in your system to hex. Remember that 1K is 1024 bytes.
2. Determine the length of your BIOS in hex.
3. Locate the line in Figure 7-8 that shows a BIOS length equal to or greater than the length of your BIOS.
4. Using the "H" command in DDT, compute the BIOS Base Address using the formula:

    Memory in system — BIOS length from Figure 7-8

5. Find the line in Figure 7-8 that shows the same BIOS Base Address as the result of the computation above. Use this line to derive the other relevant numbers.

It is helpful to use DDT to examine a CP/M image in memory to check that all of the components are correctly placed, and, in the case of the CCP and BDOS, correctly relocated.

Figure 7-9 shows an example console dialog in which DDT is used first to examine the memory image produced by MOVCPM and second to examine the image built into the PUTCPMF utility shown in Figure 7-5.

BIOS Length	BIOS Base	DDT Offset	MOVCPM 'nn'	CCP Base	BDOS Base
600	FA00	2580	64	E400	EC00
A00	F600	2980	63	E000	E800
E00	F200	2D80	62	DC00	E400
1200	EE00	3180	61	D800	E000
1600	EA00	3580	60	D400	DC00
1A00	E600	3980	59	D000	D800
1E00	E200	3D80	58	CC00	D400
2200	DE00	4180	57	C800	D000
2600	DA00	4580	56	C400	CC00
2A00	D600	4980	55	C000	C800
2E00	D200	4D80	54	BC00	C400
3200	CE00	5180	53	B800	C000
3600	CA00	5580	52	B400	BC00
3A00	C600	5980	51	B000	B800
3E00	C200	5D80	50	AC00	B400
4200	BE00	6180	49	A800	B000
4600	BA00	6580	48	A400	AC00
4A00	B600	6980	47	A000	A800
4E00	B200	6D80	46	9C00	A400
5200	AE00	7180	45	9800	A000
5600	AA00	7580	44	9400	9C00
5A00	A600	7980	43	9000	9800
5E00	A200	7D80	42	8C00	9400
6200	9E00	8180	41	8800	9000
6600	9A00	8580	40	8400	8C00
6A00	9600	8980	39	8000	8800

Apart from the MOVCPM 'nn' value all other values are in hexadecimal

Figure 7-8. CP/M addresses for different BIOS lengths

204 The CP/M Programmer's Handbook

```
                                    Call up MOVCPM requesting a '63K' system
                                    and the image to be left in memory.
A>Movcpm 63 *<cr>
CONSTRUCTING 63k CP/M vers 2.2
READY FOR "SYSGEN" OR
"SAVE 34 CPM63.COM"
                                    Save the image from location 100H up. By
                                    convention, the file name is CPMnn.COM, so
                                    in this case it will be CPM63.COM
A>Save 34 cpm63.com<cr>
                                    Call up DDT and request that it read in
                                    CPM63.COM
A>ddt cpm63.com<cr>
DDT VERS 2.2
NEXT   PC
2300   0100
                                    Display memory to show the first few bytes of
                                    the CCP. Note the two JMP (C3H) instructions,
                                    followed by 7FH, 00H, 20H's, and the Digital
                                    Research Copyright notice. These identify the
                                    code as being the CCP. Note that the first
                                    JMP instruction is to 35CH into the CCP -- you
                                    can therefore infer the base address of the
                                    CCP. In this case the JMP is to locat;on E35C,
                                    therefore this version of the CCP has been
                                    configured to execute based at E000H.
-d980,9cf<cr>
0980 C3 5C E3 C3 58 E3 7F 00 20 20 20 20 20 20 20 20 .\..X...
0990 20 20 20 20 20 20 20 20 43 4F 50 59 52 49 47 48         COPYRIGH
09A0 54 20 28 43 29 20 31 39 37 39 2C 20 44 49 47 49 T (C) 1979, DIGI
09B0 54 41 4C 20 52 45 53 45 41 52 43 48 20 20 00 00 TAL RESEARCH  ..
09C0 00 00 00 00 00 00 00 00 00 00 00 00 00 00 00 00 ................
                                    Display the first few bytes of the BDOS. Note
                                    the JMP instruction at 1186. This is the
                                    instruction to which control is transferred
                                    by the JMP in location 5.
-d1180,118F<cr>
1180 00 16 00 00 09 85 C3 11 E8 99 E8 A5 E8 AB E8 B1 ................
                                    Displaying further up in the BDOS identifies
                                    it unambiguously -- there are some ASCII error
                                    messages.
-d1230,126f<cr>
1230 E8 21 DC E8 CD E5 E8 C3 00 00 42 64 6F 73 20 45 .!......Bdos E
1240 72 72 20 4F 6E 20 20 3A 20 24 42 61 64 20 53 65 rr On  : $Bad Se
1250 63 74 6F 72 24 53 65 6C 65 63 74 24 46 69 6C 65 ctor$Select$File
1260 20 52 2F 4F 24 20 E5 CD C9 E9 3A 42 EB C6 41 32 C6  R/O$....:B..A2.
                                    Display the first few bytes of the BIOS.
                                    Notice the BIOS JMP vector -- the series of C3H
                                    instructions. Normally the first instruction
                                    in the vector can be used to infer the base
                                    address of the BIOS; in this case it is
                                    F600H. But there is no rule that says that
                                    the cold boot code must be close to the BIOS
                                    JMP vector -- so this is only a rough guide.
-d1f80<cr>
1F80 C3 B3 F6 C3 C3 F6 C3 61 F7 C3 64 F7 C3 6A F7 C3 .......a..d..j..
1F90 6D F7 C3 72 F7 C3 75 F7 C3 78 F7 C3 7D F7 C3 A7 m..r..u..x..}...
1FA0 F7 C3 AC F7 C3 BB F7 C3 C1 F7 C3 CA F7 C3 70 F7 ..............P.
1FB0 C3 B1 F7 82 F6 00 00 00 00 00 00 6E F8 73 F6 0D ...........n.s..
1FC0 F9 EE F8 82 F6 00 00 00 00 00 00 6E F8 73 F6 3C ...........n.s.<
1FD0 F9 1D F9 82 F6 00 00 00 00 00 00 6E F8 73 F6 6B ...........n.s.k
1FE0 F9 4C F9 82 F6 00 00 00 00 00 00 6E F8 73 F6 9A .L.........n.s..
1FF0 F9 7B F9 1A 00 03 07 00 F2 00 3F 00 C0 00 10 00 .{........?.....
2000 02 00 01 07 0D 13 19 05 0B 11 17 03 09 0F 15 02 ................
2010 08 0E 14 1A 06 0C 12 18 04 0A 10 16 0D 0A 0A 36 ...............6
2020 33 6B 20 43 50 2F 4D 20 76 65 72 73 20 32 2E 32 3k CP/M vers 2.2
2030 0D 0A 00 31 00 01 21 9C F6 CD D3 F7 AF 32 04 00 ...1..!......2..
-^C
```

Figure 7-9. Using DDT to check CP/M images

```
                              In contrast, load DDT and request that it
                              load the PUTCPMF5.COM program.
A>ddt putcpmf5.com<cr>
DDT VERS 2.2
NEXT  PC
2900  0100
                              Display the special bootstrap loader that
                              starts at location 0780H (compared to the
                              MDS-800 bootstrap which is at 0980H). Note
                              the sign-on message.
-d780,7af<cr>
0780 C3 40 01 0D 0A 43 50 2F 4D 20 42 6F 6F 74 73 74 .@...CP/M Bootst
0790 72 61 70 20 4C 6F 61 64 65 72 0D 0A 56 65 72 73 rap Loader..Vers
07A0 69 6F 6E 20 30 31 20 30 37 2F 32 34 2F 38 32 0D ion 01 07/24/82.
                              Confirm that the CCP is loaded in the correct
                              place. Check the address of the first JMP
                              instruction (0E35CH).
-d980,9bf<cr>
0980 C3 5C E3 C3 58 E3 7F 00 20 20 20 20 20 20 20 20 .\..X...
0990 20 20 20 20 20 20 20 20 43 4F 50 59 52 49 47 48         COPYRIGH
09A0 54 20 28 43 29 20 31 39 37 39 2C 20 44 49 47 49 T (C) 1979, DIGI
09B0 54 41 4C 20 52 45 53 45 41 52 43 48 20 20 00 00 TAL RESEARCH  ..
                              Confirm that the BDOS is also in place.
-d1180,118f<cr>
1180 00 16 00 00 09 85 C3 11 E8 99 E8 A5 E8 AB E8 B1 ................
                              Confirm that the BIOS has been loaded in the
                              correct place. Check the first JMP to get
                              some idea of the BIOS base address. Note the
                              sign-on message.
-d1f80<cr>
1F80 C3 F9 F6 C3 0C FE C3 62 F8 C3 78 F8 C3 86 F8 C3 .......b..x.....
1F90 A4 F8 C3 B4 F8 C3 C5 F8 C3 B6 FB C3 0E FB C3 3B ...............;
1FA0 FB C3 41 FB C3 48 FB C3 DE FB C3 F8 FB C3 94 F8 ..A..H..........
1FB0 C3 B0 FB ED 06 00 00 00 42 6E 25 DF 01 B6 DE 02 ........Bn%.....
1FC0 38 00 00 43 50 2F 4D 20 32 2E 32 2E 30 30 20 30 8..CP/M 2.2.00 0
1FD0 37 2F 31 35 2F 38 32 0D 0A 0A 53 69 6D 70 6C 65 7/15/82...Simple
1FE0 20 42 49 4F 53 0D 0A 0A 44 69 73 6B 20 43 6F 6E  BIOS...Disk Con
1FF0 66 69 67 75 72 61 74 69 6F 6E 20 3A 0D 0A 0A 20 figuration :...
2000 20 20 20 20 41 3A 20 30 2E 33 35 20 4D 62 79 74     A: 0.35 Mbyt
2010 65 20 35 22 20 46 6C 6F 70 70 79 0D 0A 20 20 20 e 5" Floppy..
2020 20 20 42 3A 20 30 2E 33 35 20 4D 62 79 74 65 20   B: 0.35 Mbyte
2030 35 22 20 46 6C 6F 70 70 79 0D 0A 20 20 20 20 20 5" Floppy...
-^C
A>_
```

Figure 7-9. Using DDT to check CP/M images (continued)

Putting it all Together

Figure 7-10 shows an annotated console dialog for the complete generation of a new CP/M system. Note that the following file names appear in the dialog:

```
BIOS1.ASM       Figure 6-4.
PUTCPMF5.ASM    Figure 7-5.
BOOTF5.ASM      Figure 7-7.
```

```
C>asm bootf5.ccz<cr>                    Assemble the CP/M Bootstrap Loader,
CP/M ASSEMBLER - VER 2.0                with the source code and HEX file
02E4                                    on drive C:, no listing output.
004H USE FACTOR
END OF ASSEMBLY


                                        Assemble the PUTCPMF5 program (that
                                        writes CP/M onto the disk), with
                                        the source code and HEX file on
C>asm putcpmf5.ccz<cr>                  drive C:, no listing output.
CP/M ASSEMBLER - VER 2.0
01DB
003H USE FACTOR
END OF ASSEMBLY

                                        Assemble the BIOS with the source
                                        code and HEX file on drive C:, no
C>asm bios1.ccz<cr>                     listing output.
CP/M ASSEMBLER - VER 2.0
FE6C
011H USE FACTOR
END OF ASSEMBLY

                                        Start piecing the CP/M image
                                        together. Load DDT and ask it to
                                        read in the file previously SAVEd
                                        after a MOVCPM 63 *.
C>ddt cpm63.com<cr>
DDT VERS 2.2
NEXT  PC
2300  0100
                                        Indicate the file name of
                                        PUTCPMF5.HEX, and read in without
                                        any offset (i.e. it will load at
                                        100H because of the ORG 100H it
-r<cr>                                  contains). -iputcpmf5.hex<cr>
NEXT  PC
2300  0100

                                        Indicate the file name of
                                        BOOTF5.HEX and read in with an
                                        offset of 680H to make it load at
                                        780H on up (it contains ORG 100H
-ibootf5.hex<cr>                        too).
-r680<cr>
NEXT  PC
2300  0100

                                        Indicate the file name of the BIOS
                                        HEX file, and read it in with an
                                        offset of 2980 such that it will
                                        load at 1F80H (it contains an ORG
                                        0F600H).
-ibios1.hex<cr>
-r2980<cr>
NEXT  PC
27EC  0000
                                        Exit from DDT by going to location
                                        0000H and executing a warm boot.
-g0<cr>
                                        Save the complete CP/M image on
                                        disk. Saving 40 256-byte pages from
                                        location 100H to 2900H.
C>save 40 putcpmf5.com<cr>
```

Figure 7-10.   Console dialog for system build

Chapter 7: Building a New CP/M System **207**

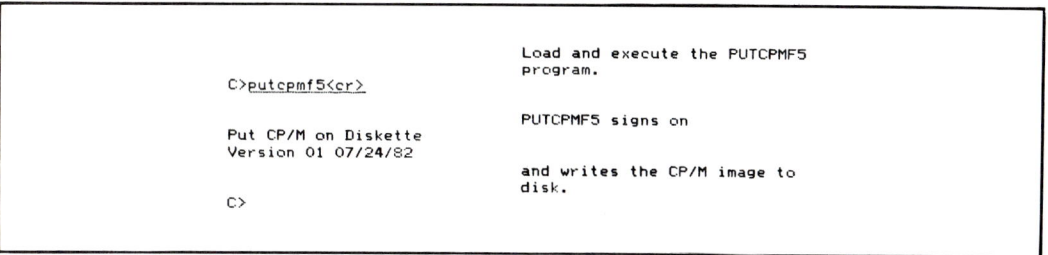

Figure 7-10. Console dialog for system build (continued)

BIOS Enhancements
Character Input/Output
Data Structures
Disk Input/Output
Custom Patches to CP/M
An Enhanced BIOS

Writing An Enhanced BIOS

This chapter describes ways in which you can enhance your BIOS to make CP/M easier to use, faster, and more versatile.

Get a standard BIOS working on your computer system, and then install the additional features. Although you can write an enhanced BIOS from the outset, it will take considerably longer to get it functioning correctly.

A complete listing of an enhanced BIOS is included at the end of this chapter. It is quite large: approximately 4500 lines of source code, with extensive comments and long variable names to make it more understandable.

The sections that follow describe the main concepts embodied in the enhanced BIOS listing.

BIOS Enhancements

BIOS enhancements fall into two classes: those that add new capabilities and those that extend existing features.

Some enhancements are normally accompanied by utility programs that allow you to select the enhancement option from the console. For example, when the BIOS is enhanced to include a *real time clock,* you need a utility program to set the clock to the correct time. Other enhancements will not require supporting utilities. For example, if the disk drivers are improved to read and write data faster, the enhancement is "transparent." As a user, you are aware of the results of the enhancement but not of the enhancement itself.

Viewed at its simplest, the BIOS deals with two broad classes of input/output:

Character input/output
    This includes the console, auxiliary, and list devices.

Disk input/output
    This can accommodate several types of floppy and hard disks.

Enhancements in these areas do not fundamentally change the way that the BDOS and CCP interact with these devices. Instead, enhancements improve the way in which the *device drivers* deal with the devices. They can improve the speed of manipulating data, the way of handling external devices, or the user's control over the behavior of the system.

The example enhanced BIOS has capabilities not found in standard CP/M systems. These can be grouped in several main categories:

Character input/output
    This area probably benefits most from enhancement. This is partly because such a wide range of peripheral devices needs to be supported and partly because this is the most visible area of interaction between you and your computer. Any improvements here will therefore be immediate and obvious to you as a user.

Error handling
    CP/M's error handling is, at best, startling in its simplicity. Enhanced error handling gives you more information about the nature of the failure, and then gives you the options of retrying the operation, ignoring the error, or aborting the program. This topic is covered in detail in Chapter 9.

System date and time
    This is the ability to maintain a time-of-day clock and the current date. It allows your programs to set and access the date and time. In addition, your system can react to the passing of time, and you can move certain operations into the time domain. For example, you can set upper limits on the

number of seconds, or milliseconds, that each operation should take, and arrange for emergency action if the operation takes too long.

Logical-to-physical device assignment
CP/M's logical-to-physical device assignment is primitive. With enhancements, you can use any character input/output device as the system console, and output data to several devices at the same time.

Disk input/output
CP/M only knows about the 128-byte sector. Even with the deblocking routines shown in Figure 6-4, overall disk performance can be slow. Performance can be improved dramatically by "track buffering" (in which entire tracks are read and written at one time) or by using a *memory disk* (that is, using large areas of RAM as though they were a disk). These have a cost, though, in increased memory requirements.

Public files
CP/M's user number system needs improvements to function well in conjunction with large hard disks.

Preserving User-Settable Options

A by-product of adding features to the BIOS is that many of these features have options that you can alter, either from the console using a utility program or from within one of your programs.

Each of these options, once set according to your preferences, or to the requirements of your hardware, do not normally change from day to day. Therefore, the BIOS should be designed so that options set by the user can be "frozen" or preserved on the disk by using a utility program, FREEZE. All of the variables recording these options are gathered into a single area and then this area is written out to the disk.

This area is called the *configuration block*. In practice, there are two configuration blocks: one short term and the other long term. The short term block is not preservable — you can set options within it, but they cannot be preserved after you switch your computer off. The system date, for example, is normally set each time you turn your computer on, and therefore is kept in the short term block. The baud rate for your printer, on the other hand, is kept in the long term block so that it can be saved permanently.

An extra BIOS entry point, CBGetAddress, has been built into the enhanced BIOS so that utility programs can locate variables in both configuration blocks. For example, when a utility needs to know where the date is kept in memory, it calls CBGetAddress using a code number (specific for date) in a register. CBGetAddress returns the address of the date in memory. If a new version of the BIOS is produced with the date in a different location, CBGetAddress will still hand the correct, although different, address back to the utility program.

Two other variables that CBGetAddress can access pertain to the configuration block itself. One is the relative address of the start of the long term configuration block. The other is the length of the long term block. These are used by the FREEZE utility when it needs to preserve the long term block on a disk. FREEZE must (1) read in the sectors containing the long term block from the CP/M BIOS image on the reserved area of the disk, (2) copy the current RAM-resident version of the long term block over the disk image version, and then (3) write the sectors back onto the disk.

Figure 8-1 shows how the long term block appears on disk and in memory. The

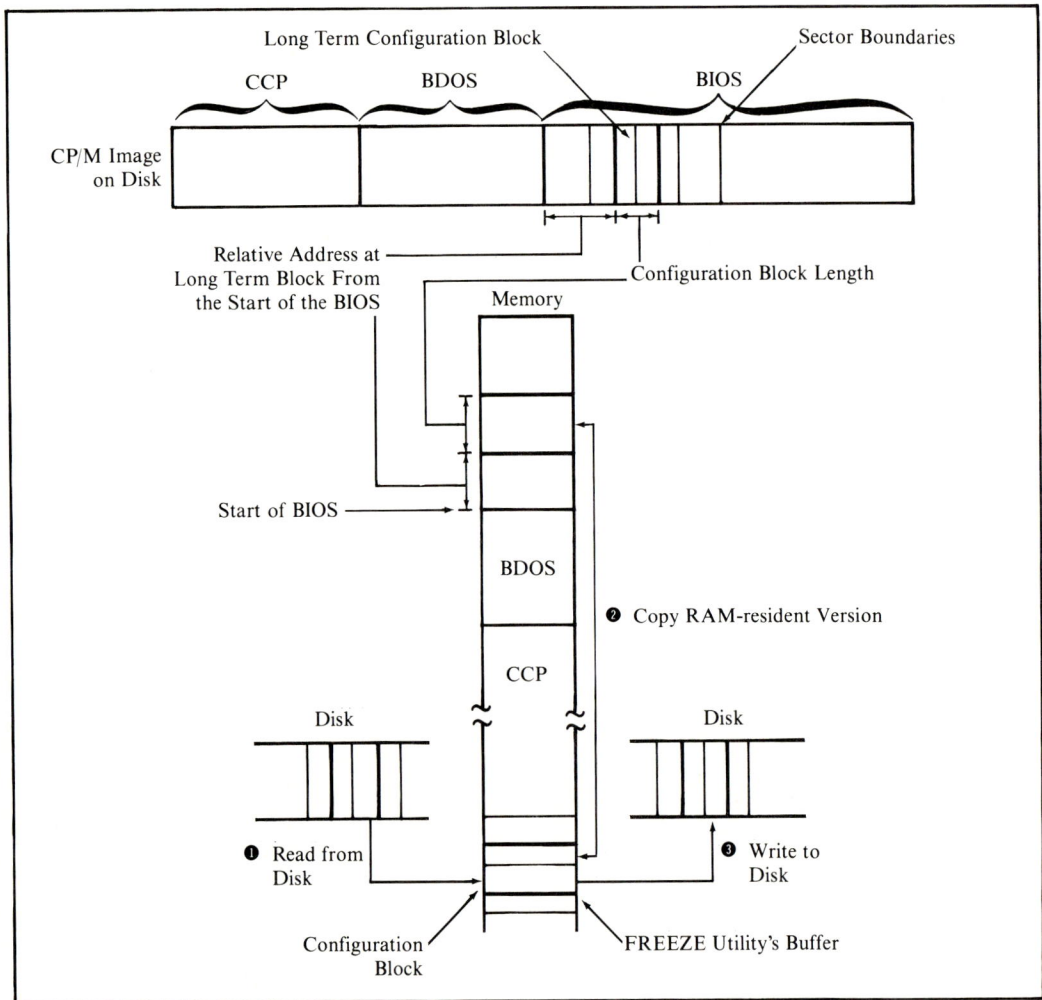

Figure 8-1. Saving the long term configuration block

size of the CCP and BDOS do not change, even if the BIOS does. Therefore, the sector containing the start of the BIOS will not change. The formula (using decimal numbers)

BIOS Start Sector + INT(Relative LTB Address / 128)

then gives the start sector number to be read in. The number of sectors to read is calculated as follows:

(Long Term Block Length + 127)/128

The relative address and length can be used to locate the long term block in the BIOS executing in RAM.

Character Input/Output

The character I/O drivers shown in the example BIOS, Figure 8-10, have been enhanced to have the following features:

- A single set of driver subroutines controlling all character devices
- Preservation of option settings
- Flexible redirection of input/output between logical and physical devices
- Interrupt-driven input drivers, to get user "type-ahead" capability
- Support of several different protocols to avoid loss of data during high-speed output to printers or other operations
- Forced input of characters into the console input stream, allowing automatic commands at system start-up
- Conversion of terminal function keys into useful character strings
- Ability to recognize "escape sequences" output to the console and to take special action as a result
- Ability to read the current time and date as though they were typed on the console
- "Timeout" signaling when the printer is busy for too long.

Each of these features is discussed in the following sections, as an introduction to the actual code example.

Single Set of Driver Subroutines

In the following examples, only a single set of subroutines is used to process the input and output for all of the physical devices in the system.

This is made possible by grouping all of the individual device's characteristics into a table called the *device table*. For example, in order to get a character from the current console device, the address of its device table will be handed over to the subroutines. These in turn will use the appropriate values from the device table when they need to access a port number or any unique attribute of that device.

In our example, the drivers assume that all of the physical devices use serial input/output. To support a device with parallel input/output, you would need to extend the device table to include a field that would enable the drivers to detect whether they were operating on a serial or parallel device. You would probably also have to add different device initialization and input/output routines more suited to the problems of dealing with a parallel port.

The device table structure consists of a series of equate (EQU) instructions. These define the relative offset of each field in the table. Each definition is expressed by referencing the *preceding* field so that you can insert additional fields without revising the definitions for all the other fields.

Individual instances of device tables are then defined as a series of define byte (DB) and define word (DW) lines. The drivers are given the base address of the device table whenever they need to do something with a device. By adding the base address to the relative address (defined by the equate), the drivers can determine the actual address in memory that contains the required value. The detailed contents of the device table are described later in this chapter.

Permanent Setting of Options

About the only options that need preserving in the long term configuration block are the values used to initialize the hardware chips. Other options can be set during automatic execution of the command file when CP/M is first loaded.

Redirection of Input/Output Between Devices

As you recall, the BDOS only "knows about" the *logical* devices console, reader, punch, and list. Using the IOBYTE at location 0003H in conjunction with the STAT utility, you can redirect the BDOS to assign the logical devices to specific physical devices. However, the redirection provided by CP/M is rather primitive. It permits only four physical devices per logical device. Input and output of a logical device must always come from the same physical device. Output data can only be sent to a single destination, or (using the CONTROL-P toggle) to the console and the list device.

The system in Figure 8-10 supports up to 16 physical devices. Any one of these devices can act as the console, reader, punch, or list device. Input can come from any single device. Output can be sent to any or all of the devices. Each logical device's input and output are separate—that is, console input can come from physical device X while the output can be sent to physical devices Y and Z.

Device redirection can be done dynamically, either from within a program or by using a system utility program. For example, if you have some special input device, your program can momentarily switch over to reading input from this device as though it were the console, and then revert back to reading data from the "real" console.

This redirection scheme is achieved by defining a 16-bit word, called the *redirection word,* in the long term configuration block for each of the following logical devices:

- Console input
- Console output
- Auxiliary (reader/punch) input
- Auxiliary (reader/punch) output
- List input (printers need to send data, too)
- List output.

Each bit in a given redirection word is assigned to a physical device. For input, the drivers use the device corresponding to the first 1 bit that they find in the redirection word. For output, the drivers send the character to be output to all of the devices for which the corresponding bit is set.

The example code does not select a different driver for each bit set — it selects a specific device table and then hands over the base address of this table to the common driver used for all character operations.

Interrupt-Driven Input Drivers

With a standard CP/M BIOS, character data is read from the hardware chips only when control is transferred to the CONIN or READER subroutines. If this character data arrives faster than the BIOS can handle, data overrun occurs and incoming characters are lost.

By using interrupts, the hardware can transfer control to the appropriate interrupt service routine whenever an incoming character arrives. This routine reads the data character and places it into a buffer area to wait for the next CONIN or READER call, which will get the character from the buffer and feed it into the incoming data stream.

User programs and the CCP are "unaware" of this process, perceiving only that data characters are available. However, users will become aware of the process; they will be able to enter data characters from the keyboard before the program is ready for them. This gives the technique its other name — "type-ahead." Although this technique does not alter the speed of execution of any programs running under CP/M, it does create the illusion of greater speed, since pauses while a program accepts data vanish completely. The user can enter data at a rate convenient to the tasks or thoughts at hand, without regard to the rate at which the program can accept that data.

The example contains the code necessary to handle arriving characters under interrupt control. In order to be of general applicability, the code assumes a "flat" interrupt structure: that is, all character input interrupts cause control to be transferred to the same address in memory. The address is determined by the actual hardware interrupt architecture.

The simplest interrupt schemes use the restart (RST) instructions built into the 8080 CPU chip. In the RST scheme, the external hardware interrupts what the CPU chip is doing and forces one of the eight RST instructions into the processor. Each RST instruction causes the processor to execute what is, in effect, a CALL instruction to a predetermined address in memory.

In more complicated systems, a specific interrupt controller chip (such as the Intel 8259A) will be used. In addition to providing very sophisticated (and complicated) prioritization of interrupts, the interrupt controller can transfer control to a *different* address depending on which physical device causes the interrupt. It does this by forcing the CPU to execute a CALL instruction to a different address for each device.

In both architectures, it is the responsibility of the BIOS writer to initialize all the hardware chips so that an interrupt occurs under the correct circumstances. The BIOS writer also must plant instructions at the correct places in memory to receive control from an RST instruction or from the fake CALL instruction emitted by the interrupt controller.

Some hardware requires that the interrupt service subroutine inform it as soon as the interrupt has been serviced and the character has been input. The example drivers provide for this.

This section deals with using interrupts for the *input* drivers, not the output drivers. All of today's microcomputers can output data much faster than external peripherals can handle. After the first few minutes of output, the computer will fill any reasonably sized buffer — and from this point there is no advantage in having a buffered output system. The computer still must slow down to the peripheral's data rate for each character, although now it is waiting to put the character in the output buffer rather than out to the peripheral.

One exception to this is where you have a large amount of "spare" memory and a "slow" printer (which most of them are). Increasing numbers of systems have more than 64K of RAM. The 8080 or Z80 can't address more than this, but a "bank switched" memory system can switch blocks of memory in and out of that 64K address space.

Using this trick, you can access memory "unknown" to CP/M, store some characters in it, switch back to the normal 64K memory, and return control to the caller of the BIOS output routine. When the physical device is ready to accept another output data character from the CPU, it will generate an interrupt. The interrupt service routine then will access the "secret" buffer, output the characters to the device, and switch back to the normal memory.

For example, if you have a printer that prints at 80 characters per second and

Chapter 8: Writing an Enhanced BIOS 217

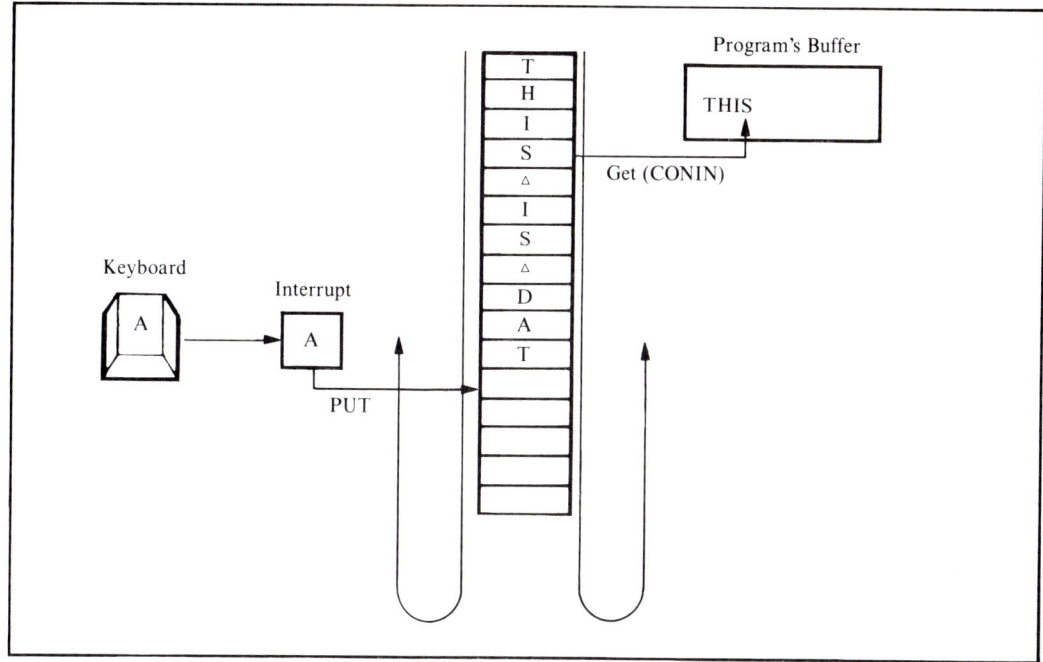

Figure 8-2. Circular buffer type-ahead

you can afford to use 64K of bank switched memory, you can squirrel away 13 minutes of printing—or even more if you design a scheme to compress blanks, storing them in the hidden buffer as a special control sequence.

From the point of view of software, interrupt-driven input drivers are divided into two major groups: the interrupt service routine that reads the characters and stacks them in a buffer, and the non-interrupt routines that get the characters from the buffer and handle the other BIOS functions such as returning console status.

The input character buffer serves as a transfer mechanism between the two groups of subroutines, although the device table also plays an important role.

The example code uses a circular buffer, as shown in Figure 8-2.

The drivers start putting data into the beginning of the buffer. When the last character in the buffer has been reached, the drivers reset to the beginning of the buffer and start over. This, of course, assumes that the non-interrupt drivers have been getting data from the front of the buffer, thus creating space for additional incoming data.

Each device table contains the address of the input buffer, a "put" pointer (for the interrupt service routine), and a "get" pointer (for the non-interrupt service routine). It also contains two character counts: the total number of characters and the number of control characters in the input buffer. You can see how the put and get pointers operate asynchronously. The put pointer is used every time an incoming character generates an interrupt. The get pointer is used for each CONIN call.

The get and put pointers are only single-byte values and are more accurately described as "relative offsets." That is, they contain a value which, when converted to a word and added to the base address of the buffer, will point directly to the appropriate position inside the buffer.

By making the buffer a binary number of characters long—32 characters, for example—a programming trick can be used to make the buffer appear circular. The device tables contain a mask value formed from the buffer's length minus one (length — 1). Whenever the get or put pointers are incremented by one (to "point" to the next character position), the updated value is ANDed with this (length — 1) mask. In this example, if the get value goes from 31 (the relative address of the last character in the buffer) to 32 (which would be "off the end"), the masking operation will reset it to zero (the relative address of the first character of the buffer). This avoids having to compare pointers to know when to reset them.

It is also simpler to use a count of the number of characters in the buffer, rather than comparing the get and put pointers, to distinguish between an empty and a full buffer. To support different serial protocols, the driver must be able to react when the buffer is within five characters of being full and when it drops below half empty. Both of these conditions are much easier to detect using a simple count that is incremented as a character is put into the buffer and decremented as a character is retrieved from the buffer.

The count of control characters is used to deal with a class of programs that incessantly "gobble" characters, thereby rendering any type-ahead useless. An example is Microsoft's BASIC interpreter. When it is interpreting a program, you can enter a CONTROL-C from the keyboard and the interpreter will come to an orderly stop. It does this by constantly making calls to CONST (console status). If it ever detects an incoming character, it makes a call to CONIN to input the character. A character that is not CONTROL-C is discarded without further ado. Thus, any characters that are input are consumed, destroying the effect of type-ahead.

To deal with this problem, the CONST routine shown in the example can be told to "lie" about the console's status. In this mode, CONST will only indicate that characters are waiting in the input buffer if a control character is received. It uses the control character count to determine whether there are control characters in the buffer; this count is incremented by the interrupt service routine when it detects one, and decremented by the CONIN routine when it gets a control character from the buffer.

Protocol Support

In this context, a protocol is a scheme to avoid loss of data that would otherwise occur if a device sent data faster than the receiving device could handle it. For example, protocols are used to prevent the CPU sending data out to a printer faster than the printer can print the characters and move the paper. The drivers also support input protocols, indicating to a transmitting device when the input buffer gets close to being full.

Two basic methods are used to implement protocols. The first uses the control lines found in the normal RS-232C serial interface cables. For data being output by the computer, the data terminal ready (DTR) signal is used, and for incoming data, the request to send (RTS) signal. These signals conform to the electrical standards for the RS-232C interface; they are considered true when they are at some positive voltage between +3 and +12 volts, and false when they are between −3 and −12 volts.

The second method uses ASCII control characters instead of control signals. Two separate protocols are supported by this method. One uses the ASCII characters XON and XOFF. Before the sending device (the computer or some peripheral device) sends a data character, it checks to see if an XOFF character has been received. If so, the sender will wait for an XON character. The receiving device will only send an XON when it is ready to receive more data.

The second protocol uses the characters ETX (end of transmission) and ACK (acknowledge). This method is normally used only when transmitting data from the computer to a buffered printer. A message length (usually half the printer's buffer size) is defined. When this number of characters has been output, the computer will send an ETX character. No further output will occur until the computer receives an ACK character from the printer.

The example drivers support the DTR high-to-send, the XON/XOFF, and the ETX/ACK protocols for output data. For input, they support RTS high-to-receive and XON/XOFF.

The input protocols are invoked when the input buffer gets within five characters of being full. Then the drivers output an XOFF character or lower the RTS signal voltage, or do both. Only when the input buffer has been emptied to 50% capacity will the drivers send XON or raise the RTS line, or both.

As an emergency measure, if the input buffer becomes completely full, notwithstanding protocols, the drivers will output a predetermined character (defined in the device table) each time they discard an incoming character. This is normally the ASCII BEL (bell) character. When you type too far ahead, the terminal will start beeping to tell you that data is being dropped.

Forced Input into the Console Stream

All application languages provide a means of reading data from the console keyboard. This makes the console input stream a useful gateway to the system. A simple enhancement to the CONIN/CONST routines makes it easy to "fool" the system into acting as if data had been input from the keyboard when in fact the data is coming in from a character string in memory.

220 The CP/M Programmer's Handbook

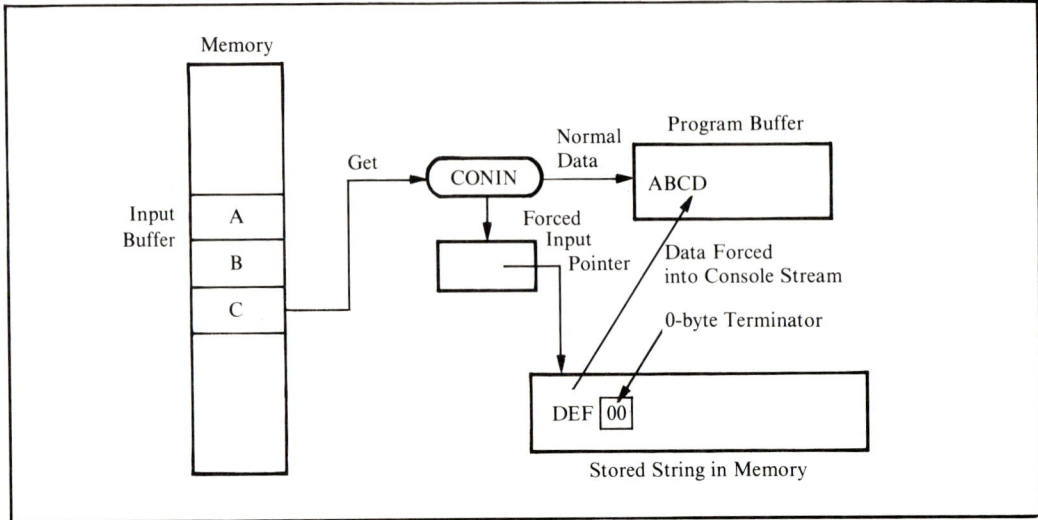

Figure 8-3.   CONIN uses forced input data if pointer points to nonzero byte

In the enhanced BIOS, both CONIN and CONST are extended to check a pointer in the long term configuration block, as shown in Figure 8-3.

If this pointer is pointing at a nonzero byte, then that byte is returned as though it had come from the console keyboard. The forced input pointer is then moved up one byte in memory. The process of forcing input continues until a zero byte is encountered.

Forced input serves several purposes. It can be used to force a command or commands into the system when the system first starts up. In conjunction with a utility program, it can allow the user to enter several CP/M commands on a single command line, injecting the characters as each of the commands is executed. It also makes possible the features described in the next two sections.

Support of Terminal Function Keys

Many terminals on the market today have special function keys on their keyboards. When you press one of these keys, the terminal will emit several characters, the first of which is normally the ASCII ESC (escape) character. The remaining one or two characters identify the specific function key that was pressed.

For these function keys to be of any practical use, an applications program must detect the incoming escape sequence and take appropriate action. The problem is that not all terminal manufacturers support the ANSI standard escape sequences.

The example drivers avoid this problem by providing a general-purpose method, shown in Figure 8-4, of detecting escape sequences and of substituting a user-defined character string that is injected into the console input stream as though it had been entered from the keyboard.

This scheme permits function keys to be used very flexibly, even for off-the-shelf programs that have not been designed specifically to accept function key input.

There is, however, one stumbling block. When an ESCAPE character is received, the progam must detect whether this is the start of a function key sequence or the user pressing the ESCAPE key on the terminal's keyboard. In the former case, the

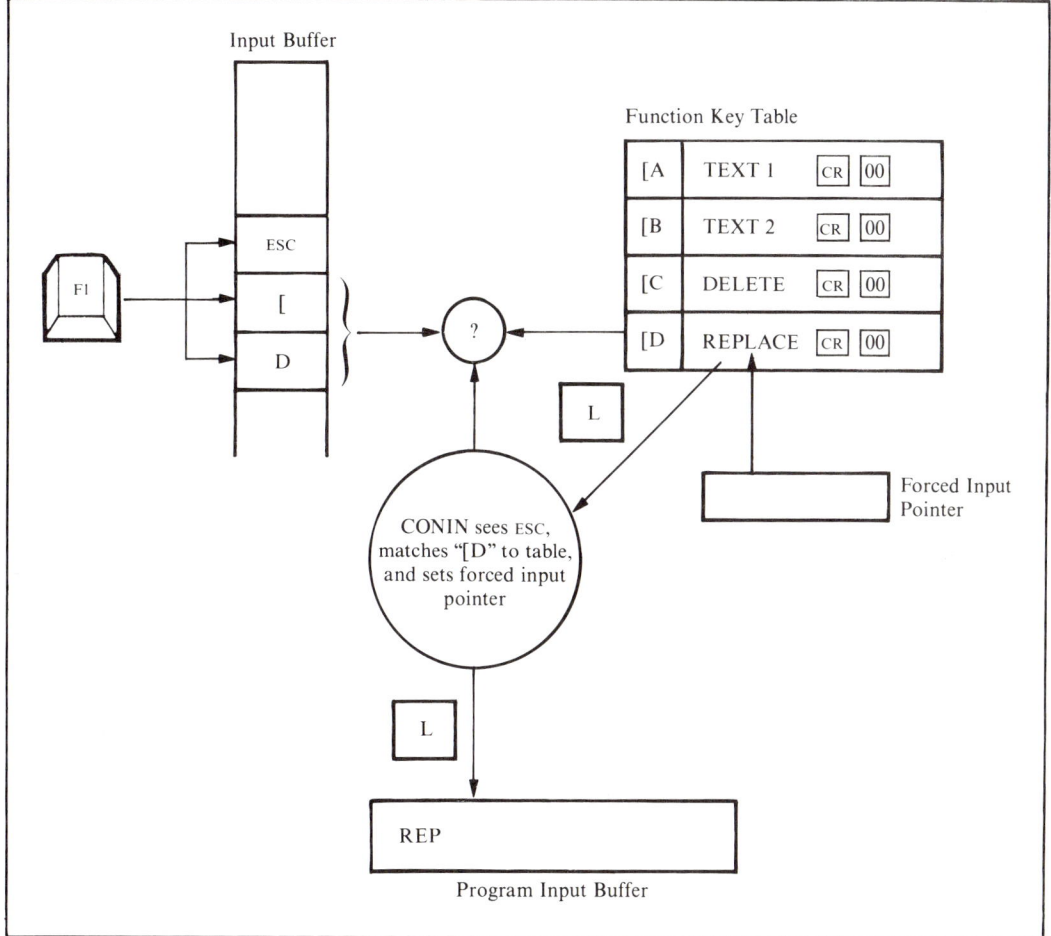

Figure 8-4. CONIN decodes terminal function keys

driver must wait to determine whether a function key string must be substituted for the escape sequence. In the latter case, the driver must input the ESCAPE character as it would other incoming data characters.

This recognition can only be done by moving into the time domain. When the CONIN routine (the non-interrupt routine) gets an ESCAPE character from the input buffer, it delays for approximately 90 milliseconds, enough time for a terminal-generated character sequence to arrive. CONIN then checks the input buffer to see if it contains at least two characters. If it does, the driver checks for a match in a function key table in the long term configuration block. If the characters match a defined function key, then the string associated with the function key will be injected into the console stream by pointing the forced input pointer at it. If the characters do not match anything in the function key table, then the ESCAPE and subsequent characters are handed over as normal data characters.

If after the 90-millisecond delay no further characters have arrived, the ESCAPE character is handed over as a normal character, on the basis that it must have been a manually entered ESCAPE character rather than part of a terminal-generated sequence.

The example drivers show the necessary code and tables for function keys that emit three characters. You could modify them easily for two-character sequences, or, if you are fortunate enough to have a keyboard that uses all eight bits of a byte, to recognize single incoming characters.

Processing Output Escape Sequences

The output side of the console driver, the CONOUT routine, can also be enhanced to recognize escape sequences. It uses a vectored JMP instruction to keep track of the current state of affairs. The CONOUT driver gets an address from the vector and transfers control to it. Normally this vector is set to direct control to the output byte routine. However, if an ESCAPE character is detected in the output stream, the vector is changed to transfer control to a routine that will recognize the character following the ESCAPE. If recognition does not occur, the driver will output an ESCAPE followed by the character that arrived after it.

If the second character is recognized, then the driver can transfer control to the correct escape-sequence processor. This processor can then take whatever action is appropriate. It must also make sure that when all processing is finished, the console output vector is set to process normal output characters again.

This technique is described in more practical detail in the next section, where it is used to preset and read the date and time. You can easily extend the recognition tables in the long term configuration block to perform any special processing that you need, ranging from altering the I/O redirection words to changing any other variable in the system or programming special hardware in your computer.

Be careful not to embed any pure binary values in the sequence of characters going out to the CONOUT routine. If you attempt to send a value of 09H (the TAB character) out via the BDOS, it will gratuitously expand the tab out to some number of blanks. If you need to send out a bit pattern, such as the I/O redirection word, split it up into a series of 7-bit long values. Then send it out with each byte having the most significant bit set to 1. A value of 09H will then become 89H, preventing the BDOS from expanding it to blanks.

Reading Date and Time From Console

For the moment, set aside the question of how the date and time get into the system. Since the date and time are stored in the short term configuration block (there being no need to save them from one work session to the next), all that the BIOS needs to be able to do is recognize a request from an applications program to read either the date or the time and then set the forced input pointer to the appropriate string in memory. Both the date and time strings are terminated by a LINE FEED followed by a 00 byte.

This sequence of events is shown in Figure 8-5.

You can see that the characters "ESC d" output to CONOUT cause it to point the forced input pointer at the date in memory. Subsequent calls to CONIN bring the characters in the date into the program as though they were being entered on the keyboard.

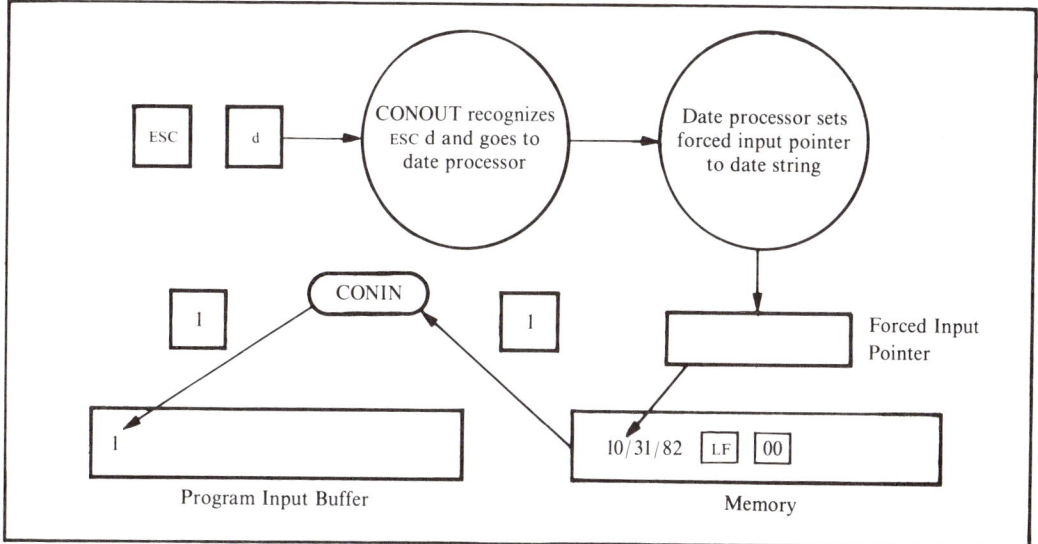

Figure 8-5. Escape sequences sent to CONOUT allow the date to be read by CONIN

"Watchdog" Timeout on Printer

There is no provision in CP/M to deal with a hardware device that for one reason or another is permanently unavailable. Unless special steps are taken in the drivers, the system will screech to a halt in a loop, reading status and testing for the peripheral to be ready.

The example enhancement code shows a scheme, using a real time clock, that can detect when a device such as a printer fails to come ready for more than 30 seconds. On detecting this situation, the code outputs a message to all of the console devices that are not also being used as printers. This type of output is needed to avoid "deadly embraces" where a printer not being ready generates a message that cannot be output because the printer is not ready.

The code that performs the timing function is known as a *watchdog timer*. Each time the real time clock "ticks," the interrupt service routine checks the watchdog count. If the count is nonzero, it is decremented. If the watchdog timer reaches zero, exceeding the time allowed, the drivers will display a message on the console indicating that the printer has been busy for too long. The user then has the option of making the printer ready and trying again to output data, ignoring the error and carrying on, or aborting the program by doing a BDOS System Reset (function 0).

Although sending an error message to the console sounds simple, it is complicated if console output is directed to the offending printer itself. The drivers attempt to solve this problem by sending the message only to those devices being used as consoles and *not* as printers. If all consoles are being used as printer devices as well, the driver will send the message to device 0 — normally the main console.

Keeping Time and Date

CP/M does not have provision for keeping the current time and date in the system. The example enhancement shows how to keep the time of day and the current date in the short term configuration block by using escape sequences output to the console (1) to set them to the correct values and (2) to "read" them from the console input stream.

The example presupposes that the system has a hardware chip that can be programmed to generate an interrupt every 1/60th of a second (16.666 milliseconds). This provides a divide-down counter to measure seconds elapsed. Of course, if your computer has a *true* real time clock that you can read and get the current time in hours, minutes, and seconds, your code will be very simple. You still will need to have the clock generate a periodic interrupt, however, in order to use the watchdog feature for timing printer and disk operations.

Actual time is kept as ASCII characters, using another ASCII control table to determine when "carry and reset to zero" should occur. By changing two bytes in this table, the time can be kept in 12- or 24-hour format.

The date is simply stored as a string. The example code does not attempt to make sure that the date is valid, nor to update when midnight rolls around. This could be done easily by the BIOS — but it would take a fairly large amount of code.

Watchdog Timer

Having a periodic source of interrupts also opens the door to building in an emergency or watchdog timer. This is nothing more than a 16-bit counter. Each time the real time clock interrupts, or ticks, the interrupt service routine checks the watchdog count. If it is already at zero, nothing more happens — the watchdog is not in use. If it is nonzero, the routine decrements the count by one. If this results in a zero value, the interrupt service routine CALLs a predetermined address. This will be the address of some emergency interrupt service routine that can then take special action, such as investigating the cause of the timeout.

The watchdog routine has a non-interrupt-level subroutine associated with it. Calling this set watchdog subroutine provides a means of setting the count to a predetermined number of real time clock "ticks" and setting the address to which control should be transferred if the count reaches zero.

Having called the set watchdog subroutine, the driver can then sit in a status loop, with interrupts enabled, waiting for some event to occur. If the event happens before the watchdog count hits zero, the driver must call the set watchdog routine again to set the count back to zero, thereby disabling the watchdog mechanism.

The watchdog timer can be used to detect printers that are busy for too long or disk drives that take too long to complete an action either because of a hardware failure or because the user has not loaded the disk into the drive.

Data Structures

As already stated, each character I/O device has its own device table that describes all of its unique characteristics.

The other major data structure is the configuration blocks — both short and long term.

This section describes each field in these data structures.

Device Table

Figure 8-6 shows the contents of a device table. More correctly, it shows a series of equates that define the offsets of each field in the device table. The drivers are given the base address of a specific device table. They then access each field by adding the required offset to this base address.

The first part of the device table is devoted to the physical aspect of the device, defining which port numbers are to be used to communicate with it. The drivers need to know several different port numbers since each one is used for a particular

```
;       The drivers use a device table for each
;       physical device they service. The equates that follow
;       are used to access the various fields within the
;       device table.
;
;                       Port numbers and status bits
0000 =          DT$Status$Port          EQU     0       ;Device status port number
0001 =          DT$Data$Port            EQU     DT$Status$Port+1
                                                        ;Device data port number
0002 =          DT$Output$Ready         EQU     DT$DataPort+1
                                                        ;Output ready status mask
0003 =          DT$Input$Ready          EQU     DT$Output$Ready+1
                                                        ;Input ready status mask
0004 =          DT$DTR$Ready            EQU     DT$Input$Ready+1
                                                        ;DTR ready to send mask
0005 =          DT$Reset$Int$Port       EQU     DT$DTR$Ready+1
                                                        ;Port number used to reset an
                                                        ;  interrupt
0006 =          DT$Reset$Int$Value      EQU     DT$Reset$Int$Port+1
                                                        ;Value output to reset interrupt
0007 =          DT$Detect$Error$Port    EQU     DT$Reset$Int$Value+1
                                                        ;Port number for error detect
0008 =          DT$Detect$Error$Value   EQU     DT$Detect$Error$Port+1
                                                        ;Mask for detecting error (parity etc.)
0009 =          DT$Reset$Error$Port     EQU     DT$Detect$Error$Value+1
                                                        ;Output to port to reset error
000A =          DT$Reset$Error$Value    EQU     DT$Reset$Error$Port+1
                                                        ;Value to output to reset error
000B =          DT$RTS$Control$Port     EQU     DT$Reset$Error$Value+1
                                                        ;Control port for lowering RTS
000C =          DT$Drop$RTS$Value       EQU     DT$RTS$Control$Port+1
                                                        ;Value, when output, to drop RTS
000D =          DT$Raise$RTS$Value      EQU     DT$Drop$RTS$Value+1
                                                        ;Value, when output, to raise RTS
;
;                       Device logical status (incl. protocols)
000E =          DT$Status               EQU     DT$Raise$RTS$Value+1
                                                        ;Status bits
0001 =          DT$Output$Suspend       EQU     0000$0001B      ;Output suspended pending
                                                                ;  protocol action
0002 =          DT$Input$Suspend        EQU     0000$0010B      ;Input suspended until
                                                                ;  buffer empties
0004 =          DT$Output$DTR           EQU     0000$0100B      ;Output uses DTR-high-to-send
0008 =          DT$Output$Xon           EQU     0000$1000B      ;Output uses Xon/Xoff
0010 =          DT$Output$Etx           EQU     0001$0000B      ;Output uses Etx/Ack
0020 =          DT$Output$Timeout       EQU     0010$0000B      ;Output uses Timeout
0040 =          DT$Input$RTS            EQU     0100$0000B      ;Input uses RTS-high-to-receive
0080 =          DT$Input$Xon            EQU     1000$0000B      ;Input uses Xon/Xoff
000F =          DT$Status$2             EQU     DT$Status+1     ;Secondary status byte
0001 =          DT$Fake$Typeahead       EQU     0000$0001B      ;Requests Input$Status to
                                                                ;  return "Data Ready" when
                                                                ;  control characters are in
                                                                ;  input buffer
;
0010 =          DT$Etx$Count            EQU     DT$Status$2+1
                                                        ;No. of chars.sent in Etx protocol
0012 =          DT$Etx$Message$Length   EQU     DT$Etx$Count+2
                                                        ;Specified message length
;
;                       Input buffer values
0014 =          DT$Buffer$Base          EQU     DT$Etx$Message$Length+2
                                                        ;Address of input buffer
0016 =          DT$Put$Offset           EQU     DT$Buffer$Base+2
                                                        ;Offset for putting chars.into buffer
0017 =          DT$Get$Offset           EQU     DT$Put$Offset+1
                                                        ;Offset for getting chars.from buffer
0018 =          DT$Buffer$Length$Mask   EQU     DT$Get$Offset+1
                                                        ;Length of buffer - 1
                                                        ;Note: Buffer length must always be
                                                        ;  a binary number; e.g. 32, 64, or 128,
                                                        ;This mask then becomes:
                                                        ;   32 ->  31 (0001$1111B)
                                                        ;   64 ->  63 (0011$1111B)
                                                        ;  128 -> 127 (0111$1111B)
```

Figure 8-6. Device table equates

```
0019 =          DT$Character$Count       EQU   ;After the get/put offset has been
                                               ; incremented it is ANDed with the mask
                                               ; to reset it to zero when the end of
                                               ; the buffer has been reached.
                                               DT$Buffer$Length$Mask+1
                                               ;Count of the number of characters
                                               ; currently in the buffer
001A =          DT$Stop$Input$Count      EQU   DT$Character$Count+1
                                               ;Stop input when the count reaches
                                               ; this value
001B =          DT$Resume$Input$Count    EQU   DT$Stop$Input$Count+1
                                               ;Resume input when the count reaches
                                               ; this value
001C =          DT$Control$Count         EQU   DT$Resume$Input$Count+1
                                               ;Count of the number of control
                                               ; characters in the buffer
001D =          DT$Function$Delay        EQU   DT$Control$Count+1
                                               ;Number of clock ticks to delay to
                                               ; allow all characters after function
                                               ; key lead-in to arrive
001E =          DT$Initialize$Stream     EQU   DT$Function$Delay+1
                                               ;Address of byte stream necessary to
                                               ; initialize this device
```

Figure 8-6. Device table equates (continued)

function. Depending upon your hardware, each port number could be different; however, with standard Intel or Zilog chips, you will often find that the same port number is used for several functions. The drivers also need to know what bit patterns to expect when they read some ports and what values to output to ports in order to obtain particular results.

The layout of the device table and the manner in which the equates are declared are designed to make it easy for you to change the contents of the table to meet your own special requirements. The fields in this first section of the device table are discussed in the sections that follow.

DT$Status$Port   The driver reads this port to determine whether the hardware chip has incoming data ready to be input to the computer or whether the chip is capable of accepting another data character for output to the physical device.

DT$Data$Port   The driver reads from this port to access the next data character from the physical device. The driver also writes to this port to output the next data character to the device.

If your computer hardware requires that the input data port be a different number from the output data port, you will have to alter the coding in the device table equates as well as make the necessary changes in the input and output subroutines in the body of the code.

DT$Output$Ready   This is the bit mask that the driver will AND with the current device status (obtained by reading the DT$Status$Port) to see whether the device is ready to accept another output character. It assumes that the device is ready if the result of the AND instruction is nonzero. You may have to change some JNZ (jump nonzero) instructions to JZ (jump zero) instructions if your hardware device uses inverted logic, with bits in the status byte set to 0 to indicate that the device can accept another character for output.

Note that this status check relates only to the output chip—it is completely separate from the question of whether the peripheral itself is ready to accept data.

DT$Input$Ready   This is the bit mask that the driver will AND with the current device status to see if there is an incoming data character. The drivers again presume that if the result of the AND is nonzero, then an incoming data character is waiting to be read from the data port. You will need to make changes similar to those for the output subroutines described in the previous section if your hardware uses inverted logic (0 bit means incoming data).

DTDTRReady   DTR stands for *data terminal ready*. It refers to one of the control lines connected from the actual peripheral device to the I/O chip (via several other integrated circuits). The drivers, as an option, will only output data to the device when the DTR signal is at a positive voltage. If the peripheral, in order to stop the flow of data characters being output to it, lowers the DTR signal to a negative voltage, the drivers will wait. Once DTR goes positive again, the drivers will resume sending data. Many hard-copy devices use this scheme to give themselves a chance to print out data received from the computer. They may have to lower DTR for several seconds, while they perform paper movement, for example.

The value in this field is a bit mask that the drivers use on the device status to determine the state of the data-terminal-ready control signal.

DT$Reset$Int$Port   Since the input side of the drivers uses interrupts, when an incoming character is ready to be input by the CPU, the hardware generates an interrupt signal, and control is transferred to the interrupt service routine. This routine "services" the interrupt by reading the incoming data character, saving it in memory, and then transferring control back to whatever was being executed when the interrupt occurred.

The more complicated interrupt controller chips (such as the Intel 8259A) must be told as soon as a given interrupt has been serviced so that they can permit servicing of any lower priority interrupts that may be waiting.

This field contains the port number that will be used to "reset" the interrupt, or more correctly, to indicate the end of the previous interrupt's servicing.

DT$Reset$Int$Value   This is the value that will be output to the DT$Reset$Int$Port to tell the hardware that the previous interrupt service has been completed.

DT$Detect$Error$Port   Before the driver attempts to read any incoming data from the DT$Data$Port, it checks to see if any hardware errors have occurred. It does so by reading status from this port.

DT$Detect$Error$Value The status byte that is input from the DT$Detect$Error$Port is ANDed with this value. If the result is nonzero, the driver assumes that an error has occurred.

DT$Reset$Error$Port If an error has occurred, the driver outputs an error reset value to this port number.

DT$Reset$Error$Value This is the value that will be output to the DT$Reset$Error$Port to reset an error.

DTRTSControl$Port The drivers use this port number to control the request-to-send line if the RTS protocol option is selected.

DT$Drop$RTS$Value This value is output to the RTS control port to lower the RTS line so that some external device will stop sending data to the computer.

DT$Raise$RTS$Value This value is output to raise the RTS line so that the external device will resume sending data to the computer.

DT$Status This is the first of two status bytes. It contains bit flags that are set to a 1 bit to indicate the following conditions:

> *DT$Output$Suspend*
> Because of protocol, the device is currently suspended from receiving any further output characters.
>
> *DT$Input$Suspend*
> Because of protocol, the device has been requested not to send any more input characters.
>
> *DT$Output$DTR*
> The driver will maintain DTR-high-to-send protocol for output data.
>
> *DT$Output$Xon*
> The driver will maintain XON/XOFF protocol for output data.
>
> *DT$Output$Etx*
> The driver will maintain ETX/ACK protocol for output data.
>
> *DT$Input$RTS*
> The driver will maintain RTS-high-to-receive protocol for input data.
>
> *DT$Input$Xon*
> The driver will maintain XON/XOFF protocol for input data.

DT$Status$2 This is another status byte, also with the following bit flag:

> *DT$Fake$Typeahead*
> CONST will "lie" about the availability of incoming console characters. It

will only indicate that data is waiting if there are control characters other than CARRIAGE RETURN, LINE FEED, or TAB in the input buffer.

DTEtxCount   This value is only used for ETX/ACK protocol. It is a count of the number of characters sent in the current message. When this count reaches the defined message length, then the driver will send an ETX character and suspend any further output.

DTEtxMessage$Length   This value is the defined message length for the ETX/ACK protocol. It is used to reset the DTEtxCount.

DT$Buffer$Base   This is the address of the first byte of the device's input buffer.

DTPutOffset   This *byte* contains the relative offset indicating where the next incoming character is to be "put" in the input buffer. This byte must then be converted into a word value and added to the DT$Buffer$Base address to get the absolute memory location.

DTGetOffset   This byte contains the relative offset indicating where the next character is to be "got" in the input buffer.

DT$Buffer$Length$Mask   This byte contains the length of the buffer minus one. The length of the buffer must always be a binary number (8, 16, 32, 64...). Therefore, one less than the length forms a mask value. Both the get and put offsets, after being incremented, are masked with this value. When the offset reaches the end of the buffer, this masking operation will "automatically" reset the offset to zero.

DT$Character$Count   This is a count of the total number of characters in the buffer. It is incremented by the interrupt service routine each time a character is placed in the buffer, and decremented by the CONIN routine each time it gets a character from the buffer.

CONST uses this value to determine whether any characters are available for input.

DT$Stop$Input$Count   When the interrupt service routines detect that the DT$Character$Count is equal to this value (normally buffer length minus five), the drivers will invoke the selected input protocol, lowering RTS or sending XOFF, to shut off the incoming data stream.

DT$Resume$Input$Count   When the CONIN routine detects that the DT$Character$Count has become equal to this value, the drivers will again invoke the selected input protocol, either raising RTS or sending XON to resume receiving input data.

DT$Control$Count   This is a count of the number of control characters in the input buffer. CARRIAGE RETURN, LINE FEED, and TAB characters are not included in this count.

It is incremented by the interrupt service routine and decremented by CONIN. CONST uses the count when the DT$Fake$Typeahead mode is active; it will only indicate that characters are waiting in the input buffer if the control count is nonzero.

DT$Function$Delay   This is the number of clock ticks that should be allowed to elapse after the first character of an incoming escape sequence has been detected. It allows time for the remaining characters in the escape sequence to arrive, assuming that these are being emitted by a terminal at maximum baud rate. Normally, this will correspond to a delay of approximately 90 milliseconds.

DT$Initialize$Stream   This is the address of the first byte of a string. This string has the following format:

```
DB  ppH          Port number
DB  nnH          Number of bytes to be output
DB  vvH,vvH...   Initialization bytes to be output to the specified port number
```

This sequence can be repeated as many times as is necessary, with a "port" number of 00H acting as a terminator.

Disk Input/Output

The example drivers show three main disk I/O enhancements:

- Full track buffering
- Using memory as an ultra-fast disk
- Improved error handling.

Full Track Buffering

The 5 1/4" diskettes used in the example system are double-sided. Each side has a separate read/write head in the disk drive. The disk controller is fast enough that, if so commanded, it can read in a complete track's worth of data from one side of the diskette in a single revolution of the diskette.

The drivers have been modified to do just this. The main disk buffer has been dramatically enlarged to accommodate nine 512-byte sectors.

In the earlier standard BIOS, CP/M was configured for tracks of 18 512-byte sectors. The data from each head on a given track was laid "end-to-end" to create the illusion of a single surface with twice as much data on it. For track buffering, performance would be reduced if each read required two revolutions of the diskette, and so in this BIOS the tables and the low-level driver logic have been changed. Each surface is separated, with even numbered tracks on head 0, odd on head 1.

The track number given to the low-level drivers serves two purposes. The least significant bit identifies the head number. When the track number is shifted one bit right, the result is the *physical* track number to which the head assembly must be positioned.

The deblocking algorithm has also been modified by deleting references to sectors. The code is now concerned only with whether the correct disk and track are in the buffer. If this is true, the correct sector must, by definition, be in the buffer.

The deblocking code no longer takes any note when the BDOS indicates that it is writing to an unallocated allocation block—knowledge it used to bypass a sector preread in the standard BIOS. The track size in this enhanced BIOS is much larger than an allocation block, and so the question is meaningless; the whole track must be preread to write just a single sector.

This enhancement really excels when the BDOS is doing directory operations, which always involve a series of sequential reads. The entire directory can be brought into memory, updated, and written back in just two disk revolutions.

One point to watch out for is what is known as "deferred writes." Imagine a program instructed to write on a sector on track 20. The drivers will read in track 20, copy the contents of the designated sector into the track buffer, and return to the program *without* actually writing the data to the disk. The program could "write" to all of the sectors on this track without any actual disk writes. During all this time, this data would exist only in memory and not on the disk drive, so if a power failure occurred, several thousand bytes of data would be lost. Writing to the directory is an exception. The drivers always physically write to the disk when the BDOS indicates that it is writing to a directory sector.

In reality, the increased risk is small. Most programs are constantly reading and writing files, so that the track buffer will be written out frequently in order to read in another track. When programs end, they close output files. This in turn triggers directory writes that force data tracks onto the disk.

If high security is a requirement for your computer, you could extend the watchdog routine to include another separate timer. You could preset this timer for, say, a ten-second delay each time you write into the track buffer but do not write the buffer to the disk. When the count expires, it would set a flag that could be tested by all of the BIOS entry points. If set, they would initiate a write of the track buffer to the disk.

Using Memory as an Ultra-Fast Disk

As you can see from the preceding section, increased performance tends to go hand in hand with increased memory requirements. This is certainly true with a "memory disk," commonly called a RAM-disk or M-disk. In fact, to have an M-disk with reasonable storage capacity, your computer must have at least 128K bytes of additional memory.

Chapter 8: Writing an Enhanced BIOS   **233**

Since the 8080 or Z80 can only address 64K of memory at one time, to get access to any of this additional memory, some part of your computer's "normal" memory must be removed from the 64K address space and the additional memory must be switched in. This is known as bank-switched memory.

Figure 8-7 shows the memory organization that is supported by the example M-disk drivers.

You can see that the system has a total of 256K bytes of RAM, organized with the top 16K, from 64K down to 48K, being "common"—that is, switched into the address space all the time. The lower 48K can be selected from five banks, numbered 0 to 4. Bank 0 is switched in for normal CP/M operations.

The M-disk parameter blocks describe a disk with eight "tracks," numbered 0 to 7. The least significant bit of the track number determines whether the base address of the track will be 0000H or 6000H. Shifting the track number right one bit gives the bank number. Each track consists of 192 sectors. To get the relative address of a sector within its "track," shift the sector number eight bits left, thus multiplying it by 128.

The M-disk is referenced by logical disk M:. A few special-case instructions are required to return the special M-disk parameter header in SELDSK.

One problem, fortunately easily solved, is that the user's DMA address coexists in the address space with the M-disk image itself. There is no direct way to move data between bank 0 and any other bank. The M-disk uses an intermediary buffer in common memory (above 48K), moving data into this, switching banks, and then moving the data down again. Figure 8-8 shows an example of this sequence, as used when reading from the M-disk.

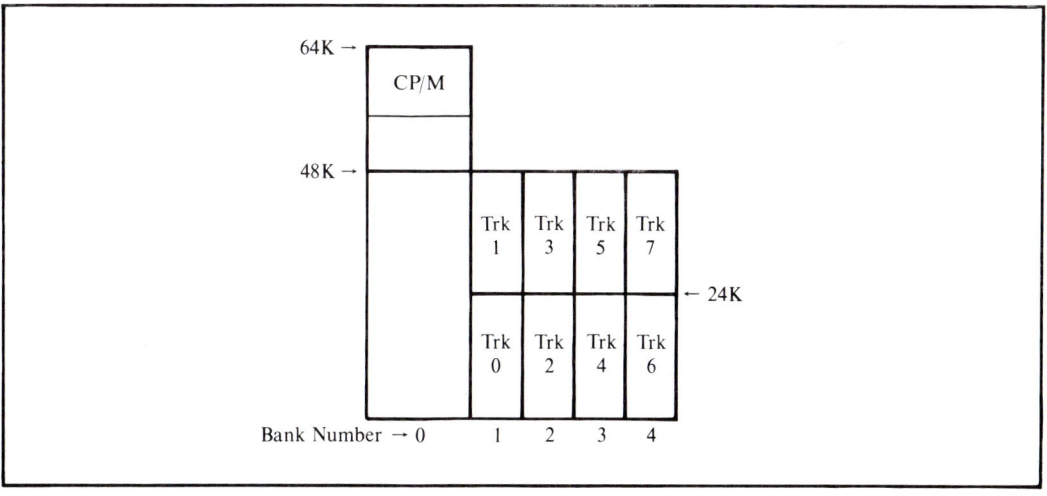

Figure 8-7.   Memory organization for M-disk

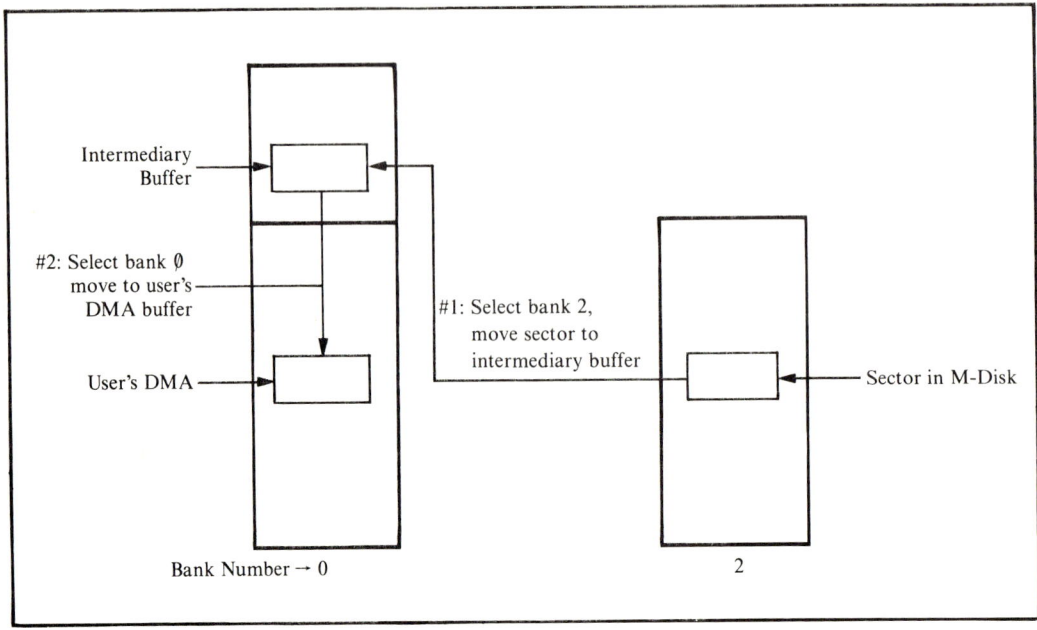

Figure 8-8. Reading a sector from the M-disk image

During cold boot initialization, the M-disk driver checks the very first directory entry (in bank 1) to see if it matches a dummy entry for a file called "M$Disk." If this entry is present, the M-disk is assumed to contain valid information. If the entry is absent, the initialization code makes this special directory entry and fills the remainder of the directory with 0E5H, making it appear empty. The dummy entry makes it appear that the "M$Disk" file is in user 15, marked System status and Read-Only — all of which are designed to prevent its accidental erasure.

Custom Patches to CP/M

Two features shown in the enhanced BIOS, one in the CCP and one in the BDOS, require changes to CP/M itself. These features are implemented by modifying the CCP and BDOS to transfer control to the BIOS at specific points, execute a few instructions in the BIOS, and then return to CP/M. The patches could be made by modifying the MOVCPM program to install the changes permanently. The changed version of MOVCPM, however, *must* be used with a specific version of the BIOS. Therefore, patching CP/M "on the fly" ensures that there will be no mismatch between the BIOS and the rest of CP/M.

Both of these patches were produced with the assistance of Digital Research.

User 0 Files Made Public

The first change permits files created in user area 0 to be accessible from all other user numbers. This feature comes into its own only with hard disk systems. On a hard disk, user numbers can partition the disk, but the frequently used utilities must then be duplicated in each user area. Allowing files in user area 0 to be public means that these files will be accessible from all the other user numbers. Hence the files need not be copied into each user area.

The public files feature alters the way that the BDOS performs the Search Next function, allowing access to files declared in user area 0 even when the current user number is not 0. However, the feature is a double-edged sword—user 0 files can be accidentally erased or damaged as well as accessed. Therefore, user 0 files should be declared as System status and Read-Only to protect them. As an additional precaution, public files can be turned off by a control flag in the long term configuration block. This flag is set to an initial state that disables public files.

Modified User Prompt

This modification makes the CCP display the current user number as well as the default disk. For example,

3B>

indicates that you are currently in user number 3, with disk B: as the default. In addition, if you have enabled public files, the prompt is preceded by the letter "P" to serve as a reminder:

P3B>

An Enhanced BIOS

The remainder of this chapter consists of the assembly language source code for the enhanced BIOS described here. It is rather a daunting listing, but will be well worth your study. The copious commentary has been written to make this study easier, and emphasis has been placed on explaining *why* as well as *what* things are done.

As with the standard BIOS, each line is numbered so that you can use the functional index in Figure 8-9 to find areas of interest in the listing. Note that the line numbers are not contiguous. They jump several hundred at the start of each major section or subroutine. This facilitates minor changes in the listing without revision of the functional index. The full listing is given in Figure 8-10.

Start Line	Functional Component or Routine
00001	Introductory Comments and Equates
00200	BIOS Jump Table with Additional Private Entries
00400	Long Term Configuration Block
00800	Interrupt Vector
00900	Device Port Numbers and Other Equates
01100	Display$Message Subroutine
01200	Enter$CPM Setup
01300	Device Table Equates
01500	Device Table Declarations
01700	General Device Initialization
01800	Specific Device Initialization
02000	Output Byte Stream
02100	CONST Routine
02200	CONIN Routine with Function Key Processing
02500	Console Output
02700	CONOUT Routine with Escape Sequence Processing
02900	AUXIST—Auxiliary Input Status Routine
03000	AUXOST—Auxiliary Output Status Routine
03100	AUXIN—Auxiliary Input Routine
03200	AUXOUT—Auxiliary Output Routine
03300	LISTST—List Status Routine
03400	LIST—List Output Routine
03500	Request User Choice—Request Action After Error
03600	Output Error Message
03656	Get Composite Status from Selected Output Devices
03800	Multiple Output of Byte to All Output Devices
04000	Check Output Device Logically (Protocol) Ready
04200	Process ETX/ACK Protocol
04400	Select Device Table from I/O Redirection Bit Map
04600	Get Input Character from Input Buffer
04800	Introductory Comments for Interrupt-Driven Drivers
04900	Character Interrupt Service Routine
05000	Service Device—Puts Character into Input Buffer
05300	Get Address of Character in Input Buffer
05400	Check if Control Character (not CR, LF, TAB)
05500	Output Data Byte
05700	Input Status Routine
05900	Set Watchdog Timer Routine
06000	Real Time Clock Interrupt Service Routine
06200	Shift HL Right One Bit Routine
06300	Introductory Comments for High-Level Disk Drivers
06400	Disk Parameter Headers
06600	Disk Parameter Blocks
06800	SELDSK—Select Disk Routine
07000	SETTRK—Set Track Routine
07100	SETSEC—Set Sector Routine

Figure 8-9. Functional index for listing in Figure 8-10

07200	SETDMA—Set DMA Routine
07300	Skew Tables for Sector Translation
07400	SECTRAN—Sector Translation Routine
07500	HOME—Home Disk to Track and Sector 0
07600	Equates for Physical Disk and Deblocking Variables
07800	READ—Sector Read Routine
07900	WRITE—Sector Write Routine
08000	Common Read/Write Code with Deblocking Algorithm
08300	Move$8 Routine—Moves Memory in 8-Byte Blocks
08500	Introductory Comments for Disk Controllers
08700	Nondeblocked Read and Write
08900	M-Disk Driver
09100	Select Memory Bank Routine
09200	Physical Read/Write to Deblocked Disks
09400	Disk Error Handling Routines
09700	Disk Control Tables for Warm Boot
09800	WBOOT—Warm Boot Routine
10000	Ghost Interrupt Service
10100	Patch CP/M for Public Files and Prompt Changes
10300	Get Configuration Block Addresses
10400	Addresses of Objects in Configuration Blocks
10500	Short Term Configuration Block
10700	Note on Why Uninitialized Buffers are at End of BIOS
10800	Cold Boot Initialization Hidden in Disk Buffer Followed by All Uninitialized Buffers

FIGURE 8-9. Functional index for listing in Figure 8-10 (continued)

```
                00001   ;       This is a skeletal example of an enhanced BIOS.
                00010   ;       It includes fragments of the standard BIOS
                00011   ;       shown as Figure 6-4 in outline, so as to
                00012   ;       avoid cluttering up the enhancements with the
                00013   ;       supporting substructure. Many of the original
                00014   ;       comment blocks have been abbreviated or deleted
                00015   ;       entirely.
                00016   ;
                00017   ;< -- NOTE:    The line numbers at the left are included
                00018   ;              to allow reference to the code from the text.
                00019   ;              There are deliberate discontinuities in the
                00020   ;              numbers to allow space for expansion.
                00021   ;
3030 =          00022   VERSION   EQU    '00'        ;Equates used in the sign-on message
3230 =          00023   MONTH     EQU    '02'
3632 =          00024   DAY       EQU    '26'
3338 =          00025   YEAR      EQU    '83'
                00026   ;
                00027   ;*******************************************************************
                00028   ;*                                                                 *
                00029   ;*      This BIOS is for a computer system with the following      *
                00030   ;*      hardware configuration :                                   *
                00031   ;*                                                                 *
                00032   ;*         -- 8080 CPU                                             *
                00033   ;*         -- 64K bytes of RAM                                     *
                00034   ;*         -- 3 serial I/O ports (using signetics 2651) for:       *
                00035   ;*            console, communications and list                     *
                00036   ;*         -- Two 5 1/4" mini floppy, double-sided, double-        *
                00037   ;*            density drives. These drives use 512-byte sectors.   *
                00038   ;*            These are used as logical disks A: and B:.           *
                00039   ;*            Full track buffering is supported.                   *
```

Figure 8-10. Enhanced BIOS listing

```
           00040  ;*              -- Two 8" standard diskette drives (128-byte sectors)  *
           00041  ;*                 These are used as logical disks C: and D:.          *
           00042  ;*              -- A memory-based disk (M-disk) is supported.          *
           00043  ;*                                                                     *
           00044  ;*              Two intelligent disk controllers are used, one for     *
           00045  ;*              each diskette type. These controllers access memory    *
           00046  ;*              directly, both to read the details of the              *
           00047  ;*              operations they are to perform and also to read        *
           00048  ;*              and write data from and to the diskettes.              *
           00049  ;*                                                                     *
           00050  ;*                                                                     *
           00051  ;***********************************************************************
           00052
           00053
           00054  ;       Equates for characters in the ASCII character set
           00055  ;
0011 =     00056  XON       EQU     11H       ;Reenables transmission of data
0013 =     00057  XOFF      EQU     13H       ;Disables transmission of data
0003 =     00058  ETX       EQU     03H       ;End of transmission
0006 =     00059  ACK       EQU     06H       ;Acknowledge
000D =     00060  CR        'EQU    0DH       ;Carriage return
000A =     00061  LF        EQU     0AH       ;Line feed
0009 =     00062  TAB       EQU     09H       ;Horizontal tab
0007 =     00063  BELL      EQU     07H       ;Sound terminal's bell
           00064  ;
           00065  ;
           00066  ;       Equates for defining memory size and the base address and
           00067  ;       length of the system components
           00068  ;
0040 =     00069  Memory$Size   EQU    64      ;Number of Kbytes of RAM
           00070  ;
           00071  ;       The BIOS length must be determined by inspection.
           00072  ;       Comment out the ORG BIOS$Entry line below by changing the first
           00073  ;       character to a semicolon (this will make the assembler start
           00074  ;       the BIOS at location 0). Then assemble the BIOS and round up to
           00075  ;       the nearest 100H the address displayed on the console at the end
           00076  ;       of the assembly.
           00077  ;
2500 =     00078  BIOS$Length   EQU    2500H   ;<-- Revised to an approximate value
           00079  ;                                 to reflect enhancements
           00080  ;
0800 =     00081  CCP$Length    EQU    0800H   ;Constant
0E00 =     00082  BDOS$Length   EQU    0E00H   ;Constant
           00083  ;
000F =     00084  Overall$Length  EQU  (CCP$Length + BDOS$Length + BIOS$Length + 1023) / 1024
           00085  ;
C400 =     00086  CCP$Entry     EQU    (Memory$Size - Overall$Length) * 1024
CC06 =     00087  BDOS$Entry    EQU    CCP$Entry + CCP$Length + 6
DA00 =     00088  BIOS$Entry    EQU    CCP$Entry + CCP$Length + BDOS$Length
           00089  ;
0005 =     00090  BDOS          EQU    0005H   ;BDOS entry point (used for making
           00091  ;                                system reset requests)
           00092  ;
           00200  ;#
           00201          ORG     BIOS$Entry      ;Assemble code at BIOS address
           00202  ;
           00203          BIOS jump vector
           00204  ;
0000 C31311  00205         JMP     BOOT    ;Cold boot -- entered from CP/M bootstrap loader
           00206  Warm$Boot$Entry:     ;   Labelled so that the initialization code can
           00207                       ;   put the warm boot entry address in location
           00208                       ;   0001H and 0002H of the base page
0003 C3750E  00209         JMP     WBOOT   ;Warm boot -- entered by jumping to location 0000H
           00210                       ;   Reloads the CCP, which could have been
           00211                       ;   overwritten by previous program in transient
           00212                       ;   program area
0006 C32D03  00213         JMP     CONST   ;Console status -- returns A = 0FFH if there is a
           00214                       ;   console keyboard character waiting
0009 C33A03  00215         JMP     CONIN   ;Console input -- returns the next console keyboard
           00216                       ;   character in A
000C C3D703  00217         JMP     CONOUT  ;Console output -- outputs the character in C to
           00218                       ;   the console device
000F C3F504  00219         JMP     LIST    ;List output -- outputs the character in C to the
           00220                       ;   list device
0012 C3CE04  00221         JMP     AUXOUT  ;Auxiliary output -- outputs the character in C to
           00222                       ;   logical auxiliary device
```

Figure 8-10. (Continued)

```
0015 C3A104        00223              JMP      AUXIN       ;Auxiliary input -- returns the next input character from
                  00224                                    ;  the logical auxiliary device in A
0018 C3160A        00225              JMP      HOME        ;Homes the currently selected disk to track 0
001B C36309        00226              JMP      SELDSK      ;Selects the disk drive specified in register C and
                  00227                                    ;  returns the address of the disk parameter header
001E C39B09        00228              JMP      SETTRK      ;Sets the track for the next read or write operation
                  00229                                    ;  from the BC register pair
0021 C3A109        00230              JMP      SETSEC      ;Sets the sector for the next read or write operation
                  00231                                    ;  from the A register
0024 C3A809        00232              JMP      SETDMA      ;Sets the direct memory address (disk read/write)
                  00233                                    ;  address for the next read or write operation
                  00234                                    ;  from the DE register pair
0027 C3370A        00235              JMP      READ        ;Reads the previously specified track and sector from
                  00236                                    ;  the selected disk into the DMA address
002A C34B0A        00237              JMP      WRITE       ;Writes the previously specified track and sector onto
                  00238                                    ;  the selected disk from the DMA address
002D C3D704        00239              JMP      LISTST      ;Returns A = 0FFH if the list device(s) are
                  00240                                    ;  logically ready to accept another output byte
0030 C3100A        00241              JMP      SECTRAN     ;Translates a logical sector into a physical one
                  00242       ;
                  00243       ;       Additional "private" BIOS entry points
                  00244       ;
0033 C38F04        00245              JMP      AUXIST      ;Returns A = 0FFH if there is input data for
                  00246                                    ;  the logical auxiliary device
0036 C39B04        00247              JMP      AUXOST      ;Returns A = 0FFH if the auxiliary device(s) are
                  00248                                    ;  logically ready to accept another output byte
0039 C3FA02        00249              JMP      Specific$CIO$Initialization
                  00250                                    ;Initializes character device whose device
                  00251                                    ;  number is in register A on entry
003C C36D08        00252              JMP      Set$Watchdog
                  00253                                    ;Sets up watchdog timer to CALL address specified
                  00254                                    ;  in HL, after BC clock ticks have elapsed
003F C33C0F        00255              JMP      CB$Get$Address
                  00256                                    ;Configuration block get address
                  00257                                    ;   Returns address in HL of data element whose
                  00258                                    ;   code number is specified in C
                  00259       ;
                  00400       ;#
                  00401       ;       Long term configuration block
                  00402       ;
                  00403       Long$Term$CB:
                  00404
                  00405       ;
                  00406       ;       Public files (files in user 0 accessible from all
                  00407       ;       other user numbers) enabled when this flag is set
                  00408       ;       nonzero.
                  00409       ;
0042 00            00410       CB$Public$Files:    DB       0           ;Default is OFF
                  00411       ;
                  00412       ;
                  00413       ;       The forced input pointer is initialized to point to the
                  00414       ;       following string of characters. These are injected into
                  00415       ;       the console input stream on system start-up.
                  00416       ;
0043 5355424D4900417 CB$Startup:        DB       'SUBMIT STARTUP',LF,0,0,0,0,0
                  00418       ;
                  00419       ;       Logical to physical device redirection
                  00420       ;
                  00421       ;               Each logical device has a 16-bit word associated
                  00422       ;               with it. Each bit in the word is assigned to a
                  00423       ;               specific physical device. For input, only one bit
                  00424       ;               can be set -- input will be read from the
                  00425       ;               corresponding physical device. Output can be
                  00426       ;               directed to several devices, so more than one
                  00427       ;               bit can be set.
                  00428       ;
                  00429       ;               The following equates are used to indicate
                  00430       ;               specific physical devices.
                  00431       ;
                  00432       ;                       1111 11
                  00433       ;                       5432 1098 7654 3210  )<- Device number
0001 =             00434       Device$0     EQU    0000$0000$0000$0001B
0002 =             00435       Device$1     EQU    0000$0000$0000$0010B
0004 =             00436       Device$2     EQU    0000$0000$0000$0100B
                  00437       ;
                  00438       ;               The following words are tested by the logical
                  00439       ;               device drivers to transfer control to
```

Figure 8-10. (Continued)

```
                    00440  ;              the appropriate physical device drivers
                    00441  ;
0058 0100           00442  CB$Console$Input:    DW      Device$0
005A 0100           00443  CB$Console$Output:   DW      Device$0
                    00444  ;
005C 0200           00445  CB$Auxiliary$Input:  DW      Device$1
005E 0200           00446  CB$Auxiliary$Output: DW      Device$1
                    00447  ;
0060 0400           00448  CB$List$Input:       DW      Device$2
0062 0400           00449  CB$List$Output:      DW      Device$2
                    00450  ;
                    00451  ;              The table below relates specific bits in the
                    00452  ;              redirection words above to specific device
                    00453  ;              tables used by the physical drivers
                    00454  ;
                    00455  CB$Device$Table$Addresses:
0064 8E02           00456          DW      DT$0
0066 AE02           00457          DW      DT$1
0068 CE02           00458          DW      DT$2
006A 000000000000   00459          DW      0,0,0,0,0,0,0,0,0,0,0,0         ;Unassigned
                    00460  ;
                    00461  ;
                    00462  ;              Device initialization byte streams
                    00463  ;
                    00464  ;              These initialization streams are output during the device
                    00465  ;              initialization phase, or on request whenever the baud rate
                    00466  ;              needs to be changed. They are defined in the long term
                    00467  ;              configuration block so as to "freeze" their contents from one
                    00468  ;              system startup until the next.
                    00469  ;
                    00470  ;              The address of each stream is contained in each device table.
                    00471  ;
                    00472  ;              The stream format is:
                    00473  ;
                    00474  ;                      DB      xx              ;Port number (00H terminates)
                    00475  ;                      DB      nn              ;Number of bytes to output to port
                    00476  ;                      DB      vv,vv,vv..      ;Values to be output
                    00477  ;
                    00478  D0$Initialize$Stream:                          ;Example data for an 8251A chip
0084 ED             00479          DB      0EDH                           ;Port number for 8251A
0085 06             00480          DB      6                              ;Number of bytes
0086 000000         00481          DB      0,0,0                          ;Dummy bytes to get chip ready
0089 42             00482          DB      0100$0010B                     ;Reset and raise DTR
008A 6E             00483          DB      01$10$11$10B                   ;1 stop, no parity, 8 bits/char,
                    00484                                                 ;  divide down of 16
008B 25             00485          DB      0010$0101B                     ;RTS high, enable Tx/Rx
                    00486                                                 ;Example data for an 8253 chip
008C DF             00487          DB      0DFH                           ;Port number for 8253 mode
008D 01             00488          DB      1                              ;Number of bytes to output
008E 76             00489          DB      01$11$011$0B                   ;Select:
                    00490                                                 ;        Counter 1
                    00491                                                 ;        Load LS byte first
                    00492                                                 ;        Mode 3, binary count
008F DE             00493          DB      0DEH                           ;Port number for counter
0090 02             00494          DB      2                              ;Number of bytes to output
                    00495  D0$Baud$Rate$Constant:                         ;Label used by utilities
0091 0700           00496          DW      0007H                          ;9600 Baud (based on 16x divider)
0093 00             00497          DB      0                              ;Port number of 00 terminates stream
                    00498
                    00499  D1$Initialize$Stream:                          ;Example data for an 8251A chip
0094 DD             00500          DB      0DDH                           ;Port number for 8251A
0095 06             00501          DB      6                              ;Number of bytes
0096 000000         00502          DB      0,0,0                          ;Dummy bytes to get chip ready
0099 42             00503          DB      0100$0010B                     ;Reset and raise DTR
009A 6E             00504          DB      01$10$11$10B                   ;1 stop, no parity, 8 bits/char,
                    00505                                                 ;  divide down of 16
009B 25             00506          DB      0010$0101B                     ;RTS high, enable Tx/Rx
                    00507
                    00508                                                 ;Example data for an 8253 chip
009C DF             00509          DB      0DFH                           ;Port number for 8253 mode
009D 01             00510          DB      1                              ;Number of bytes to output
009E B6             00511          DB      10$11$011$0B                   ;Select:
                    00512                                                 ;        Counter 2
                    00513                                                 ;        Load LS byte first
                    00514                                                 ;        Mode 3, binary count
009F DE             00515          DB      0DEH                           ;Port number for counter
00A0 02             00516          DB      2                              ;Number of bytes to output
```

Figure 8-10.   (Continued)

Chapter 8: Writing an Enhanced BIOS 241

```
                00517        D1$Baud$Rate$Constant:
00A1 3800       00518                DW      0038H                   ;1200 baud (based on 16x divider)
00A3 00         00519                DB      0                       ;Port number of 00 terminates stream
                00520
                00521        D2$Initialize$Stream:           ;Example data for an 8251A chip
00A4 DD         00522                DB      0DDH                    ;Port number for 8251A
00A5 06         00523                DB      6                       ;Number of bytes
00A6 000000     00524                DB      0,0,0                   ;Dummy bytes to get chip ready
00A9 42         00525                DB      0100$0010B              ;Reset and raise DTR
00AA 6E         00526                DB      01$10$11$10B            ;1 stop, no parity, 8 bits/char,
                00527                                                ;  divide down of 16
00AB 25         00528                DB      0010$0101B              ;RTS high, enable Tx/Rx
                00529
                00530                                        ;Example data for an 8253 chip
00AC DF         00531                DB      0DFH                    ;Port number for 8253 mode
00AD 01         00532                DB      1                       ;Number of bytes to output
00AE F6         00533                DB      11$11$011$0B            ;Select:
                00534                                        ;          Counter 3
                00535                                        ;          Load LS byte first
                00536                                        ;          Mode 3, binary count
00AF DE         00537                DB      0DEH                    ;Port number for counter
00B0 02         00538                DB      2                       ;Number of bytes to output
                00539        D2$Baud$Rate$Constant:
00B1 3800       00540                DW      0038H                   ;1200 baud (based on 16x divider)
00B3 00         00541                DB      0                       ;Port number of 00 terminates stream
                00542
                00543        ;
                00544        ;       This following table is used to determine the maximum
                00545        ;       value for each character position in the ASCII time
                00546        ;       value above (except the ":"). Note -- this table is
                00547        ;       in the long term configuration block so that the clock
                00548        ;       can be set "permanently" to either 12 or 24 hour format.
                00549        ;
                00550        ;       NOTE: The table is processed backwards -- to correspond
                00551        ;       with the ASCII time.
                00552        ;       Each character represents the value for the corresponding
                00553        ;       character in the ASCII time at which a carry-and-reset-to-zero
                00554        ;       should occur.
                00555        ;
00B4 00         00556                DB      0                       ;"Terminator"
                00557        CB$12$24$Clock:
00B5 3334       00558                DB      '34'                    ;Change to '23' for a 12-hour clock
00B7 FF         00559                DB      0FFH                    ;"Skip" character
00B8 363A       00560                DB      '6:'                    ;Maximum minutes are 59
00BA FF         00561                DB      0FFH                    ;"Skip" character
00BB 363A       00562                DB      '6:'                    ;Maximum seconds are 59
                00563        Update$Time$End:                        ;Used when updating the time
                00564        ;
                00565        ;
                00566        ;       Variables for the real time clock and watchdog
                00567        ;       timer
                00568        ;
00BD 3C         00569        RTC$Ticks$per$Second    DB      60      ;Number of real time clock
                00570                                                ;  ticks per elapsed second
00BE 3C         00571        RTC$Tick$Count          DB      60      ;Residual count before next
                00572                                                ;  second will elapse
00BF 0000       00573        RTC$Watchdog$Count      DW      0       ;Watchdog timer tick count
                00574                                                ;(0 = no watchdog timer set)
00C1 0000       00575        RTC$Watchdog$Address    DW      0       ;Address to which control
                00576                                                ;  will be transferred if the
                00577                                                ;  watchdog count hits 0
                00578
                00579        ;
                00580        ;       Function key table
                00581        ;
                00582        ;       This table consists of a series of entries, each one having the
                00583        ;       following structure:
                00584        ;
                00585        ;               DB      Second character of sequence emitted by
                00586        ;                       terminal's function key
                00587        ;       (       DB      Third character of sequence -- NOTE: this       )
                00588        ;       (               field will not be present if the source code   )
                00589        ;       (               has been configured to accept only two characters )
                00590        ;       (               in function key sequences.                      )
                00591        ;       (               NOTE: Adjust the equates for:                   )
                00592        ;       (                       Function$Key$Length                     )
                00593        ;       (                       Three$Character$Function                )
```

Figure 8-10. (Continued)

```
                  00594  ;
                  00595  ;              DB        A character string to be forced into the console
                  00596  ;                        input stream when the corresponding function key
                  00597  ;                        is pressed. The last byte of this string must be
                  00598  ;                        00H to terminate the forced input.
                  00599  ;
001B =            00600  Function$Key$Lead         EQU       1BH        ;Signals function key sequence
0003 =            00601  Function$Key$Length       EQU       3          ;Number of characters in function
                  00602                                                 ;  key input sequence (NOTE: this
                  00603                                                 ;  can only be 3 or 2 characters).
                  00604
                  00605  ;
                  00606                                                 ;The logic associated with function
                  00607                                                 ;  key recognition is made easier with
                  00608                                                 ;  the following equate
0001 =            00609  Three$Character$Function  EQU       Function$Key$Length - 2
                  00610                            ;Three$Character$Function will be TRUE if the
                  00611                            ;  function keys emit a three character
                  00612                            ;  sequence, FALSE if they emit a two character
                  00613                            ;  sequence.
                  00614
                  00615  ;       Each entry in the table must be the same length, as defined by:
                  00616  ;
0013 =            00617  CB$Function$Key$Entry$Size          EQU      16 + 1 + Function$Key$Length - 1
                  00618                                                       ^        ^                  ^
                  00619  ;                                                    :        :                  :
                  00620                   Maximum length of substitute        :        Lead character is not
                  00621                   string                              :        in table entry
                  00622                                                       For the terminating 00H
                  00623  ;
                  00624          The last entry in the table is marked by a 00-byte.
                  00625  ;
                  00626          The example values shown below are for a VT-100 terminal.
                  00627  ;
                  00628  CB$Function$Key$Table:
                  00629  ;                123456789.1234    5     6   7 <- Use to check length
00C3 4F5046756E00 00630          DB       'O','P','Function Key 1',LF,0,0
00D6 4F5146756E00 00631          DB       'O','Q','Function Key 2',LF,0,0
00E9 4F5246756E00 00632          DB       'O','R','Function Key 3',LF,0,0
00FC 4F5346756E00 00633          DB       'O','S','Function Key 4',LF,0,0
                  00634  ;
                  00635  ;                123456789.1
010F 5B4155702000 00636          DB       '[','A','Up Arrow',LF,0,0,0,0,0,0
0122 5B42446F7700 00637          DB       '[','B','Down Arrow',LF,0,0,0,0,0,0
0135 5B4352696700 00638          DB       '[','C','Right Arrow',LF,0,0,0,0,0
0148 5B444C656600 00639          DB       '[','D','Left Arrow',LF,0,0,0,0,0,0
                  00640
015B 000000000000 00641          DB       0,0,0,0,0,0,0,0,0,0,0,0,0,0,0,0,0,0,0   ;Spare entries
016E 000000000000 00642          DB       0,0,0,0,0,0,0,0,0,0,0,0,0,0,0,0,0,0,0
0181 000000000000 00643          DB       0,0,0,0,0,0,0,0,0,0,0,0,0,0,0,0,0,0,0
0194 000000000000 00644          DB       0,0,0,0,0,0,0,0,0,0,0,0,0,0,0,0,0,0,0
01A7 000000000000 00645          DB       0,0,0,0,0,0,0,0,0,0,0,0,0,0,0,0,0,0,0
01BA 000000000000 00646          DB       0,0,0,0,0,0,0,0,0,0,0,0,0,0,0,0,0,0,0
01CD 000000000000 00647          DB       0,0,0,0,0,0,0,0,0,0,0,0,0,0,0,0,0,0,0
01E0 000000000000 00648          DB       0,0,0,0,0,0,0,0,0,0,0,0,0,0,0,0,0,0,0
01F3 000000000000 00649          DB       0,0,0,0,0,0,0,0,0,0,0,0,0,0,0,0,0,0,0
0206 000000000000 00650          DB       0,0,0,0,0,0,0,0,0,0,0,0,0,0,0,0,0,0,0
                  00651
0219 FFFF         00652          DB       0FFH,0FFH          ;Terminator for utility that preprograms
                  00653                                      ;  function key sequence
                  00654  ;
                  00655  ;
                  00656  ;       Console output escape sequence control table
                  00657  ;
                  00658  ;       This table is referenced after a Function$Key$Lead character
                  00659  ;       has been detected in the CONOUT routine. The next character
                  00660  ;       to be output to the console is compared to the first byte
                  00661  ;       in each 3-byte table entry. If a match is found, then control
                  00662  ;       is transferred to the address following the byte that matched.
                  00663  ;
                  00664  CONOUT$Escape$Table:
021B 74           00665          DB       't'                ;Read current time
021C 4804         00666          DW       CONOUT$Time
021E 64           00667          DB       'd'                ;Read current date
021F 4104         00668          DW       CONOUT$Date
0221 75           00669          DB       'u'                ;Set current time
0222 5D04         00670          DW       CONOUT$Set$Time
```

Figure 8-10. (Continued)

```
0224 65          00671           DB      'e'                     ;Set current date
0225 4E04        00672           DW      CONOUT$Set$Date
                 00673
0227 00          00674           DB      0                       ;Terminator
                 00675   ;
                 00676   Long$Term$CB$End:
                 00677   ;
                 00800   ;#
                 00801   ;
                 00802   ;       Interrupt vector
                 00803   ;
                 00804   ;       Control is transferred here by the programmable interrupt
                 00805   ;       controller -- an Intel 8259A.
                 00806   ;
                 00807   ;       NOTE: The interrupt controller chip requires that the
                 00808   ;             interrupt vector table start on a paragraph
                 00809   ;             boundary. This is achieved by the following ORG line
0240             00810           ORG     ($ AND 0FFE0H) + 20H
                 00811   Interrupt$Vector:
                 00812                                   ;Interrupt number
0240 C37808      00813           JMP     RTC$Interrupt           ;0 -- clock
0243 00          00814           DB      0                       ;Skip a byte
0244 C3E806      00815           JMP     Character$Interrupt     ;1 -- character I/O
0247 00          00816           DB      0
0248 C3D80E      00817           JMP     Ghost$Interrupt         ;2 -- not used
024B 00          00818           DB      0
024C C3D80E      00819           JMP     Ghost$Interrupt         ;3 -- not used
024F 00          00820           DB      0
0250 C3D80E      00821           JMP     Ghost$Interrupt         ;4 -- not used
0253 00          00822           DB      0
0254 C3D80E      00823           JMP     Ghost$Interrupt         ;5 -- not used
0257 00          00824           DB      0
0258 C3D80E      00825           JMP     Ghost$Interrupt         ;6 -- not used
025B 00          00826           DB      0
025C C3D80E      00827           JMP     Ghost$Interrupt         ;7 -- not used
                 00828   ;
                 00900   ;#
                 00901
                 00902   ;       Device port numbers and other equates
                 00903   ;
0080 =           00904   CIO$Base$Port   EQU     80H             ;Base port number
                 00905
0080 =           00906   D0$Base$Port    EQU     CIO$Base$Port           ;Device 0
0080 =           00907   D0$Data$Port    EQU     D0$Base$Port
0081 =           00908   D0$Status$Port  EQU     D0$Base$Port + 1
0082 =           00909   D0$Mode$Port    EQU     D0$Base$Port + 2
0083 =           00910   D0$Command$Port EQU     D0$Base$Port + 3
                 00911   ;
                 00912
0084 =           00913   D1$Base$Port    EQU     CIO$Base$Port + 4       ;Device 1
0084 =           00914   D1$Data$Port    EQU     D1$Base$Port
0085 =           00915   D1$Status$Port  EQU     D1$Base$Port + 1
0086 =           00916   D1$Mode$Port    EQU     D1$Base$Port + 2
0087 =           00917   D1$Command$Port EQU     D1$Base$Port + 3
                 00918
0088 =           00919   D2$Base$Port    EQU     CIO$Base$Port + 8       ;Device 2
0088 =           00920   D2$Data$Port    EQU     D2$Base$Port
0089 =           00921   D2$Status$Port  EQU     D2$Base$Port + 1
008A =           00922   D2$Mode$Port    EQU     D2$Base$Port + 2
008B =           00923   D2$Command$Port EQU     D2$Base$Port + 3
                 00924
004E =           00925   D$Mode$Value$1  EQU     01$00$11$10B
                 00926                                   ;1 stop bit, no parity
                 00927                                   ;8 bits, Async. 16x rate
003C =           00928   D$Mode$Value$2  EQU     00$11$1100B
                 00929                                   ;Tx/Rx on internal clock
                 00930                                   ;9600 baud
0027 =           00931   D$Command$Value EQU     00$100111B
                 00932                                   ;Normal mode
                 00933                                   ;Enable Tx/Rx
                 00934                                   ;RTS and DTR active
0038 =           00935   D$Error         EQU     0011$1000B
0037 =           00936   D$Error$Reset   EQU     00$110111B
                 00937                                   ;Same as command value plus error reset
0001 =           00938   D$Output$Ready  EQU     0000$0001B
0002 =           00939   D$Input$Ready   EQU     0000$0010B
0080 =           00940   D$DTR$High      EQU     1000$0000B      ;Note: this is actually the
```

Figure 8-10. (Continued)

```
                00941                             ;    data-set-ready pin
                00942                             ;    on the chip. It is connected
                00943                             ;    to the DTR pin on the cable
0027 =          00944   D$Raise$RTS    EQU   00$1$00111B   ;Raise RTS, Tx/Rx enable
0007 =          00945   D$Drop$RTS     EQU   00$0$00111B   ;Drop RTS, Tx/Rx enable
                00946   ;
                00947   ;
                00948   ;         Interrupt controller ports (Intel 8259A)
                00949   ;
                00950   ;     Note : these equates are placed here so that they
                00951   ;            follow the definition of the interrupt vector
                00952   ;            and thus avoid 'P' (phase) errors in ASM.
                00953   ;
00D9 =          00954   IC$OCW1$Port   EQU   0D9H   ;Operational control word 1
00D8 =          00955   IC$OCW2$Port   EQU   0D8H   ;Operational control word 2
00D8 =          00956   IC$OCW3$Port   EQU   0D8H   ;Operational control word 3
00D8 =          00957   IC$ICW1$Port   EQU   0D8H   ;Initialization control word 1
00D9 =          00958   IC$ICW2$Port   EQU   0D9H   ;Initialization control word 2
                00959   ;
0020 =          00960   IC$EOI         EQU   20H    ;Nonspecific end of interrupt
                00961   ;
0056 =          00962   IC$ICW1        EQU   (Interrupt$Vector AND 1110$0000B) + 000$10110B
                00963                             ;Sets the A7 - A5 bits of the interrupt
                00964                             ; vector address plus:
                00965                             ;   Edge triggered
                00966                             ;   4-byte interval
                00967                             ;   Single 8259 in system
                00968                             ;   No ICW4 needed
0002 =          00969   IC$ICW2        EQU   Interrupt$Vector SHR 8
                00970                             ;Address bits A15 - A8 of the interrupt
                00971                             ; vector address. Note the interrupt
                00972                             ; vector is the first structure in
                00973                             ; the long term configuration block
                00974   ;
00FC =          00975   IC$OCW1        EQU   1111$1100B   ;Interrupt mask
                00976                             ;Interrupt 0 (clock) enabled
                00977                             ;Interrupt 1 (character input) enabled
                00978   ;
                01100   ;#
                01101   ;
                01102   ;
                01103   Display$Message:          ;Displays the specified message on the console.
                01104                             ;On entry, HL points to a stream of bytes to be
                01105                             ;output. A 00H-byte terminates the message.
025F 7E         01106           MOV    A,M           ;Get next message byte
0260 B7          01107           ORA    A             ;Check if terminator
0261 C8          01108           RZ                   ;Yes, return to caller
0262 4F          01109           MOV    C,A           ;Prepare for output
0263 E5          01110           PUSH   H             ;Save message pointer
0264 CDD703      01111           CALL   CONOUT        ;Go to main console output routine
0267 E1          01112           POP    H             ;Recover message pointer
0268 23          01113           INX    H             ;Move to next byte of message
0269 C35F02      01114           JMP    Display$Message ;Loop until complete message output
                01115   ;
                01200   ;#
                01201   ;
                01202   Enter$CPM:      ;This routine is entered either from the cold or warm
                01203                   ; boot code. It sets up the JMP instructions in the
                01204                   ; base page, and also sets the high-level disk driver's
                01205                   ; input/output address (the DMA address).
                01206   ;
026C 3EC3       01207           MVI    A,JMP         ;Get machine code for JMP
026E 320000     01208           STA    0000H         ;Set up JMP at location 0000H
0271 320500     01209           STA    0005H         ; and at location 0005H
                01210   ;
0274 210300     01211           LXI    H,Warm$Boot$Entry   ;Get BIOS vector address
0277 220100     01212           SHLD   0001H         ;Put address at location 0001H
                01213   ;
027A 2106CC     01214           LXI    H,BDOS$Entry  ;Get BDOS entry point address
027D 220600     01215           SHLD   6             ;Put address at location 0005H
                01216   ;
0280 018000     01217           LXI    B,80H         ;Set disk I/O address to default
0283 CDA809     01218           CALL   SETDMA        ;Use normal BIOS routine
                01219   ;
0286 FB         01220           EI                   ;Ensure interrupts are enabled
0287 3A0400     01221           LDA    Default$Disk  ;Handover current default disk to
028A 4F         01222           MOV    C,A           ; console command processor
```

Figure 8-10. (Continued)

```
028B C300C4      01223              JMP      CCP$Entry          ;Transfer to CCP
                 01224      ;
                 01300      ;#
                 01301      ;
                 01302      ;       Device table equates
                 01303      ;       The drivers use a device table for each
                 01304      ;       physical device they service. The equates that follow
                 01305      ;       are used to access the various fields within the
                 01306      ;       device table.
                 01307      ;
                 01308                                  Port numbers and status bits
0000 =           01309      DT$Status$Port     EQU      0           ;Device status port number
0001 =           01310      DT$Data$Port       EQU      DT$Status$Port+1
                 01311                                              ;Device data port number
0002 =           01312      DT$Output$Ready    EQU      DT$DataPort+1
                 01313                                              ;Output ready status mask
0003 =           01314      DT$Input$Ready     EQU      DT$Output$Ready+1
                 01315                                              ;Input ready status mask
0004 =           01316      DT$DTR$Ready       EQU      DT$Input$Ready+1
                 01317                                              ;DTR ready to send mask
0005 =           01318      DT$Reset$Int$Port  EQU      DT$DTR$Ready+1
                 01319                                              ;Port number used to reset an
                 01320                                              ;  interrupt
0006 =           01321      DT$Reset$Int$Value EQU      DT$Reset$Int$Port+1
                 01322                                              ;Value output to reset interrupt
0007 =           01323      DT$Detect$Error$Port EQU    DT$Reset$Int$Value+1
                 01324                                              ;Port number for detecting error
0008 =           01325      DT$Detect$Error$Value EQU   DT$Detect$Error$Port+1
                 01326                                              ;Mask for detecting error (parity etc.)
0009 =           01327      DT$Reset$Error$Port EQU     DT$Detect$Error$Value+1
                 01328                                              ;Output to port to reset error
000A =           01329      DT$Reset$Error$Value EQU    DT$Reset$Error$Port+1
                 01330                                              ;Value to output to reset error
000B =           01331      DT$RTS$Control$Port EQU     DT$Reset$Error$Value+1
                 01332                                              ;Control port for lowering RTS
000C =           01333      DT$Drop$RTS$Value  EQU      DT$RTS$Control$Port+1
                 01334                                              ;Value, when output, to drop RTS
000D =           01335      DT$Raise$RTS$Value EQU      DT$Drop$RTS$Value+1
                 01336                                              ;Value, when output, to raise RTS
                 01337      ;
                 01338                                  Device logical status (incl. protocols)
000E =           01339      DT$Status          EQU      DT$Raise$RTS$Value+1
                 01340                                              ;Status bits
0001 =           01341      DT$Output$Suspend  EQU      0000$0001B  ;Output suspended pending
                 01342                                              ;   protocol action
0002 =           01343      DT$Input$Suspend   EQU      0000$0010B  ;Input suspended until
                 01344                                              ;   buffer empties
0004 =           01345      DT$Output$DTR      EQU      0000$0100B  ;Output uses DTR-high-to-send
0008 =           01346      DT$Output$Xon      EQU      0000$1000B  ;Output uses XON/XOFF
0010 =           01347      DT$Output$Etx      EQU      0001$0000B  ;Output uses ETX/ACK
0020 =           01348      DT$Output$Timeout  EQU      0010$0000B  ;Output uses timeout
0040 =           01349      DT$Input$RTS       EQU      0100$0000B  ;Input uses RTS-high-to-receive
0080 =           01350      DT$Input$Xon       EQU      1000$0000B  ;Input uses XON/XOFF
                 01351      ;
000F =           01352      DT$Status$2        EQU      DT$Status+1 ;Secondary status byte
0001 =           01353      DT$Fake$Typeahead  EQU      0000$0001B  ;Requests Input$Status to
                 01354                                              ;  return "Data Ready" when
                 01355                                              ;  control characters are in
                 01356                                              ;  input buffer
                 01357      ;
0010 =           01358      DT$Etx$Count       EQU      DT$Status$2+1
                 01359                                              ;No. of chars. sent in Etx protocol
0012 =           01360      DT$Etx$Message$Length EQU   DT$Etx$Count+2
                 01361                                              ;Specified message length
                 01362      ;
                 01363                                  Input buffer values
0014 =           01364      DT$Buffer$Base     EQU      DT$Etx$Message$Length+2
                 01365                                              ;Address of Input buffer
0016 =           01366      DT$Put$Offset      EQU      DT$Buffer$Base+2
                 01367                                              ;Offset for putting chars. into buffer
0017 =           01368      DT$Get$Offset      EQU      DT$Put$Offset+1
                 01369                                              ;Offset for getting chars. from buffer
0018 =           01370      DT$Buffer$Length$Mask EQU   DT$Get$Offset+1
                 01371                                              ;Length of buffer - 1
                 01372                                              ;Note: Buffer length must always be
                 01373                                              ;  a binary number; e.g. 32, 64 or 128
```

Figure 8-10.   (Continued)

```
                01374                                           ;This mask then becomes:
                01375                                           ;   32 ->   31 (0001$1111B)
                01376                                           ;   64 ->   63 (0011$1111B)
                01377                                           ;  128 ->  127 (0111$1111B)
                01378                                           ;After the get/put offset has been
                01379                                           ;  incremented, it is ANDed with the mask
                01380                                           ;  to reset it to zero when the end of
                01381                                           ;  the buffer has been reached
0019 =          01382           DT$Character$Count     EQU      DT$Buffer$Length$Mask+1
                01383                                           ;Count of the number of characters
                01384                                           ;  currently in the buffer
001A =          01385           DT$Stop$Input$Count    EQU      DT$Character$Count+1
                01386                                           ;Stop input when the count reaches
                01387                                           ;  this value
001B =          01388           DT$Resume$Input$Count  EQU      DT$Stop$Input$Count+1
                01389                                           ;Resume input when the count reaches
                01390                                           ;  this value
001C =          01391           DT$Control$Count       EQU      DT$Resume$Input$Count+1
                01392                                           ;Count of the number of control
                01393                                           ;  characters in the buffer
001D =          01394           DT$Function$Delay      EQU      DT$Control$Count+1
                01395                                           ;Number of clock ticks to delay to
                01396                                           ;  allow all characters after function
                01397                                           ;  key lead-in to arrive
001E =          01398           DT$Initialize$Stream   EQU      DT$Function$Delay+1
                01399                                           ;Address of byte stream necessary to
                01400                                           ;  initialize this device
                01401
                01500           ;#
                01501           ;
                01502           ;       Device tables
                01503           ;
                01504           DT$0:
028E 81         01505                   DB      D0$Status$Port ;Status port (8251A chip)
028F 80         01506                   DB      D0$Data$Port   ;Data port
0290 01         01507                   DB      D$Output$Ready ;Output data ready
0291 02         01508                   DB      D$Input$Ready  ;Input data ready
0292 80         01509                   DB      D$DTR$High     ;DTR ready to send
0293 D8         01510                   DB      IC$OCW2$Port   ;Reset interrupt port (00H is an unused port)
0294 20         01511                   DB      IC$EOI         ;Reset interrupt value (nonspecific EOI)
0295 81         01512                   DB      D0$Status$Port ;Detect error port
0296 38         01513                   DB      D$Error        ;Mask: framing, overrun, parity errors
0297 83         01514                   DB      D0$Command$Port ;Reset error port
0298 37         01515                   DB      D$Error$Reset  ;Reset error: RTS high, reset, Tx/Rx enable
0299 83         01516                   DB      D0$Command$Port ;Drop/raise RTS port
029A 07         01517                   DB      D$Drop$RTS     ;Drop RTS Value (keep Tx & Rx enabled)
029B 27         01518                   DB      D$Raise$RTS    ;Raise RTS value (keep Tx & Rx enabled)
029C C0         01519                   DB      DT$Input$Xon + DT$Input$RTS   ;Protocol and status
029D 00         01520                   DB      0              ;Status #2
029E 0004       01521                   DW      1024           ;Etx/Ack message count
02A0 0004       01522                   DW      1024           ;Etx/Ack message length
02A2 2422       01523                   DW      D0$Buffer      ;Input buffer
02A4 00         01524                   DB      0              ;Put offset into buffer
02A5 00         01525                   DB      0              ;Get offset into buffer
02A6 1F         01526                   DB      D0$Buffer$Length -1 ;Buffer length mask
02A7 00         01527                   DB      0              ;Count of characters in buffer
02A8 1B         01528                   DB      D0$Buffer$Length - 5 ;Stop input when count hits this value
02A9 10         01529                   DB      D0$Buffer$Length / 2 ;Resume input when count hits this value
02AA 00         01530                   DB      0              ;Count of control characters in buffer
02AB 06         01531                   DB      6              ;Number of 16.66ms ticks to allow function
                01532                                           ;  key sequence to arrive (approx. 90ms)
02AC 8400       01533                   DW      D0$Initialize$Stream  ;Address of initialization stream
                01534           ;
                01535           DT$1:
02AE 85         01536                   DB      D1$Status$Port ;Status port (8251A chip)
02AF 84         01537                   DB      D1$Data$Port   ;Data port
02B0 01         01538                   DB      D$Output$Ready ;Output data ready
02B1 02         01539                   DB      D$Input$Ready  ;Input data ready
02B2 80         01540                   DB      D$DTR$High     ;DTR ready to send
02B3 D8         01541                   DB      IC$OCW2$Port   ;Reset interrupt port (00H is an unused port)
02B4 20         01542                   DB      IC$EOI         ;Reset interrupt value (nonspecific EOI)
02B5 85         01543                   DB      D1$Status$Port ;Detect error port
02B6 38         01544                   DB      D$Error        ;Mask: framing, overrun, parity errors
02B7 87         01545                   DB      D1$Command$Port ;Reset error port
02B8 37         01546                   DB      D$Error$Reset  ;Reset error: RTS high, reset, Tx/Rx enable
02B9 87         01547                   DB      D1$Command$Port ;Drop/raise RTS port
02BA 07         01548                   DB      D$Drop$RTS     ;Drop RTS value (keep Tx & Rx enabled)
```

Figure 8-10.   (Continued)

Chapter 8: Writing an Enhanced BIOS 247

```
02BB 27        01549          DB      D$Raise$RTS             ;Raise RTS value (keep Tx & Rx enabled)
02BC C0        01550          DB      DT$Input$Xon + DT$Input$RTS     ;Protocol and status
02BD 00        01551          DB      0                       ;Status #2
02BE 0004      01552          DW      1024                    ;Etx/Ack message count
02C0 0004      01553          DW      1024                    ;Etx/Ack message length
02C2 4422      01554          DW      D1$Buffer               ;Input buffer
02C4 00        01555          DB      0                       ;Put offset into buffer
02C5 00        01556          DB      0                       ;Get offset into buffer
02C6 1F        01557          DB      D1$Buffer$Length -1 ;Buffer length mask
02C7 00        01558          DB      0                       ;Count of characters in buffer
02C8 1B        01559          DB      D1$Buffer$Length - 5 ;Stop input when count hits this value
02C9 10        01560          DB      D1$Buffer$Length / 2 ;Resume input when count hits this value
02CA 00        01561          DB      0                       ;Count of control characters in buffer
02CB 06        01562          DB      6                       ;Number of 16.66ms ticks to allow function
               01563                                          ;  key sequence to arrive (approx. 90ms)
02CC 9400      01564          DW      D1$Initialize$Stream    ;Address of initialization stream
               01565  ;
               01566  ;
               01567  DT$2:
02CE 89        01568          DB      D2$Status$Port          ;Status port (8251A chip)
02CF 88        01569          DB      D2$Data$Port            ;Data port
02D0 01        01570          DB      D$Output$Ready          ;Output data ready
02D1 02        01571          DB      D$Input$Ready           ;Input data ready
02D2 80        01572          DB      D$DTR$High              ;DTR ready to send
02D3 D8        01573          DB      IC$OCW2$Port            ;Reset interrupt port (00H is an unused port)
02D4 20        01574          DB      IC$EOI                  ;Reset interrupt value (nonspecific EOI)
02D5 89        01575          DB      D2$Status$Port          ;Detect error port
02D6 38        01576          DB      D$Error                 ;Mask: framing, overrun, parity errors
02D7 8B        01577          DB      D2$Command$Port         ;Reset error port
02D8 37        01578          DB      D$Error$Reset           ;Reset error: RTS high, reset, Tx/Rx enable
02D9 8B        01579          DB      D2$Command$Port         ;Drop/raise RTS port
02DA 07        01580          DB      D$Drop$RTS              ;Drop RTS value (keep Tx & Rx enabled)
02DB 27        01581          DB      D$Raise$RTS             ;Raise RTS value (keep Tx & Rx enabled)
02DC C0        01582          DB      DT$Input$Xon + DT$Input$RTS     ;Protocol and status
02DD 00        01583          DB      0                       ;Status #2
02DE 0004      01584          DW      1024                    ;Etx/Ack message count
02E0 0004      01585          DW      1024                    ;Etx/Ack message length
02E2 6422      01586          DW      D2$Buffer               ;Input buffer
02E4 00        01587          DB      0                       ;Put offset into buffer
02E5 00        01588          DB      0                       ;Get offset into buffer
02E6 1F        01589          DB      D2$Buffer$Length -1 ;Buffer length mask
02E7 00        01590          DB      0                       ;Count of characters in buffer
02E8 1B        01591          DB      D2$Buffer$Length - 5 ;Stop input when count hits this value
02E9 10        01592          DB      D2$Buffer$Length / 2 ;Resume input when count hits this value
02EA 00        01593          DB      0                       ;Count of control characters in buffer
02EB 06        01594          DB      6                       ;Number of 16.66ms ticks to allow function
               01595                                          ;  Key sequence to arrive (approx. 90ms)
02EC A400      01596          DW      D2$Initialize$Stream    ;Address of initialization stream
               01597  ;
               01700  ;#
               01701  ;       General character I/O device initialization
               01702  ;
               01703  ;       This routine will be called from the main CP/M
               01704  ;       initialization code.
               01705  ;
               01706  ;       It makes repeated calls to the specific character I/O
               01707  ;       device initialization routine.
               01708  ;
               01709  General$CIO$Initialization:
02EE AF        01710          XRA     A                       ;Set device number (used to access the
               01711                                          ;  table of device table addresses in the
               01712                                          ;  configuration block)
02EF 4F        01713          MOV     C,A                     ;Match to externally CALLable interface
               01714  GCI$Next$Device:
02F0 CDFA02    01715          CALL    Specific$CIO$Initialization     ;Initialize the device
02F3 3C        01716          INR     A                       ;Move to next device
02F4 FE10      01717          CPI     16                      ;Check if all possible devices (0 - 15)
02F6 C8        01718          RZ                              ;  have been initialized
02F7 C3F002    01719          JMP     GCI$Next$Device
               01720  ;
               01800  ;#
               01801  ;
               01802  ;       Specific character I/O initialization
               01803  ;
               01804  ;       This routine outputs the specified byte values to the specified
               01805  ;       ports as controlled by the initialization streams in the
               01806  ;       configuration block. Each device table contains a pointer to
```

Figure 8-10. (Continued)

```
                01807   ;       these streams. The device table itself is selected according
                01808   ;       to the device NUMBER -- this is an entry parameter for this
                01809   ;       routine.
                01810   ;       This routine will be called either from the general device
                01811   ;       initialization routine above, or directly by a BIOS call from
                01812   ;       a system utility executing in the TPA.
                01813   ;
                01814   ;       Entry parameters
                01815   ;
                01816   ;               C = device number
                01817   ;
                01818   ;       Exit parameters
                01819   ;
                01820   ;               A = Device number (preserved)
                01821   ;
                01822   ;===========================
                01823   Specific$CIO$Initialization:           ;<=== BIOS entry point (private)
                01824   ;===========================
02FA 79         01825           MOV     A,C                    ;Get device number
02FB F5         01826           PUSH    PSW                    ;Preserve device number
02FC 87         01827           ADD     A                      ;Make device number into word pointer
02FD 4F         01828           MOV     C,A
02FE 0600       01829           MVI     B,0                    ;Make into a word
0300 216400     01830           LXI     H,CB$Device$Table$Addresses   ;Get table base
0303 09         01831           DAD     B                      ;HL -> device table address
0304 5E         01832           MOV     E,M                    ;Get LS byte
0305 23         01833           INX     H
0306 56         01834           MOV     D,M                    ;Get MS byte: DE -> device table
                01835
0307 7A         01836           MOV     A,D                    ;Check if device table address = 0
0308 B3         01837           ORA     E
0309 CA1703     01838           JZ      SCI$Exit               ;Yes, device table nonexistent
                01839
030C 211E00     01840           LXI     H,DT$Initialize$Stream
030F 19         01841           DAD     D                      ;HL -> initialization stream address
0310 5E         01842           MOV     E,M                    ;Get LS byte
0311 23         01843           INX     H
0312 56         01844           MOV     D,M                    ;Get MS byte
0313 EB         01845           XCHG                           ;HL -> initialization stream itself
0314 CD1903     01846           CALL    Output$Byte$Stream     ;Output byte stream to various
                01847                                          ;  ports
                01848   ;
                01849   SCI$Exit:
0317 F1         01850           POP     PSW                    ;Recover user's device number in C
0318 C9         01851           RET
                01852   ;
                02000   ;#      Output byte stream
                02001   ;
                02002   ;
                02003   ;       This routine outputs initialization bytes to port
                02004   ;       numbers. The byte stream has the following format:
                02005   ;
                02006   ;               DB      ppH     Port number
                02007   ;               DB      nn      Number of bytes to output
                02008   ;               DB      vvH,vvH...  Bytes to be output
                02009   ;               :
                02010   ;               :       Repeated
                02011   ;               :
                02012   ;               DB      00H     Port number of 0 terminates
                02013   ;
                02014   ;       Entry parameters
                02015   ;
                02016   ;               HL -> Byte stream
                02017   ;
                02018   Output$Byte$Stream:
                02019   OBS$Loop:
0319 7E         02020           MOV     A,M                    ;Get port number
031A B7         02021           ORA     A                      ;Check if 00H (terminator)
031B C8         02022           RZ                             ;Exit if at end of stream
031C 322503     02023           STA     OBS$Port               ;Store in port number below
031F 23         02024           INX     H                      ;HL -> count of bytes
0320 4E         02025           MOV     C,M                    ;Get count
0321 23         02026           INX     H                      ;HL -> first initialization byte
                02027   ;
                02028   OBS$Next$Byte:
0322 7E         02029           MOV     A,M                    ;Get next byte
0323 23         02030           INX     H                      ;HL -> next data byte (or port number)
```

Figure 8-10. (Continued)

Chapter 8: Writing an Enhanced BIOS **249**

```
                    02031
0324 D3             02032          DB      OUT
                    02033  OBS$Port:
0325 00             02034          DB      0                       ;<- Set up in instruction above
0326 0D             02035          DCR     C                       ;Count down on byte counter
0327 C22203         02036          JNZ     OBS$Next$Byte           ;Output next data byte
032A C31903         02037          JMP     OBS$Loop                ;Go back for next port number
                    02038  ;
                    02100  ;#
                    02101  ;       CONST - Console status
                    02102  ;
                    02103  ;       This routine checks both the forced input pointer and
                    02104  ;       the character count for the appropriate input buffer.
                    02105  ;       The A register is set to indicate whether or not there
                    02106  ;       is data waiting.
                    02107  ;
                    02108  ;       Entry parameters: none.
                    02109  ;
                    02110  ;       Exit parameters
                    02111  ;
                    02112  ;               A = 000H if there is no data waiting
                    02113  ;               A = 0FFH if there is data waiting
                    02114  ;
                    02115  ;=========================
                    02116  CONST:                                   ;<=== BIOS entry point (standard)
                    02117  ;=========================
032D 2A5800         02118          LHLD    CB$Console$Input        ;Get redirection word
0330 116400         02119          LXI     D,CB$Device$Table$Addresses
0333 CD6F06         02120          CALL    Select$Device$Table     ;Get device table address
0336 C34708         02121          JMP     Get$Input$Status        ;Get status from input device
                    02122                                          ;  and return to caller
                    02200  ;#
                    02201  ;
                    02202  ;       CONIN -- console input
                    02203  ;
                    02204  ;       This routine returns the next character for the console input
                    02205  ;       stream. Depending on the circumstances, this can be a character
                    02206  ;       from the console input buffer, or from a previously stored
                    02207  ;       string of characters to be "forced" into the input stream, for
                    02208  ;       the automatic execution of system initialization routines.
                    02209  ;       The "forced input" can come from any previously stored character
                    02210  ;       string in memory. It is used to inject the current time and date
                    02211  ;       or a string associated with a function key into the console
                    02212  ;       stream. On system startup, a string of "SUBMIT STARTUP" is
                    02213  ;       forced into the console input stream to provide a mechanism.
                    02214  ;
                    02215  ;       Normal ("unforced") input comes from whichever physical device
                    02216  ;       is specified in the console input redirection word (see the
                    02217  ;       configuration block).
                    02218  ;
0339 00             02219  CONIN$Delay$Elapsed:    DB      0       ;Flag used during function key
                    02220                                          ;  processing to indicate that
                    02221                                          ;  a predetermined delay has
                    02222                                          ;  elapsed
                    02223  ;
                    02224  ;=========================
                    02225  CONIN:                                   ;<=== BIOS entry point (standard)
                    02226  ;=========================
033A 2A8D0F         02227          LHLD    CB$Forced$Input         ;Get the forced input pointer
033D 7E             02228          MOV     A,M                     ;Get the next character of input
033E B7             02229          ORA     A                       ;Check if a null
033F CA4703         02230          JZ      CONIN$No$FI             ;Yes, no forced input
0342 23             02231          INX     H                       ;Yes, update the pointer
0343 228D0F         02232          SHLD    CB$Forced$Input         ;  and store it back
0346 C9             02233          RET
                    02234  ;
                    02235  CONIN$No$FI                              ;No forced input
0347 2A5800         02236          LHLD    CB$Console$Input        ;Get redirection word
034A 116400         02237          LXI     D,CB$Device$Table$Addresses
034D CD6F06         02238          CALL    Select$Device$Table     ;Get device table address
0350 CD9106         02239          CALL    Get$Input$Character     ;Get next character from input device
                    02240
                    02241                                          ;Function key processing
0353 FE1B           02242          CPI     Function$Key$Lead       ;Check if first character of function
                    02243                                          ;  key sequence (normally escape)
0355 C0             02244          RNZ                             ;Return to BIOS caller if not
0356 F5             02245          PUSH    PSW                     ;Save lead in character
```

Figure 8-10. (Continued)

```
0357 211D00    02246          LXI    H,DT$Function$Delay    ;Get delay time constant for
               02247                                         ;  delay while waiting for subsequent
               02248                                         ;  characters of function key sequence
               02249                                         ;  to arrive
035A 19        02250          DAD    D
035B 4E        02251          MOV    C,M                     ;Get delay value
035C 0600      02252          MVI    B,0                     ;Make into word value
035E AF        02253          XRA    A                       ;Indicate timer not yet out of time
035F 323903    02254          STA    CONIN$Delay$Elapsed
0362 217B03    02255          LXI    H,CONIN$Set$Delay$Elapsed ;Address to resume at after delay
0365 CD6D08    02256          CALL   Set$Watchdog            ;Sets up delay based on real time
               02257                                         ;  clock such that control will be
               02258                                         ;  transferred to specified address
               02259                                         ;  after time interval has elapsed
               02260   CONIN$Wait$for$Delay:                  ;Wait here until delay has elapsed
0368 3A3903    02261          LDA    CONIN$Delay$Elapsed     ;Check flag set by watchdog routine
036B B7        02262          ORA    A
036C CA6803    02263          JZ     CONIN$Wait$for$Delay
               02264   
               02265   CONIN$Check$for$Function:
036F 211900    02266          LXI    H,DT$Character$Count    ;Now check if the remaining characters
               02267                                         ;  of the sequence have been input
0372 19        02268          DAD    D
0373 7E        02269          MOV    A,M                     ;Get count of characters in buffer
0374 FE02      02270          CPI    Function$Key$Length - 1
0376 D28103    02271          JNC    CONIN$Check$Function    ;Enough characters in buffer for
               02272                                         ;  possible function key sequence
0379 F1        02273          POP    PSW                     ;Insufficient characters in buffer
               02274                                         ;  to be a function key, so return
               02275                                         ;  to caller with lead character
037A C9        02276          RET
               02277   
               02278   ;
               02279   ;      The following routine is called by the watchdog routine
               02280   ;      when the specified delay has elapsed.
               02281   ;
               02282   CONIN$Set$Delay$Elapsed:
037B 3EFF      02283          MVI    A,0FFH                  ;Indicate watchdog timer out of time
037D 323903    02284          STA    CONIN$Delay$Elapsed
0380 C9        02285          RET                             ;Return to watchdog routine
               02286   ;
               02287   ;
               02288   CONIN$Check$Function:
0381 211700    02289          LXI    H,DT$Get$Offset         ;Save the current "get pointer"
0384 19        02290          DAD    D                       ;  in the buffer
0385 7E        02291          MOV    A,M                     ;Get the pointer
0386 F5        02292          PUSH   PSW                     ;Save pointer on the stack
               02293   
0387 211700    02294          LXI    H,DT$Get$Offset         ;Check the second (and possibly third)
038A CDF007    02295          CALL   Get$Address$in$Buffer   ;  character in the sequence
038D 46        02296          MOV    B,M                     ;Get the second character
               02297   
               02298          IF     Three$Character$Function
038E C5        02299          PUSH   B                       ;Save for later use
038F 211700    02300          LXI    H,DT$Get$Offset         ;Retrieve the third character
0392 CDF007    02301          CALL   Get$Address$in$Buffer
0395 C1        02302          POP    B                       ;Recover second character
0396 4E        02303          MOV    C,M                     ;Now BC = Char 2, Char 3
               02304          ENDIF
               02305   
0397 D5        02306          PUSH   D                       ;Save device table pointer
0398 21B000    02307          LXI    H,CB$Function$Key$Table - CB$Function$Key$Entry$Size
               02308                                         ;Get pointer to function key table
               02309                                         ;  in configuration block
039B 111300    02310          LXI    D,CB$Function$Key$Entry$Size  ;Get entry size ready for loop
               02311   CONIN$Next$Function:
039E 19        02312          DAD    D                       ;Move to next (or first) entry
039F 7E        02313          MOV    A,M                     ;Get second character of sequence
03A0 B7        02314          ORA    A                       ;Check if end of function key table
03A1 CAC203    02315          JZ     CONIN$Not$Function      ;Yes -- it is not a function key
03A4 B8        02316          CMP    B                       ;Compare second characters
03A5 C29E03    02317          JNZ    CONIN$Next$Function     ;No match, so try next entry in table
               02318   
               02319          IF     Three$Character$Function
03A8 23        02320          INX    H                       ;HL -> third character
03A9 7E        02321          MOV    A,M                     ;Get third character of sequence
03AA 2B        02322          DCX    H                       ;Simplify logic for 2 & 3 char. seq.
```

Figure 8-10. (Continued)

```
03AB B9         02323           CMP     C                       ;Compare third characters
03AC C29E03     02324           JNZ     CONIN$Next$Function     ;No match, so try next entry in table
03AF 23         02325           INX     H                       ;When match found, compensate for
                02326                                           ;   extra decrement
                02327           ENDIF
                02328
03B0 23         02329           INX     H                       ;HL -> first character of substitute
                02330                                           ;   string of characters (00-byte term.)
03B1 228D0F     02331           SHLD    CB$Forced$Input         ;Make the CONIN routine inject the
                02332                                           ;   substitute string into the input
                02333                                           ;   stream
                02334
                02335                                           ;Now that a function sequence has been
                02336                                           ;   identified, the stack must be
                02337                                           ;   balanced prior to return
03B4 D1         02338           POP     D                       ;Get the device table pointer
03B5 F1         02339           POP     PSW                     ;Dump the "get" offset value
03B6 F1         02340           POP     PSW                     ;Dump the function sequence lead char.
                02341
03B7 211900     02342           LXI     H,DT$Character$Count    ;Downdate the character count
03BA 19         02343           DAD     D                       ;   to reflect the characters removed
                02344                                           ;   from the buffer
03BB 7E         02345           MOV     A,M                     ;Get the count
03BC D602       02346           SUI     Function$Key$Length -1  ; (the lead character has already
03BE 77         02347           MOV     M,A                     ;   been deducted)
03BF C33A03     02348           JMP     CONIN                   ;Return to CONIN processing to get
                02349                                           ;   the forced input characters
                02350   CONIN$Not$Function:
                02351                                           ;Attempts to recognize a function key sequence
                02352                                           ;   have failed. The "get" offset pointer must be
                02353                                           ;   restored to its previous value so that
                02354                                           ;   the character(s) presumed to be part of
                02355                                           ;   the function sequence are not lost.
                02356
03C2 D1         02357           POP     D                       ;Recover device table pointer
03C3 F1         02358           POP     PSW                     ;Recover previous "get" offset
03C4 211700     02359           LXI     H,DT$Get$Offset
03C7 19         02360           DAD     D                       ;HL -> "get" offset in table
03C8 77         02361           MOV     M,A                     ;Reset "get" offset as it was after
                02362                                           ;   the lead character was detected
03C9 F1         02363           POP     PSW                     ;Recover lead character
03CA C9         02364           RET                             ;Return the lead character to the user
                02365   ;
                02500   ;#      Console output
                02501   ;
                02502   ;
                02503   ;       This routine outputs data characters to the console device(s).
                02504   ;       It also "traps" escape sequences being output to the console,
                02505   ;       triggering specific actions according to the sequences.
                02506   ;       A primitive "state-machine" is used to step through escape
                02507   ;       sequence recognition.
                02508   ;       In addition to outputting the next character to all of the
                02509   ;       devices currently selected in the console output redirection word,
                02510   ;       it checks to see that output to the selected device has not been
                02511   ;       suspended by XON/XOFF protocol, and that DTR is high if
                02512   ;       it should be.
                02513   ;       Once the character has been output, if ETX/ACK protocol is in use,
                02514   ;       and the specified length of message has been output, an Etx
                02515   ;       character is output and the device is flagged as being suspended.
                02516   ;
                02517   ;       Entry parameters
                02518   ;
                02519   ;               C = character to be output
                02520   ;
                02521   ;       CONOUT storage variables
                02522   ;
03CB 00         02523   CONOUT$Character:       DB      0       ;Save area for character to be output
                02524
03CC DB03       02525   CONOUT$Processor:       DW      CONOUT$Normal
                02526                                           ;This is the address of the piece of
                02527                                           ;   code that will process the next
                02528                                           ;   character. The default case is
                02529                                           ;   CONOUT$Normal
03CE 0000       02530   CONOUT$String$Pointer:  DW      0       ;This points to a string (normally
                02531                                           ;   in the configuration block) that
                02532                                           ;   is being preset by characters from
                02533                                           ;   the console output stream
```

Figure 8-10. (Continued)

```
03D0 00         02534       CONOUT$String$Length:   DB      0           ;This contains the maximum number of
                02535                                                   ;  characters to be preset into a
                02536                                                   ;  from the console output stream
                02537
                02538       ;
                02539       ;       *** WARNING ***
                02540       ;       The output error message routine shares the code in this
                02541       ;       subroutine. On entry here, the data byte to be output
                02542       ;       will be on the stack, and the DE registers set up correctly.
                02543       ;
                02544       ;
                02545       CONOUT$OEM$Entry:
03D1 32CB03     02546               STA     CONOUT$Character        ;Save data byte
03D4 C3E803     02547               JMP     CONOUT$Entry2           ;HL already has special bit map
                02548       ;
                02549       ;=====================
                02550       CONOUT:                                 ;<=== BIOS entry point (standard)
                02551       ;=====================
03D7 2ACC03     02552               LHLD    CONOUT$Processor        ;Get address of processor to handle
                02553                                               ;  the next character to be output
                02554                                               ;(Default is CONOUT$Normal)
03DA E9         02555               PCHL                            ;Transfer control to the processor
                02556       ;
                02557       ;
                02558       CONOUT$Normal:                          ;Normal processor for console output
03DB 79         02559               MOV     A,C                     ;Check if possible start of escape
03DC FE1B       02560               CPI     Function$Key$Lead       ;  sequence
03DE CA1204     02561               JZ      CONOUT$Escape$Found     ;Perhaps
                02562       CONOUT$Forced:
03E1 79         02563               MOV     A,C                     ;Forced output entry point
03E2 32CB03     02564               STA     CONOUT$Character        ;Not escape sequence -- Save data byte
                02565
03E5 2A5A00     02566               LHLD    CB$Console$Output       ;Get console redirection word
                02567       ;
                02568       CONOUT$Entry2:                          ;<=== output error message entry point
                02569       ;
03E8 116400     02570               LXI     D,CB$Device$Table$Addresses     ;Addresses of dev. tables
03EB D5         02571               PUSH    D                       ;Put onto stack ready for loop
03EC E5         02572               PUSH    H
                02573
                02574       CONOUT$Next$Device:
03ED E1         02575               POP     H                       ;Recover redirection bit map
03EE D1         02576               POP     D                       ;Recover device table addresses pointer
03EF CD6F06     02577               CALL    Select$Device$Table     ;Get device table in DE
03F2 B7         02578               ORA     A                       ;Check if a device has been
                02579                                               ;  selected (i.e. bit map not all zero)
03F3 CA0D04     02580               JZ      CONOUT$Exit             ;No, exit
03F6 C5         02581               PUSH    B       ;Yes - B..      ;Save redirection bit map
03F7 E5         02582               PUSH    H                       ;Save device table addresses pointer
                02583       CONOUT$Wait:
03F8 CD0F06     02584               CALL    Check$Output$Ready      ;Check if device not suspended and
                02585                                               ;  (if appropriate) DTR is high
03FB CAF803     02586               JZ      CONOUT$Wait             ;No, wait
                02587
03FE F3         02588               DI                              ;Interrupts off to avoid
                02589                                               ;  involuntary re-entrance
03FF 3ACB03     02590               LDA     CONOUT$Character        ;Recover the data byte
0402 4F         02591               MOV     C,A                     ;Ready for output
0403 CD2608     02592               CALL    Output$Data$Byte        ;Output the data byte
0406 FB         02593               EI
                02594
0407 CD3A06     02595               CALL    Process$Etx$Protocol    ;Deal with Etx/Ack protocol
040A C3ED03     02596               JMP     CONOUT$Next$Device      ;Loop back for next device
                02597
                02598       CONOUT$Exit:
040D 3ACB03     02599               LDA     CONOUT$Character        ;Recover data character
0410 79         02600               MOV     A,C                     ;CP/M "convention"
0411 C9         02601               RET
                02602       ;
                02603       CONOUT$Escape$Found:                    ;Possible escape sequence
0412 211904     02604               LXI     H,CONOUT$Process$Escape ;Vector processing of next character
                02605       CONOUT$Set$Processor:
0415 22CC03     02606               SHLD    CONOUT$Processor        ;Set vector address
0418 C9         02607               RET                             ;Return to BIOS caller
                02700       ;#
                02701       ;
                02702       ;       Console output: escape sequence processing
```

Figure 8-10. (Continued)

```
                02703   ;
                02704   CONOUT$Process$Escape:          ;Control arrives here with character
                02705                                   ;   after escape in C
0419 211B02     02706           LXI     H,CONOUT$Escape$Table   ;Get base of recognition table
                02707   CONOUT$Next$Entry:
041C 7E         02708           MOV     A,M                     ;Check if at end of table
041D B7         02709           ORA     A
041E CA2B04     02710           JZ      CONOUT$No$Match         ;Yes, no match found
0421 B9         02711           CMP     C                       ;Compare to data character
0422 CA3B04     02712           JZ      CONOUT$Match            ;They match
0425 23         02713           INX     H                       ;Move to next entry in table
0426 23         02714           INX     H
0427 23         02715           INX     H
0428 C31C04     02716           JMP     CONOUT$Next$Entry       ;Go back and check again
                02717   ;
                02718   CONOUT$No$Match:                ;No match found, so original
                02719                                   ;  escape and following character
                02720                                   ;  must be output
042B C5         02721           PUSH    B                       ;Save character after escape
042C 0E1B       02722           MVI     C,Function$Key$Lead     ;Get escape character
042E CDE103     02723           CALL    CONOUT$Forced           ;Output to console devices
0431 C1         02724           POP     B                       ;Get character after escape
0432 CDE103     02725           CALL    CONOUT$Forced           ;Output it, too
                02726   ;
                02727   CONOUT$Set$Normal:
0435 21DB03     02728           LXI     H,CONOUT$Normal         ;Set vector back to normal
0438 C31504     02729           JMP     CONOUT$Set$Processor    ;  for subsequent characters
                02730   ;
                02731   ;
                02732   CONOUT$Match:
043B 23         02733           INX     H                       ;HL -> LS byte of subprocessor
043C 5E         02734           MOV     E,M                     ;Get LS byte
043D 23         02735           INX     H
043E 56         02736           MOV     D,M                     ;Get MS byte
043F EB         02737           XCHG                            ;HL -> subprocessor
0440 E9         02738           PCHL                            ;Goto subprocessor
                02739   ;
                02740   CONOUT$Date:                    ;Subprocessor to inject current date
                02741                                   ;  into console input stream (using
                02742                                   ;  forced input)
0441 218F0F     02743           LXI     H,Date
                02744   CONOUT$Set$Forced$Input:
0444 228D0F     02745           SHLD    CB$Forced$Input
0447 C9         02746           RET                             ;Return to BIOS' caller
                02747   ;
                02748   CONOUT$Time:                    ;Subprocessor to inject time into
                02749                                   ;  console input stream
0448 21990F     02750           LXI     H,Time$In$ASCII
044B C34404     02751           JMP     CONOUT$Set$Forced$Input
                02752   ;
                02753   CONOUT$Set$Date:                ;Subprocessor to set the date by taking
                02754                                   ;  the next 8 characters of console output
                02755                                   ;  and storing them in the date string
044E 21A30F     02756           LXI     H,Time$Date$Flags       ;Set flag to indicate that the
0451 3E02       02757           MVI     A,Date$Set              ;  date has been set by program
0453 B6         02758           ORA     M
0454 77         02759           MOV     M,A
0455 3E08       02760           MVI     A,8                     ;Set character count
0457 218F0F     02761           LXI     H,Date                  ;Set address
045A C36C04     02762           JMP     CONOUT$Set$String$Pointer
                02763   ;
                02764   ;
                02765   CONOUT$Set$Time:                ;Subprocessor to set the time by taking
                02766                                   ;  the next 8 characters of console output
                02767                                   ;  and storing them in the time string
045D 21A30F     02768           LXI     H,Time$Date$Flags       ;Set flag to indicate that the
0460 3E01       02769           MVI     A,Time$Set              ;  time has been set by program
0462 B6         02770           ORA     M
0463 77         02771           MOV     M,A
0464 3E08       02772           MVI     A,8                     ;Set character count
0466 21990F     02773           LXI     H,Time$in$ASCII         ;Set address
0469 C36C04     02774           JMP     CONOUT$Set$String$Pointer
                02775   ;
                02776   CONOUT$Set$String$Pointer:      ;HL -> string, A = count
046C 32D003     02777           STA     CONOUT$String$Length    ;Save count
046F 22CE03     02778           SHLD    CONOUT$String$Pointer   ;Save address
0472 217804     02779           LXI     H,CONOUT$Process$String ;Vector further output
```

Figure 8-10. (Continued)

```
0475 C31504   02780           JMP     CONOUT$Set$Processor
              02781   ;
              02782   CONOUT$Process$String:          ;Control arrives here for each character
              02783                                   ;  in the string in register C. The
              02784                                   ;  characters are stacked into the
              02785                                   ;  receiving string until either a 00-byte
              02786                                   ;  is encountered or the specified number
              02787                                   ;  of characters is stacked.
0478 2ACE03   02788           LHLD    CONOUT$String$Pointer   ;Get current address for stacking chars
047B 79       02789           MOV     A,C             ;Check if current character is 00H
047C B7       02790           ORA     A
047D CA3504   02791           JZ      CONOUT$Set$Normal       ;Revert to normal processing
0480 77       02792           MOV     M,A             ;Otherwise, stack character
0481 23       02793           INX     H               ;Update pointer
0482 3600     02794           MVI     M,00H           ;Stack fail-safe terminator
0484 22CE03   02795           SHLD    CONOUT$String$Pointer   ;Save updated pointer
0487 21D003   02796           LXI     H,CONOUT$String$Length  ;Downdate count
048A 35       02797           DCR     M
048B CA3504   02798           JZ      CONOUT$Set$Normal       ;Revert to normal processing
              02799                                   ;  if count hits 0
048E C9       02800           RET                     ;Return with output vectored back
              02801                                   ;  to CONOUT$Process$String
              02802   ;
              02900   ;#
              02901   ;
              02902   ;       Auxiliary input status
              02903   ;
              02904   ;       This routine checks the character count in the
              02905   ;       appropriate input buffer.
              02906   ;       The A register is set to indicate whether or not
              02907   ;       data is waiting.
              02908   ;
              02909   ;       Entry parameters: none.
              02910   ;
              02911   ;       Exit parameters
              02912   ;
              02913   ;               A = 00H if there is no data waiting
              02914   ;               A = 0FFH if there is data waiting
              02915   ;
              02916   ;==========================
              02917   AUXIST:                         ;<=== BIOS entry point (Private)
              02918   ;==========================
048F 2A5C00   02919           LHLD    CB$Auxiliary$Input      ;Get redirection word
0492 116400   02920           LXI     D,CB$Device$Table$Addresses     ; and table pointer
0495 CD6F06   02921           CALL    Select$Device$Table     ;Get device table address
0498 C34708   02922           JMP     Get$Input$Status        ;Get status from input device
              02923                                   ;  and return to caller
              02924   ;
              03000   ;#
              03001   ;
              03002   ;       Auxiliary output status
              03003   ;
              03004   ;       This routine sets the A register to indicate whether the
              03005   ;       Auxiliary device(s) is/are ready to accept output data.
              03006   ;       As more than one device can be used for auxiliary output, this
              03007   ;       routine returns a Boolean AND of all of their statuses.
              03008   ;
              03009   ;       Entry parameters: none
              03010   ;
              03011   ;       Exit parameters
              03012   ;
              03013   ;               A = 00H if one or more list devices are not ready
              03014   ;               A = 0FFH if all list devices are ready
              03015   ;
              03016   ;==========================
              03017
              03018   AUXOST:                         ;<=== BIOS entry point (Private)
              03019   ;==========================
049B 2A5E00   03020           LHLD    CB$Auxiliary$Output     ;Get list redirection word
049E C37905   03021           JMP     Get$Composite$Status
              03022   ;
              03100   ;#
              03101   ;
              03102   ;       Auxiliary input (replacement for READER)
              03103   ;
              03104   ;       This routine returns the next input character from the
```

Figure 8-10. (Continued)

```
                    03105   ;          appropriate logical auxiliary device.
                    03106   ;
                    03107   ;          Entry parameters: none.
                    03108   ;
                    03109   ;          Exit parameters
                    03110   ;
                    03111   ;                  A = data character
                    03112   ;
                    03113   ;==========================
                    03114   AUXIN:                                  ;<=== BIOS entry point (standard)
                    03115   ;==========================
04A1 2A5C00         03116           LHLD    CB$Auxiliary$Input              ;Get redirection word
04A4 116400         03117           LXI     D,CB$Device$Table$Addresses     ; and table pointer
04A7 CD6F06         03118           CALL    Select$Device$Table             ;Get device table address
04AA C39106         03119           JMP     Get$Input$Character             ;Get next input character
                    03120                                                   ; and return to caller
                    03121   ;
                    03200   ;#
                    03201   ;          Auxiliary output (replaces PUNCH)
                    03202   ;
                    03203   ;          This routine outputs a data byte to the auxiliary device(s).
                    03204   ;          It is similar to CONOUT except that it uses the watchdog
                    03205   ;          timer to detect if a device stays busy for more than
                    03206   ;          30 seconds at a time. It outputs a message to the console
                    03207   ;          if this happens.
                    03208   ;
                    03209   ;          Entry parameters
                    03210   ;
                    03211   ;                  C = data byte
                    03212   ;
04AD 0D0A07417503213        AUXOUT$Busy$Message:    DB      CR,LF,7,'Auxiliary device not Ready?',CR,LF,0
                    03214   ;
                    03215   ;======================
                    03216   AUXOUT:                                 ;<=== BIOS entry point (standard)
                    03217   ;======================
04CE 2A5E00         03218           LHLD    CB$Auxiliary$Output             ;Get aux. redirection word
04D1 11AD04         03219           LXI     D,AUXOUT$Busy$Message           ;Message to be output if time
                    03220                                                   ; runs out
04D4 C3A205         03221           JMP     Multiple$Output$Byte
                    03222   ;
                    03300   ;#
                    03301   ;
                    03302   ;          List status
                    03303   ;
                    03304   ;          This routine sets the A register to indicate whether the
                    03305   ;          List Device(s) is/are ready to accept output data.
                    03306   ;          As more than one device can be used for list output, this
                    03307   ;          routine returns a Boolean AND of all of their statuses.
                    03308   ;
                    03309   ;          Entry parameters: none
                    03310   ;
                    03311   ;          Exit parameters
                    03312   ;
                    03313   ;                  A = 000H if one or more list devices are not ready
                    03314   ;                  A = 0FFH if all list devices are ready
                    03315   ;
                    03316   ;
                    03317   ;======================
                    03318   LISTST:                                 ;<=== BIOS entry point (standard)
                    03319   ;======================
04D7 2A6200         03320           LHLD    CB$List$Output                  ;Get list redirection word
04DA C37905         03321           JMP     Get$Composite$Status
                    03322   ;
                    03400   ;#
                    03401   ;
                    03402   ;          List output
                    03403   ;
                    03404   ;          This routine outputs a data byte to the list device.
                    03405   ;          It is similar to CONOUT except that it uses the watchdog
                    03406   ;          timer to detect if the printer stays busy for more
                    03407   ;          than 30 seconds at a time. It outputs a message to the console
                    03408   ;          if this happens.
                    03409   ;
                    03410   ;          Entry parameters
                    03411   ;
                    03412   ;                  C = data byte
```

Figure 8-10. (Continued)

```
04DD 0D0A07507203413      LIST$Busy$Message:     DB        CR,LF,7,'Printer not Ready?',CR,LF,0
              03414       ;
              03415       ;======================
              03416       LIST:                             ;<=== BIOS entry point (standard)
              03417       ;======================
04F5 2A6200   03418                 LHLD      CB$List$Output          ;Get list redirection word
04F8 11DD04   03419                 LXI       D,LIST$Busy$Message     ;Message to be output if time
              03420                                                   ; runs out
04FB C3A205   03421                 JMP       Multiple$Output$Byte
              03422       ;
              03500       ;#
              03501       ;         Request user choice
              03502       ;
              03503       ;         This routine displays an error message, requesting
              03504       ;         a choice of:
              03505       ;
              03506       ;                   R -- Retry the operation that caused the error
              03507       ;                   I -- Ignore the error and attempt to continue
              03508       ;                   A -- Abort the program and return to CP/M
              03509       ;
              03510       ;         This routine accepts a character from the console,
              03511       ;         converts it to uppercase and returns to the caller
              03512       ;         with the response in the A register.
              03513       ;
              03514       RUC$Message:
04FE 0D0A     03515                 DB        CR,LF
0500 202020202003516                 DB        '     Enter R - Retry, I - Ignore, A - Abort : ',0
              03517       ;
              03518       ;
              03519       Request$User$Choice:
052F CD2D03   03520                 CALL      CONST                   ;Gobble up any type-ahead
0532 CA3B05   03521                 JZ        RUC$Buffer$Empty
0535 CD3A03   03522                 CALL      CONIN
0538 C32F05   03523                 JMP       Request$User$Choice
              03524       ;
              03525       RUC$Buffer$Empty:
053B 21FE04   03526                 LXI       H,RUC$Message           ;Display prompt
053E CD5305   03527                 CALL      Output$Error$Message
              03528       ;
0541 CD3A03   03529                 CALL      CONIN                   ;Get console character
0544 CD3B0E   03530                 CALL      A$To$Upper              ;Make uppercase for comparisons
0547 32B00D   03531                 STA       Disk$Action$Confirm     ;Save in confirmatory message
054A F5       03532                 PUSH      PSW                     ;Save for later
              03533       ;
054B 21B00D   03534                 LXI       H,Disk$Action$Confirm
054E CD5305   03535                 CALL      Output$Error$Message
              03536       ;
0551 F1       03537                 POP       PSW                     ;Recover action code
0552 C9       03538                 RET
              03539       ;
              03600       ;#
              03601       ;
              03602       ;         Output error message
              03603       ;
              03604       ;         This routine outputs an error message to all the currently
              03605       ;         selected console devices except those being used to receive
              03606       ;         LIST output as well.  This is to avoid "deadly embrace" situations
              03607       ;         where the printer's being busy for too long causes an error message
              03608       ;         to be output -- and console output is being directed to the
              03609       ;         printer as well.
              03610       ;
              03611       ;         This subroutine makes use of most of the CONOUT subroutine.
              03612       ;         For memory economy it enters CONOUT using a private
              03613       ;         entry point.
              03614       ;
              03615       ;         Entry parameters
              03616       ;
              03617       ;                   HL -> 00-byte terminated error message
              03618       ;
              03619       Output$Error$Message:
0553 E5       03620                 PUSH      H                       ;Save message address
0554 2A5A00   03621                 LHLD      CB$Console$Output       ;Get console redirection bit map
0557 EB       03622                 XCHG
0558 2A6200   03623                 LHLD      CB$List$Output          ;Get list redirection bit map
              03624                                                   ;HL = list, DE = console
              03625                                                   ;Now set to 0 all bits in the console
```

Figure 8-10. (Continued)

Chapter 8: Writing an Enhanced BIOS **257**

```
                        03626                                  ; bit map that are set to 1 in the
                        03627                                  ; list bit map
055B 7C                 03628           MOV      A,H           ;Get MS byte of list
055C 2F                 03629           CMA                    ;Invert
055D A2                 03630           ANA      D             ;Preserve only bits with 0's
055E 67                 03631           MOV      H,A           ;Save result
055F 7D                 03632           MOV      A,L           ;Repeat for LS byte of list
0560 2F                 03633           CMA
0561 A3                 03634           ANA      E
0562 6F                 03635           MOV      L,A           ;HL now has only pure console
                        03636                                  ; devices
0563 B4                 03637           ORA      H             ;Ensure that at least one device
0564 CA6A05             03638           JZ       OEM$Device$Present  ; is selected
0567 210100             03639           LXI      H,0001H       ;Otherwise use default of device 0
                        03640  OEM$Device$Present:
                        03641  OEM$Next$Character:
056A D1                 03642           POP      D             ;Recover message address into DE
056B 1A                 03643           LDAX     D             ;Get next byte of message
056C 13                 03644           INX      D             ;Update message pointer
056D B7                 03645           ORA      A             ;Check if end of message
056E C8                 03646           RZ                     ;Yes, exit
056F D5                 03647           PUSH     D             ;Save message address for later
0570 E5                 03648           PUSH     H             ;Save special bit map
                        03649                                  ;Data character is in A
0571 CDD103             03650           CALL     CONOUT$OEM$Entry    ;Enter shared code
0574 E1                 03651           POP      H             ;Recover special bit map
0575 C36A05             03652           JMP      OEM$Next$Character
                        03653  ;
                        03654  ;
                        03655  ;
                        03656  ;       Get composite status
                        03657  ;
                        03658  ;       This routine sets the A register to indicate whether the
                        03659  ;       output device(s) is/are ready to accept output data.
                        03660  ;       As more than one device can be used for output, this
                        03661  ;       routine returns a Boolean AND of all of their statuses.
                        03662  ;
                        03663  ;       Entry parameters
                        03664  ;
                        03665  ;               HL = I/O redirection bit map for output device(s)
                        03666  ;
                        03667  ;       Exit parameters
                        03668  ;
                        03669  ;               A = 000H if one or more list devices are not ready
                        03670  ;               A = 0FFH if all list devices are ready
                        03671  ;
0578 00                 03672  GCS$Status:      DB       0     ;Composite status of all devices
                        03673  ;
                        03674  ;
                        03675  Get$Composite$Status:
0579 3EFF               03676           MVI      A,0FFH        ;Assume all devices are ready
057B 327805             03677           STA      GCS$Status    ;Preset composite status byte
                        03678
057E 116400             03679           LXI      D,CB$Device$Table$Addresses  ;Addresses of dev. tables
0581 D5                 03680           PUSH     D             ;Put onto stack ready for loop
0582 E5                 03681           PUSH     H             ;Save bit map
                        03682  GCS$Next$Device:
0583 E1                 03683           POP      H             ;Recover redirection bit map
0584 D1                 03684           POP      D             ;Recover device table addresses pointer
0585 CD6F06             03685           CALL     Select$Device$Table  ;Get device table in DE
0588 B7                 03686           ORA      A             ;Check if a device has been
                        03687                                  ; selected (i.e. bit map not all zero)
0589 CA9905             03688           JZ       GCS$Exit      ;No, exit
058C C5                 03689           PUSH     B    ;Yes - B..  ;Save redirection bit map
058D E5                 03690           PUSH     H             ;Save device table addresses pointer
058E CD0F06             03691           CALL     Check$Output$Ready   ;Check if device ready
0591 217805             03692           LXI      H,GCS$Status  ;AND together with previous devices
0594 A6                 03693           ANA      M             ; status
0595 77                 03694           MOV      M,A           ;Save composite status
                        03695
0596 C38305             03696           JMP      GCS$Next$Device      ;Loop back for next device
                        03697  ;
                        03698  GCS$Exit:
0599 3A7805             03699           LDA      GCS$Status    ;Return with composite status
059C B7                 03700           ORA      A
059D C9                 03701           RET
```

Figure 8-10. (Continued)

```
                03702   ;
                03800   ;#
                03801   ;
                03802   ;       Multiple output byte
                03803   ;
                03804   ;       This routine outputs a data byte to the all of the
                03805   ;       devices specified in the I/O redirection word.
                03806   ;       It is similar to CONOUT except that it uses the watchdog
                03807   ;       timer to detect if any of the devices stays busy for more
                03808   ;       than 30 seconds at a time. It outputs a message to the console
                03809   ;       if this happens.
                03810   ;
                03811   ;       Entry parameters
                03812   ;
                03813   ;               HL = I/O redirection bit map
                03814   ;               DE -> Message to be output if time runs out
                03815   ;               C  = data byte
                03816   ;
0708 =          03817   MOB$Maximum$Busy        EQU     1800            ;Number of clock ticks (each at
                03818                                                   ;  16.666 milliseconds) for which the
                03819                                                   ;  device might be busy
059E 00         03820   MOB$Character:          DB      0               ;Character to be output
059F 0000       03821   MOB$Busy$Message:       DW      0               ;Address of message to be
                03822                                                   ;  output if time runs out
05A1 00         03823   MOB$Need$Message:       DB      0               ;Flag used to detect that the
                03824                                                   ;  watchdog timer timed out
                03825   ;
                03826   Multiple$Output$Byte:
05A2 79         03827           MOV     A,C                             ;Get data byte
05A3 320807     03828           STA     MOB$Maximum$Busy                ;Save copy
05A6 EB         03829           XCHG                                    ;HL -> timeout message
05A7 229F05     03830           SHLD    MOB$Busy$Message                ;Save for later use
05AA EB         03831           XCHG                                    ;HL = bit map again
                03832   ;
05AB 116400     03833           LXI     D,CB$Device$Table$Addresses     ;Addresses of dev. tables
05AE D5         03834           PUSH    D                               ;Save on stack ready for loop
05AF E5         03835           PUSH    H                               ;Save I/O redirection bit map
                03836   MOB$Next$Device:
05B0 E1         03837           POP     H                               ;Recover redirection bit map
05B1 D1         03838           POP     D                               ;Recover device table addresses pointer
05B2 CD6F06     03839           CALL    Select$Device$Table             ;Get device table in DE
05B5 B7         03840           ORA     A
05B6 CAEC05     03841           JZ      MOB$Exit                        ;Check if any device selected
                03842   ;
05B9 C5         03843           PUSH    B       ;<- Yes : B             ;Save device table addresses pointer
05BA E5         03844           PUSH    H                               ;Save redirection bit map
                03845   ;
                03846   MOB$Start$Watchdog:
05BB AF         03847           XRA     A                               ;Reset message needed flag
05BC 32A105     03848           STA     MOB$Need$Message
05BF 010807     03849           LXI     B,MOB$Maximum$Busy              ;Time delay
05C2 210906     03850           LXI     H,MOB$Not$Ready                 ;Address to go to
05C5 CD6D08     03851           CALL    Set$Watchdog                    ;Start timer
                03852   ;
                03853   MOB$Wait:
05C8 3AA105     03854           LDA     MOB$Need$Message                ;Check if watchdog timed out
05CB B7         03855           ORA     A
05CC C2EE05     03856           JNZ     MOB$Output$Message              ;Yes, output warning message
05CF CD0F06     03857           CALL    Check$Output$Ready              ;Check if device ready
05D2 CAC805     03858           JZ      MOB$Wait                        ;No, wait
                03859   ;
05D5 F3         03860           DI                                      ;Interrupts off to avoid
                03861                                                   ;  involuntary reentrance
05D6 010000     03862           LXI     B,0                             ;Turn off watchdog
05D9 CD6D08     03863           CALL    Set$Watchdog                    ;  (HL setting is irrelevant)
                03864   ;
05DC 3A9E05     03865           LDA     MOB$Character                   ;Get data byte
05DF 4F         03866           MOV     C,A
05E0 CD2608     03867           CALL    Output$Data$Byte                ;Output the data byte
05E3 FB         03868           EI
05E4 CD3A06     03869           CALL    Process$Etx$Protocol            ;Deal with ETX/ACK protocol
05E7 C3B005     03870           JMP     MOB$Next$Device
                03871   ;
                03872   MOB$Ignore$Exit:                                ;Ignore timeout error
05EA E1         03873           POP     H                               ;Balance the stack
05EB D1         03874           POP     D
```

Figure 8-10. (Continued)

```
                      03875  ;
                      03876  MOB$Exit:
05EC  79              03877          MOV     A,C                       ;CP/M "convention"
05ED  C9              03878          RET
                      03879  ;
                      03880  MOB$Output$Message:
05EE  2A9F05          03881          LHLD    MOB$Busy$Message          ;Display warning message
05F1  CD5305          03882          CALL    Output$Error$Message      ;  on selected console devices
                      03883  MOB$Request$Choice:
05F4  CD2F05          03884          CALL    Request$User$Choice       ;Display message and get
                      03885                                            ;  action character
05F7  FE52            03886          CPI     'R'                       ;Retry
05F9  CABB05          03887          JZ      MOB$Start$Watchdog        ;Restart watchdog and try again
05FC  FE49            03888          CPI     'I'                       ;Ignore
05FE  CAEA05          03889          JZ      MOB$Ignore$Exit
0601  FE41            03890          CPI     'A'                       ;Abort
0603  CA360E          03891          JZ      System$Reset              ;  Give BDOS function 0
0606  C3F405          03892          JMP     MOB$Request$Choice
                      03893  ;
                      03894  MOB$Not$Ready:                    ;Watchdog timer routine will call this
                      03895                                    ;  routine if the device is busy
                      03896                                    ;  for more than approximately 30 seconds
                      03897                                    ;Note: This is an interrupt service routine
0609  3EFF            03898          MVI     A,0FFH                    ;Set request to output message
060B  32A105          03899          STA     MOB$Need$Message
060E  C9              03900          RET                               ;Return to the watchdog routine
                      03901  ;
                      04000  ;#
                      04001  ;       Check output ready
                      04002  ;
                      04003  ;       This routine checks to see if the specified device is ready
                      04004  ;       to receive output data.
                      04005  ;       It does so by checking to see if the device has been suspended
                      04006  ;       for protocol reasons and if DTR is low.
                      04007  ;
                      04008  ;       NOTE: This routine does NOT check if the USART itself is ready.
                      04009  ;             This test is done in the output data byte routine itself.
                      04010  ;
                      04011  ;       Entry parameters
                      04012  ;
                      04013  ;               DE -> device table
                      04014  ;
                      04015  ;       Exit parameters
                      04016  ;
                      04017  ;               A = 000H (Zero-flag set)   : Device not ready
                      04018  ;               A = 0FFH (Zero-flag clear) : Device ready
                      04019  ;
                      04020  Check$Output$Ready:
060F  210E00          04021          LXI     H,DT$Status               ;Get device status
0612  19              04022          DAD     D                         ;HL -> status byte
0613  7E              04023          MOV     A,M                       ;Get status byte
0614  47              04024          MOV     B,A                       ;Take a copy of the status byte
0615  E601            04025          ANI     DT$Output$Suspend         ;Check if output is suspended
0617  C23806          04026          JNZ     COR$Not$Ready             ;Yes, indicate not ready
                      04027
061A  3E04            04028          MVI     A,DT$Output$DTR           ;Check if DTR must be high to send
061C  A0              04029          ANA     B                         ;Mask with device status from table
061D  CA3406          04030          JZ      COR$Ready                 ;No, device is logically ready
                      04031
0620  210000          04032          LXI     H,DT$Status$Port          ;Set up to read device status
0623  19              04033          DAD     D
0624  7E              04034          MOV     A,M                       ;Get status port number
0625  322906          04035          STA     COR$Status$Port           ;Set up instruction below
                      04036
0628  DB              04037          DB      IN
                      04038  COR$Status$Port:
0629  00              04039          DB      0                 ;<-- Set up by instruction above
062A  4F              04040          MOV     C,A                       ;Save hardware status
                      04041
062B  210400          04042          LXI     H,DT$DTR$Ready            ;Yes, set up to check chip status
062E  19              04043          DAD     D                         ;  to see if DTR is high
062F  7E              04044          MOV     A,M                       ;Get DTR high status mask
0630  A1              04045          ANA     C                         ;Test chip status
0631  CA3806          04046          JZ      COR$Not$Ready             ;DTR low, indicate not ready
                      04047  ;
                      04048  COR$Ready:
```

Figure 8-10. (Continued)

```
0634 3EFF        04049           MVI     A,0FFH                      ;Indicate device ready for output
0636 B7          04050           ORA     A
0637 C9          04051           RET
                 04052   ;
                 04053   COR$Not$Ready:                               ;Indicate device not ready for output
0638 AF          04054           XRA     A
0639 C9          04055           RET
                 04056   ;
                 04200   ;#
                 04201   ;
                 04202   ;       Process ETX/ACK protocol
                 04203   ;
                 04204   ;       This routine maintains ETX/ACK protocol.
                 04205   ;       After a specified number of data characters have been output
                 04206   ;       to the device, an ETX character is output and the device
                 04207   ;       put into output suspended state. Only when an incoming
                 04208   ;       ACK character is received (under interrupt control) will
                 04209   ;       output be resumed to the device.
                 04210   ;
                 04211   ;       Entry parameters
                 04212   ;
                 04213   ;               DE -> device table
                 04214   ;
                 04215   ;       Exit parameters
                 04216   ;
                 04217   ;               Message count downdated (and reset if necessary)
                 04218   ;
                 04219   Process$Etx$Protocol:
063A 210E00      04220           LXI     H,DT$Status                 ;Check if ETX/ACK protocol enabled
063D 19          04221           DAD     D
063E 7E          04222           MOV     A,M
063F E610        04223           ANI     DT$Output$Etx
0641 C8          04224           RZ                                  ;No, so return immediately
0642 211000      04225           LXI     H,DT$Etx$Count              ;Yes, so downdate count
0645 19          04226           DAD     D
0646 E5          04227           PUSH    H                           ;Save address of count for later
0647 4E          04228           MOV     C,M                         ;Get LS byte
0648 23          04229           INX     H
0649 46          04230           MOV     B,M                         ;Get MS byte
064A 0B          04231           DCX     B
064B 78          04232           MOV     A,B
064C B1          04233           ORA     C                           ;Check if count now zero
064D C25706      04234           JNZ     PEP$Save$Count              ;No
0650 211200      04235           LXI     H,DT$Etx$Message$Length     ;Yes, reset to message length
0653 19          04236           DAD     D
0654 4E          04237           MOV     C,M                         ;Get LS byte
0655 23          04238           INX     H
0656 46          04239           MOV     B,M                         ;Get MS byte
                 04240   PEP$Save$Count:
0657 E1          04241           POP     H                           ;Recover address of count
0658 71          04242           MOV     M,C                         ;Save count back in table
0659 23          04243           INX     H
065A 70          04244           MOV     M,B
                 04245   ;
065B B7          04246           ORA     A                           ;Reestablish whether count hit 0
065C C0          04247           RNZ                                 ;No, no further processing required
065D 0E03        04248           MVI     C,ETX                       ;Yes, send ETX to device
065F F3          04249           DI                                  ;Avoids involuntary reentrance
0660 CD2608      04250           CALL    Output$Data$Byte
0663 FB          04251           EI
0664 210E00      04252           LXI     H,DT$Status                 ;Flag device as output suspended
0667 19          04253           DAD     D
0668 F3          04254           DI                                  ;Avoid interaction with interrupts
0669 7E          04255           MOV     A,M                         ;Get status byte
066A F601        04256           ORI     DT$Output$Suspend           ;Set bit
066C 77          04257           MOV     M,A                         ;Save back in table
066D FB          04258           EI
066E C9          04259           RET
                 04260   ;
                 04400   ;#
                 04401   ;
                 04402   ;       Select device table
                 04403   ;
                 04404   ;       This routine scans a 16-bit word, and depending on which is the
                 04405   ;       first 1-bit set, selects the corresponding device table address.
                 04406   ;
```

Figure 8-10. (Continued)

```
                04407   ;               Entry parameters
                04408   ;
                04409   ;                       HL = Bit map
                04410   ;                       DE -> Table of device table addresses
                04411   ;                               The first address in the list is called
                04412   ;                               if the least significant bit of the bit map is
                04413   ;                               nonzero, and so on.
                04414   ;
                04415   ;               Exit parameters
                04416   ;
                04417   ;                       BC -> Current entry in device table addresses
                04418   ;                       DE = Selected device table address
                04419   ;                       HL = Shifted bit map
                04420   ;                               Nonzero if a 1-bit was found
                04421   ;                               Zero if bit map now entirely 0000
                04422   ;
                04423   ;               Note: If HL is 0000H on input, then the first entry in the
                04424   ;               device table addresses will be returned in DE.
                04425   ;
                04426   Select$Device$Table:
066F 7C         04427           MOV     A,H                     ;Get most significant byte of bit map
0670 B5         04428           ORA     L                       ;Check if HL completely 0
0671 C8         04429           RZ                              ;Return indicating no more bits set
0672 7D         04430           MOV     A,L                     ;Check if the LS bit is nonzero
0673 E601       04431           ANI     1
0675 C28006     04432           JNZ     SDT$Bit$Set             ;Yes, return corresponding address
0678 13         04433           INX     D                       ;No, update table pointer
0679 13         04434           INX     D
067A CDDB08     04435           CALL    SHLR                    ;Shift HL right one bit
067D C36F06     04436           JMP     Select$Device$Table     ;Check next bit
                04437   SDT$Bit$Set:
0680 E5         04438           PUSH    H                       ;Save shifted bit map
0681 42         04439           MOV     B,D                     ;Take copy of table pointer
0682 4B         04440           MOV     C,E
0683 EB         04441           XCHG
0684 5E         04442           MOV     E,M                     ;HL -> address in table
0685 23         04443           INX     H
0686 56         04444           MOV     D,M                     ;DE -> selected device table
                04445                                           ;Set up registers for another
                04446                                           ; entry
0687 E1         04447           POP     H                       ;Recover shifted bit map
0688 CDDB08     04448           CALL    SHLR                    ;Shift bit map right one bit
068B 03         04449           INX     B                       ;Update DT address table pointer to
068C 03         04450           INX     B                       ; entry
068D 3E01       04451           MVI     A,1                     ;Indicate that a one bit was found
068F B7         04452           ORA     A                       ; and registers are set up correctly
0690 C9         04453           RET
                04454   ;
                04600   ;#
                04601   ;
                04602   ;               Get input character
                04603   ;
                04604   ;               This routine gets the next input character from the device
                04605   ;               specified in the device table handed over as an input
                04606   ;               parameter.
                04607   ;
                04608   Get$Input$Character:
0691 211900     04609           LXI     H,DT$Character$Count    ;Check if any characters have
0694 19         04610           DAD     D                       ; been stored in the buffer
                04611   GIC$Wait:
0695 FB         04612           EI                              ;Ensure that incoming chars. will
                04613                                           ; be detected
0696 7E         04614           MOV     A,M                     ;Get character count
0697 B7         04615           ORA     A
0698 CA9506     04616           JZ      GIC$Wait                ;No characters, so wait
069B 35         04617           DCR     M                       ;Down date character count for
                04618                                           ; the character about to be
                04619                                           ; removed from the buffer
069C 211700     04620           LXI     H,DT$Get$Offset         ;Use the get offset to access
069F CDF007     04621           CALL    Get$Address$in$Buffer   ;Returns HL -> character
                04622                                           ; and with get offset updated
06A2 7E         04623           MOV     A,M                     ;Get the actual data character
06A3 F5         04624           PUSH    PSW                     ;Save until later
                04625
06A4 211900     04626           LXI     H,DT$Character$Count    ;Check downdated count of chars. in
06A7 19         04627           DAD     D                       ; buffer, checking if input should be
```

Figure 8-10. (Continued)

```
                    04920
0702 11CE02         04921          LXI     D,DT$2              ;Device 2
0705 CD1607         04922          CALL    Service$Device
                    04923
0708 3E20           04924          MVI     A,IC$EOI            ;Tell the interrupt controller chip
070A D3D8           04925          OUT     IC$OCW2$Port        ;  that the interrupt has been serviced
070C D1             04926          POP     D                   ;Restore registers
070D C1             04927          POP     B
070E F1             04928          POP     PSW
070F 2A8422         04929          LHLD    PI$User$Stack       ;Switch back to user's stack
0712 F9             04930          SPHL
0713 E1             04931          POP     H
0714 FB             04932          EI                          ;Reenable interrupts in the CPU
0715 C9             04933          RET                         ;Resume pre-interrupt processing
                    04934   ;
                    05000   ;#
                    05001   ;
                    05002   ;       Service device
                    05003   ;
                    05004   ;       This routine performs the device interrupt servicing,
                    05005   ;       checking to see if the device described in the specified
                    05006   ;       device table (address in DE) is actually interrupting,
                    05007   ;       and if so, inputs the character. Depending on which data character
                    05008   ;       is input, this routine will either stack it in the input buffer
                    05009   ;       (shutting off the input stream if the buffer is nearly full),
                    05010   ;       or will suspend or resume the output to the device.
                    05011   ;
                    05012   ;       Entry parameters
                    05013   ;
                    05014   ;               DE -> device table
                    05015   ;
                    05016           Service$Device:
0716 210000         05017          LXI     H,DT$Status$Port    ;Check if this device is really
0719 19             05018          DAD     D                   ;  interrupting
071A 7E             05019          MOV     A,M                 ;Get status port number
071B 321F07         05020          STA     SD$Status$Port      ;Store in instruction below
                    05021
071E DB             05022          DB      IN                  ;Input status
                    05023          SD$Status$Port:
071F 00             05024          DB      0       ;<-- Set up by instruction above
                    05025   ;
0720 210300         05026          LXI     H,DT$Input$Ready    ;Check if status indicates data ready
0723 19             05027          DAD     D
0724 A6             05028          ANA     M                   ;Mask with input ready value
0725 C8             05029          RZ                          ;No, return to interrupt service
                    05030                                      ;Check if any errors have occurred
0726 210700         05031          LXI     H,DT$Detect$Error$Port ;Set up to read error status
0729 19             05032          DAD     D                   ;  interrupting
072A 7E             05033          MOV     A,M                 ;Get status port number
072B 322F07         05034          STA     SD$Error$Port       ;Store in instruction below
                    05035
072E DB             05036          DB      IN                  ;Input error status
                    05037          SD$Error$Port:
072F 00             05038          DB      0       ;<-- Set up by instruction above
                    05039   ;
0730 210800         05040          LXI     H,DT$Detect$Error$Value ;Mask with error bit(s)
0733 19             05041          DAD     D
0734 A6             05042          ANA     M
0735 CA4707         05043          JZ      SD$No$Error         ;No bit(s) set
0738 210900         05044          LXI     H,DT$Reset$Error$Port  ;Set up to reset error
073B 19             05045          DAD     D
073C 7E             05046          MOV     A,M                 ;Get reset port number
073D 324607         05047          STA     SD$Reset$Error$Port ;Store in instruction below
0740 210A00         05048          LXI     H,DT$Reset$Error$Value
0743 19             05049          DAD     D
0744 7E             05050          MOV     A,M                 ;Get reset interrupt value
                    05051
0745 D3             05052          DB      OUT
                    05053          SD$Reset$Error$Port:
0746 00             05054          DB      0       ;<-- Set up in instruction above
                    05055
                    05056          SD$No$Error:
0747 210100         05057          LXI     H,DT$Data$Port      ;Input the data character (this may
074A 19             05058          DAD     D                   ;  be garbled if an error occurred)
074B 7E             05059          MOV     A,M                 ;Get data port number
074C 325007         05060          STA     SD$Data$Port        ;Store in instruction below
```

Figure 8-10. (Continued)

```
                05061
074F DB         05062           DB      IN              ;Input data character
                05063   SD$Data$Port:
0750 00         05064           DB      0       ;<-- Set up by instruction above
                05065
0751 47         05066           MOV     B,A             ;Take copy of data character above
0752 210E00     05067           LXI     H,DT$Status     ;Check if either XON or ETX protocols
0755 19         05068           DAD     D               ; is currently active
0756 7E         05069           MOV     A,M             ;Get protocol byte
0757 E618       05070           ANI     DT$Output$Xon + DT$Output$Etx
0759 CA8107     05071           JZ      SD$No$Protocol  ;Neither is active
075C E608       05072           ANI     DT$Output$Xon   ;Check if XON/XOFF is active
075E C26E07     05073           JNZ     SD$Check$if$Xon ;Yes, check if XON char. input
                05074                                   ;No, assume ETX/ACK active
0761 3E06       05075           MVI     A,ACK           ;Check if input character is ACK
0763 B8         05076           CMP     B
0764 C28107     05077           JNZ     SD$No$Protocol  ;No, process character as data
                05078   SD$Output$Desuspend:            ;Yes, device now ready
                05079                                   ;  to accept more data, so indicate
                05080                                   ;  output to device can resume
                05081                                   ;The noninterrupt driven output
                05082                                   ;  routine checks the suspend bit
0767 7E         05083           MOV     A,M             ;Get status/protocol byte again
0768 E6FE       05084           ANI     0FFH AND NOT DT$Output$Suspend ;Preserve all bits BUT suspend
076A 77         05085           MOV     M,A             ;Save back with suspend = 0
076B C3D907     05086           JMP     SD$Exit         ;Exit to interrupt service without
                05087                                   ;  saving data character
                05088   ;
                05089   SD$Check$if$Xon:                ;XON/XOFF protocol active, so
                05090                                   ;  if XOFF received, suspend output
                05091                                   ;  if XON received, resume output
                05092                                   ;The noninterrupt driven output
                05093                                   ;  routine checks the suspend bit
076E 3E11       05094           MVI     A,XON           ;Check if XON character input
0770 B8         05095           CMP     B
0771 CA6707     05096           JZ      SD$Output$Desuspend ;Yes, enable output to device
0774 3E13       05097           MVI     A,XOFF          ;Check if XOFF character input
0776 B8         05098           CMP     B
0777 C28107     05099           JNZ     SD$No$Protocol  ;No, process character as data
                05100   SD$Output$Suspend:              ;Device needs pause in output of
                05101                                   ;  data, so indicate output suspended
077A 7E         05102           MOV     A,M             ;Get status/protocol byte again
077B F601       05103           ORI     DT$Output$Suspend ;Set suspend bit to 1
077D 77         05104           MOV     M,A             ;Save back in device table
077E C3D907     05105           JMP     SD$Exit         ;Exit to interrupt service without
                05106                                   ;  saving the input character
                05107   ;
                05108   SD$No$Protocol:
0781 211800     05109           LXI     H,DT$Buffer$Length$Mask ;Check if there is still space
0784 19         05110           DAD     D               ;  in the input buffer
0785 7E         05111           MOV     A,M             ;Get length - 1
0786 3C         05112           INR     A               ;Update to actual length
0787 211900     05113           LXI     H,DT$Character$Count ;Get current count of characters
078A 19         05114           DAD     D               ;  in buffer
078B BE         05115           CMP     M               ;Check if count = length
078C CAEB07     05116           JZ      SD$Buffer$Full  ;Yes, output bell character
078F C5         05117           PUSH    B               ;Save data character
0790 211600     05118           LXI     H,DT$Put$Offset ;Compute address of character in
                05119                                   ;  input buffer
0793 CDF007     05120           CALL    Get$Address$In$Buffer ;HL -> character position
0796 C1         05121           POP     B               ;Recover input character
0797 70         05122           MOV     M,B             ;Save character in input buffer
                05123                                   ;Update number of characters in input
                05124                                   ;  buffer, checking if input should
                05125                                   ;  be temporarily halted
0798 211900     05126           LXI     H,DT$Character$Count
079B 19         05127           DAD     D
079C 34         05128           INR     M               ;Update character count
079D 7E         05129           MOV     A,M             ;Get updated count
079E 211A00     05130           LXI     H,DT$Stop$Input$Count ;Check if current count matches
07A1 19         05131           DAD     D               ;  buffer-full threshold
07A2 BE         05132           CMP     M
07A3 C2CE07     05133           JNZ     SD$Check$Control ;Not at threshold, check if control
                05134                                   ;  character input
07A6 210E00     05135           LXI     H,DT$Status     ;At threshold, check which means
07A9 19         05136           DAD     D               ;  for pausing input are to be used
```

Figure 8-10. (Continued)

264   The CP/M Programmer's Handbook

```
07AA 7E         05137           MOV     A,M                     ;Get status/protocol byte
07AB F602       05138           ORI     DT$Input$Suspend        ;Indicate input is suspended
07AD 77         05139           MOV     M,A                     ;Save updated status in table
07AE F5         05140           PUSH    PSW                     ;Save for later use
07AF E640       05141           ANI     DT$Input$RTS            ;Check if clear to send to be dropped
07B1 CAC307     05142           JZ      SD$Check$Input$Xon      ;No
07B4 210B00     05143           LXI     H,DT$RTS$Control$Port   ;Yes, get control port number
07B7 19         05144           DAD     D
07B8 7E         05145           MOV     A,M
07B9 32C207     05146           STA     SD$Drop$RTS$Port                ;Store in instruction below
07BC 210C00     05147           LXI     H,DT$Drop$RTS$Value
07BF 19         05148           DAD     D
07C0 7E         05149           MOV     A,M                     ;Get value needed to drop RTS
                05150           DB      OUT
07C1 D3         05151
                05152   SD$Drop$RTS$Port:
07C2 00         05153           DB      0               ;<- Set up in instruction above
                05154                                   ;Drop into input XON test
                05155   SD$Check$Input$Xon:             ;Check if XON/XOFF protocol being used
                05156                                   ; to temporarily suspend input
07C3 F1         05157           POP     PSW                     ;Recover status/protocol byte
07C4 E680       05158           ANI     DT$Input$Xon            ;Check if XON bit set
07C6 CACE07     05159           JZ      SD$Check$Control        ;No, see if control char. input
07C9 0E13       05160           MVI     C,XOFF                  ;Yes, output XOFF character
07CB CD2608     05161           CALL    Output$Data$Byte        ;Output data byte
                05162   ;
                05163   SD$Check$Control:               ;Check if control character (other than
                05164                                   ;  CR, LF, or TAB) input, and update
                05165                                   ;  count of control characters in buffer
07CE CD0808     05166           CALL    Check$Control$Char      ;Check if control character
07D1 CAD907     05167           JZ      SD$Exit                 ;No, it is not a control character
07D4 211C00     05168           LXI     H,DT$Control$Count
07D7 19         05169           DAD     D
07D8 34         05170           INR     M                       ;Update count of control chars.
                05171   ;
                05172   SD$Exit:                        ;Reset hardware interrupt system
07D9 210500     05173           LXI     H,DT$Reset$Int$Port
07DC 19         05174           DAD     D
07DD 7E         05175           MOV     A,M                     ;Get reset port number
07DE B7         05176           ORA     A                       ;Check if port specified
                05177                                   ;  (assumes it will always be NZ)
07DF C8         05178           RZ                              ;Bypass reset if no port specified
07E0 32E907     05179           STA     SD$Reset$Int$Port       ;Store in instruction below
07E3 210600     05180           LXI     H,DT$Reset$Int$Value
07E6 19         05181           DAD     D
07E7 7E         05182           MOV     A,M                     ;Get reset interrupt value
                05183
07E8 D3         05184           DB      OUT
                05185   SD$Reset$Int$Port:
07E9 00         05186           DB      0       ;<-- Set up in instruction above
07EA C9         05187           RET                     ;Return to interrupt service routine
                05188   ;
                05189   SD$Buffer$Full:                 ;Input buffer completely full
07EB 0E07       05190           MVI     C,BELL                  ;Send bell character as desperate
07ED C32608     05191           JMP     Output$Data$Byte        ;  measure. Note JMP return to
                05192                                   ;  caller will be done by subroutine
                05193   ;
                05300   ;#
                05301   ;
                05302   ;       Get address in buffer
                05303   ;
                05304   ;       This routine computes the address of the next character to
                05305   ;       access in a device buffer.
                05306   ;
                05307   ;       Entry parameters
                05308   ;
                05309   ;               DE -> appropriate device table
                05310   ;               HL = offset in the device table of either the
                05311   ;                       Get$Offset or the Put$Offset
                05312   ;
                05313   ;       Exit parameters
                05314   ;
                05315   ;               DE unchanged
                05316   ;               HL -> address in character buffer
                05317   ;
                05318   Get$Address$In$Buffer:
```

Figure 8-10.   (Continued)

```
07F0 19      05319          DAD   D                              ;HL -> get/put offset in dev. table
07F1 E5      05320          PUSH  H                              ;Preserve pointer to table
07F2 4E      05321          MOV   C,M                            ;Get offset value
07F3 0600    05322          MVI   B,0                            ;Make into word value
             05323          ;                                    ;Update offset value, resetting to
             05324          ;                                    ;  0 at end of buffer
07F5 79      05325          MOV   A,C                            ;Get copy of offset
07F6 3C      05326          INR   A                              ;Update to next position
07F7 211800  05327          LXI   H,DT$Buffer$Length$Mask
07FA 19      05328          DAD   D
07FB A6      05329          ANA   M                              ;Mask LS bits with length - 1
07FC E1      05330          POP   H                              ;Recover pointer to offset in table
07FD 77      05331          MOV   M,A                            ;Save new value (set to 0 if nec.)
07FE 211400  05332          LXI   H,DT$Buffer$Base               ;Get base address of input buffer
0801 19      05333          DAD   D                              ;HL -> address of buffer in table
0802 7E      05334          MOV   A,M                            ;Get LS byte of address
0803 23      05335          INX   H                              ;HL -> MS byte of address
0804 66      05336          MOV   H,M                            ;H = MS byte
0805 6F      05337          MOV   L,A                            ;L = LS byte
0806 09      05338          DAD   B                              ;Add on offset to base
0807 C9      05339          RET
             05340
             05341  ;
             05400  ;#
             05401  ;
             05402  ;      Check control character
             05403  ;
             05404  ;      This routine checks the character in A to see if it is a
             05405  ;      control character other than CR, LF, or TAB. The result is
             05406  ;      returned in the Z-flag.
             05407  ;
             05408  ;      Entry parameters
             05409  ;
             05410  ;              A = character to be checked
             05411  ;
             05412  ;      Exit parameters
             05413  ;
             05414  ;              Zero status if A does not contain a control character
             05415  ;                      or if it is CR, LF, or TAB
             05416  ;
             05417  ;              Nonzero if A contains a control character other than
             05418  ;                      CR, LF, or TAB.
             05419  Check$Control$Char:
0808 3E1F    05420          MVI   A,' '-1                        ;Space is first noncontrol char.
080A B8      05421          CMP   B
080B DA2408  05422          JC    CCC$No                         ;Not a control character
080E 3E0D    05423          MVI   A,CR                           ;Check if carriage return
0810 B8      05424          CMP   B
0811 CA2408  05425          JZ    CCC$No                         ;Not really a control character
0814 3E0A    05426          MVI   A,LF                           ;Check if LF
0816 B8      05427          CMP   B
0817 CA2408  05428          JZ    CCC$No                         ;Not really a control character
081A 3E09    05429          MVI   A,TAB                          ;Check if horizontal tab
081C B8      05430          CMP   B
081D CA2408  05431          JZ    CCC$No                         ;Not really a control character
0820 3E01    05432          MVI   A,1                            ;Indicate a control character
0822 B7      05433          ORA   A
0823 C9      05434          RET
             05435  CCC$No:                                      ;Indicate A does not contain
0824 AF      05436          XRA   A                              ;   a control character
0825 C9      05437          RET
             05438  ;
             05500  ;#
             05501  ;
             05502  ;      Output data byte
             05503  ;
             05504  ;      This is a simple polled output routine that outputs a single
             05505  ;      character (in register C on entry) to the device specified in
             05506  ;      the device table.
             05507  ;      Preferably, this routine would have been re-entrant; however
             05508  ;      it does have to store the port numbers. Therefore, to use it
             05509  ;      from code executed with interrupts enabled, the instruction
             05510  ;      sequence must be:
             05511  ;
             05512  ;              DI                       ;Interrupts off
             05513  ;              CALL  Output$Data$Byte
```

Figure 8-10. (Continued)

```
                    05514   ;                   EI                      ;Interrupts on
                    05515   ;
                    05516   ;           Failure to do this may cause involuntary re-entrance.
                    05517   ;
                    05518   ;           Entry parameters
                    05519   ;
                    05520   ;                   C = character to be output
                    05521   ;                   DE -> device table
                    05522   ;
                    05523   Output$Data$Byte:
0826 C5             05524           PUSH    B                           ;Save registers
0827 210200         05525           LXI     H,DT$Output$Ready           ;Get output ready status mask
082A 19             05526           DAD     D
082B 46             05527           MOV     B,M
082C 210000         05528           LXI     H,DT$Status$Port            ;Get status port number
082F 19             05529           DAD     D
0830 7E             05530           MOV     A,M
0831 323508         05531           STA     ODB$Status$Port             ;Store in instruction below
                    05532   ODB$Wait$until$Ready:
                    05533
0834 DB             05534           DB      IN                          ;Read status
                    05535   ODB$Status$Port:
0835 00             05536           DB      0       ;<-- Set up in instruction above
                    05537
0836 A0             05538           ANA     B                           ;Check if ready for output
0837 CA3408         05539           JZ      ODB$Wait$until$Ready        ;No
083A 210100         05540           LXI     H,DT$Data$Port              ;Get data port
083D 19             05541           DAD     D
083E 7E             05542           MOV     A,M
083F 324408         05543           STA     ODB$Data$Port               ;Store in instruction below
0842 79             05544           MOV     A,C                         ;Get character to output
                    05545
0843 D3             05546           DB      OUT
                    05547   ODB$Data$Port:
0844 00             05548           DB      0       ;<-- Set up in instruction above
                    05549
0845 C1             05550           POP     B                           ;Restore registers
0846 C9             05551           RET
                    05552   ;
                    05700   ;#
                    05701   ;
                    05702   ;
                    05703   ;           Input status routine
                    05704   ;
                    05705   ;           This routine returns a value in the A register indicating whether
                    05706   ;           one or more data characters is/are waiting in the input buffer.
                    05707   ;           Some products, such as Microsoft BASIC, defeat normal type-ahead
                    05708   ;           by constantly "gobbling" characters in order to see if an incoming
                    05709   ;           Control-S, -Q or -C has been received. In order to preserve
                    05710   ;           type-ahead under these circumstances, the input status return
                    05711   ;           can, as an option selected by the user, return "data waiting" only
                    05712   ;           if the input buffer contains a Control-S, -Q or -C. This fools
                    05713   ;           Microsoft BASIC into allowing type-ahead.
                    05714   ;
                    05715   ;           Entry parameters
                    05716   ;
                    05717   ;                   DE -> device table
                    05718   ;
                    05719   ;           Exit parameters
                    05720   ;
                    05721   ;                   A = 000H if no characters are waiting in the input
                    05722   ;                           buffer
                    05723   ;
                    05724   ;
                    05725   Get$Input$Status:
0847 210F00         05726           LXI     H,DT$Status$2               ;Check if fake mode enabled
084A 19             05727           DAD     D                           ;HL -> status byte in table
084B 7E             05728           MOV     A,M                         ;Get status byte
084C E601           05729           ANI     DT$Fake$Typeahead           ;Isolate status bit
084E CA5B08         05730           JZ      GIS$True$Status             ;Fake mode disabled
                    05731           ;
                    05732                                               ;Fake mode -- only indicates data
                    05733                                               ;ready if control chars. in buffer
0851 211C00         05734           LXI     H,DT$Control$Count          ;Check if any control characters
0854 19             05735           DAD     D                           ;  in the input buffer
0855 AF             05736           XRA     A                           ;Cheap 0
```

Figure 8-10.   (Continued)

```
0856 B6       05737           ORA     M                       ;Set flags according to count
0857 C8       05738           RZ                              ;Return indicating zero
              05739   GIS$Data$Ready:
0858 AF       05740           XRA     A                       ;Cheap 0
0859 3D       05741           DCR     A                       ;Set A = 0FFH and flags NZ
085A C9       05742           RET                             ;Return to caller
              05743   ;
              05744   GIS$True$Status:                        ;
              05745                                           ;True status, based on any characters
              05746                                           ;ready in input buffer
085B 2A8D0F   05747           LHLD    CB$Forced$Input         ;Check if any forced input waiting
085E 7E       05748           MOV     A,M                     ;Get next character of forced input
085F B7       05749           ORA     A                       ;Check if nonzero
0860 C25808   05750           JNZ     GIS$Data$Ready          ;Yes, indicate data waiting
              05751
0863 211900   05752           LXI     H,DT$Character$Count    ;Check if any characters
0866 19       05753           DAD     D                       ;  in buffer
0867 7E       05754           MOV     A,M                     ;Get character count
0868 B7       05755           ORA     A
0869 C8       05756           RZ                              ;Empty buffer, A = 0, Z-set
086A C35808   05757           JMP     GIS$Data$Ready
              05758   ;
              05759   ;
              05900   ;#
              05901   ;
              05902   ;       Real time clock processing
              05903   ;
              05904   ;       Control is transferred to the RTC$Interrupt routine each time
              05905   ;       the real time clock ticks. The tick count is downdated to see
              05906   ;       if a complete second has elapsed. If so, the ASCII time in
              05907   ;       the configuration block is updated.
              05908   ;
              05909   ;       With each tick, the watchdog count is downdated to see if control
              05910   ;       must be "forced" to a previously specified address on return
              05911   ;       from the RTC interrupt. The watchdog timer can be used to pull
              05912   ;       control out of what would otherwise be an infinite loop, such
              05913   ;       as waiting for the printer to come ready.
              05914   ;
              05915   ;
              05916   ;       Set watchdog
              05917   ;
              05918   ;       This is a noninterrupt level subroutine that simply sets the
              05919   ;       watchdog count and address
              05920   ;
              05921   ;       Entry parameters
              05922   ;
              05923   ;               BC = number of clock ticks before watchdog should
              05924   ;                    "time out"
              05925   ;               HL = address to which control will be transferred when
              05926   ;                    watchdog times out
              05927   ;
              05928   Set$Watchdog:
086D F3       05929           DI                              ;Avoid interference from interrupts
086E 22C100   05930           SHLD    RTC$Watchdog$Address    ;Set address
0871 60       05931           MOV     H,B
0872 69       05932           MOV     L,C
0873 22BF00   05933           SHLD    RTC$Watchdog$Count      ;Set count
0876 FB       05934           EI
0877 C9       05935           RET
              05936   ;
              05937   ;
              06000   ;#
              06001   ;
              06002                                           ;Control is received here each time the
              06003                                           ;  real time clock ticks
              06004   RTC$Interrupt:
0878 F5       06005           PUSH    PSW                     ;Save other registers
0879 228622   06006           SHLD    PI$User$HL              ;Switch to local stack
087C 210000   06007           LXI     H,0
087F 39       06008           DAD     SP                      ;Get user's stack
0880 228422   06009           SHLD    PI$User$Stack           ;Save it
0883 31B022   06010           LXI     SP,PI$Stack             ;Switch to local stack
0886 C5       06011           PUSH    B
0887 D5       06012           PUSH    D
              06013
0888 21BE00   06014           LXI     H,RTC$Tick$Count        ;Downdate tick count
```

Figure 8-10. (Continued)

```
08B8 35          06015           DCR     M
088C C2B008      06016           JNZ     RTC$Check$Watchdog      ;Is not at 0 yet
                 06017                                           ;One second has elapsed so
088F 3ABD00      06018           LDA     RTC$Ticks$per$Second    ;  reset to original value
0892 77          06019           MOV     M,A
                 06020                                           ;Update ASCII real time clock
0893 11A10F      06021           LXI     D,Time$in$ASCII$End     ;DE -> 1 character after ASCII time
0896 21BD00      06022           LXI     H,Update$Time$End       ;HL -> 1 character after control table
                 06023   RTC$Update$Digit:
0899 1B          06024           DCX     D                       ;Downdate pointer to time in ASCII
089A 2B          06025           DCX     H                       ;Downdate pointer to control table
089B 7E          06026           MOV     A,M                     ;Get next control character
089C B7          06027           ORA     A                       ;Check if end of table and therefore
089D CAB008      06028           JZ      RTC$Clock$Updated       ;  all digits of clock updated
08A0 FA9908      06029           JM      RTC$Update$Digit        ;Skip over ":" in ASCII time
08A3 1A          06030           LDAX    D                       ;Get next ASCII time digit
08A4 3C          06031           INR     A                       ;Update it
08A5 12          06032           STAX    D                       ;  and store it back
08A6 BE          06033           CMP     M                       ;Compare to maximum value
08A7 C2B008      06034           JNZ     RTC$Clock$Updated       ;No carry needed so update complete
08AA 3E30        06035           MVI     A,'0'                   ;Reset digit to ASCII 0
08AC 12          06036           STAX    D                       ;  and store back in ASCII time
08AD C39908      06037           JMP     RTC$Update$Digit        ;Go back for next digit
                 06038   ;
                 06039   RTC$Clock$Updated:
                 06040   RTC$Check$Watchdog:
08B0 2ABF00      06041           LHLD    RTC$Watchdog$Count      ;Get current watchdog count
08B3 2B          06042           DCX     H                       ;Downdate it
08B4 7C          06043           MOV     A,H                     ;Check if it is now 0FFFFH
08B5 B7          06044           ORA     A
08B6 FACB08      06045           JM      RTC$Dog$Not$Set         ;It must have been 0 beforehand
08B9 B5          06046           ORA     L                       ;Check if it is now 0
08BA C2C808      06047           JNZ     RTC$Dog$NZ              ;No, it is not out of time
                 06048
                 06049                                           ;Watchdog time elapsed, so "call"
                 06050                                           ;  appropriate routine
08BD 21C508      06051           LXI     H,RTC$Watchdog$Return   ;Set up return address
08C0 E5          06052           PUSH    H                       ;  ready for return
08C1 2AC100      06053           LHLD    RTC$Watchdog$Address    ;Transfer control as though by CALL
08C4 E9          06054           PCHL
                 06055   RTC$Watchdog$Return:                    ;Control will come back here from
                 06056                                           ;  the user's watchdog routine
08C5 C3CB08      06057           JMP     RTC$Dog$Not$Set         ;Behave as though watchdog not active
                 06058
                 06059   RTC$Dog$NZ:
08C8 22BF00      06060           SHLD    RTC$Watchdog$Count      ;Save downdated count
                 06061   RTC$Dog$Not$Set:                        ;  (Leaves count unchanged)
08CB 3E20        06062           MVI     A,IC$EOI                ;Reset the interrupt controller chip
08CD D3D8        06063           OUT     IC$OCW2$Port
                 06064
08CF D1          06065           POP     D                       ;Restore registers from local stack
08D0 C1          06066           POP     B
08D1 2A8422      06067           LHLD    PI$User$Stack           ;Switch back to user's stack
08D4 F9          06068           SPHL
08D5 2A8622      06069           LHLD    PI$User$HL              ;Recover user's registers
08D8 F1          06070           POP     PSW
08D9 FB          06071           EI                              ;Re-enable interrupts
08DA C9          06072           RET
                 06073   ;
                 06200   ;#
                 06201   ;
                 06202   ;       Shift HL Right one bit
                 06203   ;
                 06204   SHLR:
08DB B7          06205           ORA     A                       ;Clear carry
08DC 7C          06206           MOV     A,H                     ;Get MS byte
08DD 1F          06207           RAR                             ;Bit 7 set from previous carry
                 06208                                           ;Bit 0 goes into carry
08DE 67          06209           MOV     H,A                     ;Put shifted MS byte back
08DF 7D          06210           MOV     A,L                     ;Get LS byte
08E0 1F          06211           RAR                             ;Bit 7 = bit 0 of MS byte
08E1 6F          06212           MOV     L,A                     ;Put back into result
08E2 C9          06213           RET
                 06214
                 06215   ;
                 06300   ;#
```

Figure 8-10. (Continued)

Chapter 8: Writing an Enhanced BIOS

```
                06301  ;       High level diskette drivers
                06302  ;
                06303  ;       These drivers perform the following functions:
                06304  ;
                06305  ;       SELDSK  Select a specified disk and return the address of
                06306  ;               the appropriate disk parameter header
                06307  ;       SETTRK  Set the track number for the next read or write
                06308  ;       SETSEC  Set the sector number for the next read or write
                06309  ;       SETDMA  Set the DMA (read/write) address for the next read or write
                06310  ;       SECTRAN Translate a logical sector number into a physical
                06311  ;       HOME    Set the track to 0 so that the next read or write will
                06312  ;               be on Track 0
                06313  ;
                06314  ;       In addition, the high level drivers are responsible for making
                06315  ;       the 5 1/4" floppy diskettes that use a 512-byte sector appear
                06316  ;       to CP/M as though they used a 128-byte sector. They do this
                06317  ;       by using blocking/deblocking code. This blocking/deblocking
                06318  ;       code is described in more detail later in this listing,
                06319  ;       just prior to the code itself.
                06320  ;
                06321  ;
                06322  ;
                06323  ;       Disk parameter tables
                06324  ;
                06325  ;       As discussed in Chapter 3, these describe the physical
                06326  ;       characteristics of the disk drives. In this example BIOS,
                06327  ;       there are two types of disk drives; standard single-sided,
                06328  ;       single-density 8", and double-sided, double-density 5 1/4"
                06329  ;       mini-diskettes.
                06330  ;
                06331  ;       The standard 8" diskettes do not need to use the blocking/
                06332  ;       deblocking code, but the 5 1/4" drives do. Therefore an additional
                06333  ;       byte has been prefixed onto the disk parameter block to
                06334  ;       tell the disk drivers what each logical disk's physical
                06335  ;       diskette type is, and whether or not it needs deblocking.
                06336  ;
                06337  ;
                06338  ;       Disk definition tables
                06339  ;
                06340  ;       These consist of disk parameter headers, with one entry
                06341  ;       per logical disk driver, and disk parameter blocks with
                06342  ;       either one parameter block per logical disk, or the same
                06343  ;       parameter block for several logical disks.
                06344  ;
                06400  ;#
                06401  ;
                06402  Disk$Parameter$Headers:                 ;Described in Chapter 3
                06403  ;
                06404                          ;Logical disk A: (5 1/4" diskette)
08E3 AE09       06405          DW      Floppy$5$Skewtable      ;5 1/4" skew table
08E5 000000000006406          DW      0,0,0                   ;Reserved for CP/M
08EB B022       06407          DW      Directory$Buffer
08ED 3409       06408          DW      Floppy$5$Parameter$Block
08EF B023       06409          DW      Disk$A$Workarea
08F1 1024       06410          DW      Disk$A$Allocation$Vector
                06411  ;
                06412                          ;Logical disk B: (5 1/4" diskette)
08F3 AE09       06413          DW      Floppy$5$Skewtable      ;Shares same skew table as A:
08F5 000000000006414          DW      0,0,0                   ;Reserved for CP/M
08FB B022       06415          DW      Directory$Buffer        ;Shares same buffer as A:
08FD 3409       06416          DW      Floppy$5$Parameter$Block ;Same DPB as A:
08FF D023       06417          DW      Disk$B$Workarea         ;Private work area
0901 2624       06418          DW      Disk$B$Allocation$Vector ;Private allocation vector
                06419  ;
                06420                          ;Logical disk C: (8" floppy)
0903 F609       06421          DW      Floppy$8$Skewtable      ;8" skew table
0905 000000000006422          DW      0,0,0                   ;Reserved for CP/M
090B B022       06423          DW      Directory$Buffer        ;Shares same buffer as A:
090D 4409       06424          DW      Floppy$8$Parameter$Block
090F F023       06425          DW      Disk$C$Workarea         ;Private work area
0911 3C24       06426          DW      Disk$C$Allocation$Vector ;Private allocation vector
                06427  ;
                06428                          ;Logical disk D: (8" floppy)
0913 AE09       06429          DW      Floppy$5$Skewtable      ;Shares same skew table as A:
0915 000000000006430          DW      0,0,0                   ;Reserved for CP/M
091B B022       06431          DW      Directory$Buffer        ;Shares same buffer as A:
```

Figure 8-10. (Continued)

```
091D 4409        06432           DW      Floppy$8$Parameter$Block        ;Same DPB as C:
091F 0024        06433           DW      Disk$D$Workarea                 ;Private work area
0921 5B24        06434           DW      Disk$D$Allocation$Vector        ;Private allocation vector
                 06435
                 06436                           ;Logical disk M: (memory disk)
                 06437   M$Disk$DPH:
0923 0000        06438           DW      0                               ;No skew required
0925 000000000006439            DW      0,0,0                            ;Reserved for CP/M
092B B022        06440           DW      Directory$Buffer
092D 5409        06441           DW      M$Disk$Parameter$Block
092F 0000        06442           DW      0                               ;Disk cannot be changed, therefore
                 06443                                                   ;  no work area is required
0931 7A24        06444           DW      M$Disk$Allocation$Vector
                 06445   ;
                 06446   ;
                 06447   ;       Equates for disk parameter block
                 06448   ;
                 06449   ;       Disk Types
                 06450   ;
0001 =           06451   Floppy$5         EQU    1                       ;5 1/4" mini floppy
0002 =           06452   Floppy$8         EQU    2                       ;8" floppy (SS SD)
0003 =           06453   M$Disk           EQU    3                       ;Memory disk
                 06454   ;
                 06455   ;       Blocking/deblocking indicator
                 06456   ;
0080 =           06457   Need$Deblocking  EQU    1000$0000B              ;Sector size > 128 bytes
                 06458   ;
                 06600   ;#
                 06601
                 06602   ;       Disk parameter blocks
                 06603   ;
                 06604   ;       5 1/4" mini floppy
                 06605   ;
                 06606                                                   ;Extra byte prefixed to indicate
                 06607                                                   ; disk type and blocking required
0933 81          06608           DB      Floppy$5 + Need$Deblocking
                 06609                                                   ;The parameter block has been amended
                 06610                                                   ; to reflect the new layout of one
                 06611                                                   ; track per diskette side, rather
                 06612                                                   ; than viewing one track as both
                 06613                                                   ; sides on a given head position.
                 06614                                                   ;It has also been adjusted to reflect
                 06615                                                   ; one "new" track more being used for
                 06616                                                   ; the CP/M image, with the resulting
                 06617                                                   ; change in the number of allocation
                 06618                                                   ; blocks and the number of reserved
                 06619                                                   ; tracks.
                 06620   Floppy$5$Parameter$Block:
0934 2400        06621           DW      36                              ;128-byte sectors per track
0936 04          06622           DB      4                               ;Block shift
0937 0F          06623           DB      15                              ;Block mask
0938 01          06624           DB      1                               ;Extent mask
0939 AB00        06625           DW      171                             ;Maximum allocation block number
093B 7F00        06626           DW      127                             ;Number of directory entries - 1
093D C0          06627           DB      1100$0000B                      ;Bit map for reserving 1 alloc. block
093E 00          06628           DB      0000$0000B                      ; for file directory
093F 2000        06629           DW      32                              ;Disk-changed work area size
0941 0300        06630           DW      3                               ;Number of tracks before directory
                 06631   ;
                 06632   ;
                 06633   ;       Standard 8" Floppy
                 06634                                                   ;Extra byte prefixed to DPB for
                 06635                                                   ; this version of the BIOS
0943 02          06636           DB      Floppy$8                        ;Indicates disk type and the fact
                 06637                                                   ; that no deblocking is required
                 06638   Floppy$8$Parameter$Block:
0944 1A00        06639           DW      26                              ;Sectors per track
0946 03          06640           DB      3                               ;Block shift
0947 07          06641           DB      7                               ;Block mask
0948 00          06642           DB      0                               ;Extent mask
0949 F200        06643           DW      242                             ;Maximum allocation block number
094B 3F00        06644           DW      63                              ;Number of directory entries - 1
094D C0          06645           DB      1100$0000B                      ;Bit map for reserving 2 alloc. blocks
094E 00          06646           DB      0000$0000B                      ; for file directory
094F 1000        06647           DW      16                              ;Disk-changed work area size
0951 0200        06648           DW      2                               ;Number of tracks before directory
```

Figure 8-10. (Continued)

Chapter 8: Writing an Enhanced BIOS

```
                  06649    ;
                  06650    ;        M$Disk
                  06651    ;
                  06652                                   ;The M$Disk presumes that 4 x 48K memory
                  06653                                   ; banks are available. The following
                  06654                                   ; table describes the disk as having
                  06655                                   ; 8 tracks: two tracks per memory bank
                  06656                                   ; with each track having 192 128-byte
                  06657                                   ; sectors.
                  06658                                   ; The track number divided by 2 will be
                  06659                                   ; used to select the bank
0953 03           06660           DB      M$Disk          ;Type is M$Disk, no deblocking
                  06661    M$Disk$Parameter$Block:
0954 C000         06662           DW      192             ;Sectors per "track". Each track is
                  06663                                   ; 24K of memory
0956 03           06664           DB      3               ;Block shift (1024 byte allocation)
0957 07           06665           DB      7               ;Block mask
0958 00           06666           DB      0               ;Extent mask
0959 C000         06667           DW      192             ;Maximum allocation block number
095B 3F00         06668           DW      63              ;Number of directory entries -1
095D C0           06669           DB      1100$0000B      ;Bit map for reserving 2 allocation blocks
095E 00           06670           DB      0000$0000B      ; for file directory
095F 0000         06671           DW      0               ;Disk cannot be changed, therefore no
                  06672                                   ; work area
0961 0000         06673           DW      0               ;No reserved tracks
                  06674    ;
0004 =            06675    Number$of$Logical$Disks       EQU     4
                  06676    ;
                  06800    ;#
                  06801    ;
                  06802    SELDSK:          ;Select disk in register C
                  06803                     ;C = 0 for drive A, 1 for B, etc.
                  06804                     ;Return the address of the appropriate
                  06805                     ; disk parameter header in HL, or 0000H
                  06806                     ; if the selected disk does not exist.
                  06807    ;
0963 210000       06808           LXI     H,0             ;Assume an error
0966 79           06809           MOV     A,C             ;Check if requested disk valid
                  06810
0967 FE0C         06811           CPI     'M' - 'A'       ;Check if memory disk
0969 CA9509       06812           JZ      SELDSK$M$Disk   ;Yes
                  06813
096C FE04         06814           CPI     Number$of$Logical$Disks
096E D0           06815           RNC                     ;Return if > maximum number of disks
                  06816    ;
096F 322D0A       06817           STA     Selected$Disk   ;Save selected disk number
                  06818                                   ;Set up to return DPH address
0972 6F           06819           MOV     L,A             ;Make disk into word value
0973 2600         06820           MVI     H,0
                  06821                                   ;Compute offset down disk parameter
                  06822                                   ; header table by multiplying by
                  06823                                   ; parameter header length (16 bytes)
0975 29           06824           DAD     H               ;*2
0976 29           06825           DAD     H               ;*4
0977 29           06826           DAD     H               ;*8
0978 29           06827           DAD     H               ;*16
0979 11E308       06828           LXI     D,Disk$Parameter$Headers   ;Get base address
097C 19           06829           DAD     D               ;DE -> appropriate DPH
097D E5           06830           PUSH    H               ;Save DPH address
                  06831    ;
                  06832                                   ;Access disk parameter block to
                  06833                                   ; extract special prefix byte that
                  06834                                   ; identifies disk type and whether
                  06835                                   ; deblocking is required
                  06836                                   ;
097E 110A00       06837           LXI     D,10            ;Get DPB pointer offset in DPH
0981 19           06838           DAD     D               ;DE -> DPB address in DPH
0982 5E           06839           MOV     E,M             ;Get DPB address in DE
0983 23           06840           INX     H
0984 56           06841           MOV     D,M
0985 EB           06842           XCHG                    ;DE -> DPB
                  06843
                  06844    SELDSK$Set$Disk$Type:
0986 2B           06845           DCX     H               ;DE -> prefix byte
0987 7E           06846           MOV     A,M             ;Get prefix byte
0988 E60F         06847           ANI     0FH             ;Isolate disk type
```

Figure 8-10. (Continued)

272 The CP/M Programmer's Handbook

```
098A 32360A    06848           STA     Selected$Disk$Type     ;Save for use in low level driver
098D 7E        06849           MOV     A,M                    ;Get another copy of prefix byte
098E E680      06850           ANI     Need$Deblocking        ;Isolate deblocking flag
0990 32350A    06851           STA     Selected$Disk$Deblock  ;Save for use in low level driver
0993 E1        06852           POP     H                      ;Recover DPH pointer
0994 C9        06853           RET
               06854   ;
               06855   SELDSK$M$Disk:                         ;M$Disk selected
0995 212309    06856           LXI     H,M$Disk$DPH           ;Return correct parameter header
0998 C38609    06857           JMP     SELDSK$Set$Disk$Type   ;Resume normal processing
               06858   ;
               07000   ;#
               07001   ;
               07002   ;       Set logical track for next read or write
               07003   ;
               07004   SETTRK:
099B 60        07005           MOV     H,B                    ;Selected track in BC on entry
099C 69        07006           MOV     L,C
099D 222E0A    07007           SHLD    Selected$Track         ;Save for low level driver
09A0 C9        07008           RET
               07009   ;
               07100   ;#
               07101   ;
               07102   ;       Set logical sector for next read or write
               07103   ;
               07104   ;
               07105   SETSEC:                                ;Logical sector in C on entry
09A1 79        07106           MOV     A,C
09A2 32300A    07107           STA     Selected$Sector        ;Save for low level driver
09A5 C9        07108           RET
               07109   ;
               07200   ;#
               07201   ;
               07202   ;       Set disk DMA (Input/Output) address for next read or write
               07203   ;
09A6 0000      07204   DMA$Address:    DW      0              ;DMA address
               07205   ;
               07206   SETDMA:                                ;Address in BC on entry
09A8 69        07207           MOV     L,C                    ;Move to HL to save
09A9 60        07208           MOV     H,B
09AA 22A609    07209           SHLD    DMA$Address            ;Save for low level driver
09AD C9        07210           RET
               07211   ;
               07300   ;#
               07301   ;
               07302   ;       Translate logical sector number to physical
               07303   ;
               07304   ;       Sector translation tables
               07305   ;       These tables are indexed using the logical sector number,
               07306   ;       and contain the corresponding physical sector number.
               07307   ;
               07308           Floppy$5$Skewtable:    ;Each physical sector contains four
               07309                                  ;128-byte sectors.
               07310   ;              Physical 128b     Logical 128b      Physical 512-byte
09AE 00010203  07311           DB     00,01,02,03      ;00,01,02,03      0  )
09B2 10111213  07312           DB     16,17,18,19      ;04,05,06,07      4  )
09B6 20212223  07313           DB     32,33,34,35      ;08,09,10,11      8  )
09BA 0C0D0E0F  07314           DB     12,13,14,15      ;12,13,14,15      3  ) Head
09BE 1C1D1E1F  07315           DB     28,29,30,31      ;16,17,18,19      7  ) 0
09C2 08090A0B  07316           DB     08,09,10,11      ;20,21,22,23      2  )
09C6 18191A1B  07317           DB     24,25,26,27      ;24,25,26,27      6  )
09CA 04050607  07318           DB     04,05,06,07      ;28,29,30,31      1  )
09CE 14151617  07319           DB     20,21,22,23      ;32,33,34,35      5  )
               07320   ;
09D2 24252627  07321           DB     36,37,38,39      ;36,37,38,39      0  ]
09D6 34353637  07322           DB     52,53,54,55      ;40,41,42,43      4  ]
09DA 44454647  07323           DB     68,69,70,71      ;44,45,46,47      8  ]
09DE 30313233  07324           DB     48,49,50,51      ;48,49,50,51      3  ] Head
09E2 40414243  07325           DB     64,65,66,67      ;52,53,54,55      7  ] 1
09E6 2C2D2E2F  07326           DB     44,45,46,47      ;56,57,58,59      2  ]
09EA 3C3D3E3F  07327           DB     60,61,62,63      ;60,61,62,63      6  ]
09EE 28292A2B  07328           DB     40,41,42,43      ;64,65,66,67      1  ]
09F2 38393A3B  07329           DB     56,57,58,59      ;68,69,70,71      5  ]
               07330   ;
               07331   ;
               07332           Floppy$8$Skewtable:    ;Standard 8" Driver
```

Figure 8-10. (Continued)

```
                07333          ;             01,02,03,04,05,06,07,08,09,10     Logical sectors
09F6 01070D131907334           DB            01,07,13,19,25,05,11,17,23,03    ;Physical sectors
                07335          ;
                07336          ;             11,12,13,14,15,16,17,18,19,20     Logical sectors
0A00 090F15020807337           DB            09,15,21,02,08,14,20,26,06,12    ;Physical sectors
                07338          ;
                07339          ;             21,22,23,24,25,26                 Logical sectors
0A0A 1218040A1007340           DB            18,24,04,10,16,22                ;Physical sectors
                07341
                07400          ;#
                07401          ;
                07402          SECTRAN:                  ;Translate logical sector into physical
                07403                                    ;On entry, BC = logical sector number
                07404                                    ;              DE -> appropriate skew table
                07405                                    ;
                07406                                    ;on exit, HL = physical sector number
0A10 EB         07407          XCHG                      ;HL -> skew table base
0A11 09         07408          DAD     B                 ;Add on logical sector number
0A12 6E         07409          MOV     L,M               ;Get physical sector number
0A13 2600       07410          MVI     H,0               ;Make into a 16-bit value
0A15 C9         07411          RET
                07412          ;
                07500          ;#
                07501          ;
                07502          ;
                07503          HOME:                     ;Home the selected logical disk to track 0
                07504                                    ;Before doing this, a check must be made to see
                07505                                    ;   if the physical disk buffer has information in
                07506                                    ;   it that must be written out.  This is indicated by
                07507                                    ;   a flag, Must$Write$Buffer, that is set in the
                07508                                    ;   deblocking code.
                07509
0A16 3A2C0A     07510          LDA     Must$Write$Buffer ;Check if physical buffer must
0A19 B7         07511          ORA     A                 ;  be written to a disk
0A1A C2200A     07512          JNZ     HOME$No$Write
0A1D 322B0A     07513          STA     Data$In$Disk$Buffer ;No, so indicate that buffer
                07514                                      ;  is now unoccupied
                07515          HOME$No$Write:
0A20 0E00       07516          MVI     C,0               ;Set to track 0 (logically,
0A22 CD9B09     07517          CALL    SETTRK            ;  no actual disk operation occurs)
0A25 C9         07518          RET
                07519
                07520          ;
                07600          ;#
                07601          ;     Data written to or read from the mini-floppy drive is transferred
                07602          ;     via a physical buffer that is one complete track in length,
                07603          ;     9 * 512 bytes.  It is declared at the end of the BIOS, and has
                07604          ;     some small amount of initialization code "hidden" in it.
                07605          ;
                07606          ;     The blocking/deblocking code attempts to minimize the amount
                07607          ;     of actual disk I/O by storing the disk and track
                07608          ;     currently residing in the physical buffer.
                07609          ;     If a read request occurs of a 128-byte CP/M "sector"
                07610          ;     that already is in the physical buffer, no disk access occurs
                07611          ;     If a write request occurs if and the 128-byte CP/M 'sector'
                07612          ;     is already in the physical buffer, no disk access will occur,
                07613          ;     UNLESS the BDOS indicates that it is writing to the directory.
                07614          ;     Directory writes cause an immediate write to disk of the entire
                07615          ;     track in the physical buffer.
                07616          ;
                07617          ;
0800 =          07618          Allocation$Block$Size   EQU   2048
0009 =          07619          Physical$Sec$Per$Track  EQU   9         ;Adjusted to reflect a "new"
                07620                                                  ;  track is only one side of the
                07621                                                  ;  disk
0200 =          07622          Physical$Sector$Size    EQU   512       ;This is the actual sector size
                07623                                                  ;  for the 5 1/4" mini-floppy diskettes
                07624                                                  ;The 8" diskettes and memory disk
                07625                                                  ;  use 128-byte sectors
                07626                                                  ;Declare the physical disk buffer for the
                07627                                                  ;  5 1/4" diskettes
0004 =          07628          CPM$Sec$Per$Physical    EQU   Physical$Sector$Size/128
0024 =          07629          CPM$Sec$Per$Track       EQU   CPM$Sec$Per$Physical*Physical$Sec$Per$Track
1200 =          07630          Bytes$Per$Track         EQU   Physical$Sec$Per$Track*Physical$Sector$Size
0003 =          07631          Sector$Mask             EQU   CPM$Sec$Per$Physical-1
0002 =          07632          Sector$Bit$Shift        EQU   2         ;LOG2(CPM$Sec$Per$Physical)
```

Figure 8-10. (Continued)

```
               07633   ;
               07634   ;                        ;These are the values handed over by the BDOS
               07635   ;                        ;  when it calls the write operation.
               07636   ;                        ;The allocated/unallocated indicates whether the
               07637   ;                        ;  BDOS wishes to write to an unallocated allocation
               07638   ;                        ;  block (it only indicates this for the first
               07639   ;                        ;  128-byte sector write), or to an allocation block
               07640   ;                        ;  that has already been allocated to a file.
               07641   ;                        ;The BDOS also indicates if it wishes to write to
               07642   ;                        ;  the file directory.
               07643   ;
0000 =         07644   Write$Allocated          EQU    0
0001 =         07645   Write$Directory          EQU    1
0002 =         07646   Write$Unallocated        EQU    2           ;<== ignored for track buffering
               07647   ;
0A26  00       07648   Write$Type:              DB     0           ;Contains the type of write
               07649                                                ;  indicated by the BDOS
               07650   ;
               07651   ;
               07652   In$Buffer$Dk$Trk:                            ;Variables for physical sector currently
               07653                                                ;  in Disk$Buffer in memory
0A27  00       07654   In$Buffer$Disk:          DB     0           ;) These are moved and compared
0A28  0000     07655   In$Buffer$Track:         DW     0           ;) as a group, so do not alter
               07656                                                ;  these lines
0A2A  00       07657   In$Buffer$Disk$Type:     DB     0           ;Disk type for sector in buffer
               07658   ;
0A2B  00       07659   Data$In$Disk$Buffer:     DB     0           ;When nonzero, the disk buffer has
               07660                                                ;  data from the disk in it
0A2C  00       07661   Must$Write$Buffer:       DB     0           ;Nonzero when data has been written
               07662                                                ;  into Disk$Buffer but not yet
               07663                                                ;  written out to disk
               07664   ;
               07665   Selected$Dk$Trk:                             ;Variables for selected disk, track and sector
               07666                                                ;  (Selected by SELDSK, SETTRK and SETSEC)
0A2D  00       07667   Selected$Disk:           DB     0           ;) These are moved and compared
0A2E  0000     07668   Selected$Track:          DW     0           ;) as a group so do not alter order
               07669
0A30  00       07670   Selected$Sector:         DB     0           ;Not part of group but needed here
               07671
0A31  00       07672   Selected$Physical$Sector: DB    0           ;Selected physical sector derived
               07673                                                ;  from selected (CP/M) sector by
               07674                                                ;  shifting it right the number of
               07675                                                ;  bits specified by Sector$Bit$Shift
               07676
               07677   ;
               07678
0A32  00       07679   Disk$Error$Flag:         DB     0           ;Nonzero to indicate an error
               07680                                                ;  that could not be recovered
               07681                                                ;  by the disk drivers. The BDOS
               07682                                                ;  will output a "Bad Sector" message
0A33  00       07683   Disk$Hung$Flag:          DB     0           ;Nonzero if a watchdog timeout
               07684                                                ;  occurs
0258 =         07685   Disk$Timer               EQU    600         ;Number of 16.66 ms clock ticks
               07686                                                ;  for a 10 second timeout
               07687   ;
               07688                                                ;Flags used inside the deblocking code
               07689
0A34  00       07690   Read$Operation:          DB     0           ;Nonzero when a CP/M 128-byte
               07691                                                ;  sector is to be read
0A35  00       07692   Selected$Disk$Deblock:   DB     0           ;Nonzero when the selected disk
               07693                                                ;  needs deblocking (set in SELDSK)
0A36  00       07694   Selected$Disk$Type:      DB     0           ;Indicates 8" or 5 1/4" floppy or
               07695                                                ;  M$Disk selected. (set in SELDSK)
               07696   ;
               07800   ;#
               07801   ;
               07802   ;       Read in the 128-byte CP/M sector specified by previous calls
               07803   ;       to Select Disk, Set Track and Sector. The sector will be read
               07804   ;       into the address specified in the previous Set DMA Address call.
               07805   ;
               07806   ;       If reading from a disk drive using sectors larger than 128 bytes,
               07807   ;       deblocking code will be used to "unpack" a 128-byte sector from
               07808   ;       the physical sector.
               07809   READ:
0A37  3A350A   07810           LDA     Selected$Disk$Deblock       ;Check if deblocking needed
0A3A  B7       07811           ORA     A                            ;  (flag was set in SELDSK call)
```

Figure 8-10. (Continued)

Chapter 8: Writing an Enhanced BIOS **275**

```
0A3B CA2F0B    07812           JZ      Read$No$Deblock         ;No, use normal nondeblocked
               07813
               07814                                           ;The deblocking algorithm used is such
               07815                                           ;  that a read operation can be viewed
               07816                                           ;  until the actual data transfer as though
               07817                                           ;  it was the first write to an unallocated
               07818                                           ;  allocation block
0A3E 3E01      07819           MVI     A,1                     ;Indicate that a read actually
0A40 32340A    07820           STA     Read$Operation          ;  is to be performed
               07821
0A43 3E00      07822           MVI     A,Write$Allocated       ;Fake deblocking code into believing
0A45 32260A    07823           STA     Write$Type              ;  that this is a write to an
               07824                                           ;  allocated allocation block
0A48 C35C0A    07825           JMP     Perform$Read$Write      ;Use common code to execute read
               07826   ;
               07900   ;#
               07901   ;       Write a 128-byte sector from the current DMA address to
               07902   ;       the previously selected disk, track and sector.
               07903   ;
               07904   ;       On arrival here, the BDOS will have set register C to indicate
               07905   ;       whether this write operation is to an already allocated allocation
               07906   ;       block (which means a preread of the sector may be needed), or
               07907   ;       to the directory (in which case the data will be written to the
               07908   ;       disk immediately).
               07909   ;
               07910   ;       Only writes to the directory take place immediately. In all other
               07911   ;       cases, the data will be moved from the DMA address into the disk
               07912   ;       buffer, and only be written out when circumstances force the
               07913   ;       transfer. The number of physical disk operations can therefore
               07914   ;       be reduced considerably.
               07915   ;
               07916   WRITE:
0A4B 3A350A    07917           LDA     Selected$Disk$Deblock   ;Check if deblocking is required
0A4E B7        07918           ORA     A                       ;  (flag set in SELDSK call)
0A4F CA2A0B    07919           JZ      Write$No$Deblock
               07920
0A52 AF        07921           XRA     A                       ;Indicate that a write operation
0A53 32340A    07922           STA     Read$Operation          ;  is required (i.e NOT a read)
0A56 79        07923           MOV     A,C                     ;Save the BDOS write type
0A57 E601      07924           ANI     1                       ;  but only distinguish between
               07925                                           ;  write to allocated block or
0A59 32260A    07926           STA     Write$Type              ;  directory write
               07927   ;
               07928   ;
               08000   ;#
               08001   ;
               08002   Perform$Read$Write:     ;Common code to execute both reads and
               08003                           ;  writes of 128-byte sectors.
0A5C AF        08004           XRA     A                       ;Assume that no disk errors will
0A5D 32320A    08005           STA     Disk$Error$Flag         ;  occur
               08006
0A60 3A300A    08007           LDA     Selected$Sector         ;Convert selected 128-byte sector
0A63 1F        08008           RAR                             ;  into physical sector by dividing by 4
0A64 1F        08009           RAR
0A65 E63F      08010           ANI     3FH                     ;Remove any unwanted bits
0A67 32310A    08011           STA     Selected$Physical$Sector
               08012   ;
0A6A 212B0A    08013           LXI     H,Data$In$Disk$Buffer   ;Check if disk buffer already has
0A6D 7E        08014           MOV     A,M                     ;  data in it
0A6E 3601      08015           MVI     M,1                     ;(Unconditionally indicate that
               08016                                           ;  the buffer now has data in it)
0A70 B7        08017           ORA     A                       ;Did it indeed have data in it?
0A71 CA870A    08018           JZ      Read$Track$into$Buffer  ;No, proceed to read a physical
               08019                                           ;  track into the buffer
               08020   ;
               08021                                           ;The buffer does have a physical track
               08022                                           ;  in it. Check if it is the right one
               08023
0A74 11270A    08024           LXI     D,In$Buffer$Dk$Trk      ;Check if track in buffer is the
0A77 212D0A    08025           LXI     H,Selected$Dk$Trk       ;  same as that selected earlier
0A7A CDE10A    08026           CALL    Compare$Dk$Trk          ;Compare ONLY disk and track
0A7D CA910A    08027           JZ      Track$In$Buffer         ;Yes, it is already in buffer
               08028
               08029                                           ;No, it will have to be read in
               08030                                           ;  over current contents of buffer
0A80 3A2C0A    08031           LDA     Must$Write$Buffer       ;Check if buffer has data in that
```

Figure 8-10.   (Continued)

```
0A83 B7      08032         ORA     A                   ; must be written out first
0A84 C4E50B  08033         CNZ     Write$Physical      ;Yes, write it out
             08034  ;
             08035  Read$Track$into$Buffer:
0A87 CDCE0A  08036         CALL    Set$In$Buffer$Dk$Trk ;Set in buffer variables from
             08037                                     ;   selected disk, track
             08038                                     ;   to reflect which track is in the
             08039                                     ;   buffer now
0A8A CDEA0B  08040         CALL    Read$Physical       ;Read the track into the buffer
0A8D AF      08041         XRA     A                   ;Reset the flag to reflect buffer
0A8E 322C0A  08042         STA     Must$Write$Buffer   ;   contents
             08043  ;
             08044  Track$In$Buffer:                   ;Selected track and
             08045                                     ;   disk is already in the buffer
             08046                                     ;Convert the selected CP/M (128-byte)
             08047                                     ;   sector into a relative address down
             08048                                     ;   the buffer
0A91 3A300A  08049         LDA     Selected$Sector     ;Get selected sector number
0A94 6F      08050         MOV     L,A                 ;Multiply by 128 by shifting 16-bit value
0A95 2600    08051         MVI     H,0                 ;left 7 bits
0A97 29      08052         DAD     H                   ;* 2
0A98 29      08053         DAD     H                   ;* 4
0A99 29      08054         DAD     H                   ;* 8
0A9A 29      08055         DAD     H                   ;* 16
0A9B 29      08056         DAD     H                   ;* 32
0A9C 29      08057         DAD     H                   ;* 64
0A9D 29      08058         DAD     H                   ;* 128
             08059  ;
0A9E 11400F  08060         LXI     D,Disk$Buffer       ;Get base address of disk buffer
0AA1 19      08061         DAD     D                   ;Add on sector number * 128
             08062                                     ;HL -> 128-byte sector number start
             08063                                     ;   address in disk buffer
0AA2 EB      08064         XCHG                        ;DE -> sector in disk buffer
0AA3 2AA609  08065         LHLD    DMA$Address         ;Get DMA address set in SETDMA call
0AA6 EB      08066         XCHG                        ;Assume a read operation, so
             08067                                     ;   DE -> DMA address
             08068                                     ;   HL -> sector in disk buffer
0AA7 0E10    08069         MVI     C,128/8             ;Because of the faster method used
             08070                                     ;   to move data in and out of the
             08071                                     ;   disk buffer, (eight bytes moved per
             08072                                     ;   loop iteration) the count need only
             08073                                     ;   be 1/8 of normal
             08074                                     ;At this point,
             08075                                     ;   C = loop count
             08076                                     ;   DE -> DMA address
             08077                                     ;   HL -> sector in disk buffer
0AA9 3A340A  08078         LDA     Read$Operation      ;Determine whether data is to be moved
0AAC B7      08079         ORA     A                   ;   out of the buffer (read) or into the
0AAD C2B50A  08080         JNZ     Buffer$Move         ;   buffer (write)
             08081                                     ;Writing into buffer
             08082                                     ;   (A must be 0 get here)
0AB0 3C      08083         INR     A                   ;Set flag to force a write
0AB1 322C0A  08084         STA     Must$Write$Buffer   ;   of the disk buffer later on.
0AB4 EB      08085         XCHG                        ;Make DE -> sector in disk buffer
             08086                                     ;     HL -> DMA address
             08087  ;
             08088  ;
             08089  Buffer$Move:
0AB5 CDF80A  08090         CALL    Move$8              ;Moves 8 bytes * C times from (HL)
             08091                                     ;   to (DE)
             08092  
             08093  ;
0AB8 3A260A  08094         LDA     Write$Type          ;If write to directory, write out
0ABB FE01    08095         CPI     Write$Directory     ;   buffer immediately
0ABD 3A320A  08096         LDA     Disk$Error$Flag     ;Get error flag in case delayed write or read
0AC0 C0      08097         RNZ                         ;Return if delayed write or read
             08098  ;
0AC1 B7      08099         ORA     A                   ;Check if any disk errors have occured
0AC2 C0      08100         RNZ                         ;Yes, abandon attempt to write to directory
             08101  ;
0AC3 AF      08102         XRA     A                   ;Clear flag that indicates buffer must be
0AC4 322C0A  08103         STA     Must$Write$Buffer   ;   written out
0AC7 CDE50B  08104         CALL    Write$Physical      ;Write buffer out to physical track
0ACA 3A320A  08105         LDA     Disk$Error$Flag     ;Return error flag to caller
0ACD C9      08106         RET
             08107  ;
```

Figure 8-10. (Continued)

```
                08108   ;
                08109   ;
                08110   Set$In$Buffer$Dk$Trk:              ;Indicate selected disk, track
                08111                                      ;   now residing in buffer
OACE  3A2D0A    08112           LDA     Selected$Disk
OAD1  32270A    08113           STA     In$Buffer$Disk
                08114
OAD4  2A2E0A    08115           LHLD    Selected$Track
OAD7  22280A    08116           SHLD    In$Buffer$Track
                08117
OADA  3A360A    08118           LDA     Selected$Disk$Type
OADD  322A0A    08119           STA     In$Buffer$Disk$Type  ;Also reflect disk type
                08120
OAE0  C9        08121           RET
                08122   ;
                08123   ;
                08124   Compare$Dk$Trk:                    ;Compares just the disk and track
                08125                                      ;   pointed to by DE and HL
OAE1  0E03      08126           MVI     C,3                ;Disk (1), track (2)
                08127   Compare$Dk$Trk$Loop:
OAE3  1A        08128           LDAX    D                  ;Get comparitor
OAE4  BE        08129           CMP     M                  ;Compare with comparand
OAE5  C0        08130           RNZ                        ;Abandon comparison if inequality found
OAE6  13        08131           INX     D                  ;Update comparitor pointer
OAE7  23        08132           INX     H                  ;Update comparand pointer
OAE8  0D        08133           DCR     C                  ;Count down on loop count
OAE9  C8        08134           RZ                         ;Return (with zero flag set)
OAEA  C3E30A    08135           JMP     Compare$Dk$Trk$Loop
                08136   ;
                08137   ;
                08138   Move$Dk$Trk:                       ;Moves the disk, track
                08139                                      ;   variables pointed at by HL to
                08140                                      ;   those pointed at by DE
OAED  0E03      08141           MVI     C,3                ;Disk (1), Track (2)
                08142   Move$Dk$Trk$Loop:
OAEF  7E        08143           MOV     A,M                ;Get source byte
OAF0  12        08144           STAX    D                  ;Store in destination
OAF1  13        08145           INX     D                  ;Update pointers
OAF2  23        08146           INX     H
OAF3  0D        08147           DCR     C                  ;Count down on byte count
OAF4  C8        08148           RZ                         ;Return if all bytes moved
OAF5  C3EF0A    08149           JMP     Move$Dk$Trk$Loop
                08150   ;
                08300   ;#
                08301   ;
                08302   ;       Move eight bytes
                08303   ;
                08304   ;       This routine moves eight bytes in a block, C times, from
                08305   ;       (HL) to (DE). It uses "drop through" coding to speed
                08306   ;       up execution.
                08307   ;
                08308   ;       Entry Parameters
                08309   ;
                08310   ;               C = number of 8-byte blocks to move
                08311   ;               DE -> destination address
                08312   ;               HL -> source address
                08313   ;
                08314   Move$8:
OAF8  7E        08315           MOV     A,M                ;Get byte from source
OAF9  12        08316           STAX    D                  ;Put into destination
OAFA  13        08317           INX     D                  ;Update pointers
OAFB  23        08318           INX     H
OAFC  7E        08319           MOV     A,M                ;Get byte from source
OAFD  12        08320           STAX    D                  ;Put into destination
OAFE  13        08321           INX     D                  ;Update pointers
OAFF  23        08322           INX     H
OB00  7E        08323           MOV     A,M                ;Get byte from source
OB01  12        08324           STAX    D                  ;Put into destination
OB02  13        08325           INX     D                  ;Update pointers
OB03  23        08326           INX     H
OB04  7E        08327           MOV     A,M                ;Get byte from source
OB05  12        08328           STAX    D                  ;Put into destination
OB06  13        08329           INX     D                  ;Update pointers
OB07  23        08330           INX     H
OB08  7E        08331           MOV     A,M                ;Get byte from source
OB09  12        08332           STAX    D                  ;Put into destination
```

Figure 8-10. (Continued)

```
0B0A 13      08333           INX    D              ;Update pointers
0B0B 23      08334           INX    H
0B0C 7E      08335           MOV    A,M            ;Get byte from source
0B0D 12      08336           STAX   D              ;Put into destination
0B0E 13      08337           INX    D              ;Update pointers
0B0F 23      08338           INX    H
0B10 7E      08339           MOV    A,M            ;Get byte from source
0B11 12      08340           STAX   D              ;Put into destination
0B12 13      08341           INX    D              ;Update pointers
0B13 23      08342           INX    H
0B14 7E      08343           MOV    A,M            ;Get byte from source
0B15 12      08344           STAX   D              ;Put into destination
0B16 13      08345           INX    D              ;Update pointers
0B17 23      08346           INX    H
             08347
0B18 0D      08348           DCR    C              ;Count down on loop counter
0B19 C2F80A  08349           JNZ    Move$8         ;Repeat until done
0B1C C9      08350           RET
             08351
             08352   ;
             08500   ;#
             08501   ;
             08502   ;       Introduction to the disk controllers on this computer system
             08503   ;
             08504   ;       There are two "smart" disk controllers on this system, one
             08505   ;       for the 8" floppy diskette drives, and one for the 5 1/4"
             08506   ;       mini-diskette drives.
             08507   ;
             08508   ;       The controllers are "hard-wired" to monitor certain locations
             08509   ;       in memory to detect when they are to perform some disk
             08510   ;       operation. The 8" controller looks at location 0040H, and
             08511   ;       the 5 1/4" controller looks at location 0045H. These are
             08512   ;       called their disk control bytes. If the most significant
             08513   ;       bit of a disk control byte is set, the controller will then
             08514   ;       look at the word following the respective control bytes.
             08515   ;       This word must contain the address of a valid disk control
             08516   ;       table that specifies the exact disk operation to be performed.
             08517   ;
             08518   ;       Once the operation has been completed, the controller resets
             08519   ;       its disk control byte to 00H, and this indicates completion
             08520   ;       to the disk driver code.
             08521   ;
             08522   ;       The controller also sets a return code in a disk status block.
             08523   ;       Both controllers use the same location (0043H) for this.
             08524   ;       If the first byte of this status block is less than 80H, then
             08525   ;       a disk error has occurred. For this simple BIOS, no further details
             08526   ;       of the status settings are relevant. Note that the disk controller
             08527   ;       has built-in retry logic, reads and writes are attempted ten
             08528   ;       times before the controller returns an error.
             08529   ;
             08530   ;       The disk control table layout is shown below. Note that the
             08531   ;       controllers have the capability for control tables to be
             08532   ;       chained together so that a sequence of disk operations can
             08533   ;       be initiated. In this BIOS this feature is not used. However,
             08534   ;       the controller requires that the chain pointers in the
             08535   ;       disk control tables be pointed back to the main control bytes
             08536   ;       in order to indicate the end of the chain.
             08537   ;
0040 =       08538   Disk$Control$8       EQU    40H      ;8" control byte
0041 =       08539   Command$Block$8      EQU    41H      ;Control table pointer
             08540   ;
0043 =       08541   Disk$Status$Block    EQU    43H      ;8" AND 5 1/4" status block
             08542   ;
0045 =       08543   Disk$Control$5       EQU    45H      ;5 1/4" control byte
0046 =       08544   Command$Block$5      EQU    46H      ;Control table pointer
             08545   ;
             08546   ;
             08547   ;          Floppy Disk Control Tables
             08548   ;
0B1D 00      08549   Floppy$Command:      DB     0        ;Command
0001 =       08550   Floppy$Read$Code     EQU    01H
0002 =       08551   Floppy$Write$Code    EQU    02H
0B1E 00      08552   Floppy$Unit:         DB     0        ;Unit (drive) number = 0 or 1
0B1F 00      08553   Floppy$Head:         DB     0        ;Head number = 0 or 1
0B20 00      08554   Floppy$Track:        DB     0        ;Track number
0B21 00      08555   Floppy$Sector:       DB     0        ;Sector number
```

Figure 8-10. (Continued)

```
0B22 0000      08556        Floppy$Byte$Count:              DW      0       ;Number of bytes to read/write
0B24 0000      08557        Floppy$DMA$Address:             DW      0       ;Transfer address
0B26 0000      08558        Floppy$Next$Status$Block:       DW      0       ;Pointer to next status block
               08559                                                        ;   if commands are chained.
0B28 0000      08560        Floppy$Next$Control$Location:   DW      0       ;Pointer to next control byte
               08561                                                        ;   if commands are chained
               08562        ;
               08700        ;#
               08701        ;
               08702        ;
               08703        Write$No$Deblock:                       ;Write contents of disk buffer to
               08704                                                ;  correct sector
0B2A 3E02      08705                MVI     A,Floppy$Write$Code     ;Get write function code
0B2C C3310B    08706                JMP     Common$No$Deblock       ;Go to common code
               08707        Read$No$Deblock:                        ;Read previously selected sector
               08708                                                ;  into disk buffer.
0B2F 3E01      08709                MVI     A,Floppy$Read$Code      ;Get read function code
               08710        Common$No$Deblock:
0B31 321D0B    08711                STA     Floppy$Command          ;Set command function code
               08712                                                ;Set up nondeblocked command table
               08713
0B34 3A360A    08714                LDA     Selected$Disk$Type      ;Check if memory disk operation
0B37 FE03      08715                CPI     M$Disk
0B39 CA7A0B    08716                JZ      M$Disk$Transfer ;Yes, it is M$Disk
               08717
               08718        No$Deblock$Retry:               ;Re-entry point to retry after error
0B3C 218000    08719                LXI     H,128           ;Bytes per sector
0B3F 22220B    08720                SHLD    Floppy$Byte$Count
0B42 AF        08721                XRA     A               ;8" floppy only has head 0
0B43 321F0B    08722                STA     Floppy$Head
               08723                                        ;
0B46 3A2D0A    08724                LDA     Selected$Disk   ;8" floppy controller only knows about
               08725                                        ;   units 0 and 1 so Selected$Disk must
               08726                                        ;   be converted
0B49 E601      08727                ANI     01H             ;Turn into 0 or 1
0B4B 321E0B    08728                STA     Floppy$Unit     ;Set unit number
               08729                                        ;
0B4E 3A2E0A    08730                LDA     Selected$Track
0B51 32200B    08731                STA     Floppy$Track    ;Set track number
               08732                                        ;
0B54 3A300A    08733                LDA     Selected$Sector
0B57 32210B    08734                STA     Floppy$Sector   ;Set sector number
               08735                                        ;
0B5A 2AA609    08736                LHLD    DMA$Address     ;Transfer directly between DMA Address
0B5D 22240B    08737                SHLD    Floppy$DMA$Address      ; and 8" controller.
               08738                                        ;
               08739                                        ;The disk controller can accept chained
               08740                                        ;   disk control tables, but in this case,
               08741                                        ;   they are not used, so the "Next" pointers
               08742                                        ;   must be pointed back at the initial
               08743                                        ;   control bytes in the base page.
0B60 214300    08744                LXI     H,Disk$Status$Block             ;Point next status back at
0B63 22260B    08745                SHLD    Floppy$Next$Status$Block        ;  main status block
               08746                                                        ;
0B66 214000    08747                LXI     H,Disk$Control$8                ;Point next control byte
0B69 22280B    08748                SHLD    Floppy$Next$Control$Location    ;  back at main control byte
               08749                                                        ;
0B6C 211D0B    08750                LXI     H,Floppy$Command        ;Point controller at control table
0B6F 224100    08751                SHLD    Command$Block$8
               08752                                                ;
0B72 214000    08753                LXI     H,Disk$Control$8        ;Activate controller to perform
0B75 3680      08754                MVI     M,80H                   ;  operation
0B77 C33B0C    08755                JMP     Wait$For$Disk$Complete
               08756
               08757        ;
               08900        ;#
               08901        ;       Memory disk driver
               08902        ;
               08903        ;       This routine must use an intermediary buffer, since the
               08904        ;       DMA address in bank ("track") 0 occupies the same
               08905        ;       place in the overall address space as the M$Disk itself.
               08906        ;       The M$Disk$Buffer is above the 48K mark, and therefore
               08907        ;       remains in the address space regardless of which bank/track
               08908        ;       is selected.
               08909        ;
               08910        ;
```

Figure 8-10. (Continued)

```
                    08911  ;       For writing, the 128-byte sector must be processed:
                    08912  ;
                    08913  ;               1. Move sector DMA$Address -> M$Disk$Buffer
                    08914  ;               2. Select correct track (+1 to get bank number)
                    08915  ;               3. Move sector M$Disk$Buffer -> M$Disk image
                    08916  ;               4. Select bank 0
                    08917  ;
                    08918  ;       For reading, the processing is:
                    08919  ;
                    08920  ;               1. Select correct track/bank
                    08921  ;               2. Move sector M$Disk image -> M$Disk$Buffer
                    08922  ;               3. Select Bank 0
                    08923  ;               4. Move sector M$Disk$Buffer -> DMA$Address
                    08924  ;
                    08925  ;       If there is any risk of any interrupt causing control
                    08926  ;       to be transferred to an address below 48K, interrupts must
                    08927  ;       be disabled when any bank other than 0 is selected.
                    08928  ;
                    08929  M$Disk$Transfer:
0B7A 3A300A         08930          LDA     Selected$Sector  ;Compute address in memory
0B7D 6F             08931          MOV     L,A              ; by muliplying sector * 128
0B7E 2600           08932          MVI     H,0
0B80 29             08933          DAD     H                ;* 2
0B81 29             08934          DAD     H                ;* 4
0B82 29             08935          DAD     H                ;* 8
0B83 29             08936          DAD     H                ;* 16
0B84 29             08937          DAD     H                ;* 32
0B85 29             08938          DAD     H                ;* 64
0B86 29             08939          DAD     H                ;* 128
                    08940
0B87 3A2E0A         08941          LDA     Selected$Track   ;Compute which half of bank sector
                    08942                                   ; is in by using LS bit of track
0B8A 47             08943          MOV     B,A              ;Save copy for later
0B8B E601           08944          ANI     1                ;Isolate lower/upper indicator
0B8D CA940B         08945          JZ      M$Disk$Lower$Half
                    08946
0B90 110060         08947          LXI     D,(48 * 1024) / 2   ;Upper half, so bias address
0B93 19             08948          DAD     D
                    08949
                    08950  M$Disk$Lower$Half:                ;HL -> sector in memory
0B94 78             08951          MOV     A,B              ;Recover selected track
0B95 1F             08952          RAR                      ;Divide by 2 to get bank number
0B96 3C             08953          INR     A                ;Bank 1 is first track
0B97 47             08954          MOV     B,A              ;Preserve for later use
                    08955
0B98 3A1D0B         08956          LDA     Floppy$Command   ;Check if reading or writing
0B9B FE02           08957          CPI     Floppy$Write$Code
0B9D CABE0B         08958          JZ      M$Disk$Write     ;Writing
                    08959                                   ;Reading
                    08960
0BA0 CDDD0B         08961          CALL    Select$Bank      ;Select correct memory bank
0BA3 113023         08962          LXI     D,M$Disk$Buffer  ;DE -> M$Disk$Buffer, HL -> M$Disk image
0BA6 0E10           08963          MVI     C,128/8          ;Number of 8-byte blocks to move
0BA8 CDF80A         08964          CALL    Move$8
                    08965
0BAB 0600           08966          MVI     B,0              ;Revert to normal memory bank
0BAD CDDD0B         08967          CALL    Select$Bank
                    08968
0BB0 2AA609         08969          LHLD    DMA$Address      ;Get user's DMA address
0BB3 113023         08970          LXI     D,M$Disk$Buffer
0BB6 EB             08971          XCHG                     ;DE -> User's DMA, HL -> M$Disk buffer
0BB7 0E10           08972          MVI     C,128/8          ;Number of 8-byte blocks to move
0BB9 CDF80A         08973          CALL    Move$8
                    08974
0BBC AF             08975          XRA     A                ;Indicate no error
0BBD C9             08976          RET
                    08977
                    08978  M$Disk$Write:                    ;Writing
0BBE E5             08979          PUSH    H                ;Save sector's address in M$Disk image
0BBF 2AA609         08980          LHLD    DMA$Address      ;Move sector into M$Disk$Buffer
0BC2 113023         08981          LXI     D,M$Disk$Buffer
0BC5 0E10           08982          MVI     C,128/8          ;Number of 8-byte blocks to move
0BC7 CDF80A         08983          CALL    Move$8           ;(Does not use B register)
                    08984                                   ;B = memory bank to select
0BCA CDDD0B         08985          CALL    Select$Bank
                    08986
```

Figure 8-10.   (Continued)

Chapter 8: Writing an Enhanced BIOS **281**

```
             OBCD D1           08987           POP      D                      ;Recover sector's M$Disk image address
             OBCE 213023       08988           LXI      H,M$Disk$Buffer
             OBD1 0E10         08989           MVI      C,128/8
             OBD3 CDF80A       08990           CALL     Move$8                 ;Move into M$Disk image
                               08991
             OBD6 0600         08992           MVI      B,0                    ;Select bank 0
             OBD8 CDDD0B       08993           CALL     Select$Bank
                               08994           ;
             OBDB AF           08995           XRA      A                      ;Indicate no error
             OBDC C9           08996           RET
                               08997           ;
                               09100           ;#
                               09101           ;       Select bank
                               09102           ;
                               09103           ;       This routine switches in the required memory bank.
                               09104           ;       Note that the hardware port that controls bank selection
                               09105           ;       also has other bits in it. These are preserved across
                               09106           ;       bank selections.
                               09107           ;
                               09108           ;       Entry parameter
                               09109           ;
                               09110           ;               B = bank number
                               09111           ;
    0040 =                     09112           Bank$Control$Port    EQU     40H
    00F8 =                     09113           Bank$Mask            EQU     1111$1000B       ;To preserve other bits
                               09114           ;
                               09115           Select$Bank:
             OBDD DB40         09116           IN       Bank$Control$Port      ;Get current setting in port
             OBDF E6F8         09117           ANI      Bank$Mask              ;Preserve all other bits
             OBE1 B0           09118           ORA      B                      ;Set bank code
             OBE2 D340         09119           OUT      Bank$Control$Port      ;Select the bank
             OBE4 C9           09120           RET
                               09121           ;
                               09200           ;#
                               09201           ;
                               09202           ;
                               09203           Write$Physical:                 ;Write contents of disk buffer to
                               09204                                           ;   correct sector
             OBE5 3E02         09205           MVI      A,Floppy$Write$Code    ;Get write function code
             OBE7 C3EC0B       09206           JMP      Common$Physical ;Go to common code
                               09207           Read$Physical:                  ;Read previously selected sector
                               09208                                           ;  into disk buffer
             OBEA 3E01         09209           MVI      A,Floppy$Read$Code     ;Get read function code
                               09210           ;
                               09211           Common$Physical:
             OBEC 321D0B       09212           STA      Floppy$Command  ;Set command table
                               09213           ;
                               09214           ;
                               09215           Deblock$Retry:                  ;Re-entry point to retry after error
             OBEF 3A2A0A       09216           LDA      In$Buffer$Disk$Type    ;Get disk type currently in buffer
             OBF2 FE01         09217           CPI      Floppy$5               ;Confirm it is a 5 1/4" floppy
             OBF4 CAFD0B       09218           JZ       Correct$Disk$Type      ;Yes
             OBF7 3E01         09219           MVI      A,1
             OBF9 32320B       09220           STA      Disk$Error$Flag        ;No, indicate disk error
             OBFC C9           09221           RET
                               09222           Correct$Disk$Type:              ;Set up disk control table
                               09223           ;
             OBFD 3A270A       09224           LDA      In$Buffer$Disk         ;Convert disk number to 0 or 1
             0C00 E601         09225           ANI      1                      ;  for disk controller
             0C02 321E0B       09226           STA      Floppy$Unit
                               09227
             0C05 2A280A       09228           LHLD     In$Buffer$Track        ;Set up head and track number
             0C08 7D           09229           MOV      A,L                    ;Even numbered tracks will be on
             0C09 E601         09230           ANI      1                      ;  head 0, odd numbered on head 1
             0C0B 321F0B       09231           STA      Floppy$Head            ;Set head number
                               09232
             0C0E 7D           09233           MOV      A,L                    ;Note: this is single byte value
             0C0F 1F           09234           RAR                             ;  /2 for track (carry off from ANI above)
             0C10 32200B       09235           STA      Floppy$Track
                               09236
             0C13 3E01         09237           MVI      A,1                    ;Start with sector 1 as a whole
             0C15 32210B       09238           STA      Floppy$Sector          ;  track will be transferred
                               09239           ;
             0C18 210012       09240           LXI      H,Bytes$Per$Track      ;Set byte count for complete
             0C1B 22220B       09241           SHLD     Floppy$Byte$Count      ;  track to be transferred
                               09242           ;
```

Figure 8-10. (Continued)

```
OC1E 21A40F    09243           LXI     H,Disk$Buffer              ;Set transfer address to be
OC21 22240B    09244           SHLD    Floppy$DMA$Address         ;   disk buffer
               09245           ;
               09246                                              ;As only one control table is in
               09247                                              ;   use, close the status and busy
               09248                                              ;   chain pointers back to the
               09249                                              ;   main control bytes
OC24 214300    09250           LXI     H,Disk$Status$Block
OC27 22260B    09251           SHLD    Floppy$Next$Status$Block
OC2A 214500    09252           LXI     H,Disk$Control$5
OC2D 22280B    09253           SHLD    Floppy$Next$Control$Location
               09254           ;
OC30 211D0B    09255           LXI     H,Floppy$Command           ;Set up command block pointer
OC33 224600    09256           SHLD    Command$Block$5
               09257           ;
OC36 214500    09258           LXI     H,Disk$Control$5           ;Activate 5 1/4" disk controller
OC39 3680      09259           MVI     M,80H
               09260           ;
               09261   Wait$For$Disk$Complete:                    ;Wait until disk status block indicates
               09262                                              ;   operation has completed, then check
               09263                                              ;   if any errors occurred.
               09264                                              ;On entry HL -> disk control byte
OC3B AF        09265           XRA     A                          ;Ensure hung flag clear
OC3C 32330A    09266           STA     Disk$Hung$Flag
               09267           ;
OC3F 21570C    09268           LXI     H,Disk$Timed$Out           ;Set up watchdog timer
OC42 015802    09269           LXI     B,Disk$Timer               ;Time delay
OC45 CD6D08    09270           CALL    Set$Watchdog
               09271   Disk$Wait$Loop:
OC48 7E        09272           MOV     A,M                        ;Get control byte
OC49 B7        09273           ORA     A
OC4A CA5D0C    09274           JZ      Disk$Complete              ;Operation done
               09275           ;
OC4D 3A330A    09276           LDA     Disk$Hung$Flag             ;Also check if time expired
OC50 B7        09277           ORA     A
OC51 C2B40D    09278           JNZ     Disk$Error                 ;Will be set to 40H
               09279           ;
OC54 C3480C    09280           JMP     Disk$Wait$Loop
               09281           ;
               09282   Disk$Timed$Out:                            ;Control arrives here from watchdog
               09283                                              ;   routine itself -- so this is effectively
               09284                                              ;   part of the interrupt service routine.
OC57 3E40      09285           MVI     A,40H                      ;Set disk hung error code
OC59 32330A    09286           STA     Disk$Hung$Flag             ;   into error flag to pull
               09287                                              ;   control out of loop
OC5C C9        09288           RET                                ;Return to watchdog routine
               09289           ;
               09290   Disk$Complete:
OC5D 010000    09291           LXI     B,0                        ;Reset watchdog timer
               09292                                              ;HL is irrelevant here
OC60 CD6D08    09293           CALL    Set$Watchdog
               09294           ;
OC63 3A4300    09295           LDA     Disk$Status$Block          ;Complete, now check status
OC66 FE80      09296           CPI     80H                        ;Check if any errors occurred
OC68 DAB40D    09297           JC      Disk$Error                 ;Yes
               09298           ;
               09299   Disk$Error$Ignore:                         ;No
OC6B AF        09300           XRA     A
OC6C 32320A    09301           STA     Disk$Error$Flag            ;Clear error flag
OC6F C9        09302           RET
               09303           ;
               09304           ;
               09400           ;#
               09401           ;       Disk error message handling
               09402           ;
               09403           ;
               09404   Disk$Error$Messages:                       ;This table is scanned, comparing the
               09405                                              ;   disk error status with those in the
               09406                                              ;   table. Given a match, or even when
               09407                                              ;   then end of the table is reached, the
               09408                                              ;   address following the status value
               09409                                              ;   points to the correct message text.
OC70 40        09410           DB      40H
OC71 9D0C      09411           DW      Disk$Msg$40
OC73 41        09412           DB      41H
OC74 A20C      09413           DW      Disk$Msg$41
```

Figure 8-10.   (Continued)

```
0C76 42          09414           DB      42H
0C77 AC0C        09415           DW      Disk$Msg$42
0C79 21          09416           DB      21H
0C7A BC0C        09417           DW      Disk$Msg$21
0C7C 22          09418           DB      22H
0C7D C10C        09419           DW      Disk$Msg$22
0C7F 23          09420           DB      23H
0C80 C80C        09421           DW      Disk$Msg$23
0C82 24          09422           DB      24H
0C83 DA0C        09423           DW      Disk$Msg$24
0C85 25          09424           DB      25H
0C86 E60C        09425           DW      Disk$Msg$25
0C88 11          09426           DB      11H
0C89 F90C        09427           DW      Disk$Msg$11
0C8B 12          09428           DB      12H
0C8C 070D        09429           DW      Disk$Msg$12
0C8E 13          09430           DB      13H
0C8F 140D        09431           DW      Disk$Msg$13
0C91 14          09432           DB      14H
0C92 220D        09433           DW      Disk$Msg$14
0C94 15          09434           DB      15H
0C95 310D        09435           DW      Disk$Msg$15
0C97 16          09436           DB      16H
0C98 3D0D        09437           DW      Disk$Msg$16
0C9A 00          09438           DB      0                       ;<== Terminator
0C9B 4D0D        09439           DW      Disk$Msg$Unknown        ;Unmatched code
                 09440           ;
0003 =           09441           DEM$Entry$Size  EQU     3       ;Disk error message table entry size
                 09442           ;
                 09443           ;       Message texts
                 09444           ;
0C9D 48756E670009445    Disk$Msg$40:    DB      'Hung',0         ;Timeout message
0CA2 4E6F74205209446    Disk$Msg$41:    DB      'Not Ready',0
0CAC 577269746509447    Disk$Msg$42:    DB      'Write Protected',0
0CBC 446174610009448    Disk$Msg$21:    DB      'Data',0
0CC1 466F726D6109449    Disk$Msg$22:    DB      'Format',0
0CC8 4D6973736909450    Disk$Msg$23:    DB      'Missing Data Mark',0
0CDA 427573205409451    Disk$Msg$24:    DB      'Bus Timeout',0
0CE6 436F6E747209452    Disk$Msg$25:    DB      'Controller Timeout',0
0CF9 447269766509453    Disk$Msg$11:    DB      'Drive Address',0
0D07 486561642009454    Disk$Msg$12:    DB      'Head Address',0
0D14 547261636B09455    Disk$Msg$13:    DB      'Track Address',0
0D22 536563746F09456    Disk$Msg$14:    DB      'Sector Address',0
0D31 427573204109457    Disk$Msg$15:    DB      'Bus Address',0
0D3D 496C6C656709458    Disk$Msg$16:    DB      'Illegal Command',0
0D4D 556E6B6E6F09459    Disk$Msg$Unknown:    DB  'Unknown',0
                 09460           ;
                 09461           Disk$EM$1:
0D55 070D0A      09462           DB      BELL,CR,LF
0D58 4469736B2009463    DB      'Disk ',0
                 09464           ;
                 09465                           ;Error text output next
                 09466           ;
                 09467           Disk$EM$2:              ;Main disk error message -- part 2
0D5E 204572726F09468    DB      ' Error ('
0D66 0000        09469   Disk$EM$Status: DB  0,0     ;Status code in Hex.
0D68 290D0A202009470    DB      ')',CR,LF,'   Drive '
0D76 00          09471   Disk$EM$Drive:  DB  0       ;Disk drive code, A,B...
0D77 2C2048656109472    DB      ', Head '
0D7E 00          09473   Disk$EM$Head:   DB  0       ;Head number
0D7F 2C20547261 09474    DB      ', Track '
0D87 0000        09475   Disk$EM$Track:  DB  0,0     ;Track number
0D89 2C20536563 09476    DB      ', Sector '
0D92 0000        09477   Disk$EM$Sector: DB  0,0     ;Sector number
0D94 2C204F7065 09478    DB      ', Operation - '
0DA2 00          09479   DB      0       ;Terminator
                 09480           ;
0DA3 526561642E09481    Disk$EM$Read:   DB  'Read.',0    ;Operation names
0DA9 577269746509482    Disk$EM$Write:  DB  'Write.',0
                 09483           ;
                 09484           ;
                 09485           Disk$Action$Confirm:
0DB0 00          09486           DB      0       ;Set to character entered by user
0DB1 0D0A00      09487           DB      CR,LF,0
                 09488           ;
                 09489           ;       Disk error processor
```

Figure 8-10. (Continued)

```
                09490   ;
                09491   ;       This routine builds and outputs an error message.
                09492   ;       The user is then given the opportunity to:
                09493   ;
                09494   ;               R -- retry the operation that caused the error
                09495   ;               I -- ignore the error and attempt to continue
                09496   ;               A -- abort the program and return to CP/M.
                09497   ;
                09498   Disk$Error:
0DB4 F5         09499           PUSH    PSW                     ;Preserve error code from controller
0DB5 21660D     09500           LXI     H,Disk$EM$Status        ;Convert code for message
0DB8 CD440E     09501           CALL    CAH                     ;Converts A to hex.
                09502   ;
0DBB 3A270A     09503           LDA     In$Buffer$Disk          ;Convert disk id. for message
0DBE C641       09504           ADI     'A'                     ;Make into letter
0DC0 32760D     09505           STA     Disk$EM$Drive
                09506   ;
0DC3 3A1F0B     09507           LDA     Floppy$Head             ;Convert head number
0DC6 C630       09508           ADI     '0'
0DC8 327E0D     09509           STA     Disk$EM$Head
                09510   ;
0DCB 3A200B     09511           LDA     Floppy$Track            ;Convert track number
0DCE 21870D     09512           LXI     H,Disk$EM$Track
0DD1 CD440E     09513           CALL    CAH
                09514   ;
0DD4 3A210B     09515           LDA     Floppy$Sector           ;Convert sector number
0DD7 21920D     09516           LXI     H,Disk$EM$Sector
0DDA CD440E     09517           CALL    CAH
                09518   ;
0DDD 21550D     09519           LXI     H,Disk$EM$1             ;Output first part of message
0DE0 CD5305     09520           CALL    Output$Error$Message
                09521   ;
0DE3 F1         09522           POP     PSW                     ;Recover error status code
0DE4 47         09523           MOV     B,A                     ;For comparisons
0DE5 216D0C     09524           LXI     H,Disk$Error$Messages   - DEM$Entry$Size
                09525                                           ;HL -> table - one entry
0DE8 110300     09526           LXI     D,DEM$Entry$Size        ;Get entry size for loop below
                09527   Disk$Error$Next$Code:
0DEB 19         09528           DAD     D                       ;Move to next (or first) entry
                09529   ;
0DEC 7E         09530           MOV     A,M                     ;Get code number from table
0DED B7         09531           ORA     A                       ;Check if end of table
0DEE CAF80D     09532           JZ      Disk$Error$Matched      ;Yes, pretend a match occurred
0DF1 B8         09533           CMP     B                       ;Compare to actual code
0DF2 CAF80D     09534           JZ      Disk$Error$Matched      ;Yes, exit from loop
0DF5 C3EB0D     09535           JMP     Disk$Error$Next$Code    ;Check next code
                09536   ;
                09537   Disk$Error$Matched:
0DF8 23         09538           INX     H                       ;HL -> address of text
0DF9 5E         09539           MOV     E,M                     ;Get address into DE
0DFA 23         09540           INX     H
0DFB 56         09541           MOV     D,M
0DFC EB         09542           XCHG                            ;HL -> text
0DFD CD5305     09543           CALL    Output$Error$Message    ;Display explanatory text
                09544   ;
0E00 215E0D     09545           LXI     H,Disk$EM$2             ;Display second part of message
0E03 CD5305     09546           CALL    Output$Error$Message
                09547   ;
0E06 21A30D     09548           LXI     H,Disk$EM$Read          ;Choose operation text
                09549                                           ; (assume a read)
0E09 3A1D0B     09550           LDA     Floppy$Command          ;Get controller command
0E0C FE01       09551           CPI     Floppy$Read$Code
0E0E CA140E     09552           JZ      Disk$Error$Read         ;Yes
0E11 21A90D     09553           LXI     H,Disk$EM$Write         ;No, change address in HL
                09554   Disk$Error$Read:
0E14 CD5305     09555           CALL    Output$Error$Message    ;Display operation type
                09556   ;
                09557   Disk$Error$Request$Action:              ;Ask the user what to do next
0E17 CD2F05     09558           CALL    Request$User$Choice     ;Display prompt and wait for input
                09559                                           ; Returns with A = uppercase char.
0E1A FE52       09560           CPI     'R'                     ;Retry?
0E1C CA2C0E     09561           JZ      Disk$Error$Retry
0E1F FE41       09562           CPI     'A'                     ;Abort
0E21 CA360E     09563           JZ      System$Reset
0E24 FE49       09564           CPI     'I'                     ;Ignore
0E26 CA6B0C     09565           JZ      Disk$Error$Ignore
```

Figure 8-10. (Continued)

```
0E29 C3170E      09566              JMP     Disk$Error$Request$Action
                 09567      ;
                 09568      Disk$Error$Retry:               ;The decision on where to return
                 09569                                      ;  depends on whether the operation
                 09570                                      ;  failed on a deblocked or
                 09571                                      ;  nondeblocked drive.
0E2C 3A350A      09572              LDA     Selected$Disk$Deblock
0E2F B7          09573              ORA     A
0E30 C2EF0B      09574              JNZ     Deblock$Retry
0E33 C33C0B      09575              JMP     No$Deblock$Retry
                 09576      ;
                 09577      System$Reset:                   ;This is a radical approach, but
                 09578                                      ;  it does cause CP/M to restart.
0E36 0E00        09579              MVI     C,0             ;System reset
0E38 CD0500      09580              CALL    BDOS
                 09581
                 09582      ;
                 09583      ;
                 09584      ;    A to upper
                 09585      ;
                 09586      ;    Converts the contents of the A register to an upper-
                 09587      ;    case letter if it is currently a lowercase letter.
                 09588      ;
                 09589      ;    Entry parameters
                 09590      ;
                 09591      ;            A = character to be converted
                 09592      ;
                 09593      ;    Exit parameters
                 09594      ;
                 09595      ;            A = converted character
                 09596      ;
                 09597      A$To$Upper:
0E3B FE61        09598              CPI     'a'             ;Compare to lower limit
0E3D D8          09599              RC                      ;No need to convert
0E3E FE7B        09600              CPI     'z' + 1         ;Compare to upper limit
0E40 D0          09601              RNC                     ;No need to convert
0E41 E65F        09602              ANI     5FH             ;Convert to uppercase
0E43 C9          09603              RET
                 09604      ;
                 09605      ;    Convert A register to hexadecimal
                 09606      ;
                 09607      ;    This subroutine converts the A register to hexadecimal.
                 09608      ;
                 09609      ;    Entry parameters
                 09610      ;
                 09611      ;            A = value to be converted and output
                 09612      ;            HL -> buffer area to receive two characters of output
                 09613      ;
                 09614      ;    Exit parameters
                 09615      ;
                 09616      ;            HL -> byte following last hex byte output
                 09617      ;
                 09618      CAH:
0E44 F5          09619              PUSH    PSW             ;Take a copy of the value to be converted
0E45 0F          09620              RRC                     ;Shift A right four places
0E46 0F          09621              RRC
0E47 0F          09622              RRC
0E48 0F          09623              RRC
0E49 CD4D0E      09624              CALL    CAH$Convert     ;Convert to ASCII
0E4C F1          09625              POP     PSW             ;Get original value again
                 09626                                      ;Drop into subroutine, which converts
                 09627                                      ;  and returns to caller
                 09628      CAH$Convert:
0E4D E60F        09629              ANI     0000$1111B      ;Isolate LS four bits
0E4F C630        09630              ADI     '0'             ;Convert to ASCII
0E51 FE3A        09631              CPI     '9' + 1         ;Compare to maximum
0E53 DA580E      09632              JC      CAH$Numeric     ;No need to convert to A -> F
0E56 C607        09633              ADI     7               ;Convert to a letter
                 09634      CAH$Numeric:
0E58 77          09635              MOV     M,A             ;Save character
0E59 23          09636              INX     H               ;Update character pointer
0E5A C9          09637              RET
                 09638
                 09639      ;
                 09640      ;
                 09700      ;#
```

Figure 8-10.   (Continued)

```
                09701   ;
                09702   ;       Disk control table images for warm boot
                09703   ;
                09704   Boot$Control$Part1:
0E5B 01         09705           DB      1                       ;Read function
0E5C 00         09706           DB      0                       ;Unit (drive) number
0E5D 00         09707           DB      0                       ;Head number
0E5E 00         09708           DB      0                       ;Track number
0E5F 02         09709           DB      2                       ;Starting sector number
0E60 0010       09710           DW      8*512                   ;Number of bytes to read
0E62 00C4       09711           DW      CCP$Entry               ;Read into this address
0E64 4300       09712           DW      Disk$Status$Block       ;Pointer to next status block
0E66 4500       09713           DW      Disk$Control$5          ;Pointer to next control table
                09714   Boot$Control$Part2:
0E68 01         09715           DB      1                       ;Read function
0E69 00         09716           DB      0                       ;Unit (drive) number
0E6A 01         09717           DB      1                       ;Head number
0E6B 00         09718           DB      0                       ;Track number
0E6C 01         09719           DB      1                       ;Starting sector number
0E6D 0006       09720           DW      3*512                   ;Number of bytes to read
0E6F 00D4       09721           DW      CCP$Entry + (8*512)     ;Read into this address
0E71 4300       09722           DW      Disk$Status$Block       ;Pointer to next status block
0E73 4500       09723           DW      Disk$Control$5          ;Pointer to next control table
                09724   ;
                09725   ;
                09726   ;
                09800   ;#
                09801   ;
                09802   WBOOT:                   ;Warm boot entry
                09803                            ;On warm boot, the CCP and BDOS must be reloaded
                09804                            ;   into memory. In this BIOS, only the 5 1/4"
                09805                            ;   diskettes will be used, therefore this code
                09806                            ;   is hardware specific to the controller. Two
                09807                            ;   prefabricated control tables are used.
0E75 318000     09808           LXI     SP,80H
0E78 115B0E     09809           LXI     D,Boot$Control$Part1    ;Execute first read of warm boot
0E7B CD8A0E     09810           CALL    Warm$Boot$Read          ;Load drive 0, track 0,
                09811                                           ;   head 0, sectors 2 - 8
0E7E 11680E     09812           LXI     D,Boot$Control$Part2    ;Execute second read
0E81 CD8A0E     09813           CALL    Warm$Boot$Read          ;Load drive 0, track 0,
                09814                                           ;   head 1, sectors 1 - 3
0E84 CDDF0E     09815           CALL    Patch$CPM               ;Make custom enhancements patches
0E87 C36C02     09816           JMP     Enter$CPM               ;Set up base page and enter CCP
                09817   ;
                09818   Warm$Boot$Read:          ;On entry, DE -> control table image
                09819                            ;This control table is moved into
                09820                            ;   the main disk control table and
                09821                            ;   then the controller activated.
0E8A 211D0B     09822           LXI     H,Floppy$Command        ;HL -> actual control table
0E8D 224600     09823           SHLD    Command$Block$5         ;Tell the controller its address
                09824                                           ;Move the control table image
                09825                                           ;   into the control table itself.
0E90 0E0D       09826           MVI     C,13                    ;Set byte count
                09827   Warm$Boot$Move:
0E92 1A         09828           LDAX    D                       ;Get image byte
0E93 77         09829           MOV     M,A                     ;Store into actual control table
0E94 23         09830           INX     H                       ;Update pointers
0E95 13         09831           INX     D
0E96 0D         09832           DCR     C                       ;Count down on byte count
0E97 C2920E     09833           JNZ     Warm$Boot$Move          ;Continue until all bytes moved
                09834   ;
0E9A 214500     09835           LXI     H,Disk$Control$5        ;Activate controller
0E9D 3680       09836           MVI     M,80H
                09837   Wait$For$Boot$Complete:
0E9F 7E         09838           MOV     A,M                     ;Get status byte
0EA0 B7         09839           ORA     A                       ;Check if complete
0EA1 C29F0E     09840           JNZ     Wait$For$Boot$Complete  ;No
                09841                                           ;Yes, check for errors
0EA4 3A4300     09842           LDA     Disk$Status$Block
0EA7 FE80       09843           CPI     80H
0EA9 DAAD0E     09844           JC      Warm$Boot$Error         ;Yes, an error occurred
0EAC C9         09845           RET
                09846   ;
                09847   Warm$Boot$Error:
0EAD 21B60E     09848           LXI     H,Warm$Boot$Error$Message
0EB0 CD5F02     09849           CALL    Display$Message
```

Figure 8-10. (Continued)

Chapter 8: Writing an Enhanced BIOS 287

```
0EB3 C3750E      09850            JMP      WBOOT               ;Restart warm boot
                 09851       ;
                 09852       Warm$Boot$Error$Message:
0EB6 0D0A57617209853            DB       CR,LF,'Warm Boot Error - retrying...',CR,LF,0
                 09854       ;
                 09855       ;
                 10000       ;#
                 10001       ;
                 10002       Ghost$Interrupt:        ;Control will only arrive here under the most
                 10003                               ; unusual circumstances, as the interrupt
                 10004                               ; controller will have been programmed to
                 10005                               ; suppress unused interrupts.
                 10006       ;
0ED8 F5          10007            PUSH     PSW                 ;Save pre-interrupt registers
0ED9 3E20        10008            MVI      A,IC$EOI            ;Indicate end of interrupt
0EDB D3D8        10009            OUT      IC$OCW2$Port
0EDD F1          10010            POP      PSW
0EDE C9          10011            RET
                 10012       ;
                 10013       ;
                 10100       ;#
                 10101       ;
                 10102       ;     Patch CP/M
                 10103       ;
                 10104       ;     This routine makes some very special patches to the
                 10105       ;     CCP and BDOS in order to make some custom enhancements
                 10106       ;
                 10107       ;     Public files:
                 10108       ;           On large hard disk systems it is extremely useful
                 10109       ;           to partition the disk using the user number features.
                 10110       ;           However, it becomes wasteful of disk space because
                 10111       ;           multiple copies of common programs must be stored in
                 10112       ;           each user area. This patch makes User 0 public --
                 10113       ;           accessible from any other user area.
                 10114       ;           *** WARNING ***
                 10115       ;           Files in User 0 MUST be set to system and read/only
                 10116       ;           status to avoid their being accidentally damaged.
                 10117       ;           Because of the side effects associated with public
                 10118       ;           files, the patch can be turned on or off using
                 10119       ;           a flag in the long term configuration block.
                 10120       ;
                 10121       ;     User prompt:
                 10122       ;           When using CP/M's USER command and user numbers
                 10123       ;           in general, it is all too easy to become confused
                 10124       ;           and forget which user number you are "in." This
                 10125       ;           patch modifies the CCP to display a prompt which
                 10126       ;           shows not only the default disk id., but also the
                 10127       ;           current user number, and an indication of whether
                 10128       ;           public files are enabled:
                 10129       ;
                 10130       ;                      P3B>   or   3B>
                 10131       ;                      ^
                 10132       ;                      When public files are enabled.
                 10133       ;
                 10134       ;     Equates for public files
                 10135       ;
D35E =           10136       PF$BDOS$Exit$Point      EQU    BDOS$Entry + 758H
D37C =           10137       PF$BDOS$Char$Matches    EQU    BDOS$Entry + 776H
D361 =           10138       PF$BDOS$Resume$Point    EQU    BDOS$Entry + 75BH
000D =           10139       PF$BDOS$Unused$Bytes    EQU    13
                 10140       ;
                 10141       ;
                 10142       ;     Equates for user prompt
                 10143       ;
C788 =           10144       UP$CCP$Exit$Point       EQU    CCP$Entry + 388H
C78B =           10145       UP$CCP$Resume$Point     EQU    CCP$Entry + 38BH
C513 =           10146       UP$CCP$Get$User         EQU    CCP$Entry + 113H
C5D0 =           10147       UP$CCP$Get$Disk$Id      EQU    CCP$Entry + 1D0H
C48C =           10148       UP$CCP$CONOUT           EQU    CCP$Entry + 8CH
                 10149       ;
                 10150       ;
                 10151       ;     Set up the intervention points
                 10152       ;
                 10153       Patch$CPM:
0EDF 3EC3        10154            MVI      A,JMP               ;Set up opcode
0EE1 325ED3      10155            STA      PF$BDOS$Exit$Point
```

Figure 8-10. (Continued)

```
OEE4 3288C7   10156           STA     UP$CCP$Exit$Point
OEE7 21F40E   10157           LXI     H,Public$Patch
OEEA 225FD3   10158           SHLD    PF$BDOS$Exit$Point + 1
OEED 21110F   10159           LXI     H,Prompt$Patch      ;Get address of intervening code
OEF0 2289C7   10160           SHLD    UP$CCP$Exit$Point + 1
              10161
OEF3 C9       10162           RET                         ;Return to enter CP/M
              10163   ;
              10164   ;
              10165   ;
              10166   Public$Patch:                       ;Control arrives here from the BDOS
              10167                                       ;The BDOS is in the process of scanning
              10168                                       ;  down the target file name in the
              10169                                       ;  search next function
              10170                                       ;  HL -> the name of the file searched for
              10171                                       ;  DE -> directory entry
              10172                                       ;  B = character count
              10173
OEF4 3A4200   10174           LDA     CB$Public$Files     ;Check if public files are to be enabled
OEF7 B7       10175           ORA     A
OEF8 CA0B0F   10176           JZ      No$Public$Files     ;No
              10177
OEFB 78       10178           MOV     A,B                 ;Get character count
OEFC B7       10179           ORA     A                   ;Check if looking at first byte
              10180                                       ;  (that contains the user number)
OEFD C20B0F   10181           JNZ     No$Public$Files     ;No, ignore this patch
              10182
OF00 1A       10183           LDAX    D                   ;Get user number from directory entry
OF01 FEE5     10184           CPI     0E5H                ;Check if active directory entry
OF03 CA0B0F   10185           JZ      No$Public$Files     ;Yes, ignore this patch
              10186
OF06 7E       10187           MOV     A,M                 ;Get user number
OF07 B7       10188           ORA     A                   ;Check if User 0
OF08 CA7CD3   10189           JZ      PF$BDOS$Char$Matches    ;Force character match
              10190
              10191   No$Public$Files:                    ;Replaced patched out code
OF0B 78       10192           MOV     A,B                 ;Check if count indicates that
OF0C FE0D     10193           CPI     PF$BDOS$Unused$Bytes    ;  registers are pointing at
              10194                                       ;  unused bytes field of FCB
OF0E C361D3   10195           JMP     PF$BDOS$Resume$Point    ;Return to BDOS
              10196   ;
              10197   Prompt$Patch:                       ;Control arrives here from the CCP
              10198                                       ;The CCP is just about to get the
              10199                                       ;  drive id. when control gets here.
              10200                                       ;The CCP's version of CONOUT is used
              10201                                       ;  so that the CCP can keep track of
              10202                                       ;  the cursor position.
              10203
OF11 3A4200   10204           LDA     CB$Public$Files     ;Check if public files are enabled
OF14 B7       10205           ORA     A
OF15 CA1D0F   10206           JZ      UP$Private$Files    ;No
              10207
OF18 3E50     10208           MVI     A,'P'
OF1A CD8CC4   10209           CALL    UP$CCP$CONOUT       ;Use CCP's CONOUT routine
              10210
              10211   UP$Private$Files:
OF1D CD13C5   10212           CALL    UP$CCP$Get$User     ;Get current user number
OF20 FE0A     10213           CPI     9 + 1               ;Check if one or two digits
OF22 D2300F   10214           JNC     UP$2$Digits
OF25 C630     10215           ADI     '0'                 ;Convert to ASCII
              10216   UP$1$Digit:
OF27 CD8CC4   10217           CALL    UP$CCP$CONOUT       ;Output the character
OF2A CDD0C5   10218           CALL    UP$CCP$Get$Disk$Id  ;Get disk identifier
OF2D C38BC7   10219           JMP     UP$CCP$Resume$Point ;Return to CCP
              10220   ;
              10221   UP$2$Digits:
OF30 C626     10222           ADI     '0' - 10            ;Subtract 10 and convert to ASCII
OF32 F5       10223           PUSH    PSW                 ;Save converted second digit
OF33 3E31     10224           MVI     A,'1'               ;Output leading '1'
OF35 CD8CC4   10225           CALL    UP$CCP$CONOUT
OF38 F1       10226           POP     PSW                 ;Recover second digit
OF39 C3270F   10227           JMP     UP$1$Digit          ;Output remainder of prompt and return to
              10228                                       ;  the CCP
              10229
              10230   ;
              10300   ;#
```

Figure 8-10. (Continued)

```
                    10301   ;
                    10302   ;       Configuration block get address
                    10303   ;
                    10304   ;       This routine is called by utility programs running in the TPA.
                    10305   ;       Given a specific code number, it returns the address of a specific
                    10306   ;       object in the configuration block.
                    10307   ;
                    10308   ;       By using this routine, utility programs need not know the exact
                    10309   ;       layout of the configuration block.
                    10310   ;
                    10311   ;       Entry parameters
                    10312   ;
                    10313   ;               C = Object identity code (in effect, this is the
                    10314   ;                   subscript of the object's address in the
                    10315   ;                   table below)
                    10316   ;
                    10317   ;===========================
                    10318   CB$Get$Address:                         ;<=== BIOS entry point (private)
                    10319   ;===========================
OF3C  F5            10320           PUSH    PSW                     ;Save user's registers
OF3D  C5            10321           PUSH    B
OF3E  D5            10322           PUSH    D
                    10323
OF3F  69            10324           MOV     L,C                     ;Make code into a word
OF40  2600          10325           MVI     H,0
OF42  29            10326           DAD     H                       ;Convert code into word offset
OF43  114F0F        10327           LXI     D,CB$Object$Table       ;Get base address of table
OF46  19            10328           DAD     D                       ;HL -> object's address in table
OF47  5E            10329           MOV     E,M                     ;Get LS byte
OF48  23            10330           INX     H
OF49  56            10331           MOV     D,M                     ;Get MS byte
OF4A  EB            10332           XCHG                            ;HL = address of object
                    10333
OF4B  D1            10334           POP     D                       ;Recover user's registers
OF4C  C1            10335           POP     B
OF4D  F1            10336           POP     PSW
                    10337
OF4E  C9            10338           RET
                    10339   ;
                    10400   ;#
                    10401   ;
                    10402   CB$Object$Table:
                    10403                                           ;       Code
                    10404                                           ;       vv
OF4F  8F0F          10405           DW      Date                    ;01 date in ASCII
OF51  990F          10406           DW      Time$In$ASCII           ;02 time in ASCII
OF53  A30F          10407           DW      Time$Date$Flags         ;03 flags indicated if time/date set
OF55  8D0F          10408           DW      CB$Forced$Input         ;04 forced input pointer
OF57  4300          10409           DW      CB$Startup              ;05 system startup message
                    10410                                           ;   Redirection words
OF59  5800          10411           DW      CB$Console$Input        ;06
OF5B  5A00          10412           DW      CB$Console$Output       ;07
OF5D  5C00          10413           DW      CB$Auxiliary$Input      ;08
OF5F  5E00          10414           DW      CB$Auxiliary$Output     ;09
OF61  6000          10415           DW      CB$List$Input           ;10
OF63  6200          10416           DW      CB$List$Output          ;11
                    10417
OF65  6400          10418           DW      CB$Device$Table$Addresses ;12
OF67  B500          10419           DW      CB$12$24$Clock          ;13 Selects 12/24 hr. format clock
OF69  BD00          10420           DW      RTC$Ticks$per$Second    ;14
OF6B  BF00          10421           DW      RTC$Watchdog$Count      ;15
OF6D  C100          10422           DW      RTC$Watchdog$Address    ;16
OF6F  C300          10423           DW      CB$Function$Key$Table   ;17
OF71  1B02          10424           DW      CONOUT$Escape$Table     ;18
                    10425
OF73  8400          10426           DW      D0$Initialize$Stream    ;19
OF75  9100          10427           DW      D0$Baud$Rate$Constant   ;20
OF77  9400          10428           DW      D1$Initialize$Stream    ;21
OF79  A100          10429           DW      D1$Baud$Rate$Constant   ;22
OF7B  A400          10430           DW      D2$Initialize$Stream    ;23
OF7D  B100          10431           DW      D2$Baud$Rate$Constant   ;24
OF7F  4002          10432           DW      Interrupt$Vector        ;25
OF81  890F          10433           DW      LTCB$Offset             ;26
OF83  8B0F          10434           DW      LTCB$Length             ;27
OF85  4200          10435           DW      CB$Public$Files         ;30
```

Figure 8-10. (Continued)

```
OF87 A421      10436            DW      Multi$Command$Buffer    ;31
               10437     ;
               10500     ;#
               10501     ;       The short term configuration block.
               10502     ;
               10503     ;       This contains variables that can be set once CP/M
               10504     ;       has been initiated, but that are never preserved
               10505     ;       from one loading of CP/M to the next. This part of
               10506     ;       the configuration block form the last initialized bytes
               10507     ;       in the BIOS.
               10508     ;
               10509     ;       The two values below are used by utility programs that
               10510     ;       need to read in the long term configuration block from disk.
               10511     ;       The BIOS starts on a 256-byte page boundary, and therefore
               10512     ;       will always be on a 128-byte sector boundary in the reserved
               10513     ;       area on the disk. A utility program can then, using the
               10514     ;       CB$Get$Address Private BIOS call, determine how many 128-byte
               10515     ;       sectors need to be read in by the formula:
               10516     ;
               10517     ;               (LCTB$Offset + LTCB$Length) / 128
               10518     ;
               10519     ;       The LTCB$Offset is the offset from the start of the BIOS to
               10520     ;       where the first byte of the long term configuration block
               10521     ;       starts. Using the offset and the length, the utility can
               10522     ;       copy the RAM version of the LTCB over the disk image
               10523     ;       that it has read from the disk, and then write the
               10524     ;       updated LTCB back onto the disk.
               10525     ;
OF89 BED9      10526     LTCB$Offset:    DW      BIOS$Entry - Long$Term$CB
OF8B E601      10527     LTCB$Length:    DW      Long$Term$CB$End - Long$Term$CB
               10528     ;
               10529     ;       Forced input pointer
               10530     ;
               10531     ;       If CONIN ever finds that this pointer is pointing to a nonzero
               10532     ;       byte, then this byte will be injected into the console input
               10533     ;       stream as though it had been typed on the console. The
               10534     ;       pointer is then updated to the next byte in memory.
               10535     ;
OF8D 4300      10536     CB$Forced$Input:        DW      CB$Startup
               10537     ;
               10538     ;
               10539     Date:                   ;Current system date
OF8F 31302F31371054O             DB      '10/17/82',LF   ;Unless otherwise set to the contrary
               10541                                     ;  this is the release date of the system
               10542                                     ;Normally, it will be set by the DATE utility
OF98 00        10543             DB      0               ;00-byte terminator
               10544
               10545     Time$in$ASCII:          ;Current system time
OF99 3030      10546     HH:     DB      '00'            ;Hours
OF9B 3A        10547             DB      ':'
OF9C 3030      10548     MM:     DB      '00'            ;Minutes
OF9E 3A        10549             DB      ':'
OF9F 3030      10550     SS:     DB      '00'            ;Seconds
               10551     Time$in$ASCII$End:              ;Used when updating the time
OFA1 0A        10552             DB      LF
OFA2 00        10553             DB      0               ;00-byte terminator
               10554     ;
               10555     ;
               10556     Time$Date$Flags:        ;This byte contains two flags that are  used
               10557                             ;  to indicate whether the time and/or date
               10558                             ;  have been set either programmatically or
               10559                             ;  by using the TIME and DATE utilities. These
               10560                             ;  flags can be tested by utility programs that
               10561                             ;  need to have the correct time and date set.
OFA3 00        10562             DB      0
0001 =         10563     Time$Set        EQU     0000$0001B
0002 =         10564     Date$Set        EQU     0000$0010B
               10565
               10566     ;
               10700     ;#
               10701     ;       Uninitialized buffer areas
               10702     ;
               10703     ;       With the exception of the main Disk$Buffer, which contains a few
               10704     ;       bytes of code, all of the other uninitialized variables
               10705     ;       occur here. This has the effect of reducing the number of
               10706     ;       bytes that need be stored in the CP/M image on the disk,
```

Figure 8-10. (Continued)

Chapter 8: Writing an Enhanced BIOS 291

```
                10707   ;         since uninitialized areas do not need to be kept on the disk.
                10708   ;
                10709   ;
                10800   ;#
                10801   ;
                10802   ;         The cold boot initialization code is only needed once.
                10803   ;         It can be overwritten once it has been executed.
                10804   ;         Therefore, it is "hidden" inside the main disk buffer.
                10805   ;
                10806   ;
0FA4            10807   Disk$buffer:    DS          Physical$Sector$Size * Physical$Sec$Per$Track
                10808                                           ;Save the location counter
21A4 =          10810   After$Disk$Buffer   EQU     $           ;$ = current value of location counter
                10811   ;
0FA4            10812                               ORG         Disk$Buffer      ;Wind the location counter back
                10813   ;
                10814   Initialize$Stream:      ;This stream of data is used by the
                10815                           ;  Initialize subroutine. It has the following
                10816                           ;  format:
                10817                           ;
                10818                           ;     DB      Port number to be initialized
                10819                           ;     DB      Number of byte to be output
                10820                           ;     DB      xx,xx,xx,xx data to be output
                10821                           ;     :
                10822                           ;     :
                10823                           ;     DB      Port number of 00H terminates
                10824                           ;
                10825                           ;
                10826   ;
                10827   ;       Initialization stream declared here
0FA4 D8         10828           DB      IC$ICW1$Port    ;Program the 8259 interrupt controller
0FA5 01         10829           DB      1
0FA6 56         10830           DB      IC$ICW1
                10831
0FA7 D9         10832           DB      IC$ICW2$Port
0FA8 01         10833           DB      1
0FA9 02         10834           DB      IC$ICW2
                10835
0FAA D9         10836           DB      IC$OCW1$Port
0FAB 01         10837           DB      1
0FAC FC         10838           DB      IC$OCW1
                10839
0FAD 83         10840           DB      83H             ;Program the 8253 clock generator
0FAE 01         10841           DB      1
0FAF 34         10842           DB      00$11$010$0B    ;Counter 0, periodic interrupt, mode 2
                10843
0FB0 80         10844           DB      80H             ;RTC uses channel 0
0FB1 02         10845           DB      2
0FB2 0146       10846           DW      17921           ;19721 * 930 nanoseconds =
                10847                                   ;  16.666 milliseconds). 60 ticks/sec.
0FB4 00         10848           DB      0               ;Port number of 0 terminates
                10849   ;
                10850   ;
                10851   Signon$Message:
0FB5 43502F4D2010852            DB      'CP/M 2.2.'
0FBE 3030       10853           DW      VERSION         ;Current version number
0FC0 20         10854           DB      ' '
0FC1 3032       10855           DW      MONTH           ;Current date
0FC3 2F         10856           DB      '/'
0FC4 3236       10857           DW      DAY
0FC6 2F         10858           DB      '/'
0FC7 3833       10859           DW      YEAR
0FC9 0D0A0A     10860           DB      CR,LF,LF
0FCC 456E68616E10861            DB      'Enhanced BIOS',CR,LF,LF
0FDC 4469736B2010862            DB      'Disk Configuration :',CR,LF,LF
0FF3 202020202010863            DB      '    A: 0.35 Mbyte 5" Floppy',CR,LF
1011 202020202010864            DB      '    B: 0.35 Mbyte 5" Floppy',CR,LF,LF
1030 202020202010865            DB      '    C: 0.24 Mbyte 8" Floppy',CR,LF
104E 202020202010866            DB      '    D: 0.24 Mbyte 8" Floppy',CR,LF
106C 202020202010867            DB      '    M: 0.19 Mbyte Memory Disk',CR,LF,LF
                10868   ;
108D 00         10869           DB      0
                10870   ;
                10871   ;       Messages for M$Disk
                10872   ;
```

Figure 8-10. (Continued)

```
                       10873 M$Disk$Setup$Message:
108E 2020202020 10874         DB      '     M$Disk already contains valid information.',CR,LF,0
                       10875 M$Disk$Not$Setup$Message:
10C0 2020202020 10876         DB      '     M$Disk has been initialized to empty state.',CR,LF,0
                       10877 ;
                       10878 M$Disk$Dir$Entry:        ;Dummy directory entry used to determine
                       10879                          ;  if the M$Disk contains valid information
10F3 0F          10880         DB      15             ;User 15
10F4 4D24446973  10881         DB      'M$Disk '
10FC A0A020      10882         DB      ' '+80H,' '+80H,' '     ;System and read/only
10FF 00000000    10883         DB      0,0,0,0
1103 00000000000010884         DB      0,0,0,0,0,0,0,0,0,0,0,0,0,0,0,0
                       10885 ;
0004 =           10886 Default$Disk     EQU     0004H  ;Default disk in base page
                       10887 ;
                       10888 BOOT:                    ;Entered directly from the BIOS JMP Vector
                       10889                          ;Control will be transferred here by the CP/M
                       10890                          ;  bootstrap loader
                       10891 ;
                       10892                          ;Initialize system
                       10893                          ;This routine uses the Initialize$Stream
                       10894                          ;  declared above
                       10895
1113 F3          10896         DI                     ;Disable interrupts to prevent any
                       10897                          ;  side effects during initialization
1114 21A40F      10898         LXI     H,Initialize$Stream    ;HL -> data stream
1117 CD1903      10899         CALL    Output$Byte$Stream     ;Output it to the specified
                       10900                          ;  ports
                       10901
111A CDEE02      10902         CALL    General$CIO$Initialization ;Initialize character devices
                       10903
111D 21B50F      10904         LXI     H,Signon$Message       ;Display sign-on message on console
1120 CD5F02      10905         CALL    Display$Message
                       10906 ;
1123 CDDF0E      10907         CALL    Patch$CPM      ;Make necessary patches to CCP and BDOS
                       10908                          ;  for custom enhancements
                       10909
                       10910                          ;Initialize M$Disk
                       10911                          ;If the M$Disk directory has the
                       10912                          ;  special reserved file name "M$disk"
                       10913                          ;  (with lowercase letters and marked
                       10914                          ;  SYS and R/O), then the M$Disk is
                       10915                          ;  assumed to contain valid data.
                       10916                          ;If the "M$Disk" file is absent, the
                       10917                          ;  M$Disk Directory entry is moved into
                       10918                          ;  the M$Disk image, and the remainder of
                       10919                          ;  the directory set to 0E5H.
1126 0601        10920         MVI     B,1            ;Select bank 1
1128 CDDD0B      10921         CALL    Select$Bank    ;  which contains the M$Disk directory
                       10922
                       10923                          ;Check if M$Disk directory entry present
112B 210000      10924         LXI     H,0            ;Start address for first directory
112E 11F310      10925         LXI     D,M$Disk$Dir$Entry
1131 0E20        10926         MVI     C,32           ;Length to compare
                       10927 M$Disk$Test:
1133 1A          10928         LDAX    D              ;Get byte from initialized variable
1134 BE          10929         CMP     M              ;Compare with M$Disk image
1135 C24F11      10930         JNZ     M$Disk$Not$Setup       ;Match fails
1138 13          10931         INX     D
1139 23          10932         INX     H
113A 0D          10933         DCR     C
113B CA4111      10934         JZ      M$Disk$Setup   ;All bytes match
113E C33311      10935         JMP     M$Disk$Test
                       10936 ;
                       10937 M$Disk$Setup:
1141 218E10      10938         LXI     H,M$Disk$Setup$Message ;Inform user
                       10939 ;
                       10940 M$Disk$Setup$Done:
1144 CD5F02      10941         CALL    Display$Message
                       10942
1147 AF          10943         XRA     A              ;Set default disk drive to A:
1148 320400      10944         STA     Default$Disk
114B FB          10945         EI                     ;Interrupts can now be enabled
                       10946
114C C36C02      10947         JMP     Enter$CPM      ;Go into CP/M
                       10948 ;
```

Figure 8-10. (Continued)

Chapter 8: Writing an Enhanced BIOS

```
                    10949           M$Disk$Not$Setup:
114F 110000         10950                   LXI     D,0                     ;Move M$Disk directory entry into
1152 21F310         10951                   LXI     H,M$Disk$Dir$Entry      ;  M$Disk image
1155 0E04           10952                   MVI     C,32/8                  ;Number of 8-byte blocks to move
1157 CDF80A         10953                   CALL    Move$8
                    10954           ;
                    10955                                                   ;DE -> next byte after M$Disk directory
                    10956                                                   ;  entry in image
115A 3EE5           10957                   MVI     A,0E5H                  ;Set up to do memory fill
115C 12             10958                   STAX    D                       ;Store first byte in "source" area
115D 62             10959                   MOV     H,D                     ;Set HL to DE +1
115E 6B             10960                   MOV     L,E
115F 23             10961                   INX     H
1160 0EFC           10962                   MVI     C,((2 * 1024) - 32) / 8 ;Two allocation blocks
                    10963                                                   ;  less 32 bytes for M$Disk entry
1162 CDF80A         10964                   CALL    Move$8                  ;Use Move$8 to do fill operation
                    10965           ;
1165 21C010         10966                   LXI     H,M$Disk$Not$Setup$Message
1168 C34411         10967                   JMP     M$Disk$Setup$Done       ;Output message and enter CP/M
                    10968           ;
                    10969           ;
116B 00             10970                   DB      0                       ;Dummy
                    10971           Last$Initialized$Byte:                  ;<== address of last initialized byte
                    10972           ;
                    10973           ;       End of cold boot initialization code
                    10974           ;
21A4                10975                   ORG     After$Disk$Buffer       ;Reset location counter
                    10976           ;
21A4                10977           Multi$Command$Buffer:   DS      128     ;This can be used to insert long
                    10978                                                   ;  command sequences into the
                    10979                                                   ;  console input stream by setting
                    10980                                                   ;  the forced input pointer here
                    10981           ;
0020 =              10982           D0$Buffer$Length        EQU     32      ;Must be binary number
2224                10983           D0$Buffer:      DS      D0$Buffer$Length
                    10984           ;
0020 =              10985           D1$Buffer$Length        EQU     32      ;Must be binary number
2244                10986           D1$Buffer:      DS      D1$Buffer$Length
                    10987           ;
0020 =              10988           D2$Buffer$Length        EQU     32      ;Must be binary number
2264                10989           D2$Buffer:      DS      D2$Buffer$Length
                    10990           ;
                    10991           ;       Data areas for the character drivers
                    10992           ;
2284                10993           PI$User$Stack:  DS      2               ;Storage area for user's stack pointer
                    10994                                                   ;  when an interrupt occurs
2286                10995           PI$User$HL:     DS      2               ;Save area for user's HL
2288                10996                           DS      40              ;Stack area for use by interrupt service
                    10997           PI$Stack:                               ;  routines to avoid overflowing the
                    10998                                                   ;  user's stack area
                    10999           ;
22B0                11000           Directory$Buffer:       DS      128     ;Disk directory buffer
                    11001           ;
2330                11002           M$Disk$Buffer:          DS      128     ;Intermediary buffer for
                    11003                                                   ;  M$Disk
                    11004           ;
                    11005           ;       Disk work areas
                    11006           ;
                    11007           ;       These are used by the BDOS to detect any unexpected
                    11008           ;       change of diskettes. The BDOS will automatically set
                    11009           ;       such a changed diskette to read-only status.
                    11010           ;
23B0                11011           Disk$A$Workarea:        DS      32      ; A:
23D0                11012           Disk$B$Workarea:        DS      32      ; B:
23F0                11013           Disk$C$Workarea:        DS      16      ; C:
2400                11014           Disk$D$Workarea:        DS      16      ; D:
                    11015           ;
                    11016           ;
                    11017           ;       Disk allocation vectors
                    11018           ;
                    11019           ;       These are used by the BDOS to maintain a bit map of
                    11020           ;       which allocation blocks are used and which are free.
                    11021           ;       One byte is used for eight allocation blocks, hence the
                    11022           ;       expression of the form (allocation blocks/8)+1.
                    11023           ;
2410                11024           Disk$A$Allocation$Vector        DS      (174/8)+1       ; A:
```

Figure 8-10. (Continued)

```
2426        11025    Disk$B$Allocation$Vector     DS      (174/8)+1      ; B:
             11026    ;
243C        11027    Disk$C$Allocation$Vector     DS      (242/8)+1      ; C:
245B        11028    Disk$D$Allocation$Vector     DS      (242/8)+1      ; D:
             11029    ;
247A        11030    M$Disk$Allocation$Vector     DS      (192/8)+1      ; M$Disk
             11031
2493        11032            END         ;of enhanced BIOS listing
```

Figure 8-10. (Continued)

Classes of Errors
BIOS Error-Handling Functions
Practical Error Handling
Character I/O Errors
Disk Errors
Improving Error Messages

Dealing with Hardware Errors

This chapter describes the enhancements you can make to improve CP/M's somewhat primitive error handling. It covers the general classes of errors that the BIOS may have to handle. It describes some of the underlying philosophical aspects of errors, how to detect them, and how to correct them or otherwise make the best of the situation.

At the end of the chapter are some example error-handling subroutines. Some of these have already been shown in the previous chapter as part of the enhanced BIOS (Figure 8-10); they are repeated here so that you can see them in isolation.

Classes of Errors

Basically, the user perceives only two classes of errors—those that are user-correctable and those that are not. There is a third, almost invisible class of errors—those that are recoverable by the hardware or software without the user's intervention.

The possible sources for hardware errors vary wildly from one computer system to another, since error detection is heavily dependent on the particular logic in the hardware. The BIOS can detect some hardware-related errors—mainly errors caused when something takes too long to happen, such as when a recalcitrant printer does not react in a specified length of time.

The BDOS has no built-in hardware detection code. It can detect *system* errors, such as an attempt to write to a disk file that is marked "Read-Only" in the file directory or attempts to access files that are not on the disk. These BDOS-detected errors, however, generally are unrelated to the well-being of the hardware. For example, a disk controller with a hardware problem could easily overwrite a sector of the directory, thereby deleting several files. This error would not show up until the user tried to use one of the now-departed files.

BIOS Error-Handling Functions

The error-handling code in the BIOS has to serve the following functions:

- Detection
- Analysis
- Indication
- Correction.

Error Detection

Clearly, before any later steps can be taken, an error must be detected. This can be done by the software alone or by the BIOS interacting with error-detecting logic in the hardware. In general, the only errors that the BIOS can detect unassisted are caused when certain operations take longer to complete than expected. Because the writer of the BIOS knows the operating environment of the specific peripherals in the system, the code can predict how long a particular operation should take and can signal an error when this time is exceeded. This would include such problems as printers that fail to react within a specified time period.

The BIOS can work in cooperation with the hardware to determine whether the hardware itself has detected an error. Armed with the hardware's specifications, the BIOS can input information on controller or device status to trigger error-detecting logic. How this should be done depends heavily on the peripheral devices in your computer system and the degree to which these devices have "smart" controllers capable of processing independently of the computer. Unfortunately, many manufacturers document the significance of individual status bits that indicate errors, but not combinations of errors, or what to do when a particular error occurs.

Error Analysis

Given that your BIOS has detected an error, it must first determine the class of error; that is, whether or not the error can be corrected by simply trying the operation again. Some errors appear at first to be correctable, but retrying the operation several times still fails to complete it. An example would be a check-sum error while reading a disk sector. If several attempts to read the sector all yield an error, then it becomes a "fatal" error. The code in your BIOS must be capable of initial classification and then subsequent reclassification if remedial action fails.

Other types of errors can be classified immediately as fatal errors—nothing can be done to save the situation. For example, if the floppy disk controller indicates that it cannot find a particular sector number on a diskette (due to an error in formatting), there is nothing that the BIOS can do other than inform the user of the problem and supply other helpful information.

Analysis of errors may require some basic research, such as inducing failures in the hardware and observing combinations of error indicators. For example, some printers (interfaced via a parallel port) indicate that they are "Out of Paper" or "Busy" when, in fact, they are switched off. The BIOS should detect this condition and tell the user to switch the printer on, not load more paper.

Error Indication

An incomplete or cryptic error message is infuriating. It is the functional equivalent of saying, "There has been an error. See if you can guess what went wrong!"

An error message, to be complete, should inform the recipient of the following:

- The fact that an error has occurred.
- Whether or not automatic recovery has been attempted and failed.
- The details of the error, if need be in technical terms to assist a hardware engineer.
- What possible choices the user has now.

To put these points into focus, consider the error message that can be output by CP/M after you have attempted to load a program by entering its name into the CCP. What you see on the console is the following dialog:

```
A>myprog<cr>
BAD LOAD
A>
```

All you know is that there has been an error, and you must guess what it is, even though the specific cause of the error was known to CP/M when it output the message. This error message is output by the CCP when it attempts to load a

".COM" file larger than the current transient program area. The message "BAD LOAD" is only understandable *after* you know what the error is. Even then, it does not tell you what went wrong, whether there is anything you can do about it, and how to go about doing it.

To be complete, this error message could say something like this:

```
A>myprog<cr>
     "MYPROG.COM" exceeds the available memory space by
     1,024 bytes, and therefore cannot be loaded under the
     current version of CP/M.
```

Notice how the message tells you what the problem is, and even quantifies it so that you can determine its severity (you need to get 1K more memory or reduce the program's size). It also tells you how you stand—you cannot load this program under the current version of CP/M, so retrying the operation is futile.

Not many systems programmers like to output messages like the example above. They argue that such a message is too long and too much work for something that does not happen often. Admittedly, the message *is* too long. It could be shortened to read

```
(131) Program 1,024 bytes too large to load.
```

This conveys the same information; the number in parentheses can serve as a reference to a manual where the full impact of the message should be described.

The major problem with the way error messages are designed is that they usually are written by programmers to be read by nontechnical lay users, and programmers are notoriously bad at guessing what nonexperts need to know.

Error indications you design should address the following issues, from the point of view of the user:

- The cause of the error
- The severity of the error
- The corrective action that has and can be taken.

Examine the error messages in the error processor for the example BIOS in Figure 8-10, from line 03600 onward. Although these are an improvement on the BDOS all-purpose

```
BDOS Error on A: Bad Sector
```

even these messages do not really meet all of the requirements of a good error message system.

Another often overlooked aspect of errors is that most hardware errors form a pattern. This pattern is normally only discernible to the trained eye of a hardware maintenance engineer. When these engineers are called to investigate a problem, they will quiz the user to determine whether a given failure is an isolated incident or part of an ongoing pattern. This is why an error message should contain additional technical details. For example, a disk error message should include the track and sector used in the operation that resulted in an error. Only with these details can the engineer piece together the context of a failure or group of failures.

Error Correction

Given that a lucid error message has been displayed on the console, the user is still confronted with the question: "Now what do I do?" Not only can this be difficult for the user to answer, but also the particular solution decided upon can be hard for the BIOS to execute.

Normally, there are three possible options in response to errors:

- Try the operation again
- Ignore the error and attempt to continue
- Abort the program causing the error and return to CP/M.

For some errors, retrying can be effective. For example, if you forget to put the printer on-line and get a "Printer Timeout" error message, it is easy to put the printer back on-line and ask the BIOS to try again to send data to the printer.

Seldom can you ignore an error and hope to get sensible results from the machine; many disk controllers do not even transfer data between themselves and the disk drive if an error has been detected. Only ignorant users, or brave ones in desperation, ignore errors.

Aborting the program causing the error is a drastic measure, although it does escape from what could otherwise be a "deadly embrace" situation. For example, if you misassign the printer to an inactive serial port and turn on printer echoing (with the CONTROL-P toggle), you will send the system into an endless series of "Printer Timeout" messages. If you abort the program, the error handler in the BIOS executes a System Reset function (function 0) in the BDOS, CP/M warm boots, and control is returned to the CCP. In the process, the printer toggle is reset and the circle is broken.

Practical Error Handling

This section discusses several errors, describing their causes and the way in which the BIOS and the user can handle them when they occur.

Character I/O Errors

At the BIOS level, most detectable errors related to character input or output will be found by the hardware chips.

Parity Error

Parity, in this context, refers to the number of bits set to 1 in an 8-bit character. The otherwise unused eighth bit in ASCII characters can be set to make this number always odd, or alternatively, always even. Your computer hardware can be programmed to count the number of 1 bits in each character and to generate an error if the number is odd (odd parity) or, alternatively, if it is even (even parity). If the hardware on the other end of the line is programmed to operate in the same mode, parity checking provides a primitive error-detection mechanism — you can tell that a character is bad, but not what it should have been.

CP/M does not provide a standard mechanism for reporting a parity error, so your only option is to reset the hardware and substitute an ASCII DEL (7FH; delete) character in the place of the erroneous character.

If your BIOS is operating in a highly specialized environment, you may need to count the number of such parity errors so that a utility program can report on the overall performance of the system.

Framing Error

When an 8-bit ASCII character is transmitted over a serial line, the eight bits are transmitted serially, one after the other. A *start* bit is transmitted first, followed by the data character and then a *stop* bit. If the hardware fails to find the stop and start bits in the correct positions, a *framing error* will occur. Again, the only option available to the BIOS is to reset the hardware chip and substitute an ASCII DEL.

Overrun Error

This error occurs when incoming data characters arrive faster than the program can handle them, so that the last characters overrun those being processed by the hardware chip. This error can normally be avoided by the use of serial line protocols, such as those in the example BIOS in Figure 8-10.

An *overrun error* implies that the protocol has broken down. As with the parity and framing errors, almost the only option is to reset the hardware and substitute a DEL character.

Printer Timeout Error

This is one of the few errors where the BIOS can sensibly attempt an error recovery. The error occurs when the BIOS tries to output a character to a serial printer and finds that the printer is not ready for more than, say, 30 seconds. The most common cause of this error is that the user forgets to put the printer on-line. Many printers require that they be off-line during a manual form feed, and users will often forget to push the on-line button afterward.

After a 30-second delay, the BIOS can send a message to the console device(s) informing the user of the error and asking the user to choose the appropriate course of action. Note that console output can be directed to more than one device.

Parallel Printers

Printers connected to your system by means of a parallel port can indicate their status to the computer much more easily than can serial printers. They can communicate such error states as "Out of Paper," "End of Ribbon," and "Off-line."

These single-error indicators can also be used in combination to indicate whether the printer cable is connected, or even whether the printer is receiving power. You need to experiment, deliberately putting the printer into these states and reading status in order to identify them. It is misleading to indicate to the inexperienced user that the printer is "Out of Paper" when the problem is that the data cable has inadvertently become disconnected.

However, each of these errors can be dealt with in the same way as the serial printer's timeout problem: display an error message and request the user's choice of action.

Example Printer Error Routine

Figure 9-1 shows an example of a program that handles printer errors. It consists of several subroutines, including

- The error detection classification and indication routine
- The error correction routine.

It uses other subroutines that are omitted from the figure to avoid obscuring the logic. These subroutines are listed in full in the example BIOS in Figure 8-10.

```
;       This example shows, in outline form, how to handle the
;       situation when a serial printer remains busy for too long.
;       It is intended that this generic example show how to
;       deal with this class of errors.
;
;       The example presupposes the existence of a clock interrupt
;       every 16.666 milliseconds (1/60th of a second), and that
;       control will be transferred to the Real Time Clock service
;       routine each time the clock "ticks".
;
;       Figure 8-10 shows a more complete example, installed in a real
;       BIOS.
;
0000 =          B$System$Reset          EQU     0       ;BDOS system reset function
0005 =          BDOS                    EQU     5       ;BDOS entry point
                ;
0000 00         Printer$Timeout$Flag:   DB      0       ;This flag is set by the interrupt
                                                        ;   service subroutine that is called
                                                        ;   when the watchdog timer subroutine
                                                        ;   count hits zero (after having
                                                        ;   counted down a 30-second delay)

0708 =          Printer$Delay$Count     EQU     1800    ;Given a clock period of 16.666 ms
                                                        ;   this represents a delay of 30 secs
```

Figure 9-1.   Serial printer error handling

```
                ;
000D =          CR              EQU     0DH             ;Carriage return
000A =          LF              EQU     0AH             ;Line feed
                ;
                Printer$Busy$Message:
0001 0D0A               DB      CR,LF
0003 5072696E74         DB      'Printer has been busy for too long.',CR,LF
0028 436865636B         DB      'Check that it is on-line and ready.',CR,LF,0
                ;
004E 00         Printer$Character:      DB      0       ;Save area for the data character
                                                        ;   to be output
                ;
                ;
                LIST:                                   ;<=== Main BIOS entry point
                        ;......                         ;<=== I/O redirection code occurs here

004F 79                 MOV     A,C                     ;Save the data character
0050 324E00             STA     Printer$Character

                Printer$Retry:
0053 010807             LXI     B,Printer$Delay$Count   ;This is the count of the number
                                                        ;  of clock ticks before the watchdog
                                                        ;  subroutine call
0056 217E00             LXI     H,Printer$Timed$Out     ;<== this address
0059 CDA300             CALL    Set$Watchdog            ;Sets the watchdog running

                Printer$Wait:
005C CDA300             CALL    Get$Printer$Status      ;See if the printer is ready to
                                                        ;  accept a character for output
                                                        ;  This includes checking if the printer
                                                        ;  is "Busy" because the driver is
                                                        ;  waiting for XON, ACK, or DTR to
                                                        ;  come high
005F C26C00             JNZ     Printer$Ready           ;The printer is now ready

0062 3A0000             LDA     Printer$Timeout$Flag    ;Check if the watchdog timer has
                                                        ;  hit zero (if it does, the
                                                        ;  watchdog routine will call
                                                        ;  the Printer$Timed$Out code
                                                        ;  that sets this flag)
0065 B7                 ORA     A
0066 C28400             JNZ     Display$Busy$Message    ;Yes, so display message to
                                                        ;  indicate an error has occurred
0069 C35C00             JMP     Printer$Wait            ;Otherwise, check if printer is
                                                        ;  now not busy

                Printer$Ready:                          ;The printer is now ready to output
                                                        ;  a character, but before doing so,
                                                        ;  the watchdog timer must be reset
006C F3                 DI                              ;Ensure no false timeout occurs
006D 010000             LXI     B,0                     ;This is done by setting the count
0070 CDA300             CALL    Set$Watchdog            ;  to zero
0073 FB                 EI

0074 3A4E00             LDA     Printer$Character       ;Get character to output
0077 11A300             LXI     D,Printer$Device$Table  ;DE -> device table for printer
007A CDA300             CALL    Output$Data$Byte        ;Output the character to the printer

007D C9                 RET                             ;Return to the BIOS's caller
                ;
                ;
                Printer$Timed$Out:                      ;Control arrives here from the
                                                        ;  watchdog routine if the
                                                        ;  watchdog count ever hits zero
                                                        ;  This is an interrupt service
                                                        ;  routine
                                                        ;All registers have been saved
                                                        ;  before control arrives here
007E 3EFF               MVI     A,0FFH                  ;Set printer timeout flag
0080 320000             STA     Printer$Timeout$Flag
0083 C9                 RET                             ;Return back to the watchdog
                                                        ;Interrupt service routine
```

Figure 9-1. (Continued)

Chapter 9: Dealing with Hardware Errors **303**

```
                ;
                Display$Busy$Message:             ;Printer has been busy for
0084 AF             XRA     A                    ;    30 seconds or more
0085 320000         STA     Printer$Timeout$Flag ;Reset timeout flag

0088 210100         LXI     H,Printer$Busy$Message  ;Output error message
008B CDA300         CALL    Output$Error$Message

008E CDA300         CALL    Request$User$Choice  ;Displays a Retry, Abort, Ignore?
                                                 ;   prompt, accepts a character from
                                                 ;   the keyboard, and returns with the
                                                 ;   character, converted to upper
                                                 ;   case in the A register
0091 FE52           CPI     'R'                  ;Check if Retry
0093 CA5300         JZ      Printer$Retry
0096 FE41           CPI     'A'
0098 CA9E00         JZ      Printer$Abort        ;Check if Abort
009B FE49           CPI     'I'
009D C8             RZ                           ;Check if Ignore
                ;
                Printer$Abort:
009E 0E00           MVI     C,B$System$Reset     ;Issue system reset
00A0 C30500         JMP     BDOS                 ;No need to give call as
                                                 ;   control will not be returned
                ;
                ;
                ;       Dummy subroutines
                ;       These are shown in full in Figure 8-10. The line numbers in
                ;       Figure 8-10 are shown in the comment field below
                ;
                Printer$Device$Table:    ;Line 01300 (example layout)
                Request$User$Choice:     ;Line 03400
                Output$Error$Message:    ;Line 03500
                Get$Printer$Status:      ;Line 03900 (similar code)
                Output$Data$Byte:        ;Line 05400 (similar code)
                Set$Watchdog:            ;Line 05800
```

Figure 9-1.   Serial printer error handling (continued)

Disk Errors

Disks are much more complicated than character I/O devices. Errors are possible in the electronics and in the disk medium itself. Most of the errors concerned with electronics need only be reported in enough detail to give a maintenance engineer information about the problem. This kind of error is rarely correctable by retrying the operation. In contrast, media errors often can be remedied by retrying the operation or by special error processing software built into the BIOS. This chapter discusses this class of errors.

Media errors occur when the BIOS tries to read a sector from the disk and the hardware detects a check-sum failure in the data. This is known as a *cyclical redundancy check* (CRC) error. Some disk controllers execute a read-after-write check, so a CRC error can also occur during an attempt to write a sector to the disk.

304 The CP/M Programmer's Handbook

With floppy diskettes, the disk driver should retry the operation at least ten times before reporting the error to the user. Then, because diskettes are inexpensive and replaceable, the user can choose to discard the diskette and continue with a new one.

With hard disks, the media cannot be exchanged. The only way of dealing with bad sectors is to replace them logically, substituting other sectors in their place.

There are two fundamentally different ways of doing this. Figure 9-2 shows the scheme known as sector sparing—substituting sectors on an outer track for a sector that is bad.

The advantage of this scheme is that it is dynamic. If a sector is found to be bad in a read-after-write check, even after several retries, then the data intended for the failing sector can be written to a spare sector. The failing sector's number is placed into a spare-sector directory on the disk. Thereafter, the disk drivers will be redirected to the spare sector every time an attempt is made to read or write the bad sector.

The disadvantage of this system is that the read/write heads on the disk must move out to the spare sector and then back to access the next sector. This can be a problem if you attempt to make a high-speed backup on a streaming tape drive (one that writes data to a tape in a single stream rather than in discrete blocks). The delay caused by reading the spare sector interrupts the data flow to the streaming tape drive.

You need a special utility program to manipulate the spare-sector directory, both to substitute for a failing sector manually and to attempt to rewrite a spare sector back onto the bad sector.

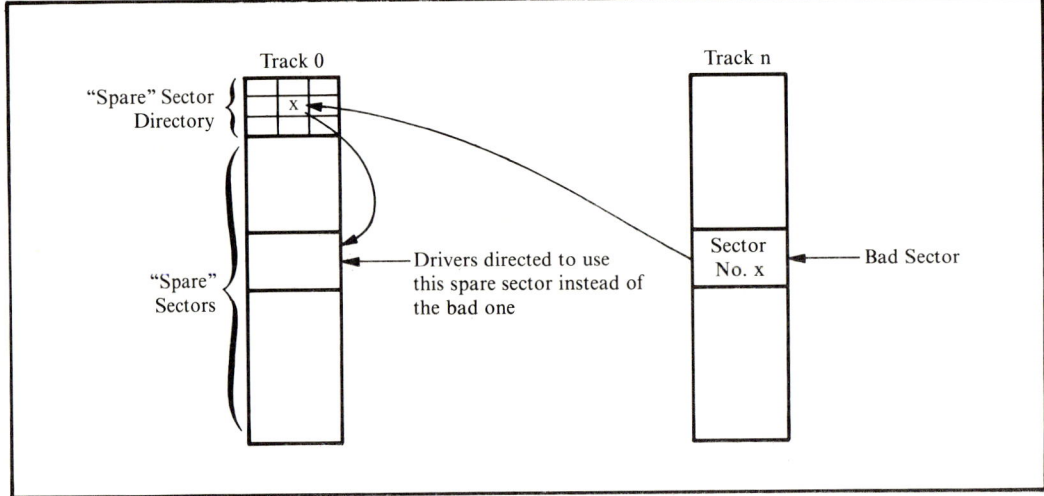

Figure 9-2.   Sector sparing

Figure 9-3 shows another scheme for dealing with bad sectors. In this method, bad sectors are skipped rather than having sectors substituted for them.

The advantage of sector skipping is that the heads do not have to perform any long seeks. The failing sector is skipped, and the next sector is used in its place. Because of this, sector skipping can give much better performance. Data can be read off the disk fast enough to keep a streaming tape drive "fed" with data.

The disadvantage of sector skipping is that it does not lend itself to dynamic operation. The bad sector table is best built during formatting. Once data has been written to the disk, if a sector goes bad, all subsequent sectors on the disk must be "moved down one" to make space to skip the bad sector. On a large hard disk, this could take several minutes.

Example Bad Sector Management

Sector sparing and sector skipping use similar logic. Both require a spare-sector directory on each physical disk, containing the sector numbers of the bad sectors. This directory is read into memory during cold start initialization. Thereafter, all disk read and write operations refer to the memory-resident table to see if they are about to access a bad sector.

For sector sparing, if the sector about to be read or written is found in the spare directory, its position in the directory determines which spare sector should be read.

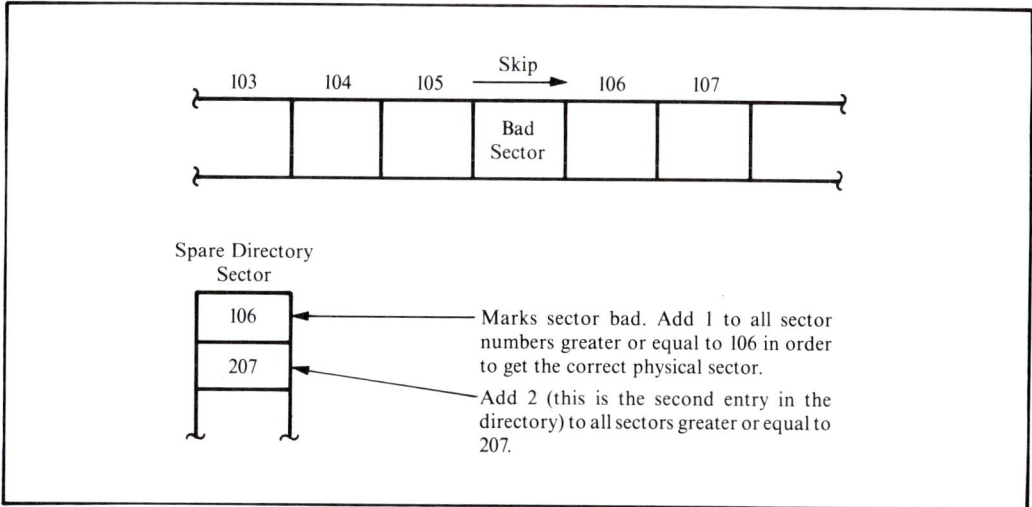

Figure 9-3. Sector skipping

In the case of sector skipping, every access to the disk makes the driver check the bad sector directory. The directory is used to tell how many bad sectors exist between the start of the disk and the failing bad sector. This number must be added to the requested track and sector to compensate for all the bad sectors.

The physical low-level drivers need four entry points:

- Read the specified sector without using bad sector management. This is used to read in the spare directory itself.

- Write the specified sector without using bad sector management. This is used to write the spare directory onto the disk, both to initialize it and to update it.

- Read and write the sector using bad sector management. These entry points are used for normal disk input/output.

Figure 9-4 shows the code necessary for both sector sparing and (using conditional code) sector skipping.

```
                    ;       This example shows the modifications to be made in order
                    ;       to implement bad sector management using sector sparing
                    ;       and sector skipping.
                    ;
0000 =              False              EQU     0
FFFF =              True               EQU     Not False
                    ;
0000 =              Sector$Sparing     EQU     False
FFFF =              Sector$Skipping    EQU     Not Sector$Sparing
                    ;
                    ;
                    ;       Additional equates and definitions
                    ;
                    Spare$Directories:                 ;Table of spare directory addresses
                                                       ;Note: The directories themselves
                                                       ;  are declared at the end of the
                                                       ;  BIOS
0000 D500                  DW      Spare$Directory$0   ;Physical disk 0
0002 9701                  DW      Spare$Directory$1   ;Physical disk 1
                    ;
                    Spare$Dir$In$Memory:               ;Flags used to indicate whether spare
0004 00                    DB      0                   ;  directory for a given physical disk
0005 00                    DB      0                   ;  has been loaded into memory. Set by SELDSK
                    ;
                    ;
0000 =              Spare$Track        EQU     0       ;Track containing spare directory
                                                       ;  sectors
0004 =              Spare$Sector       EQU     4       ;Sector containing directory
0005 =              First$Spare$Sector EQU     Spare$Sector + 1
                    ;
                    ;       Variables set by SELDSK
                    ;
                    Selected$Spare$Directory:
0006 0000                  DW      0                   ;Pointer to directory
0008 00             Selected$Disk:       DB    0       ;Logical disk number
0009 00             Disk$Type:           DB    0       ;Floppy/hard disks
000A 00             Deblocking$Required: DB    0       ;Deblocking flag
000B 00             Selected$Physical$Disk: DB 0       ;Physical disk number
                    ;
000C 0000           Disk$Track:          DW    0       ;) These variables are part of the command
000E 00             Disk$Sector:         DB    0       ;) block handed over to the disk controller
```

Figure 9-4.   Bad sector management

```
                ;
8000 =          Maximum$Track           EQU     32768       ;Used as a terminator
0012 =          Sectors$Per$Track       EQU     18
0000 =          First$Sector$On$Track   EQU     0
                ;
                Disk$Parameter$Headers:
                        ;--------------------------
                        ;Standard DPH Declarations
                        ;--------------------------
                ;
                ;
                ;       Equates for disk parameter block
                ;
                ;       The special disk parameter byte that precedes each disk
                ;       parameter block, needs to be rearranged so that a
                ;       physical disk drive number can be added.
                ;
                ;       Disk types
                ;
                ;                                 vvvv--- Physical disk number
0010 =          Floppy$5        EQU     0$001$0000B     ;5 1/4" mini floppy
0020 =          Floppy$8        EQU     0$010$0000B     ;8" floppy (SS SD)
0030 =          M$Disk          EQU     0$011$0000B     ;Memory disk
0040 =          H$Disk$10       EQU     0$100$0000B     ;Hard disk - 10 megabyte
                ;
0070 =          Disk$Type$$Mask         EQU     0$111$0000B     ;Masks to isolate values
000F =          Physical$Disk$Mask      EQU     0$000$1111B
                ;
                ;       Blocking/deblocking indicator
                ;
0080 =          Need$Deblocking EQU     1$000$0000B     ;Sector size > 128 bytes
                ;
                ;       Disk parameter blocks
                ;
                        ;--------------------------
                        ; Standard DPB's for A: and B:
                        ;--------------------------
                ;
                                        ;Logical disk C:
                                        ;Extra byte indicates disk type
                                        ; deblocking requirements and physical
                                        ; disk drive.
000F C0                 DB      H$Disk$10 + Need$Deblocking + 0 ; Physical drive 0
                Hard$5$Parameter$Block$C:
                        ;--------------------------
                        ;Standard format parameter block
                        ;--------------------------
                ;
                ;
0010 C0                 DB      H$Disk$10 + Need$Deblocking + 0 ; Physical drive 0
                Hard$5$Parameter$Block$D:
                        ;--------------------------
                        ;Standard format parameter block
                        ;--------------------------
                ;
                ;
0004 =          Number$of$Logical$Disks         EQU     4
                ;
                ;
                SELDSK:                 ;Select disk in register C
                                        ;C = 0 for drive A, 1 for B, etc.
                                        ;Return the address of the appropriate
                                        ; disk parameter header in HL, or 0000H
                                        ; if the selected disk does not exist.
                                        ;
0011 210000             LXI     H,0             ;Assume an error
0014 79                 MOV     A,C             ;Check if requested disk valid

0015 FE04               CPI     Number$of$Logical$Disks
0017 D0                 RNC                     ;Return if > maximum number of disks
```

Figure 9-4. (Continued)

```
0018 320800         STA     Selected$Disk       ;Save selected disk number
                                                ;Set up to return DPH address
001B 6F             MOV     L,A                 ;Make disk into word value
001C 2600           MVI     H,0
                                                ;Compute offset down disk parameter
                                                ; header table by multiplying by
                                                ; parameter header length (16 bytes)
001E 29             DAD     H                   ;*2
001F 29             DAD     H                   ;*4
0020 29             DAD     H                   ;*8
0021 29             DAD     H                   ;*16
0022 110F00         LXI     D,Disk$Parameter$Headers    ;Get base address
0025 19             DAD     D                   ;DE -> appropriate DPH
0026 E5             PUSH    H                   ;Save DPH address

                                                ;Access disk parameter block in order
                                                ; to extract special prefix byte that
                                                ; identifies disk type and whether
                                                ; deblocking is required
                                                ;
0027 110A00         LXI     D,10                ;Get DPB pointer offset in DPH
002A 19             DAD     D                   ;DE -> DPB address in DPH
002B 5E             MOV     E,M                 ;Get DPB address in DE
002C 23             INX     H
002D 56             MOV     D,M
002E EB             XCHG                        ;DE -> DPB

          SELDSK$Set$Disk$Type:
002F 2B             DCX     H                   ;DE -> prefix byte
0030 7E             MOV     A,M                 ;Get prefix byte
0031 E670           ANI     Disk$Type$Mask      ;Isolate disk type
0033 320900         STA     Disk$Type           ;Save for use in low-level driver
0036 7E             MOV     A,M                 ;Get another copy of prefix byte
0037 E680           ANI     Need$Deblocking     ;Isolate deblocking flag
0039 320A00         STA     Deblocking$Required ;Save for use in low-level driver

                                                ;Additional code to check if spare
                                                ; directory for given disk has already
                                                ; been read in.

003C 7E             MOV     A,M                 ;Get physical disk number
003D E60F           ANI     Physical$Disk$Mask
003F 320B00         STA     Selected$Physical$Disk   ;Save for low-level drivers

0042 5F             MOV     E,A                 ;Make into word
0043 1600           MVI     D,0
0045 210400         LXI     H,Spare$Dir$In$Memory    ;Make pointer into table
0048 19             DAD     D

0049 7E             MOV     A,M                 ;Get flag
004A B7             ORA     A
004B C27700         JNZ     Dir$In$Memory       ;Spare directory already in memory
004E 34             INR     M                   ;Set flag

004F 210000         LXI     H,Spare$Directories ;Create pointer to spare
0052 19             DAD     D                   ; spare directory (added twice
0053 19             DAD     D                   ; as table has word entries)
                                                ;HL -> word containing directory addr.
0054 5E             MOV     E,M
0055 23             INX     H
0056 56             MOV     D,M                 ;Spare directory address in DE
0057 EB             XCHG                        ;HL -> spare directory
0058 220600         SHLD    Selected$Spare$Directory ;Save for use in physical
                                                ; drivers later on

005B 110000         LXI     D,Spare$Track       ;Track containing spare directory
005E 3A0B00         LDA     Selected$Physical$Disk
0061 47             MOV     B,A
0062 3E04           MVI     A,Spare$Sector      ;Sector containing spare directory
0064 0E18           MVI     C,Spare$Length/8    ;Number of bytes in spare directory / 8
0066 CDD500         CALL    Absolute$Read       ;Read in spare directory - without
                                                ; using bad sector management
```

Figure 9-4.   (Continued)

```
0069 2A0600          LHLD    Selected$Spare$Directory ;Set end marker
006C 11C000          LXI     D,Spare$Length           ;  at back end of spare directory
006F 19              DAD     D
0070 110080          LXI     D,Maximum$Track          ;Use maximum track number
0073 73              MOV     M,E
0074 23              INX     H
0075 3602            MVI     M,D

            Dir$In$Memory:
0077 E1              POP     H                        ;Recover DPH pointer
0078 C9              RET
            ;
            ;
            ;   In the low-level disk drivers, the following code must be
            ;   inserted just before the disk controller is activated to
            ;   execute a read or a write command.
            ;
0079 2A0C00          LHLD    Disk$Track               ;Get track number from disk
                                                      ;  controller command table
007C EB              XCHG                             ;DE = track
007D 2A0600          LHLD    Selected$Spare$Directory ;HL -> spare directory
0080 2B              DCX     H                        ;Back up one entry
0081 2B              DCX     H
0082 2B              DCX     H                        ;  (3 bytes)

0083 3A0E00          LDA     Disk$Sector              ;Get sector number
0086 4F              MOV     C,A                      ;Save for later

0087 06FF            MVI     B,0FFH                   ;Set counter (biased -1)

            Check$Next$Entry:
0089 23              INX     H                        ;Update to next (or first) entry
            Check$Next$Entry1:
008A 23              INX     H
            Check$Next$Entry2:
008B 23              INX     H

008C 04              INR     B                        ;Update count

                     IF      Sector$Sparing
                                                      ;If sparing is used, the
                                                      ;  end of the table is indicated
                                                      ;  by an entry with the track number
                                                      ;  = to maximum track number
                     LXI     D,Maximum$Track          ;Get maximum track number
                     CALL    CMPM                     ;Compare DE to (HL), (HL+1)
                     JZ      Not$Bad$Sector           ;End of table reached
                     ENDIF

                                                      ;Note: For sector skipping
                                                      ;  the following search loop will
                                                      ;  terminate when the requested track
                                                      ;  is less than that in the table.
                                                      ;This will always happen when the
                                                      ;  maximum track number is encountered
                                                      ;  at the end of the table.
008D EB              XCHG                             ;DE -> table entry
008E 2A0C00          LHLD    Disk$Track               ;Get requested track
0091 EB              XCHG                             ;DE = req. track, HL -> table entry
0092 CDCD00          CALL    CMPM                     ;Compare req. track to table entry

                     IF      Sector$Sparing
                                                      ;Use the following code for
                                                      ;  sector sparing
                     JNZ     Check$Next$Entry         ;Track does not match
                     INX     H                        ;HL -> MS byte of track
                     INX     H                        ;HL -> sector
                     MOV     A,C                      ;Get requested sector
                     CMP     M                        ;Compare to table entry
                     JNZ     Check$Next$Entry2        ;Sector does not match

                                                      ;Track and sector match, so
                                                      ;  substitute spare track and
                                                      ;  appropriate sector
```

Figure 9-4. (Continued)

```
                    LXI     H,Spare$Track       ;Get track number used for spare
                                                ;  sectors
                    SHLD    Disk$Track          ;Substitute track
                    MVI     A,First$Spare$Sector ;Get first sector number
                    ADD     B                   ;Add on matched directory
                                                ;  entry number
                    STA     Disk$Sector         ;Substitute sector
                    ENDIF

                    IF      Sector$Skipping     ;Use the following code for
                                                ;  sector skipping
                                                ;The object is to find the
                                                ;  entry in the table which
                                                ;  is greater or equal to the
                                                ;  requested sector/track
0095 CA9E00         JZ      Tracks$Match        ;Possible match of track and sector
0098 D2AC00         JNC     Compute$Increment   ;Requested track < table entry
009B C38900         JMP     Check$Next$Entry    ;Requested track > table entry

            Tracks$Match:
009E 23             INX     H                   ;HL -> MS byte of track
009F 23             INX     H                   ;HL -> sector
00A0 77             MOV     M,A                 ;Get sector from table
00A1 B9             CMP     C                   ;Compare with requested sector
00A2 CAAB00         JZ      Sectors$Match       ;Track/sector matches
00A5 D2AC00         JNC     Compute$Increment   ;Req. trk/sec < spare trk/sec
00A8 C38B00         JMP     Check$Next$Entry2   ;Move to next table entry

            Sectors$Match:
00AB 04             INR     B                   ;If track and sectors match with
                                                ;  a table entry, then an additional
                                                ;  sector must be skipped

            Compute$Increment:
                                                ;B contains number of cumulative
                                                ;  number of sectors to skip
00AC 79             MOV     A,C                 ;Get requested sector
00AD 80             ADD     B                   ;Skip required number
00AE 0612           MVI     B,Sectors$Per$Track ;Determine final sector number
                                                ;  and track increment
00B0 CDC300         CALL    DIV$A$BY$B          ;Returns C = quotient, A = remainder
00B3 320E00         STA     Disk$Sector         ;A = new sector number

00B6 59             MOV     E,C                 ;Make track increment a word
00B7 1600           MVI     D,0
00B9 2A0C00         LHLD    Disk$Track          ;Get requested track
00BC 19             DAD     D                   ;Add on increment
00BD 220C00         SHLD    Disk$Track          ;Save updated track
                    ENDIF

            Not$Bad$Sector:
                                                ;Either track/sector were not bad,
                                                ;  or requested track and sector have
                                                ;  been updated.
00C0 C3D500         JMP     Read$Write$Disk     ;Go to physical disk read/write
            ;
                    IF      Sector$Skipping
                                                ;Subroutine required for skipping
                                                ;  routine
            ;
            ;
            ;       DIV$A$BY$B
            ;       Divide A by B
            ;
            ;       This routine divides A by B, returning the quotient in C
            ;       and the remainder in A.
            ;
            ;       Entry parameters
            ;
            ;               A = dividend
            ;               B = divisor
            ;
            ;       Exit parameters
```

Figure 9-4. (Continued)

```
                        ;
                        ;               A = remainder
                        ;               C = quotient
                        ;
                        DIV$A$BY$B:
00C3 0E00                       MVI     C,0             ;Initialize quotient
                        DIV$A$BY$B$Loop:
00C5 0C                         INR     C               ;Increment quotient
00C6 90                         SUB     B               ;Subtract divisor
00C7 F2C500                     JP      DIV$A$BY$B$Loop ;Repeat if result still +ve
00CA 0D                         DCR     C               ;Correct quotient
00CB 80                         ADD     B               ;Correct remainder
00CC C9                         RET
                                ENDIF
                        ;
                        ;       CMPM
                        ;       Compare memory
                        ;
                        ;       This subroutine compares the contents of DE to (HL) and (HL+1)
                        ;       returning with the flags as though the subtraction (HL) - DE
                        ;       were performed.
                        ;
                        ;       Entry parameters
                        ;
                        ;               HL -> word in memory
                        ;               DE = value to be compared
                        ;
                        ;       Exit parameters
                        ;
                        ;               Flags set for (HL) - DE
                        ;
                        CMPM:
00CD 7E                         MOV     A,M             ;Get MS byte
00CE BA                         CMP     D
00CF C0                         RNZ                     ;Return now if MS bytes unequal
00D0 23                         INX     H               ;HL -> LS byte
00D1 7E                         MOV     A,M             ;Get LS byte
00D2 BB                         CMP     E
00D3 2B                         DCX     H               ;Return with HL unchanged
00D4 C9                         RET

                        ;
                        ;
                        Absolute$Read:
                                                ;The absolute read (and write) routines
                                                ;  access the specified sector and track
                                                ;  without using bad sector management.
                        ;       Entry parameters
                        ;
                        ;               HL -> Buffer
                        ;               DE = Track
                        ;               A = Sector
                        ;               B = Physical disk drive number
                        ;               C = Number of bytes to read / 8
                        ;
                        ;       Set up disk controller command block with parameters in
                        ;       registers, then initiate read operation by falling through
                        ;       into Read$Write$Disk code below.
                        ;
                        Read$Write$Disk:

                                ;---------------------------------------------------
                                ;The remainder of the low level disk drivers follow,
                                ; reading the required sector and track.
                                ;---------------------------------------------------

                        ;
                        ;       Spare directory declarations
                        ;
                        ;       Note: The disk format utility creates an initial spare
                        ;       directory with track/sector entries for those track/sectors
                        ;       that it finds are bad. It fills the remainder of the
                        ;       directory with 0FFH's (these serve to terminate the
                        ;       searching of the directory).
```

Figure 9-4. (Continued)

```
                ;
                ;
    00C0 =      Spare$Length     EQU      64 * 3        ;64 Entries, 3 bytes each
                                                        ;  Byte 0,1 = track
                                                        ;  Byte 2 = sector

                Spare$Directory$0:
    00D5        DS       Spare$Length                   ;Spare directory itself
    0195        DS       2                              ;Set to maximum track number by SELDSK as
                                                        ;  a safety precaution. The FORMAT utility
                                                        ;  puts the maximum track number into all
                                                        ;  unused entries in the spare directory.

                Spare$Directory$1:
    0197        DS       Spare$Length                   ;Spare directory itself
    0257        DS       2                              ;End marker
```

Figure 9-4. Bad sector management (continued)

Improving Error Messages

The final extension to BIOS error handling discussed here is in disk-driver error-message handling. The subroutine shown in the example BIOS in Figure 8-10, although a significant improvement on the messages normally output by the BDOS, did not advise the user of the most suitable course of action for each error. Figure 9-5 shows an improved version of the error message processor.

```
                ;     This shows slightly more user-friendly error processor
                ;     for disk errors than that shown in the enhanced BIOS
                ;     in Figure 8-10.
                ;     This version outputs a recommended course of action
                ;     depending on the nature of the error detected.
                ;     Code that remains unchanged from Figure 8-10 has been
                ;     abbreviated.
                ;
                ;     Dummy equates and data declarations needed to get
                ;     an error free assembly of this example.
                ;
    0001 =      Floppy$Read$Code         EQU      01H    ;Read command for controller
    0002 =      Floppy$Write$Code        EQU      02H    ;Write command for controller
                ;
    0000 00     Disk$Hung$Flag:          DB       0      ;Set NZ when watchdog timer times
                                                         ;  out
    0258 =      Disk$Timer               EQU      600    ;10-second delay (16.66ms tick)
                ;
    0043 =      Disk$Status$Block        EQU      43H    ;Address in memory where controller
                                                         ;  returns status
                                                         ;Values from controller command table
    0001 00     Floppy$Command:          DB       0
    0002 00     Floppy$Head:             DB       0
    0003 00     Floppy$Track:            DB       0
    0004 00     Floppy$Sector:           DB       0
```

Figure 9-5. User-friendly disk-error processor

```
0005 00.            Deblocking$Required:    DB      0       ;Flag set by SELDSK according
                                                            ;   to selected disk type
0006 00             Disk$Error$Flag:        DB      0       ;Error flag returned to BDOS
                    ;
0007 00             In$Buffer$Disk:         DB      0       ;Logical disk Id. relating to current
                                                            ;   disk sector in deblocking buffer
                    ;
                    ;       Equates for Messages
                    ;
0007 =              BELL    EQU     07H     ;Sound terminal bell
000D =              CR      EQU     0DH     ;Carriage return
000A =              LF      EQU     0AH     ;Line feed
                    ;
0005 =              BDOS    EQU     5       ;BDOS entry point (for system reset)
                    ;
                    ;
                    ;
                    No$Deblock$Retry:
                    ;-----------------------------------------------------------
                    ; Omitted code to set up disk controller command table
                    ; and initiate the disk operation
                    ;-----------------------------------------------------------
0008 C31500                 JMP     Wait$For$Disk$Complete
                    ;
                    ;
                    Write$Physical:                 ;Write contents of disk buffer to
                                                    ;   correct sector
000B 3E02                   MVI     A,Floppy$Write$Code     ;Get write function code
000D C31200                 JMP     Common$Physical ;Go to common code
                    Read$Physical:                  ;Read previously selected sector
                                                    ;   into disk buffer
0010 3E01                   MVI     A,Floppy$Read$Code      ;Get read function code
                    Common$Physical:
0012 320100                 STA     Floppy$Command  ;Set command table
                    ;
                    Deblock$Retry:                  ;Re-entry point to retry after error
                    ;-----------------------------------------------------------
                    ; Omitted code sets up disk controller command block
                    ; and initiates the disk operation
                    ;-----------------------------------------------------------
                    Wait$For$Disk$Complete:         ;Wait until disk status block indicates
                                                    ;  operation has completed, then check
                                                    ;  if any errors occurred
                                                    ;On entry HL -> disk control byte
0015 AF                     XRA     A                       ;Ensure hung flag clear
0016 320000                 STA     Disk$Hung$Flag

0019 213100                 LXI     H,Disk$Timed$Out        ;Set up watchdog timer
001C 015802                 LXI     B,Disk$Timer            ;Time delay
001F CD3B03                 CALL    Set$Watchdog
                    Disk$Wait$Loop:
0022 7E                     MOV     A,M                     ;Get control byte
0023 B7                     ORA     A
0024 CA3700                 JZ      Disk$Complete           ;Operation done

0027 3A0000                 LDA     Disk$Hung$Flag          ;Also check if timed out
002A B7                     ORA     A
002B C29F02                 JNZ     Disk$Error              ;Will be set to 40H

002E C32200                 JMP     Disk$Wait$Loop

                    Disk$Timed$Out:                 ;Control arrives here from watchdog
                                                    ; routine itself -- so this is effectively
                                                    ; part of the interrupt service routine.
0031 3E40                   MVI     A,40H                   ;Set disk hung error code
0033 320000                 STA     Disk$Hung$Flag          ;  into error flag to pull
                                                            ;  control out of loop
0036 C9                     RET                             ;Return to watchdog routine
```

Figure 9-5.   (Continued)

```
                    Disk$Complete:
0037 010000         LXI         B,0                         ;Reset watchdog timer
                                                            ;HL is irrelevant here
003A CD3B03         CALL        Set$Watchdog

003D 3A4300         LDA         Disk$Status$Block           ;Complete -- now check status
0040 FE80           CPI         80H                         ;Check if any errors occurred
0042 DA9F02         JC          Disk$Error                  ;Yes
                ;
                    Disk$Error$Ignore:
0045 AF             XRA         A                           ;No
0046 320600         STA         Disk$Error$Flag             ;Clear error flag
0049 C9             RET

                ;
                ;   Disk error message handling
                ;
                ;
                    Disk$Error$Messages:        ;This table is scanned, comparing the
                                                ;  disk error status with those in the
                                                ;  table. Given a match, or even when
                                                ;  the end of the table is reached, the
                                                ;  address following the status value
                                                ;  points to the correct advisory message text.
                                                ;  Following this is the address of an
                                                ;  error description message.
004A 40             DB          40H
004B B0019500       DW          Disk$Advice1,Disk$Msg$40
004F 41             DB          41H
0050 C9019A00       DW          Disk$Advice2,Disk$Msg$41
0054 42             DB          42H
0055 E301A400       DW          Disk$Advice3,Disk$Msg$42
0059 21             DB          21H
005A 0702B400       DW          Disk$Advice4,Disk$Msg$21
005E 22             DB          22H
005F 1B02B900       DW          Disk$Advice5,Disk$Msg$22
0063 23             DB          23H
0064 1B02C000       DW          Disk$Advice5,Disk$Msg$23
0068 24             DB          24H
0069 3D02D200       DW          Disk$Advice6,Disk$Msg$24
006D 25             DB          25H
006E 3D02DE00       DW          Disk$Advice6,Disk$Msg$25
0072 11             DB          11H
0073 5302F100       DW          Disk$Advice7,Disk$Msg$11
0077 12             DB          12H
0078 5302FF00       DW          Disk$Advice7,Disk$Msg$12
007C 13             DB          13H
007D 53020C01       DW          Disk$Advice7,Disk$Msg$13
0081 14             DB          14H
0082 53021A01       DW          Disk$Advice7,Disk$Msg$14
0086 15             DB          15H
0087 53022901       DW          Disk$Advice7,Disk$Msg$15
008B 16             DB          16H
008C 53023501       DW          Disk$Advice7,Disk$Msg$16
0090 00             DB          0                           ;<== Terminator
0091 53024501       DW          Disk$Advice7,Disk$Msg$Unknown  ;Unmatched code
                ;
0005 =              DEM$Entry$Size  EQU     5               ;Entry size in error message table
                ;
                ;
                ;   Message texts
                ;
0095 48756E6700Disk$Msg$40:  DB  'Hung',0        ;Timeout message
009A 4E6F742052Disk$Msg$41:  DB  'Not Ready',0
00A4 5772697465Disk$Msg$42:  DB  'Write Protected',0
00B4 4461746100Disk$Msg$21:  DB  'Data',0
00B9 466F726D61Disk$Msg$22:  DB  'Format',0
00C0 4D69737369Disk$Msg$23:  DB  'Missing Data Mark',0
00D2 4275732054Disk$Msg$24:  DB  'Bus Timeout',0
00DE 436F6E7472Disk$Msg$25:  DB  'Controller Timeout',0
00F1 4472697665Disk$Msg$11:  DB  'Drive Address',0
00FF 4865616420Disk$Msg$12:  DB  'Head Address',0
010C 547261636BDisk$Msg$13:  DB  'Track Address',0
```

Figure 9-5. (Continued)

```
011A 536563746FDisk$Msg$14:    DB      'Sector Address',0
0129 4275732041Disk$Msg$15:    DB      'Bus Address',0
0135 496C6C6567Disk$Msg$16:    DB      'Illegal Command',0
0145 556E6B6E6FDisk$Msg$Unknown:  DB   'Unknown',0
                ;
                Disk$EM$1:                      ;Main disk error message -- part 1
014D 070D0A                    DB      BELL,CR,LF
0150 4469736B20                 DB      'Disk ',0
                ;
                                                ;Error text output next
                Disk$EM$2:                      ;Main disk error message -- part 2
0156 204572726F                 DB      ' Error ('
015E 0000       Disk$EM$Status: DB      0,0       ;Status code in hex
0160 290D0A2020                 DB      ')',CR,LF,'     Drive '
016E 00         Disk$EM$Drive:  DB      0         ;Disk drive code, A,B...
016F 2C20486561                 DB      ', Head '
0176 00         Disk$EM$Head:   DB      0         ;Head number
0177 2C20547261                 DB      ', Track '
017F 0000       Disk$EM$Track:  DB      0,0       ;Track number
0181 2C20536563                 DB      ', Sector '
018A 0000       Disk$EM$Sector: DB      0,0       ;Sector number
018C 2C204F7065                 DB      ', Operation - '
019A 00                         DB      0         ;Terminator
                ;
019B 526561642EDisk$EM$Read:    DB      'Read.',0     ;Operation names
01A1 5772697465Disk$EM$Write:   DB      'Write.',0
                ;
01A8 0D0A202020Disk$Advice0:    DB      CR,LF,'     ',0
01B0 436865636BDisk$Advice1:    DB      'Check disk loaded, Retry',0
01C9 506F737369Disk$Advice2:    DB      'Possible hardware problem',0
01E3 5772697465Disk$Advice3:    DB      'Write enable if correct disk, Retry',0
0207 5265747279Disk$Advice4:    DB      'Retry several times',0
021B 5265666F72Disk$Advice5:    DB      'Reformat disk or use another disk',0
023D 4861726477Disk$Advice6:    DB      'Hardware error, Retry',0
0253 4861726477Disk$Advice7:    DB      'Hardware or Software error, Retry',0
                ;
0275 2C206F7220Disk$Advice9:    DB      ', or call for help if error persists',CR,LF
                ;
                Disk$Action$Confirm:
029B 00                         DB      0         ;Set to character entered by user
029C 0D0A00                     DB      CR,LF,0
                ;
                ;       Disk error processor
                ;
                ;       This routine builds and outputs an error message.
                ;       The user is then given the opportunity to:
                ;
                ;               R -- retry the operation that caused the error
                ;               I -- ignore the error and attempt to continue
                ;               A -- abort the program and return to CP/M
                ;
                Disk$Error:
029F F5                         PUSH    PSW                     ;Preserve error code from controller
02A0 215E01                     LXI     H,Disk$EM$Status        ;Convert code for message
02A3 CD3B03                     CALL    CAH                     ;Converts A to hex

02A6 3A0700                     LDA     In$Buffer$Disk          ;Convert disk id. for message
02A9 C641                       ADI     'A'
02AB 326E01                     STA     Disk$EM$Drive           ;Make into letter

02AE 3A0200                     LDA     Floppy$Head             ;Convert head number
02B1 C630                       ADI     '0'
02B3 327601                     STA     Disk$EM$Head

02B6 3A0300                     LDA     Floppy$Track            ;Convert track number
02B9 217F01                     LXI     H,Disk$EM$Track
02BC CD3B03                     CALL    CAH

02BF 3A0400                     LDA     Floppy$Sector           ;Convert sector number
02C2 218A01                     LXI     H,Disk$EM$Sector
02C5 CD3B03                     CALL    CAH

02C8 214D01                     LXI     H,Disk$EM$1             ;Output first part of message
02CB CD3B03                     CALL    Output$Error$Message
```

Figure 9-5. (Continued)

```
02CE F1              POP     PSW                         ;Recover error status code
02CF 47              MOV     B,A                         ;For comparisons
02D0 214500          LXI     H,Disk$Error$Messages - DEM$Entry$Size
                                                         ;HL -> table -- one entry
02D3 110500          LXI     D,DEM$Entry$Size            ;For loop below
             Disk$Error$Next$Code:
02D6 19              DAD     D                           ;Move to next (or first) entry
02D7 7E              MOV     A,M                         ;Get code number from table
02D8 B7              ORA     A                           ;Check if end of table
02D9 CAE302          JZ      Disk$Error$Matched          ;Yes, pretend a match occurred
02DC B8              CMP     B                           ;Compare to actual code
02DD CAE302          JZ      Disk$Error$Matched          ;Yes, exit from loop
02E0 C3D602          JMP     Disk$Error$Next$Code        ;Check next code
             ;
             Disk$Error$Matched:
02E3 23              INX     H                           ;HL -> advisory text address
02E4 5E              MOV     E,M
02E5 23              INX     H
02E6 56              MOV     D,M                         ;DE -> advisory test
02E7 D5              PUSH    D                           ;Save for later

02E8 23              INX     H                           ;HL -> message text address
02E9 5E              MOV     E,M                         ;Get address into DE
02EA 23              INX     H
02EB 56              MOV     D,M

02EC EB              XCHG                                ;HL -> text
02ED CD3B03          CALL    Output$Error$Message        ;Display explanatory text

02F0 215601          LXI     H,Disk$EM$2                 ;Display second part of message
02F3 CD3B03          CALL    Output$Error$Message

02F6 219B01          LXI     H,Disk$EM$Read              ;Choose operation text
                                                         ; (assume a read)
02F9 3A0100          LDA     Floppy$Command              ;Get controller command
02FC FE01            CPI,    Floppy$Read$Code
02FE CA0403          JZ      Disk$Error$Read             ;Yes
0301 21A101          LXI     H,Disk$EM$Write             ;No, change address in HL
             Disk$Error$Read:
0304 CD3B03          CALL    Output$Error$Message        ;Display operation type

0307 21A801          LXI     H,Disk$Advice0              ;Display leading blanks
030A CD3B03          CALL    Output$Error$Message

030D E1              POP     H                           ;Recover advisory text pointer
030E CD3B03          CALL    Output$Error$Message

0311 217502          LXI     H,Disk$Advice9              ;Display trailing component
0314 CD3B03          CALL    Output$Error$Message
             ;
             Disk$Error$Request$Action:                  ;Ask the user what to do next
0317 CD3B03          CALL    Request$User$Choice         ;Display prompt and get single
                                                         ; character response (folded to
                                                         ; uppercase)
031A FE52            CPI     'R'                         ;Retry
031C CA2C03          JZ      Disk$Error$Retry
031F FE41            CPI     'A'                         ;Abort?
0321 CA3603          JZ      System$Reset
0324 FE49            CPI     'I'                         ;Ignore?
0326 CA4500          JZ      Disk$Error$Ignore
0329 C31703          JMP     Disk$Error$Request$Action
             ;
             Disk$Error$Retry:                           ;The decision on where to return to
                                                         ; depends on whether the operation
                                                         ; failed on a deblocked or
                                                         ; nondeblocked drive
032C 3A0500          LDA     Deblocking$Required
032F B7              ORA     A
0330 C21500          JNZ     Deblock$Retry
0333 C30800          JMP     No$Deblock$Retry
```

Figure 9-5.   (Continued)

```
                    ;
                    System$Reset:                           ;This is a radical approach, but
                                                            ;  it does cause CP/M to restart
       0336 0E00            MVI     C,0                     ;System reset
       0338 CD0500          CALL    BDOS
                    ;
                    ;       Omitted subroutines (listed in full in Figure 8-10)
                    ;
                    Set$Watchdog:           ;Set watchdog timer (to number of "ticks" in BC, and
                                            ;  to transfer control to (HL) if timer hits zero).
                    CAH:                    ;Convert A to two ASCII hex characters, storing
                                            ;  the output in (HL) and (HL+1)
                    Output$Error$Message:   ;Display the 00-byte terminated error message
                                            ;  pointed to by HL. Output is directed only to
                                            ;  those console devices not being used for list
                                            ;  output as well.
                    Request$User$Choice:    ;Display prompt "Enter R, A, I..." and return
                                            ;  single keyboard character (uppercase) in A
       033B C9              RET             ;Dummy
```

Figure 9-5. User-friendly disk-error processor (continued)

Basic Debugging Techniques
Debug Subroutines
Software Tools for Debugging
Bringing Up CP/M for the First Time
Debugging the CP/M Bootstrap
  Loader
Debugging the BIOS
Live Testing a New BIOS

Debugging A New CP/M System

This chapter deals with some of the problems you will face bringing up CP/M on a computer system for the first time or enhancing it once it is up and running on your system.

In the first case, when CP/M does not yet run on your computer, you may be writing the complete BIOS yourself, although you can model what you do on the example BIOS provided on the CP/M release diskette and the example code from Chapter 6.

In the second case, you can extend the existing BIOS by adding code—from the examples in Chapters 8 and 9, code from computer magazines, or code you create yourself. To do this, you will need access to the BIOS source code—a problem if the manufacturer of your computer does not make it available. In general, however, the BIOS source code is included with the system or can be obtained at nominal or no cost. If you cannot obtain the source code, you can, of course, take the bull by the horns and reimplement CP/M on your system. This may require many hours of disassembling the current BIOS machine code to find out how to access all the various ports and how to control the devices to which they are connected.

Although the BIOS is the major component of a new CP/M implementation, remember that it is only the beginning—you can spend the same amount of time and effort getting the bootstrap loader and all the utilities to function.

Basic Debugging Techniques

Before getting involved in the details of how to debug a CP/M implementation, it is worth considering the nature of the task. Some quotations that are appropriate here:

"Program testing can be used to show the presence of bugs, but never to show their absence." —Dijkstra

"We call them bugs because to call them mistakes would be psychologically unacceptable." —Hopkins

"Constants aren't, variables won't." —Osborne

Debugging is the name we give to the process of executing programs and ascertaining whether the programs are running correctly. "Correctly" means in accordance with the mental model we have built of how the program should behave, subject to the constraints imposed by the physical hardware. Therein lies the first of the problems; you and the hardware are the arbiters of correct performance. The hardware is usually unforgiving; if there is a flaw in the way you program it, it will either be dramatically "uncooperative" or not work at all. As for how you perceive the system, several fairly simple tests, along with attempts to use the system for useful work for a few days, will shake the system down fairly well. The most difficult problems will be with intermittent failures or logical contradictions.

Computers are deterministic. That is, if you start from a known state and perform a known series of operations, the computer will always yield the same results. To achieve a known state is not so difficult—resetting the system and clearing memory will do it. Performing a known series of operations just means running the program again, although if you are using interrupts, you cannot truthfully say that exactly the same operations are being performed, because the interrupts will not happen at *exactly* the same time as before.

The "Orville Wright" Approach

Your role in debugging a new CP/M system is comparable to the popular, though untrue, idea of the way the Wright brothers developed flying machines:

build a machine, take it to the top of a hill, throw it off, and, when it crashes, examine the debris to discover what went wrong.

Each time you do an assembly and test, you are building the aircraft and lobbing it off the edge of a cliff. Each time it crashes, you examine the wreckage and try to determine the possible cause.

This is a highly inferential process. With the wreckage as a starting point, you use inference and intuition to extrapolate the real problem and the correction for it.

Built-In Debug Code

The single most important concept that you will need in testing CP/M systems is the same as that used in the modern day "black box" flight recorder. This device is essentially a multi-channel tape recorder that records all of the relevant conditions of the aircraft, its height, altitude, throttle settings, flap settings, and even the voice communications among crew members. If the airplane crashes, investigators can replay the information and understand what happened during the flight.

Applying this concept to debugging CP/M means that you must build into your code some method for recording what it is doing, so that if the system crashes, you can see what it was doing. Make the code tell you what went wrong.

The debug code should be designed at the same time as the rest of the program. Plan the debugging code while the design is still on the drawing board. The source code for debugging should be a permanent part of the BIOS. Use conditional assembly to "IF" out most of the debug code from the final version, or make the code sensitive to a flag in the configuration block so that you can re-enable the debug code at a moment's notice if the system begins to behave strangely.

The more meaningful the debug output data, the less you will have to guess at what is wrong, and therefore the less painful and time-consuming the debugging process will be. Make the output intelligible to others who may use it or yourself several months hence. Data that tells you what is happening is more useful than internal hexadecimal values, particularly if someone else must interpret it or relay it to you over the telephone.

Debug Subroutines

Many programmers do their debugging on a casual "catch as catch can" basis because they are overwhelmed by the task of building the necessary tools. Others are too eager to start on a new program to take a few extra hours or days to build debug subroutines.

To help solve this problem, the following section provides some ready-made debugging tools that can be used "as is." Each of these routines has been thoroughly debugged (there's nothing worse than debug code with bugs in it!) and has been used in actual program testing.

Overall Design Philosophy

Some common methods run through the examples that follow. These include displaying meaningful "captions" (including the specific address that called the debug routine), grouping all debugging code together, preserving the contents of all registers, and setting up the stack area in a standard way.

Debug Code Captions When the contents of registers or memory are output as part of a debugging process, a caption of explanatory text describing the values should be displayed. For example, rather than displaying the contents of the A register like this,

```
A = 1F
```

you can use a meaningful caption such as:

```
Transaction Code A = 1F.
```

When you write additional debugging code, especially if you need to add it to an existing routine, it is cumbersome to have to write the call to the debug routine and then search through the source code to find a convenient place to put an ASCII caption string. A caption string several pages removed from the point where it is referenced makes for problems when you want to relate the debug output on the screen or listing to the source code itself. Therefore, all of the routines that follow allow you to declare the caption strings "in-line" like this:

```
IF          DEBUG
CALL        Debug$Routine
DB          'Caption string here',CR,LF,0
ENDIF
MVI         .....           ;Next instruction
```

All of the following routines that output a caption recognize one specific 8-bit value in the caption string. If they encounter a value of 0ADH (mnemonic for ADdress), they will output the address of the byte following the call to the debug routine. For example,

```
0210        CALL        Debug$Routine
0213        DB          0ADH,'Caption string',0
```

will cause the routine to display the following:

```
0213 Caption string
```

This identifies the point in your program from which the debug routine was called, and thus avoids any possible ambiguity between different calls to the same debug routine with similar captions.

Grouping Debug Code Grouping all the debug code together lends itself to using conditional assembly with IF/ENDIF statements.

Setting Up the Stack Area All of the following routines preserve the CPU registers so that there are no side effects from using them. All of them assume that they can use the stack pointer and that there is sufficient room in the stack area. Hence you will need to declare adequate stack space for your main code and for the debug routines. Fill the stack area with a known pattern like this:

```
       DW    9999H,9999H,9999H,9999H,9999H,9999H,9999H,9999H
       DW    9999H,9999H,9999H,9999H,9999H,9999H,9999H,9999H
       DW    9999H,9999H,9999H,9999H,9999H,9999H,9999H,9999H
Stack$Area:              ;Label the upper end of the area
```

Then, during debugging, you can examine the stack area and determine how much of it is unused. For example, if you looked at the stack area you might see something like this:

```
                       "Low-water mark"
                              v
99 99 99 99 99 99 99 99 99 99 99 99 09 15 43 42
01 29 00 00 1A 2B 10 FF FF 39 02 ED 11 01 37 44
DD 00 00 11 1A 23 31 00 41 AE FE 00 01 10 70 C9
```

Stack area overflow can give arcane bugs; the program seems to leap off into space in a nondeterministic way. By setting up the stack area in this way, you can recognize an overflow condition easily.

Debug Initialization Before you can execute any of the debug subroutines in this chapter, you must make a call to the initialization subroutine, DB$Init. The DB$Init routine sets up some of the internal variables needed by the debug package. You may need to add some of your own initialization code here.

Console Output

Normally, you can use the CONOUT functions either via the BDOS (Function 2), or via the BIOS by calling the jump vector directly. You cannot do this when you need to debug console routines themselves, nor when you need to debug interrupt service routines. In the latter case, if an interrupt pulled control out of the CONOUT routine in the BIOS, you would get unwanted re-entrancy if the debug code again entered the CONOUT driver to display a caption. Therefore, the debug routines have been written to call their own local CONOUT routine, which is called DB$CONOUT. DB$CONOUT can be changed to call the BDOS, the BIOS, or a "private" polled output routine.

A counterpart DB$CONIN routine for console input is provided for essentially the same reasons.

Controlling Debug Output

All output of debug routines in this chapter is controlled by a single master flag, DB$Flag. If this flag is nonzero, debug output will occur; if zero, all output is suppressed.

This flag can be set and cleared from any part of the program you are testing. It is especially useful when you need to debug a subroutine that is called many times from many different places. You can write additional code to enable debug output when certain conditions prevail; for example, when a particular track or sector is about to be written or when a character input buffer is almost full.

Two subroutines, DB$On and DB$Off, are shown that access the debug control flag. These, as their names suggest, turn debug output on and off.

Turning the debug output on and off from within the program can create a confusing display of debug output, lacking any apparent continuity. DB$Off gives you the option of outputting a character string indicating that debug output has been turned off.

Pass Counters

Another method of controlling debug output is to use a *pass counter,* enabling debug output only after control has passed through a particular point in the code a specific number of times.

Two subroutines are provided for this purpose. DBSetPass sets the pass counter to a specific value. DB$Pass decrements this pass count each time control is transferred to it. When the pass count hits zero, the debug control flag DB$Flag is nonzero and debug output begins.

Using pass counter techniques can save you time and effort in tracking down a problem that occurs only after the code has been running for several minutes.

Displaying Contents of Registers and Memory

Figure 10-2 shows a series of display subroutines, the primary one of which is DB$Display. It takes several parameters, depending on the information you want displayed. The generic call to DB$Display is as follows:

```
CALL      DB$Display
DB        Code      <- Indicates the data to be
                       displayed
{DW       Optional additional parameters}
DB        'Caption string',0
```

The codes that can be used in this call are shown in Table 10-1.

The only function that uses additional parameters is DB$Memory. This displays bytes from memory in hexadecimal and ASCII, using the start and finish addresses following the call. Here is an example:

```
CALL    DB$Display
DB      DB$Memory
DW      Start$Address,End$Address
DB      'Caption string',0
```

Table 10-1. Codes for DB$Display

Code	Value displayed
8-bit registers	
DB$F	Condition Flags
DB$A	Register A
DB$B	Register B
DB$C	Register C
DB$D	Register D
DB$E	Register E
DB$H	Register H
DB$L	Register L
Memory	
DB$Memory	Bytes starting and ending at the addresses specified by the two word values following the code value.
16-bit registers	
DB$BC	Register pair BC
DB$DE	Register pair DE
DB$HL	Register pair HL
DB$SP	Stack Pointer
Byte values	
DBBBC	Byte addressed by BC
DBBDE	Byte addressed by DE
DBBHL	Byte addressed by HL
Word values	
DBWBC	Word addressed by BC
DBWDE	Word addressed by DE
DBWHL	Word addressed by HL

Debugging Program Logic

In addition to displaying the contents of registers and memory, you need to display the program's execution path, not in terms of addresses, but in terms of the *problem*. You can do this by displaying debug messages that indicate what decisions have been made by the program as it executes. For example, if your BIOS checks a particular value to see whether the system should read or write on a particular device, the debug routine should display a message like this:

```
Entering Disk Read Routine
```

This is more meaningful than just displaying the function code for the drivers — although you may want to display this as well, in case it has been set to some strange value.

Two subroutines are provided to display debug messages. They are DB$MSG and DB$MSGI. Both of these display text strings are terminated with a byte of 00H. You can see the difference between the two subroutines if you examine the way they are called.

DB$MSG is called like this:

```
LXI   H,Message$Text       ;HL -> text string
CALL  DB$MSG
```

DB$MSGI is called like this:

```
CALL  DB$MSG
DB    0DH,0AH,'Message Text',0 ;In-line
```

DB$MSGI is more convenient to use. If you decide that you need to add a message, you can declare the message immediately following the call. This also helps when you look at the listing, since you can see the complete text at a glance.

Use DB$MSG when the text of the message needs to be selected from a table. Get the address of the text into HL and then call DB$MSG to display it.

Creating Your Own Debug Displays

If you need to build your own special debug display routines, you may find it helpful to incorporate some of the small subroutines in the debug package. The following are the subroutines you may want to use:

DB$CONOUT

Displays the character in the C register.

DB$CONIN

Returns the next keyboard character in A.

DB$CONINU

Returns the next keyboard character in A, converting lowercase letters to uppercase.

DB$DHLH
   Displays contents of HL in hexadecimal.

DB$DAH
   Displays contents of A in hexadecimal.

DB$CAH
   Converts contents of A to hexadecimal and stores in memory pointed at by HL.

DB$Nibble$To$Hex
   Converts the least significant four bits of A into an ASCII hexadecimal character in A.

DB$CRLF
   Displays a CARRIAGE RETURN/LINE FEED.

DB$Colon
   Displays the string " : ".

DB$Blank
   Displays a single space character.

DB$Flag$Save$On
   Saves the current state of the debug output control flag and then sets the flag "on" to enable debug output.

DB$Flag$Restore
   Restores the debug output control flag to the state it was in when the DB$Flag$Save$On routine was last called.

DB$GHV
   Gets a hexadecimal value from the keyboard, displaying a prompt message first. From one to four characters can be specified as the maximum number of characters to be input.

DBATo$Upper
   If the A register contains a lowercase letter, this converts it to an uppercase letter.

Debugging I/O Drivers

Debugging low-level device drivers creates special problems. The major one is that you do not normally want to read and write via actual hardware ports while you are debugging the code—either because doing so would cause strange things to happen to the hardware during the debugging, or because you are developing and debugging the drivers on a system different from the target hardware on which the drivers are to execute.

Before considering the solution, remember that the input and output instructions (IN and OUT) are each two bytes long. The first byte is the operation code

(0DBH for input, 0D3H for output), and the second byte is the port number to "input from" or "output to."

Debug subroutines are provided here to intercept all IN and OUT instructions, displaying the port number and either accepting a hexadecimal value from the console and putting it into the A register (in the case of IN), or displaying the contents of the A register (for the OUT instruction).

IN and OUT instructions can be "trapped" by changing the operation code to one of two RST (restart) instructions. An RST is effectively a single-byte CALL instruction, calling down to a predetermined address in low memory. The debug routines arrange for JMP instructions in low memory to receive control when the correct RST is executed. The code that receives control can pick up the port number, display it, and then accept a hex value for the A register (for IN) or display the current contents of the A register (for OUT). The example subroutines shown later in this chapter use RST 4 in place of IN instructions, RST 5 for OUT.

Wherever you plan to use IN, use the following code:

```
IF          Debug
RST         4
ENDIF
IF          NOT Debug
DB          IN
ENDIF
DB          Port$Number
```

Note that you can use the IN operation code as the operand of a DB statement. The assembler substitutes the correct operation code.

Use the following code wherever you need to use an OUT instruction:

```
IF          Debug
RST         5
ENDIF
IF          NOT Debug
DB          OUT
ENDIF
DB          Port$Number
```

When the RST 4 (IN) instruction is executed, the debug subroutine displays

```
1AB3 : Input from Port 01 : _
```

The "1AB3" is the address in memory of the byte containing the port number. It serves to pinpoint the IN instruction in memory. You can then enter one or two hexadecimal digits. These will be converted and put into the A register before control returns to the main program at the instruction following the byte containing the port number.

When the RST 5 (OUT) instruction is encountered, the debug subroutine displays

```
1AB5 : Output to Port 01 : FF
```

This identifies where the OUT instruction would normally be as well as the port number and the contents of the A register when the RST 5 (OUT) is executed.

Debugging Interrupt Service Routines

You can use a technique similar to that of the RST instruction just described to "fake" an interrupt. You preset the low-memory address for the RST instruction you have chosen for the jump into the interrupt service routine under test.

When the RST instruction is executed, control will be transferred into the interrupt service routine just as though an interrupt had occurred. You will need to intercept any IN or OUT instructions as described above—otherwise the code probably will go into an endless loop.

Before executing the RST instruction to fake the interrupt, load all the registers with known values. For example:

```
MVI     A,0AAH
LXI     B,0BBCCH
LXI     D,0DDEEH
LXI     H,01122H
RST     6          ;Fake interrupt
NOP
```

When control returns from the service routine, you can check to see that it restored all of the registers to their correct values. An interrupt service routine that does not restore all the registers can produce bugs that are very hard to find.

Check, too, that the stack pointer register has been restored and that the service routine did not require too many bytes on the stack.

You also can use the CALL instruction to transfer control to the interrupt service routine in order to fake an interrupt. RST and CALL achieve the same effect, but RST is closer to what happens when a real interrupt occurs. As it is a single-byte instruction, it also is easier to patch in.

Subroutine Listings

Figure 10-1 is a functional index to the source code listing for the debug subroutines shown in Figure 10-2. The listing's commentary defines precisely how each debug subroutine is called.

Figure 10-3 shows the output from the debug testbed.

Software Tools for Debugging

In addition to building in debugging subroutines, you will need one of the following proprietary debug programs:

DDT (Dynamic Debugging Tool)
This program, included with the standard CP/M release, allows you to load programs, set and display memory and registers, trace through your program instruction by instruction, or execute it at full speed, but stopping

Start Line	Functional Component or Routines
00001	Debug subroutine's Testbed
00100	Test register display
00200	Test memory dump display
00300	Test register pair display
00400	Test byte indirect display
00500	Test DB$On/Off
00600	Test DBSetPass and DB$Pass
00700	Test debug input/output
00800	Debug subroutines themselves
01100	DB$Init - initialization
01200	DB$CONINU - get uppercase keyboard character
01300	DB$CONIN - get keyboard character
01400	DB$CONOUT - display character in C
01500	DB$On - enable debug output
01600	DB$Off - disable debug output
01700	DBSetPass - set pass counter
01800	DB$Pass - execute pass point
01900	DB$Display - main debug display routine
02200	Main display processing subroutines
02500	DB$Display$CALLA - display CALL's address
02600	DB$DHLH - display HL in hexadecimal
02700	DB$DAH - display A in hexadecimal
02800	DB$CAH - convert A to hexadecimal in memory
02900	DB$Nibble$To$Hex - convert LS 4 bits of A to hex.
02930	DB$CRLF - display Carriage Return, Line Feed
02938	DB$Colon - display " : "
02946	DB$Blank - display " "
03100	DB$MSGI - display in-line message
03147	DB$MSG - display message addressed by HL
03300	DB$Input - debug INput routine
03500	DB$Output - debug OUTput routine
03700	DB$Flag$Save$On - save debug flag and enable
03800	DB$Flag$Restore - restore debug control flag
03900	DB$GHV - get hexadecimal value from keyboard
04100	DBATo$Upper - convert A to upper case

Figure 10-1. Functional index for Figure 10-2

at certain addresses (called breakpoints). It also has a built-in mini-assembler and disassembler so you do not have to hand assemble any temporary code "patches" you add.

SID (Symbolic Interactive Debug)

Similar to DDT in many ways, SID has enhancements that are helpful if you use Digital Research's MAC (Macro Assembler) or RMAC (Relocating Macro Assembler). Both of these assemblers can be told to output a file

Chapter 10: Debugging a New CP/M System

```
00001
00002
00003          ;
00004          ;       Debug Subroutines
00005          ;
00006          ;<---- NOTE:
00007          ;      The line numbers at the extreme left are included purely
00008          ;      to reference the code from the text.
00009          ;      There are deliberately induced discontinuities
00010          ;      in the numbers in order to allow space for expansion.
00011          ;
00012          ;      Because of the need to test these routines thoroughly,
00013          ;      and in case you wish to make any changes, the testbed
00014          ;      routine for the debug package itself has been left in
00015          ;      in this figure.
00016          ;
00017          ;      Debug testbed
00018          ;
00019   0100          ORG     100H
00020          START:
00021   0100 316B03   LXI     SP,Test$Stack       ;Set up local stack
00022   0103 CDEA04   CALL    DB$Init             ;Initialize the debug package
00023   0106 CD1505   CALL    DB$On               ;Enable debug output
00024                                             ;Simple test of A register display
00025   0109 3EAA     MVI     A,0AAH              ;Preset a value in the A register
00026   010B 01CCBB   LXI     B,0BBCCH            ;Prefill all other registers, partly
00027   010E 11EEDD   LXI     D,0DDEEH            ;  to check the debug display, but
00028   0111 2111FF   LXI     H,0FF11H            ;  also to check register save/restore
00100          ;#
00101          ;      Test register display
00102          ;
00103   0114 B7      ORA     A                    ;Set M-flag, clear Z-flag, set E-flag
00104   0115 37      STC                          ;Set carry
00105   0116 CD5205  CALL    DB$Display           ;Call the debug routine
00106   0119 00      DB      DB$F
00107   011A 466C616773  DB  'Flags',0
00108          ;
00109   0120 CD5205  CALL    DB$Display           ;Call the debug routine
00110   0123 02      DB      DB$A
00111   0124 4120526567  DB  'A Register',0
00112          ;
00113   012F CD5205  CALL    DB$Display           ;Call the debug routine
00114   0132 04      DB      DB$B
00115   0133 4220526567  DB  'B Register',0
00116          ;
00117   013E CD5205  CALL    DB$Display           ;Call the debug routine
00118   0141 06      DB      DB$C
00119   0142 4320526567  DB  'C Register',0
00120          ;
00121   014D CD5205  CALL    DB$Display           ;Call the debug routine
00122   0150 08      DB      DB$D
00123   0151 4420526567  DB  'D Register',0
00124          ;
00125   015C CD5205  CALL    DB$Display           ;Call the debug routine
00126   015F 0A      DB      DB$E
00127   0160 4520526567  DB  'E Register',0
00128          ;
00129   016B CD5205  CALL    DB$Display           ;Call the debug routine
00130   016E 0C      DB      DB$H
00131   016F 4820526567  DB  'H Register',0
00132          ;
00133   017A CD5205  CALL    DB$Display           ;Call the debug routine
00134   017D 0E      DB      DB$L
00135   017E 4C20526567  DB  'L Register',0
00200          ;#
00201          ;      Test Memory Dump Display
00202          ;
00203   0189 CD5205  CALL    DB$Display
00204   018C 18      DB      DB$M                 ;Dump memory
00205   018D 08012801 DW     108H,128H            ;Check start/end at nonmultiples
00206   0191 4D656D6F72 DB   'Memory Dump #1',0   ;  of 10H
00207          ;
00208   01A0 CD5205  CALL    DB$Display
00209   01A3 18      DB      DB$M                 ;Dump memory
00210   01A4 00011F01 DW     100H,11FH            ;Check start and end on displayed
00211   01A8 4D656D6F72 DB   'Memory Dump #2',0   ;  line boundaries
00212          ;
```

Figure 10-2.   Debug subroutines

```
00213   01B7 CD5205              CALL    DB$Display
00214   01BA 18                  DB      DB$M                    ;Dump memory
00215   01BB 01010001            DW      101H,100H               ;Check error handling where
00216   01BF 4D656D6F72          DB      'Memory Dump #3',0      ;  start > end address
00217                    ;
00218   01CE CD5205              CALL    DB$Display
00219   01D1 18                  DB      DB$M                    ;Dump memory
00220   01D2 00010001            DW      100H,100H               ;Check end-case of single byte
00221   01D6 4D656D6F72          DB      'Memory Dump #4',0      ;  output
00300                    ;#
00301                    ;       Test register pair display
00302                    ;
00303   01E5 CD5205              CALL    DB$Display              ;Call the debug routine
00304   01E8 10                  DB      DB$BC
00305   01E9 4243205265          DB      'BC Register',0
00306                    ;
00307   01F5 CD5205              CALL    DB$Display              ;Call the debug routine
00308   01F8 12                  DB      DB$DE
00309   01F9 4445205265          DB      'DE Register',0
00310                    ;
00311   0205 CD5205              CALL    DB$Display              ;Call the debug routine
00312   0208 14                  DB      DB$HL
00313   0209 484C205265          DB      'HL Register',0
00314                    ;
00315   0215 CD5205              CALL    DB$Display              ;Call the debug routine
00316   0218 16                  DB      DB$SP
00317   0219 5350205265          DB      'SP Register',0
00318                    ;
00319   0225 013203              LXI     B,Byte$BC               ;Set up registers for byte tests
00320   0228 113303              LXI     D,Byte$DE
00321   022B 213403              LXI     H,Byte$HL
00400                    ;#
00401                    ;       Test byte indirect display
00402                    ;
00403   022E CD5205              CALL    DB$Display              ;Call the debug routine
00404   0231 1A                  DB      DB$B$BC
00405   0232 4279746520          DB      'Byte at (BC)',0
00406                    ;
00407   023F CD5205              CALL    DB$Display              ;Call the debug routine
00408   0242 1C                  DB      DB$B$DE
00409   0243 4279746520          DB      'Byte at (DE)',0
00410                    ;
00411   0250 CD5205              CALL    DB$Display              ;Call the debug routine
00412   0253 1E                  DB      DB$B$HL
00413   0254 4279746520          DB      'Byte at (HL)',0
00414                    ;
00415   0261 013503              LXI     B,Word$BC               ;Set up the registers for word tests
00416   0264 113703              LXI     D,Word$DE
00417   0267 213903              LXI     H,Word$HL
00418                    ;
00419   026A CD5205              CALL    DB$Display              ;Call the debug routine
00420   026D 20                  DB      DB$W$BC
00421   026E 576F726420          DB      'Word at (BC)',0
00422                    ;
00423   027B CD5205              CALL    DB$Display              ;Call the debug routine
00424   027E 22                  DB      DB$W$DE
00425   027F 576F726420          DB      'Word at (DE)',0
00426                    ;
00427   028C CD5205              CALL    DB$Display              ;Call the debug routine
00428   028F 24                  DB      DB$W$HL
00429   0290 576F726420          DB      'Word at (HL)',0
00500                    ;#
00501                    ;       Test DB$On/Off
00502                    ;
00503   029D CD1D05              CALL    DB$Off                  ;Disable debug output
00504   02A0 CDD607              CALL    DB$MSGI                 ;Display in-line message
00505   02A3 0D0A546869          DB      0DH,0AH,'This message should NOT appear',0
00506                    ;
00507   02C4 CD1505              CALL    DB$On
00508   02C7 CDD607              CALL    DB$MSGI
00509   02CA 0D0A446562          DB      0DH,0AH,'Debug output has been re-enabled.',0
00600                    ;#
00601                    ;       Test pass count logic
00602                    ;
```

Figure 10-2. (Continued)

Chapter 10: Debugging a New CP/M System

```
00603    02EE CD1D05           CALL    DB$Off              ;Disable debug output
00604    02F1 CD2405           CALL    DB$Set$Pass         ;Set pass count
00605    02F4 1E00             DW      30
00606                  ;
00607    02F6 3E22             MVI     A,34                ;Set loop counter greater than pass
00608                                                      ;  counter
00609                  Test$Pass$Loop:
00610    02F8 CD3505           CALL    DB$Pass             ;Decrement pass count
00611    02FB CDD607           CALL    DB$MSGI             ;Display in-line message
00612    02FE 0D0A546869       DB      0DH,0AH,'This message should display 5 times',0
00613    0324 3D               DCR     A
00614    0325 C2F802           JNZ     Test$Pass$Loop
00700                  ;#
00701                  ;      Test debug input/output
00702                  ;
00703    0328 CD1D05           CALL    DB$Off              ;Check that debug IN/OUT
00704                                                      ;  must still occur when debug
00705                                                      ;  output is disabled.
00706    032B E7               RST     4                   ;Debug input
00707    032C 11               DB      11H                 ;Port number
00708    032D EF               RST     5                   ;Debug output (value return from input)
00709    032E 22               DB      22H                 ;Port number
00710                  ;
00711    032F C30000           JMP     0                   ;Warm boot at end of testbed
00712                  ;
00713                  ;
00714                  ;      Dummy values for byte and word displays
00715    0332 BC      Byte$BC:         DB      0BCH
00716    0333 DE      Byte$DE:         DB      0DEH
00717    0334 F1      Byte$HL:         DB      0F1H
00718                  ;
00719    0335 0C0B    Word$BC:         DW      0B0CH
00720    0337 0E0D    Word$DE:         DW      0D0EH
00721    0339 010F    Word$HL:         DW      0F01H
00722                  ;
00723    033B 9999999999        DW      9999H,9999H,9999H,9999H,9999H,9999H,9999H
00724    034B 9999999999        DW      9999H,9999H,9999H,9999H,9999H,9999H,9999H
00725    035B 9999999999        DW      9999H,9999H,9999H,9999H,9999H,9999H,9999H
00726                  Test$Stack:
00727                  ;
00728                  ;
00729                  ;
00730    0400                  ORG     400H                ;To avoid unnecessary listings
00731                                                      ;  when only the testbed changes
00732                  ;--------------------------------------------------------------
00800                  ;#
00801                  ;
00802                  ;      Debug subroutines
00803                  ;
00804                  ;
00805                  ;      Equates for DB$Display codes
00806                  ;      These equates are the offsets down the table of addresses
00807                  ;      for various subroutines to be used.
00808                  ;
00809    0000 =        DB$F    EQU     00                  ;Flags
00810    0002 =        DB$A    EQU     02                  ;A register
00811    0004 =        DB$B    EQU     04                  ;B
00812    0006 =        DB$C    EQU     06                  ;C
00813    0008 =        DB$D    EQU     08                  ;D
00814    000A =        DB$E    EQU     10                  ;E
00815    000C =        DB$H    EQU     12                  ;H
00816    000E =        DB$L    EQU     14                  ;L
00817    0010 =        DB$BC   EQU     16                  ;BC
00818    0012 =        DB$DE   EQU     18                  ;DE
00819    0014 =        DB$HL   EQU     20                  ;HL
00820    0016 =        DB$SP   EQU     22                  ;Stack pointer
00821    0018 =        DB$M    EQU     24                  ;Memory
00822    001A =        DB$B$BC EQU     26                  ;(BC)
00823    001C =        DB$B$DE EQU     28                  ;(DE)
00824    001E =        DB$B$HL EQU     30                  ;(HL)
00825    0020 =        DB$W$BC EQU     32                  ;(BC+1),(BC)
00826    0022 =        DB$W$DE EQU     34                  ;(DE+1),(DE)
00827    0024 =        DB$W$HL EQU     36                  ;(HL+1),(HL)
00828                  ;
00829                  ;
00830                  ;      Equates
00831    0020 =        RST4    EQU     20H      ;Address for RST 4 - IN instruction
```

Figure 10-2. (Continued)

```
00832   0028 =           RST5            EQU     28H             ;Address for RST 5 - OUT instruction
00833                    ;
00834   0001 =           B$CONIN         EQU     1               ;BDOS CONIN function code
00835   0002 =           B$CONOUT        EQU     2               ;BDOS CONOUT function code
00836   000A =           B$READCONS      EQU     10              ;BDOS read console function code
00837   0005 =           BDOS            EQU     5               ;BDOS entry point
00838                    ;
00839   0000 =           False           EQU     0
00840   FFFF =           True            EQU     NOT False
00841                    ;
00842                                                            ;Equates to specify how DB$CONOUT
00843                                                            ;  and DB$CONIN should perform
00844                                                            ;  their input/output
00845   0000 =           DB$Polled$IO    EQU     False           ;)
00846   0000 =           DB$BIOS$IO      EQU     False           ;) Only one must be true
00847   FFFF =           DB$BDOS$IO      EQU     True            ;)
00848                    ;
00849                                                            ;Equates for polled I/O
00850   0001 =           DB$Status$Port  EQU     01H             ;Console status port
00851   0002 =           DB$Data$Port    EQU     02H             ;Console data port
00852                    ;
00853   0002 =           DB$Input$Ready  EQU     0000$0010B      ;Incoming data ready
00854   0001 =           DB$Output$Ready EQU     0000$0001B      ;Ready for output
00855                    ;
00856                                                            ;Data for BIOS I/O
00857   0400 C3          BIOS$CONIN:     DB      JMP             ;The initialization routine sets these
00858   0401 0000                        DW      0               ;  two JMP addresses into the BIOS
00859   0403 C3          BIOS$CONOUT:    DB      JMP
00860   0404 0000                        DW      0
00861                    ;
00862                    ;       Main debug variables and constants
00863                    ;
00864   0406 00          DB$Flag:        DB      0               ;Main debug control flag
00865                                                            ;  When this flag is nonzero, all debug
00866                                                            ;  output will be made. When zero, all
00867                                                            ;  debug output will be suppressed.
00868                                                            ;  It is altered either directly by the user
00869                                                            ;  or using the routines DB$On, DB$Off and
00870                                                            ;  DB$Pass.
00871                    ;
00872   0407 0000        DB$Pass$Count:  DW      0               ;Pass counter
00873                                                            ;  When this is nonzero, calls to DB$Pass
00874                                                            ;  decrement it by one. When it reaches
00875                                                            ;  zero, the debug control flag, DB$Flag,
00876                                                            ;  is set nonzero, thereby enabling
00877                                                            ;  debug output.
00878                    ;
00879                    DB$Save$HL:                             ;Save area for HL
00880   0409 00          DB$Save$L:      DB      0
00881   040A 00          DB$Save$H:      DB      0
00882                    ;
00883   040B 0000        DB$Save$SP:     DW      0               ;Save area for stack pointer
00884   040D 0000        DB$Save$RA:     DW      0               ;Save area for return address
00885   040F 0000        DB$Call$Address: DW     0               ;   Starts out the same as DB$Save$RA
00886                                                            ;   but DB$Save$RA gets updated during
00887                                                            ;   debug processing. This value is
00888                                                            ;   output ahead of the caption
00889                    DB$Start$Address:                       ;Start address for memory display
00890   0411 0000                        DW      0
00891                    DB$End$Address:                         ;End address for memory display
00892   0413 0000                        DW      0
00893                    DB$Display$Code:                        ;Display code requested
00894   0415 00                          DB      0
00895                    ;
00896                    ;                                       ;Stack area
00897                    ;
00898   0416 9999999999                  DW      9999H,9999H,9999H,9999H,9999H,9999H,9999H,9999H
00899   0426 9999999999                  DW      9999H,9999H,9999H,9999H,9999H,9999H,9999H
00900   0436 9999999999                  DW      9999H,9999H,9999H,9999H,9999H,9999H,9999H
00901   0446 00          DB$Save$E:      DB      0               ;E register
00902   0447 00          DB$Save$D:      DB      0               ;D register
00903   0448 00          DB$Save$C:      DB      0               ;C register
00904   0449 00          DB$Save$B:      DB      0               ;B register
00905   044A 00          DB$Save$F:      DB      0               ;Flags
00906   044B 00          DB$Save$A:      DB      0               ;A register
00907                    DB$Stack:                               ;Debug stack area
00908                                                            ;  The registers in the stack area are PUSHed
00909                                                            ;  onto the stack and accessed directly.
```

Figure 10-2.   (Continued)

```
00910          ;
00911          ;          Register caption messages
00912          ;
00913          ;          The table below, indexed by the Display$Code is used to access
00914          ;          the register caption string.
00915          ;
00916                     DB$Register$Captions:
00917  044C 7204          DW      DB$F$RC         ;Flags
00918  044E 7804          DW      DB$A$RC         ;A register
00919  0450 7A04          DW      DB$B$RC         ;B
00920  0452 7C04          DW      DB$C$RC         ;C
00921  0454 7E04          DW      DB$D$RC         ;D
00922  0456 8004          DW      DB$E$RC         ;E
00923  0458 8204          DW      DB$H$RC         ;H
00924  045A 8404          DW      DB$L$RC         ;L
00925  045C 8604          DW      DB$BC$RC        ;BC
00926  045E 8904          DW      DB$DE$RC        ;DE
00927  0460 8C04          DW      DB$HL$RC        ;HL
00928  0462 8F04          DW      DB$SP$RC        ;Stack pointer
00929  0464 9204          DW      DB$M$RC         ;Memory
00930  0466 A604          DW      DB$B$BC$RC      ;(BC)
00931  0468 AB04          DW      DB$B$DE$RC      ;(DE)
00932  046A B004          DW      DB$B$HL$RC      ;(HL)
00933  046C B504          DW      DB$W$BC$RC      ;(BC+1),(BC)
00934  046E C104          DW      DB$W$DE$RC      ;(DE+1),(DE)
00935  0470 CD04          DW      DB$W$HL$RC      ;(HL+1),(HL)
00936          ;
00937  0472 466C616773 DB$F$RC:    DB    'Flags',0     ;Flags
00938  0478 4100       DB$A$RC:    DB    'A',0         ;A register
00939  047A 4200       DB$B$RC:    DB    'B',0         ;B
00940  047C 4300       DB$C$RC:    DB    'C',0         ;C
00941  047E 4400       DB$D$RC:    DB    'D',0         ;D
00942  0480 4500       DB$E$RC:    DB    'E',0         ;E
00943  0482 4800       DB$H$RC:    DB    'H',0         ;H
00944  0484 4C00       DB$L$RC:    DB    'L',0         ;L
00945  0486 424300     DB$BC$RC:   DB    'BC',0        ;BC
00946  0489 444500     DB$DE$RC:   DB    'DE',0        ;DE
00947  048C 484C00     DB$HL$RC:   DB    'HL',0        ;HL
00948  048F 535000     DB$SP$RC:   DB    'SP',0        ;Stack pointer
00949  0492 5374617274 DB$M$RC:    DB    'Start, End Address ',0 ;Memory
00950  04A6 2842432900 DB$B$BC$RC: DB    '(BC)',0      ;(BC)
00951  04AB 2844452900 DB$B$DE$RC: DB    '(DE)',0      ;(DE)
00952  04B0 28484C2900 DB$B$HL$RC: DB    '(HL)',0      ;(HL)
00953  04B5 2842432B31 DB$W$BC$RC: DB    '(BC+1),(BC)',0 ;(BC+1),(BC)
00954  04C1 2844452B31 DB$W$DE$RC: DB    '(DE+1),(DE)',0 ;(DE+1),(DE)
00955  04CD 28484C2B31 DB$W$HL$RC: DB    '(HL+1),(HL)',0 ;(HL+1),(HL)
00956          ;
00957          ;
00958          ;          Flags message
00959  04D9 43785A784D DB$Flags$Msg: DB  'CxZxMxExIx',0 ;Compatible with DDT's display
00960          ;
00961          ;          Flags masks used to test user's flag byte
00962          ;
00963                    DB$Flag$Masks:
00964  04E4 01           DB      0000$0001B      ;Carry
00965  04E5 40           DB      0100$0000B      ;Zero
00966  04E6 80           DB      1000$0000B      ;Minus
00967  04E7 04           DB      0000$0100B      ;Even parity
00968  04E8 10           DB      0001$0000B      ;Interdigit carry (aux carry)
00969  04E9 00           DB      0               ;Terminator
01100          ;#
01101          ;         DB$Init
01102          ;         This routine initializes the debug package.
01103          ;
01104                    DB$Init:
01105                    IF      DB$BIOS$IO      ;Use BIOS for CONIN/CONOUT
01106                    LHLD    1               ;Get warm boot address from base
01107                                             ; page. H = BIOS jump vector page
01108                    MVI     L,09H           ;Get CONIN offset in jump vector
01109                    SHLD    BIOS$CONIN + 1  ;Set up address
01110                    MVI     L,0CH           ;Get CONOUT offset in jump vector
01111                    SHLD    BIOS$CONOUT + 1
01112                    ENDIF
01113
01114                                            ;Set up JMP instructions to receive control
01115                                            ; when an RST instruction is executed
01116  04EA 3EC3         MVI     A,JMP           ;Set JMP instructions at RST points
```

Figure 10-2. (Continued)

```
01117   04EC 322000          STA     RST4
01118   04EF 322800          STA     RST5
01119   04F2 211A08          LXI     H,DB$Input       ;Address of fake input routine
01120   04F5 222100          SHLD    RST4 + 1
01121   04F8 216C08          LXI     H,DB$Output      ;Address of fake output routine
01122   04FB 222900          SHLD    RST5 + 1
01123
01124   04FE C9              RET
01200                ;#
01201                ;       DB$CONINU
01202                ;       This routine returns the next character from the console,
01203                ;       but converting "a" to "z" to uppercase letters.
01204                ;
01205                DB$CONINU:
01206   04FF CD0505          CALL    DB$CONIN         ;Get character from keyboard
01207   0502 C31B09          JMP     DB$A$To$Upper    ;Fold to upper and return
01300                ;#
01301                ;       DB$CONIN
01302                ;       This routine returns the next character from the console.
01303                ;       According to the setting of equates, it uses simple
01304                ;       polled I/O, the BDOS (function 2) or the BIOS.
01305                ;
01306                ;       Exit parameters
01307                ;
01308                ;               A = character from console
01309                ;
01310                DB$CONIN:
01311                        IF      DB$Polled$IO     ;Simple polled input
01312                        IN      DB$Status$Port   ;Check if incoming data
01313                        ANI     DB$Input$Ready
01314                        JZ      DB$CONIN         ;No
01315                        IN      DB$Data$Port     ;Input data character
01316                        PUSH    PSW              ;Save data character
01317                        MOV     C,A              ;Ready for output
01318                        CALL    DB$CONOUT        ;Echo it back
01319                        POP     PSW              ;Recover data character
01320                        RET
01321                        ENDIF
01322
01323                        IF      DB$BDOS$IO       ;Use BDOS for input
01324   0505 0E01             MVI     C,B$CONIN       ;Read console
01325   0507 C30500           JMP     BDOS            ;BDOS returns to our caller
01326                        ENDIF
01327
01328                        IF      DB$BIOS$IO       ;Use BIOS for input
01329                        JMP     BIOS$CONIN       ;This was set up during BIOS
01330                                                 ; initialization
01331                        ENDIF
01332
01400                ;#
01401                ;       DB$CONOUT
01402                ;       This routine outputs the character in the C register to the
01403                ;       console, using simple polled I/O, the BDOS or the BIOS.
01404                ;
01405                ;       Entry parameters
01406                ;               A = byte to be output
01407                ;
01408                DB$CONOUT:
01409   050A 3A0604          LDA     DB$Flag          ;Check if debug output enabled
01410   050D B7              ORA     A
01411   050E C8              RZ                       ;Ignore output if disabled
01412
01413                        IF      DB$Polled$IO     ;Use simple polled output
01414                        IN      DB$Status$Port   ;Check if ready for output
01415                        ANI     DB$Output$Ready
01416                        JZ      DB$CONOUT        ;No
01417                        MOV     A,C              ;Get data byte
01418                        OUT     DB$Data$Port
01419                        RET
01420                        ENDIF
01421
01422                        IF      DB$BDOS$IO       ;Use BDOS for output
01423   050F 59               MOV     E,C             ;Move into correct register
01424   0510 0E02             MVI     C,B$CONOUT
01425   0512 C30500           JMP     BDOS            ;BDOS returns to our caller
01426                        ENDIF
01427
01428                        IF      DB$BIOS$IO       ;Use BIOS for output
```

Figure 10-2. (Continued)

```
01429                           MOV     A,C                 ;Move into correct register
01430                           JMP     BIOS$CONOUT         ;Set up during debug initialization
01431                           ENDIF
01500           ;#
01501           ;
01502           ;       DB$On
01503           ;       This routine enables all debug output by setting the
01504           ;       DB$Flag nonzero.
01505           ;
01506           DB$On:
01507  0515 F5          PUSH    PSW                 ;Preserve registers
01508  0516 3EFF        MVI     A,0FFH
01509  0518 320604      STA     DB$Flag
01510  051B F1          POP     PSW                 ;Set control flag on
01511  051C C9          RET
01600           ;#
01601           ;
01602           ;       DB$Off
01603           ;       This routine disables all debug output by setting the
01604           ;       DB$Flag to zero.
01605           ;
01606           DB$Off:
01607  051D F5          PUSH    PSW                 ;Preserve registers
01608  051E AF          XRA     A
01609  051F 320604      STA     DB$Flag
01610  0522 F1          POP     PSW                 ;Clear control flag
01611  0523 C9          RET
01700           ;#
01701           ;
01702           ;       DB$Set$Pass
01703           ;       This routine sets the pass counter. Subsequent calls to DB$Pass
01704           ;       decrement the count, and when it reaches 0, debug output
01705           ;       is enabled.
01706           ;
01707           ;       Calling sequence
01708           ;
01709           ;               CALL    DB$Set$Pass
01710           ;               DW      Pass$Count$Value
01711           ;
01712           DB$Set$Pass:
01713  0524 220904      SHLD    DB$Save$HL          ;Preserve user's HL
01714  0527 E1          POP     H                   ;Recover return address
01715  0528 D5          PUSH    D                   ;Preserve user's DE
01716  0529 5E          MOV     E,M                 ;Get LS byte of count
01717  052A 23          INX     H                   ;Update pointer
01718  052B 56          MOV     D,M                 ;Get MS byte
01719  052C 23          INX     H                   ;HL points to return address
01720  052D EB          XCHG                        ;HL = pass counter
01721  052E 220704      SHLD    DB$Pass$Count       ;Set debug pass counter
01722  0531 EB          XCHG                        ;HL points to return address
01723  0532 D1          POP     D                   ;Recover user's DE
01724  0533 E3          XTHL                        ;Recover user's HL and set
01725                                               ; return address on top of stack
01726  0534 C9          RET
01800           ;#
01801           ;
01802           ;       DB$Pass
01803           ;       This routine decrements the debug pass counter -
01804           ;       if the result is negative, it takes no further action.
01805           ;       If the result is zero, it sets the debug control flag nonzero
01806           ;       to enable debug output.
01807           ;
01808           DB$Pass:
01809  0535 F5          PUSH    PSW                 ;Save user's registers
01810  0536 E5          PUSH    H
01811  0537 2A0704      LHLD    DB$Pass$Count       ;Get pass count
01812  053A 2B          DCX     H
01813  053B 7C          MOV     A,H                 ;Check if count now negative
01814  053C B7          ORA     A
01815  053D FA4705      JM      DB$Pass$x           ;Yes, take no further action
01816  0540 220704      SHLD    DB$Pass$Count       ;Save downdated count
01817  0543 B5          ORA     L                   ;Check if count now zero
01818  0544 CA4A05      JZ      DB$Pass$ED          ;Yes, enable debug
01819           DB$Pass$x:
01820  0547 E1          POP     H                   ;Recover user's registers
01821  0548 F1          POP     PSW
01822  0549 C9          RET
```

Figure 10-2. (Continued)

```
01823                          ;
01824                          DB$Pass$Ed:                          ;Enable debug
01825          054A 3EFF                MVI    A,0FFH
01826          054C 320604             STA    DB$Flag              ;Set debug control flag
01827          054F C34705             JMP    DB$Pass$x
01900                          ;#
01901                          ;
01902                          ;       DB$Display
01903                          ;       This is the primary debug display routine.
01904                          ;
01905                          ;       Calling sequence
01906                          ;
01907                          ;               CALL    DB$Display
01908                          ;               DB      Display$Code
01909                          ;               DB      'Caption String',0
01910                          ;
01911                          ;       Display code identifies which register(s) are to be
01912                          ;       displayed.
01913                          ;
01914                          ;       When the display code specifies a block of memory
01915                          ;       the sequence is:
01916                          ;
01917                          ;               CALL    DB$Display
01918                          ;               DB      Display$Code
01919                          ;               DW      Start$Address,End$Address
01920                          ;               DB      'Caption String',0
01921                          ;
01922                          DB$Display:
01923                          ;
01924                          DB$Display$Enabled:
01925          0552 220904             SHLD   DB$Save$HL            ;Save user's HL
01926
01927          0555 E3                 XTHL                          ;Get return address from stack
01928          0556 220D04             SHLD   DB$Save$RA            ;This gets updated by debug code
01929          0559 E5                 PUSH   H                     ;Save return address temporarily
01930          055A 2B                 DCX    H                     ;Subtract 3 to address call instruction
01931          055B 2B                 DCX    H                     ;  itself
01932          055C 2B                 DCX    H
01933          055D 220F04             SHLD   DB$Call$Address       ;Save actual address of CALL
01934          0560 E1                 POP    H                     ;Recover return address
01935
01936          0561 F5                 PUSH   PSW                   ;Temporarily save flags to avoid
01937                                                               ;  them being changed by DAD SP
01938          0562 210000             LXI    H,0                   ;Preserve stack pointer
01939          0565 39                 DAD    SP
01940          0566 23                 INX    H                     ;Correct for extra PUSH PSW needed
01941          0567 23                 INX    H                     ;  to save the flags
01942          0568 220B04             SHLD   DB$Save$SP
01943          056B F1                 POP    PSW                   ;Recover flags
01944
01945          056C 314C04             LXI    SP,DB$Stack           ;Switch to local stack
01946
01947          056F F5                 PUSH   PSW                   ;Save other user's registers
01948          0570 C5                 PUSH   B                     ;The stack area is specially laid
01949          0571 D5                 PUSH   D                     ;  out to access these registers
01950
01951          0572 2A0D04             LHLD   DB$Save$RA            ;Get return address
01952          0575 7E                 MOV    A,M                   ;Get display code
01953          0576 321504             STA    DB$Display$Code
01954          0579 23                 INX    H                     ;Update return address
01955
01956          057A FE18                CPI    DB$M                  ;Check if memory to be displayed
01957          057C C29105             JNZ    DB$Not$Memory
01958          057F 5E                 MOV    E,M                   ;Get DE = start address
01959          0580 23                 INX    H
01960          0581 56                 MOV    D,M
01961          0582 23                 INX    H
01962          0583 EB                 XCHG                          ;HL = start address
01963          0584 221104             SHLD   DB$Start$Address
01964          0587 EB                 XCHG                          ;HL -> end address
01965          0588 5E                 MOV    E,M                   ;Get DE = end address
01966          0589 23                 INX    H
01967          058A 56                 MOV    D,M
01968          058B 23                 INX    H
01969          058C EB                 XCHG                          ;HL = end address, DE -> caption
01970          058D 221304             SHLD   DB$End$Address
01971          0590 EB                 XCHG                          ;HL -> caption string
```

Figure 10-2. (Continued)

Chapter 10: Debugging a New CP/M System

```
01972                    DB$Not$Memory:
01973             ;
01974             ;      Output preamble and caption string
01975             ;      The format for everything except memory display is:
01976             ;
01977             ;         nnnn : Caption String : RC = vvvv
01978             ;                ^                ^
01979             ;           Call Address         :   Value
01980             ;                          Register Caption (A, B, C...)
01981             ;
01982             ;      A carriage return, line feed is output at the start of the
01983             ;      message - but NOT at the end.
01984             ;
01985             ;      Memory displays look like :
01986             ;
01987             ; nnnn : Caption String : Start, End  ssss, eeee
01988             ; ssss : hh hh hh hh hh hh hh hh hh hh hh hh hh hh hh hh : cccc cccc cccc cccc
01989             ;
01990
01991   0591 E5            PUSH    H                      ;Save pointer to caption string
01992   0592 CDC107        CALL    DB$CRLF                ;Display carriage return, line feed
01993   0595 CD7C07        CALL    DB$Display$CALLA       ;Display DB$Call$Address in hex.
01994
01995   0598 E1            POP     H                      ;Recover pointer to caption string
01996                    DB$Display$Caption:              ;HL -> caption string
01997   0599 7E            MOV     A,M                    ;Get character
01998   059A 23            INX     H
01999   059B B7            ORA     A                      ;Check if end of string
02000   059C CAA805        JZ      DB$End$Caption         ;Yes
02001
02002   059F E5            PUSH    H                      ;Save string pointer
02003   05A0 4F            MOV     C,A                    ;Ready for output
02004   05A1 CD0A05        CALL    DB$CONOUT              ;Display character
02005   05A4 E1            POP     H                      ;Recover string pointer
02006   05A5 C39905        JMP     DB$Display$Caption     ;Go back for next character
02007             ;
02008                    DB$End$Caption:
02009   05A8 220D04        SHLD    DB$Save$RA             ;Save updated return address
02010
02011   05AB CDC807        CALL    DB$Colon               ;Display ´ : ´
02012
02013                                                     ;Display register caption
02014   05AE 3A1504        LDA     DB$Display$Code        ;Get user´s display code
02015   05B1 5F            MOV     E,A                    ;Make display code into word
02016   05B2 1600          MVI     D,0
02017   05B4 D5            PUSH    D                      ;Save word value for later
02018
02019   05B5 FE18          CPI     DB$M                   ;Memory display is a special case
02020   05B7 CACF05        JZ      DB$Display$Mem$Caption ;Yes
02021
02022   05BA 214C04        LXI     H,DB$Register$Captions ;Make pointer to address in table
02023   05BD 19            DAD     D                      ;HL -> word containing address of
02024                                                     ;  register caption
02025   05BE 5E            MOV     E,M                    ;Get LS byte of address
02026   05BF 23            INX     H
02027   05C0 56            MOV     D,M
02028   05C1 EB            XCHG                           ;DE -> register caption string
02029                                                     ;HL -> register caption string
02030   05C2 CDEE07        CALL    DB$MSG                 ;Display message addressed by HL
02031   05C5 CDD607        CALL    DB$MSGI                ;Display in-line message
02032   05C8 203D2000      DB      ´ = ´,0
02033   05CC C3ED05        JMP     DB$Select$Routine      ;Go to correct processor
02034             ;
02035                    DB$Display$Mem$Caption:          ;The memory display requires a special
02036                                                     ;  caption with the start and end
02037                                                     ;  addresses
02038   05CF 219204        LXI     H,DB$M$RC              ;Display specific caption
02039   05D2 CDEE07        CALL    DB$MSG
02040   05D5 CDC807        CALL    DB$Colon               ;Display ´ : ´
02041
02042   05D8 2A1104        LHLD    DB$Start$Address       ;Display start address
02043   05DB CD8707        CALL    DB$DHLH                ;Display HL in hex.
02044
02045   05DE CDD607        CALL    DB$MSGI                ;Display in-line message
02046   05E1 2C2000        DB      ´, ´,0
02047
02048   05E4 2A1304        LHLD    DB$End$Address         ;Get end address
```

Figure 10-2. (Continued)

```
02049   05E7 CD8707          CALL    DB$DHLH         ;Display HL in hex.
02050   05EA CDC107          CALL    DB$CRLF         ;Display carriage return, line feed
02051                                                ;Drop into select routine
02052                DB$Select$Routine:
02053   05ED D1              POP     D               ;Recover word value Display$Code
02054   05EE 210A06          LXI     H,DB$Display$Table
02055   05F1 19              DAD     D               ;HL -> address of code to process
02056                                                ;    display requirements
02057   05F2 5E              MOV     E,M             ;Get LS byte of address
02058   05F3 23              INX     H               ;Update pointer
02059   05F4 56              MOV     D,M             ;Get MS byte of address
02060   05F5 EB              XCHG                    ;HL -> code
02061
02062   05F6 11FB05          LXI     D,DB$Exit       ;Fake link on stack
02063   05F9 D5              PUSH    D
02064   05FA E9              PCHL                    ;"CALL" display processor
02065                ;
02066                DB$Exit:                        ;Return to the user
02067   05FB D1              POP     D               ;Recover user's registers saved
02068   05FC C1              POP     B               ;   on local debug stack
02069   05FD F1              POP     PSW
02070   05FE 2A0B04          LHLD    DB$Save$SP      ;Revert to user's stack
02071   0601 F9              SPHL
02072   0602 2A0D04          LHLD    DB$Save$RA      ;Get updated return address (bypasses
02073                                                ;   in-line parameters)
02074   0605 E3              XTHL                    ;Replace on top of user's stack
02075   0606 2A0904          LHLD    DB$Save$HL      ;Get user's HL
02076   0609 C9              RET                     ;Transfer to correct return address
02077
02078
02079                DB$Display$Table:
02080   060A 3006            DW      DP$F            ;Flags
02081   060C 5A06            DW      DP$A            ;A register
02082   060E 5A06            DW      DP$B            ;B
02083   0610 6006            DW      DP$C            ;C
02084   0612 6606            DW      DP$D            ;D
02085   0614 6C06            DW      DP$E            ;E
02086   0616 7206            DW      DP$H            ;H
02087   0618 7806            DW      DP$L            ;L
02088   061A 7E06            DW      DP$BC           ;BC
02089   061C 8406            DW      DP$DE           ;DE
02090   061E 8A06            DW      DP$HL           ;HL
02091   0620 9006            DW      DP$SP           ;Stack pointer
02092   0622 9606            DW      DP$M            ;Memory
02093   0624 4907            DW      DP$B$BC         ;(BC)
02094   0626 5007            DW      DP$B$DE         ;(DE)
02095   0628 5707            DW      DP$B$HL         ;(HL)
02096   062A 5E07            DW      DP$W$BC         ;(BC+1),(BC)
02097   062C 6807            DW      DP$W$DE         ;(DE+1),(DE)
02098   062E 7207            DW      DP$W$HL         ;(HL+1),(HL)
02200                ;#
02201                ;       Debug display processing routines
02202                ;
02203                DP$F:                           ;Flags
02204                                                ;The flags are displayed in the same way that
02205                                                ;   DDT uses: C1ZOMOEOIO
02206   0630 3A4A04          LDA     DB$Save$F       ;Get flags
02207   0633 47              MOV     B,A             ;Preserve copy
02208   0634 21DA04          LXI     H,DB$Flags$Msg + 1    ;HL -> first 0/1 in message
02209   0637 11E404          LXI     D,DB$Flag$Masks ;DE -> table of flag mask values
02210                DB$F$Next:
02211   063A 1A              LDAX    D               ;Get next flag mask
02212   063B B7              ORA     A               ;Check if end of table
02213   063C CA4E06          JZ      DB$F$Display    ;Yes, display the results
02214
02215   063F A0              ANA     B               ;Check if this flag is set
02216   0640 3E31            MVI     A,'1'           ;Assume yes
02217   0642 C24706          JNZ     DB$F$NZ         ;Yes,it is set
02218   0645 3E30            MVI     A,'0'           ;No,it is clear
02219                DB$F$NZ:
02220   0647 77              MOV     M,A             ;Store '0' or '1' in message text
02221   0648 23              INX     H               ;Update pointer to next 0/1
02222   0649 23              INX     H
02223   064A 13              INX     D               ;Update flag mask pointer
02224   064B C33A06          JMP     DB$F$Next
02225                DB$F$Display:                   ;Display results
02226   064E 21D904          LXI     H,DB$Flags$Msg
```

Figure 10-2. (Continued)

```
02227       0651 C3EE07        JMP      DB$MSG           ;Display message and return
02228                   ;
02229                   DP$A:                   ;A register
02230       0654 3A4B04        LDA      DB$Save$A        ;Get saved value
02231       0657 C39107        JMP      DB$DAH           ;Display it and return
02232                   ;
02233                   DP$B:                   ;B
02234       065A 3A4904        LDA      DB$Save$B        ;Get saved value
02235       065D C39107        JMP      DB$DAH           ;Display it and return
02236                   ;
02237                   DP$C:                   ;C
02238       0660 3A4804        LDA      DB$Save$C        ;Get saved value
02239       0663 C39107        JMP      DB$DAH           ;Display it and return
02240                   ;
02241                   DP$D:                   ;D
02242       0666 3A4704        LDA      DB$Save$D        ;Get saved value
02243       0669 C39107        JMP      DB$DAH           ;Display it and return
02244                   ;
02245                   DP$E:                   ;E
02246       066C 3A4604        LDA      DB$Save$E        ;Get saved value
02247       066F C39107        JMP      DB$DAH           ;Display it and return
02248                   ;
02249                   DP$H:                   ;H
02250       0672 3A0A04        LDA      DB$Save$H        ;Get saved value
02251       0675 C39107        JMP      DB$DAH           ;Display it and return
02252                   ;
02253                   DP$L:                   ;L
02254       0678 3A0904        LDA      DB$Save$L        ;Get saved value
02255       067B C39107        JMP      DB$DAH           ;Display it and return
02256                   ;
02257                   DP$BC:                  ;BC
02258       067E 2A4804        LHLD     DB$Save$C        ;Get saved word value
02259       0681 C38707        JMP      DB$DHLH          ;Display it and return
02260                   ;
02261                   DP$DE:                  ;DE
02262       0684 2A4604        LHLD     DB$Save$E        ;Get saved word value
02263       0687 C38707        JMP      DB$DHLH          ;Display it and return
02264                   ;
02265                   DP$HL:                  ;HL
02266       068A 2A0904        LHLD     DB$Save$HL       ;Get saved word value
02267       068D C38707        JMP      DB$DHLH          ;Display it and return
02268                   ;
02269                   DP$SP:                  ;Stack Pointer
02270       0690 2A0B04        LHLD     DB$Save$SP       ;Get saved word value
02271       0693 C38707        JMP      DB$DHLH          ;Display it and return
02272                   ;
02273                   DP$M:                   ;Memory
02274       0696 2A1304        LHLD     DB$End$Address   ;Increment end address to make
02275       0699 23            INX      H                ;  arithmetic easier
02276       069A 221304        SHLD     DB$End$Address
02277
02278       069D 2A1104        LHLD     DB$Start$Address
02279       06A0 CD3A07        CALL     DB$M$Check$End   ;Compare HL to End$Address
02280       06A3 DAD106        JC       DB$M$Address$OK  ;End > start
02281       06A6 CDD607        CALL     DB$MSGI          ;Error start > end
02282       06A9 0D0A2A2A20    DB       0DH,0AH,'** ERROR - Start Address > End **',0
02283       06CD C9            RET
02284                   ;
02285                   DB$M$Next$Line:
02286       06CE CDC107        CALL     DB$CRLF          ;Output carriage return, line feed
02287                   DB$M$Address$OK:                  ;Bypass CR,LF for first line
02288       06D1 CDD607        CALL     DB$MSGI          ;Indent line
02289       06D4 202000        DB       ' ',0
02290       06D7 2A1104        LHLD     DB$Start$Address ;Get start of line address
02291       06DA CD8707        CALL     DB$DHLH          ;Display in hex
02292
02293       06DD CDC807        CALL     DB$Colon         ;Display ':'
02294
02295       06E0 2A1104        LHLD     DB$Start$Address
02296                   DB$M$Next$Hex$Byte:
02297       06E3 E5            PUSH     H                ;Save memory address
02298       06E4 CDD007        CALL     DB$Blank         ;Output a blank
02299       06E7 E1            POP      H                ;Recover current byte address
02300       06E8 7E            MOV      A,M              ;Get byte from memory
02301       06E9 23            INX      H                ;Update memory pointer
02302       06EA E5            PUSH     H                ;Save for later
02303       06EB CD9107        CALL     DB$DAH           ;Display in hex.
02304       06EE E1            POP      H                ;Recover memory updated address
```

Figure 10-2. (Continued)

342 The CP/M Programmer's Handbook

```
02305      06EF CD3A07            CALL    DB$M$Check$End          ;Compare HL vs.end address
02306      06F2 CAFE06            JZ      DB$M$Display$ASCII      ;Yes, end of area
02307      06F5 7D                MOV     A,L                     ;Check if at start of new line,
02308      06F6 E60F              ANI     0000$1111B              ;  (is address XXX0H?)
02309      06F8 CAFE06            JZ      DB$M$Display$ASCII      ;Yes
02310      06FB C3E306            JMP     DB$M$Next$Hex$Byte      ;No, loop back for another
02311                             ;
02312                     DB$M$Display$ASCII:                     ;Display bytes in ASCII
02313      06FE CDC807            CALL    DB$Colon                ;Display ´ : ´
02314      0701 2A1104            LHLD    DB$Start$Address        ;Start ASCII as beginning of line
02315                     DB$M$Next$ASCII$Byte:
02316      0704 7E                MOV     A,M                     ;Get byte from memory
02317      0705 E5                PUSH    H                       ;Save memory address
02318      0706 E67F              ANI     0111$1111B              ;Remove parity
02319      0708 4F                MOV     C,A                     ;Prepare for output
02320      0709 FE20              CPI     ´ ´                     ;Check if non-graphic
02321      070B D21007            JNC     DB$M$Display$Char       ;Char >= space
02322      070E 0E2E              MVI     C,´.´                   ;Display non-graphic as ´.´
02323                     DB$M$Display$Char:
02324      0710 FE7F              CPI     7FH                     ;Check if DEL (may be non-graphic)
02325      0712 C21707            JNZ     DB$M$Not$DEL            ;No, it is graphic
02326      0715 0E2E              MVI     C,´.´                   ;Force to ´.´
02327                             ;
02328                     DB$M$Not$DEL:
02329      0717 CD0A05            CALL    DB$CONOUT               ;Display character
02330      071A E1                POP     H                       ;Recover memory address
02331      071B 23                INX     H                       ;Update memory pointer
02332      071C 221104            SHLD    DB$Start$Address        ;Update memory copy
02333      071F CD3A07            CALL    DB$M$Check$End          ;Check if end of memory dump
02334      0722 CA3707            JZ      DB$M$Exit               ;Yes, done
02335      0725 7D                MOV     A,L                     ;Check if end of line
02336      0726 E60F              ANI     0000$1111B              ;  by checking address = XXX0H
02337      0728 CACE06            JZ      DB$M$Next$Line          ;Yes, start next line
02338      072B 7D                MOV     A,L                     ;Check if extra blank needed
02339      072C E603              ANI     0000$0011B              ;  if address is multiple of 4
02340      072E C20407            JNZ     DB$M$Next$ASCII$Byte    ;No -- go back for next character
02341      0731 CDD007            CALL    DB$Blank                ;Yes, output blank
02342      0734 C30407            JMP     DB$M$Next$ASCII$Byte    ;Go back for next character
02343                             ;
02344                             ;
02345                     DB$M$Exit:
02346      0737 C3C107            JMP     DB$CRLF                 ;Output carriage return, line feed
02347                             ;                               ;  and return
02348                             ;
02349                     DB$M$Check$End:                         ;Compares HL vs End$Address
02350      073A D5                PUSH    D                       ;Save DE (defensive programming)
02351      073B EB                XCHG                            ;DE = current address
02352      073C 2A1304            LHLD    DB$End$Address          ;Get end address
02353      073F 7A                MOV     A,D                     ;Compare MS bytes
02354      0740 BC                CMP     H
02355      0741 C24607            JNZ     DB$M$Check$End$X        ;Exit now as they are unequal
02356      0744 7B                MOV     A,E                     ;Compare LS bytes
02357      0745 BD                CMP     L
02358                     DB$M$Check$End$X:
02359      0746 EB                XCHG                            ;HL = current address
02360      0747 D1                POP     D                       ;Recover DE
02361      0748 C9                RET                             ;Return with condition flags set
02362                             ;
02363                     DP$B$BC:                ;(BC)
02364      0749 2A4804            LHLD    DB$Save$C               ;Get saved word value
02365      074C 7E                MOV     A,M                     ;Get byte addressed by it
02366      074D C39107            JMP     DB$DAH                  ;Display it and return
02367                             ;
02368                     DP$B$DE:                ;(DE)
02369      0750 2A4604            LHLD    DB$Save$E               ;Get saved word value
02370      0753 7E                MOV     A,M                     ;Get byte addressed by it
02371      0754 C39107            JMP     DB$DAH                  ;Display it and return
02372                             ;
02373                     DP$B$HL:                ;(HL)
02374      0757 2A0904            LHLD    DB$Save$HL              ;Get saved word value
02375      075A 7E                MOV     A,M                     ;Get byte addressed by it
02376      075B C39107            JMP     DB$DAH                  ;Display it and return
02377                             ;
02378                     DP$W$BC:                ;(BC+1),(BC)
02379      075E 2A4804            LHLD    DB$Save$C               ;Get saved word value
02380      0761 5E                MOV     E,M                     ;Get word addressed by it
02381      0762 23                INX     H
```

Figure 10-2. (Continued)

```
02382   0763 56                  MOV     D,M
02383   0764 EB                  XCHG                    ;HL = word to be displayed
02384   0765 C38707              JMP     DB$DHLH         ;Display it and return
02385                       ;
02386                       DP$W$DE:                ;(DE+1),(DE)
02387   0768 2A4604              LHLD    DB$Save$E       ;Get saved word value
02388   076B 5E                  MOV     E,M             ;Get word addressed by it
02389   076C 23                  INX     H
02390   076D 56                  MOV     D,M
02391   076E EB                  XCHG                    ;HL = word to be displayed
02392   076F C38707              JMP     DB$DHLH         ;Display it and return
02393                       ;
02394                       DP$W$HL:                ;(HL+1),(HL)
02395   0772 2A0904              LHLD    DB$Save$HL      ;Get saved word value
02396   0775 5E                  MOV     E,M             ;Get word addressed by it
02397   0776 23                  INX     H
02398   0777 56                  MOV     D,M
02399   0778 EB                  XCHG                    ;HL = word to be displayed
02400   0779 C38707              JMP     DB$DHLH         ;Display it and return
02401                       ;
02500                       ;#
02501                       ;       DB$Display$CALLA
02502                       ;       This routine displays the DB$Call$Address in hexadecimal,
02503                       ;       followed by " : ".
02504                       ;
02505                       DB$Display$CALLA:
02506   077C E5                  PUSH    H               ;Save caller's HL
02507   077D 2A0F04              LHLD    DB$Call$Address ;Get the call address
02508   0780 CD8707              CALL    DB$DHLH         ;Display HL in hex.
02509   0783 E1                  POP     H               ;Recover caller's HL
02510   0784 C3C807              JMP     DB$Colon        ;Display " : " and return
02511                       ;
02600                       ;#
02601                       ;
02602                       ;       DB$DHLH
02603                       ;       Display HL in hex.
02604                       ;
02605                       ;       Entry parameters
02606                       ;
02607                       ;               HL = value to be displayed
02608                       ;
02609                       DB$DHLH:
02610   0787 E5                  PUSH    H               ;Save input value
02611   0788 7C                  MOV     A,H             ;Get MS byte first
02612   0789 CD9107              CALL    DB$DAH          ;Display A in hex.
02613   078C E1                  POP     H               ;Recover input value
02614   078D 7D                  MOV     A,L             ;Get LS byte
02615   078E C39107              JMP     DB$DAH          ;Display it and return
02616                       ;
02700                       ;#
02701                       ;
02702                       ;       DB$DAH
02703                       ;       Display A register in hexadecimal
02704                       ;
02705                       ;       Entry parameters
02706                       ;
02707                       ;               A = value to be converted and output
02708                       ;
02709                       DB$DAH:
02710   0791 F5                  PUSH    PSW             ;Take a copy of the value to be converted
02711   0792 0F                  RRC                     ;Shift A right four places
02712   0793 0F                  RRC
02713   0794 0F                  RRC
02714   0795 0F                  RRC
02715   0796 CDB407              CALL    DB$Nibble$To$Hex  ;Convert LS 4 bits to ASCII
02716   0799 CD0A05              CALL    DB$CONOUT       ;Display the character
02717   079C F1                  POP     PSW             ;Get original value again
02718   079D CDB407              CALL    DB$Nibble$To$Hex  ;Convert LS 4 bits to ASCII
02719   07A0 C30A05              JMP     DB$CONOUT       ;Display and return to caller
02800                       ;#
02801                       ;
02802                       ;       DB$CAH
02803                       ;       Convert A register to hexadecimal ASCII and store in
02804                       ;       specified address.
02805                       ;
02806                       ;       Entry parameters
02807                       ;
```

Figure 10-2. (Continued)

344 The CP/M Programmer's Handbook

```
02808                   ;               A = value to be converted and output
02809                   ;               HL -> buffer area to receive two characters of output
02810                   ;
02811                   ;       Exit parameters
02812                   ;
02813                   ;               HL -> byte following last hex.byte output
02814                   ;
02815                   DB$CAH:
02816   07A3 F5         PUSH    PSW                     ;Take a copy of the value to be converted
02817   07A4 0F         RRC                             ;Shift A right four places
02818   07A5 0F         RRC
02819   07A6 0F         RRC
02820   07A7 0F         RRC
02821   07A8 CDB407     CALL    DB$Nibble$To$Hex        ;Convert to ASCII hex.
02822   07AB 77         MOV     M,A                     ;Save in memory
02823   07AC 23         INX     H                       ;Update pointer
02824   07AD F1         POP     PSW                     ;Get original value again
02825   07AE CDB407     CALL    DB$Nibble$To$Hex        ;Convert to ASCII hex.
02826   07B1 77         MOV     M,A                     ;Save in memory
02827   07B2 23         INX     H                       ;Update pointer
02828   07B3 C9         RET
02900                   ;#
02901                   ;
02902                   ;       Minor subroutines
02903                   ;
02904                   ;
02905                   ;       DB$Nibble$To$Hex
02906                   ;       This is a minor subroutine that converts the least
02907                   ;       significant four bits of the A register into an ASCII
02908                   ;       hex. character in A and C
02909                   ;
02910                   ;       Entry parameters
02911                   ;
02912                   ;               A = nibble to be converted in LS 4 bits
02913                   ;
02914                   ;       Exit parameters
02915                   ;
02916                   ;               A,C = ASCII hex. character
02917                   ;
02918                   DB$Nibble$To$Hex:
02919   07B4 E60F       ANI     0000$1111B              ;Isolate LS four bits
02920   07B6 C630       ADI     '0'                     ;Convert to ASCII
02921   07B8 FE3A       CPI     '9' + 1                 ;Compare to maximum
02922   07BA DABF07     JC      DB$NTH$Numeric          ;No need to convert to A -> F
02923   07BD C607       ADI     7                       ;Convert to a letter
02924                   DB$NTH$Numeric:
02925   07BF 4F         MOV     C,A                     ;For convenience of other routines
02926   07C0 C9         RET
02927
02928
02929                   ;
02930                   ;       DB$CRLF
02931                   ;       Simple routine to display carriage return, line feed.
02932                   ;
02933                   DB$CRLF:
02934   07C1 CDD607     CALL    DB$MSGI                 ;Display in-line message
02935   07C4 0D0A00     DB      0DH,0AH,0
02936   07C7 C9         RET
02937                   ;
02938                   ;       DB$Colon
02939                   ;       Simple routine to display ' : '.
02940                   ;
02941                   DB$Colon:
02942   07C8 CDD607     CALL    DB$MSGI                 ;Display in-line message
02943   07CB 203A2000   DB      ' : ',0
02944   07CF C9         RET
02945                   ;
02946                   ;       DB$Blank
02947                   ;       Simple routine to display ' '.
02948                   ;
02949                   DB$Blank:
02950   07D0 CDD607     CALL    DB$MSGI                 ;Display in-line message
02951   07D3 2000       DB      ' ',0
02952   07D5 C9         RET
03100                   ;#
03101                   ;
03102                   ;       Message processing subroutines
```

Figure 10-2. (Continued)

```
03103          ;
03104          ;       DB$MSGI (message in-line)
03105          ;       Output null-byte terminated message that follows the
03106          ;       CALL to MSGOUTI
03107          ;
03108          ;       Calling sequence
03109          ;
03110          ;               CALL    DB$MSGI
03111          ;               DB      'Message',0
03112          ;               ... next instruction
03113          ;
03114          ;       Exit parameters
03115          ;               HL -> instruction following message
03116          ;
03117          ;
03118          DB$MSGI:
03119                                          ;Get return address of stack, save
03120                                          ; user's HL on top of stack
03121  07D6 E3         XTHL                    ;HL -> message
03122
03123  07D7 F5         PUSH    PSW             ;Save all user's registers
03124  07D8 C5         PUSH    B
03125  07D9 D5         PUSH    D
03126          DB$MSGI$Next:
03127  07DA 7E         MOV     A,M             ;Get next data byte
03128  07DB 23         INX     H               ;Update message pointer
03129  07DC B7         ORA     A               ;Check if null byte
03130  07DD C2E507     JNZ     DB$MSGIC        ;No, continue
03131
03132  07E0 D1         POP     D               ;Recover user's registers
03133  07E1 C1         POP     B
03134  07E2 F1         POP     PSW
03135  07E3 E3         XTHL                    ;Recover user's HL from stack, replacing
03136                                          ;  it with updated return address
03137  07E4 C9         RET                     ;Return to address after 00-byte
03138                                          ;  after in-line message
03139          DB$MSGIC:
03140  07E5 E5         PUSH    H               ;Save message pointer
03141  07E6 4F         MOV     C,A             ;Ready for output
03142  07E7 CD0A05     CALL    DB$CONOUT
03143  07EA E1         POP     H               ;Recover message pointer
03144  07EB C3DA07     JMP     DB$MSGI$Next    ;Go back for next char.
03145
03146          ;
03147          ;       DB$MSG
03148          ;       Output null-byte terminated message
03149          ;
03150          ;       Calling sequence
03151          ;
03152          ;       MESSAGE:        DB      'Message',0
03153          ;               :
03154          ;               LXI     H,MESSAGE
03155          ;               CALL    DB$MSG
03156          ;
03157          ;       Exit parameters
03158          ;               HL -> null byte terminator
03159          ;
03160          ;
03161          DB$MSG:
03162  07EE F5         PUSH    PSW             ;Save user's registers
03163  07EF C5         PUSH    B
03164  07F0 D5         PUSH    D
03165          DB$MSG$Next:
03166  07F1 7E         MOV     A,M             ;Get next byte for output
03167  07F2 B7         ORA     A               ;Check if 00-byte terminator
03168  07F3 CA0008     JZ      DB$MSG$X        ;Exit
03169  07F6 23         INX     H               ;Update message pointer
03170  07F7 E5         PUSH    H               ;Save updated pointer
03171  07F8 4F         MOV     C,A             ;Ready for output
03172  07F9 CD0A05     CALL    DB$CONOUT
03173  07FC E1         POP     H               ;Recover message pointer
03174  07FD C3F107     JMP     DB$MSG$Next     ;Go back for next character
03175          ;
03176          DB$MSG$X:
03177  0800 D1         POP     D               ;Recover user's registers
03178  0801 C1         POP     B
03179  0802 F1         POP     PSW
```

Figure 10-2.   (Continued)

```
03180      0803 C9                      RET
03300                    ;#
03301                    ;
03302                    ;      Debug input routine
03303                    ;
03304                    ;      This routine helps debug code in which input instructions
03305                    ;      would normally occur. The opcode of the IN instruction
03306                    ;      must be replaced by a value of 0E7H (RST 4).
03307                    ;
03308                    ;      This routine picks up the port number contained in the byte
03309                    ;      following the RST 4, converts it to hexadecimal, and
03310                    ;      displays the message:
03311                    ;
03312                    ;                  Input from port XX :
03313                    ;
03314                    ;      It then accepts two characters (in hex.) from the keyboard,
03315                    ;      converts these to binary in A, and then returns control
03316                    ;      to the byte following the port number
03317                    ;
03318                    ;      *******
03319                    ;      WARNING - This routine uses both DB$CONOUT and BDOS calls
03320                    ;      *******
03321                    ;
03322      0804 496E707574DBIN$Message:  DB       'Input from Port '
03323      0814 5858203A20DBIN$Port:     DB       'XX : ',0
03324                    ;
03325                 DB$Input:
03326
03327      081A 220904              SHLD    DB$Save$HL         ;Save user's HL
03328      081D E1                  POP     H                  ;Recover address of port number
03329      081E 2B                  DCX     H                  ;Backup to point to RST
03330      081F 220F04              SHLD    DB$Call$Address    ;Save for later display
03331      0822 23                  INX     H                  ;Restore to point to port number
03332                                                          ;Note: A need not be preserved
03333      0823 7E                  MOV     A,M                ;Get port number
03334      0824 23                  INX     H                  ;Update return address to bypass port number
03335      0825 220D04              SHLD    DB$Save$RA         ;Save return address
03336      0828 C5                  PUSH    B                  ;Save remaining registers
03337      0829 D5                  PUSH    D
03338      082A F5                  PUSH    PSW                ;Save port number for later
03339
03340
03341      082B CDB108              CALL    DB$Flag$Save$On    ;Save current state of debug flag
03342                                                          ;  and enable debug output
03343
03344      082E CDC107              CALL    DB$CRLF            ;Display carriage return, line feed
03345      0831 CD7C07              CALL    DB$Display$CALLA   ;Display call address
03346      0834 F1                  POP     PSW                ;Recover port number
03347      0835 211408              LXI     H,DBIN$Port
03348      0838 CDA307              CALL    DB$CAH             ;Convert to hex, and store in message
03349      083B 210408              LXI     H,DBIN$Message     ;Output prompting message
03350      083E CDEE07              CALL    DB$MSG
03351      0841 0E02                MVI     C,2                ;Get 2 digit hex. value
03352      0843 CDCF08              CALL    DB$GHV             ;Returns value in HL
03353      0846 7D                  MOV     A,L                ;Get just single byte
03354
03355      0847 CDBF08              CALL    DB$Flag$Restore    ;Restore debug output to previous state
03356
03357      084A D1                  POP     D                  ;Recover registers
03358      084B C1                  POP     B
03359      084C 2A0904              LHLD    DB$Save$HL         ;Get previous HL
03360      084F E5                  PUSH    H                  ;Put on top of stack
03361      0850 2A0D04              LHLD    DB$Save$RA         ;Get return address
03362      0853 E3                  XTHL                       ;TOS = return address, HL = previous value
03363      0854 C9                  RET
03500                    ;#
03501                    ;
03502                    ;      Debug output routine
03503                    ;
03504                    ;      This routine helps debug code in which output instructions
03505                    ;      would normally occur. The opcode of the OUT instruction
03506                    ;      must be replaced by a value of 0EFH (RST 5).
03507                    ;
03508                    ;      This routine picks up the port number contained in the byte
03509                    ;      following the RST 5, converts it to hexadecimal, and
03510                    ;      displays the message:
03511                    ;
```

Figure 10-2. (Continued)

```
03512                           ;              Output to port XX : AA
03513                           ;
03514                           ;       where AA is the contents of the A register prior to the
03515                           ;       RST 5 being executed.
03516                           ;       Control is then returned to the byte following the port number.
03517                           ;
03518                           ;       *******
03519                           ;       WARNING - This routine uses both DB$CONOUT and BDOS calls
03520                           ;       *******
03521                           ;
03522                           ;
03523      0855 4F75747075  DBO$Message:   DB      'Output to Port '
03524      0864 5858203A20  DBO$Port:      DB      'XX : '
03525      0869 414100      DBO$Value:     DB      'AA',0
03526                           ;
03527                           ;
03528                       DB$Output:
03529      086C 220904          SHLD    DB$Save$HL        ;Save user's HL
03530      086F E1              POP     H                 ;Recover address of port number
03531      0870 2B              DCX     H                 ;Backup to point to RST
03532      0871 220F04          SHLD    DB$Call$Address   ;Save for later display
03533      0874 23              INX     H                 ;Restore to point at port number
03534      0875 32B404          STA     DB$Save$A         ;Preserve value to be output
03535      0878 7E              MOV     A,M               ;Get port number
03536      0879 23              INX     H                 ;Update return address to bypass port number
03537      087A 220D04          SHLD    DB$Save$RA        ;Save return address
03538      087D C5              PUSH    B                 ;Save remaining registers
03539      087E D5              PUSH    D
03540      087F F5              PUSH    PSW               ;Save port number for later
03541
03542      0880 CDB108          CALL    DB$Flag$Save$On   ;Save current state of debug flag
03543                           ;                          and enable debug output
03544
03545      0883 CDC107          CALL    DB$CRLF           ;Display carriage return, line feed
03546      0886 CD7C07          CALL    DB$Display$CALLA  ;Display call address
03547      0889 F1              POP     PSW               ;Recover port number
03548      088A 216408          LXI     H,DBO$Port
03549      088D CDA307          CALL    DB$CAH            ;Convert to hex.and store in message
03550
03551      0890 3A4B04          LDA     DB$Save$A
03552      0893 216908          LXI     H,DBO$Value       ;Convert value to be output
03553      0896 CDA307          CALL    DB$CAH            ;Convert to hex.and store in message
03554
03555      0899 215508          LXI     H,DBO$Message     ;Output prompting message
03556      089C CDEE07          CALL    DB$MSG
03557
03558      089F CDBF08          CALL    DB$Flag$Restore   ;Restore debug flag to previous state
03559
03560      08A2 D1              POP     D                 ;Recover registers
03561      08A3 C1              POP     B
03562      08A4 2A0904          LHLD    DB$Save$HL        ;Get previous HL
03563      08A7 E5              PUSH    H                 ;Put on top of stack
03564      08A8 2A0D04          LHLD    DB$Save$RA        ;Get return address
03565      08AB E3              XTHL                      ;TOS = return address, HL = previous value
03566      08AC 3A4B04          LDA     DB$Save$A         ;Recover A (NOTE: FLAG NOT RESTORED)
03567      08AF C9              RET
03700                           ;#
03701                           ;
03702                           ;       DB$Flag$Save$On
03703                           ;       This routine is only used for DB$IN/OUT.
03704                           ;       It saves the current state of the debug control flag,
03705                           ;       D$Flag, and then enables it to make sure that
03706                           ;       DB$IN/OUT output always goes out.
03707                           ;
03708      08B0 00          DB$Flag$Previous:  DB  0      ;Previous flag value
03709                           ;
03710                       DB$Flag$Save$On:
03711      08B1 F5              PUSH    PSW               ;Save caller's registers
03712      08B2 3A0604          LDA     DB$Flag           ;Get current value
03713      08B5 32B008          STA     DB$Flag$Previous  ;Save it
03714      08B8 3EFF            MVI     A,0FFH            ;Set flag
03715      08BA 320604          STA     DB$Flag
03716      08BD F1              POP     PSW
03717      08BE C9              RET
03800                           ;#
03801                           ;
```

Figure 10-2. (Continued)

```
03802                           ;       DB$Flag$Restore
03803                           ;       This routine is only used for DB$IN/OUT.
03804                           ;       It restores the debug control flag, DB$Flag, to
03805                           ;       its former state.
03806                           ;
03807                           DB$Flag$Restore:
03808     08BF F5                        PUSH    PSW
03809     08C0 3AB008                    LDA     DB$Flag$Previous        ;Get previous setting
03810     08C3 320604                    STA     DB$Flag                 ;Set debug control flag
03811     08C6 F1                        POP     PSW
03812     08C7 C9                        RET
03813
03814                           ;
03900                           ;#
03901                           ;
03902                           ;       Get hex. value
03903                           ;
03904                           ;       This subroutine outputs a prompting message, and then reads
03905                           ;       the keyboard in order to get a hexadecimal value.
03906                           ;       It is somewhat simplistic in that the first non-hex value
03907                           ;       terminates the input. The maximum number of digits to be
03908                           ;       converted is specified as an input parameter. If more than the
03909                           ;       maximum number is entered, only the last four are significant.
03910                           ;
03911                           ;****************************************************************
03912                           ;                       W A R N I N G
03913                           ;       DB$GHV will always use the BDOS to perform a read console
03914                           ;       function (#10). Be careful if you use this routine from
03915                           ;       within an executing BIOS.
03916                           ;****************************************************************
03917                           ;
03918                           ;       Entry parameters
03919                           ;
03920                           ;               HL -> 00-byte terminated message to be output
03921                           ;               C = number of hexadecimal digits to be input
03922                           ;
03923                           ;
03924                           DB$GHV$Buffer:                          ;Input buffer for console characters
03925                           DB$GHV$Max$Count:
03926     08C8 00                        DB      0                       ;Set to the maximum number of chars.
03927                           ;                                       ; to be input
03928                           DB$GHV$Input$Count:
03929     08C9 00                        DB      0                       ;Set by the BDOS to the actual number
03930                           ;                                       ; of chars. entered
03931                           DB$GHV$Data$Bytes
03932     08CA                           DS      5                       ;Buffer space for the characters
03933                           ;
03934                           ;
03935                           DB$GHV:
03936     08CF 79                        MOV     A,C                     ;Get maximum characters to be input
03937     08D0 FE05                      CPI     5                       ;Check against maximum count
03938     08D2 DAD708                    JC      DB$GHV$Count$OK         ;Carry set if A < 5
03939     08D5 3E04                      MVI     A,4                     ;Force to only four characters
03940                           DB$GHV$Count$OK:
03941     08D7 32C808                    STA     DB$GHV$Max$Count        ;Set up maximum count in input buffer
03942     08DA CDEE07                    CALL    DB$MSG                  ;Output prompting message
03943     08DD 11C808                    LXI     D,DB$GHV$Buffer         ;Accept characters from console
03944     08E0 0E0A                      MVI     C,B$READCONS            ;Function code
03945     08E2 CD0500                    CALL    BDOS
03946
03947     08E5 0E02                      MVI     C,B$CONOUT              ;Output a line feed
03948     08E7 1E0A                      MVI     E,0AH
03949     08E9 CD0500                    CALL    BDOS
03950
03951     08EC 210000                    LXI     H,0                     ;Initial value
03952     08EF 11CA08                    LXI     D,DB$GHV$Data$Bytes     ;DE -> data characters
03953     08F2 3AC908                    LDA     DB$GHV$Input$Count      ;Get count of characters input
03954     08F5 4F                        MOV     C,A                     ;Keep count in C
03955                           DB$GHV$Loop:
03956     08F6 0D                        DCR     C                       ;Downdate count
03957     08F7 F8                        RM                              ;Return when all done (HL has value)
03958     08F8 1A                        LDAX    D                       ;Get next character from buffer
03959     08F9 13                        INX     D                       ;Update buffer pointer
03960     08FA CD1B09                    CALL    DB$A$To$Upper           ;Convert A to uppercase if need be
03961     08FD FE30                      CPI     '0'                     ;Check if less than 0
03962     08FF D8                        RC                              ;Yes, terminate
03963     0900 FE3A                      CPI     '9' + 1                 ;Check if > 9
03964     0902 DA1009                    JC      DB$GHV$Hex$Digit        ;No, it must be numeric
```

Figure 10-2. (Continued)

Chapter 10: Debugging a New CP/M System **349**

```
03965      0905 FE41              CPI      'A'                    ;Check if < 'A'
03966      0907 D8                RC                              ;Yes, terminate
03967      0908 FE47              CPI      'F' + 1                ;Check if > 'F'
03968      090A D0                RNC                             ;Yes, terminate
03969      090B D637              SUI      'A' - 10               ;Convert A through F to numeric
03970      090D C31209            JMP      DB$GHV$Shift$Left$4    ;Combine with current result
03971                             ;
03972                             DB$GHV$Hex$Digit:
03973      0910 D630              SUI      '0'                    ;Convert to binary
03974                             DB$GHV$Shift$Left$4:
03975      0912 29                DAD      H                      ;Shift HL left four bits
03976      0913 29                DAD      H
03977      0914 29                DAD      H
03978      0915 29                DAD      H
03979      0916 85                ADD      L                      ;Add binary value in LS 4 bits of A
03980      0917 6F                MOV      L,A                    ;Put back into HL total
03981      0918 C3F608            JMP      DB$GHV$Loop            ;Loop back for next character
04100                             ;#
04101                             ;
04102                             ;        A to upper
04103                             ;        Converts the contents of the A register to an uppercase
04104                             ;        letter if it is currently a lowercase letter
04105                             ;
04106                             ;        Entry parameters
04107                             ;
04108                             ;                A = character to be converted
04109                             ;
04110                             ;        Exit parameters
04111                             ;
04112                             ;                A = converted character
04113                             ;
04114                             DB$A$To$Upper:
04115      091B FE61              CPI      'a'                    ;Compare to lower limit
04116      091D D8                RC                              ;No need to convert
04117      091E FE7B              CPI      'z' + 1                ;Compare to upper limit
04118      0920 D0                RNC                             ;No need to convert
04119      0921 E65F              ANI      5FH                    ;Convert to uppercase
04120      0923 C9                RET
```

Figure 10-2. Debug subroutines (continued)

```
B>ddt fig10-2.hex<cr>
DDT VERS 2.0
NEXT  PC
0924  0000
-g100<cr>

0116 : Flags : Flags = C1ZOM1E1IO
0120 : A Register : A = AA
012F : B Register : B = BB
013E : C Register : C = CC
014D : D Register : D = DD
015C : E Register : E = EE
016B : H Register : H = FF
017A : L Register : L = 11
0189 : Memory Dump #1 : Start, End Address : 0108, 0128
  0108 :  05 3E AA 01 CC BB 11 EE : .>*. L;.n
  0110 :  DD 21 11 FF B7 37 CD 52 05 00 46 6C 61 67 73 00 : ]!.. 77MR ..Fl ags.
  0120 :  CD 52 05 02 41 20 52 65 67 : MR.. A Re g

01A0 : Memory Dump #2 : Start, End Address : 0100, 011F
  0100 :  31 6B 03 CD EA 04 CD 15 05 3E AA 01 CC BB 11 EE : 1k.M j.M. .>*. L;.n
  0110 :  DD 21 11 FF B7 37 CD 52 05 00 46 6C 61 67 73 00 : ]!.. 77MR ..Fl ags.

01B7 : Memory Dump #3 : Start, End Address : 0101, 0100
** ERROR - Start Address > End **
01CE : Memory Dump #4 : Start, End Address : 0100, 0100
  0100 :  31 : 1
```

Figure 10-3. Console output from debug testbed run

```
01E5 : BC Register : BC = BBCC
01F5 : DE Register : DE = DDEE
0205 : HL Register : HL = FF11
0215 : SP Register : SP = 0369
022E : Byte at (BC) : (BC) = BC
023F : Byte at (DE) : (DE) = DE
0250 : Byte at (HL) : (HL) = F1
026A : Word at (BC) : (BC+1),(BC) = 0B0C
027B : Word at (DE) : (DE+1),(DE) = 0D0E
028C : Word at (HL) : (HL+1),(HL) = 0F01
Debug output has been re-enabled.
This message should display 5 times
This message should display 5 times
This message should display 5 times
This message should display 5 times
This message should display 5 times
032B : Input from Port 11 : aa

032D : Output to Port 22 : AA
```

Figure 10-3. Console output from debug tested run (continued)

containing all of the symbols in your program, along with their respective addresses. Once the program has been loaded by SID, you can refer to the memory image of your program not by address, but by the actual symbol name from your source code. SID also supports the "pass count" concept when using breakpoints.

ZSID (Z80 Symbolic Debug)

This is the Z80 CPU's version of SID. The mini-assembler/disassembler uses Zilog instruction mnemonics rather than those used by Intel.

Bringing Up CP/M for the First Time

It is much harder to bring up CP/M on a new computer system than to debug an enhanced version on a system already running CP/M. You will often find yourself staring at a programmatic "brick wall" with no adequate debugging tools to assist you.

For example, you install the CP/M system on a diskette (using another CP/M-based computer system), put the diskette into the new computer, and press the RESET button. The disk head loads on the disk, and then—nothing! You cannot use any programs such as DDT or SID because you do not yet have CP/M up and running on the new computer. Or can you?

The answer is, wherever possible, debug the code for the new machine on an existing CP/M system. You may have to "fake" some aspects of the new bootstrap or BIOS so that the act of testing it on the host machine does not interact with the CP/M already running on it.

This scheme permits you to be fairly sure of your program logic before loading the diskette into the new machine. It will help pin down problems caused by hardware problems on the new computer.

Chapter 10: Debugging a New CP/M System **351**

The hardest situation of all is if you have only the new computer and the release diskettes from Digital Research. Your only option is to find a way of reading the CP/M image on the release diskette into memory, hand patch in new console and disk drivers (not a trivial task), write the patched image back onto a diskette, and resort to Orville Wright testing.

If you value your time, it is always more cost-effective to use another system with CP/M already installed. This is true even if the two systems do not have the same diskette format. You can still do the bootstrap and build the CP/M image on the host machine. Then download the image directly into the memory of the new machine and write it out to a diskette.

This *downloading* process does require, however, that the new computer have a read-only memory (ROM) monitor program. Depending on the capability of this ROM monitor program, you may have to hand patch into the new machine's memory a primitive "download" program that reads 8-bit characters from a serial port, stacking them up in memory and returning control to the monitor program when you press a keyboard character on the new machine's console. In fact, some ROM monitor programs have a downloading program built in.

Debugging the CP/M Bootstrap Loader

The CP/M bootstrap loader, as you may recall, is written on one of the outermost tracks on a diskette or hard disk. On a standard 8-inch single-sided, single-density diskette, CP/M's bootstrap loader is stored on the first sector of the first track. The loader is brought into memory by firmware that gets control of the CPU when you turn your machine on or press the RESET button.

The bootstrap has to be compact, as the diskette space on which it is stored is limited: no more than 128 bytes for standard 8-inch diskettes. This tends to rule out the use of the debug subroutines already described, so you have to fall back to more primitive techniques.

Testing the Bootstrap Under CP/M

A bootstrap is best developed on a CP/M-based system. The task is easiest of all if you already have CP/M running on your new machine and are simply preparing an enhanced version of the bootstrap loader. In this case, you can test most of the code as though it were a user program running in the transient program area (TPA).

Most bootstraps get loaded into memory at location 0000H, so at the front of the code to be debugged you must put a temporary origin line that reads

```
ORG     100H
```

If you omit this and ask DDT to load the HEX file output by the assembler, it will load at the true origin, 0000H, and wipe out the contents of the base page for the version of CP/M that you are running. This will cause a system crash; you will have to press the RESET button and reload CP/M. When this happens, DDT does not tell you directly that anything is amiss; it just displays a "?" after your request to load the HEX file. You will discover that the system has "gone away" only when you try to do something else.

You also will need to adjust the addresses into which the bootstrap tries to load the CP/M image. If you do not, you will overwrite the version of CP/M presently running.

With these adjustments made, you can load the bootstrap under DDT and watch it execute, confirming that it does load the correct image into the correct addresses for debugging and transfer control to the BIOS jump vector. When everything appears to be functioning correctly, use the IF instruction to disable the debug code, reassemble the bootstrap, and write it onto a diskette. Then put the diskette into drive A and press RESET.

Was the Bootstrap Loaded?

At this point you must establish whether the bootstrap is being loaded into memory when the machine is turned on or RESET is pressed. The best way of doing this, and one that you can leave in place permanently, is to output a sign-on message as soon as the loader gets control. This requires hardware set up to prepare the USART (Universal Synchronous/Asynchronous Receive/Transmit) chip to output data, although some manufacturers write this initialization code into the firmware that loads the bootstrap. A suitable sign-on message would be the following:

```
CP/M Bootstrap Loader : Vn 1.0 11/18/82
```

If you do not see this message, assume that control is *not* being transferred to the bootstrap loader. This will be useful in the future if someone should call you with a complaint that CP/M cannot be loaded. If this message does not appear, they probably do not have CP/M on the disk.

Did the Bootstrap Load CP/M?

This is a harder question to answer than whether the bootstrap itself has been loaded, especially if the bootstrap loader sign-on is displayed and then the system crashes. A sign-on message early in the BIOS cold boot processing can confirm the correct transfer of control into the BIOS.

If the problems with the bootstrap program are severe, you may have to adapt the memory-dump debugging subroutine, dumping the contents of memory to the console in order to see what information the bootstrap loader is placing in memory. Display 100H bytes starting from the front of the BIOS jump vector. This table has an immediately recognizable pattern of 0C3H values every three bytes.

You should also check to see that the bootstrap is loading the correct number of sectors from the disk into memory. If it loads too few, CP/M may sign on only to crash a few moments later because it attempts either to execute code or access a constant at the end of the BIOS. If the bootstrap loads too many sectors from the disk, the excess may "wrap around" the top of memory and overwrite the bootstrap itself, down at location 0000H, before it has completed its task. In this case, you would see only the sign-on for the bootstrap, not for the BIOS.

Debugging the BIOS

Rather than try to debug the BIOS as a single piece of code, debug it as a series of separate functional modules.

Notwithstanding current "top-down" philosophies of dealing with overall structure first, it can be quicker to debug the low-level subroutines in a device driver first. This gives you a solid base on which to build.

The BIOS can be divided up into its constituent modules as follows:

Character input
    Interrupt service
    Non-interrupt service

Character output

Interrupt routines
    Real time clock
    Watchdog timers

Disk drivers
    High-level (deblocking)
    Low-level (physical I/O)

Plan to write a *testbed* program for each of these modules. This testbed code serves two purposes; first, it provides a means of transferring control into the module under test in a controlled way. Second, it includes the necessary modules or dummy modules to "fool" the module under test into responding as if it were running in a complete BIOS under CP/M.

Using the testbed, you can check every part of the module's logic except the part that may be time-critical. Problems caused by timing, such as interrupts disabled for too long or code that is too slow or too fast for a particular peripheral controller chip, tend to show up only when you are testing on the final hardware and when you are running your new BIOS under CP/M.

What You Should Test for in the BIOS

Describing fully how to debug each module in the BIOS ould fill several books. Remember that you are trying to establish the *absence* of errors using a technique that, by its very nature, tends to show only their *presence*.

There are two basic approaches to debugging. One is the plodding method, checking every aspect of the code to ensure that every feature really does work. The second is to try to do something useful with the code.

Plan to use both. Start with the plodding method, testing each feature under control of the testbed until you are sure that it is working *in vitro*. When all of the BIOS modules have been tested individually, build a CP/M system and try to do some useful work with it. Trying to use the system for actual work testing *in vitro* can be a good test.

Feature Checklist

Make a list of the specific features included in the various BIOS modules. Then devise specific test sequences that will show that each of the features is working correctly.

The same testbed code can often test all of the features of a driver module. If it cannot, create a new testbed for the more exotic features.

Keep the testbed routines. Experience shows that they are most often needed shortly after you have erased them. Even after you have tested the BIOS, the testbed routines will come in handy if you decide to enhance a particular driver later on. You can extract the driver code from the BIOS, glue it together with the testbed, and test the new feature code in isolation from the BIOS.

The following sections show example testbeds for the various drivers, along with example checklists. These checklists were used to test the example BIOS routines shown in earlier chapters.

Character Drivers

Figure 10-4 shows the code for an example testbed routine for character I/O drivers in the BIOS. This code would be followed by the actual character I/O drivers, exactly as they would appear in the BIOS except that all IN and OUT instructions would be replaced with RST 4's and 5's respectively (see Figure 10-2) so that you could enter input values and inspect output values on the console.

This example contains the initialization code for the debug package shown in Figure 10-2 and the code setting up an RST 6 used to "fake" incoming character interrupts.

The main testbed loop consists of a faked incoming character interrupt followed by optional calls to CONIN or CONOUT, the return of control to DDT, or a loop back to fake another character interrupt. You can only return control to DDT if you used DDT to load the testbed and driver programs in the first place.

Chapter 10: Debugging a New CP/M System

```
                    ;       Testbed for character I/O drivers in the BIOS
                    ;
                    ;       The complete source file consists of three components:
                    ;
                    ;               1. The testbed code shown here
                    ;               2. The character I/O drivers destined for the BIOS
                    ;               3. The debug package shown in Figure 10-2.
                    ;
FFFF =              TRUE    EQU     0FFFFH
0000 =              FALSE   EQU     NOT TRUE

FFFF =              DEBUG   EQU     TRUE            ;For conditional assembly of RST
                                                    ;  instructions in place of IN and
                                                    ;  OUT instructions in the drivers
0030 =              RST6    EQU     30H             ;Use RST 6 for fake incoming character
                                                    ;  interrupt
0100                        ORG     100H
                    START:
0100 31D101                 LXI     SP,Test$Stack   ;Use a local stack
0103 CDD101                 CALL    DB$Init         ;Initialize the debug package
0106 3EC3                   MVI     A,JMP           ;Set up RST 6 with JMP opcode
0108 323000                 STA     RST6
010B 21D101                 LXI     H,Character$Interrupt  ;Set up RST 6 JMP address
010E 223100                 SHLD    RST6 + 1
                    ;
                    ;       Make repeated entry to character interrupt routine
                    ;       to ensure that characters can be captured and stored in
                    ;       an input buffer
                    ;
                    Testbed$Loop:
0111 3EAA                   MVI     A,0AAH          ;Set registers to known pattern
0113 01CCBB                 LXI     B,0BBCCH
0116 11EEDD                 LXI     D,0DDEEH
0119 2111FF                 LXI     H,0FF11H
011C F7                     RST     6               ;Fake interrupt for incoming character

011D CDD101                 CALL    DB$MSGI         ;Display in-line message
0120 0D0A456E74             DB      0DH,0AH,'Enter I to Input Char., O to Output, D to enter
0152 444454203A             DB      'DDT : ',0

0159 CDD101                 CALL    DB$CONINU       ;Get uppercase character
015C FE49                   CPI     'I'             ;CONIN?
015E CA7201                 JZ      Go$CONIN
0161 FE44                   CPI     'D'             ;DDT?
0163 CA6E01                 JZ      Go$DDT
0166 FE4F                   CPI     'O'             ;CONOUT?
0168 CA9101                 JZ      Go$CONOUT
016B C31101                 JMP     Testbed$Loop    ;Loop back to interrupt again
                    Go$DDT:
016E FF                     RST     7               ;Enter DDT (RST 7 set up by DDT)
016F C31101                 JMP     Testbed$Loop
                    Go$CONIN:
0172 CDD101                 CALL    CONST           ;Get console status
0175 CA1101                 JZ      Testbed$Loop    ;No data waiting
0178 CDD101                 CALL    CONIN           ;Get data from buffer

017B CDD101                 CALL    DB$Display      ;Display character returned
017E 02                     DB      DB$A            ;  in A register
017F 434F4E494E             DB      'CONIN returned',0

018E C37201                 JMP     Go$CONIN        ;Repeat CONIN loop until no chars.
                                                    ;  waiting
                    Go$CONOUT:
0191 CDD101                 CALL    CONST           ;Get console status
0194 CA1101                 JZ      Testbed$Loop    ;No data waiting
0197 CDD101                 CALL    CONIN
019A 4F                     MOV     C,A             ;Ready for output
019B CDD101                 CALL    CONOUT          ;Output to console
019E C39101                 JMP     Go$CONOUT       ;Repeat while there is still data
                    ;
01A1 9999999999              DW     9999H,9999H,9999H,9999H,9999H,9999H,9999H
01B1 9999999999              DW     9999H,9999H,9999H,9999H,9999H,9999H,9999H
01C1 9999999999              DW     9999H,9999H,9999H,9999H,9999H,9999H,9999H
```

Figure 10-4. Testbed for character I/O drivers in the BIOS

```
                Test$Stack:
                ;
                ;       Dummy routines for those shown in other figures
                ;
                ;       BIOS routines (Figure 8-10)
                ;
                CONST:                  ;BIOS console status
                CONIN:                  ;BIOS console input
                CONOUT:                 ;BIOS console output;
                Character$Interrupt:    ;Interrupt service routine for incoming chars.
                ;
                ;       Debug routines (Figure 10-2)
                ;
                DB$Init:                ;Debug initialization
                DB$MSGI:                ;Display message in-line
                DB$CONINU:              ;Get uppercase character from keyboard
                DB$Display:             ;Main debug display routine
      0002 =    DB$A       EQU    02   ;Display code for DB$Display
```

Figure 10-4.   Testbed for character I/O drivers in the BIOS (continued)

Executing an RST 7 without using DDT will cause a system crash, as DDT sets up the necessary JMP instruction at location 0038H in the base page.

The faked incoming character interrupt transfers control directly to the interrupt service routine in the BIOS (see the example in Figure 8-10, line 04902, label Character$Interrupt). This reads the status ports of each of the character devices; you can enter the specific status byte values that you want. If you enter a value that indicates that a data character is "incoming," you will be prompted for the actual 8-bit data value to be "input." You can make the interrupt service routine appear to be inputting characters and stacking characters up in the input buffer. For debugging purposes, reduce the size of the input buffer to eight bytes. Making it larger means you will have to input more characters to test the buffer threshold logic. To check the interrupt service routine, you will pass through the main testbed loop doing nothing but faking incoming character interrupts and entering status and data values. The data characters will then be stacked up in the input buffer.

To check the correct functioning of the interrupt service routines, you can stay in control with DDT from the outset. Alternatively, you can just use DDT to load the testbed/driver HEX file, loop around inputting several characters, and then request that the testbed return control to DDT. Then you can use DDT to inspect the contents of the device table(s) and input buffers.

Another possibility is to create debugging routines that display the contents of the device table in a meaningful way, with each field captioned like this:

```
DEVICE TABLE 0
    Status Port      81    Data Port         80
    Output Ready     01    Input Ready       02
    DTR high         40
    Reset Int. Prt   D8    Reset Int. Val.   20
    :
    :
    Status Byte 1
        Output Suspended
        Output Xon Enabled
    :
```

```
:
Buffer Base  0E8C
Put Offset      05        Get Offset       01
Char. Count     04        Control Count    00
Data Buffer
41 42 43 44 45 00 00 00
```

This display device table routine will require a fair amount of effort to code and debug—but it will pay dividends. You can obtain a complete "snapshot" of the device table without having to decode hexadecimal memory dumps and individual bits. Constant values in the device tables are also displayed, so that if a bug in your code corrupts the table, you will know about it immediately.

The next section shows examples of the specific tests you need to make, along with a description of the strategy you can use.

Interrupt Service Routine Checklist In a functioning BIOS, control is transferred to the interrupt service module whenever an incoming character causes an interrupt. In the example BIOS in Figure 8-10 (line 4900), the code scans each character device in turn to determine which one is causing the interrupt.

When you are debugging the interrupt service routines using the "fake" input/output instructions, you will have to enter specific status byte values. Refer to the device table declarations in Figure 8-10, line 1500, to determine what values you must enter to make the service routine think that an incoming character is arriving or that data terminal ready (DTR) is high or low.

Start the debugging process using the first device table. Then repeat the tests on the other device tables.

The following is a checklist of features that should be checked in debugging the interrupt service routine:

Are all registers restored correctly on exit from the interrupt servicing?

Using DDT, start execution from the beginning of the testbed. Set a breakpoint (with the G100,nnnn command) to get control back immediately before the CALL Character$Interrupt. Use the X command to display all of the registers, and then, by using the G,nnnn command, you set a breakpoint at the instruction that immediately follows the CALL Character$Interrupt. The character drivers will prompt you for the status values. Enter 00 (which indicates that no character is incoming). Display the registers again—their values should be the same. Remember to check the value of the stack pointer and the amount of the stack area that has been used.

NOTE: Do not be too surprised if you lose control of the machine when you first try this test. You may have some fundamental logic errors initially. If the system crashes, reset it, reload CP/M, and then start the test again. This time, rather than setting the second breakpoint at the instruction following the CALL Character$Interrupt, venture down into the Character$Interrupt code and go through the code a few instructions at a time, setting breakpoints before any instructions that could cause a transfer of control. Find out how far you are getting into the driver before it either jumps off into space or settles into a loop.

Does the service routine push a significant number of bytes onto the stack after an interrupt has occurred?

When you get control back after the CALL Character$Interrupt, use the D (dump) command to dump the stack area's memory on the console. Check how far down the stack came by looking for the point where the constants that used to fill the stack area are overwritten by other data.

The example BIOS in Figure 8-10 saves only the contents of the HL register pair on the pre-interrupt stack. It then switches over to a private BIOS stack to save the contents of the rest of the registers and service the interrupt.

Are data characters added to the input buffer correctly?

"Input" a noncontrol character via the Character$Interrupt routine. Then check the contents of the appropriate device table. The character count and the put offset should both be set to one. Then check the contents of the input buffer itself; does it contain the character that you "input?"

Are control characters added to the input buffer correctly?

"Input" a control character such as 01H. Do not use ETX, ACK, XON, or XOFF (03H, 06H, 11H, and 13H, respectively); these may cause side effects if you have errors in the protocol handling logic. Check that the character is stored in the next byte of the input buffer and that the character and control counts are set to two and one, respectively. The put offset should also be set to two.

When the input buffer full threshold is reached, does the driver output the correct protocol character?

Set the first status byte in the first device table to enable input XON or RTS protocol, or both. Then go round the main testbed loop putting characters into the input buffer. Check the console display to see if the drivers output the correct values when the buffer is almost full (the default threshold is when five bytes remain). The driver should then drop the RTS line or output an XOFF character or both, according to the input protocol that you enabled.

When the input buffer is completely full, does the driver respond correctly?

This is an extension of the test above. Input one more character than can fit into the buffer. Check to see that the drivers do not stack the character into the input buffer and that a BELL character (07H) is output to the data port.

Are protocol characters XON/XOFF recognized and the necessary control flags set or reset?

Reload the testbed and drivers. Set the status byte to enable the output XON/XOFF protocol. Then use the Character$Interrupt routine to input an XOFF character (13H). Check to see that the XOFF character has not been put into the input buffer. Instead, the status byte should be set to indicate that output has indeed been suspended.

Input an XON and check to see that the output suspended flag has been reset.

Does the driver detect and reset hardware errors correctly?

Proceed as though you were going to input a character into the input buffer, but instead enter a status byte value that indicates that a hardware error has occurred (enter the value given in the device table for DT$Detect$Error$Value).

Check that the driver detects the error status and outputs the correct error-reset value to the appropriate control port.

Non-interrupt Service Routine Checklist   In a "live" BIOS, non-interrupt service routines are accessed via the CONIN and CONST entry points in the BIOS jump vector. During debugging, the testbed can call the CONIN and CONST code directly.

Is input redirection functioning? Does control arrive in the driver with the correct device table selected?

This is best tested directly with DDT. Use the Gnnnn,bbbb command to transfer control into the CONIN code with a breakpoint at the RET instruction at the end of the Select$Device$Table routine (see Figure 8-10, line 04400). Check that the DE register pair is pointing at device table 0. If it is not, you will have to restart the test. Use the Tn command to make DDT trace through the Select$Device$Table subroutine to find the bug.

Are characters returned correctly from the buffer?

Use the testbed to "input" a character or two. Then use the testbed to make several entries into CONIN. Check the characters returned from the buffer.

Are the data character and control character counts correctly decremented?

After each character has been removed from the buffer by CONIN, use DDT to examine the device table and check that the data character and control character counts have been decremented correctly. Also check that the get pointer has moved up the input buffer.

When the buffer "almost empty" threshold is reached, does the driver emit the correct protocol character or manipulate the request to send (RTS) line correctly?

Use DDT to enable the input RTS or XON protocol or both. Then input characters into the input buffer until it reaches the buffer full threshold (the default is when only five spare bytes remain in the buffer). Confirm that "buffer almost full" processing occurs. Then make repetitive calls to CONIN to flush data out of the buffer. Check that the "buffer emptying" processing occurs when the correct threshold is reached. For RTS protocol, the driver should output a raise RTS value to the specified RTS control port. For XON, the driver should output an XON character to the data port (after first having read the status port to ensure that the hardware can output the character).

Does the driver handle buffer "wraparound" correctly?

Input characters to the input buffer until it becomes completely full. Then make a single CONIN call to remove the first character from the buffer. Follow this by inputting one more character to the buffer. Check that the get pointer is set to one and the put pointer set to zero.

Next, make successive CONIN calls to empty the buffer. Then input one more character to the buffer. Check that this last character is put into the first byte of the input buffer.

Can the driver handle "forced input" correctly?

Using DDT, set the forced input pointer to point to a 00-byte-terminated string; for example, use one of the function key decode default strings. (In Figure 8-10, the forced input pointer is initialized to point to a "startup string"—this is declared at the beginning of the configuration block at line 00400.)

Using DDT, call the CONST routine and check that it returns with A = 0FFH (indicating that there appears to be input data waiting).

Make successive calls to CONIN and confirm that the data bytes in the forced input string are returned. Check that the forcing of input ends when the 00H-byte is detected.

Does the console status routine operate correctly when it checks for data characters in the buffer, control characters in the buffer, and forced input?

Input a single noncontrol character, such as 41H, into the input buffer. Using DDT, check that the second status byte in the device table has the fake type-ahead flag set to zero. Call the CONST routine—it should return with A = 0FFH (meaning that there is data in the buffer). Then set the fake type-ahead bit in the second status byte and call CONST again. It should return with A = 00H (meaning that there is now "no data" in the buffer). Input a single control character into the buffer. Now CONST should return with A = 0FFH because there is a control character in the buffer.

Does the driver recognize escape sequences incoming from keyboard function keys?

This is a difficult feature to test when the real time clock routine is not running. The driver uses the watchdog timer to wait until all characters in the escape sequence have arrived. You will therefore have to modify the code in CONIN so that the watchdog timer appears to time out immediately, rather than waiting for the real time clock to tick. To make this change, refer to Figure 8-10, line 2200; this is the start of the CONIN routine. Look for the label CONIN$Wait$For$Delay. A few instructions later there is a JNZ CONIN$Wait$For$Delay. Using DDT, set all three bytes of this JNZ to 00H.

Then, using the testbed, input the complete escape sequence into the input buffer. For example, input hexadecimal values 1B, 4F, 51 (ESCAPE, O, P), which correspond to the characters emitted on a VT-100 terminal when FUNCTION KEY 1 (PF1) is pressed.

Next, use the testbed to make successive calls to CONIN. You should see the text associated with the function key (FUNCTION KEY 1, LINE FEED) being returned by CONIN.

Repeat this test using different function key sequences, including a sequence that does not correspond to any of the preset function keys. Check that the escape sequence itself is returned by CONIN without being changed into another string.

Can the driver differentiate between a function key and the same escape sequence generated by discrete key strokes?

This is almost the same test as above. Make the same patch to the CONIN code, only this time do not enter the complete escape sequence into the buffer. Enter only the hex characters 1B and 4F. Make sure that the CONIN routine does not substitute another string in place of this quasi-escape sequence.

This test only mimics the results of manually entering an escape sequence. You could not press the keys on a terminal fast enough to get all three characters into the input buffer within the time allowed by the watchdog timer.

Character Output Checklist *Can the driver output a character?*

The CONOUT option in the testbed calls CONIN first to get a character. To start with, you may want to use DDT to set the C register to some graphic ASCII character such as 41H (A), and transfer control into CONOUT directly. Check that CONOUT reads the USART's status, waits for the output ready value, and then outputs the data to the data port. Note that the testbed will output all characters waiting in the input buffer (or forced input) when you select its CONOUT option. This is a convenience for advanced testing of the drivers — for initial testing you may want to modify the testbed to make only one call to CONIN and CONOUT and then return to the top of the testbed loop.

Does the driver suspend output when a protocol control flag indicates that output is to be suspended?

Using DDT, set the status byte in the device table to enable output XON/XOFF protocol. Then input an XOFF character and confirm that the output suspended bit in the status byte is set. Output a single character, and using DDT, confirm that the driver will remain in a status loop waiting for the output suspended bit to be cleared. Clear the bit using DDT and check that the character is output correctly.

When using ETX/ACK protocol, does the driver output an ETX after the specified number of characters have been output, then indicate that output is suspended?

For debugging purposes, alter the ETX message count value in the device table to three bytes. Then output three bytes of data via CONOUT. Check that the driver sends an ETX character (03H) after the three bytes have been output and that the output suspended flag in the status byte has been set.

Then input an ACK character (06H). Check that this character is not stored in the input buffer and that the output suspended flag is cleared.

Does the driver recognize and output escape sequences?

Input an ESCAPE, "t" (1BH, 74H) into the input buffer. Then output them via CONOUT. Using DDT, check that the CONOUT routine recognizes that an escape sequence is being output and selects the correct processing routine. In this case, the forced input pointer should be set to point at the ASCII time of day in the configuration block.

Does each of the escape sequence processors function correctly? Can the time and date be set to specified values using escape sequences?

Repeat the test above using all of the other escape sequences to make sure that they can be recognized and that they function correctly.

Real Time Clock Routines

A separate testbed program, shown in Figure 10-5, is used to check these routines. It calls the interrupt service routine directly to simulate a real time clock "tick," and then displays the time of day in ASCII on the console.

As you can see, the testbed makes a call into the debug package's initialization routine, DB$Init, and then uses an RST 6 to generate fake clock "ticks."

There is a JMP instruction in the testbed that bypasses a call to Set$Watchdog. Remove this JMP, either by editing it out or by using DDT to change it to NO OPERATIONs (NOP, 00H) when you are ready to test the watchdog routines.

Real Time Clock Test Checklist   *Is the clock running at all?*

Using DDT, trace through the interrupt service routine logic. Check that the seconds are being updated.

Chapter 10: Debugging a New CP/M System

```
                ;       Testbed for real time clock driver in the BIOS.
                ;
                ;       The complete source file consists of three components:
                ;
                ;               1. The testbed code shown here
                ;               2. The real time clock driver destined for the BIOS.
                ;               3. The debug package shown in Figure 10-2.
                ;
FFFF =          TRUE    EQU     0FFFFH
0000 =          FALSE   EQU     NOT TRUE

FFFF =          DEBUG   EQU     TRUE            ;For conditional assembly of RST
                                                ; instructions in place of IN and
                                                ; OUT instructions in the drivers.
0030 =          RST6    EQU     30H             ;Use RST 6 for fake clock tick.

0100                    ORG     100H
                START:
0100 318B01             LXI     SP,Test$Stack   ;Use local stack
0103 CD8B01             CALL    DB$Init         ;Initialize the debug package
0106 3EC3               MVI     A,JMP           ;Set up RST 6 with JMP opcode
0108 323000             STA     RST6
010B 218B01             LXI     H,RTC$Interrupt ;Set up RST 6 JMP address
010E 223100             SHLD    RST6 + 1

0111 C31D01             JMP     Testbed$Loop    ;<=== REMOVE THIS JMP WHEN READY TO
                                                ;     TEST WATCHDOG ROUTINES

0114 013200             LXI     B,50            ;50 ticks before timeout
0117 214201             LXI     H,WD$Timeout    ;Address to transfer to
011A CD8B01             CALL    Set$Watchdog    ;Set the watchdog timer
                ;
                ;
                ;       Make repeated entry to RTC interrupt routine
                ;       to ensure that clock is correctly updated
                ;
                Testbed$Loop:
011D 3EAA               MVI     A,0AAH          ;Set registers to known pattern
011F 01CCBB             LXI     B,0BBCCH
0122 11EEDD             LXI     D,0DDEEH
0125 2111FF             LXI     H,0FF11H
0128 F7                 RST     6               ;Fake interrupt clock
0129 CD8B01             CALL    DB$MSGI         ;Display in-line message
012C 436C6F636B         DB      'Clock =',0

0134 218B01             LXI     H,Time$In$ASCII ;Get address of clock in driver
0137 CD8B01             CALL    DB$MSG          ;Display current clock value
                                                ; (Note: Time$In$ASCII already has
                                                ; a line feed character in it)
013A CD8B01             CALL    DB$MSGI         ;Display in-line message
013D 0D00               DB      0DH,0           ;Carriage return
013F C31D01             JMP     Testbed$Loop
                ;
                ;       Control arrives here when the watchdog timer times
                ;       out
                WD$Timeout:
0142 CD8B01             CALL    DB$MSGI
0145 0D0A576174         DB      0DH,0AH,'Watchdog timed out',0
015A C9                 RET                     ;Return to watchdog routine
                ;
015B 9999999999         DW      9999H,9999H,9999H,9999H,9999H,9999H,9999H,9999H
016B 9999999999         DW      9999H,9999H,9999H,9999H,9999H,9999H,9999H,9999H
017B 9999999999         DW      9999H,9999H,9999H,9999H,9999H,9999H,9999H,9999H
                Test$Stack:
                ;
                ;       Dummy routines for those shown in other figures
                ;
                ;       BIOS routines (Figure 8-10)
                RTC$Interrupt:                  ;Interrupt service routine for clock tick
                Set$Watchdog:                   ;Set watchdog timer
                Time$In$ASCII:                  ;ASCII string of HH:MM:SS, LF, 0
                ;
                ;       Debug routines (Figure 10-2)
                ;
                DB$Init:                        ;Debug initialization
                DB$MSGI:                        ;Display message in-line
                DB$MSG:                         ;Display message
```

Figure 10-5.   Testbed for real-time-clock driver in the BIOS

Are the hours, minutes, and seconds carrying over correctly?

Let the testbed code run at full speed. You should see the time being updated on the console display—although it will be updated much more rapidly than real time.

Use DDT to set the minutes to 58 and then let the clock run again. Does it correctly show the hour and reset the minutes to 00? Then set the hours to 11 and the minutes to 58 and let the clock run. Do minutes carry over into hours and are hours reset to 0?

Repeat these tests with the clock update constants set for 24-hour format.

Is the clock interrupt service routine restoring the registers correctly?

Using DDT, check that the registers are still set correctly on return from the clock interrupt service routine.

How much of a load on the pre-interrupt stack is the service routine imposing?

Check the "low water mark" of the preset values remaining in the testbed stack area to see how much of a load the interrupt service routine is imposing on the stack.

Can the watchdog timer be set to a nonzero value? Can it be set back to zero?

Using the second part of the testbed, call the Set$Watchdog routine, and then monitor the testbed's execution as the watchdog timer times out. Check that the registers and stack pointer are set correctly when control is transferred to the timeout routine. Also check that control is returned properly from this routine, and thence from the interrupt service routine.

Disk Drivers

It is only feasible to check the low-level disk drivers in isolation from a real BIOS, as the BDOS interface to the deblocking code is very difficult to simulate. The testbed shown in Figure 10-6 serves only as a time-saver. It does not test the interface to the subroutines. Use DDT to set up the disk, track, and sector numbers, and then monitor the calls into SELDSK, SETTRK, SETSEC, SETDMA, and the read/write routines.

Unless you have the same disk controller on the host system as you do on the target machine, you will have to use the fake input/output system described earlier in this chapter, rather than attempt to read and write on real disks.

You can see that the testbed, after initializing the debugging package, makes calls to SELDSK, SETTRK, SETSEC, and SETDMA. It then calls a low-level read or write routine. The low-level routine called depends on which driver you wish to debug. For the standard floppy diskette driver shown in Figure 8-10, use ReadNoDeblock and WriteNoDeblock. For the 5 1/4-inch diskettes, use Read$Physical and Write$Physical. You will have to use DDT to set up some of the variables required by the low-level drivers that would normally be set up by the deblocking code.

```
                ;       Testbed for disk I/O drivers in the BIOS
                ;
                ;       The complete source file consists of three components:
                ;
                ;               1. The testbed code shown here
                ;               2. The Disk I/O drivers destined for the BIOS
                ;               3. The debug package shown in Figure 10-2.
                ;
FFFF =          TRUE    EQU     0FFFFH
0000 =          FALSE   EQU     NOT TRUE

FFFF =          DEBUG   EQU     TRUE            ;For conditional assembly of RST
                                                ;  instructions in place of IN and
                                                ;  OUT instructions in the drivers.
0100                    ORG     100H
                START:
0100 314704             LXI     SP,Test$Stack   ;Use a local stack
0103 CD4704             CALL    DB$Init         ;Initialize the debug package
                ;
                ;       Make calls to SELDSK, SETTRK, SETSEC and SETDMA,
                ;       then either a read or write routine.
                ;
                Testbed$Loop:
0106 314704             LXI     SP,Test$Stack   ;Use local stack

0109 3A1202             LDA     Logical$Disk    ;Set up for SELDSK call
010C 4F                 MOV     C,A
010D CD4704             CALL    SELDSK

0110 CD4704             CALL    DB$Display      ;Display return value in HL
0113 14                 DB      DB$HL
0114 53454C4453         DB      'SELDSK returned',0

0124 223201             SHLD    DPH$Start       ;Set up to display disk parameter header
0127 111000             LXI     D,16            ;Compute end address
012A 19                 DAD     D
012B 223401             SHLD    DPH$End         ;Store into debug call

012E CD4704             CALL    DB$Display      ;Display DPH
0131 18                 DB      DB$M            ;Memory
                DPH$Start:
0132 0000               DW      0
                DPH$End:
0134 0000               DW      0
0136 53656C6563         DB      'Selected DPH',0

0143 2A1302             LHLD    Track           ;Call SETTRK
0146 E5                 PUSH    H
0147 C1                 POP     B               ;SETTRK needs track in BC
0148 CD4704             CALL    SETTRK

014B 3A1502             LDA     Sector          ;Call SETSEC
014E 4F                 MOV     C,A             ;SETSEC need sector in C
014F CD4704             CALL    SETSEC

0152 011702             LXI     B,Test$Buffer   ;Set DMA address
0155 CD4704             CALL    SETDMA
0158 3A1602             LDA     Write$Disk      ;Check if reading or writing
015B B7                 ORA     A
015C C2D101             JNZ     Test$Write

015F CD4704             CALL    Read$No$Deblock ;*** or Read$Physical depending on which
                                                ;*** drivers you are testing
0162 CD4704             CALL    DB$Display      ;Display return code
0165 02                 DB      DB$A
0166 5465737420         DB      'Test Read returned',0

0179 CD0102             CALL    Check$Ripple    ;Check if ripple pattern in buffer
017C CA0601             JZ      Testbed$Loop    ;Yes, it is correct

017F CD4704             CALL    DB$MSGI         ;Indicate problem
0182 14                 DB      DB$HL           ;Display HL (points to offending byte)
0183 526970706C         DB      'Ripple pattern incorrect. HL -> failure.',0

01AC CD4704             CALL    DB$Display      ;Display test buffer
01AF CD1800             CALL    DB$M            ;Memory
01B2 1702               DW      Test$Buffer
```

Figure 10-6. Testbed for disk I/O drivers in the BIOS

```
01B4 0002                DW      Test$Buffer$Size
01B6 436F6E7465          DB      'Contents of Test$Buffer',0

01CE C30601              JMP     Testbed$Loop

              Test$Write:
01D1 CDF201              CALL    Fill$Ripple        ;Fill the test buffer with ripple pattern
01D4 CD4704              CALL    Write$No$Deblock;*** or Write$Physical depending on which
                                                    ;*** drivers you are testing

01D7 CD4704              CALL    DB$Display         ;Display return code
01DA 02                  DB      DB$A
01DB 5465737420          DB      'Test Write returned',0

01EF C30601              JMP     Testbed$Loop

              Fill$Ripple:                           ;Fills the Test$Buffer with a pattern
                                                    ;  formed by putting into each byte, the
                                                    ;  least significant 8-bits of the byte's
                                                    ;  address.
01F2 010002              LXI     B,Test$Buffer$Size
01F5 211702              LXI     H,Test$Buffer
              FR$Loop:
01F8 75                  MOV     M,L                ;Set pattern value into buffer
01F9 23                  INX     H                  ;Update buffer pointer
01FA 0B                  DCX     B                  ;Down date count
01FB 79                  MOV     A,C                ;Check if count zero
01FC B0                  ORA     B
01FD C2F801              JNZ     FR$Loop            ;Repeat until zero
0200 C9                  RET
              ;
              Check$Ripple:                         ;Check that the buffer is filled with the
                                                    ;  correct ripple pattern.
                                                    ;  Returns with zero status if this is true,
                                                    ;  nonzero status if the ripple is not
                                                    ;  correct. HL point to the offending byte
                                                    ;  (which should  = L)
0201 010002              LXI     B,Test$Buffer$Size
0204 211702              LXI     H,Test$Buffer
              CR$Loop:
0207 7D                  MOV     A,L                ;Get correct value
0208 BE                  CMP     M                  ;Compare to that in the buffer
0209 C0                  RNZ                        ;Mismatch, nonzero already indicated
020A 23                  INX     H                  ;Update buffer pointer
020B 0B                  DCX     B                  ;Downdate count
020C 79                  MOV     A,C                ;Check count zero
020D B0                  ORA     B
020E C20702              JNZ     CR$Loop            ;Repeat until zero
0211 C9                  RET                        ;Zero flag will already be set
              ;
              ;     Testbed variables
              ;
0212 00       Logical$Disk:    DB      0            ;A = 0, B = 1,...
0213 0000     Track:           DW      0            ;Disk track number
0215 00       Sector:          DB      0            ;Disk sector number
0216 00       Write$Disk:      DB      0            ;NZ to write to disk

0200 =        Test$Buffer$Size    EQU   512         ;<=== Alter as required
0217          Test$Buffer:     DS      Test$Buffer$Size
              ;
0417 9999999999          DW      9999H,9999H,9999H,9999H,9999H,9999H,9999H,9999H
0427 9999999999          DW      9999H,9999H,9999H,9999H,9999H,9999H,9999H,9999H
0437 9999999999          DW      9999H,9999H,9999H,9999H,9999H,9999H,9999H,9999H
              Test$Stack:
              ;
              ;     Dummy routines for those shown in other figures
              ;
              ;     BIOS routines (Figure 8-10)
              ;
              SELDSK:                  ;Select logical disk
              SETTRK:                  ;Set track number
              SETSEC:                  ;Set sector number
              SETDMA:                  ;Set DMA address
              Read$No$Deblock:
              Read$Physical:           ;Driver read routines
              Write$No$Deblock:
              Write$Physical:          ;Driver write routines
```

Figure 10-6. (Continued)

```
          ;
          ;          Debug routines (Figure 10-2)
          ;
          DB$Init:              ;Debug initialization
          DB$MSGI:              ;Display message in-line
          DB$Display:           ;Main debug display routine
0002 =    DB$A       EQU   02   ;Display codes for DB$Display
0014 =    DB$HL      EQU   20
0018 =    DB$M       EQU   24
```

Figure 10-6. Testbed for disk I/O drivers in the BIOS (continued)

Before issuing the write call, the testbed fills the disk buffer with a known pattern. This pattern is checked on return from a read operation.

For both reading and writing, the testbed shows the contents of the A register. If you have added the enhanced disk error handling described in the previous chapter, the return value in A must *always* be zero.

Disk Driver Checklist *Does SELDSK return the correct address and set up the required system variables?*

Check that the correct disk parameter header address is returned for legitimate logical disks. Check, too, that it returns an address of 0000H for illegal disks.

Check that any custom processing, such as setting the disk type and deblocking requirements from extra bytes on the disk parameter blocks, is performed correctly.

Does the SETTRK and SETSEC processing function correctly?

Using DDT, check that the correct variables are set to the specified values.

Does the driver read in the spare-sector directory correctly?

Set up to execute a physical read and, using DDT, trace the logic of the READ entry point. Check that the spare-sector directory would be loaded into the correct buffer. If you are using fake input/output, use DDT to patch in a typical spare-sector directory with two or three "spared-out" sectors.

Does the driver produce the correct spare sector in place of a bad one?

Continuing with the physical read operation, check that, for "good" track/sectors, the sector-sparing logic returns the original track and sector number, and for "bad" track/sectors, it substitutes the correct spare track and sector. If you are using sector skipping, check that the correct number of sectors is skipped.

Can a sector be read in from the disk?

Continuing further with the physical read, check that the correct sector is read from the specified disk and track. If you are using real I/O (as opposed to faking it), the "ripple pattern" set by the testbed can be used, or you can fill the disk buffer area with some known pattern (using DDT's F command) so you can tell if any data gets read in.

Make sure you do not have any disks or diskettes in the computer system that are not write-protected — you may inadvertently write on a disk rather than read it during the early stages of testing.

Can a sector be written to the disk?

Using DDT, set up to write to a particular disk, track, and sector. Remove any write protection that you put on the target disk during earlier testing. You can either use the testbed's ripple pattern or fill the disk buffer area with a distinctive pattern. Write this data onto the disk, fill the buffer area with a *different* pattern, and read in the sector that you wrote. Check that the disk buffer gets changed back to the pattern written to the disk.

Does the driver display error messages correctly?

Rather than deliberately damaging a diskette to create errors, use DDT to temporarily sabotage the disk driver's logic. Make it return each of the possible error codes in turn, checking each time that the correct error message is displayed.

For each error condition in turn, check that the disk driver performs the correct recovery action, including interacting with the user and offering the choice of retrying, ignoring the error, or aborting the program.

Live Testing a New BIOS

Given that the drivers have passed all of the testing outlined above, you are ready to pull all of the BIOS pieces together and build a CP/M image.

For your initial testing, disable the real time clock, and use simple, polled I/O for the console driver if you can. It is important to get *something* up and running as soon as possible, and it is easier to do this without possible side effects from interrupts.

Prepare a complete listing of the BIOS and plan to spend at least an hour checking through it. Take a dry run through the console and disk driver — if there are any serious bugs left in these two drivers, CP/M may not start up. Remember that once the BIOS cold boot code has been executed and control is handed over to the CCP, the BDOS will be requested to log in the system disk, and this involves reading in the disk's directory.

Pay special attention to checking some of the major data structures. Make certain that everything is at a reasonable place in memory; for example, if the last address used by the BIOS is greater than 0FFFFH, you will need to move the entire CP/M image down in memory.

Then build a system disk, load it into the machine, and press the RESET button. You should see the bootstrap sign on, then the BIOS, and after a pause of about one second, the A> prompt (or 0A> if you have included the special feature that patches the CCP).

If you see both sign-on messages but do not get an A> prompt, a likely cause of the problem is in the disk drivers. Alternatively, the directory area on the disk may be full of random data rather than 0E5H's.

If you cannot see what is wrong with the system, you might try faking the disk drivers to return a 128-byte block of 0E5H's for each read operation. The CCP should then sign on.

Once you do have the A> prompt, you can proceed with the system checkout. Start by checking that the warm boot logic works. Type a CONTROL-C. There should be a slight pause, and the A> prompt should be output again.

Next, check that you can read the disk directory by using the DIR command. If you have an empty directory, you should get a NO FILE response. If you get strange characters instead, you either forgot to initialize the directory area or the disk parameter block is directing CP/M to the wrong part of the disk for the file directory. If the system crashes, there is a problem with the disk driver.

Check that you can write on the disk by entering the command SAVE 1 TEST. Then use the DIR command to confirm that file TEST shows up in the file directory. If it does, use the ERA command ERA TEST and do another DIR command to confirm that TEST has indeed been erased.

If TEST either does not show up on the disk or cannot be erased, then you have a problem with the disk driver WRITE routine.

Put a standard CP/M release diskette into drive B and use the DIR command to check that you can access the drive and display a disk directory. If you do, then load the DDT utility and exit from it by using a G0 (G, zero) command. This further tests if the disk drivers are functioning correctly.

To test the deblocking logic (if you are using disks that require deblocking), use the command:

```
PIP A:=B:*.*[V]
```

This copies all files from drive B to drive A using the verify option. It is a particularly good test of the system, and if you have any problems with the high-level disk drivers and deblocking code, you will get a Verify Error message from PIP. You can also get this message if you have hardware problems with the computer's memory, so run a memory test if you cannot find anything obviously wrong with the deblocking algorithm.

To completely test the deblocking code, you need to use PIP to copy a file of text larger than the amount of memory available. Thus, you may have to create a large text file using a text editor just to provide PIP with test data.

With the disk driver functioning correctly, rebuild the system with the real time clock enabled. Bring up the new system and check that the ASCII time of day is being updated in the configuration block; use DDT to inspect this in memory. Set the clock to the current time, let it run for five minutes, and see if it is still accurate. You may have to adjust one of the initialization time constants for the device that is providing the periodic interrupts for the clock.

Rebuild the system yet again, this time with the real interrupt-driven console input and the real console output routines. Check that the system comes up properly and that the initial forced-input startup string appears on the console.

Check that when you type characters on the keyboard they are displayed as you type them. If not, there could be a problem with either the CONIN or CONOUT routines. Experimentally type in enough characters to fill the input buffer. If the terminal's bell starts to sound, the interrupt service routine is probably not the culprit. Check the CONOUT routine again.

Check that the function key decode logic is working correctly. With the A> prompt displayed, press a function key. The CONIN driver should inject the correct function key string and it should appear on the terminal. For example, with the BIOS in Figure 8-10, pressing PF1 on the VT-100 terminal should produce this on the display:

```
A>Function Key1
Function?
A>
```

The CCP does not recognize "Function" as a legitimate command name, nor is there such a COM file — hence the question mark.

Using DDT, write a small program that outputs ESCAPE, "t" to the console, and check that the ASCII time of day string appears on the console. This checks that the escape sequence has been recognized.

Library Functions
Reading or Writing Using the BIOS
    Accessing the File Directory
Utility Programs Enhancing
    Standard CP/M
Utility Programs for the Enhanced BIOS

Additional Utility Programs

This chapter contains the narrated source code for several useful utility programs. Two groups of such programs are included—those that supplement Digital Research's standard utility programs, and those that work in conjunction with features shown in the enhanced BIOS (Figure 8-10).

To avoid unnecessary detail, the programs shown in this chapter are all written in the C language. C is a good language to use for such purposes since it can show the overall logic of a program without the clutter of details common in assembly language.

In order to reuse as much source code as possible, this chapter includes a "library" of all the general-purpose C functions that can be called from within any of the utility programs. This file, called "LIBRARY.C", is shown in Figure 11-1. Once a utility program has been compiled, the necessary functions from the library can be linked with the utility's binary output to form the ".COM" file.

372 The CP/M Programmer's Handbook

```
/* Library of commonly-used functions */

#include <LIBRARY.H>      /* Standard defines and structures */

/*      Configuration block access       */

/*===============================================================*/
char
*get_cba(code)                /* Get configuration block address */
/*===============================================================*/
/* This function makes a call to a "private" entry in the BIOS
   jump vector to return the address of a specific data object in
   the BIOS. The code indicates which object is required.
   Each program using this function could make a direct call to
   the BIOS using the biosh() function provided by BDS C. This
   function provides a common point to which debugging code can
   be added to display the addresses returned. */

/* Entry parameters */
int code;            /* Code that specifies the object
                        whose address is required */
/* Exit Parameters
   Address returned by the BIOS routine */

{
char *retval;        /* Value returned by the BIOS */

        retval = biosh(CBGADDR,code);
 /* printf("\nget_cba : code %d address %4x",code,retval); */
        return retval;
} /* End of get_cba(code) */



/*      Character manipulation functions        */


/*===============================================================*/
strscn(string,key)                /* String scan */
/*===============================================================*/
/* This function scans a 00-terminated character string looking
   for a key string in it. If the key string is found within the
   string, the function returns a pointer to it. Otherwise it
   returns a value of zero. */
/* Entry parameters */
char *string;                /* String to be searched */
char *key;                   /* Key string to be searched for */

/* Exit parameters
    Pointer to key string within searched string, or
    zero if key not found
*/

{
while (*string)         /* For all non-null chars. in string */
    {
    if ((*string == *key) &&
        (sstrcmp(string,key) == 0)    /* First char. matches */
                                      /* Perform substring
                                         compare on rest */
       )
            return string;            /* Substring matches,
                                         return pointer */
    string++;                         /* Move to next char. in string */
    }
return 0;                             /* Indicate no match found */
} /* End of strscn */


/*===============================================================*/
ustrcmp(string1,string2)              /* Uppercase string compare */
/*===============================================================*/
/* This function is similar to the normal strcmp function;
   it differs only in that the characters are compared as if they
   were all uppercase characters -- the strings are left
   unaltered. */
```

a

b

c

Figure 11-1. LIBRARY.C, commonly used functions, in C language

```
/* Entry Parameters */
char *string1;          /* Pointer to first string */
char *string2;          /* Pointer to second string */

/* Exit parameters
   0 - if string 1 = string 2
   -ve integer if string 1 > string 2
   +ve integer if string 1 < string 2
*/
{
int count;              /* Used to access chars. in both strings */

count = 0;              /* Start with the first character of both */

        /* While string 1 characters are non-null, and
           match their counterparts in string 2. */
while (string1[count] == string2[count])
        {
        if (string1[++count] == '\0')   /* Last char. in string 1 */
                return 0;               /* Indicate equality */
        }
return string2[count] - string1[count]; /* "Compare" chars. */

} /* End of sstrcmp */


/*================================================================*/
sstrcmp(string,substring)               /* Substring compare */
/*================================================================*/
/* This function compares two strings. The first, string, need not
   be 00-terminated. The second, substring, must be 00-terminated.
   It is similar to the standard function strcmp, except that the
   length of the substring controls how many characters are compared. */

/* Entry parameters */
char *string;           /* Pointer to main string */
char *substring;        /* Pointer to substring */

/* Exit parameters
   0 - substring matches corresponding characters in string
   -ve integer if char. in string is > char. in substring
   +ve integer if char. in string is < char. in substring
*/
{
int count;      /* Used to access chars. in string and substring */

count = 0;      /* Start with the first character of each */

        /* While substring characters are non-null, and
           match their counterparts in string. */
while (string[count] == substring[count])
        {
        if (substring[++count] == '\0') /* Last char in substring */
                return 0;               /* Indicate equality */
        }
return substring[count] - string[count];        /* "Compare" chars. */

} /* End of sstrcmp */


/*================================================================*/
usstrcmp(string,substring)              /* Uppercase substring compare */
/*================================================================*/
/* This function compares two strings. The first, string, need not
   be 00-terminated. The second, substring, must be 00-terminated.
   It is similar to the substring compare above except all
   characters are made uppercase. */

/* Entry parameters */
char *string;           /* Pointer to main string */
char *substring;        /* Pointer to substring */

/* Exit parameters
   0 -- substring matches corresponding characters in string
```

Figure 11-1. (Continued)

```
            -ve integer if char. in string is > char. in substring
            +ve integer if char. in string is < char. in substring
*/
{
int count;      /* Used to access chars in string and substring */

count = 0;      /* Start with the first character of each */

                /* While substring characters are non-null, and
                    match their counterparts in string. */
while (toupper(string[count]) == toupper(substring[count]))
        {
        if (substring[++count] == '\0')  /* Last char. in substring */
                return 0;                /* Indicate equality */
        }
return substring[count] - string[count];        /* "Compare" chars. */
} /* End of usstrcmp */


/*==============================================================*/
comp_fname(scb,name)            /* Compare file names */
/*==============================================================*/
/* This function compares a possibly ambiguous file name
    to the name in the specified character string. The number of
    bytes compared is determined by the number of characters in
    the mask.
    This function can be used to compare file names and types,
    or, by appending an extra byte to the mask, the file names,
    types, and extent numbers.
    For file directory entries, an extra byte can be prefixed to
    the mask and the function used to compare user number, file
    name, type, and extent.
    Note that a "?" in the first character of the mask will NOT
    match with a value of 0xE5 (this value is used to indicate
    an inactive directory entry). */

/* Entry parameters */
struct _scb *scb;       /* Pointer to search control block */
char *name;             /* Pointer to file name */

/* Exit parameter
    NAME_EQ if the names match the mask
    NAME_LT if the name is less than the mask
    NAME_GT if the name is greater than the mask
    NAME_NE if the name is not equal to the mask (but the outcome
        is ambiguous because of the wildcards in the mask)
*/
{
int count;              /* Count of the number of chars. processed */
short ambiguous;        /* NZ when the mask is ambiguous */
char *mask;             /* Pointer to bytes at front of SCB */

/* Set pointer to characters at beginning of search control block */
mask = scb;

        /* Ambiguous match on user number, matches
            only users 0 - 15, and not inactive entries */
if (mask[0] == '?')
        {
        if (name[0] == 0xE5)
                return NAME_NE; /* Indicate inequality */
        }
else    /* First char. of mask is not "?" */
        {
        if (mask[0] != name[0]) /* User numbers do not match */
                return NAME_NE; /* Indicate inequality */
        }

/* No, check the name (and, if the length is such, the extent) */
for (count = 1;                 /* Start with first name character */
     count <= scb -> scb_length; /* For all required characters */
     count++)                   /* Move to next character */
        {
        if (mask[count] == '?') /* Wildcard character in mask */
```

Figure 11-1. (Continued)

```c
                        {
                        ambiguous = 1;  /* Indicate ambiguous name in mask */
                        continue;       /* Do not make any comparisons */
                        }
            if (mask[count] != (name[count] & 0x7F))
                        {               /* Mask char. not equal to FCB char. */
                        if (ambiguous)  /* If previous wildcard, indicate NE */
                                return NAME_NE;
                        else
                                /* Compare chars. to determine relationship */
                                return (mask[count] > name[count]) ?
                                        NAME_LT : NAME_GT);
                        }
            }
            /* If control reaches here, then all characters of the
               mask and name have been processed, and either there
               were wildcards in the mask, or they all matched. */
    return NAME_EQ;         /* Indicate mask and name are "equal" */

} /* End of comp_fname */


/*================================================================*/
conv_fname(fcb,fn)                  /* Convert file name for output */
/*================================================================*/
/* This function converts the contents of a file control
   block into a printable string "D:FILENAME.TYP." */

/* Entry parameters */
struct _fcb *fcb;                   /* Pointer to file control block */
char *fn;                           /* Pointer to area to receive name */

{
            /* If the disk specification in the
               FCB is 0, use the current disk */
    *fn++ = (fcb -> fcb_disk) ? (fcb -> fcb_disk + ('A'-1)) :
                    (bdos(GETDISK) + 'A');

    *fn++ = ':';                            /* Insert disk id. delimiter */

    movmem(&fcb -> fcb_fname,fn,8);         /* Move file name */
    fn += 8;                                /* Update pointer */
    *fn++ = '.';                            /* Insert file name/type delimiter */
    movmem(&fcb -> fcb_fname+8,fn,3);       /* Move file type */
    *fn++ &= 0x7F;                          /* Remove any attribute bits */
    *fn++ &= 0x7F;                          /* Remove any attribute bits */
    *fn++ &= 0x7F;                          /* Remove any attribute bits */
    *fn = '\0';                             /* Terminator */

} /* End of conv_fname */


/*================================================================*/
conv_dfname(disk,dir,fn)            /* Convert directory file name for output */
/*================================================================*/
/* This function converts the contents of a file directory entry
   block into a printable string "D:FILENAME.TYP," */

/* Entry parameters */
short disk;                         /* Disk id. (A = 0, B = 1) */
struct _dir *dir;                   /* Pointer to file control block */
char *fn;                           /* Pointer to area to receive name */

{
            /* Convert user number and disk id. */
    sprintf(fn,"%2d/%c:",dir -> de_userno,disk + 'A');
    fn += 5;                                /* Update pointer to file name */

    movmem(&dir -> de_fname,fn,8);          /* Move file name */
    fn += 8;                                /* Update pointer */
    *fn++ = '.';                            /* Insert file name/type delimiter */

    movmem(&dir -> de_fname+8,fn,3);        /* Move file type */
    *fn++ &= 0x7F;                          /* Remove any attribute bits */
    *fn++ &= 0x7F;                          /* Remove any attribute bits */
    *fn++ &= 0x7F;                          /* Remove any attribute bits */
    *fn = '\0';                             /* Terminator */
```

Figure 11-1. (Continued)

```c
        } /*  End of conv_dfname  */

/*================================================================*/
get_nfn(amb_fname,next_fname)    /* Get next file name */
/*================================================================*/
/* This function sets the FCB at "next_fname" to contain the
     directory entry found that matches the ambiguous file name
     in "amb_fname."
     On the first entry for a given file name, the most significant
     bit in the FCB's disk field must be set to one (this causes a
     search first BDOS call to be made). */

/* Entry parameters */
struct _fcb *amb_fname; /* Ambiguous file name */
struct _fcb *next_fname;/* First byte must have ms bit set for
                           first time entry)*/

/* Exit parameters
     0 = No further name found
     1 = Further name found (and set up in next_fname)
*/
{
char bdos_func;          /* Set to either search first or next */
char *pfname;            /* Pointer to file name in directory entry */

          /* Initialize tail-end of next file FCB to zero */
setmem(&next_fname -> fcb_extent,FCBSIZE-12,0);

bdos_func = SEARCHF;     /* Assume a search first must be given */

if (!(next_fname -> fcb_disk & 0x80))    /* If not first time */
          {
                  /* search first on previous name */
          srch_file(next_fname,SEARCHF);
          bdos_func = SEARCHN;                /* Then do a search next */
          }
else      /* First time */
          next_fname -> fcb_disk &= 0x7F; /* Reset first-time flag */

          /* Refresh next_fname from ambiguous file name
             (move disk, name, type) */
movmem(amb_fname,next_fname,12);

          /* If first time, issue search first, otherwise
             issue a search next call. "srch_file" returns
             a pointer to the directory entry that matches
             the ambiguous file name, or 0 if no match */
if (!(pfname = srch_file(next_fname,bdos_func)) )
          {
          return 0;      /* Indicate no match */
          }
          /* Move file name and type */
movmem(pfname,&next_fname -> fcb_fname,11);
return 1;                /* Indicate match found */

} /*  End of get_nfn  */


/*================================================================*/
char *srch_file(fcb,bdos_code)   /* Search for file */
/*================================================================*/
/* This function issues either a search first or search next
     BDOS call. */

/* Entry Parameters */
struct _fcb *fcb;        /* pointer to file control block */
short bdos_code;         /* either SEARCHF or SEARCHN */

/* Exit parameters
     0 = no match found
     NZ = pointer to entry matched (currently in buffer)
*/
```

Figure 11-1. (Continued)

```
{
unsigned r_code;        /* Return code from search function
                           This is either 255 for no match, or 0, 1, 2, or 3
                           being the ordinal of the 32-byte entry in the
                           buffer that matched the name  */
char *dir_entry;        /* Pointer to directory entry */

        /* The BDS C compiler always sets the BDOS DMA
              to location 0x80 */

r_code = bdos(bdos_code,fcb);  /* Issue the BDOS call */
if (r_code == 255)             /* No match found */
        return 0;

        /* Set a pointer to the matching
              entry by multiplying return code by 128
              and adding onto the buffer address (0x80),
              also add 1 to point to first character of name */

return (r_code << 5) + 0x81;

}/* End of srch_file */


/*================================================================*/
rd_disk(drb)            /* Read disk (via BIOS) */
/*================================================================*/
/* This function uses the parameters previously set up in the
     incoming request block, and, using the BIOS directly,
     executes the disk read. */

/* Entry parameters */
struct _drb *drb;       /* Disk request block (disk, track, sector, buffer) */

/* Exit parameters
     0 = No data available
     1 = Data available
*/
{
if (!set_disk(drb))     /* Call SELDSK, SETTRK, SETSEC */
        return 0;       /* If SELDSK fails, indicate
                           no data available */
if (bios(DREAD))        /* Execute BIOS read */
        return 0;       /* Indicate no data available if error returned */

return 1;               /* Indicate data available */

} /*  End of rd_disk */



/*================================================================*/
wrt_disk(drb)           /* Write disk (via BIOS) */
/*================================================================*/
/* This function uses the parameters previously set up in the
     incoming request block, and, using the BIOS directly,
     executes the disk write. */

/* Entry parameters */
struct _drb *drb;       /* Disk request block (disk, track, sector, buffer) */

/* Exit parameters
     0 = Error during write
     1 = Data written OK
*/
{
if (!set_disk(drb))     /* Call SELDSK, SETTRK, SETSEC, SETDMA */
        return 0;       /* If SELDSK fails, indicate no data written */
if (bios(DWRITE))       /* Execute BIOS write */
        return 0;       /* Indicate error returned */

return 1;               /* Indicate data written */

} /*  End of wrt_disk */
```

Figure 11-1. (Continued)

```
/*================================================================*/
short set_disk(drb)         /* Set disk parameters */
/*================================================================*/
/* This function sets up the BIOS variables in anticipation of
   a subsequent disk read or write. */

/* Entry parameters */
struct _drb *drb;           /* Disk request block (disk, track, sector, buffer) */

/* Exit parameters
   0 = Invalid disk (do not perform read/write)
   1 = BIOS now set up for read/write
*/
{
        /* The sector in the disk request block contains a
           LOGICAL sector. If necessary (as determined by the
           value in the disk parameter header), this must be
           converted into the PHYSICAL sector.
           NOTE: skewtab is declared as a pointer to a pointer to
           a short integer (single byte). */
short **skewtab;            /* Skewtab -> disk parameter header -> skew table */
short phy_sec;              /* Physical sector */

        /* Call the SELDSK BIOS entry point. If this returns
           a 0, then the disk is invalid. Otherwise, it returns
           a pointer to the pointer to the skew table */
if ( !(skewtab = biosh(SELDSK,drb -> dr_disk)).)
        return 0;           /* Invalid disk */

bios(SETTRK,drb -> dr_track);   /* Set track */

        /* Note that the biosh function puts the sector into
           registers BC, and a pointer to the skew table in
           registers HL. It returns the value in HL on exit
           from the BIOS */
phy_sec = biosh(SECTRN,drb -> dr_sector,*skewtab); /* Get physical sector */
bios(SETSEC,phy_sec);       /* Set sector */
bios(SETDMA,drb -> dr_buffer);  /* Set buffer address */

return 1;                   /* Indicate no problems */

} /* End of setp_disk */


/*      Directory Management Functions          */


/*================================================================*/
get_nde(dir_pb)             /* Get next directory entry */
/*================================================================*/
/* This function returns a pointer to the next directory entry.
   If the directory has not been opened, it opens it.
   When necessary, the next directory sector is read in.
   If the current sector has been modified and needs to be written back
   onto the disk, this will be done before reading in the next sector. */

/* Entry parameters */
struct _dirpb *dir_pb;      /* Pointer to the disk parameter block */

/* Exit Parameters
   Returns a pointer to the next directory entry in the buffer.
   The directory open and write sector flags in the parameter
   block are reset as necessary.
*/
{
if(!dir_pb -> dp_open)      /* Directory not yet opened */
        {
        if (!open_dir(dir_pb))  /* Initialize and open directory */
                {
                err_dir(O_DIR,dir_pb);      /* Report error on open */
                exit();
                }
        /* Deliberately set the directory entry pointer to the end
           of the buffer to force a read of a directory sector */
```

Figure 11-1. (Continued)

```
                dir_pb -> dp_entry = dir_pb -> dp_buffer + DIR_BSZ;
                dir_pb -> dp_write = 0;         /* Reset write-sector flag */
                }

            /* Update the directory entry pointer to the next entry in
                  the buffer. Check if the pointer is now "off the end"
                  of the buffer and another sector needs to be read. */
        if (++dir_pb -> dp_entry < dir_pb -> dp_buffer + DIR_BSZ)
                {
                return dir_pb -> dp_entry;      /* Return pointer to next entry */
                }

            /* Need to move to next sector and read it in */

            /* Do not check if at end of directory or move to
                  the next sector if the directory has just been
                  opened (but the opened flag has not yet been set) */
        if (!dir_pb -> dp_open)
                dir_pb -> dp_open = 1;  /* Indicate that the directory is now open */
        else
                {
            /* Check if the sector currently in the buffer needs to be
                  written back out to the disk (having been changed) */
                if (dir_pb -> dp_write)
                        {
                        dir_pb -> dp_write = 0;         /* Reset the flag */
                        if(!rw_dir(W_DIR,dir_pb))       /* Write the directory sector */
                                {
                                err_dir(W_DIR,dir_pb);  /* Report error on writing */
                                exit();
                                }
                        }

            /* Count down on number of directory entries left to process,
                  always four 32-byte entries per 128-byte sector */
                dir_pb -> dp_entrem -= 4;

            /* Set directory-end flag true if number of entries now < 0 */
                if (dir_pb -> dp_entrem == 0)           /* now at end of directory */
                        {
                        dir_pb -> dp_end = 1;           /* Indicate end */
                        dir_pb -> dp_open = 0;          /* Indicate directory now closed */
                        return 0;                       /* Indicate no more entries */
                        }

            /* Update sector (and if need be track and sector) */
                if (++dir_pb -> dp_sector == dir_pb -> dp_sptrk)
                        {
                        ++dir_pb -> dp_track;           /* Update track */
                        dir_pb -> dp_sector = 0;        /* Reset sector */
                        }
                }
        if(!rw_dir(R_DIR,dir_pb))       /* Read next directory sector */
                {
                err_dir(R_DIR,dir_pb);  /* Report error on reading */
                exit();
                }

        /* Reset directory-entry pointer to first entry in buffer */
        return dir_pb -> dp_entry = dir_pb -> dp_buffer;

}  /* End of get_nde */


/*==============================================================*/
open_dir(dir_pb)           /* Open directory */
/*==============================================================*/
/* This function "opens" up the file directory
     on a specified disk for subsequent processing
     by rw_dir, next_dir functions. */

/* Entry parameters */
struct _dirpb *dir_pb;  /* Pointer to directory parameter block */
```

Figure 11-1. (Continued)

```c
/* Exit parameters
     0 = Error, directory not opened
     1 = Directory open for processing
*/
{
struct _dpb *dpb;              /* CP/M disk parameter block */

        /* Get disk parameter block address for the disk specified in
            the directory parameter block */
if ((dpb = get_dpb(dir_pb -> dp_disk)) == 0)
        return 0;              /* Return indicating no DPB for this disk */

        /* Set the remaining fields in the parameter block */
dir_pb -> dp_sptrk = dpb -> dpb_sptrk;   /* Sectors per track */
dir_pb -> dp_track = dpb -> dpb_trkoff;  /* Track offset of the directory */
dir_pb -> dp_sector = 0;                 /* Beginning of directory */
dir_pb -> dp_nument = dpb -> dpb_maxden+1; /* No. of directory entries */
dir_pb -> dp_entrem = dir_pb -> dp_nument; /* Entries remaining to process */
dir_pb -> dp_end = 0;                    /* Indicate not at end */

        /* Set number of allocation blocks per directory entry to
            8 or 16 depending on the number of allocation blocks */
dir_pb -> dp_nabpde = (dpb -> dpb_maxabn > 255 ? 8 : 16);
        /* Set number of allocation blocks (one more than number of
            highest block) */
dir_pb -> dp_nab = dpb -> dpb_maxabn;

        /* Set the allocation block size based on the block shift.
            The possible values are: 3 = 1k, 4 = 2K, 5 = 4K, 6 = 8K, 7 = 16K.
            So a value of 16 is shifted right by (7 - bshift) bits. */
dir_pb -> dp_absize = 16 >> (7 - dpb -> dpb_bshift);

return 1;              /* Indicate that directory now opened */

} /* End of open_dir */


/*================================================================*/
rw_dir(read_op,dir_pb)    /* Read/write directory */
/*================================================================*/
/* This function reads/writes the next 128-byte
    sector from/to the currently open directory. */

/* Entry parameters */
short read_op;                 /* True to read, false (0) to write */
struct _dirpb *dir_pb;         /* Directory parameter block */

/* Exit parameters
     0 = error -- operation not performed
     1 = operation completed
*/
{
struct _drb drb;               /* Disk request (for BIOS read/write) */

drb.dr_disk = dir_pb -> dp_disk;      /* Set up disk request */
drb.dr_track = dir_pb -> dp_track;
drb.dr_sector = dir_pb -> dp_sector;
drb.dr_buffer = dir_pb -> dp_buffer;

if (read_op)
        {
        if (!rd_disk(&drb))    /* Issue read command */
                return 0;      /* Indicate error -- no data available */
        }
else
        {
        if (!wrt_disk(&drb))   /* Issue write command */
                return 0;      /* Indicate error -- no data written */
        }
return 1;                      /* Indicate operation complete */

} /* End of rd_dir */
```

Figure 11-1.   (Continued)

Chapter 11: Additional Utility Programs

```
/*================================================================*/
err_dir(opcode,dir_pb)            /* Display directory error */
/*================================================================*/
/* This function displays an error message to report an error
   detected in the directory management functions open_dir and rw_dir. */
/* Entry parameters */
short opcode;                     /* Operation being attempted */
struct _dirpb *dir_pb;            /* Pointer to directory parameter block */

{
printf("\n\007Error during ");

switch(opcode)
    {
    case R_DIR:
            printf("Reading");
            break;
    case W_DIR:
            printf("Writing");
            break;
    case O_DIR:
            printf("Opening");
            break;
    default:
            printf("Unknown Operation (%d) on",opcode);
    }
printf(" Directory on disk %c:. ",dir_pb -> dp_disk + 'A');

} /* End of err_dir */


/*================================================================*/
setscb(scb,fname,user,extent,length)   /* Set search control block */
/*================================================================*/
/* This function sets up a search control block according
   to the file name specified. The file name can take the
   following forms:

        filename
        filename.typ
        d:filename.typ
        *:filename.typ (meaning "all disks")
        ABCD...NOP:filename.typ (meaning "just the specified disks")

   The function sets the bit map according to which disks should be
   searched. For each selected disk, it checks to see if an error is
   generated when selecting the disk (i.e. if there are disk tables
   in the BIOS for the disk). */

/* Entry parameters */
struct _scb *scb;       /* Pointer to search control block */
char *fname;            /* Pointer to the file name */
short user;             /* User number to search for */
short extent;           /* Extent number to search for */
int length;             /* Number of bytes to compare */

/* Exit parameters
   None.
*/

{
int disk;               /* Disk number currently being checked */
unsigned adisks;        /* Bit map for active disks */

adisks = 0;             /* Assume no disks to search */

if (strscn(fname,":"))  /* Check if ":" in file name */
    {
    if (*fname == '*')  /* Check if "all disks" */
        {
        adisks = 0xFFFF;        /* Set all bits */
        }
    else                /* Set specific disks */
        {
        while(*fname != ':')    /* Until ":" reached */
```

Figure 11-1. (Continued)

```
                              {
                              /* Build the bit map by getting the next disk
                                 id. (A - P), converting it to a number in
                                 the range 0 - 15, shifting a 1-bit left
                                 that many places, and OR-ing it into the
                                 current active disks. */
                              adisks |= 1 << (toupper(*fname) - 'A');
                              ++fname;          /* Move to next character */
                              }
                    ++fname;                    /* Bypass colon */
                    }
          }
     else      /* Use only current default disk */
          {
                    /* Set just the bit corresponding to the current disk */
          adisks = 1 << bdos(GETDISK);
          }
     setfcb(scb,fname);     /* Set search control block as though it
                               were a file control block. */

     /* Make calls to the BIOS SELDSK routine to make sure that
        all of the active disk drives have disk tables for them
        in the BIOS. If they don't, turn off the corresponding
        bits in the bit map. */

     for (disk = 0;          /* Start with disk A: */
          disk < 16;         /* Until disk P: */
          disk++)            /* Use next disk */
          {
          if ( !((1 << disk) & adisks))
               continue;               /* Avoid selecting unspecified disks */
          if (biosh(SELDSK,disk) == 0) /* Make BIOS SELDSK call */
               {                       /* Returns 0 if invalid disk */
               /* Turn OFF corresponding bit in mask
                   by AND-ing it with bit mask having
                   all the other bits set = 1 */
               adisks &= ((1 << disk) ^ 0xFFFF);
               }
          }
     scb -> scb_adisks = adisks;       /* Set bit map in SCB */
     scb -> scb_userno = user;         /* Set user number */
     scb -> scb_extent = extent;       /* Set extent number */
     scb -> scb_length = length;       /* Set number of bytes to compare */

     } /* End setscb */


/*================================================================*/
dm_clr(disk_map)                    /* Disk map clear (to zeros) */
/*================================================================*/
/* This function clears all elements of the disk map to zero. */

/* Entry Parameters */
unsigned disk_map[16][18];          /* Address of array of unsigned integers */

/* Exit parameters
     None.
*/
     {
          /* WARNING -- The 576 in the setmem call below is based on
             the disk map array being [16][18] -- i.e. 288 unsigned
             integers, hence 576 bytes. */
     setmem(disk_map,576,'\0');     /* Fill array with zeros */

     } /* End of dm_clr */


/*================================================================*/
dm_disp(disk_map,adisks)            /* Disk map display */
/*================================================================*/
/* This function displays the elements of the disk map, showing
   the count in each element. A zero value-element is shown as
   blanks. For example:
```

Figure 11-1.   (Continued)

```
         0   1   2   3   4   5   6   7   8   9  10  11  12  13  14  15 Used Free
    A:  123     20  98         202     199 101 211                         954  70
        Lines will only be printed for active disks (as indicated by
        the bit map). */

    /* Entry parameters */
    unsigned disk_map[16][18];      /* Pointer to disk map array */
    unsigned adisks;                /* Bit map of active disks */

    {
    #define USED_COUNT 16           /* "User" number for used entities */
    #define FREE_COUNT 17           /* "User" number for free entities */

    int disk;                       /* Current disk number */
    int userno;                     /* Current user number */
    unsigned dsum;                  /* Sum of entries for given disk */

    printf("\n     0   1   2   3   4   5   6   7   8   9  10  11  12  13  14  15 Used Free");

    for (disk = 0;                  /* Start with disk A: */
         disk < 16;                 /* Until disk P: */
         disk++)                    /* Next disk */
        {
        if (!(adisks & (1 << disk)))    /* Check if disk is active */
                continue;               /* No -- so bypass this one */

        printf("\n%c: ",disk + 'A');    /* Display disk number */

        dsum = 0;                   /* Reset sum for this disk */
        for (userno = 0;            /* Start with user 0 */
             userno < 16;           /* Until user 15 */
             userno++)              /* Next user number */
            {
            dsum += disk_map[disk][userno]; /* Build sum */
            }

        if (dsum)       /* Check if any output for this disk,
                           and if not, display d: None */
            {
            /* Print either number or blanks */
            for (userno = 0;            /* Start with user 0 */
                 userno < 16;           /* Until user 15 */
                 userno++)              /* Next user number */
                {
                if (disk_map[disk][userno])
                        printf("%4d",disk_map[disk][userno]);
                else
                        printf("    ");
                }
            }
        else            /* No output for this disk */
            {
            printf( " -- None -- ");
            }
        printf("  %4d %4d",disk_map[disk][USED_COUNT],disk_map[disk][FREE_COUNT]);
        }

    } /* End dm_disp */


    /*================================================================*/
    get_dpb(disk)           /* Get disk parameter block address */
    /*================================================================*/
    /* This function returns the address of the disk parameter
       block (located in the BIOS). */

    /* Entry parameters */
    char disk;              /* Logical disk for which DPB address is needed */

    /* Exit parameters
            0 = Invalid logical disk
            NZ = Pointer to disk parameter block
    */

    {
    if (biosh(SELDSK,disk) == 0)        /* Make BIOS SELDSK call */
            return 0;                   /* Invalid disk */
```

Figure 11-1. (Continued)

```
        bdos(SETDISK,disk);              /* Use BDOS SETDISK function */
        return bdos(GETDPARM);           /* Get the disk parameter block */

    } /* End of get_dpb   */


        /*      Code table functions    */

    /* Most programs that interact with a user must
        accept parameters from the user by name and translate
        the name into some internal code value.
        They also must be able to work in reverse, examining
        the setting of a variable, and determining what (ASCII
        name) it has been set to.

        An example is setting baud rates. The user may want to
        enter "19200," and have this translated into a number
        to be output to a chip. Alternatively, a previously
        set baud rate variable may have to be examined and the
        string "19200" generated to display its current
        setting to the user.

        A code table is used to make this task easier.
        Each element in the table logically consists of:
            A code value (unsigned integer)
            An ASCII character string (actually a pointer to it) */

    /*==============================================================*/
    ct_init(entry,code,string)         /* Initialize code table */
    /*==============================================================*/
    /* This function initializes a specific entry in a code table
        with a code value and string pointer.

        NOTE: By convention, the last entry in a given
        code table will have a code value of CT_SNF (string not found). */

    /* Entry parameters */
    struct _ct *entry;                 /* Pointer to code table entry */
    int code;                          /* Code value to store in entry */
    char *string;                      /* Pointer to string for entry */

    /* Exit parameters
        None.
    */
    {
    entry -> _ct_code = code;          /* Set _ct_code */
    entry -> _ct_sp = string;          /* Set string pointer */
    } /* end of ct_inti */

    /*==============================================================*/
    unsigned
    ct_parc(table,string)              /* Parameter - return code */
    /*==============================================================*/
    /* This function searches the specified table for a
        matching string, and returns the code value that corresponds to it.
        If only one match is found in the table, then this function returns
        that code value. If no match or more than one match is found,
        it returns the error value, CT_SNF (string not found).
        This function is specifically designed for processing
        parameters on a command tail.
        Note that the comparison is done after conversion to uppercase
        (i.e. "STRING" matches "string"). A substring compare is used so
        that only the minimum number of characters for an unambiguous
        response need be entered. For example, if the table contained:

                Code    Value
                1       "APPLES"
                2       "ORANGES"
                3       "APRICOTS"

        A response of "O" would return code = 2, but "A" or "AP" would
        be ambiguous. "APR" or "APP" would be required. */

    struct _ct *table;                 /* Pointer to table */
    char *string;                      /* Pointer to key string */
```

Figure 11-1.   (Continued)

```
{
int mcode;                          /* Matched code to return */
int mcount;                         /* Count of number of matches found */

mcode = CT_SNF;                     /* Assume error */
mcount = 0;                         /* Reset match count */

while(table -> _ct_code != CT_SNF)  /* Not at end of table */
        {
        /* Compare keyboard response to table entry using
           uppercase substring compare. */
        if (usstrcmp(table -> _ct_sp,string) == 0)
                {
                mcount++;           /* Update match count */
                mcode = table -> _ct_code;    /* Save code */
                }
        table++;                    /* Move to next entry */
        }
if (mcount == 1)                    /* Only one match found */
        return mcode;               /* Return matched code */
else                                /* Illegal or ambiguous */
        return CT_SNF;

} /* End ct_parc */


/*================================================================*/
unsigned
ct_code(table,string)    /* Return code for string */
/*================================================================*/
/* This function searches the specified table for the
   specified string. If a match occurs, it returns the
   corresponding code value. Otherwise it returns CT_SNF
   (string not found).
   Unlike ct_parc, this function compares every character in the
   key string, and will return the code on the first match found. */

/* Entry parameters */
struct _ct *table;       /* Pointer to table */
char *string;            /* Pointer to string */

/* Exit parameters
   Code value -- if string found
   CT_SNF -- if string not found
*/
{
while(table -> _ct_code != CT_SNF)        /* For all entries in table */
        {
        if (ustrcmp(table -> _ct_sp,string) == 0) /* Compare strings */
                return table -> _ct_code;         /* Return code */
        table++;                                  /* Move to next entry */
        }
return CT_SNF;                                    /* String not found */

} /* End ct_code */


/*================================================================*/
ct_disps(table) /*   Displays all strings in specified table */
/*================================================================*/
/* This function displays all of the strings in a given table.
   It is used to indicate valid responses for operator input. */

/* Entry parameters */
struct _ct *table;                /* Pointer to table */

/* Exit Parameters
        None.
*/
{
while(table -> _ct_code != CT_SNF)        /* Not end of table */
        {
        printf("\n\t\t%s",table -> _ct_sp);     /* Print string */
        table++;                                /* Move to next entry */
        }
```

Figure 11-1. (Continued)

```
        putchar('\n');                          /* Add final return */
    } /* End of ct_disps */


    /*================================================================*/
    ct_index(table,string) /* Returns index for a given string */
    /*================================================================*/
    /* This function searches the specified table, and returns
       the INDEX of the entry containing a matching string.
       All characters of the string are used for the comparison,
       after they have been made uppercase. */

    /* Entry parameters */
    struct _ct *table;                  /* Pointer to table */
    char *string;                       /* Pointer to string */

    /* Exit parameters
       Index of entry matching string, or
       CT_SNF if string not found.
    */
    {
    int index;                          /* Current value of index */

    index = 0;                          /* Initialize index */

    while(table -> _ct_code != CT_SNF)  /* Not at end of table */

            {
            if (ustrcmp(table -> _ct_sp,string) == 0)
                    return index;       /* Return index */
            table++;                    /* Move to next table entry */
            index++;                    /* Update index */
            }
    return CT_SNF;         /* String not found */

    }


    /*================================================================*/
    char *ct_stri(table,index)          /* Get string according to index */
    /*================================================================*/
    /* This function returns a pointer to the string in the
       table entry specified by the index. */

    /* Entry parameters */
    struct _ct *table;                  /* Pointer to table */
    int index;                          /* Index into table */

    {
    struct _ct *entry;                  /* Entry pointer */
            entry = table[index];       /* Point to entry */
            return entry -> _ct_sp;     /* Return pointer to string */

    } /* End of ct_stri */


    /*================================================================*/
    char *ct_strc(table,code)  /* Get string according to code value */
    /*================================================================*/
    /* This function searches the specified table and returns a
       pointer to the character string in the entry with the
       matching code value or a pointer to a string of "unknown"
       if the code value is not found. */

    /* Entry parameters */
    struct _ct *table;                  /* Pointer to table */
    unsigned  code;                     /* Code value */

    {
    while(table -> _ct_code != CT_SNF)  /* Until end of table */
            {
            if (table -> _ct_code == code)  /* Check code matches */
                    return table -> _ct_sp; /* Yes, return ptr. to str. */
            table++;                    /* No, move to next entry */
```

Figure 11-1. (Continued)

```
        }
    return "Unknown";
    }


    /*      Bit vector functions    */

    /* These functions manipulate bit vectors. A bit vector is a group
        of adjacent bits, packed eight per byte. Each bit vector has the
        structure defined in the LIBRARY.H file.

        Bit vectors are used primarily to manipulate the operating
        system's allocation vectors and other values that can best
        be represented as a series of bits. */

    /*==============================================================*/
    bv_make(bv,bytes)           /* Make a bit vector and clear to zeros */
    /*==============================================================*/
    /* This function uses C's built-in memory allocation, alloc,
        to allocate the necessary amount of memory, and then
        sets the vector to zero-bits. */

    /* Entry parameters */
    struct _bv *bv;             /* Pointer to a bit vector */
    unsigned bytes;             /* Number of bytes in bit vector */

    /* Exit parameter
        NZ = vector created
        0 = insufficient memory to create vector
    */
    {
    if(!(bv -> bv_bits = alloc(bytes)))     /* Request memory */
            return 0;                       /* Request failed */
    bv -> bv_bytes = bytes;                 /* Set length */
    bv -> bv_end = bv -> bv_bits + bytes;   /* Set pointer to end */
    bv_fill(bv,0);                          /* Fill with 0's */
    return 1;

    } /* End bv_make */


    /*==============================================================*/
    bv_fill(bv,value)           /* Fill bit vector with value */
    /*==============================================================*/
    /* This function fills the specified bit vector with the
        specified value.
        This function exist only for consistency's sake and
        to isolate the main body of code from standard
        functions like setmem. */

    /* Entry parameters */
    struct _bv *bv;             /* Pointer to bit vector */
    char value;                 /* Value to fill vector with */

    /* Exit parameters
        None.
    */

    {
    /*       address       length      value */
    setmem(bv -> bv_bits,bv -> bv_bytes,value);
    }

    /*==============================================================*/
    bv_set(bv,bitnum)           /* Set the specified bit number */
    /*==============================================================*/
    /* This function sets the specified bit number in the bit vector
        to one-bit. */

    /* Entry parameters */
    struct _bv *bv;             /* Pointer to bit vector */
    unsigned bitnum;            /* Bit number to be set */
```

bb

cc

dd

ee

Figure 11-1. (Continued)

```
/* Exit parameters
    None.
*/
{
unsigned byte_offset;         /* Byte offset into the bit vector */

if ((byte_offset = bitnum >> 3) > bv -> bv_bytes)
        return 0;     /* Bitnum is "off the end" of the vector */

/* Set the appropriate bit in the vector. The byte offset
   has already been calculated. The bit number in the byte
   is calculated by AND ing the bit number with 0x07.
   The specified bit is then OR ed into the vector */

bv -> bv_bits[byte_offset] |= (1 << (bitnum & 0x7));

return 1;             /* Indicate completion */

/* End of bv_set */

/*================================================================*/
bv_test(bv,bitnum)                /* Test the specified bit number */
/*================================================================*/
/* This function returns a value that reflects the current
   setting of the specified bit. */

/* Entry parameters */
struct _bv *bv;               /* Pointer to bit vector */
unsigned bitnum;              /* Bit number to be set */

/* Exit parameters
    None.
*/
{
unsigned byte_offset;         /* Byte offset into the bit vector */

if ((byte_offset = bitnum >> 3) > bv -> bv_bytes)
        return 0;     /* Bitnum is "off the end" of the vector */

/* Set the appropriate bit in the vector. The byte offset
   has already been calculated. The bit number in the byte
   is calculated by AND ing the bit number with 0x07.
   The specified bit is then OR ed into the vector */

return bv -> bv_bits[byte_offset] & (1 << (bitnum & 0x7));

} /* End of bv_tests */

/*================================================================*/
bv_nz(bv)                     /* Test bit vector nonzero */
/*================================================================*/
/* This function tests each byte in the specified vector,
   and returns indicating whether any bits are set in
   the vector. */

/* Entry parameters */
struct _bv *bv;               /* Pointer to bit vector */

/* Exit Parameters
    NZ = one or more bits are set in the vector
    0 = all bits are off
*/
{
char *bits;                   /* Pointer to bits in bit vector */

bits = bv -> bv_bits;         /* Set working pointer */

while (bits != bv -> bv_end)  /* For entire bit vector */
    {
    if (*bits++)              /* If nonzero */
            return bits--;    /* Return pointer to NZ byte */
```

ee

ff

gg

Figure 11-1. (Continued)

Chapter 11: Additional Utility Programs **389**

```
              }
        return 0;                     /* Indicate vector is zero */

    } /* End of by_nz */                                              } gg


    /*================================================================*/
    bv_and(bv3,bv1,bv2)               /* bv3 = bv1 & bv2 */
    /*================================================================*/
    /* This function performs a boolean AND between the bytes
       of bit vector 1 and 2, storing the result in bit vector 3. */

    /* Entry parameters */
    struct _bv *bv1;                  /* Pointer to input bit vector */
    struct _bv *bv2;                  /* Pointer to input bit vector */

    /* Exit parameters */
    struct _bv *bv3;                  /* Pointer to output bit vector */

    {
    char *bits1, *bits2, *bits3;      /* Working pointers to bit vectors */     hh

    bits1 = bv1 -> bv_bits;           /* Initialize working pointers */
    bits2 = bv2 -> bv_bits;
    bits3 = bv3 -> bv_bits;

            /* AND ing will proceed until the end of any one of the bit
               vectors is reached */
    while (bits1 != bv1 -> bv_end &&
           bits2 != bv2 -> bv_end &&
           bits3 != bv3 -> bv_end)
            {
                  *bits3++ = *bits1++ & *bits2++; /* bv3 = bv1 & bv2 */
            }
    } /* End of bv_and */


    /*================================================================*/
    bv_or(bv3,bv1,bv2)                /* bv3 = bv1 or bv2 */
    /*================================================================*/
    /* This function performs a boolean inclusive OR between the bytes
       of bit vectors 1 and 2, storing the result in bit vector 3. */

    /* Entry parameters */
    struct _bv *bv1;                  /* Pointer to input bit vector */
    struct _bv *bv2;                  /* Pointer to input bit vector */

    /* Exit parameters */
    struct _bv *bv3;                  /* Pointer to output bit vector */

    {
    char *bits1, *bits2, *bits3;      /* Working pointers to bit vectors */     ii

    bits1 = bv1 -> bv_bits;           /* Initialize working pointers */
    bits2 = bv2 -> bv_bits;
    bits3 = bv3 -> bv_bits;

            /* The OR ing will proceed until the end of any one of the bit
               vectors is reached. */
    while (bits1 != bv1 -> bv_end &&
           bits2 != bv2 -> bv_end &&
           bits3 != bv3 -> bv_end)
            {
                  *bits3++ = *bits1++ | *bits2++; /* bv3 = bv1 or bv2 */
            }
    } /* End of bv_or */


    /*================================================================*/
    bv_disp(title,bv)                 /* Bit vector display */
    /*================================================================*/
    /* This function displays the contents of the specified bit vector
       in hexadecimal. It is normally only used for debugging. */

    /* Entry parameters */
    char *title;                      /* Title for the display */               jj
    struct _bv *bv;                   /* Pointer to the bit vector */
```

Figure 11-1. (Continued)

```
/* Exit parameters
      None.
*/

{
char *bits;                     /* Working pointer */
unsigned byte_count;            /* Count used for formatting display */
unsigned bit_count;             /* Count for processing bits in a byte */
char byte_value;                /* Value to be displayed */

printf("\nBit Vector : %s",title);   /* Display title */

bits = bv -> bv_bits;           /* Set working pointer */
byte_count = 0;                 /* Initialize count */

while (bits != bv -> bv_end)    /* For the entire vector */
    {
    if (byte_count % 5 == 0)    /* Check if new line */
                                /* Display bit number */
            printf("\n%4d : ",byte_count << 3);

    byte_value = *bits++;       /* Get the next byte from the vector */

    for (bit_count = 0; bit_count < 8; bit_count++)
        {
        /* Display the leftmost bit, then shift the value
            left one bit */
        if (bit_count == 4) putchar(' '); /* Separator */
        putchar((byte_value & 0x80) ? '1' : '0');
        byte_value <<= 1;       /* Shift value left */
        }
    printf(" ");                /* Separator */

    byte_count++;   /* Update byte count */
    }
} /* End of bv_disp */

/* End of LIBRARY.C */
```

Figure 11-1.   (Continued)

Associated with the library of functions is another section of source code called "LIBRARY.H", shown in Figure 11-2. This "header" file must be included at the beginning of each program that calls any of the library functions.

For reasons of clarity, this chapter describes the simplest functions first, followed by the more complex, and finally by the utility programs that use the functions.

Several functions in the library and some definitions in the library header are not used by the utilities shown in this chapter. They have been included to illustrate techniques and because they might be useful in other utilities you could write.

```
#define LIBVN "1.0"     /* Library version number */

/* This file contains groups of useful definitions.
   It should be included at the beginning of any program
   that uses the functions in LIBRARY.C */


/* Definition to make minor language modification to C. */
#define short char              /* Short is not supported directly */
```

Figure 11-2.   LIBRARY.H, code to be included at the beginning of any program that calls LIBRARY functions in Figure 11-1

```
/* One of the functions (bv_make) in the library uses the BDS C
   function, alloc, to allocate memory. The following definitions
   are provided for alloc. */

struct _header                     /* Header for block of memory allocated */
      {
       struct _header *_ptr;       /* Pointer to the next header in the chain */
       unsigned _size;             /* Number of bytes in the allocated block */
      };
struct _header _base;              /* Declare the first header of the chain */
struct _header *_allocp;           /* Used by alloc() and free() functions */


/* BDOS function call numbers */

#define SETDISK  14      /* Set (select) disk */
#define SEARCHF  17      /* Search first */
#define SEARCHN  18      /* Search next */
#define DELETEF  19      /* Delete file */
#define GETDISK  25      /* Get default disk (currently logged in) */
#define SETDMA   26      /* Set DMA (Read/Write) Address */
#define GETDPARM 31      /* Get disk parameter block address */
#define GETUSER  32      /* Get current user number */
#define SETUSER  32      /* Set current user number */


/* Direct BIOS calls
     These definitions are for direct calls to the BIOS.
     WARNING:   Using these makes program less transportable.
     Each symbol is related to its corresponding jump in the
     BIOS jump vector.
     Only the more useful entries are defined. */

#define CONST    2       /* Console status */
#define CONIN    3       /* Console input */
#define CONOUT   4       /* Console output */
#define LIST     5       /* List output */
#define AUXOUT   6       /* Auxiliary output */
#define AUXIN    7       /* Auxiliary input */

#define HOME     8       /* Home disk */
#define SELDSK   9       /* Select logical disk */
#define SETTRK   10      /* Set track */
#define SETSEC   11      /* Set sector */
#define SETDMA   12      /* Set DMA address */
#define DREAD    13      /* Disk read */
#define DWRITE   14      /* Disk write */
#define LISTST   15      /* List status */
#define SECTRN   16      /* Sector translate */
#define AUXIST   17      /* Auxiliary input status */
#define AUXOST   18      /* Auxiliary output status */

                         /* "Private" entries in jump vector */
#define CIOINIT  19      /* Specific character I/O initialization */
#define SETDOG   20      /* Set watchdog timer */
#define CBGADDR  21      /* Configuration block, get address */


/* Definitions for accessing the configuration block */

#define CB_GET   21      /* BIOS jump number to access routine */
#define DEV_INIT 19      /* BIOS jump to initialize device */

#define CB_DATE  0       /* Date in ASCII */
#define CB_TIMEA 1       /* Time in ASCII */
#define CB_DTFLAGS 2     /* Date, time flags */
#define TIME_SET 0x01    /* This bit NZ means date has been set */
#define DATE_SET 0x02    /* This bit NZ means time has been set */

#define CB_FIP   3       /* Forced input pointer */
#define CB_SUM   4       /* System start-up message */

#define CB_CI    5       /* Console input */
#define CB_CO    6       /* Console output */
#define CB_AI    7       /* Auxiliary input */
#define CB_AO    8       /* Auxiliary output */
```

Figure 11-2. (Continued)

```
#define CB_LI    9              /* List input */
#define CB_LO    10             /* List output */

#define CB_DTA   11             /* Device table addresses */
#define CB_C1224 12             /* Clock 12/24 format flag */
#define CB_RTCTR 13             /* Real time clock tick rate (per second) */

#define CB_WDC   14             /* Watchdog count */
#define CB_WDA   15             /* Watchdog address */

#define CB_FKT   16             /* Function key table */
#define CB_COET  17             /* Console output escape table */

#define CB_D0_IS  18            /* Device 0 initialization stream */
#define CB_D0_BRC 19            /* Device 0 baud rate constant */

#define CB_D1_IS  20            /* Device 1 initialization stream */
#define CB_D1_BRC 21            /* Device 1 baud rate constant */

#define CB_D2_IS  22            /* Device 2 initialization stream */
#define CB_D2_BRC 23            /* Device 2 baud rate constant */

#define CB_IV    24             /* Interrupt vector */
#define CB_LTCBO 25             /* Long term config. block offset */
#define CB_LTCBL 26             /* Long term config. block length */

#define CB_PUBF  27             /* Public files flag */
#define CB_MCBUF 28             /* Multi-command buffer */
#define CB_POLLC 29             /* Polled console flag */


        /* Device numbers and names for physical devices */
        /* NOTE: Change these definitions for your computer system */

#define T_DEVN  0               /* Terminal */
#define M_DEVN  1               /* Modem */
#define P_DEVN  2               /* Printer */

#define MAXPDEV 2               /* Maximum physical device number */

        /* Names for the physical devices */

#define PN_T "TERMINAL"
#define PN_M "MODEM"
#define PN_P "PRINTER"

        /* Structure and definitions for function keys */

#define FK_ILENGTH 2            /* No. of chars. input when func. key pressed
                                   NOTE: This does NOT include the ESCAPE. */
#define FK_LENGTH  16           /* Length of string (not including fk_term) */
#define FK_ENTRIES 18           /* Number of function key entries in table */

struct _fkt                     /* Function key table */
        {
        char fk_input[FK_ILENGTH];    /* Lead-in character is not in table */
        char fk_output[FK_LENGTH];    /* Output character string */
        char fk_term;                 /* Safety terminating character */
        };

/* Definitions and structure for device tables */

        /* Protocol bits */
        /* Note: if the most significant bit is
           set = 1, then the set_proto function
           will logically OR in the value. This
           permits Input DTR to co-exist with
           XON or ETX protocol. */

#define DT_ODTR 0x8004          /* Output DTR high to send (OR ed in) */
#define DT_OXON 0x0008          /* Output XON */
#define DT_OETX 0x0010          /* Output ETX/ACK */

#define DT_IRTS 0x8040          /* Input RTS (OR-ed in) */
#define DT_IXON 0x0080          /* Input XON */
```

Figure 11-2. (Continued)

```
#define ALLPROTO 0xDC          /* All protocols combined */

struct _dt                     /* Device table */
    {
    char dt_f1[14];            /* Filler */
    char dt_st1;               /* Status byte 1 -- has protocol flags */
    char dt_st2;               /* Status byte 2 */
    unsigned dt_f2;            /* Filler */
    unsigned dt_etxml;         /* ETX/ACK message length */
    char dt_f3[12];            /* Filler */
    } ;

/* Values returned by the comp_fname (compare file name) */

#define NAME_EQ 0              /* Names equal */
#define NAME_LT 1              /* Name less than mask */
#define NAME_GT 2              /* Name greater than mask */
#define NAME_NE 3              /* Name not equal (and comparison ambiguous) */

/* Structure for standard CP/M file control block */

#define FCBSIZE 36             /* Define the overall length of an FCB */

struct _fcb
    {
    short fcb_disk;            /* Logical disk (0 = default) */
    char fcb_fname[11];        /* File name, type (with attributes) */
    short fcb_extent;          /* Current extent */
    unsigned fcb_s12;          /* Reserved for CP/M */
    short fcb_reccnt;          /* Record count used in current extent */
    union                      /* Allocation blocks can be either */
        {                      /* Single or double bytes */
        short fcbab_short[16];
        unsigned fcbab_long[8];
        } _fcbab;
    short fcb_currec;          /* Current record within extent */
    char fcb_ranrec[3];        /* Record for random read/write */
    };

/* Parameter block used for calls to the directory management routines */

#define DIR_BSZ 128            /* Directory buffer size */

struct _dirpb
    {
    short dp_open;             /* 0 to request directory to be opened */
    short dp_end;              /* NZ when at end of directory */
    short dp_write;            /* NZ to write current sector to disk */
    struct _dir *dp_entry;     /* Pointer to directory entry in buffer */
    char dp_buffer [DIR_BSZ];  /* Directory sector buffer */
    char dp_disk;              /* Current logical disk */
    int dp_track;              /* Start track */
    int dp_sector;             /* Start sector */
    int dp_nument;             /* Number of directory entries */
    int dp_entrem;             /* Entries remaining to process */
    int dp_sptrk;              /* Number of sectors per track */
    int dp_nabpde;             /* Number of allocation blocks per dir. entry */
    unsigned dp_nab;           /* Number of allocation blocks */
    int dp_absize;             /* Allocation block size (in Kbytes) */
    };

/* The err_dir function is used to report errors found by the
   directory management routines, open_dir and rw_dir.
   Err_dir needs a parameter to define the operation being
   performed when the error occurred. The following definitions
   represent the operations possible. */

#define W_DIR  0               /* Writing directory */
#define R_DIR  1               /* Reading directory */
#define O_DIR  2               /* Opening directory */
```

Figure 11-2. (Continued)

```
/* Disk parameter block maintained by CPM */
struct _dpb
    {
    unsigned dpb_sptrk;     /* Sectors per track */
    short dpb_bshift;       /* Block shift */
    short dpb_bmask;        /* Block mask */
    short dpb_emask;        /* Extent mask */
    unsigned dpb_maxabn;    /* Maximum allocation block number */
    unsigned dpb_maxden;    /* Maximum directory entry number */
    short dpb_rab0;         /* Allocation blocks reserved for */
    short dpb_rab1;         /*    directory blocks */
    unsigned dpb_diskca;    /* Disk changed workarea */
    unsigned dpb_trkoff;    /* Track offset */
    };                                                              ⎤
                                                                    ⎥ n
                                                                    ⎦

/* Disk directory entry format */
struct _dir {
    char de_userno;         /* User number or 0xE5 if free entry */
    char de_fname[11];      /* File name [8] and type [3] */
    int de_extent;          /* Extent number of this entry */
    int de_reccnt;          /* Number of 128-byte records used in last
                                    allocation block */
    union                   /* Allocation blocks can be either */
        {                   /*    single or double bytes */
        short de_short[16];
        unsigned de_long[8];
        } _dirab;                                                   ⎤
    };                                                              ⎥ o
                                                                    ⎦

/* Disk request parameters for BIOS-level read/writes */
struct _drb
    {
    short dr_disk;          /* Logical disk A = 0, B = 1... */
    unsigned dr_track;      /* Track (for SETTRK) */
    unsigned dr_sector;     /* Sector (for SETSEC) */
    char *dr_buffer;        /* Buffer address (for SETDMA) */
    } ;                                                             ⎤
                                                                    ⎥ p
                                                                    ⎦

/* Search control block used by directory scanning functions */
struct _scb
        {
        short scb_userno;       /* User number(s) to match */
        char scb_fname[11];     /* File name and type */
        short scb_extent;       /* Extent number */
        char unused[19];        /* Dummy bytes to make this look like
                                        a file control block */
        short scb_length;       /* Number of bytes to compare */
        short scb_disk;         /* Current disk to be searched */
        unsigned scb_adisks;    /* Bit map of disks to be searched.
                                        the rightmost bit is for disk A:. */
        } ;                                                         ⎤
                                                                    ⎥ q
                                                                    ⎦

/* Code table related definitions */
#define CT_SNF 0xFFFF       /* String not found */

struct _ct                  /* Define structure of code table */
        {
        unsigned _ct_code;      /* Code value */
        char *_ct_sp;           /* String pointer */
        };                                                          ⎤
                                                                    ⎥ r
                                                                    ⎦
```

Figure 11-2. (Continued)

```
/* Structure for bitvectors */
struct _bv
        {
        unsigned bv_bytes;      /* Number of bytes in the vector */
        char *bv_bits;          /* Pointer to the first byte in the vector */
        char *bv_end;           /* Pointer to byte following bit vector */
        } ;


/* End of LIBRARY.H */
```
s

Figure 11-2. (Continued)

Library Functions

This section describes the library functions and the sections from the header file that must be included at the beginning of each utility program.

A Minor Change to C Language

One minor problem with the BDS C Compiler is that it does not support "short" integers, or integers that are only a single byte long. It is convenient to declare certain values as short to serve as a reminder of the standard type definition. Therefore, the BDS C compiler must be "fooled" by declaring these values to be single characters. To do this, the library header file contains the declaration

`#define short char.`

shown in Figure 11-2, section a.

The "#define" tells the first part of the C compiler, the preprocessor, to substitute the string "char" (which declares a character variable) whenever it encounters the string "short" (which would ordinarily declare a short integer in standard C).

Note that character strings enclosed in "/*" and "*/" are regarded as comments and are ignored by the compiler.

BDOS Calls

The standard library of functions that comes with the BDS C compiler includes a function to make BDOS calls, called "bdos." It takes two parameters, and a typical call is of the following form:

`bdos(c,de);`

The "c" parameter represents the value that will be placed into the C register. This is the BDOS function code number. The "de" is the value that will be placed in the DE register pair.

The library header contains definitions (#define declarations) for BDOS functions 14 through 32, making these functions easier to use (Figure 11-2, c). Function 32 (Get/Set Current User Number) has two definitions; the "de" parameter is used to differentiate whether a get or a set function is to be performed.

BIOS Calls

The BDS C standard library also contains two functions that make direct BIOS calls. These are "bios" and "biosh." They differ only in that the bios function returns the value in the A register on return from the BIOS routine, whereas biosh, as its name implies, returns the value in the HL register pair. Examples of their use are

```
bios(jump_number,bc);
```

and

```
biosh(jump_number,bc,de);
```

Both functions take as their first parameter the number of the jump instruction in the BIOS jump vector to which control is to be transferred. For example, the console-status entry point is the third JMP in the vector. Numbering from 0, this would be jump number 2.

The library header file contains #defines for BIOS jumps 2 through 21 (Figure 11-2, d). The last group of these #defines (19 through 21) is for the "private" additions to the standard BIOS jump vectors described in Chapter 8.

Remember, though, that using direct BIOS calls makes programs more difficult to move from one system to another.

BIOS Configuration Block Access

As you may recall, the configuration block is a collection of data structures in the BIOS. These structures are used either to store the current settings of certain user-selectable options, or to point to other important data structures in the BIOS.

One of the "private" jumps appended to the standard BIOS jump vector transfers control to a routine that returns the address in memory of a specified data structure. For example, if a utility program needs to locate the word in the BIOS that determines from which physical device the console input is to read, it can transfer control to jump 21 in the BIOS jump vector (actually the 22nd jump) with a code value of 5 in the C register. This jump transfers control to the CBGet-Address code, which on its return will set HL to the address of the console input redirection vector. The utility program can then read from or write into this variable. The library header file contains #define declarations relating the code values to mnemonic names (Figure 11-2, e).

You will need to refer to the source code in Figure 8-10 to determine whether the address returned by the BIOS function is the address of the data element or the address of a higher-level table that in turn points to the data element.

In order to access the current system date, for example, you would include the following code:

```
char *ptr_to_date;           /* declare date pointer*/
ptr_to_date = biosh(CB_DATE); /* get address */
```

The ptr_to_date can then be used to access the date directly.

During initial debugging of a utility, it is useful to be able to intercept all such accesses to the configuration block, partly to reassure yourself that the utility program is working as it should, and partly to ensure that the BIOS routine is returning the correct addresses to the data structures. Therefore, the utility library contains a function, "get_cba," that gets a configuration block address (Figure 11-1, a).

At first, it appears that get_cba is declared as a function that returns a pointer to characters. This is not strictly true. Sometimes the address it returns will point to characters, sometimes to integers, and sometimes to structures (such as the function key table).

The "printf" instruction has been left in the function in anticipation of debugging a utility. If you need to see some debug output whenever the get_cba function is used, delete the "/*" and "*/" surrounding the "printf" and recompile the library.

BIOS Function Key Table Access

The BIOS shown in Figure 8-10 contains code to recognize when an incoming escape sequence indicates that one of the terminal's function keys has been pressed. Instead of returning just the escape sequence, the console driver injects a previously programmed string of characters into the console input stream. For example, on a DEC VT-100 terminal, when the PF1 function key is pressed, the terminal emits the following character sequence: ESCAPE, "O", "P". The function key table contains the "OP" and a 00H-byte-terminated string of characters to be injected into the console input stream. In Figure 8-10, the example string is "FUNCTION KEY 1", LINE FEED. The library header file contains a declaration for the structure of the function key table (Figure 11-2, h).

Note the use of "#define" to declare the length of the incoming characters emitted by the terminal as well as the length of the output string.

In order to access a function key table entry, you must declare a pointer to a "_fkt" structure like this:

```
struct _fkt *ptr_to_fkt;       /* Declare pointer */
ptr_to_fkt = get_cba(CB_FKT); /* Set pointer */
printf("Display the first string : %s",
     ptr_to_fkt -> fk_output);
++ptr_to_fkt;                  /* Move to next entry */
```

The get_cba function is used to return the address of the first entry in the function key table and set a pointer to it. Then the printf function (part of the standard BDS C library) is used to print out the first string, which gets substituted for the "%s" in the quoted string. Note that the statement

```
++ptr_to_fkt
```

does not just add one to the pointer to the function key table—it adds whatever it takes to move the pointer to the next *entry* in the table.

BIOS Device Table Access

The device tables are important structures for the serial devices served by the console, auxiliary, and list device drivers in the BIOS. They are declared at line 1500 in Figure 8-10.

The get_cba function does not return a pointer to a specific device table, but a pointer to a table of device table addresses. Each entry in the address table corresponds to a specific device number. If there is no device table for a specific device number, then the corresponding entry in the table will be set to zero. the library header file contains definitions for the device table (Figure 11-2, i).

The device tables contain, among other things, the current serial line protocols used to synchronize the transmission and reception of data by the device drivers and the physical devices. An example utility, PROTOCOL, is shown later in the chapter. The example #define declarations and structure definition shown here are modeled on the requirements of this utility. The only relevant bytes are the two status bytes dt_st1 and dt_st2 and the message length used with the ETX/ACK protocol, dt_etxml. The #defines shown are for the specific bits in the device table's status bytes. The PROTOCOL utility uses the most significant bit to indicate whether a given protocol setting can coexist with others.

To access these fields, use the following code:

```
struct _ppdt
    {
    char *pdt[16];        /* Array of 16 pointers to device tables */
    } *ppdt;               /* Pointer to array of 16 pointers */
struct _dt *dt;           /* Pointer to device table */

ppdt = get_cba(CB_DTA);   /* Set pointer to array of pointers */
dt = ppdt -> pdt[device_no]; /* Set pointer to specified device
                                 table */
if (!dt)
    printf("\nError - no device table for this device.");

dt -> dt_etxml = 0;       /* Clear ETX message length */
```

BIOS Disk Parameter Block Access

Several of the utility programs shown in this chapter must access the file directory on a given logical disk. The disk parameter block (DPB) indicates the size and location of the file directory. The library header contains a structure definition that describes the DPB (Figure 11-2, n).

Chapter 11: Additional Utility Programs **399**

To locate the DPB, you can make a direct BIOS call to the SELDSK routine, which returns the address of the disk parameter header (DPH). You then can access the DPB pointer in the DPH. Alternatively, using the BDOS, you can make the required disk the default disk and then request the address of its DPB. The code for the latter method is shown in the get_dpb function included in the utility library (Figure 11-1, u).

The get_dpb function uses a BIOS SELDSK function first to see if the specified disk is legitimate. Only then does it use the BDOS.

Reading or Writing a Disk Using the BIOS

When you write a program that uses direct BIOS calls, you increase the possibility of problems in moving the program from one system to another. However, in certain circumstances it is necessary to use the BIOS. Reading and writing the file directory is one of these; the BDOS cannot be used to access the directory directly. The library header contains a structure declaration for a parameter block that contains the details of an "absolute" disk read or write (Figure 11-2, p).

Note the pointer to the 128-byte data buffer used to hold one of CP/M's "records."

The disk read and write functions are rd_disk (Figure 11-1, k) and wrt_disk (Figure 11-1, l). Both of them take a _drb as an input parameter, and both call the set_disk function to make the individual BIOS calls to SELDSK, SETTRK, and SETSEC.

Of special note is the code in set_disk (Figure 11-1, m) that converts a logical sector into a physical sector using the sector translation table and the SECTRAN entry point in the BIOS.

File Directory Entry Access

All of the utility programs that access a disk directory share the same basic logic regardless of their specific task. This logic can be described best in pseudo-code:

```
while (not at the end of the directory)
    {
    access the next directory entry
    if (this entry matches the current search criteria)
        {
        process the entry
        }
    }
```

There are two ways of implementing this logic. The first uses the BIOS to read the directory. Entries are presented to the utility exactly as they occur in the file directory. The second uses the BDOS functions Search First and Search Next and accesses the directory file-by-file rather than by entry. This latter method is more suited to utilities that process files rather than entries. The ERASE utility, described later in this chapter, illustrates this second method.

Three groups of functions are provided in the library: to access the next entry in the directory, to match the name in the current entry against a search key, and to assist with processing the directory.

Directory Accessing Functions

A number of functions involve access to the file directory. The first group of such functions performs the following:

get_nde (get next directory entry; Figure 11-1, n)
    This function returns a pointer to the next directory entry, or returns zero if the end of the directory has been reached.

open_dir (open directory; Figure 11-1, o)
    This function is called by get_nde to open up a directory for processing.

rw_dir (read/write directory; Figure 11-1, p)
    This function reads or writes the current directory sector.

err_dir (error on directory; Figure 11-1, q)
    This general-purpose routine displays an error message if the BIOS indicates that it had problems either reading or writing the directory.

All of these functions use a directory parameter block to coordinate their activity. The library header contains the definitions for this structure (Figure 11-2, l), as well as #define declarations for operation codes used by the directory-accessing functions (Figure 11-2, m).

Before calling get_nde, the calling program needs to set dp_open to zero (forcing a call to open_dir) and the dp_disk field to the correct logical disk. The open_dir function sets up all of the remaining fields, using get_dpb to access the disk parameter block for the disk specified in dp_disk.

Of the remaining flags, dp_end will be set to true, when the end of the directory is reached, and dp_write must be nonzero for rw_dir to write the current sector back onto the disk.

The get_nde function includes all of the necessary logic to move from one directory entry to the next, reading in the next sector when necessary, and writing out the previous sector if the dp_write flag has been set to a nonzero value by the calling program. It also counts down on the number of directory entries processed, detecting and indicating the end of the directory.

The code at the beginning of the function calls open_dir if the dp_open flag is false. Note the code at the end of open_dir that sets the number of allocation blocks per directory entry (dp_nabpde). This number is computed from the maximum allocation block number in the disk parameter block. If it is larger than 255, each allocation block must occupy a word, and there will be eight blocks per directory entry. If there are 255 or fewer allocation blocks, each will be one byte long and there will be 16 per entry. The allocation block size, in Kbytes, is computed from a simple formula.

In the early stages of debugging utilities, comment out the line that makes the call to wrt_disk. This will prevent the directory from being overwritten. You then can test even those utilities that attempt to erase entries from the directory without any risk of damaging any data on the disk.

The last function in this group, err_dir, is a common error handling function for taking care of errors while reading or writing the directory.

Directory Matching Functions

The second group of functions that access the file directory matches each directory entry against specific search criteria. These include the following functions:

setscb (set search control block; Figure 11-1, r)
    A search control block (SCB) is a structure that defines the entries in the directory that are to be selected for processing.

comp_fname (compare file name; Figure 11-1, f)
    This function compares the file name in the current directory entry with the one specified in the search control block.

The library header contains the structure definition for the search control block (Figure 11-2, q). This SCB is a hybrid structure. The first part of it is a cross between a file control block (FCB) and a directory entry. The last three fields, scb_length, scb_disk, and scb_adisks, are peculiar to the search control block. Note that its overall length is the same as an FCB's so that the standard BDS C function set_fcb can be used. This function sets the file name and type into an FCB, replacing "*" with as many "?" characters as are required, and clears all unused bytes to zero.

The scb_length field indicates to the comp_fname (compare file name) function how many bytes of the structure are to be compared. This field will be set to 12 to compare the user number, file name, and type, or to 13 to include the extent number.

Note that scb_disk is the *current* disk to be searched, whereas scb_adisks is a bit map with a 1 bit corresponding to each of the 16 possible logical disks that must be searched.

The search control block is initialized by the setscb function.

Note the form of the file name that setscb expects to receive. This is described in the comments at the beginning of the function.

Several of the utility programs use their own special versions of setscb, renaming it ssetscb (special setscb) to avoid the library version being linked into the programs.

The complementary function comp_fname is used to compare the first few bytes of the current directory entry to the corresponding bytes of the SCB.

The comp_fname function performs a specialized string match of the user number, the file name, the file type, and, optionally, the extent number. A "?" character in the search control block file name, type, and extent will match with any character in the file directory entry. However, in the SCB user number, a "?" will only match a number in the range 0 to 15; it will not match a directory entry that has the user number byte set to E5H (or 0xE5, as hexadecimal notation in C).

This function also returns one of several values to indicate the result of the comparison. These values are defined in the library header file (Figure 11-2, j).

Directory Processing Functions

The final group of functions that access the directory are those that help process the directory entries themselves. These functions use a structure definition to access each directory entry (Figure 11-2, o).

A union statement is used for the allocation block numbers. These can be single- or two-byte entries, depending on the maximum number of allocation blocks that must be represented. The union statement tells the BDS C compiler whether there will be a 16-byte array of short integers (characters) or an array of eight unsigned two-byte integers.

The functions contained in this group can be divided into three subgroups:

- Those that deal with converting directory entries for display on the console.
- Those that deal with a "disk map"—a convenient array for representing logical disks and the user numbers they contain.
- Those that deal with "bit vectors"—a convenient representation of which allocation blocks on a logical disk are in use or available.

The library contains only one function to convert a directory-entry file name into a suitable form for display on the console. This is the conv_dfname function (Figure 11-1, h). It takes the information from the specified directory entry (or, as a convenience, a search control block) and formats it into a string of the form

`uu/d:filename.typ`

The "uu" specifies the user number and the "d" specifies the disk identification.

The repetitive code at the end of the function is necessary to make sure that the characters in the file type do not have their high-order bits set. These bits are the file attributes. If they are set, they can render the characters nondisplayable on some terminals.

The second subgroup of functions, those that manipulate a "disk map," produce an array that looks like this:

```
Disks
  :
  v  User Numbers -->                                   -Totals-
  A  0  1  2  3  4  5  6  7  8  9 10 11 12 13 14 15 Used Free
  B
  :
  :
  P
```

This disk map is used by several utility programs. For example, the SPACE utility displays a disk map that shows, for each logical disk in the system, and for each user on each logical disk, how many Kbytes of disk space are in use. The totals at the right show the total of used and free space. In another example, the FIND utility shows how many files on each disk and in each user number match the search name.

Each utility program that uses a disk map is coded:

```
unsigned disk_map[16][18];
```

Two functions are provided in the library to deal with the disk map:

dm_clr (disk map clear; Figure 11-1, s)
    This function fills the entire disk map with zeros.

dm_disp (disk map display; Figure 11-1, t)
    This function displays the horizontal and vertical caption lines for the disk map and then converts each element of the disk map to a decimal number.

The first function, dm_clr, uses one of the standard BDS C functions to set a block of memory to a specific value. It presumes that the disk map is 16 × 18 elements, each two bytes long.

The second function, dm_disp, prints horizontal lines only for those disks specified in the bit map parameter. Here is an example of its output:

```
        0  1  2  3  4 ...  10 11 12 13 14 15 Used Free
A:      1  1                                   15  241
B:     66 20 74 50  3                         245  779
C:     -- None --                               0 1024
(NOTE: All user groups would be shown on the terminal.)
```

The final subgroup deals with processing "bit vectors." A bit vector is a string of bits packed eight bits per byte. Each bit is addressed by its relative number along the vector; the first bit is number 0.

An example of why bit vectors are used is a utility program that needs to scan the directory of a disk and build a structure showing which allocation blocks are in use. It can do this by accessing each active directory element and, for each nonzero allocation block number, setting the corresponding bit number in a bit vector.

The library header has a structure definition for a bit vector (Figure 11-2, s).

This vector contains the overall length of the bit vector in bytes, and two pointers. The first points to the start of the vector, the second to the end. The bytes that contain the vector bits themselves are allocated by the alloc function—one of the standard BDS C functions.

The following bit vector functions are provided in the library:

bv_make (bit vector make; Figure 11-1, cc)
 This function allocates memory for the bit vector (using the standard mechanism provided by BDS C) and sets all of the bits to zero.

bv_fill (bit vector fill; Figure 11-1, dd)
 This fills a specified vector, setting each byte to a specified value.

bv_set (bit vector set; Figure 11-1, ee)
 This sets the specified bit of a vector to one.

bv_test (bit vector test; Figure 11-1, ff)
 This function returns a value of zero or one, reflecting the setting of the specified bit in a bit vector.

bv_nz (bit vector nonzero; Figure 11-1, gg)
 This returns zero or a nonzero value to reflect whether *any* bits are set in the specified bit vector.

bv_and (bit vector AND; Figure 11-1, hh)
 This function performs a Boolean AND between two bit vectors and places the result into a third vector.

bv_or (bit vector OR; Figure 11-1, ii)
 This is similar to bv_and, except that it performs an inclusive OR on the two input vectors.

bv_disp (bit vector display; Figure 11-1, jj)
 This function displays a caption line and then prints out the contents of the specified bit vector as a series of zeros and ones. Each byte is formatted to make the output easier to read.

The bv_make function uses the alloc function to allocate a block from the unused part of memory between the end of a program and the base of the BDOS. It requires that two data structures be declared at the beginning of the program. These structures are declared in the library header file (Figure 11-2, b).

The bv_fill function uses the standard BDS C setmem function.

The bv_set function converts the bit number into a byte offset by shifting the bit number right three places. The least significant three bits of the original bit number specify which bit in the appropriate byte needs to be ORed in.

The bv_test function is effectively the reverse of bv_set. It accesses the specified bit and returns its value to the calling program.

The bv_nz function scans the entire bit vector looking for the first nonzero byte. If the entire vector is zero, it returns a value of zero. Otherwise, it returns a pointer to the first nonzero byte.

Both bv__and and bv__or functions take three bit vectors as parameters. The first vector is used to hold the result of either ANDing or ORing the second and third vectors together. Both of these functions assume that the output vector has already been created using bv_make. The shortest of the three vectors will terminate the bv_and or bv_or function; that is, these functions will terminate when they reach the end of the first (shortest) vector.

The final function, bv_disp, displays the title line specified by the calling program, and then displays all of the bits in the vector, with the bit number of the first bit on each line shown on the left.

None of the utility programs uses bv_disp—it has been left in the library purely as an aid to debugging.

Here is an example of bv_disp's output:

```
Bit Vector : Allocation Blocks in Use
    0 : 0000 0000  0001 1000  1000 0001  1111 1111  1111 1111
   40 : 1111 1111  1111 1111  1111 1111  1110 1011  0000 0000
   80 : 1100 0000  1111 1100  1111 1001  1100 0000  1001 1111
  120 : 1110 1100  0001 1111  0000 0000  1101 1000  0001 1110
  160 : 1111 1111  1110 1111  1110 1111  0000 0111  0000 0111
  200 : 1111 0010
```

Checking User-Specified Parameters

The C language provides a mechanism for accessing the parameters specified in the "command tail." It provides a count of the number of parameters entered, "argc" (argument count), and an array of pointers to each of the character strings, "argv" (argument vector). At the beginning of the main function of each program you must define these two variables like this:

```
main(argc,argv)
{
int argc;        /* Argument count */
char *argv[];    /* Array of pointers to char. strings */
:
: /* Remainder of main function */
:
}
```

Consider the minimum case—a command line with just the program name on it:

```
A>command
```

The convention is that the first argument on the line is the name of the program itself. Hence argc would be set to one, and argv[0] would be a pointer to the program name, "command."

Next consider a more complex case — a command line with parameters like the following:

```
A>command param1 123
```

In this case, argc will be three; argv[1] will be a pointer to param1; and argv[1][0] will access the 0 (the first) character of argv[1]—in this case the character "p."

To detect whether the second parameter is present and numeric, the code will be

```
if (isdigit(argv[1][0]))
    {
        /* Process digit */
    }
else
    {
        /* Parameter either not present or has
           alpha character at the front */
    }
```

In most of the utilities, you will get a much "friendlier" program if the user need only specify enough characters of a parameter to distinguish the value entered from the other possible values. For example, consider a program that can have as a parameter one of the following values: 300, 600, 1200, 2400, 4800, 9600, or 19200. It would be convenient if the user needed to type only the first digit, rather than having to enter redundant keystrokes. However, the values 1200 and 19200 would then be ambiguous. The user would have to enter 12 or 19. Novice users often prefer to specify the entire parameter for clarity and security.

The standard C library provides a character string comparison function, strcmp. Unfortunately, this function does not provide for the partial matching just described. Therefore, the library includes two special functions that do make this possible: sstrcmp (substring compare, Figure 11-1, d) and usstrcmp (uppercase substring compare, Figure 11-1, e). The latter function is necessary when you need to compare a substring that could contain lowercase characters; it converts characters to uppercase before the comparison.

To assist with character string manipulation, two additional functions have been included in the library. These are strscn (string scan, Figure 11-1, b) and ustrcmp (uppercase string compare, Figure 11-1, c).

Using Code Tables

A code table is a simple structure used by all of the utility programs that accept parameters that can have any of several values. The library header contains a structure definition for a code table (Figure 11-2, r).

A code table entry contains an unsigned code value and a pointer to a character string. It is used in the utility programs wherever there is a need to relate some arbitrary code number or bit pattern to an ASCII character string. For example,

Chapter 11: Additional Utility Programs **407**

to program a serial port baud-rate-generator chip to various baud rates requires different time constants for each rate. Users do not need to know what these numbers are; they only need to be able to specify the baud rate as an ASCII string.

Thus, a code table is set up as follows:

Baud Rate Constant	User's Name
0x35	"300"
0x36	"600"
0x37	"1200"
0x3A	"2400"
0x3C	"4800"
0x3E	"9600"
0x3F	"19200"

A utility program now needs to be able to perform various operations using the code table:

- Given the input parameter on the command tail, the utility must check whether the ASCII string is in the code table, display all of the legal options on the console if it is not, and return the code value for subsequent processing if it is.

- Given the current baud rate constant (held in the BIOS), the utility must scan the code table and display the corresponding ASCII string to tell the user the current baud rate setting.

The library includes specialized functions to do this, plus some additional functions to make code tables more generally usable. These functions are

ct_init (code table initialize; Figure 11-1, v)
    This function initializes a specific entry in a code table, setting the code value and the pointer to the character string.

ct_parc (code table parameter return code; Figure 11-1, w)
    This performs an uppercase substring match on the specified key string, returning either an error (the value CT_SNF—string not found) or a code value.

ct_code (code table return code; Figure 11-1, x)
    This function is similar to ct_parc in that it scans a code table and returns the corresponding code. It differs in the way that the comparison is done. The entire search string is compared with the string in the code table entry. A match only occurs when all characters are the same.

ct_disps (code table display strings; Figure 11-1, y)
    This function displays all strings in a given code table. It is used either when the user has entered an invalid string, or when the utility program is requested to show what options are available for a parameter.

ct_index (code table return index; Figure 11-1, z)
    This function, given a string, searches the code table and returns the *index*

of the entry that has a string matching the search string. The index is not the code value; it is the number of the entry in the table.

ct_stri (code table string index; Figure 11-1, aa)
: This function, given an entry index number, returns a pointer to the string in that entry.

ct_strc (code table string code; Figure 11-1, bb)
: This function, given a code number, returns a pointer to the string in the entry that has a matching code number.

Accessing a Directory via the BDOS

One problem associated with accessing the file directory directly, as illustrated by earlier functions, is that the program is presented with directory entries in exactly the order that they occur in the directory. For some programs, such as those that process groups of files, it is better to use the BDOS Search First and Search Next functions to access the directory.

Using the BDOS, the program can process the first file name to match an ambiguous search key, then go back to the BDOS to get the name of the next file, and so on. The library header contains a structure definition for a standard CP/M file control block (Figure 11-2, k).

Notice that the first byte of the FCB is a disk number rather than the user number of the directory entry. Note also the use of a union statement to describe the allocation block numbers.

The standard BDS C library contains a function, setfcb, that is given the address of an FCB and a pointer to a string containing a file name. It converts any "*" in the name to the appropriate number of "?", and fills the remainder of the FCB with zeros.

The example library contains the following functions designed for BDOS file directory access:

get_nfn (get next file name; Figure 11-1, i)
: This function is given a pointer to an ambiguous file name and a pointer to an FCB. It returns with the FCB set up to access the next file that matches the ambiguous file name.

srch_file (search for file; Figure 11-1, j)
: This function, used by get_nfn, issues either a Search First or a Search Next BDOS call.

conv_fname (convert file name; Figure 11-1, g)
: This function converts a file name from an FCB into a form suitable for display on the console. It is similar to the conv_dfname function described earlier except that it outputs only the disk, file name, and type (not the user number) in the form

```
d:filename.typ
```

Chapter 11: Additional Utility Programs **409**

To signal the get_nfn function that you want the first file name, you must set the most significant bit of the first byte, the disk number.

Here is an example showing how to use the get_nfn function:

```
struct _fcb fcb;            /* Declare a file control block */
setmem(fcb,FCB_SIZE,0);     /* Clear FCB to zeros */
fcb.fcb_disk = 0x80;        /* Mark FCB for "first time" */
while (get_nfn(fcb,"B:XYZ*.*"))
                            /* Until get_nfn returns a zero */
    {
                            /* Open the file using FCB */
    while                   (/* Not at end of file */)
        {
                            /* Process next record or
                               Character in file*/
        }
                            /* Close the file */
    }
```

The quoted string "B:XYZ*.*" could also be just a pointer to a string, or a parameter on the command line, argv[n].

The last function for BDOS processing of the file directory, conv_fname, is used to convert a file name for output to a terminal. Again, the repetitive code at the end clears the file attribute bits to avoid any side effects from the terminal.

Utility Programs Enhancing Standard CP/M

This group of utilities is designed to enhance those supplied by Digital Research. They do not take advantage of any special features of the enhanced BIOS in Figure 8-10 and can be used on *any* CP/M Version 2.2 installation.

With the exception of the ERASE utility, all of the utilities scan down the file directory using BIOS calls, as described earlier in this chapter.

ERASE — A Safer Way to Erase Files

There are two disadvantages to the Console Command Processor's built-in ERA command. First, it will unquestioningly erase groups of files. Second, if you have a file name with nongraphic or lowercase characters, you cannot use the ERA command, as the CCP converts the command tail characters to uppercase and terminates a file name on encountering any strange character in the string.

The ERASE utility shown in Figure 11-3 erases groups of files, but it asks the user for confirmation before it erases each file.

Rather than use the BIOS to access each directory entry, it uses the get_nfn function, which then calls the BDOS. Thus ERASE functions equally well for files that have multiple entries in the directory. It can use the BDOS Delete File function to erase all extents of a given file.

Here is an example console dialog showing ERASE in operation:

```
P3A>erase<CR>
ERASE Version 1.0 02/23/83 (Library 1.0)
Usage :
        ERASE {d:}file_name.typ


P3A>erase *.com<CR>
ERASE Version 1.0 02/23/83 (Library 1.0)

Searching for file(s) matching A:????????.COM.
        Erase A:UNERASE .COM y/n? n
        Erase A:TEMP1   .COM y/n? y <== Will be Erased!
        Erase A:TEMP2   .COM y/n? n
        Erase A:TEMP3   .COM y/n? n
        Erase A:TEMP4   .COM y/n? y <== Will be Erased!
        Erase A:ERASE   .COM y/n? n

Erasing files now...
        File A:TEMP1    .COM erased.
        File A:TEMP4    .COM erased.
```

```c
#define VN "1.0 02/24/83"

/* ERASE
    This utility erases the specified file(s) logically
    by using a BDOS delete function. */

#include <LIBRARY.H>

struct _fcb amb_fcb;        /* Ambiguous name file control block */
struct _fcb fcb;            /* Used for BDOS search functions */

char file_name[20];         /* Formatted for display: d:FILENAME.TYP */
short cur_disk;             /* Current logical disk at start of program */
                            /* ERASE saves the FCB's of the all the
                               files that need to be erased in the
                               following array   */
#define MAXERA 1024
struct _fcb era_fcb[MAXERA];
int ecount;                 /* Count of number of files to be erased */
int count;                  /* Used to access era_fcb during erasing */


main(argc,argv)
short argc;                 /* Argument count */
char *argv[];               /* Argument vector (pointer to an array of char.  */
{
printf("\nERASE Version %s (Library %s)",VN,LIBVN);
chk_use(argc);              /* Check usage */
cur_disk = bdos(GETDISK);   /* Get current default disk */

ecount = 0;                 /* Initialize count of files to erase */

setfcb(amb_fcb,argv[1]);    /* Set ambiguous file name */
if (amb_fcb.fcb_disk)       /* Check if default disk to be used */
    {
    bdos(SETDISK,amb_fcb.fcb_disk + 1);     /* Set to specified disk */
    }
```

Figure 11-3. ERASE.C, a utility that requests confirmation before erasing

```
        /* Convert ambiguous file name for output */
conv_fname(amb_fcb,file_name);
printf("\n\nSearching for file(s) matching %s.",file_name);

        /* Set the file control block to indicate a "first" search */
fcb.fcb_disk != 0x80;   /* OR in the ms bit */

        /* While not at the end of the directory, set the FCB
           to the next name that matches */
while(get_nfn(amb_fcb,fcb))
        {
        conv_fname(fcb,file_name);
                /* Ask whether to erase file or not */
        printf("\n\tErase %s y/n? ",file_name);
        if (toupper(getchar()) == 'Y')
                {
                printf(" <== Will be erased!");
                        /* add current fcb to array of FCB's */
                movmem(fcb,&era_fcb[ecount++],FCBSIZE);
                        /* Check that the table is not full */
                if (ecount == MAXERA)
                        {
                        printf("\nWarning : Internal table now full. No more files can be erased");
                        printf("\n    until those already specified have been erased.");
                        break;  /* Break out of while loop */
                        }
                }
        }       /* All directory entries processed */
if (ecount)
        printf("\n\nErasing files now...");

        /* now process each FCB in the array, erasing the files */
for (count = 0;          /* Starting with the first file in the array */
     count < ecount;     /* Until all active entries processed */
     count++)            /* Move to next FCB */
        {
        conv_fname(&era_fcb[count],file_name);
        if (bdos(DELETEF,&era_fcb[count]) == -1)        /* error? */
                printf("\n\007Error trying to erase %s",file_name);
        else            /* File erased */
                printf("\n\tFile %s erased.",file_name);
        }
bdos(SETDISK,cur_disk); /* reset to current disk */
}


chk_use(argc)           /* Check usage */
/* This function checks that the correct number of
   parameters has been specified, outputting instructions if not. */


/* Entry parameter */
int argc;       /* Count of the number of arguments on the command line */

{
        /* The minimum value of argc is 1 (for the program name itself),
           so argc is always one greater than the number of parameters
           on the command line */

if (argc != 2)
        {
        printf("\nUsage :");
        printf("\n\tERASE {d:}file_name.typ");
        exit();
        }

}
```

Figure 11-3.   (Continued)

UNERASE — Restore Erased Files

UNERASE, as its name implies, can be used to "revive" an accidentally erased file. Only files whose allocation blocks have not been reallocated to other files can be revived. The UNERASE utility shown in Figure 11-4 builds a bit vector of all the allocation blocks used by active directory entries. Then it builds a bit vector for all the allocation blocks required by the file to be UNERASEd. If a Boolean AND between the two vectors yields a nonzero vector, then one or more blocks that originally belonged to the erased file are now allocated to other files on the disk.

```
#define VN "1.0 02/12/83"

/* UNERASE --
   This utility does the inverse of ERASE: it restores
   specified files to the directory by changing the first byte of
   their directory entries from 0xE5 back to the specified user
   number. */

#include <LIBRARY.H>

struct _dirpb dir_pb;           /* Directory management parameter block */
struct _dir *dir_entry;         /* Pointer to directory entry */
struct _scb scb;                /* Search control block */
struct _scb scba;               /* SCB set up to match all files */
struct _dpb dpb;                /* CP/M's disk parameter block */
struct _bv inuse_bv;            /* Bit vector for blocks in use */
struct _bv file_bv;             /* Bit vector for file to be unerased */
struct _bv extents;             /* Bit vector for those extents unerased */

char file_name[20];             /* Formatted for display : un/d:FILENAME.TYP */

short cur_disk;                 /* Current logical disk at start of program
                                   NZ = show map of number of files */
int count;                      /* Used to access the allocation block numbers
                                   in each directory entry */
int user;                       /* User in which the file is to be revived */

main(argc,argv)
short argc;                     /* Argument count */
char *argv[];                   /* Argument vector (pointer to an array of chars.) */

{
printf("\nUNERASE Version %s (Library %s)",VN,LIBVN);
chk_use(argc);                  /* Check usage */
cur_disk = bdos(GETDISK);       /* Get current default disk */

        /* Using a special version of the set search-control-block utility,
           set the disk, name, type (no ambiguous names), the user number
           to match only erased entries, and the length to compare
           the user, name, and type.
           This special version also returns the disk_id taken from
           the file name on the command line.  */
if ((dir_pb.dp_disk = ssetscb(scb,argv[1],0xE5,12)) == 0)
        {       /* Use default disk */
        dir_pb.dp_disk = cur_disk;
        }
else
        {       /* make disk A = 0, B = 1 (for SELDSK) */
        dir_pb.dp_disk--;
        }
printf("\nSearching disk %d.",dir_pb.dp_disk);

if(strscn(scb,"?"))             /* Check if ambiguous name */
        {
        printf("\nError -- UNERASE can only revive a single file at a time.");
        exit();
```

Figure 11-4. UNERASE.C, a utility program that "revives" erased files

```
                }
        /* Set up a special search control block that will match with
           all existing files. */
ssetscb(scba,"*.*",'?',12);     /* Set file name and initialize SCB */

if (argc == 2)                  /* No user number specified */
        user = bdos(GETUSER,0xFF);      /* Get current user number */
else
{
        user = atoi(argv[2]);           /* Get specified number */
        if (user > 15)
                {
                printf("\nUser number can only be 0 - 15.");
                exit();
                }
}

/* Build a bit vector that shows the allocation blocks
   currently in use. SCBA has been set up to match all
   active directory entries on the disk. */
build_bv(inuse_bv,scba);

/* Build a bit vector for the file to be restored showing
   which allocation blocks will be needed for the file. */
if (!build_bv(file_bv,scb))
        {
        printf("\nNo directory entries found for file %s.",
                argv[1]);
        exit();
        }
/* Perform a boolean AND of the two bit vectors. */
bv_and(file_bv,inuse_bv,file_bv);

/* Check if the result is nonzero -- if so, then one or more
   of the allocation blocks required by the erased file is
   already in use for an existing file and the file cannot
   be restored. */
if (bv_nz(file_bv))
{
        printf("\n--- This file cannot be restored as some parts of it");
        printf("\n    have been re-used for other files! ---");
        exit();
}


/* Continue on to restore the file by changing all the entries
   in the directory to have the specified user number.
   Note: There may be several entries in the directory for
   the same file name and type, and even with the same extent
   number. For this reason, a bit map is kept of the extent
   numbers unerased -- duplicate extent numbers will not be
   unerased. */

/* Set up the bit vector for up to 127 unerased extents */
bv_make(extents,16);            /* 16 * 8 bits */

/* Set the directory to "closed", and force the get_nde
   function to open it. */
dir_pb.dp_open = 0;

/* While not at the end of the directory, return a pointer to
   the next entry in the directory. */
while(dir_entry = get_nde(dir_pb))
{
        /* Check if user = 0xE5 and name, type match */
if (comp_fname(scb,dir_entry) == NAME_EQ)
        {
                /* Test if this extent has already been
                   unerased */
        if (bv_test(extents,dir_entry -> de_extent))
                {               /* Yes it has */
                printf("\n\t\tExtent #%d of %s ignored.",
                        dir_entry -> de_extent,argv[1]);
                continue;       /* Do not unerase this one */
                }
```

Figure 11-4. (Continued)

```
            else                  /* Indicate this extent unerased */
                {
                bv_set(extents,dir_entry -> de_extent);
                dir_entry -> de_userno = user; /* Unerase entry */
                dir_pb.dp_write = 1;    /* Need to write sector back */
                printf("\n\tExtent #%d of %s unerased.",
                        dir_entry -> de_extent,argv[1]);
                }
        }
    }
printf("\n\nFile %s unerased in User Number %d.",
argv[1],user);

bdos(SETDISK,cur_disk); /* Reset to current disk */
}


build_bv(bv,scb)            /* Build bit vector (from directory) */
/* This function scans the directory of the disk specified in
    the directory parameter block (declared as a global variable),
    and builds the specified bit vector, showing all the allocation
    blocks used by files matching the name in the search control
    block. */

/* Entry parameters */
struct _bv *bv;             /* Pointer to the bit vector */
struct _scb *scb;           /* Pointer to search control block */
/* Also uses : directory parameter block (dir_pb) */

/* Exit parameters
    The specified bit vector will be created, and will have 1-bits
    set wherever an allocation block is found in a directory
    entry that matches the search control block.
    It also returns the number of directory entries matched. */
{
unsigned abno;              /* Allocation block number */
struct _dpb *dpb;           /* Pointer to the disk parameter block in the BIOS */
int mcount;                 /* Match count of dir. entries matched */

mcount = 0;                 /* Initialize match count */
dpb = get_dpb(dir_pb.dp_disk); /* Get disk parameter block address */

/* make the bit vector with one byte for each eight allocation
    blocks + 1 */
if (!(bv_make(bv,(dpb -> dpb_maxabn >>3)+1)))
        {
        printf("\nError -- Insufficient memory to make a bit vector.");
        exit();
        }

/* Set directory to "closed" to force the get_nde
    function to open it. */
dir_pb.dp_open = 0;

/* Now scan the directory building the bit vector */
while(dir_entry = get_nde(dir_pb))
        {
                /* Compare user number (which can legitimately be
                    0xE5), the file name and the type). */
                if (comp_fname(scb,dir_entry) == NAME_EQ)
                        {
                        ++mcount;               /* Update match count */
                        for (count = 0;         /* Start with the first alloc. block */
                            count < dir_pb.dp_nabpde;  /* For number of alloc. blks. per dir. entry */
                            count++)
                                {
                                /* Set the appropriate bit number for
                                    each nonzero allocation block number */
                                if (dir_pb.dp_nabpde == 8)    /* assume 8 2-byte numbers */
                                        {
                                        abno = dir_entry -> _dirab.de_long[count];
                                        }
                                else            /* Assume 16 1-byte numbers */
                                        {
```

Figure 11-4. (Continued)

```
                                    abno = dir_entry -> _dirab.de_short[count];
                                    }
                                 if (abno) bv_set(bv,abno); /* Set the bit */
                                 }
                     }
                }
     return mcount;             /* Return number of dir. entries matched */
     }


     chk_use(argc)              /* Check usage */
     /* This function checks that the correct number of
        parameters has been specified, outputting instructions
        if not. */

     /* Entry parameter */
     int argc;        /* Count of the number of arguments on the command line */
     {

     /* The minimum value of argc is 1 (for the program name itself),
        so argc is always one greater than the number of parameters
        on the command line */

     if (argc == 1 || argc > 3)
            {
            printf("\nUsage :");
            printf("\n\tUNERASE {d:}filename.typ {user}");
                  printf("\n\tOnly a single unambiguous file name can be used.)");
            exit();
            }
     } /* end chk_use */


     ssetscb(scb,fname,user,length)  /* Special version of set search control block */
     /* This function sets up a search control block according
        to the file name, type, user number, and number of bytes
        to compare.
        The file name can take the following forms :
              filename
              filename.typ
              d:filename.typ

        It sets the bit map according to which disks should be searched.
        For each selected disk, it checks to see if an error is generated
        when selecting the disk (i.e. if there are disk tables in the BIOS
        for the disk). */

     /* Entry parameters */
     struct _scb *scb;          /* Pointer to search control block */
     char *fname;               /* Pointer to the file name */
     short user;                /* User number to be matched */
     int length;                /* Number of bytes to compare */

     /* Exit parameters
        Disk number to be searched. (A = 1, B = 2...)
     */
     {
     short disk_id;             /* Disk number to search */

     setfcb(scb,fname);         /* Set search control block as though it
                                    were a file control block. */
     disk_id = scb -> scb_userno;  /* Set disk_id before it gets overwritten
                                      by the user number */
     scb -> scb_userno = user;  /* Set user number */
     scb -> scb_length = length; /* Set number of bytes to compare */
     return disk_id;
     } /* end setscb */
```

Figure 11-4. (Continued)

A further complication occurs if two or more directory entries of the erased file have the same extent number. This can happen if the file has been created and erased several times. Under these circumstances, UNERASE revives the first entry with a given extent number that it encounters, and displays a message on the console both when an extent is revived and when one is ignored.

Because of the complicated nature of the UNERASE process, the utility can process only a single, unambiguous file name.

The following console dialog shows UNERASE in operation:

```
P3A>dir *.com<CR>
A: UNERASE  COM : TEMP2    COM : TEMP3    COM : ERASE    COM

P3A>unerase<CR>
UNERASE Version 1.0 02/12/83 (Library 1.0)
Usage :
        UNERASE {d:}filename.typ {user}
        Only a single unambiguous file name can be used.

P3A>unerase temp1.com<CR>
UNERASE Version 1.0 02/12/83 (Library 1.0)
Searching disk A.
        Extent #0 of TEMP1.COM unerased.
            Extent #0 of TEMP1.COM ignored.

File TEMP1.COM unerased in User Number 3.

P3A>dir *.com<CR>
A: UNERASE  COM : TEMP1    COM : TEMP2    COM : TEMP3    COM
A: ERASE    COM

P3A>unerase temp5.com<CR>
UNERASE Version 1.0 02/12/83 (Library 1.0)
Searching disk A.
No directory entries found for file TEMP5.COM.
```

FIND — Find "Lost" Files

The FIND utility shown in Figure 11-5 searches all user numbers on specified logical disks, matching each entry against an ambiguous file name. It can then display either a disk map showing how many matching files were found in each user number for each disk, or the user number, file name, and type for each matched directory entry.

You can use FIND to locate a specific file or group of files, as shown in the following console dialog:

```
P3B>find<CR>
FIND Version 1.0 02/11/83 (Library 1.0)
Usage :
        FIND d:filename.typ {NAMES}
            *:filename.typ (All disks)
            ABCD..OP:filename.typ (Selected Disks)
        NAMES option shows actual names rather than map.

P3B>find ab:*.*<CR>
FIND Version 1.0 02/11/83 (Library 1.0)
```

```
            Searching disk : A
            Searching disk : B
                        Numbers show files in each User Number.
                                --- User Numbers ---        Dir. Entries
                        0   1   2   3   4   5  ...  11  12  13  14  15   Used Free
            A:          1   1       8                                      23  233
            B:         66  20  74  55   3                                 252  772

            P3B>find *:*.com<CR>
            FIND Version 1.0 02/11/83 (Library 1.0)
            Searching disk : A
            Searching disk : B
            Searching disk : C
                                --- User Numbers ---        Dir. Entries
                        0   1   2   3   4   5  ...  11  12  13  14  15   Used Free
            A:                      5                                      23  233
            B:         61   5   4  13                                     252  772
            C:         -- None --                                          16  112


            P3B>find *.com names<CR>
            FIND Version 1.0 02/11/83 (Library 1.0)
            Searching disk : B
            0/B:CC        .COM    0/B:CC2       .COM    0/B:CLINK    .COM    2/B:CLIB     .COM
            1/B:CPM61     .COM    1/B:MOVCPM    .COM    1/B:PSWX     .COM    0/B:SUBMIT   .COM
            2/B:CDB       .COM    1/B:CPM60     .COM    0/B:DDT      .COM    0/B:EREMOTE  .COM
            0/B:SPEEDSP   .COM    0/B:PIP       .COM    0/B:PROTOSP  .COM    0/B:RX       .COM
            0/B:TXA       .COM    0/B:EPUB      .COM    0/B:EPRIV    .COM    0/B:WSC      .COM
            0/B:X         .COM    0/B:CRCK      .COM    0/B:XSUB     .COM    0/B:DU       .COM
            0/B:QERA      .COM    0/B:FINDALL   .COM    0/B:MOVEF    .COM    0/B:REMOTE   .COM
            0/B:LOCAL     .COM    0/B:DUMP      .COM    0/B:MRESET   .COM    0/B:ELOCAL   .COM
            0/B:PUTCPMF5. COM     0/B:TEST      .COM    0/B:FDUMP    .COM    0/B:INVIS    .COM
            0/B:L80       .COM    0/B:LIST      .COM    0/B:PUB      .COM    0/B:LOAD     .COM
            0/B:MAC       .COM    0/B:SCRUB     .COM    0/B:RXA      .COM    0/B:STAT     .COM
            0/B:TX        .COM    0/B:ERASEALL. COM     0/B:WM       .COM    0/B:MSFORMAT.COM
            0/B:STATUS    .COM    0/B:UNERA     .COM    0/B:MSINIT   .COM    0/B:VIS      .COM
            0/B:WSVTIP    .COM    0/B:XD        .COM    0/B:NEWVE    .COM    0/B:DDUMP    .COM
            0/B:FORMATMA. COM     0/B:PRIV      .COM    0/B:FCOMP    .COM    0/B:DDUMPA   .COM
            0/B:PUTSYS1C. COM     0/B:DDUMPNI   .COM    0/B:DSTAT    .COM    0/B:ASM      .COM
            2/B:CDBTEST   .COM    0/B:OLDSYS    .COM    0/B:E        .COM    2/B:F/C      .COM
            3/B:ERASE     .COM    3/B:FUNKEY    .COM    3/B:DATE     .COM    3/B:FIND     .COM
            Press Space Bar to continue....
            3/B:SPACE     .COM    3/B:UNERASE   .COM    3/B:MAKE     .COM    3/B:MOVE     .COM
            1/B:PUTSYSWX.COM      3/B:TIME      .COM    3/B:ASSIGN   .COM    3/B:SPEED    .COM
            3/B:PROTOCOL.COM      0/B:PRINTC    .COM    3/B:T        .COM
```

```
#define VN "1.0 02/11/83"

/* FIND - This utility can display either a map showing on which disks
   and in which user numbers files matching the specified ambiguous
   file name are found, or the actual names matched. */

#include <LIBRARY.H>

struct _dirpb dir_pb;         /* Directory management parameter block */
struct _dir *dir_entry;       /* Pointer to directory entry (somewhere in
                                 dir_pb) */
struct _scb scb;              /* Search control block */
char file_name[20];           /* Formatted for display : un/d:FILENAME.TYP */
```

Figure 11-5. FIND.C, a utility program that locates specific files or groups of files

```
        short cur_disk;                 /* Current logical disk at start of program */
        int mcount;                     /* Match count (no. of file names matched) */
        int dmcount;                    /* Per disk match count */
        int lcount;                     /* Line count (for lines displayed) */

        int map_flag;                   /* 0 = show file names of matched files,
                                           NZ = show map of number of files */

                /* The array below is used to tabulate the results for each
                        disk drive, and for each user number on the drive.
                        In addition, two extra "users" have been added for "free"
                        and "used" values. */
        unsigned disk_map[16][18];      /* Disk A -> P, users 0 -> 15, free, used */
        #define USED_COUNT 16           /* "User" number for used entities */
        #define FREE_COUNT 17           /* "User" number for free entities */


        main(argc,argv)
        short argc;                     /* Argument count */
        char *argv[];                   /* Argument vector (pointer to an array of chars.) */
        {
        printf("\nFIND Version %s (Library %s)",VN,LIBVN);
        chk_use(argc);                  /* Check usage */
        cur_disk = bdos(GETDISK);       /* Get current default disk */

        dm_clr(disk_map);               /* Reset disk map */

                /* Set search control block
                        disks, name, type, user number, extent number,
                        and number of bytes to compare -- in this case, match all users,
                        but only extent 0 */
        setscb(scb,argv[1],'?',0,13);   /* Set disks, name, type */

        map_flag = usstrcmp("NAMES",argv[2]);   /* Set flag for map option */

        lcount = dmcount = mcount = 0;          /* Initialize counts */

        for (scb.scb_disk = 0;          /* Starting with logical disk A: */
             scb.scb_disk < 16;         /* Until logical disk P: */
             scb.scb_disk++)            /* Move to next logical disk */
        {

                /* Check if current disk has been selected for search */
        if (!(scb.scb_adisks & (1 << scb.scb_disk)))
                continue;               /* No,so bypass this disk */
        printf("\nSearching disk : %c",(scb.scb_disk + 'A'));
        lcount++;                       /* Update line count */

        dir_pb.dp_disk = scb.scb_disk;  /* Set to disk to be searched*/
        dmcount = 0;                    /* Reset disk matched count */

        if (!map_flag)                  /* If file names are to be displayed */
                putchar('\n');          /* Move to column 1 */

        /* Set the directory to "closed", and force the get_nde
           function to open it */
        dir_pb.dp_open = 0;

                /* While not at the end of the directory, set a pointer to the
                   next directory entry */
        while(dir_entry = get_nde(dir_pb))
                {
                /* Check if entry in use, to update
                   the free/used counts */

                if (dir_entry -> de_userno == 0xE5)     /* Unused */
                        disk_map[scb.scb_disk][FREE_COUNT]++;
                else    /* In use */
                        disk_map[scb.scb_disk][USED_COUNT]++;

                /* Select only those active entries that are the
                   first extent (numbered 0) of a file that matches
                   the name supplied by the user */
```

Figure 11-5.   (Continued)

```
            if (
                (dir_entry -> de_userno != 0xE5) &&
                (dir_entry -> de_extent == 0) &&
                (comp_fname(scb,dir_entry) == NAME_EQ)
               )
                {
                mcount++;           /* Update matched counts */
                dmcount++;          /* Per disk count */

                if (map_flag)       /* Check map option */
                    {
                                    /* Update disk map */
                    disk_map[scb.scb_disk][dir_entry -> de_userno]++;
                    }
                else                /* Display names */
                    {
                    conv_dfname(scb.scb_disk,dir_entry,file_name);
                    printf("%s   ",file_name);
                                    /* Check if need to start new line */
                    if (!(dmcount % 4))
                            {
                            putchar('\n');
                                    if (++lcount > 18)
                                            {
                                            lcount = 0;
                                            printf("\nPress Space Bar to continue....");
                                            getchar();
                                            putchar('\n');
                                            }
                            }
                    }
                }
            } /* End of directory */
        } /* All disks searched */
if (map_flag)
    {
    printf("\n                  Numbers show files in each user number.");
    printf("\n                         --- User Numbers ---                    Dir. Entries");

    dm_disp(disk_map,scb.scb_adisks);       /* Display disk map */
    }

if (mcount == 0)
    printf("\n --- File Not Found --- ");

bdos(SETDISK,cur_disk); /* Reset to current disk */
}


chk_use(argc)           /* check usage */
/* This function checks that the correct number of
   parameters has been specified, outputting instructions
   if not.
*/

/* Entry parameter */
int argc;       /* Count of the number of arguments on the command line */
{

/* The minimum value of argc is 1 (for the program name itself),
   so argc is always one greater than the number of parameters
   on the command line */

if (argc == 1 !! argc > 3)
    {
    printf("\nUsage :");
    printf("\n\tFIND d:filename.typ {NAMES}");
    printf("\n\t    *:filename.typ (All disks)");
    printf("\n\t     ABCD..OP:filename.typ (Selected Disks)");
    printf("\n\tNAMES option shows actual names rather than map.");
    exit();
    }

}
```

Figure 11-5.   (Continued)

SPACE — Show Used Disk Space

The SPACE utility shown in Figure 11-6 scans the specified logical disks and displays a disk map that shows, for each user number on each logical disk, how many K bytes of storage have been used. It also displays the total number of K bytes used and free on each logical disk.

Here is an example console dialog showing SPACE in operation:

```
P3B>space<CR>
SPACE Version 1.0 02/11/83 (Library 1.0)
Usage :
        SPACE *         (All disks)
        SPACE ABCD..OP (Selected Disks)

P3B>space *<CR>
SPACE Version 1.0 02/11/83 (Library 1.0)
Searching disk : A
Searching disk : B
Searching disk : C
                 Numbers show space used in kilobytes.
                         --- User Numbers ---            Space (Kb)
         0   1   2   3   4   5  ...  10  11  12  13  14  15  Used Free
     A:  18 202     38                                        258 1196
     B: 692 432 656 548  36                                  2364  996
     C: 140                                                   140  204
```

```
#define VN "1.0 02/11/83"

/* SPACE -- This utility displays a map showing on the amount of space
   (expressed as relative percentages) occupied in each user number
   for each logical disk.It also shows the relative amount of space
   free. */

#include <LIBRARY.H>

struct _dirpb dir_pb;        /* Directory management parameter block */
struct _dir *dir_entry;      /* Pointer to directory entry */
struct _scb scb;             /* Search control block */
struct _dpb dpb;             /* CP/M's disk parameter block */

char file_name[20];          /* Formatted for display : un/d:FILENAME.TYP */

short cur_disk;              /* Current logical disk at start of program
                                NZ = show map of number of files */
int count;                   /* Used to access the allocation block numbers
                                in each directory entry */
int user;                    /* Used to access the disk map when calculating */

/* The array below is used to tabulate the results for each
   disk drive, and for each user number on the drive.
   In addition, two extra "users" have been added for "free"
   and "used" values.
*/
unsigned disk_map[16][18];   /* Disk A -> P, users 0 -> 15, free, used */
#define USED_COUNT 16        /* "User" number for used entities */
#define FREE_COUNT 17        /* "User" number for free entities */


main(argc,argv)
short argc;                  /* Argument count */
char *argv[];                /* Argument vector (pointer to an array of chars.) */
{
```

Figure 11-6. SPACE.C, a utility that displays how much disk storage is used or available

```
printf("\nSPACE Version %s (Library %s)",VN,LIBVN);
chk_use(argc);              /* Check usage */
cur_disk = bdos(GETDISK);   /* Get current default disk */

dm_clr(disk_map);           /* Reset disk map */

ssetscb(scb,argv[1]);       /* Special version : set disks,
                                name, type */

for (scb.scb_disk = 0;      /* Starting with logical disk A: */
     scb.scb_disk < 16;     /* Until logical disk P: */
     scb.scb_disk++)        /* Move to next logical disk */
    {
    /* Check if current disk has been selected for search */
    if (!(scb.scb_adisks & (1 << scb.scb_disk)))
            continue;       /* No, so bypass this disk */

    printf("\nSearching disk : %c",(scb.scb_disk + 'A'));
    dir_pb.dp_disk = scb.scb_disk; /* Set to disk to be searched */

    /* Set the directory to "closed", and force the get_nde
       function to open it */
    dir_pb.dp_open = 0;

    /* While not at the end of the directory, set a pointer
       to the next entry in the directory */
    while (dir_entry = get_nde(dir_pb))
        {
        if (dir_entry -> de_userno == 0xE5)
                continue;       /* Bypass inactive entries */

        for (count = 0;         /* Start with the first alloc. block */
             count < dir_pb.dp_nabpde; /* For number of alloc. blks. per dir. entry */
             count++)
            {
            if (dir_pb.dp_nabpde == 8)   /* Assume 8 2-byte numbers */
                {
                disk_map[scb.scb_disk][dir_entry -> de_userno]
                    += (dir_entry -> _dirab.de_long[count] > 0 ? 1 : 0);
                }
            else    /* Assume 16 1-byte numbers */
                {
                disk_map[scb.scb_disk][dir_entry -> de_userno]
                    += (dir_entry -> _dirab.de_short[count] > 0 ? 1 : 0);
                }
            }       /* All allocation blocks processed */
        }   /* End of directory for this disk */

    /* Compute the storage used by multiplying the number of
       allocation blocks counted by the number of Kbytes in
       each allocation block. */
    for (user = 0;      /* Start with user 0 */
         user < 16;     /* End with user 15 */
         user ++)       /* Move to next user number */
        {
        /* Compute size occupied in Kbytes */
        disk_map[scb.scb_disk][user] *= dir_pb.dp_absize;
                        /* Build up sum for this disk */
        disk_map[scb.scb_disk][USED_COUNT] += disk_map[scb.scb_disk][user];
        }

    /* Free space = (# of alloc. blks * # of kbyte per blk)
                    - used Kbytes
                    - (directory entries * 32) / 1024 ... or divide by 32 */
    disk_map[scb.scb_disk][FREE_COUNT] = (dir_pb.dp_nab * dir_pb.dp_absize)
                    - disk_map[scb.scb_disk][USED_COUNT]
                    - (dir_pb.dp_nument >> 5);    /* Same as / 32 */
    }       /* All disks processed */

printf("\n                    Numbers show space used in kilobytes.");
printf("\n                       --- User Numbers ---                   Space (Kb)");

dm_disp(disk_map,scb.scb_adisks);   /* Display disk map */
```

Figure 11-6. (Continued)

```
        bdos(SETDISK,cur_disk);   /* Reset to current disk */
        }

        ssetscb(scb,ldisks)       /* Special version of set search control block */

        /* This function sets up a search control block according
            to just the logical disks specified. The disk are specified as
            a single string of characters without any separators. An
            asterisk means "all disks." For example --

                ABGH       (disks A:, B:, G: and H: )
                *          (all disks for which SELDSK has tables)

            It sets the bit map according to which disks should be searched.
            For each selected disk, it checks to see if an error is generated
            when selecting the disk (i.e. if there are disk tables in the BIOS
            for the disk).
            The file name, type, and extent number are all set to "?" to match
            all possible entries in the directory. */

        /* Entry parameters */
        struct _scb *scb;         /* Pointer to search control block */
        char *ldisks;             /* Pointer to the logical disks */

        /* Exit parameters
            None.
        */
        {
        int disk;                 /* Disk number currently being checked */
        unsigned adisks;          /* Bit map for active disks */

        adisks = 0;               /* Assume no disks to search */

        if (*ldisks)              /* Some values specified */
            {
            if (*ldisks == '*')   /* Check if "all disks" */
                {
                adisks = 0xFFFF;      /* Set all bits */
                }
            else                  /* Set specific disks */
                {
                while(*ldisks)    /* Until end of disks reached */
                    {
                    /* Build the bit map by getting the next disk
                        id. (A - P), converting it to a number
                        in the range 0 - 15, and shifting a 1-bit
                        left that many places and OR ing it into
                        the current active disks.
                    */
                    adisks != 1 << (toupper(*ldisks) - 'A');
                    ++ldisks;         /* Move to next character */
                    }
                }
            }
        else        /* Use only current default disk */
            {
            /* Set just the bit corresponding to the current disk */
            adisks = 1 << bdos(GETDISK);
            }

            /* Set the user number, file name, type, and extent to "?"
                so that all active directory entries will match */
                    /*         0123456789012           */
        strcpy(&scb -> scb_userno,"?????????????");

                /* Make calls to the BIOS SELDSK routine to make sure that
                    all of the active disk drives have disk tables for them
                    in the BIOS. If they don't, turn off the corresponding
                    bits in the bit map. */

        for (disk = 0;            /* Start with disk A: */
             disk < 16;           /* Until disk P: */
             disk++)              /* Use next disk */
            {
            if ( !((1 << disk) & adisks))
                continue;                 /* Avoid selecting unspecified disks */
```

Figure 11-6. (Continued)

```
                if (biosh(SELDSK,disk) == 0)     /* Make BIOS SELDSK call */
                    {                            /* Returns 0 if invalid disk */
                    /* Turn OFF corresponding bit in mask
                       by AND-ing it with bit mask having
                       all the other bits set = 1. */
                    adisks &= ((1 << disk) ^ 0xFFFF);
                    }
            }
    scb -> scb_adisks = adisks;      /* Set bit map in scb */

    } /* End ssetscb */


    chk_use(argc)               /* Check usage */
    /* This function checks that the correct number of
       parameters has been specified, outputting instructions
       if not. */

    /* Entry parameter */
    int argc;       /* Count of the number of arguments on the command line */
    {
            /* The minimum value of argc is 1 (for the program name itself),
               so argc is always one greater than the number of parameters
               on the command line */
    if (argc != 2)
            {
            printf("\nUsage :");
            printf("\n\tSPACE *          (All disks)");
            printf("\n\tSPACE ABCD..OP (Selected Disks)");
            exit();
            }
    } /* End chk_use */
```

Figure 11-6.   (Continued)

MOVE — Move Files Between User Numbers

The MOVE utility shown in Figure 11-7 moves files from one user number to another on the same logical disk. The movement is achieved by changing the user number in all the relevant directory entries. This is much faster than copying the files. It also avoids having multiple copies of the same file on the disk.

Here is a console dialog showing MOVE in operation:

```
P3B>move<CR>
MOVE Version 1.0 02/10/83 (Library 1.0)
Usage :
        MOVE d:filename.typ to_user {from_user} {NAMES}
             *:filename.typ (All disks)
             ABCD..OP:filename.typ (Selected Disks)
        NAMES option shows names of files moved.

P3B>dir *.com<CR>
B: ERASE    COM : FUNKEY   COM : DATE     COM : FIND     COM
B: SPACE    COM : UNERASE  COM : MAKE     COM : MOVE     COM
B: TIME     COM : ASSIGN   COM : SPEED    COM : PROTOCOL COM

P3B>move *.com 0 names<CR>
MOVE Version 1.0 02/10/83 (Library 1.0)

Moving file(s)   3/B:????????.COM -> User 0.
```

```
          0/B:ERASE    .COM   0/B:FUNKEY  .COM   0/B:DATE   .COM   0/B:FIND    .COM
          0/B:SPACE    .COM   0/B:UNERASE .COM   0/B:MAKE   .COM   0/B:MOVE    .COM
          0/B:TIME     .COM   0/B:ASSIGN  .COM   0/B:SPEED  .COM   0/B:PROTOCOL.COM

     P3B>user 0<CR>
     P0B>dir
          B: ERASE     COM :  FUNKEY   COM :  DATE    COM :  FIND      COM
          B: SPACE     COM :  UNERASE  COM :  MAKE    COM :  MOVE      COM
          B: TIME      COM :  ASSIGN   COM :  SPEED   COM :  PROTOCOL  COM
```

```
#define VN "1.0 02/10/83"

/* MOVE -- This utility transfers file(s) from one user number to
   another, but on the SAME logical disk. Files are not actually
   copied -- rather, their directory entries are changed. */

#include <LIBRARY.H>

struct _dirpb dir_pb;         /* Directory management parameter block */
struct _dir *dir_entry;       /* Pointer to directory entry */
struct _scb scb;              /* Search control block */

#define DIR_BSZ 128           /* Directory buffer size */
char dir_buffer[DIR_BSZ];     /* Directory buffer */

char file_name[20];           /* Formatted for display : un/d:FILENAME.TYP */
short name_flag;              /* NZ to display names of files moved */

short cur_disk;               /* Current logical disk at start of program */
int from_user;                /* User number from which to move files */
int to_user;                  /* User number to which files will be moved */

int mcount;                   /* Match count (no. of file names matched) */
int dmcount;                  /* Per-disk match count */
int lcount;                   /* Line count (for lines displayed) */

main(argc,argv)
short argc;                   /* Argument count */
char *argv[];                 /* Argument vector (pointer to an array of chars.) */
{
printf("\nMOVE Version %s (Library %s)",VN,LIBVN);

chk_use(argc);                /* Check usage */

to_user = atoi(argv[2]);      /* Convert user no. to integer */
        /* Set and check destination user number */
if(to_user > 15)
        {
        printf("\nError -- the destination user number cannot be greater than 15.");
        }

        /* Set the current user number */
from_user = bdos(GETUSER,0xFF);

        /* Check if source user number specified */
if (isdigit(argv[3][0]))
        {
                /* Set and check source user number */
        if((from_user = atoi(argv[3])) > 15)
                {
                printf("\nError -- the source user number cannot be greater than 15.");
                exit();
                }
                /* Set name suppress flag from parameter #4 */
        name_flag = usstrcmp("NAMES",argv[4]);
        }
else                          /* No source user specified */
        {
```

Figure 11-7. MOVE.C, a utility program that changes files' user numbers

```
                /* Set name suppress flag from parameter #3 */
        name_flag = usstrcmp("NAMES",argv[3]);
        }

        /* To simplify the logic below, name_flag must be made
              NZ if it is equal to NAME_EQ, O if it is any other value */
name_flag = (name_flag == NAME_EQ ? 1 : 0);

if (to_user == from_user)         /* To = from */
        {
        printf("\nError - 'to' user number is the same as 'from' user number.");
        exit();
        }

        /* Set the search control block file name, type, user number,
              extent number, and length -- length matches user number, file
              name, and type. As the extent number does not enter into the
              comparison, all extents of a given file will be found. */
setscb(scb,argv[1],from_user,'?',13);

cur_disk = bdos(GETDISK);           /* Get current default disk */
lcount = dmcount = mcount = 0;      /* Initialize counts */

for (scb.scb_disk = 0;              /* Starting with logical disk A: */
     scb.scb_disk < 16;             /* Until logical disk P: */
     scb.scb_disk++)                /* Move to next logical disk */
        {
                /* Check if current disk has been selected for search */
        if (!(scb.scb_adisks & (1 << scb.scb_disk)))
                continue;           /* No, so bypass this disk */
                /* convert search user number and name for output */
        conv_dfname(scb.scb_disk,scb,file_name);
        printf("\n\nMoving file(s) %s -> User %d.",file_name,to_user);

        lcount++;                   /* Update line count */

        dir_pb.dp_disk = scb.scb_disk;  /* Set to disk to be searched*/
        dmcount = 0;                    /* Reset disk matched count */

        if (name_flag)              /* If file names are to be displayed */
                putchar('\n');      /* Move to column 1 */

                /* Set the directory to "closed" to force the get_nde
                      function to open it. */
        dir_pb.dp_open = 0;

                /* While not at the end of the directory, set a pointer
                      to the next directory entry */
        while(dir_entry = get_nde(dir_pb))
                {
                        /* Match those entries that have the correct
                              user number, file name, type, and any
                              extent number. */
                if (
                    (dir_entry -> de_userno != 0xE5) &&
                    (comp_fname(scb,dir_entry) == NAME_EQ)
                   )
                        {
                        dir_entry -> de_userno = to_user;     /* Move to new user */
                                /* Request sector to be written back */
                        dir_pb.dp_write = 1;

                        mcount++;           /* Update matched counts */
                        dmcount++;          /* Per-disk count */

                        if (name_flag)      /* Check map option */
                                {
                                conv_dfname(scb.scb_disk,dir_entry,file_name);
                                        printf("%s   ",file_name);

                                /* Check if need to start new line */
                                if (!(dmcount % 4))
                                        {
                                        putchar('\n');
                                        if (++lcount > 18)
```

Figure 11-7.   (Continued)

```
                                                    {
                                                    lcount = 0;
                                                    printf("\nPress Space Bar to continue....");
                                                    getchar();
                                                    putchar('\n');
                                                    }
                                        }
                                    }
                                }
                            }
                        }
    if (mcount == 0)
            printf("\n --- No Files Moved --- ");

    bdos(SETDISK,cur_disk); /* Reset to current disk */
}


chk_use(argc)              /* Check usage */
/* This function checks that the correct number of
   parameters has been specified, outputting instructions
       if not */
/* Entry parameter */
int argc;         /* Count of the number of arguments on the command line */
{

/* The minimum value of argc is 1 (for the program name itself),
   so argc is always one greater than the number of parameters
   on the command line */

    if (argc == 1 || argc > 5)
            {
            printf("\nUsage :");
            printf("\n\tMOVE d:filename.typ to_user {from_user} {NAMES}");
            printf("\n\t       *:filename.typ (All disks)");
            printf("\n\t       ABCD..OP:filename.typ (Selected Disks)");
            printf("\n\tNAMES option shows names of files moved.");
            exit();
            }

}
```

Figure 11-7. (Continued)

Other Utilities

The utility programs described in this section are by no means a complete set. You may want to develop many other specialized utility programs. Some possibilities are:

FILECOPY

A more specialized version of PIP could copy ambiguously specified groups of files. Of special importance would be the ability to read a file containing the names of the files to be copied. A useful option would be the ability to detect the setting of the unused file attribute bit and copy only files that have been changed.

PROTECT/UNPROTECT

This pair of utilities would allow you to "hide" files in user numbers greater than 15. Files so hidden could not be accessed other than by UNPROTECTing them, thereby moving them back into the normal user number range.

RECLAIM
> This utility would read all sectors on a disk (using the BIOS). Any bad sectors encountered could then be logically removed by creating an entry in the file directory, with allocation block numbers that would effectively "reserve" the blocks containing the bad sectors.

OWNER
> This utility, given a track or sector number, would access the directory and determine which file or files were using that part of the disk. This is useful if you have a bad sector or track on a disk. You then can determine which files have been damaged.

Utility Programs for the Enhanced BIOS

This section describes several utility programs that work with the enhanced BIOS shown in Figure 8-10. Several of these utilities work directly with the physical devices on the computer system, which can vary from computer to computer. The library header contains #define declarations for device numbers and names for physical devices (Figure 11-2, f and Figure 11-2, g).

These #define statements are used to build a physical-device code table. If you have more physical devices or want to change the names by which you refer to the devices, you will need to change these definitions.

All of these utilities share some common features in the way that they are invoked. If they are called without any parameters, they display instructions on the console regarding what parameters are available. If they are called with the word "SHOW" (or "S", "SH", and so forth) as a parameter, they display the current settings of whatever attribute the utility controls.

MAKE — Make Files "Invisible" or "Visible"

The MAKE utility shown in Figure 11-8 is designed to operate in conjunction with the public files option implemented in the enhanced BIOS of Figure 8-10. It has two modes of operation—making files "invisible" or "visible."

An invisible file is one in user 0 which has been set to Read-Only and System status. When the public files option is enabled, these files cannot be seen when you use the DIR command, nor can they be erased accidentally.

A visible file is one that has been set to Read/Write and Directory status.

When files are made invisible, they are transferred from the current user number to user 0. When files are made visible, they are transferred from user 0 to the current user number.

Here is an example console dialog showing MAKE in operation:

```
P3B>make<CR>
MAKE Version 1.0 02/12/83 (Library 1.0)
```

```
Usage :
        MAKE d:filename.typ INVISIBLE {NAMES}
                            VISIBLE
               *:filename.typ (All disks)
               ABCD..OP:filename.typ (Selected Disks)
        NAMES option shows names of files processed.

P3B>dir *.com<CR>
B: ERASE     COM : UNERASE  COM : ASSIGN    COM : PROTOCOL COM

P3B>make *.com invisible names<CR>
MAKE Version 1.0 02/12/83 (Library 1.0)

Moving files from User 3 to 0 and making them Invisible.
Searching disk : B

        0/B:ERASE    .COM made Invisible in User 0.
        0/B:UNERASE  .COM made Invisible in User 0.
        0/B:ASSIGN   .COM made Invisible in User 0.
        0/B:PROTOCOL.COM made Invisible in User 0.

P3B>make erase.com visible names<CR>
MAKE Version 1.0 02/12/83 (Library 1.0)

Moving files from User 0 to 3 and making them Visible.
Searching disk : B

        3/B:ERASE    .COM made Visible in User 3.
```

```
#define VN "1.0 02/12/83"

/* MAKE - This utility is really two very similar programs;
   which one depends on the parameter specified on the command
   line.

   INVISIBLE finds all of the specified files, moves them
   to user number 0, and sets them to be System and Read Only
   status. These files can then be accessed from user numbers
   other than 0 when the public files feature is enabled in the
   BIOS.

   VISIBLE is the opposite in that the specified files are
   moved to the current user number and changed to Directory
   and Read/Write status. */

#include <LIBRARY.H>

struct _dirpb dir_pb;           /* Directory management parameter block */
struct _dir *dir_entry;         /* Pointer to directory entry */
struct _scb scb;                /* Search control block */
short to_user;                  /* User number to which files will be set */
short from_user;                /* User number from which files will be moved */

char file_name[20];             /* Formatted for display : un/d:FILENAME.TYP */
short name_flag;                /* NZ to display names of files moved */

short cur_disk;                 /* Current logical disk at start of program */

int mcount;                     /* Match count (no. of file names matched) */

short invisible;                /* NZ when parameter specifies invisible */
char *operation;                /* Pointer to either "invisible" or "visible" */

main(argc,argv)
short argc;                     /* Argument count */
char *argv[];                   /* Argument vector (pointer to an array of chars.) */
```

Figure 11-8. MAKE.C, a utility that makes files "invisible" and protected or makes them "visible," accessible, and unprotected

```
{
printf("\nMAKE Version %s (Library %s)",VN,LIBVN);
chk_use(argc);                  /* Check usage */
cur_disk = bdos(GETDISK);       /* Get current default disk */
mcount = 0;                     /* Initialize count */

        /* Set the invisible flag according to the parameter */
invisible = usstrcmp("VISIBLE",argv[2]);

        /* Set the from_user and to_user numbers depending on which
           program is to be built, and the parameters specified. */
if (invisible)
        {
        from_user = bdos(GETUSER,0xFF); /* Get current user number */
        to_user = 0;            /* Always move files to user 0 */
        operation = "Invisible";        /* Set pointer to string */
        }
else    /* visible */
        {
        from_user = 0;                  /* Always move from user 0 */
        to_user = bdos(GETUSER,0xFF);   /* Get current user */
        operation = "Visible";          /* Set pointer to string */
        }

        /* Set search control block disks, name, type, user number,
           extent number, and number of bytes to compare -- in this
           case, match the "from" user, all extents. */
setscb(scb,argv[1],from_user,'?',13);   /* Set disks, name, type */

name_flag = usstrcmp("NAMES",argv[3]);  /* Set name-suppress flag from param. 3 */

        /* To simplify the logic below, name_flag must be made
           NZ if it is equal to NAME_EQ, 0 if it is any other value */
name_flag = (name_flag == NAME_EQ ? 1 : 0);

        /* Convert search user number and name for output */
conv_dfname(scb.scb_disk,scb,file_name);
printf("\n\nMoving files from User %d to %d and making them %s.",
        from_user,to_user,operation);

for (scb.scb_disk = 0;          /* Starting with logical disk A: */
     scb.scb_disk < 16;         /* Until logical disk P: */
     scb.scb_disk++)            /* Move to next logical disk */
        {
            /* Check if current disk has been selected for search */
            if (!(scb.scb_adisks & (1 << scb.scb_disk)))
                continue;       /* No -- so bypass this disk */

            printf("\nSearching disk : %c",(scb.scb_disk + 'A'));

            dir_pb.dp_disk = scb.scb_disk; /* Set to disk to be searched*/

            if (name_flag)      /* If file names are to be displayed */
                putchar('\n');  /* Move to column 1 */

            /* Set the directory to "closed", and force the get_nde
                function to open it. */
            dir_pb.dp_open = 0;

            /* While not at the end of the directory,
                set a pointer to the next directory entry. */
            while(dir_entry = get_nde(dir_pb))
                {
                    /* Match those entries that have the correct
                        user number, file name, type, and any
                        extent number. */
                    if (
                       (dir_entry -> de_userno != 0xE5) &&
                       (comp_fname(scb,dir_entry) == NAME_EQ)
                       )
                        {
```

Figure 11-8. (Continued)

```
                        mcount++;        /* Update matched counts */

                        if (invisible)
                                {        /* Set ms bits */
                                dir_entry -> de_fname[8] != 0x80;
                                dir_entry -> de_fname[9] != 0x80;
                                }
                        else    /* Visible */
                                {        /* Clear ms bits */
                                dir_entry -> de_fname[8] &= 0x7F;
                                dir_entry -> de_fname[9] &= 0x7F;
                                }

                                /* Move to correct user number */
                        dir_entry -> de_userno = to_user;

                                /* Indicate sector to be written back */
                        dir_pb.dp_write = 1;

                                /* Check if name to be displayed */
                        if (name_flag)
                                {
                                conv_dfname(scb.scb_disk,dir_entry,file_name);
                                printf("\n\t%s made %s in User %d.",
                                        file_name,operation,to_user);
                                }
                        }
                }       /* All directory entries processed */
        }               /* All disks processed */

if (mcount == 0)
        printf("\n --- No Files Processed --- ");

bdos(SETDISK,cur_disk); /* Reset to current disk */
}


chk_use(argc)           /* Check usage */
/* This function checks that the correct number of
   parameters has been specified, outputting instructions
   if not.
*/
/* Entry parameter */
int argc;       /* Count of the number of arguments on the command line */
{
        /* The minimum value of argc is 1 (for the program name itself),
           so argc is always one greater than the number of parameters
           on the command line */

if (argc == 3 || argc == 4)
        return;
else
        {
        printf("\nUsage :");
        printf("\n\tMAKE d:filename.typ INVISIBLE {NAMES}");
        printf("\n\t                    VISIBLE");
        printf("\n\t    *:filename.typ (All disks)");
        printf("\n\t    ABCD..OP:filename.typ (Selected Disks)");
        printf("\n\tNAMES option shows names of files processed.");
        exit();
        }

}
```

Figure 11-8. (Continued)

SPEED — Set Baud Rates

The SPEED utility shown in Figure 11-9 sets the baud rate for a specific serial device. Here is an example console dialog that shows several of the options:

```
P3B>speed<CR>
SPEED 1.0 02/17/83
The SPEED utility sets the baud rate speed for each physical device.
Usage is :   SPEED physical-device baud-rate, or
             SPEED SHOW     (to show current settings)

Valid physical devices are:
             TERMINAL
             PRINTER
             MODEM

Valid baud rates are:
             300
             600
             1200
             2400
             4800
             9600
             19200


P3B>speed show<CR>
SPEED 1.0 02/17/83
Current Baud Rate settings are :
        TERMINAL set to 9600 baud.
        PRINTER set to 9600 baud.
        MODEM set to 9600 baud.


P3B>speed m 19<CR>
SPEED 1.0 02/17/83
Current Baud Rate settings are :
        TERMINAL set to 9600 baud.
        PRINTER set to 9600 baud.
        MODEM set to 19200 baud.


P3B>speed xyz 12<CR>
SPEED 1.0 02/17/83
Physical Device 'XYZ' is invalid or ambiguous.
Legal Physical Devices are :
             TERMINAL
             PRINTER
             MODEM
```

```
#define VN "\nSPEED 1.0 02/17/83"

/* This utility sets the baud rate speed for each of the physical
   devices. */

#include <LIBRARY.H>

struct _ct ct_pdev[MAXPDEV + 2];        /* Physical device table */

        /* Hardware specific items */
```

Figure 11-9.   SPEED.C, a utility that sets the baud rate for a specific device

```
#define B300     0x35           /* Baud rates for serial ports */
#define B600     0x36           /* 300 baud */
#define B1200    0x37           /* 600 baud */
#define B2400    0x3A           /* 1200 baud */
#define B4800    0x3C           /* 2400 baud */
#define B9600    0x3E           /* 4800 baud */
#define B19200   0x3F           /* 9600 baud */
struct _ct ct_br[10];           /* 19200 baud */
                                /* Code table for baud rates (+ spare entries) */

        /* Parameters on the command line */
#define PDEV argv[1]    /* Physical device */
#define BAUD argv[2]    /* Baud rate */


main(argc,argv)
int argc;
char *argv[];
{
printf(VN);        /* Display sign-on message */
setup();           /* Set up code tables */
chk_use(argc);     /* Check correct usage */

        /* Check if request to show current settings */
if (usstrcmp("SHOW",argv[1]))
        {          /* No -- assume setting is required */
        set_baud(get_pdev(PDEV),get_baud(BAUD)); /* Set baud rate */
        }

show_baud();       /* Display current settings */

} /* end of program */

setup()            /* set up the code tables for this program */
{
        /* Initialize the physical device table */
ct_init(ct_pdev[0],T_DEVN,PN_T);     /* Terminal */
ct_init(ct_pdev[1],P_DEVN,PN_P);     /* Printer */
ct_init(ct_pdev[2],M_DEVN,PN_M);     /* Modem */
ct_init(ct_pdev[3],CT_SNF,"*");  /* Terminator */

        /* Initialize the baud rate table */
ct_init(ct_br[0],B300,"300");
ct_init(ct_br[1],B600,"600");
ct_init(ct_br[2],B1200,"1200");
ct_init(ct_br[3],B2400,"2400");
ct_init(ct_br[4],B4800,"4800");
ct_init(ct_br[5],B9600,"9600");
ct_init(ct_br[6],B19200,"19200");
ct_init(ct_br[7],CT_SNF,"*");    /* Terminator */
}

unsigned
get_pdev(ppdev)         /* Get physical device */
/* This function returns the physical device code
   specified by the user in the command line. */
char *ppdev;            /* Pointer to character string */
{
unsigned retval;                    /* Return value */

retval = ct_parc(ct_pdev,ppdev);    /* Get code for ASCII string */
if (retval == CT_SNF)               /* If string not found */
        {
        printf("\n\007Physical Device '%s' is invalid or ambiguous.",
                ppdev);
        printf("\nLegal Physical Devices are : ");
        ct_disps(ct_pdev);          /* Display all values */
        exit();
        }
return retval;                      /* Return code */
}

unsigned
get_baud(pbaud)
/* This function returns the baud rate time constant for
   the baud rate specified by the user in the command line */
```

Figure 11-9. (Continued)

```
        char *pbaud;              /* Pointer to character string */
        {
        unsigned retval;                    /* Return value */
        retval = ct_parc(ct_br,pbaud);      /* Get code for ASCII string */
        if (retval == CT_SNF)               /* If string not found */
                {
                printf("\n\007Baud Rate '%s' is invalid or ambiguous.",
                        pbaud);
                printf("\nLegal Baud Rates are : ");
                ct_disps(ct_br);            /* Display all values */
                exit();
                }
        return retval;              /* Return code */
        }

        set_baud(pdevc,baudc)       /* Set the baud rate of the specified device */
        int pdevc;                  /* Physical device code */
        short baudc;                /* Baud rate code */
                                    /* On some systems this may have to be a
                                       two-byte (unsigned) value   */
        {
        short *baud_rc;             /* Pointer to the baud rate constant */
                                    /* On some systems this may have to be a
                                       two-byte (unsigned) value   */
        /* Note: the respective codes for accessing the baud rate constants
            via the get_cba (get configuration block address) function are:
                Device #0 = 19,  #1 = 21, #2 = 23. This function uses this
            mathematical relationship   */

                /* Set up pointer to the baud rate constant */
        baud_rc = get_cba(CB_D0_BRC + (pdevc << 1));

                /* Then set the baud rate constant */
        *baud_rc = baudc;

                /* Then call the BIOS initialization routine */
        bios(CIOINIT,pdevc);
        }

        show_baud()                 /* Show current baud rate */
        {
        int pdevn;                  /* Physical device number */
        short baudc;                /* Baud rate code */
                                    /* On some systems this may have to be a
                                       two-byte (unsigned) value   */
        short *baud_rc;             /* Pointer to the baud rate constant */
                                    /* On some systems this may have to be a
                                       two-byte (unsigned) value   */
        /* Note: the respective codes for accessing the baud rate constants
            via the get_cba (get configuration block address) function are:
                Device #0 = 19,  #1 = 21, #2 = 23. This function uses this
            mathematical relationship   */

        printf("\nCurrent baud rate settings are :");

        for (pdevn = 0; pdevn <= MAXPDEV; pdevn ++)    /* All physical devices */
                {
                        /* Set up pointer to the baud rate constant --
                           the code for the get_cba function is computed
                           by adding the physical device number *2 to
                           the Baud Rate code for device #0 */

                baud_rc = get_cba(CB_D0_BRC + (pdevn << 1));

                        /* Then set the baud rate constant */
                baudc = *baud_rc;

                printf("\n\t%s set to %s baud.",
                        ct_strc(ct_pdev,pdevn),  /* Get ptr. to device name */
                        ct_strc(ct_br,baudc) );  /* Get ptr. to baud rate */
                }
        }

        chk_use(argc)               /* Check correct usage */
        int argc;                   /* Argument count */
        {
```

Figure 11-9. (Continued)

```
if (argc == 1)
        {
        printf("\nThe SPEED utility sets the baud rate speed for each physical device.");
        printf("\nUsage is :  SPEED physical-device baud rate, or");
        printf("\n             SPEED SHOW     (to show current settings)");
        printf("\n\nValid physical devices are: ");
        ct_disps(ct_pdev);
        printf("\nValid baud rates are: ");
        ct_disps(ct_br);
        exit();
        }
}
```

Figure 11-9.   (Continued)

PROTOCOL — Set Serial Line Protocols

The PROTOCOL utility shown in Figure 11-10 is used to set the protocol for a specific serial device.

The drivers for each physical device can support several serial line protocols. The protocols are divided into two groups, depending on whether they apply to data output by or input to the computer.

Note that the output DTR and input RTS protocols can coexist with other protocols. The strategy is first to set the required character-based protocol and then to set the DTR/RTS protocol. There is an example of this in the following console dialog:

```
P3B>protocol<CR>
PROTOCOL Vn 1.0 02/17/83
PROTOCOL sets the physical device's serial protocols.
        PROTOCOL physical-device direction protocol {message-length}

Legal physical devices are :
        TERMINAL
        PRINTER
        MODEM

Legal direction/protocols are :
        Output DTR
        Output XON
        Output ETX
        Input RTS
        Input XON

    Message length can be specifed with Output ETX.


    P3B>protocol show<CR>
    PROTOCOL Vn 1.0 02/17/83
        Protocol for TERMINAL - None.
        Protocol for PRINTER - Output XON
        Protocol for MODEM - Input RTS


        P3B>protocol m o e 128<CR>
        PROTOCOL Vn 1.0 02/17/83
            Protocol for TERMINAL - None.
            Protocol for PRINTER - Output XON
```

```
Protocol for MODEM - Output ETX  Message Length 128 bytes.


P3B>protocol m o d<CR>
PROTOCOL Vn 1.0 02/17/83
        Protocol for TERMINAL - None.
        Protocol for PRINTER - Output XON
        Protocol for MODEM - Output DTR Output ETX  Message Length
            128 bytes.
```

```c
#define VN "\nPROTOCOL Vn 1.0 02/17/83"
/* PROTOCOL -- This utility sets the serial port protocol for the
   specified physical device.  Alternatively, it displays the
   current protocols for all of the serial devices. */

#include <LIBRARY.H>

        /* Code tables used to relate ASCII strings to code values */
struct _ct ct_iproto[3];        /* Code table for input protocols */
struct _ct ct_oproto[4];        /* Code table for output protocols */
struct _ct ct_dproto[7];        /* Code table for displaying protocols */
struct _ct ct_pdev[MAXPDEV + 2];/* Physical device table */
struct _ct ct_io[3];            /* Input, output */

        /* Parameters on the command line */
#define PDEV   argv[1]          /* Physical device */
#define IO     argv[2]          /* Input/output */
#define PROTO  argv[3]          /* Protocol */
#define PROTOL argv[4]          /* Protocol message length */

main(argc,argv)
int argc;
char *argv[];
{
printf(VN);             /* Display sign-on message */
setup();                /* Set up code tables */
chk_use(argc);          /* Check correct usage */

        /* Check if request to show current settings */
if (usstrcmp("SHOW",argv[1]))
        {               /* No -- assume a set is required */
        set_proto(get_pdev(PDEV),       /* Physical device */
                        /* Input/output and protocol */
                get_proto(get_io(IO),PROTO),
                PROTOL);        /* Protocol message length */
        }
show_proto();

} /* end of program */

setup()                 /* Set up the code tables for this program */
{
        /* Initialize the physical device table */
ct_init(ct_pdev[0],0,PN_T);     /* Terminal */
ct_init(ct_pdev[1],1,PN_P);     /* Printer */
ct_init(ct_pdev[2],2,PN_M);     /* Modem */
ct_init(ct_pdev[3],CT_SNF,"*"); /* Terminator */

        /* Initialize the input/output table */
ct_init(ct_io[0],0,"INPUT");
ct_init(ct_io[1],1,"OUTPUT");
ct_init(ct_io[2],CT_SNF,"*");           /* Terminator */

        /* Initialize the output protocol table */
ct_init(ct_oproto[0],DT_ODTR,"DTR");
ct_init(ct_oproto[1],DT_OXON,"XON");
ct_init(ct_oproto[2],DT_OETX,"ETX");
```

Figure 11-10. PROTOCOL.C, a utility that sets the protocol governing input and output of a specified serial device

```
        ct_init(ct_oproto[3],CT_SNF,"*");       /* Terminator */

                /* Initialize the input protocol table */
        ct_init(ct_iproto[0],DT_IRTS,"RTS");
        ct_init(ct_iproto[1],DT_IXON,"XON");
        ct_init(ct_iproto[2],CT_SNF,"*");        /* Terminator */

                /* Initialize the display protocol */
        ct_init(ct_dproto[0],DT_ODTR,"Output DTR");
        ct_init(ct_dproto[1],DT_OXON,"Output XON");
        ct_init(ct_dproto[2],DT_OETX,"Output ETX");
        ct_init(ct_dproto[3],DT_IRTS,"Input RTS");
        ct_init(ct_dproto[4],DT_IXON,"Input XON");
        ct_init(ct_dproto[5],CT_SNF,"*");
}

unsigned
get_pdev(ppdev)             /* Get physical device */
/* This function returns the physical device code
   specified by the user in the command line. */
char *ppdev;                /* Pointer to character string */
{
unsigned retval;            /* Return value */

        retval = ct_parc(ct_pdev,ppdev);/* Get code for ASCII string */
        if (retval == CT_SNF)       /* If string not found */
                {
                printf("\n\007Physical Device '%s' is invalid or ambiguous.",
                        ppdev);
                printf("\nLegal Physical Devices are : ");
                ct_disps(ct_pdev);   /* Display all values */
                exit();
                }
        return retval;              /* Return code */
}

unsigned
get_io(pio)                 /* Get input/output parameter */
char *pio;                  /* Pointer to character string */
{
unsigned retval;            /* Return value */

        retval = ct_parc(ct_io,pio);    /* Get code for ASCII string */
        if (retval == CT_SNF)       /* If string not found */
                {
                printf("\n\007Input/Output direction '%s' is invalid or ambiguous.",
                        pio);
                printf("\nLegal values are : ");
                ct_disps(ct_io);     /* Display all values */
                exit();
                }
        return retval;              /* Return code */
}

unsigned
get_proto(output,pproto)
/* This function returns the protocol code for the
   protocol specified by the user in the command line. */
int output;                 /* =1 for output, =0 for input */
char *pproto;               /* Pointer to character string */

{
unsigned retval;            /* Return value */

        if (output)                 /* OUTPUT specified */
                {
                        /* Get code for ASCII string */
                retval = ct_parc(ct_oproto,pproto);
                if (retval == CT_SNF)    /* If string not found */
                        {
                        printf("\n\007Output Protocol '%s' is invalid or ambiguous.",
                                pproto);
                        printf("\nLegal Output Protocols are : ");
                        ct_disps(ct_oproto);   /* Display valid protocols */
                        exit();
                        }
```

Figure 11-10.   (Continued)

```
        }
  else                          /* INPUT specified */
        {
                /* Get code for ASCII string */
        retval = ct_parc(ct_iproto,pproto);
        if (retval == CT_SNF)           /* If string not found */
                {
                printf("\n\007Input Protocol '%s' is invalid or ambiguous.",
        pproto);
                printf("\nLegal Input Protocols are : ");
                ct_disps(ct_iproto);    /* Display valid protocols */
                exit();
                }
        }
  return retval;                        /* Return code */
  }


  set_proto(pdevc,protoc,pplength)/* Set the protocol for physical device */
  int pdevc;                            /* Physical device code */
  unsigned protoc;                      /* Protocol byte */
  char *pplength;                       /* Pointer to protocol length */
  {
  struct _ppdt
        {
        char *pdt[16];          /* Array of 16 pointers to the device tables */
        } ;
  struct _ppdt *ppdt;                   /* Pointer to the device table array */
  struct _dt *dt;                       /* Pointer to a device table */

  ppdt = get_cba(CB_DTA); /* Set pointer to array of pointers */
  dt = ppdt -> pdt[pdevc];

  if (!dt)                      /* Check if pointer in array is valid */
        {
        printf("\nError -- Array of Device Table Addresses is not set for device #%d.",
                pdevc);
        exit();
        }

  if (protoc & 0x8000)  /* Check if protocol byte to be set
                                directly or to be OR ed in */
        {                       /* OR ed */
        dt -> dt_st1 |= (protoc & 0x7F);
        }
  else
        {               /* Set directly */
        dt -> dt_st1 = (protoc & 0x7F);
        }

  if ((protoc & 0x7F) == DT_OETX) /* If ETX/ACK, check for message
                                length */
        {
        if (isdigit(*pplength))         /* Check if length present */
                {
                        /* Convert length to binary and set device
                                table field. */
                dt -> dt_etxml = atoi(pplength);
                }
        }
  }


  show_proto()          /* Show the current protocol settings */
  {
  struct _ppdt
        {
        char *pdt[16];          /* Array of 16 pointers to the device tables */
        } ;
  struct _ppdt *ppdt;                   /* Pointer to the device table array */
  struct _dt *dt;                       /* Pointer to a device table */
  int pdevc;                            /* Physical device code */
  struct _ct *dproto;                   /* Pointer to display protocols */

  ppdt = get_cba(CB_DTA); /* Set pointer to array of pointers */

                /* For all physical devices */
```

Figure 11-10.   (Continued)

```
for (pdevc = 0; pdevc <= MAXPDEV; pdevc++)
    {
                /* Set pointer to device table */
        dt = ppdt -> pdt[pdevc];

        if (dt) /* Check if pointer in array is valid */
            {
            printf("\n\tProtocol for %s - ",ct_strc(ct_pdev,pdevc));
                    /* Check if any protocols set */
            if (!(dt -> dt_st1 & ALLPROTO))
                {
                printf("None.");
                continue;
                }
                    /* Set pointer to display protocol table */
            dproto = ct_dproto;
            while (dproto -> _ct_code != CT_SNF)
                {
                        /* Check if protocol bit set */
                if (dproto -> _ct_code & dt -> dt_st1)
                    {       /* Display protocol */
                    printf("%s ",dproto -> _ct_sp);
                    }
                ++dproto;       /* Move to next entry */
                }
                /* Check if ETX/ACK protocol and
                    message length to be displayed */
            if (dt -> dt_st1 & DT_OETX)
                printf(" Message length %d bytes.",
                        dt -> dt_etxml);
            }
    }
}

chk_use(argc)           /* Check for correct usage */
int argc;               /* Argument count on commmand line */
{
    if (argc == 1)
        {
        printf("\nPROTOCOL sets the physical device's serial protocols.");
        printf("\n\tPROTOCOL physical-device direction protocol {message-length}");
        printf("\n\nLegal physical devices are :");
        ct_disps(ct_pdev);
        printf("\nLegal direction/protocols are :");
        ct_disps(ct_dproto);
        printf("\n\tMessage length can be specifed with Output ETX.\n");
        exit();
        }
}
```

Figure 11-10. (Continued)

ASSIGN — Assign Physical to Logical Devices

The ASSIGN utility shown in Figure 11-11 sets the necessary bits in the physical input/output redirection bits in the BIOS. It assigns a logical device's input and output to physical devices. Input can only be derived from a single physical device, while output can be directed to multiple devices.

Here is an example console dialog showing ASSIGN in action:

```
P3B>assign<CR>
ASSIGN Vn 1.0 02/17/83
ASSIGN sets the Input/Output redirection.
        ASSIGN logical-device INPUT physical-device
        ASSIGN logical-device OUTPUT physical-dev1 {phy_dev2..}
        ASSIGN SHOW     (to show current assignments)
```

Chapter 11: Additional Utility Programs **439**

```
            Legal logical devices are :
                    CONSOLE
                    AUXILIARY
                    LIST

            Legal physical devices are :
                    TERMINAL
                    PRINTER
                    MODEM


        P3B>assign show<CR>
        ASSIGN Vn 1.0 02/17/83
        Current Device Assignments are :
                CONSOLE INPUT is assigned to -  TERMINAL
                CONSOLE OUTPUT is assigned to -  TERMINAL
                AUXILIARY INPUT is assigned to -  MODEM
                AUXILIARY OUTPUT is assigned to -  MODEM
                LIST INPUT is assigned to -  PRINTER
                LIST OUTPUT is assigned to -  PRINTER

        P3B>assign a o t m p<CR>
        ASSIGN Vn 1.0 02/17/83
        Current Device Assignments are :
                CONSOLE INPUT is assigned to -  TERMINAL
                CONSOLE OUTPUT is assigned to -  TERMINAL
                AUXILIARY INPUT is assigned to -  MODEM
                AUXILIARY OUTPUT is assigned to -  TERMINAL PRINTER MODEM
                LIST INPUT is assigned to -  PRINTER
                LIST OUTPUT is assigned to -  PRINTER
```

```c
#define VN "\nASSIGN Vn 1.0 02/17/83"

#include <LIBRARY.H>

struct _ct ct_pdev[MAXPDEV + 2];        /* Physical device table */


        /* Names of logical devices */
#define LN_C    "CONSOLE"
#define LN_A    "AUXILIARY"
#define LN_L    "LIST"
struct _ct ct_ldev[4];          /* Logical device table */

struct _ct ct_io[3];            /* Input, output */

        /* Parameters on the command line */
#define LDEV argv[1]    /* Logical device */
#define IO argv[2]      /* Input/output */

main(argc,argv)
int argc;
char *argv[];
{
printf(VN);     /* Display sign-on message */
setup();        /* Set up code tables */
chk_use(argc);  /* Check correct usage */

        /* Check if request to show current settings */
if (usstrcmp("SHOW",argv[1]))
        {               /* No, assume a set is required */
```

Figure 11-11. ASSIGN.C, a utility that assigns a logical device's input and output to two physical devices

```c
                /* NOTE : the number of physical devices to
                   process is given by argc - 3 */
        set_assign(get_ldev(LDEV),get_io(IO),argc - 3,argv);
        }
show_assign();

}

setup()                 /* Set up the code tables for this program */
{
        /* Initialize the physical device table */
ct_init(ct_pdev[0],0,PN_T);       /* Terminal */
ct_init(ct_pdev[1],1,PN_P);       /* Printer */
ct_init(ct_pdev[2],2,PN_M);       /* Modem */
ct_init(ct_pdev[3],CT_SNF,"*");   /* Terminator */

        /* Initialize the logical device table */
ct_init(ct_ldev[0],0,LN_C);       /* Terminal */
ct_init(ct_ldev[1],1,LN_A);       /* Auxiliary */
ct_init(ct_ldev[2],2,LN_L);       /* List */
ct_init(ct_ldev[3],CT_SNF,"*");   /* Terminator */

        /* Initialize the input/output table */
ct_init(ct_io[0],0,"INPUT");
ct_init(ct_io[1],1,"OUTPUT");
ct_init(ct_io[2],CT_SNF,"*");              /* Terminator */

}

unsigned
get_ldev(pldev)          /* Get logical device */
/* This function returns the logical device code
   specified by the user in the command line. */
char *pldev;             /* Pointer to character string */
{
unsigned retval;                   /* Return value */
retval = ct_parc(ct_ldev,pldev);   /* Get code for ASCII string */
if (retval == CT_SNF)              /* If string not found */
        {
        printf("\n\007Logical device '%s' is invalid or ambiguous.",
                pldev);
        printf("\nLegal logical devices are : ");
        ct_disps(ct_ldev);         /* Display all values */
        exit();
        }
return retval;                     /* Return code */
}

unsigned
get_io(pio)              /* Get input/output parameter */
char *pio;               /* Pointer to character string */
{
unsigned retval;                   /* Return value */

retval = ct_parc(ct_io,pio);       /* Get code for ASCII string */
if (retval == CT_SNF)              /* If string not found */
        {
        printf("\n\007Input/output direction '%s' is invalid or ambiguous.",
                pio);
        printf("\nLegal values are : ");
        ct_disps(ct_io);           /* Display all values */
        exit();
        }
return retval;                     /* Return code */
}

set_assign(ldevc,output,argc,argv)    /* Set assignment (I/O redirection) */
int ldevc;                         /* Logical device code */
int output;                        /* I/O redirection code */
int argc;                          /* count of arguments to process */
char *argv[];                      /* Replica of parameter to main function */
{
unsigned *redir;                   /* Pointer to redirection word */
int pdevc;                         /* Physical device code */
unsigned rd_val;                   /* Redirection value */

        /* Get the address of the I/O redirection word. */
```

Figure 11-11.   (Continued)

```
              This code assumes that get_cba code values
              are ordered:
                   Device #0, input & output
                   Device #1, input & output
                   Device #2, input & putput

              The get_cba code is computed by multiplying the
              logical device code by 2 (that is, shift left 1)
              and added onto the code for Device #0, input
              Then the output variable (0 = input, 1 = output)
              is added on   */
redir = get_cba(CB_CI + (ldevc << 1) + output);

rd_val = 0;      /* Initialize redirection value */

        /* For output, assignment can be made to several physical
           devices, so this code may be executed several times  */
do
        {
                /* Get code for ASCII string */
                /* NOTE: the physical device parameters start
                   with parameter #3 (argv[3]). However argc
                   is a decreasing count of the number of physical
                   devices to be processed. Therefore, argc + 2
                   causes them to be processed in reverse order
                   (i.e. from right to left on the command line) */

        pdevc = ct_parc(ct_pdev,argv[argc + 2]);

        if (pdevc == CT_SNF)            /* If string not found */
                {
                printf("\n\007Physical device '%s' is invalid or ambiguous.",
                argv[argc + 2]);
                printf("\nLegal physical devices are : ");
                ct_disps(ct_pdev);       /* Display all values */
                exit();
                }
                /* Repeat this loop for as long as there are
                   more parameters (for output only) */
        else
                {
                /* Build new redirection value by OR ing in
                   a one-bit shifted left pdevc places. */
                rd_val != (1 << pdevc);
                }
        } while (--argc && output);

*redir = rd_val;        /* Set the value into the config. block */
}

show_assign()                   /* Show current baud rate */
{
int rd_code;                    /* Redirection code for get_cba */
int ldevn;                      /* Logical device number */
int pdevn;                      /* Physical device number */
unsigned rd_val;                /* Redirection value */
unsigned *prd_val;              /* Pointer to the redirection value */

/* Note: the respective codes for accessing the redirection values
   via the get_cba (get configuration block address) function are:
        Device #0 console input  -- 5
        Device #0 console putput -- 6
        Device #1 auxiliary input -- 7
        Device #1 auxiliary output -- 8
        Device #2 list input -- 9
        Device #2 list output -- 10

   This function uses this mathematical relationship  */

printf("\nCurrent device assignments are :");

        /* For all get_cba codes */
for (rd_code = CB_CI; rd_code <= CB_LO; rd_code++)
        {
                /* Set pointer to redirection value */
        prd_val = get_cba(rd_code);
                /* Get the input redirection value */
```

Figure 11-11. (Continued)

```
                rd_val = *prd_val;       /* This also performs byte reversal */

                    /* Display device name. The rd_code is converted to a
                        device number by subtracting the first code number
                        from it and dividing by 2 (shift right one place).
                        The input/output direction is derived from the
                        least significant bit of the rd_code. */

                printf("\n\t%s %s is assigned to - ",
                        ct_strc(ct_ldev,(rd_code - CB_CI) >> 1),
                        ct_strc(ct_io,((rd_code & 0x01) ^ 1)));

                    /* For all physical devices */
                for (pdevn = 0; pdevn < 16; pdevn++)
                    {
                        /* Check if current physical device is assigned
                            by AND ing with a 1-bit shifted left pdevn times */
                        if (rd_val & (1 << pdevn))        /* Is device active? */
                            {    /* Display physical device name */
                                printf(" %s",ct_strc(ct_pdev,pdevn) );
                            }
                    }
            }
    }

chk_use(argc)           /* Check for correct usage */
int argc;               /* Argument count on commmand line */
{
if (argc == 1)
    {
    printf("\nASSIGN sets the Input/Output redirection.");
    printf("\n\tASSIGN logical-device INPUT physical-device");
    printf("\n\tASSIGN logical-device OUTPUT physical-dev1 {phy_dev2..}");
    printf("\n\tASSIGN SHOW     (to show current assignments)");
    printf("\n\nLegal logical devices are :");
    ct_disps(ct_ldev);
    printf("\nLegal physical devices are :");
    ct_disps(ct_pdev);
    exit();
    }
}
```

Figure 11-11.   (Continued)

DATE — Set the System Date

The DATE utility shown in Figure 11-12 sets the system date in the configuration block, along with a flag that indicates that the DATE utility has been used. Other utility programs can use this flag as a primitive test of whether the system date is current.

Here is an example console dialog:

```
P3B>date<CR>
DATE Vn 1.0 02/18/83
DATE sets the system date. Usage is :
        DATE mm/dd/yy
        DATE SHOW (to display current date)

P3B>date show<CR>
DATE Vn 1.0 02/18/83
        Current Date is 12/18/82

P3B>date 2/23/83<CR>
DATE Vn 1.0 02/18/83
        Current Date is 02/23/83
```

```
#define VN "\nDATE Vn 1.0 02/18/83"

/* This utility accepts the current date from the command tail,
   validates it, and set the internal system date in the BIOS.
   Alternatively, it can be requested just to display the current
   system date. */

#include <LIBRARY.H>

char *date;               /* Pointer to the date in the config. block */
char *date_flag;          /* Pointer to date-set flag */
int mm,dd,yy;             /* Variables to hold month, day, year */
int mcount;               /* Match count of numeric values entered */
int count;                /* Count used to add leading 0's to date */

main(argc,argv)
int argc;
char *argv[];
{
printf(VN);               /* Display sign-on message */
date = get_cba(CB_DATE);  /* Set pointer to date */
date_flag = get_cba(CB_DTFLAGS);/* Set pointer to date-set flag */

if (argc != 2)            /* Check if help requested (or needed) */
        show_use();       /* Display correct usage and exit */

if (usstrcmp("SHOW",argv[1]))  /* Check if not SHOW option */
        {
                          /* Convert specified time into month, day, year */
        mcount = sscanf(argv[1],"%d/%d/%d",&mm,&dd,&yy);
        if (mcount != 3)           /* Input not numeric */
                show_use();        /* Display correct usage and exit */

                 /* NOTE: The following validity checking is
                          simplistic, but could be expanded to accommodate
                          more context-sensitive checking; days in the month,
                          leap years, etc. */
        if (mm > 12 || mm < 1) /* Check valid month, day, year */
                {
                printf("\nMonth = %d is illegal.",mm);
                show_use();        /* Display correct usage and exit */
                }
        if (dd > 31 || dd < 1)
                {
                printf("\nDay = %d is illegal.",dd);
                show_use();        /* Display correct usage and exit */
                }
        if (yy > 90 || yy < 83) /* <=== NOTE ! */
                {
                printf("\nYear = %d is illegal.",yy);
                show_use();        /* Display correct usage and exit */
                }

                 /* Convert integers back into a formatted string */
        sprintf(date,"%2d/%2d/%2d",mm,dd,yy);
        date[8] = 0x0A;            /* Terminate with line feed */
        date[9] = '\0';            /* New string terminator */

                 /* Change " 1/ 2/ 3" into "01/02/03" */
        for (count = 0; count < 7; count+=3)
                {
                if (date[count] == ' ')
                        date[count] = '0';
                }

                 /* Turn flag on to indicate that user has set date */
        *date_flag |= DATE_SET;
        }
printf("\n\tCurrent Date is %s",date);
}

show_use()                /* Display correct usage and exit */
{
printf("\nDATE sets the system date. Usage is :");
printf("\n\tDATE mm/dd/yy");
printf("\n\tDATE SHOW (to display current date)\n");
exit();
}
```

Figure 11-12.   DATE.C, a utility that makes the current date part of the system

TIME — Set the System Time

The TIME utility shown in Figure 11-13 sets the current system time. Like DATE, TIME sets a flag so that other utilities can test that the system time is likely to be current.

Here is an example console dialog:

```
P3B>time<CR>
TIME Vn 1.0 02/18/83
TIME sets the system time. Usage is :
        TIME hh{:mm{:ss}}
        TIME SHOW (to display current time)


P3B>time show<CR>
TIME Vn 1.0 02/18/83
        Current Time is 13:08:44


P3B>time 5:47<CR>
TIME Vn 1.0 02/18/83
        Current Time is 05:47:00
```

```
#define VN "\nTIME Vn 1.0 02/18/83"

/* This utility accepts the current time from the command tail,
   validates it, and sets the internal system time in the BIOS.
   Alternatively, it can just display the current system time. */

#include <LIBRARY.H>

char *time;           /* Pointer to the time in the config. block */
char *time_set;       /* Pointer to the time set flag */
int hh,mm,ss;         /* Variables to hold hours, minutes, seconds */
int mcount;           /* Match count of numeric values entered */
int count;            /* Count used to add leading zeros to time */

main(argc,argv)
int argc;
char *argv[];
{
printf(VN);           /* Display sign-on message */
time = get_cba(CB_TIMEA);      /* Set pointer to time */
time_flag = get_cba(CB_DTFLAGS);        /* Set pointer to the
                                           time-set flag */
hh = mm = ss = 0;     /* Initialize the time if seconds or
                         minutes are not specified */

if (argc != 2)        /* Check if help requested (or needed) */
        show_use();   /* Display correct usage and exit */

if (usstrcmp("SHOW",argv[1]))   /* Check if not SHOW option */
        {
        /* Convert time into hours, minutes, seconds */
        mcount = sscanf(argv[1],"%d:%d:%d",&hh,&mm,&ss);
        if (!mcount)                 /* Input not numeric */
                show_use();          /* Display correct usage and exit */

        if (hh > 12)                 /* Check valid hours, minutes, seconds */
                {
                printf("\n\007Hours = %d is illegal.",hh);
                show_use();          /* Display correct usage and exit */
                }
```

Figure 11-13.   TIME.C, a utility that makes the current time part of the system

```
            if (mm > 59)
                {
                printf("\n\007Minutes = %d is illegal.",mm);
                show_use();     /* Display correct usage and exit */
                }
            if (ss > 59)
                {
                show_use();     /* Display correct usage and exit */
                printf("\n\007Seconds = %d is illegal.",ss);
                }

                /* Convert integers back into formatted string */
            sprintf(time,"%2d:%2d:%2d",hh,mm,ss);
            time[8] = 0x0A;            /* Terminate with line feed */
            time[9] = '\0';            /* New string terminator */

                /* Convert " 1: 2: 3" into "01:02:03" */
            for (count = 0; count < 7; count+=3)
                {
                if (time[count] == ' ')
                    time[count] = '0';
                }
                /* Turn bit on to indicate that the time has been set */
            *time_flag != TIME_SET;
            }
        printf("\n\tCurrent Time is %s",time);
        }
    show_use()                  /* Display correct usage and exit */
        {
        printf("\nTIME sets the system time. Usage is :");
        printf("\n\tTIME hh{:mm{:ss}}");
        printf("\n\tTIME SHOW (to display current time)\n");
        exit();
        }
```

Figure 11-13. TIME.C, a utility that makes the current time part of the system (continued)

FUNKEY — Set the Function Keys

The FUNKEY utility shown in Figure 11-14 sets the character strings associated with specific function keys. In the specified character string, the character "<" is converted into a LINE FEED character. Here is an example console dialog:

```
P3B>funkey<CR>
FUNKEY sets a specific function key string.
        FUNKEY key-number "string to be programmed<"
                (Note : '<' is changed to line feed.)
                (       key-number is from 0 to 17.)
                (       string can be up to 16 chars.)
        FUNKEY SHOW     (displays settings for all keys)


P3B>funkey show<CR>
FUNKEY Vn 1.0 02/18/83
        Key #0 = 'Function Key 1<'
        Key #1 = 'Function Key 2<'

P3B>funkey 0 "PIP B:=A:*.*[V]<"<CR>

P3B>funkey show<CR>
FUNKEY Vn 1.0 02/18/83
        Key #0 = 'PIP B:=A:*.*[V]<'
        Key #1 = 'Function Key 2<'
```

```
#define VN "\nFUNKEY Vn 1.0 02/18/83"

#include <LIBRARY.H>

int fnum;                       /* Function key number to be programmed */
char fstring[20];               /* String for function key */
struct _fkt *pfk;               /* Pointer to function key table */

main(argc,argv)
int argc;
char *argv[];
{
if (argc == 1 !! argc > 3)
        show_use();

pfk = get_cba(CB_FKT);  /* Set pointer to function key table */
if (usstrcmp("SHOW",argv[1]))
        {
        if (!isdigit(argv[1][0]))
                {
                printf("\n\007'%s' is an illegal function key.",
                        argv[1]);
                show_use();
                }

        fnum = atoi(argv[1]);    /* Convert function key number */
        if (fnum > FK_ENTRIES)
                {
                printf("\n\007Function key number %d too large.",fnum);
                show_use();
                }

        if (get_fs(fstring) > FK_LENGTH)
                {
                printf("\n\007Function key string is too long.");
                show_use();
                }


        pfk += fnum;    /* Update pointer to string */
                        /* Copy string into function key table */
                        /* Check if function key input present */
        if (!(pfk -> fk_input[0]))
                {
                printf("\n\007Error : Function Key #%d is not set up to be programmed.",fnum);
                show_use();
                }
        strcpy(pfk -> fk_output,fstring);
        }
else            /* SHOW function specified */
        {
        printf(VN);             /* Display sign-on message */
        show_fun();
        }
}
get_fs(string)          /* Get function string from command tail */
char string[];          /* Pointer to character string */
{
char *tail;             /* Pointer to command tail */
short tcount;           /* Count of TOTAL characters in command tail */
int slen;               /* String length */

tail = 0x80;            /* Command line is in memory at 0080H */
tcount = *tail++;       /* Set TOTAL count of characters in command tail */
slen = 0;               /* Initialize string length */

while(tcount--)         /* For all characters in the command tail */
        {
        if (*tail++ == '"')     /* Scan for first quotes */
                break;
```

Figure 11-14. FUNKEY.C, a utility that sets the character strings associated with specific function keys

```
            }
    if (!tcount)            /* No quotes found */
            {
            printf("\n\007No leading quotes found.");
            show_use();
            }
    ++tcount;               /* Adjust tail count */
    while(tcount--)         /* For all remaining characters in tail */
            {
            if (*tail == '"')
                    {
                    string[slen] = '\0';  /* Add terminator */
                    break;        /* Exit from loop */
                    }
            string[slen] = *tail++; /* Move char. from tail into string */
            if (string[slen] == '<')
                    string[slen] = 0x0A;
            ++slen;
            }
    if (!tcount)            /* No terminating quotes found */
            {
            printf("\n\007No trailing quotes found.");
            show_use();
            }
    return slen;            /* Return string length */
    }

show_fun()                  /* Display settings for all function keys */
    {
    struct _fkt *pfkt;      /* Local pointer to function keys */
    int count;              /* Count to access function keys */
    char *lf;               /* Pointer to "<" character (LINE FEED) */

    pfkt = get_cba(CB_FKT); /* Set pointer to function key table */
    for (count = 0; count <= FK_ENTRIES; count++)
            {
            if (pfkt -> fk_input[0])        /* Key is programmed */
                    {
                                    /* Check if at physical end of table */
                    if (pfkt -> fk_input == 0xFF)
                            break;  /* Yes -- break out of for loop */
                    strcpy(fstring,pfkt -> fk_output);
                                    /* Convert all 0x0A chars to "<" */
                    while (lf = strscn(fstring,"\012"))
                            {
                            *lf = '<';
                            }
                    printf("\n\tKey #%d = '%s'",count,fstring);
                    }
            ++pfkt;         /* Move to next entry */
            }
    }

show_use()
    {
    printf("\nFUNKEY sets a specific function key string.");
    printf("\n\tFUNKEY key-number \042string to be programmed<\042 ");
    printf("\n\t             (Note : '<' is changed to line feed.)");
    printf("\n\t     (          key-number is from 0 to %d.)",
            FK_ENTRIES-1);
    printf("\n\t     (          string can be up to %d chars.)",
            FK_LENGTH);
    printf("\n\tFUNKEY SHOW       (displays settings for all keys)");
    exit();
    }
```

Figure 11-14. (Continued)

Other Utilities

Because of space limitations, not all of the possible utility programs for the BIOS features can be shown in this chapter. Others that would need to be developed in order to have a complete set are

PUBLIC/PRIVATE
This pair of utilities would turn the public files flag on or off, making the files in user 0 available from other user numbers or not, respectively.

SETTERM
This program would program the CONOUT escape table, setting the various escape sequences as required. It could also program the characters in the function key table that match with those emitted by the terminal currently in use.

SAVESYS
This utility would save the current settings in the long term configuration block.

LOADSYS
This would load the long term configuration block from a previously saved image.

DO
This utility would copy the command tail into the multi-command buffer, changing "\" into LINE FEED, and then set the forced input pointer to the multi-command buffer. As a result, characters from the multi-command buffer would be fed into the console input stream as though they had been typed one command at a time.

SPARE
This utility would work in conjunction with the hard-disk bad-sector management in your disk drivers. It would spare out bad sectors or tracks on the hard disk. This done, all subsequent references to the sectors or tracks would be redirected to a different part of the disk.

Error Messages Displayed
Miscellaneous Errors

Error Messages

This chapter lists the error messages that emanate from standard CP/M and its utility programs. It does not include any error messages from the BIOS; these messages, if any, are the individualized product of the programmers who wrote the various versions of the BIOS.

The error messages are shown in alphabetical order, followed (in parentheses) by the name of the program or CP/M component outputting the message. Messages are shown in uppercase even if the actual message you will see contains lowercase letters. Additional characters that are displayed to "pretty up" the message have been omitted. For example, the message "** ABORTED **" will be listed as "ABORTED".

Following each message is an explanation and, where possible, some information to help you deal with the error.

The last section of the chapter deals with known errors or peculiarities in CP/M and its utilities. Read this section so that you will recognize these problems when they occur.

Error Messages Displayed

? (CCP)

The CCP displays a question mark if you enter a command name and there is no corresponding "command.COM" file on the disk.

It is also displayed if you omit the number of pages required as a parameter in the SAVE command.

? (DDT)

DDT outputs a question mark under several circumstances. You must use context (and some guesswork) to determine what has gone wrong. Here are some specific causes of problems:

- DDT cannot find the file that you have asked it to load into memory. Exit from DDT and investigate using DIR or STAT (the file may be set to System status and therefore invisible with DIR).

- There is a problem with the data in the HEX file that you have asked DDT to load. The problem could be a bad check-sum on a given line or an invalid field somewhere in the record. Try typing the HEX file out on a console, or use an editor to examine it. It is rare to have only one or two bad bits or bytes in a HEX file; large amounts of the file are more likely to have been corrupted. Therefore, you may be able to spot the trouble fairly readily. If you have the source code for the program, reassemble it to produce another copy of the HEX file. If you do not have the source code, there is no reliable way around this problem unless you are prepared to hand-create the HEX file—a difficult and tedious task.

- DDT does not recognize the instruction you have entered when using the "A" (assemble) command to convert a source code instruction into hexadecimal. Check the line that you entered. DDT does not like tabs in the line (although it appears to accept them) or hexadecimal numbers followed by "H". Check that the mnemonic and operands are valid, too.

??= (DDT)

This cryptic notation is used by DDT when you are using the "L" (list disassembled) command to display some part of memory in DDT's primitive assembly language form. DDT cannot translate all of the 256 possible values of a byte. Some of them are not used in the 8080 instruction set. When DDT encounters an untranslatable value, it displays this message as the instruction code, followed by the actual value of the byte in hexadecimal.

You will see this if you try to disassemble code written for the Z80 CPU, which uses unassigned 8080 instructions. You will also see it if you try to disassemble bytes that contain ASCII text strings rather than 8080 instructions.

ABORTED (STAT)

If you enter any keyboard character while STAT is working its way down the file directory setting files to $DIR (Directory), $SYS (System), $R/W (Read/Write), or $R/O (Read-Only) status, then it will display this message, stop what it is doing, and execute a warm boot.

By contrast, if you enter the command

```
A>stat *.*<cr>
```

to display all of the files on a disk, there is no way that the process can be aborted.

ABORTED (PIP)

This message is displayed if you press any keyboard character while PIP is copying a file to the list device.

BAD DELIMITER (STAT)

If your BIOS uses the normal IOBYTE method of assigning physical devices to logical devices, you use STAT to perform the assignment. The command has this format:

```
STAT RDR:=PTR:
```

STAT displays this message if it cannot find the "=" in the correct place.

BAD LOAD (CCP)

This is probably the most obscure error message that emanates from CP/M. You will get this message if you attempt to load a COM file that is larger than the transient program area. Your only recourse is to build a CP/M system that has a larger TPA.

BAD PARAMETER (PIP)

PIP accepts certain parameters in square brackets at the end of the command line. This message is displayed if you enter an invalid parameter or an illegal numeric value following a parameter letter.

BDOS ERROR ON d: BAD SECTOR (BDOS)

The BDOS displays this message if the READ and WRITE functions in your BIOS ever return indicating an error. The only safe response to this message is to type CONTROL-C. CP/M will then execute a warm boot. If you type CARRIAGE RETURN, the error will be ignored—with unpredictable results.

A well-implemented BIOS should include disk error recovery and control so that the error will never be communicated to the BDOS. If the BIOS gives you the option of ignoring an error, do so only when you are reasonably sure of the outcome or have adequate backup copies so that you can recreate your files.

BDOS ERROR ON d: FILE R/O (BDOS)

You will see this message if you attempt to erase (ERA) a file that has been set to Read-Only status. Typing any character on the keyboard causes the BDOS to perform a warm boot operation. Note that the BDOS does not tell you *which* file is creating the problem. This can be a problem when you use ambiguous file names in the ERA command. Use the STAT command to display all the files on the disk; it will tell you which files are Read-Only.

This message is also displayed if a program tries to delete a Read-Only file. Again, it can be difficult to determine which file is causing the problem. Your only recourse is to use STAT to try to infer which of the Read-Only files might be causing the problems.

BDOS ERROR ON d: R/O (BDOS)

This looks similar to the previous message, but it refers to an entire logical disk instead of a Read-Only file. However, it is rarely output because you have declared a disk to be Read-Only. Usually, it occurs because you changed diskettes without typing a CONTROL-C; CP/M will detect the new diskette and, without any external indication, will set the disk to Read-Only status.

If you or a program attempts to write any data to the disk, the attempt will be trapped by the BDOS and this message displayed. Typing any character on the keyboard causes a warm boot—then you can proceed.

BDOS ERROR ON d: SELECT (BDOS)

The BDOS displays this message if you or a program attempts to select a logical disk for which the BIOS lacks the necessary tables. The BDOS uses the value returned by SELDSK to determine whether a logical disk "exists" or not.

If you were trying to change the default disk to a nonexistent one, you will have to press the RESET button on your computer. There is no way out of this error.

However, if you were trying to execute a command that accessed the nonexistent disk, then you can type a CONTROL-C and CP/M will perform a warm boot.

BREAK x AT y (ED)

This is another cryptic message whose meaning you cannot guess. The list that follows explains the possible values of "x." The value "y" refers to the command ED was executing when the error occurred.

x	Meaning
#	Search failure. ED did not find the string you asked it to search for.
?	Unrecognized command.
0	File not found.
>	ED's internal buffer is full.
E	Command aborted.
F	Disk or directory full. You will have to determine which is causing the problem.

CANNOT CLOSE, READ/ONLY? (SUBMIT)

SUBMIT displays this message if the disk on which it is trying to write its output file, "$$$.SUB", is physically write protected. Do not confuse this with the disk being *logically* write protected.

The standard version of SUBMIT writes the output file onto the current default disk, so if your current default disk is other than drive A:, you may be able to avoid this problem if you switch the default to A: and then enter a command of the form

```
A>submit b:subfile<cr>
```

CANNOT CLOSE DESTINATION FILE (PIP)

PIP displays this message if the destination disk is physically write protected. Check the destination disk. If it is write protected, remove the protection and repeat the operation.

If the disk is not protected, you have a hardware problem. The directory data written to the disk is being written to the wrong place, even the wrong disk, or is not being recorded on the medium.

CANNOT CLOSE FILES (ASM)

ASM displays this message if it cannot close its output files because the disk is physically write protected, or if there is a hardware problem that prevents data being written to the disk. See the paragraph above.

CANNOT READ (PIP)

PIP displays this message if you attempt to read information from a logical device that can only output. For example:

```
A>pip diskfile=LST:<cr>
```

PIP also will display this message if you confuse it sufficiently, as with the following instruction:

```
A>pip file1=file2;file3<cr>
```

CANNOT WRITE (PIP)

PIP displays this message if you attempt to output (write) information to a logical device that can only be used for input, such as the RDR: (reader, the anachronistic name for the auxiliary input device).

CHECKSUM ERROR (LOAD)

LOAD displays this message if it encounters a line in the input HEX file that does not have the correct check sum for the data on the line.

LOAD also displays information helpful in pinpointing the problem:

```
CHECKSUM ERROR
LOAD ADDRESS    0110   <- First address on line in file
ERROR ADDRESS 0112   <- Address of next byte to be loaded
BYTES READ:
0110:
0110: 00 33 22 2B 02 21 27 02      <- Bytes preceding error
```

Note that LOAD does not display the check-sum value itself. Use TYPE or an editor to inspect the HEX file in order to see exactly what has gone wrong.

CHECKSUM ERROR (PIP)

If you ask PIP to copy a file of type HEX, it will check each line in the file, making sure that the line's check sum is valid. If it is not, PIP will display this message. Unfortunately, PIP does not tell you which line is in error—you must determine this by inspection or recreate the HEX file and try again.

COMMAND BUFFER OVERFLOW (SUBMIT)

SUBMIT displays this message if the SUB file you specified is too large to be processed. SUBMIT's internal buffer is only 2048 bytes. You must reduce the size of the SUB file; remove any comment lines, or split it into two files with the last line of the first file submitting the second to give a nested SUBMIT file.

COMMAND TOO LONG (SUBMIT)

The longest command line that SUBMIT can process is 125 characters. There is no way around this error other than reducing the length of the offending line. You will have to find this line by inspection—SUBMIT does not identify the line.

One way that you can remove a few characters from a command line is to rename the COM file you are invoking to a shorter name, or use abbreviated names for parameters if the program will accept these.

CORRECT ERROR, TYPE RETURN OR CTL-Z (PIP)

This message is a carryover from the days when PIP used to read hexadecimal data from a high-speed paper tape reader. If PIP detected the end of a physical roll of paper tape, it would display this message. The user could then check to see if the paper tape had torn or had really reached its end. If there was more tape to be read, the user could enter a CARRIAGE RETURN to resume reading tape or enter a CONTROL-Z to serve as the end-of-file character.

Needless to say, it is unlikely that you will see this message if you do not have a paper tape reader.

DESTINATION IS R/O, DELETE (Y/N)? (PIP)

PIP displays this message if you try to overwrite a disk file that has been set to Read-Only status. If you type "Y" or "y", PIP will overwrite the destination file. It leaves the destination file in Read/Write status with its Directory/System status unchanged. Typing any character other than "Y" or "y" makes PIP abandon the copy and display the message

```
** NOT DELETED**
```

You can avoid this message altogether if you specify the "w" option on PIP's command line. For example:

```
A>pip destfile=srcfile[w]<cr>
```

PIP will then overwrite Read-Only files without question.

DIRECTORY FULL (SUBMIT)

This message is displayed if the BDOS returns an error when SUBMIT tries to create its output file, "$$$.SUB". As a rough and ready approximation, use "STAT *.*" to see how many files and extents you have on the disk. Erase any unwanted ones. Then use "STAT DSK:" to find out the maximum number of directory entries possible for the disk.

You may also see this message if the file directory has become corrupted or if the disk formatting routine leaves the disk with the file directory full of some pattern other than E5H.

You can assess whether the directory has been corrupted by using "STAT USR:". STAT then displays which user numbers contain files. If the directory is corrupt, you will normally see user numbers greater than 15.

It is not easy to repair a corrupted directory. "ERA *.*" erases only the files for the current user number, so you will have to enter the command 16 times, once for each user number from 0 to 15. Alternatively, you can reformat the disk.

DISK OR DIRECTORY FULL (ED)

Self-explanatory.

DISK READ ERROR (PIP)
DISK WRITE ERROR (SUBMIT)
DISK WRITE ERROR (PIP)

These messages will normally be preceded by a BIOS error message. They will only be displayed if the BIOS returns indicating an error. As was described earlier, this is unlikely if the BIOS has any kind of error recovery logic.

END OF FILE, CTL-Z? (PIP)

PIP displays this message if, while copying a HEX file, it encounters a CONTROL-Z (end of file). Again, the underlying idea is based on the concept of physical paper tape. When you saw this message, you could look at the tape in the reader, and if it really was at the end of the roll, enter a CONTROL-Z on the keyboard to terminate the file. Given any other character, PIP would read the next piece of tape.

ERROR : CANNOT CLOSE FILES (LOAD)

LOAD displays this message if you have physically write protected the disk on which it is trying to write the output COM file.

ERROR : CANNOT OPEN SOURCE (LOAD)

LOAD displays this message if it cannot open the HEX file that you specified in the command tail.

ERROR : DISK READ (LOAD)
ERROR : DISK WRITE (LOAD)

These two messages would normally be preceded by a BIOS error message. If your BIOS includes disk error recovery, you would not normally see these messages; the error would have been handled by the BIOS.

ERROR : INVERTED LOAD ADDRESS (LOAD)

LOAD displays this message if it detects a load address less than 0100H in the input HEX file. It also displays the actual address input from the file, so you can examine the HEX file looking for this address to determine the likely cause of the problem.

Note that DDT, when asked to load the same HEX file, will do so without any error—and will probably damage the contents of the base page in so doing.

ERROR : NO MORE DIRECTORY SPACE (LOAD)

Self-explanatory.

ERROR ON LINE N (SUBMIT)

SUBMIT displays this message if it encounters a line in the SUB file that it does not know how to process. Most likely you have a file that has type .SUB but does not contain ASCII text.

The first line of the SUB file is number 001.

FILE EXISTS (CCP)

The CCP displays this message if you attempt to use the REN command to rename an existing file to a name already given to another file.

Use "STAT *.*" to display all of the files on the disk. DIR will show only those files that have Directory status, and you may not be able to see the file causing the problem.

FILE IS READ/ONLY (ED)

ED displays this message if you attempt to edit a file that has been set to Read-Only status.

FILE NOT FOUND (STAT)
FILENAME NOT FOUND (PIP)

STAT and PIP display their respective messages if you specify a nonexistent file. This applies to both specific and ambiguous file names.

INVALID ASSIGNMENT (STAT)

STAT can be used to assign physical devices to logical devices using the IOBYTE system described earlier. It will display this message if you enter an illogical assignment. Use the "STAT VAL:" command to display the valid assignments.

INVALID CONTROL CHARACTER (SUBMIT)

SUBMIT is supposed to be able to handle a control character in the SUB file—the notation being "^x", where "x" is the control letter. In fact, the standard release version of SUBMIT cannot handle this notation. A patch is available from Digital Research to correct this problem.

Given that this patch has been installed, SUBMIT will display this message if a character other than "A" to "Z" is specified after the circumflex character.

INVALID DIGIT (PIP)

PIP displays this message if it encounters non-numeric data where it expects a numeric value.

INVALID DISK ASSIGNMENT (STAT)

STAT displays this message if you try to set a logical disk to Read-Only status and you specify a parameter other than "R/O." Note that there is no leading "$" in this case (as there is when you want to set a file to Read-Only).

INVALID DRIVE NAME (USE A, B, C, OR D) (SYSGEN)

SYSGEN displays this message if you attempt to load the CP/M system from, or write the system to, a disk drive other than A, B, C, or D.

INVALID FILE INDICATOR (STAT)

STAT outputs this message if you specify an erroneous file attribute. File attributes can only be one of the following:

$DIR	Directory
$SYS	System
$R/O	Read-Only
$R/W	Read/Write

INVALID FORMAT (PIP)

PIP displays this message if you enter a badly formatted command; for example, a "+" character instead of an "=" (on some terminals these are on the same key).

INVALID HEX DIGIT (LOAD)

LOAD displays this message if it encounters a nonhexadecimal digit in the input HEX file, where only a hex digit can appear. LOAD then displays additional information to tell you where in the file the problem occurred:

```
INVALID HEX DIGIT
LOAD ADDRESS   0110   <- First address on line in file
ERROR ADDRESS  0112   <- Address of byte containing non-hex
BYTES READ:
0110:
0110:  00 33        <- Bytes preceding error
```

INVALID MEMORY SIZE (MOVCPM)

MOVCPM displays this message if you enter an invalid memory size for the CP/M system size you want to construct.

INVALID SEPARATOR (PIP)

PIP displays this message if you try to concatenate files using something other than a comma between file names.

INVALID USER NUMBER (PIP)

PIP displays this message if you enter a user number outside the range 0 to 15 with the "[gn]" option (where "n" is the user number).

NO 'SUB' FILE PRESENT (SUBMIT)

SUBMIT displays this message if it cannot find a file with the file name that you specified and with a type of .SUB.

NO DIRECTORY SPACE (ASM)
NO DIRECTORY SPACE (PIP)

Self-explanatory.

NO FILE (CCP)

The CCP displays this message if you use the REN (rename) command and it cannot find the file you wish to rename.

NO FILE (PIP)

PIP displays this message if it cannot find the file that you specified.

NO MEMORY (ED)

ED displays this message if it runs out of memory to use for storing the text that you are editing.

NO SOURCE FILE ON DISK (SYSGEN)

This error message is misleading. SYSGEN does not read source code files. The message should read "INPUT FILE NOT FOUND".

NO SOURCE FILE PRESENT (ASM)

In this case, ASM really does mean that the source code file cannot be found. Remember that ASM uses a strange form of specifying its parameters. ASM uses the file name that you enter and then searches for a file of that name, but with file type .ASM. The three characters of the file type that you specify are used to represent the logical disks on which the source, hex, and list files, respectively, are to be placed.

NO SPACE (CCP)

The CCP displays this message if you use the SAVE command and there is insufficient room on the disk to accommodate the file.

NOT A CHARACTER SOURCE (PIP)

PIP displays this message if you attempt to copy characters from a character output device, such as the auxiliary output device (known to PIP as PUN:).

OUTPUT FILE WRITE ERROR (ASM)

ASM will display this message if the BDOS returns an error from a disk write operation. If your BIOS has disk error recovery logic, you should never see this message.

PARAMETER ERROR (SUBMIT)

SUBMIT uses the "$" to mark points where parameter values are to be substituted. If you have a single "$" followed by an alphabetic character, SUBMIT will display this message. Use "$$" to represent a real "$".

PERMANENT ERROR, TYPE RETURN TO IGNORE (SYSGEN)

SYSGEN displays this message if the BIOS returns an error from a disk read or write operation. If your BIOS has disk error recovery logic, you should never see this message.

QUIT NOT FOUND (PIP)

PIP displays this message when it cannot find the string specified in the "[Qcharacter string^Z]" option, meaning "Quit copying when you encounter this string."

READ ERROR (CCP)

The CCP displays this message if the BIOS returns an error from a disk read or write operation. If your BIOS includes disk error recovery logic, you should not see this error message.

RECORD TOO LONG (PIP)

PIP displays this message if it encounters a line longer than 80 characters while copying a HEX file. Inspect the HEX file using the TYPE command or an editor.

REQUIRES CP/M 2.0 OR NEWER FOR OPERATION (PIP)
REQUIRES CP/M VERSION 2.0 OR LATER (XSUB)

Self-explanatory.

SOURCE FILE INCOMPLETE (SYSGEN)

SYSGEN displays this message if the file that you have asked it to read is too short. Use STAT to check the length of the file.

SOURCE FILE NAME ERROR (ASM)

ASM displays this message if you specify an ambiguous file name: that is, one that contains either "*" or "?".

SOURCE FILE READ ERROR (ASM)

ASM displays this message if it encounters problems reading the input source code file. Check the input file using the TYPE command or an editor.

START NOT FOUND (PIP)

PIP displays this message when it cannot find the string specified in the "[Scharacter string^Z]" option, meaning "Start copying when you encounter this string."

SYMBOL TABLE OVERFLOW (ASM)

ASM displays this message when you have too many symbols in the source code file. Your only recourse is to split the source file into several pieces and arrange for ORG (origin) statements to position the generated object code so that the pieces fit together.

SYNCRONIZATION ERROR (MOVCPM)

Apart from the spelling error, this message is designed to be cryptic. MOVCPM displays it when the Digital Research serial number embedded in MOVCPM does not match the serial number in the version of CP/M that you are currently running.

SYSTEM FILE NOT ACCESSIBLE (ED)

ED displays this message if you attempt to edit a file that has been set to System status. Use STAT to set the file to Directory status.

TOO MANY FILES (STAT)

STAT displays this message if there is insufficient memory available to sort and display all of the files on the specified disk. Try limiting the number of files it has to sort by judicious use of ambiguous file names.

UNRECOGNIZED DESTINATION (PIP)

PIP displays this message if you specify an "illegal" destination device.

VERIFY ERROR (PIP)

If you use the "[v]" (verify) option of PIP when copying to a disk file, PIP will write a sector to the disk, read it back, and compare the data. PIP displays this message if the data does not match.

If there is a problem with your disk system, you should have seen some form of disk error message preceding this one. If there is no preceding message, then you have a problem with the main memory on your system.

Wrong CP/M Version (Requires 2.0) (STAT)

Self-explanatory.

(XSUB ACTIVE) (XSUB)

This is not really an error message, but you may mistake it for one. XSUB is the eXtended SUBMIT program. Without it, SUBMIT can only feed command lines to the Console Command Processor. XSUB allows character-by-character input into any program that uses the BDOS to read console input.

XSUB is initiated by being the first command in a SUB file. Once initiated it stays in memory until the end of the SUB file has been reached. Until that happens, XSUB will output this message every time a warm boot occurs as a reminder that it is still in memory.

XSUB Already Present (XSUB)

XSUB will display this message if it is already active and you attempt to load it again.

Miscellaneous Errors

This section deals with errors that are not accompanied by any error message. It is included here to help you recognize a problem after it has already occurred.

The errors are shown grouped by product.

ASM: Fails to Detect Unterminated IF Clause

If you use the IF pseudo-operation, it must be followed by a matching ENDIF. ASM fails to detect the case that the end of the source file is encountered *before* the ENDIF.

If the condition specified on the IF line is false, you could have a situation in which ASM would ignore the majority of the source file without comment.

ASM: Creates HEX File That Cannot Be Loaded

If you omit the ORG statement at the front of a source file, ASM will assemble the code origined at location 0000H. This file will crash the system if you try to load it with DDT. The message "ERROR: INVERTED ADDRESS" will be shown from LOAD.

CP/M: Signs On and Then Dies Without A> Prompt

After the BIOS has signed on, it transfers control to the Console Command Processor. The CCP then attempts to log in the system disk, reading the file directory and building the allocation vector. If your file directory has been badly corrupted, it can cause the system to crash. Use another system disk and try to display the directory on the bad disk.

DDT: Loads HEX File and Then Crashes the System

DDT does not check the addresses specified in a HEX file. If you have forgotten to put an ORG statement at the front of the source file, or more subtly, if your source program has "wrapped around" by having addresses up at 0FFFFH and "above," the assembler will start assembling at 0000H again.

DIR: Shows Odd-Looking File Names

If you have odd-looking file names, or the vertical lines of ":" that DIR uses to separate the file names are misaligned, then the file directory has been corrupted. One strategy is to format a new disk, copy all of the valid files to it, and discard the corrupted disk.

DIR: Shows More than One Entry with the Same Name

This can happen if you use a program that creates a new file without asking the BDOS to delete any existing files of the same name. It can also happen if you use the custom MOVE utility carelessly.

To remedy the situation proceed as follows:

- Use PIP to copy the specific file to another disk. Do not use an ambiguous file name; specify the duplicated file name exactly. PIP will copy the first instance of the file it encounters in the directory.
- Use the ERA command to erase the duplicated file. *This will erase both copies of the file.*
- Use PIP to copy back the first instance of the file.

STAT: User Numbers > 15

If you use the "STAT USR:" command to display which user numbers contain active files, and user numbers greater than 15 are displayed, then the file directory on the disk has been corrupted.

Use PIP to copy the valid files from legitimate user numbers, and then discard the corrupted disk.

SUBMIT: Fails to Start Submit Procedure

There are several reasons why SUBMIT will not initiate a SUB file:

- You are using the standard release version of SUBMIT and your current default disk is other than drive A:. SUBMIT builds its "$$$.SUB" file on the default disk, but the CCP only looks on drive A: for "$$$.SUB". Use the following procedure to modify SUBMIT to build its "$$$.SUB" file on drive A:

```
A>DDT SUBMIT.COM<cr>
DDT VERS 2.2
NEXT  PC
0600  0100
-s5bb                   <- Change 5bb
05BB 01 00<cr>          <- from 00 (default drive)
05BC 24 .<cr>                to 01 (drive A:)
-^C
A>SAVE 5 SUBMIT.COM<cr>
A>_
```

- If you forgot to terminate the last line of the SUB file with a CARRIAGE RETURN.

- If your SUB file contains a line with nothing but a CARRIAGE RETURN on it (that is, a blank line).

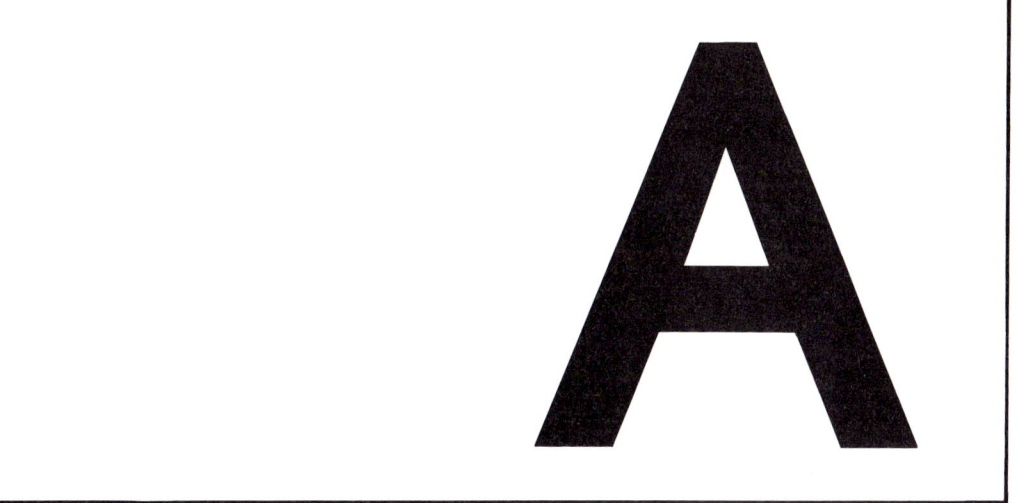

ASCII Character Set

The American Standard Code for Information Interchange (ASCII) consists of a set of 96 displayable characters and 32 nondisplayed characters. Most CP/M systems use at least a subset of the ASCII character set. When CP/M stores characters on a diskette as text, the ASCII definitions are used.

Several of the CP/M utility programs use the ASCII Character Code. Text created using ED is stored as ASCII characters on diskette. DDT, when displaying a "dump" of the contents of memory, displays both the hexadecimal and ASCII representations of memory's contents.

ASCII does not use an entire byte of information to represent a character. ASCII is a seven-bit code, and the eighth bit is often used for *parity.* Parity is an error-checking method which assures that the character received is the one transmitted. Many microcomputers and microcomputer devices ignore the *parity bit,* while others require one of the following two forms of parity:

Even Parity
    The number of binary 1's in a byte is always an even number. If there is an odd number of 1's in the character, the parity bit will be a 1; if there is an even number of 1's in the character, the parity bit is made a 0.

Odd Parity
    The number of binary 1's in a byte is always an odd number. If there is an

even number of 1's in the character, the parity bit will be a 1; if there is an odd number of 1's in the character, the parity bit is made a 0.

Alternative ways of *coding* the information stored by the computer include the 8-bit EBCDIC (Extended Binary Coded Decimal Interchange Code), used by IBM, and a number of *packed binary* schemes, primarily used to represent numerical information.

Table A-1. ASCII Character Codes

b4	b3	b2	b1	Row \ Col.	0	1	2	3	4	5	6	7
				b7 →	0	0	0	0	1	1	1	1
				b6 →	0	0	1	1	0	0	1	1
				b5 →	0	1	0	1	0	1	0	1
0	0	0	0	0	NUL	DLE	SP	0	@	P	`	p
0	0	0	1	1	SOH	DC1	!	1	A	Q	a	q
0	0	1	0	2	STX	DC2	"	2	B	R	b	r
0	0	1	1	3	ETX	DC3	#	3	C	S	c	s
0	1	0	0	4	EOT	DC4	$	4	D	T	d	t
0	1	0	1	5	ENQ	NAK	%	5	E	U	e	u
0	1	1	0	6	ACK	SYN	&	6	F	V	f	v
0	1	1	1	7	BEL	ETB	'	7	G	W	g	w
1	0	0	0	8	BS	CAN	(	8	H	X	h	x
1	0	0	1	9	HT	EM	)	9	I	Y	i	y
1	0	1	0	10	LF	SUB	*	:	J	Z	j	z
1	0	1	1	11	VT	ESC	+	;	K	[	k	{
1	1	0	0	12	FF	FS	,	<	L	\	l	|
1	1	0	1	13	CR	GS	-	=	M	]	m	}
1	1	1	0	14	SO	RS	.	>	N	^	n	~
1	1	1	1	15	SI	US	/	?	O	_	o	DEL

NUL	Null	DC1	Device control 1
SOH	Start of heading	DC2	Device control 2
STX	Start of text	DC3	Device control 3
ETX	End of text	DC4	Device control 4
EOT	End of transmission	NAK	Negative acknowledge
ENQ	Enquiry	SYN	Synchronous idle
ACK	Acknowledge	ETB	End of transmission block
BEL	Bell or alarm	CAN	Cancel
BS	Backspace	EM	End of medium
HT	Horizontal tabulation	SUB	Substitute
LF	Line feed	ESC	Escape
VT	Vertical tabulation	FS	File separator
FF	Form feed	GS	Group separator
CR	Carriage return	RS	Record separator
SO	Shift out	US	Unit separator
SI	Shift in	SP	Space
DLE	Data link escape	DEL	Delete

Appendix A: ASCII Character Set

Table A-2. ASCII Character Codes in Ascending Order

Hexadecimal	Binary	ASCII	Hexadecimal	Binary	ASCII
00	000 0000	NUL	30	011 0000	0
01	000 0001	SOH	31	011 0001	1
02	000 0010	STX	32	011 0010	2
03	000 0011	ETX	33	011 0011	3
04	000 0100	EOT	34	011 0100	4
05	000 0101	ENQ	35	011 0101	5
06	000 0110	ACK	36	011 0110	6
07	000 0111	BEL	37	011 0111	7
08	000 1000	BS	38	011 1000	8
09	000 1001	HT	39	011 1001	9
0A	000 1010	LF	3A	011 1010	:
0B	000 1011	VT	3B	011 1011	;
0C	000 1100	FF	3C	011 1100	<
0D	000 1101	CR	3D	011 1101	=
0E	000 1110	SO	3E	011 1110	>
0F	000 1111	SI	3F	011 1111	?
10	001 0000	DLE	40	100 0000	
11	001 0001	DC1	41	100 0001	A
12	001 0010	DC2	42	100 0010	B
13	001 0011	DC3	43	100 0011	C
14	001 0100	DC4	44	100 0100	D
15	001 0101	NAK	45	100 0101	E
16	001 0110	SYN	46	100 0110	F
17	001 0111	ETB	47	100 0111	G
18	001 1000	CAN	48	100 1000	H
19	001 1001	EM	49	100 1001	I
1A	001 1010	SUB	4A	100 1010	J
1B	001 1011	ESC	4B	100 1011	K
1C	001 1100	FS	4C	100 1100	L
1D	001 1101	GS	4D	100 1101	M
1E	001 1110	RS	4E	100 1110	N
1F	001 1111	US	4F	100 1111	O
20	010 0000	SP	50	101 0000	P
21	010 0001	!	51	101 0001	Q
22	010 0010	"	52	101 0010	R
23	010 0011	#	53	101 0011	S
24	010 0100	$	54	101 0100	T
25	010 0101	%	55	101 0101	U
26	010 0110	&	56	101 0110	V
27	010 0111	'	57	101 0111	W
28	010 1000	(	58	101 1000	X
29	010 1001	)	59	101 1001	Y
2A	010 1010	*	5A	101 1010	Z
2B	010 1011	+	5B	101 1011	[
2C	010 1100	,	5C	101 1100	\
2D	010 1101	-	5D	101 1101	]
2E	010 1110	.	5E	101 1110	^
2F	010 1111	/	5F	101 1111	_

Table A-2. ASCII Character Codes in Ascending Order (Continued)

Hexadecimal	Binary	ASCII	Hexadecimal	Binary	ASCII
60	110 0000		70	111 0000	p
61	110 0001	a	71	111 0001	q
62	110 0010	b	72	111 0010	r
63	110 0011	c	73	111 0011	s
64	110 0100	d	74	111 0100	t
65	110 0101	e	75	111 0101	u
66	110 0110	f	76	111 0110	v
67	110 0111	g	77	111 0111	w
68	110 1000	h	78	111 1000	x
69	110 1001	i	79	111 1001	y
6A	110 1010	j	7A	111 1010	z
6B	110 1011	k	7B	111 1011	{
6C	110 1100	l	7C	111 1100	|
6D	110 1101	m	7D	111 1101	}
6E	110 1110	n	7E	111 1110	~
6F	110 1111	o	7F	111 1111	DEL

B

CP/M Command Summary

This appendix summarizes the command line format and the function of each CP/M built-in and transient command. The commands are listed in alphabetical order.

ASM Command Lines

ASM filename\<cr\>   Assembles the file filename.ASM; uses the currently logged disk for all files.

ASM filename.opt\<cr\>   Assembles the file filename.ASM on drive o: (A:,B:,...,P:). Writes HEX file on drive p: (A:,B:,...,P:), or skips if p: is Z:.
   Writes PRN file on drive t: (A:,B:,...,P:), sends to console if p: is X:, or skips if p: is Z:.

DDT Command Lines

DDT<cr>   Loads DDT and waits for DDT commands.

DDT x:filename.typ<cr>   Loads DDT into memory and also loads filename.typ from drive x: into memory for examination, modification, or execution.

DDT Command Summary

Assss   Enters assembly language statements beginning at hexadecimal address ssss.

D   Displays the contents of the next 192 bytes of memory.

Dssss,ffff   Displays the contents of memory starting at hexadecimal address ssss and finishing at hexadecimal address ffff.

Fssss,ffff,cc   Fills memory with the 8-bit hexadecimal constant cc starting at hexadecimal address ssss and finishing with hexadecimal address ffff.

G   Begins execution at the address contained in the program counter.

G,bbbb   Sets a breakpoint at hexadecimal address bbbb, then begins execution at the address contained in the program counter.

G,bbbb,cccc   Sets breakpoints at hexadecimal addresses bbbb and cccc, then begins execution at the address contained in the program counter.

Gssss   Begins execution at hexadecimal address ssss.

Gssss,bbbb   Sets a breakpoint at hexadecimal address bbbb, then begins execution at hexadecimal address ssss.

Hx,y   Hexadecimal sum and difference of x and y.

Ifilename.typ   Sets up the default file control block using the name filename.typ.

L   Lists the next eleven lines of assembly language program disassembled from memory.

Lssss   Lists eleven lines of assembly language program disassembled from memory starting at hexadecimal address ssss.

Lssss,ffff   Lists the assembly language program disassembled from memory starting at hexadecimal address ssss and finishing at hexadecimal address ffff.

Appendix B: CP/M Command Summary

Mssss,ffff,dddd Moves the contents of the memory block starting at hexadecimal address ssss and ending at hexadecimal address ffff to the block of memory starting at hexadecimal address dddd.

R Reads a file from disk into memory (use "I" command first).

Rnnnn Reads a file from disk into memory beginning at the hexadecimal address nnnn higher than normal (use "I" command first).

Sssss Displays the contents of memory at hexadecimal address ssss and optionally changes the contents.

Tnnnn Traces the execution of (hexadecimal) nnnn program instructions.

Unnnn Executes (hexadecimal) nnnn program instructions, then stops and displays the CPU register's contents.

X Displays the CPU register's contents.

Xr Displays the contents of CPU or Flag r and optionally changes them.

DIR Command Lines

DIR x:\<cr\> Displays directory of all files on drive x:. Drive x: is optional; if omitted, the currently logged drive is used.

DIR x:filename.typ\<cr\> Displays directory of all files on drive x: whose names match the ambiguous or unambiguous filename.typ. Drive x: is optional; if omitted, the currently logged drive is used.

DUMP Command Line

DUMP x:filename.typ \<cr\> Displays the hexadecimal representations of each byte stored in the file filename.typ on drive x:. If filename.typ is ambiguous, displays the first file which matches the ambiguous file name.

ED Command Line

ED x:filename.typ \<cr\> Invokes the editor, which then searches for filename.typ on drive x: and creates a temporary file x:filename.$$$ to store the edited text. The filename.typ is unambiguous. Drive x: is optional; if omitted, the currently logged drive is assumed.

ED Command Summary

NOTE: Non-alphabetic commands follow the "Z" command.

nA	Append lines. Moves "n" lines from original file to edit buffer. 0A moves lines until edit buffer is at least half full.
+/−B	Begin/Bottom. Moves CP. +B moves CP to beginning of edit buffer −B moves CP to end of edit buffer.
+/−nC	Move by characters. Moves CP by "n" character positions. + moves forward − moves backward.
+/−nD	Delete characters. Deletes "n" characters before or after the CP in the edit buffer. + deletes before the CP − deletes after the CP.
E	End. Ends edit, closes files, and returns to CP/M; normal end.
nFstring^Z	Find string. Finds the "n"th occurrence of string, beginning the search after the CP.
H	Move to head of edited file. Ends edit, renames files, and then edits former temporary file.
I\<cr\>	Enter insert mode. Text from keyboard goes into edit buffer after the CP; exit with CONTROL-Z.
Istring^Z	Insert string. Inserts string in edit buffer after the CP.
Istring\<cr\>	Insert line. Inserts string and CRLF in the edit buffer after the CP.
nJfindstring^Zinsertstring^Zendstring^Z	Juxtaposition. Beginning after the CP, finds findstring, inserts insertstring after it, then deletes all following characters up to but not including endstring; repeats until performed "n" times.
+/−nK	Kill lines. Deletes "n" lines. + deletes after the CP − deletes before the CP.
+/−nL	Move by lines. Moves the CP to the beginning of the line it is in, then moves the CP "n" lines forward or backward. + moves forward − moves backward.
nMcommandstring^Z	Macro command. Repeats execution of the ED commands in

commandstring "n" times. "n"= 0, "n"= 1, or "n" absent repeats execution until error occurs.

nNstring^Z Find string with autoscan. Finds the "n"th occurrence of string, automatically appending from original file and writing to temporary file as necessary.

O Return to original file. Empties edit buffer, empties temporary file, returns to beginning of original file, ignores previous ED commands.

+/−nP Move CP and print pages. Moves the CP forward or backward one page, then displays the page following the CP. "nP" displays "n" pages, pausing after each.

Q Quit edit. Erases temporary file and block move file, if any, and returns to CP/M; original file is not changed.

R<cr> Read block move file. Copies the entire block move file X$$$$$$$.LIB from disk and inserts it in the edit buffer after the CP.

Rfilename<cr> Read library file. Copies the entire file filename with extension LIB from the disk and inserts it in the edit buffer after the CP.

nSfindstring^Zreplacestring^Z Substitute string. Starting at the CP, repeats "n" times: finds findstring and replaces it with replacestring.

+/−nT Type lines. Displays "n" lines.
　　+ displays the "n" lines after the CP
　　− displays the "n" lines before the CP.

　　If the CP is not at the beginning of a line
　　　0T displays from the beginning of the line to the CP
　　　T displays from the CP to the end of the line
　　　0TT displays the entire line without moving the CP.

+/−U Uppercase translation. After +U command, alphabetic input to the edit buffer is translated from lowercase to uppercase; after −U, no translation occurs.

0V Edit buffer free space/size. Displays the decimal number of free (empty) bytes in the edit buffer and the total size of the edit buffer.

+/−V Verify line numbers. After +V, a line number is displayed with each line displayed; ED's prompt is then preceded by the number of the line containing the CP. After −V, line numbers are not displayed, and ED's prompt is "*".

nW — Write lines. Writes first "n" lines from the edit buffer to the temporary file; deletes these lines from the edit buffer.

nX — Block transfer (Xfer). Copies the "n" lines following the CP from the edit buffer to the temporary block move file X$$$$$$$.LIB; adds to previous contents of that file.

nZ — Sleep. Delays execution of the command which follows it. Larger "n" gives longer delay, smaller "n" gives shorter delay.

n: — Move CP to line number "n." Moves the CP to the beginning of the line number "n" (*see* "+/−V").

:m — Continue through line number "m." A command prefix which gives the ending point for the command which follows it. The beginning point is the location of the CP (*see* "+/−V").

+/−n — Move and display one line. Abbreviated form of +/−nLT.

ERA Command Lines

ERA x:filename.typ\<cr\> — Erases the file filename.typ on the disk in drive x:. The filename and/or typ can be ambiguous. Drive x: is optional; if omitted, the currently logged drive is used.

ERA x:*.*\<cr\> — Erases all files on the disk in drive x:. Drive x: is optional; if omitted, the currently logged drive is used.

Line Editing Commands

CONTROL-C — Restarts CP/M if it is the first character in command line. Called *warm start*.

CONTROL-E — Moves to the beginning of next line. Used for typing long commands.

CONTROL-H or BACKSPACE — Deletes one character and erases it from the screen (CP/M version 2.0 and newer).

CONTROL-J or LINE FEED — Same as CARRIAGE RETURN (CP/M version 2.0 and newer).

CONTROL-M — Same as CARRIAGE RETURN (\<cr\>).

CONTROL-P — Turns on the list device (usually your printer). Type it again to turn off the list device.

Appendix B: CP/M Command Summary **475**

CONTROL-R Repeats current command line (useful with version 1.4); it verifies the line is corrected after you delete several characters (CP/M version 1.4 and newer).

CONTROL-S Temporarily stops display of data on the console. Press any key to continue.

CONTROL-U or CONTROL-X Cancels current command line (CP/M version 1.4 and newer).

RUBOUT (RUB) or DELETE (DEL) Deletes one character and echoes (repeats) it.

Load Command Line

LOAD x:filename<cr> Reads the file filename.HEX on drive x: and creates the executable program file filename.COM on drive x:.

MOVCPM Command Lines

MOVCPM<cr> Prepares a new copy of CP/M which uses all of memory; gives control to the new CP/M, but does not save it on disk.

MOVCPM nn<cr> Prepares a new copy of CP/M which uses "nn" K bytes of memory; gives control to the new CP/M, but does not save it on disk.

MOVCPM * * <cr> Prepares a new copy of CP/M that uses all of memory, to be saved with SYSGEN or SAVE.

MOVCPM nn * <cr> Prepares a new copy of CP/M that uses "nn" K bytes of memory, to be saved with SYSGEN or SAVE.
    The "nn" is an integer decimal number. It can be 16 through 64 for CP/M 1.3 or 1.4. For CP/M 2.0 and newer "nn" can be 20 through 64.

PIP Command Lines

PIP<cr> Loads PIP into memory. PIP prompts for commands, executes them, then prompts again.

PIP pipcommandline<cr> Loads PIP into memory. PIP executes the command pipcommandline, then exits to CP/M.

PIP Command Summary

x:new.typ=y:old.typ[p]<cr> Copies the file old.typ on drive y: to the file new.typ on drive x:, using parameters p.

x:new.typ=y:old1.typ[p],z:old2.typ[q]<cr> Creates a file new.typ on drive x: that consists of the contents of file old1.typ on drive y: using parameters p followed by the contents of file old2.typ on drive z: using parameters q.

x:filename.typ=dev:[p]<cr>   Copies data from device dev: to the file filename.typ on drive x:.

dev:=x:filename.typ[p]<cr>   Copies data from filename.typ on drive x: to device dev:.

dst:=src:[p]<cr>   Copies data to device dst: from device src:.

PIP Parameter Summary

B	Specifies block mode transfer.
Dn	Deletes all characters after the "n"th column.
E	Echoes the copying to the console as it is being performed.
F	Removes form feed characters during transfer.
Gn	Directs PIP to copy a file from user area "n."
H	Checks for proper Intel Hex File format.
I	Ignores any *:00* records in Intel Hex File transfers.
L	Translates uppercase letters to lowercase.
N	Adds a line number to each line transferred.
O	Object file transfer (ignores end-of-file markers).
Pn	Issues page feed after every "n"th line.
Qs^Z	Specifies quit of copying after the string "s" is encountered.
R	Directs PIP to copy from a system file.
Ss^Z	Specifies start of copying after the string "s" is encountered.
Tn	Sets tab stops to every "n"th column.
U	Translates lowercase letters to uppercase.
V	Verifies copy by comparison after copy finished.
W	Directs PIP to copy onto an R/O file.
Z	Zeroes the "parity" bit on ASCII characters.

PIP Destination Devices

CON:	PUN:	LST:	Logical devices
TTY:	PTP:	LPT:	
CRT:	UP1:	UL1:	
UC1:	UP2:		Physical devices
OUT:	PRN:		Special PIP devices

PIP Source Devices

CON:	RDR:		Logical devices
TTY:	PTR:		
CRT:	UR1:		
UC1:	UR2:		Physical devices
NUL:	EOF:	INP:	Special PIP devices

REN Command Line

REN newname.typ=oldname.typ\<cr\>   Finds the file oldname.typ and renames it newname.typ.

SAVE Command Line

SAVE nnn x:filename.typ\<cr\>   Saves a portion of the Transient Program Area of memory in the file filename.typ on drive x: where nnn is a decimal number representing the number of pages of memory. Drive x: is the option drive specifier.

STAT Command Lines

STAT\<cr\>   Displays attributes and amount of free space for all diskette drives accessed since last warm or cold start.

STAT x:\<cr\>   Displays amount of free space on the diskette in drive x:.

STAT x:filename.typ\<cr\> (CP/M 2.0 and newer)   Displays size and attributes of file(s) filename.typ on drive x:. filename.typ may be ambiguous. x: is optional; if omitted, currently logged drive is assumed.

STAT x:filename.typ $atr\<cr\>   Assigns the attribute atr to the file(s) filename.typ on drive x:. File filename.typ may be ambiguous. Drive x: is optional; if omitted, currently logged drive is assumed.

STAT DEV:\<cr\>   Reports which physical devices are currently assigned to the four logical devices.

STAT VAL:\<cr\>   Reports the possible device assignments and partial STAT command line summary.

STAT log:=phy:\<cr\>   Assigns the physical device phy: to the logical device log: (may be more than one assignment on the line; each should be set off by a comma).

STAT USR:\<cr\> (CP/M 2.0 and newer)   Reports the current user number as well as all user numbers for which there are files on currently logged disks.

STAT x:DSK<cr> (CP/M 1.4 and newer) Assigns a temporary write-protect status to drive x:.

SUBMIT Command Lines

SUBMIT filename<cr> Creates a file $$$.SUB which contains the commands listed in filename.SUB; CP/M then executes commands from this file rather than the keyboard.

SUBMIT filename parameters<cr> Creates a file $$$.SUB which contains commands from the file filename.SUB; certain parts of the command lines in filename.SUB are replaced by parameters during creation of $$$.SUB. CP/M then gets commands from this file rather than the keyboard.

SYSGEN Command Line

SYSGEN<cr> Loads the SYSGEN program to transfer CP/M from one diskette to another.

TYPE Command Line

TYPE x:filename.typ<cr> Displays the contents of file filename.typ from drive x: on the console.

USER Command Line

USER n<cr> Sets the User Number to "n," where "n" is an integer decimal number from 0 to 15, inclusive.

x: Command Line

x:<cr> Changes the currently logged disk drive to drive x:. Drive x: can be "A" through "P."

Summary of BDOS Calls

Table C-1. BDOS Function Definitions for CP/M-80 Version 2.2

Function		Entry Parameter(s)	Exit Parameter(s)	Explanation
No.	Name			
00	SYSTEM RESET	None	None	Restarts CP/M-80 by returning control to the the CCP after reinitializing the disk subsystem.
01	CONSOLE INPUT	None	A = ASCII character	Returns the next character typed to the character calling program.
				Any non-printable character is echoed to the screen (like BACKSPACE, TAB, or CARRIAGE RETURN). Execution does not return to the calling program until a character has been typed. Standard CCP control characters are recognized and their actions performed (CONTROL-P begins or ends printer echoing and so on).

Table C-1. (Continued)

Function		Entry Parameter(s)	Exit Parameter(s)	Explanation
No.	Name			
02	CONSOLE OUTPUT	E = ASCII character	None	Displays the character in the E register on the console device. Standard CCP control characters are recognized and their actions performed (CONTROL-P begins or ends printer echoing and so on.).
03	READER INPUT	None	A = ASCII character	Returns the next character received from the reader device to the calling program. Execution does not return to the calling program until a character is received.
04	PUNCH OUTPUT	E = ASCII character	None	Transmits the character in the E register to the punch device.
05	LIST OUTPUT	E = ASCII character	None	Transmits the character in the E register to the list device.
06	DIRECT CONSOLE IN	E = FF hex	A = ASCII	If register E contains an FF hex, the console device is interrogated to see if a character is ready. If no character is ready, a 00 is returned to the calling program in register A; otherwise the character detected is returned in register A. If register E contains any character other than an FF hex, that character is passed to the console display. All CCP control characters are ignored. The user must protect the program against nonsensical characters being sent from or received by the console device.
	DIRECT CONSOLE OUT	E = ASCII character	None	
07	GET IOBYTE	None	A = IOBYTE	Places a copy of the byte stored at location 0003 hex in the A register before returning control to the calling program.
08	SET IOBYTE	E = IOBYTE	None	Places a copy of the value in register E into the memory location of 0003 hex before returning control to the calling program.
09	PRINT STRING	DE = String address	None	Sends the string of characters stored beginning at the address stored in the DE register pair to the console device. All characters in subsequent addresses are sent until BDOS encounters a memory location which contains a 24 hex (an ASCII "$"). The CCP control characters are checked for and performed if encountered.

NOTE: CP/M-80 always copies the contents of the H register in the A register if nothing is to be specifically returned in the A register. Some manufacturers, specifically Microsoft, make use of such information to reduce movement of information between the H and A registers.

Appendix C: Summary of BDOS Calls

Table C-1. (Continued)

Function No.	Function Name	Entry Parameter(s)	Exit Parameter(s)	Explanation
0A	READ CONSOLE BUFFER	DE = Buffer address	Data in buffer	This function performs essentially the same as the CCP would in that it takes the characters the user types and stores them into the buffer that begins at the address stored in the DE register pair. The first byte in the buffer pointed to by the DE pair must be the maximum length of the command; BDOS will place the number of characters encountered in the second byte, with the typed command beginning with the third byte pointed to by the DE pair. All standard CCP editing characters are recognized during the command entry.
0B	GET CONSOLE STATUS	None	A = Status	BDOS checks the status of the console device and returns a 00 hex if no character is ready, FF hex if a character has been typed.
0C	GET VERSION NUMBER	None	HL = Version	If the byte returned in the H register is 00 hex then CP/M is present, if 01, then MP/M is present. The byte returned in the L register is 00 if the version is previous to CP/M 2.0, 20 hex if the version is 2.0, 21 hex if 2.1 and so on.
0D	RESET DISK SYSTEM	None		Used to tell CP/M to reset the disk subsystem. Should be used any time diskettes are changed.
0E	SELECT DISK	E = Disk number	None	Selects the disk to be used for subsequent disk operations. A 00 hex in the E register indicates disk A, a 01 hex indicates disk B, etc.
0F	OPEN FILE	DE = FCB address	A = 'Found'/ not found code	Used to activate a file on the current disk drive and current user area. BDOS scans the first 14 bytes of the designated FCB block and attempts to find a match to the filename in the block. A 3F hex (ASCII "?") can be used in any of the filename positions to indicate a "don't care" character. If a match is found, the relevant information about that file is filled into the rest of the FCB by CP/M-80. A value of 00 hex to 03 in register A upon return indicates the open operation was successful, while an FF hex indicates that the file could not be found. If question marks are used to identify a file, the first matching entry is used.

NOTE: CP/M-80 always copies the contents of the H register in the A register if nothing is to be specifically returned in the A register. Some manufacturers, specifically Microsoft, make use of such information to reduce movement of information between the H and A registers.

Table C-1. (Continued)

Function No.	Function Name	Entry Parameter(s)	Exit Parameter(s)	Explanation
10	CLOSE FILE	DE = FCB address	A = 'Found'/ not found code	Performs the opposite of the open file function. A close file function must be performed upon completion of use of any file which has had information written into it.
11	SEARCH FOR FIRST	DE = FCB address	A = 'Found'/ not found code	Performs the same as the open file function with the difference being that the current disk buffer is filled with the 128-byte record which is the directory entry of the matched file.
12	SEARCH FOR NEXT	None	A = 'Found'/ not found code	Performs the same as search for first function except that the search continues on from the last matched entry.
13	DELETE FILE	DE = FCB address	A = 'Found'/ not found code	Changes a flag on the directory entry for the file pointed to by the FCB so that CP/M-80 no longer recognizes it as a valid file. No information is actually erased when this function is performed, although subsequent writes to diskette may use some of the area previously associated with the "deleted" file.
14	READ SEQUEN- TIAL	DE = FCB address	A = Error code	If a file has been activated for use by an open file or make file function, the read sequential function reads the next 128-byte block into memory at the current DMA address. The value of 00 hex is returned in the A register if the read was successful, while any nonzero value in the A register indicates failure.
15	WRITE SEQUEN- TIAL	DE = FCB address	A = Error code	If a file has been activated for use by an open file or make file function, the write sequential function writes the 128-byte block of memory at the current DMA address to the next 128-byte record of the named file.
16	MAKE FILE	DE = FCB address	A = DIR code	Creates a new file with the information (name) indicated by the FCB. CP/M-80 does not check to see if the file indicated already exists, so you must first check to see if the file exists (or delete it). A newly created file need not be opened, as the make file function also performs the necessary opening operations.
17	RENAME FILE	DE = FCB address	A = DIR code	Changes the name of the file referenced by the first 16 bytes of the FCB to the name in the second 16 bytes.

NOTE: CP/M-80 always copies the contents of the H register in the A register if nothing is to be specifically returned in the A register. Some manufacturers, specifically Microsoft, make use of such information to reduce movement of information between the H and A registers.

Appendix C: Summary of BDOS Calls

Table C-1. (Continued)

Function		Entry Parameter(s)	Exit Parameter(s)	Explanation
No.	Name			
18	RETURN LOGIN VECTOR	None	HL = Disk login	The bits in the HL register are used to specify which disk drives are active. The first bit in the L register refers to drive A, the last bit in the H register corresponds to drive P, the highest possible drive. A bit value of 1 indicates active status, a zero denotes an inactive drive.
19	RETURN CURRENT DISK	None	A = Current disk	The numbers 0 through 15 are used to represent the current default disk drive upon return from this function.
1A	SET DMA ADDRESS	DE = DMA	None	Used to select the 128-byte memory block to be used for buffering all disk transfers. Upon system or disk reset, cold or warm start, the buffer is reset to 0080 hex on a normal CP/M-80 system.
1B	GET ALLOC ADDRESS	None	HL = Allocation address	Returns the starting address of the allocation vector, a table which is maintained in memory for each on-line disk drive that indicates the portions of the diskette which are in use.
1C	WRITE PROTECT DISK	None	None	Provides temporary write protection for the diskette in the current default disk drive.
1D	GET R/O VECTOR	None	HL = Disk R/O	Returns a 16-bit value in the HL registers which indicate which drives on the system are write protected. The drives are assigned as in the LOGIN VECTOR, with a value 1 indicating write-protection.
1E	SET FILE ATTRI- BUTES	DE = FCB address	A = DIR code	Sets the file attributes that indicate system/ directory and R/O or R/W file status for the file pointed to by the FCB address.
1F	GET DISK PARMS	None	HL = DPB address	Retrieves the disk parameter block for the current active disk drive. These parameters can be used to determine space available on a diskette or to change the characteristics of the disk drive under user control.
20	GET USER CODE SET USER CODE	E = FF E = User code	A = Current User or None	If the E register contains an FF hex, the current user number is returned in the A register. To reset the user number, the appropriate user code is placed in the E register. While the USER command allows user numbers in the range 0-15, this BDOS function can set user numbers in the range of 0-31.

NOTE: CP/M-80 always copies the contents of the H register in the A register if nothing is to be specifically returned in the A register. Some manufacturers, specifically Microsoft, make use of such information to reduce movement of information between the H and A registers.

Table C-1. (Continued)

Function		Entry Parameter(s)	Exit Parameter(s)	Explanation
No.	Name			
21	READ RANDOM	DE = FCB address	A = Error code	Reads the random record number contained in the 33rd, 34th, and 35th byte (a 24-bit address) of the FCB pointed to.
22	WRITE RANDOM	DE = FCB address	A = Error code	Writes information from the current DMA address to the random record pointed to by the number contained in the 33rd, 34th, and 35th bytes of the indicated FCB.
23	COMPUTE FILE SIZE	DE = FCB address	RRF set	Returns the current size of the random record file in the three bytes that constitute the random record field of the FCB. If the third byte contains a 1, then the file contains the maximum record count of 65536, otherwise the value in the first two bytes is a 16-bit value that represents the file size.
24	SET RANDOM RECORD	DE = FCB address	RRF set	Returns the next random record (fills in the random record field of the FCB) after the last sequentially read record. Digital Research suggests that this function is most appropriate to file indexing.
25	RESET DRIVE	DE = Reset drive bits	A = Error code	Forces the specified drives to be reset to the drive bits initial non-logged status.
28	WRITE RANDOM (ZERO)	DE = FCB address	A = Error code	Writes a record of all zeros to diskette before a record is written; useful for identifying unused random records (an unused record would contain zeros instead of data).

NOTE: CP/M-80 always copies the contents of the H register in the A register if nothing is to be specifically returned in the A register. Some manufacturers, specifically Microsoft, make use of such information to reduce movement of information between the H and A registers.

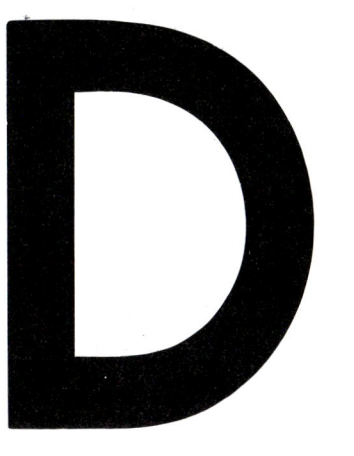

Summary of BIOS Calls

Table D-1. CP/M-80 BIOS Routine Definitions

Label in Jump Table	Entry Parameter(s)	Exit Parameter(s)	Explanation
COLDSTART	None	C = 0	Your routine should perform all the necessary start-up operations, including initializing all the values in the base page. Before exiting, the C register must be set to zero.
WARMSTART	None	C = Drive	Your routine should perform all the necessary restart operations but does not need to reinitialize the base page. The C register, on exit, should contain the current drive number.
CONSOLE STATUS (CONST)	None	A = Status	
CONSOLE* INPUT	None	A = Character	

Table D-1. (Continued)

Label in Jump Table	Entry Parameter(s)	Exit Parameter(s)	Explanation
READER* INPUT	None	A = Character	Your routine should wait for a character to be entered at the appropriate device and then return the character in the A register.
CONSOLE* OUTPUT	C = Character	None	
LIST* OUTPUT	C = Character	None	
PUNCH* OUTPUT	C = Character	None	Your routine should take the character in the C register and display it on the appropriate device.
HOME DISK	None	None	The head of the disk drive should be returned to the home position (track 0, sector 0).
SELECT DISK	C = Drive	HL = DHA	Your routine should select the drive indicated by the number in the C register. The HL register on return should contain the address of the disk parameter header.
SET TRACK	C = Track	None	The track indicated by the C register value should be set as the next track to be accessed by the disk drive.
SET SECTOR	C = Sector	None	The sector indicated by the C register value should be set as the next track to be accessed by the disk drive.
SET DMA ADDRESS	BC = DMA address	None	The DMA address indicated by the BC register pair should be set as the address to use for all information transfers from memory to diskette and vice versa.
READ DISK	None	A = Status	Read the current track and sector and transfer the data to the DMA address already set. A 01 hex should be returned if there was an error during transfer.
WRITE DISK	None	A = Status	Write the current track and sector from the data at the DMA address.
SECTOR TRANSLATION	BC = Logical sector DE = Sector map address	HL = Physical sector	A special routine used for systems which maintain data in other than 128-byte blocks. The logical sector on entry is changed to reflect the appropriate actual sector on the diskette.
LIST STATUS	None	A = Status	Your routine should interrogate the appropriate device to see if a character is ready and return a 00 hex in the A register if not ready, or a FF hex if ready.

*All console and device I/O should be done by first looking at the IOBYTE (0003 hex) to determine which device is selected.

Index

A

ANSI Standard Escape sequences:
Support via BIOS, 220

ASCII:
Updating the time in ASCII, 224

ASM:
Assembler, 185
Manual, 6

AUX:
Logical Auxiliary (Reader/Punch) device, 56

Allocation block:
Choosing size, 18
Concepts, 18
In file directory entry, 26
Maximum number in disk parameter block, 34
Prereading used block prior to writing, 155
Reserving in disk parameter block, 35

Allocation vector:
Finding address of, 119
Pointer in disk parameter header, 32

Ambiguous file names:
Avoidance in Rename File, 116
Concepts and restrictions, 24
Example processing, 401
Suggestion for utility program, 426
Used in BDOS Open File, 99
Used in DIR, 50
Used in ERA, 52
Used in Search for First Name Match, 103

Argc, argv:
C Functions for command parameters, 405

Assign:
C program, assigns logical to physical devices, 439

Attributes:
In file directory entry, 26

Available RAM:
Finding amount available, 65

B

BASIC:
Problems with "gobbling" characters, 218

BDOS:
Accessing file directory, C functions, 408
Entry Point, in base page, 59
Errors detected, 296

BDOS Function:
0, System Reset, 71
1, Read Console Byte, 72
2, Write Console Byte, 73
3, Read Reader Byte, 75
4, Write Punch Byte, 77
5, Write List Byte, 77
6, Direct Console I/O, 79
7, Get IOBYTE Setting, 80
8, Set IOBYTE, 86
9, Display $-Terminated String, 88
10, Read Console String, 90
11, Read Console Status, 94
12, Get CP/M Version Number, 94
13, Reset Disk System, 95
14, Select Logical Disk, 97
15, Open File, 98
16, Close File, 102
17, Search for First Name Match, 103
18, Search for Next File Name Match, 107
19, Erase (Delete) File, 108
20, Read Sequential, 109
21, Write Sequential, 110
22, Create (Make) File, 112
23, Rename File, 115
24, Get Active Disks, 116
25, Get Current Default Disk, 118
26, Set DMA (Read/Write) Address, 118
27, Get allocation vector, 119
28, Set Logical Disk Read-Only, 120
29, Get Read-Only Disks, 120
30, Set File Attributes, 121
31, Get Disk Parameter Block Address, 125
32, Set/Get User Number, 131
33, Read Random, 131
34, Write Random, 133
35, Get File Size, 142
36, Set Random Record Number, 142
37, Reset Logical Disk Drive, 143
40, Write Random with Zero-fill, 144

BDOS Function codes: 69
In LIBRARY.H, 391
Initialization concepts, 12
Interface to other software, 15
Introduction to function calls, 20
Making a function request, 68
Making calls in C, 395

487

BDOS Function codes *(continued)*
Naming conventions, 68
Register conventions for function requests, 70
Use of Function 0 after hardware error, 299
Use of Function 0 after printer error, 224
Use of location 0005H, 14
What the BDOS does, 67

BDOS Error:
Bad Sector, 98, 154
R/O, 120
Select, 98, 153

BIOS:
Blocking/Deblocking, 152
Bootstrap functions, 148
CONIN, console input, 151
CONOUT, console output, 151
CONST, console input status, 150
Character drivers, debugging, 354
Components, 147
Configuration Block, accessing from C, 396
Debugging, 353
Debugging interrupts service routines, 357
Device table, accessing from C, 398
Different types of disk write, 155
Direct BIOS calls, example code, 156
Direct calls, examples, 65
Direct calls to read/write disk from C, 399
Disk Parameter Block, accessing from C, 398
Enhanced BIOS listing, 235
Enhanced data structures, 225
Enhancements, 209
Enhancements to support different protocols, 218
Entry points, 148
Example code for standard BIOS, 158
Feature checklist for debugging, 354
Finding the jump vector in RAM, 56
Function key table, accessing from C, 397
HOME disk heads, 153
Hardware error handling functions, 296
Host Buffer, HSTBUF, 152
Initialization concepts, 12
Interface to other software, 15
Jump numbers in LIBRARY.H, 391
Jump vector, 15, 56
Keeping the current date, 224
Keeping the current time, 224
LIST, list output, 151
LISTST, list device output status, 156
Live testing, 368
Logical Input/Output, 15
Making calls in C, 396

BIOS *(continued)*
PUNCH (Auxiliary) output, 151
Preparing a special version, 184
READ sector, 154
READER input, 152
SECTRAN, logical to physical sector translation, 156
SELDSK, select disk, 153
SETDMA, set DMA address, 154
SETSEC, set sector, 153
SETTRK, set track, 153
Sequence of operations for sector write, 155
Support of function keys, 210
Using PIP to test, 369
WRITE sector, 155
What needs to be tested, 354
When to avoid direct calls, 15

Backspace:
CONTROL-H, 47

Bad sector management: 303
In the BIOS, 154
Suggestion for utility program, 426, 448

Base page:
Current user number, 59
Example memory dumps, 61
Set by the CCP for loaded program, 54

Basic Debugging for a BIOS: 320

Basic Disk Operating System:
See BDOS

Baud rates:
Speed, C program to set Baud rates, 431

Bit Bucket:
If no Punch driver used, 77

Bit map:
See Allocation vector

Bit vector:
As used in C functions, 402
Boolean AND, bv_and, Code, 389, Narrative, 404
Definition of structure in LIBRARY.H, 395
Display, bv_disp, Code, 389, Narrative, 404
Fill, bv_fill, Code, 387, Narrative, 404
Inclusive OR, bv_or, Code, 389, Narrative, 404
Make, bv_make, Code, 387, Narrative, 404
Set bit, bv_set, Code, 387, Narrative, 404
Test bit, bv_test, Code, 388, Narrative, 404
Test bit non-zero, Code, 388, Narrative, 404

Block mask:
In disk parameter block, 33

Block shift:
In disk parameter block, 33

Blocking/Deblocking:
Concepts, 36

Blocking/Deblocking *(continued)*
Disk write types from BDOS to BIOS, 155
In the BIOS, 152

Bootstrap loader:
Building a new version, 184
Debugging, 351
Example code, 197
Overview, 8

Buffer overflow:
Debugging character driver, 358

Buffer thresholds:
Debugging character driver, 359

Buffer wraparound:
Debugging character driver, 360

Building a new CP/M system:
Example console dialog, 206
The major steps, 183

Building an index file:
Using Set Random Record Number, 143

Building your first CP/M system: 138

Built-in commands:
In the CCP, 46

Built-in debug code: 321

Bv_and:
Bit vector, boolean AND, Code, 389, Narrative, 404

Bv_disp:
Bit vector, display, Code, 389, Narrative, 404

Bv_fill:
Bit vector, fill, Code, 387, Narrative, 404

Bv_make:
Bit vector, make, Code, 387, Narrative, 404

Bv_nz:
Bit vector, test bit non-zero, Code, 388, Narrative, 404

Bv_or:
Bit vector, inclusive OR, Code, 389, Narrative, 404

Bv_set:
Bit vector, set bit, Code, 387, Narrative, 404

Bv_test:
Bit vector, test bit, Code, 388, Narrative, 404

C

C Language:
Reference manuals, 4
Use for utility programs, 371

C programs:
ASSIGN, assigns logical to physical devices, 439
DATE, sets the date, 442
ERASE, a safer way to erase files, 409

C programs *(continued)*
FIND, finds lost files, 416
FUNKEY, sets the function keys, 445
MAKE, makes files visible/invisible, 427
MOVE, moves files between user numbers, 423
PROTOCOL, sets serial line protocols, 434
SPACE, shows used/free disk space, 420
SPEED, sets Baud rates, 431
TIME, sets the time, 442
UNERASE, restores erased files, 412

CBIOS.ASM:
An ingredient for a new system, 185

CCP:
Base page, set for program loaded, 185
Built-in commands, 50
Command Line Editing, 46
Control characters and their effects, 47
Default DMA buffer in base page, 61
Details, 45
ERA, erase (delete) files, 51
Example memory dumps of base page, 61
Functions, 46
Initialization concepts, 12
Interface to other software, 15
Logical devices, 56
Modifying the prompt to show the user number, 235
Overview, 12
Overwriting to gain memory, 45
Program loading, 54
Prompt, 46
REN, rename file, 52
Reloading on warm boot, 45
Resident commands, 14
Returning without warm boot, 66
SAVE, save memory image on disk, 53
Setting of command tail in base page, 60
Setting of default FCB's in base page, 60
TYPE, type an ASCII file, 52
USER, changing user number, 53

CCPM:
Example of Get CP/M Version Number, 95

CDISK:
Example of Reset Disk System, 96

COM file structure: 194

COM files:
Loaded by the CCP, 46

CON:
Logical console, 16

CONIN:
Accessing the date and time, 223

CONIN *(continued)*
Console input, in the BIOS, 151
Recognizing incoming function key characters, 221
Use with forced input, 219

CONOUT:
Console output, in the BIOS, 151
Escape sequences to input date and time, 223
Processing output escape sequences, 222

CONST:
Console input status, in the BIOS, 50
Problems with programs that "gobble" characters, 218
Use with forced input, 219

CP/M:
Bringing up a new system, 350

CP/M 128-byte "records": 41

CP/M file system:
Concepts, 17

CP/M records as 128-byte sectors: 71

CRC:
See Cyclic Redundancy Check

CRF:
Example of Random Write, 135

Cancel command line:
CONTROL-U, 49

Captions:
For debug subroutines, 322

CARRIAGE RETURN:
CONTROL-M, 48

Changed diskette:
Size of buffer for detection, in disk parameter block, 36
Work area in disk parameter header, 32

Changing disks:
Need to force disk log-in, 96

Changing user number:
USER, 53

Character drivers:
Example testbed, 355

Character I/O:
Enhancements, 213
In the BIOS, 150
Interrupts for input, 215
Practical handling of errors, 299

Choosing allocation block size: 18

Circular buffer:
For interrupt-driven input, 217
Structure in device table, 226

Close File:
BDOS Function 16, 102

Code table:
Definition of structure in LIBRARY.H, 394
Display all strings, ct_disps, Code, 385, Narrative, 407
Get string for code, ct_strc, Code, 386, Narrative, 407
Get string for index, ct_stri, Code, 386, Narrative, 407
Initialize, ct_init, Code, 384, Narrative, 407
Prompt and return code, ct_parc, Code, 384, Narrative, 407
Return code, ct_code, Code, 385, Narrative, 407
Return index, ct_index, Code, 386, Narrative, 407
Used for command tail parameters, 406

Cold Boot:
BIOS functions, 149
Concepts, 12

Command line:
Canceling, CONTROL-U, 49
Deleting last character typed, 49
Repeating, CONTROL-R, 49

Command Line Editing:
By the CCP, 46

Command tail:
Code tables, C functions, 405
Example program to process parameters, 63
In base page, 60
Input to the CCP, 46
Processing, C functions, 405

Communications:
Using Reader/Punch (Auxiliary), 151

Comp_fname:
Compare file name, Code, 374, Narrative, 401

Compare file name:
Comp_fname, Code, 374, Narrative, 401

Configuration Block:
Accessing from C, 396
Concepts, 211
Suggestion for utility program, 448
Variable codes in LIBRARY.H, 391

Console Command Processor:
See CCP

Console output:
From debug subroutines, 323
Temporary pause, CONTROL-S, 47

Console output to printer:
CONTROL-P, 48

Console status:
Debugging character driver, 360

Control characters:
Used in CCP command line editing, 47

Default disk:
Changing, 50
In base page, 59
In CCP prompt, 46

Default File Control Blocks:
In base page, 60

Deferred writes:
In conjunction with track buffering, 231

Delete character:
Rubout/Del, 49

Deleting files:
ERA, 51

Device table:
Accessing from C, 398
Displaying for debugging, 356
Structure, 225

Digital Research:
Manuals, 6

Direct BIOS calls:
Example code, 156
Examples, 65
When to avoid, 15

Directory code:
As returned by BDOS calls, 71
As returned from Create (Make) File, 114
As returned from Rename File, 116
Returned by BDOS Close File, 103
Returned by BDOS Open File, 99
Returned by Search for First Name Match, 103
Returned by Search for Next Name Match, 107

Directory entry: 99
Definition in LIBRARY.H, 394

Directory Parameter Block:
Definition in LIBRARY.H, 393

Disk Drivers:
Debugging, 364

Disk I/O:
Enhancements, 231
In the BIOS, 152

Disk Map:
In file directory entry, 26

Disk Parameter Block:
Accessing from C, 398
Adding extra information, 41
Block shift, mask, and extent mask, 33
Definition in LIBRARY.H, 394
Details, 33
Finding the address of, 125
Maximum allocation block number, 34

Disk Parameter Block *(continued)*
Number of directory entries — 1, 35
Number of tracks before directory, 36
Pointer in disk parameter header, 31
Reserving allocation blocks for file directory, 35
Sectors per track, 33
Size of buffer for detecting changed diskettes, 36
Worked example for hard disk, 39

Disk Parameter Header:
Details, 28
Disk buffer, 31
Disk parameter block, 31
Pointer to allocation vector, 32
Sector skewing, 28
Work area for changed diskette detection, 32

Disk buffer:
In disk parameter header, 31

Disk definition tables:
Concept, 18
Details, 27

Disk drivers:
Example testbed code, 365

Disk errors:
Strategy, 303

Disk full:
Error returned from Sequential Write, 112

Disk layout:
CP/M on diskettes, 189

Disk map:
As used in C functions, 402

Disk map clear:
Dm_clr, Code, 382, Narrative, 403

Disk map display:
Dm_disp, Code, 382, Narrative, 403

Diskette:
Layout of standard CP/M diskette, 37

Diskette format:
Concepts, 9

Display $-Terminated String:
BDOS Function 9, 88

Display directory error:
Err_dir, Code, 381, Narrative, 400

Displaying an ASCII file:
TYPE, 52

Displaying current user number: 54

Dm_clr:
Disk map clear, Code, 382, Narrative, 403

Dm_disp:
Disk map display, Code, 382, Narrative, 403

Control characters *(continued)*
CONTROL-C:
Used to abort after BDOS error, 98
CONTROL-P:
Errors generated, 299
CONTROL-Z:
If no Reader driver in BIOS, 75
Used to indicate end of file, 110
Used to terminate prior to BDOS Close File, 103

Conv_dfname:
Convert directory file name, Code, 375, Narrative, 402

Conv_fname:
Convert file name, Code, 375, Narrative, 408

Convert directory file name:
Conv_dfname, Code, 375, Narrative, 402

Convert file name:
Conv_fname, Code, 375, Narrative, 408

Create (Make) file:
BDOS Function 22, 112

Ct_code:
Code table, return code, Code, 385, Narrative, 407

Ct_disps:
Code table, display all strings, Code, 385, Narrative, 407

Ct_index:
Code table, return index, Code, 386, Narrative, 407

Ct_init:
Code table, initialize, Code, 384, Narrative, 407

Ct_parc:
Code table, prompt and return code, Code, 384, Narrative, 407

Ct_strc:
Code table, get string for code, Code, 386, Narrative, 407

Ct_stri:
Code table, get string for index, Code, 386, Narrative, 407

Current default drive: 97

Current logical disk:
In base page, 59

Current record number:
In FCB, unchanged for Random Read, 132
In FCB, unchanged for Random Write, 132

Current user number:
Displaying, 54
In base page, 59

Customization:
Of CP/M, an overview, 8

Cyclic Redundancy Check:
As used in disk errors, 303

D

DDT:
Dynamic Debug Tool, 185, 329
Manual, 6
I Command used for building new CP/M system, 195
R Command used for building new CP/M system, 195
Used for checking CP/M images, 204
Used for debugging character drivers, 354
Used to create CP/M memory image, 194
Used to debug disk drivers, 364

DESPOOL:
Use of LISTST BIOS entry, 156

DIR:
Display directory of files, 50

DMA buffer:
Default in base page, 60

DPB:
See Disk Parameter Block

DPH:
See Disk Parameter Header

DTR:
PROTOCOL, C program to set protocols, 434
See Data Terminal Ready

Data storage area:
Concept, 17

Data Terminal Ready:
Explanation of DTR protocol, 219

DATE:
C program, sets the date, 442

Date:
Keeping the current date in the BIOS, 224
Reading the date from the console driver, 223

Debug output:
Controlling when it occurs, 324

Debug subroutines: 322
Overall design philosophy, 322

Debugging a new CP/M system, 319

Debugging checklist:
Character output, 361
Disk drivers, 367
Interrupt service routines, 359
Non-interrupt service routine, 359
Real Time Clock, 362

Default DMA Address: 118

Default DMA buffer:
In base page, 60

Index **493**

DO:
Suggestion for utility program, 448
DPB:
See Disk Parameter Block
DPH:
See Disk Parameter Header

E

ED:
Editor, manual, 6
ERA:
Erase (delete) files, 51
Echoing of keyboard characters:
Read Console Byte, 72
End of File:
Detection using Read Sequential, 110
Erase (Delete) File:
BDOS Function 19, 108
ERASE:
C program, a safer way to erase files, 409
Erased files:
Unerasing them, 26
Erasing a file:
ERA, 51
Logical deletion only, 23
Err_dir:
Display directory error, Code, 381, Narrative, 400
Error messages:
Debugging disk drivers, 368, Chapter 12
Errors:
Dealing with hardware errors, 295
Example printer error routine, 301
Handling disk errors, 303
Hardware, analysis, 297
Hardware, correction, 299
Hardware, detection strategy, 296
Hardware, indication, 297
Improved disk error messages, 312
Practical handling, character I/O, 299
Escape sequences:
Function keys, debugging character driver, 360
Incoming, debugging character driver, 360
Processing output sequences, 222
Recognizing function key sequences, 222
Suggestion for utility program, 448
Support via device table, 226
Etx/Ack:
Debugging character drivers, 358, 362
Explanation of protocol, 219

Etx/Ack *(continued)*
Protocol, C program to set protocols, 434
Example programs:
Ordering diskette, 4
Extent:
In file directory entry, 26
Of files, concepts, 18
Extent mask:
In disk parameter block, 33

F

FCB:
Default FCB's in base page, 60
See File Control Block
FDOS:
Rarely used term for BDOS/CCP combined
File Attributes: 99
Setting, 121
See File status
File Control Block:
Creating one from an ASCII file name, 100
Concepts, 18
Definition in LIBRARY.H, 393
Structure, 41
Used for random file operations, 43
Used for sequential file operations, 43
Used in BDOS Open File, 99
Used in BDOS Requests, 71
File Directory:
Accessing entries directly, 399
Processing, C functions, 402
File Organizations:
Concepts, 41
File Protection:
Special characters in file name, 114
File changed:
File status bit in file directory entry, 26
File directory:
Accessing, C functions, 400
Accessing, via BDOS & C functions, 408
Concept, 17
Details, 18
Disk map, 26
Displaying contents, DIR, 50
Entry structure, 22
Erasing files, ERA, 51
File extent, 26
File name and type in entry, 27
Matching names, C functions, 401
Number of entries − 1, in disk parameter block, 35

File directory *(continued)*
Number of tracks before, 36
Record number, 27
Status (attribute) bits, 26
User number in entry, 22
File extent:
Concepts, 18
In file directory entry, 26
Manipulation to achieve Random I/O, 110-12
Opening extent 0 for Random I/O, 133-34
File name/type:
In file directory entry, 23
File protection:
Suggestion for utility program, 426
File status:
In file directory entry, 26
File system:
Concepts, 17
File type:
Conventions for actual types, 24
Filecopy:
Suggestion for utility program, 426
Files:
Creating, sequence of operations, 20
Displaying a directory, DIR, 50
Find:
C program, finds lost files, 416
Flushing buffers:
Prior to BDOS Close File, 103
Forced input:
Concepts, 219
Debugging character driver, 360
Suggestion for utility program, 448
Framing error:
Character I/O, handling, 300
Function Key table:
Accessing from C, 397
Function keys:
Structure in LIBRARY.H, 392
Support with enhanced BIOS, 220
Testing in a live BIOS, 370
FUNKEY:
C program, sets the function keys, 445

G

GETC:
Example of Read Sequential, 111
GETDPB:
Example of Get Disk Parameter Block Address, 126

GFA:
Example of Get File Attributes, 122
GNF:
Example of Search First/Next File Name Match, 104
Get CP/M Version Number:
BDOS Function 12, 94
Get Current Default Disk:
BDOS Function 25, 118
Get Disk Parameter Block Address:
BDOS Function 31, 125
Get Disk Parameter Block Address:
Get_dpb, Code, 383
Get File Size:
BDOS Function 35, 142
Get IOBYTE Setting:
BDOS Function 7, 80
Get Read-Only Disks:
BDOS Function 29, 120
Get allocation vector:
BDOS Function 27, 119
Get configuration block address:
Get_cba, 372
Get next directory entry:
Get_nde, Code, 378, Narrative, 400
Get next file name:
Get_nfn, Code, 376, Narrative, 408
Get_cba:
Get configuration block address, 372
Get_dpb:
Get Disk Parameter Block Address, Code, 383
Get_nde:
Get next directory entry, Code, 378, Narrative, 400
Get_nfn:
Get next file name, Code, 376, Narrative, 408

H

HEX file structure: 195
HOME:
Home disk heads, in the BIOS, 153
HSTBUF:
In the BIOS, 152
Hard disk:
Division into several logical disks, 39
Special considerations, 36
Hardware errors:
Dealing with, 295, Chapter 9
Hardware reset:
Debugging character driver, 359

Index **495**

Heath/Zenith:
Special version of CP/M, 55
Host Buffer:
In the BIOS, 152
Host sector size:
In the BIOS, 152

I

I/O Redirection:
Assign, C program to assign physical devices, 439
Concepts, 214
IOBYTE Structure, 57
IF/ENDIF directives:
Used for debug subroutines, 323
IOBYTE:
Equates for bit fields, 86
Structure, 57
Use for polling communications line, 75
Use with Direct Console I/O for communications, 80
Initialization of debug subroutines: 323
Input redirection:
Debugging character driver, 359
Input/Output:
Fake I/O for debugging purposes, 327
Interactions:
Between CCP, BDOS, and BIOS, 15
Interlace:
See Sector skewing
Interrupt service routines:
Debugging checklist, 357
Interrupts:
Architecture, 216
Circular buffers, 217
Dealing with buffer overflow, 219
Debugging service routines, 329
Use for character input drivers, 215

J

Johnson-Laird Inc.:
Ordering diskette, 4
Jump vector:
Use for entering the BIOS, 15

L

LIBRARY.C:
Utility function library, 372
LIBRARY.H:
Header for LIBRARY.C functions, 390
LIST:
List output, in the BIOS, 151

LISTST:
List device output status, in the BIOS, 156
LST:
Logical list device, 56
Line editing:
Using Read Console String, 91
Line feed:
CONTROL-J, 48
List Device Errors:
Problems with BDOS Function 5, 78
Loading CP/M:
Overview, 11
Loading programs:
Via the CCP, 54
Loadsys:
Suggestion for utility program, 448
Location 0000H:
Use for warm boot, 13
Location 0005H:
Simple examples of use, 20
Use for BDOS function calls, 14
Logging in a disk:
Using BDOS Reset Disk System, 96
Logical deletion of files, 23
ERA, 51
Logical devices:
CON:, LST:, AUX:, RDR:, PUN:, 56
Logical disk:
As represented in File Control Block, 42
Division of hard disk into several logical disks, 39
Selecting, 97
Logical Input/Output:
As afforded by the BIOS, 15
Logical records:
Concepts, 41
Logical sectors to physical: 28
SECTRAN, in the BIOS, 156
Login Vector:
See BDOS Function 24, 116
Lowercase letters in file name: 114
M-disk:
Using memory as an ultra-fast disk, 232
M80:
Macro Assembler, 185
MAC:
Macro Assembler, 185
MAKE:
C program, makes files visible/invisible, 427

MOVE:
C program, moves files between user numbers, 423
MOVCPM:
In conjunction with patches to CP/M, 234
Relocating the CCP and BDOS, 201
Use in building a new CP/M system, 182
MSGOUT:
Example of Write Console Byte, 74
MSGOUTI:
Example of Write Console Byte, 74
Manuals:
From Digital Research, 6
Maximum allocation block number:
In disk parameter block, 34
Memory:
Displaying in debug subroutines, 324
Finding size of area available for programs, 65
Use of hidden memory for buffers, 216
Used as an ultra-fast disk, 232
Memory dumps:
Base page, 61
Memory image:
Checking a new system, 204
Of new CP/M system, 185
Memory layout:
For example BIOS, 190
For input to SYSGEN, 187
With CP/M loaded, 13
Messages:
As an aid to debugging, 326

N

Notation:
For example console dialog, 3
Number of file directory entries:
In disk parameter block, 35

O

OM:
Example of Display $-Terminated String, 89
OPENF:
Example of Open File, 100
Open File:
BDOS Function 15, 98
Open directory:
Open_dir, Code, 378, Narrative, 400
Open_dir:
Open directory, Code, 378, Narrative, 400
Orville Wright approach to debugging: 320

Output Escape sequence:
Debugging character output driver, 362
Overrun error:
Character I/O, handling, 300
Overwriting the CCP:
To gain memory, 45
Owner:
Suggestion for utility program, 426

P

PIP:
Used to test a new BIOS, 369
PROM Bootstrap:
Used to load CP/M, 11
PUN:
Logical Punch, 56
PUNCH:
Punch (Auxiliary) output, in the BIOS, 151
PUTC:
Example of Write Sequential, 113
PUTCPM:
Example program, 191
Writing a utility, 189
Parallel printers:
Error handling, 301
Parameters:
Example program to process command tail, 63
Parity error:
Character I/O, handling, 300
Pass counters:
Use in debug subroutines, 324
Patching CP/M:
General techniques, 234
Performance:
Effect of sector skewing, 29
Physical end of line:
CONTROL-E, 47
Physical sectors:
Relative, on a hard disk, 38
Polled Reader Input:
Problems and solutions, 75
Polled communications:
Using Direct Console I/O, 80
Printer echo:
CONTROL-P, 48
Printer errors:
Example routine, 301
Use of watchdog timer, 224

Printer timeout error:
Handling, 300
Program loading:
Via the CCP, 54
Program termination:
Returning to CP/M, 66
Prompt:
From the CCP, 46
Protect/Unprotect:
Suggestion for utility program, 426
PROTOCOL:
C program, sets serial line protocols, 434
Protocol:
See also Data Terminal Ready, Request to Send, Xon/Xoff, Etx/Ack
Definitions in LIBRARY.H, 392
Support in enhanced BIOS, 218
Support via device table, 226
Xon/Xoff, used by TYPE, 52
Public files:
Patches to create this feature, 235
Suggestion for utility program, 448
Public/Private:
Suggestion for utility program, 448

R

RAM-disk:
Using memory as an ultra-fast disk, 232
RCS:
Example of Direct Console I/O, 81
RDR:
Logical Reader, 56
READ:
Read Sector, in the BIOS, 154
READER:
Reader input, in the BIOS, 152
REN:
Rename file, 52
RF:
Example of Rename File, 117
RL$RDR:
Example of Read Reader Byte, 76
RMAC:
Relocatable Macro Assembler, 185
RO:
Example of Random File I/O, 136
RSA:
Example of Read Console String, 92

RST7:
Use for debugging drivers, 356
RTS:
See also Buffer thresholds, Request to Send
Protocol, C program to set protocols, 434
Random Read:
Using Read Sequential, 110
Random Write:
Using Write Sequential, 112
Random files:
Concepts, 43
Creating an empty file, 144
Problem of sparse files, 44
Virtual size, 142
Random record number:
In FCB, set for Random Read, 132
In FCB, set for Random Write, 132
Rd_disk:
Read disk (via BIOS), Code, 377, Narrative, 400
Read Console Byte:
BDOS Function 1, 72
Read Console Status:
BDOS Function 11, 94
Read Console String:
BDOS Function 10, 90
Read Random:
BDOS Function 33, 131
Read Reader Byte:
BDOS Function 3, 75
Read Sequential:
BDOS Function 20, 109
Read disk (via BIOS):
Rd_disk, Code, 377, Narrative, 400
Read-Only:
Automatic setting after changing diskettes, 32
File status bit in file directory entry, 26
Read-Only Disks: 120
Read-Only File:
Attribute bit, 121
Read/write directory:
Rw_dir, Code, 380, Narrative, 400
Reading/Writing disk:
Direct BIOS calls from C, 399
Real Time Clock:
Debugging, 362
Example testbed code, 363
TIME, C program to set the time, 444

Reclaim:
Suggestion for utility program, 426

Record number:
In file directory entry, 26
Manipulation to achieve Random I/O, 110, 112

Registers:
Displaying in debug subroutines, 324

Relative page offset:
Use for making direct BIOS calls, 65

Relative physical sectors:
On a hard disk, 38

Release diskettes:
Files from Digital Research, 6

Rename File:
BDOS Function 23, 115

Renaming a file:
REN, 52

Repeat command line:
CONTROL-R, 48

Request to Send:
Explanation of RTS protocol, 219

Reserved area:
Concept, 17

Reset:
Signal used to start loading of CP/M, 11

Reset Disk System:
BDOS Function 13, 95

Reset Logical Disk Drive:
BDOS Function 37, 143

Resident CCP commands: 14

Restoring registers:
In interrupt service routine, 356

Rw_dir:
Read/write directory, Code, 380, Narrative, 400

S

SAVE:
Save memory image in disk file, 53
Use in building new CP/M system, 194

SECTRAN:
Logical sector to physical, in the BIOS, 156

SELDSK:
Debugging disk drivers, 367
Select disk, in the BIOS, 153

SETDMA:
Set DMA Address, in the BIOS, 154

SETSEC:
Set Sector, in the BIOS, 153

SETTRK:
Set Track, in the BIOS, 153

SETTRK/SEC:
Debugging disk drivers, 367

SFA:
Example of Set File Attributes, 122

SID:
Debugging tool, 330

STAT:
Use for displaying current user number, 54

SYSGEN:
System Generator, 185
Writing a new system to disk, 186

Savesys:
Suggestion for utility program, 448

Saving memory on disk:
SAVE, 53

Search First/Next:
Example use together, 107

Search for file:
Srch_file, Code, 376, Narrative, 408

Search for Next File Name Match:
BDOS Function 18, 107
Require for Search for First, 104

Sector interlace:
See Sector skewing

Sector size:
Host, in the BIOS, 152

Sector skewing:
Effect on performance, 29
For CP/M image on disk, 190
In disk parameter header, 28

Sector skipping:
Concepts, 304

Sector sparing:
Concepts, 304

Sectors:
Use in allocation blocks, 18

Sectors per track:
In disk parameter block, 33

Select Logical Disk:
BDOS Function 14, 97

Sequential Files:
Concepts, 43

Set DMA (Read/Write) Address:
BDOS Function 26, 118
Required by Search for First Name Match, 104

Index

Set File Attributes:
BDOS Function 30, 121
Set IOBYTE:
BDOS Function 8, 86
Set Logical Disk Read-Only:
BDOS Function 28, 120
Set Random Record Number:
BDOS Function 36, 142
Set disk parameters for rd/wrt_disk:
Set_disk, Code, 378, Narrative, 400
Set search control block:
Setscb, Code, 381, Narrative, 401
Set/Get User Number:
BDOS Function 32, 131
Set_disk:
Set disk parameters for rd/wrt_disk, Code, 378, Narrative, 401
Setscb:
Set search control block, Code, 381, Narrative, 401
Setterm:
Suggestion for utility program, 448
Shadow PROM:
Used to load CP/M, 11
Short:
Minor change to C Language, 395
Single-density, single-sided:
Diskette format, 10
Single disk reset, 143
Skewing:
See Sector skewing
Skipping:
Skipping bad sectors on disk, 304
SPACE:
C program, shows used/free disk space, 420
Spare:
Suggestion for utility program, 448
Spare directory:
Debugging disk drivers, 367
Sparing:
Use of spare sectors on disk, 304
Sparse Random Files:
Problem, 44
Special version of CP/M:
Heath/Zenith, 55
SPEED:
C program, sets baud rates, 431
Srch_file:
Search for file, Code, 376, Narrative, 408

Sstrcmp:
Substring compare, 373
Stack:
Filling with known pattern, 323
Stack overflow:
In interrupt service routine, 358
Standard BIOS:
Example code, 158
String scan:
Strscn, 372
String scan, uppercase:
Ustrscn, 372
Strscn:
String scan, 372
Structure:
Of CP/M, 5
Subroutine:
CCPM, Check if CP/M Version 2, 95
CDISK, Change Disk, 96
CRF, Create Random File, 135
DB$Blank, Display a blank, 344
DB$CAH, Convert A to ASCII Hex., 343
DB$CRLF, Display Carriage Return, Line Feed, 344
DB$Colon, Display a colon, 344
DB$Conin, Debug console input, 336
DB$Conout, Debug console output, 336
DB$DAH, Display A in Hex., 343
DB$DHLH, Display HL in Hex., 343
DB$Display$CALLA, Display call address, 343
DB$Display, Main debug display, 338
DB$GHV, Get Hex. Value, 348
DB$Init, Debug initialize, 335
DB$Input, Debug Port Input, 346
DB$MEMORY, Debug display of memory/registers, 325
DB$MSG, Display Message, 345
DB$MSGI, Display Message (In-line), 345
DB$Off, Turn debug output off, 337
DB$On, Turn debug output on, 337
DB$Output, Debug Port Output, 347
DB$Pass, Decrement the pass counter, 337
DBSetPass, Set pass counter, 337
DIVHL, Divide HL by DE, 129
FOLD, Fold lowercase to upper, 93
FSCMP, Folded String Compare, 93
GAB, Get Allocation Block given Track/Sector, 128
GDTAS, Get Directory Track/Sector, 127
GETC, Get Character from Sequential File, 111
GETDPB, Get Disk Parameter Block Address, 126
GFA, Get File Attributes, 122
GMTAS, Get Maximum Track/Sector, 127

Subroutine *(continued)*
GNF, Get Next File matching ambiguous name, 104
GNTAS, Get Next Track/Sector, 128
GTAS, Get Track/Sector from Allocation block No., 126
MSGOUT, Message Output, 74
MSGOUTI, Message Output In-Line, 74
MULHL, Multiply HL by DE, 129
OM, Output Message selected by A register, 89
OPENF, Open File given ASCII file name, 100
PUTC, Put Character to Sequential File, 113
RCS, Read Console String, 81
RF, Rename File, 117
RL$RDR, Read Line from Reader, 76
RO, Random File I/O (non-128-byte records), 136
RSA, Return Subprocessor Address, 93
SDLR, Shift DE,HL one bit right, 141
SFA, Set File Attributes, 122
SHLR, Shift HL right one bit, 130
SUBHL, Subtract DE from HL, 130
TERM, Terminal Emulator, 87
TOUPPER, Fold lowercase to upper, 84
WL$LST, Write Line to List Device, 79
WL$PUN, Write Line to Punch, 78

Substring compare:
Sstrcmp, 373
Uppercase: Usstrcmp, 373

System file:
Attribute bit, 121
File status bit in file directory entry, 26
Not displayed by DIR, 51

System Reset:
BDOS Function 0, 71

T

TERM:
Example of Set/Get IOBYTE, 87
TIME:
C program, sets the time, 442
TYPE:
Type an ASCII file, 52
Tab:
Interaction of tab characters and escape sequences, 222
Tab expansion:
Supported by Write Console Byte, 73
Using Display $-Terminated String, 89
Termination of programs, returning to CCP: 45
Testbed:
Use for new drivers, 353

Time:
Correct display during debugging, 364
Keeping the current time in the BIOS, 224
Reading the time from the console driver, 223
Top of RAM:
Finding, via base page, 60
Track buffering:
Enhancement to disk I/O, 231
Track offset:
See Tracks before directory
Tracks before directory:
In disk parameter block, 36
Transient Program Area:
Finding available size, 65
Typeahead:
Concepts, 217
Dealing with buffer overflow, 219

U

Undo command line:
CONTROL-U, 49
UNERASE:
C program, restores erased files, 412
User Number:
Changing under program control, 131
Changing using USER, 53
Displaying, 54
In base page, 59
In file directory entry, 22
Patches to make this appear in CCP prompt, 235
Suggestion for utility program, 426
Usstrcmp:
Uppercase substring compare, 373
Ustrcmp:
Uppercase string scan, 372
Utility programs: 371

V

Variable record lengths:
Processing in Random Files, 133, 134

W

WL$LST:
Example of Write List Byte, 79
WL$PUN:
Example of Write Punch Byte, 78
WRITE:
Write sector, in the BIOS, 155
Warm Boot:
After BDOS Error, 98

Warm Boot *(continued)*
BIOS functions, 150
Initiated by CONTROL-C, 47
Initiated by pressing a key, 94
Initiated by System Reset BDOS Function, 72
JMP at location 0000H, 55
Reloading the CCP, 45
Resetting Read-Only disks, 120
Setting default DMA Address, 118
Technique for avoiding, 66
Use of location 0000H, 13

Watchdog timer:
Concepts, 225
Debugging Real Time Clock, 364
Use for detecting printer errors, 224

Write Console Byte:
BDOS Function 2, 73

Write List Byte:
BDOS Function 5, 77

Write Punch Byte:
BDOS Function 4, 77

Write Random:
BDOS Function 34, 133

Write Random with Zero-fill:
BDOS Function 40, 144

Write Sequential:
BDOS Function 21, 110

Write disk (via BIOS):
Wrt_disk, Code, 377, Narrative, 400

Wrt_disk:
Write disk (via BIOS), Code, 377, Narrative, 400

X

Xoff:
CONTROL-S, 48

Xon:
CONTROL-Q, 49

Xon/Xoff:
Debugging character driver, 358, 362
Explanation of protocol, 240
PROTOCOL, C program to set protocols, 434
Supported by Read Console Byte, 72
Use by TYPE, 53

Z

ZSID:
Z80 Symbolic Interactive Debugger, 185, 350